WRITING FOR LIFE

WRITING FOR LIFE
A WRITER'S READER

Marilyn Mayer Culpepper
Perry E. Gianakos
Michigan State University

Macmillan Publishing Company
NEW YORK

Macmillan Publishing Company
866 Third Avenue, New York, New York 10022

Library of Congress Cataloging-in-Publication Data

Culpepper, Marilyn Mayer.
  Writing for life.

  Bibliography: p.
  Includes indexes.
    1. College readers. 2. English language — Rhetoric.
  I. Gianakos, Perry E.   II. Title.
  PE1417.C77   1988   808'.0427   87-21901
  ISBN 0-02-341850-8

Printing: 1 2 3 4 5 6 7   Year: 8 9 0 1 2 3 4

ISBN 0-02-341850-8

For Tom and my parents
For my parents and Aunt Z.

To the Instructor

Writing for Life is designed to accomplish a number of objectives:

- To awaken students to the pleasures and liberating effects of reading,
- To help college students improve their reading and writing skills and to develop confidence in their own inherent abilities,
- To emphasize that writing will be an important part not only of their college days but also of their professional lives,
- To provide a wide variety of examples of effective writing and to guide students in examining the techniques that make the writings successful,
- To help students discover how to employ effectively these techniques in their own writing,
- To stimulate thinking by confronting students with new ideas and/or leading them to evaluate old concepts and values.

In sum, we hope to foster the student's growth emotionally as well as cognitively.

We have based our text on the belief that the best ways to learn to write are to read widely and to write extensively. The more good writing a reader is exposed to, the more ingrained becomes the feel for the various elements that characterize successful writing. Consciously or unconsciously, readers tend to absorb a taste for good prose, which in time influences their own writing. The more students write, the more comfortable they feel with the language, the more clearly they are able to express their ideas, and eventually the more effective is their communication. Although this assimilation obviously takes time, we hope to stimulate students to a lifetime commitment to reading and writing.

Throughout the book we have sought to be practical. To prepare students exclusively for their college years is to ignore the greater part of their lives. Therefore, the models are drawn from numerous academic disciplines and professions and involve techniques applicable to students' writing needs both during and after college. Most importantly, this book insists that anyone can learn to write, that most writers are cultivated rather than born writers.

We have sought to make *Writing for Life* unique. To that end, we chose selections not because they fit a certain theme or depict a particular mode of development. Instead, we have collected examples of successful writing representing a great diversity of styles and dealing with vital concerns (education, family, health, work, careers) that students can relate to.

The selections are primarily expository. Many are untraditional, coming from a wide range of sources: classic American writers, self-taught prison convicts, young black men and women, established political figures. Others are taken from professional literature and the everyday reading fare of educated Americans — newspapers and magazines. Many are new, but we have not ignored the proven, reliable standbys.

We have attempted to make this text as flexible as possible, because we recognize that instructors are diverse in their approach to teaching and students differ in their acquisition of writing skills. Our overall organization focuses on motivating students, expanding their worlds, and acquainting them with writing in the world of work. This arrangement allows instructors to order the readings differently. Some may devise alternate arrangements to more closely incorporate the supplementary readings. Others may wish to reverse Units II and III.

As a supplement to our primary approach, we have indexed the selections according to rhetorical modes. In addition, we have included an abbreviated index of selections notable for rhetorical concerns, such as well-defined theses, clear organization, challenging introductions or conclusions, or engaging style. This latter index can be used in a traditional approach to teaching writing or as a reference for students with problems in these special areas.

As instructional features, this text offers the following: (1) survey introductions precede each major unit; (2) headnotes direct attention to particular writing techniques in each selection; (3) questions on content, structures, and strategies, and suggestions for discussion and writing follow each selection (questions and writing suggestions for the supplementary readings may be found in the Instructor's Manual); (4) essay topics synthesize ideas from several articles at the end of each major unit; and (5) a condensed survey of the writing process provides for study or review. We have also drawn up a number of suggestions, or exercises, for short assignments to be completed in student journals or notebooks. We hope that aside from encouraging students to write more often — even daily — these short writing assignments (from a paragraph to a page or two) will help to correlate more closely journal writing with the readings and writing for the course. The exercises should invite students *to relax, to experiment, to discover,* and *to expand,* free from the worries of requirements or grades. These journal entries should also lessen the instructor's burden of grading every paper yet allow random reading of student writing throughout or at the conclusion of the course.

The text is accompanied by an Instructor's Manual that also contains several pages of exercises that may be photocopied and used in class to exemplify a lesson, or may be given to students with special problems.

Acknowledgments

For their help in the early stages of this book, we would like to thank Robert K. Reddy, Robert Runck, Bev Kolz, Paul O'Connell, and Jennifer Crewe; and for her helpful and patient guidance, our editor, Barbara Heinssen. We wish also to thank our Michigan State University colleagues: Pauline Adams, Chris Birdwell, Roger Bresnahan, Bern Engel, Maxine Eyestone, Michael Holaday, Pat Julius, Thomas Kishler, Adele Newson, Douglas Noverr, Ed Stieve, Sharon Thomas, Jerry West, and Robert Wright. We are grateful to the department of American Thought and Language for providing support and released time. For their criticisms and suggestions, we are deeply indebted to our reviewers: Lucien L. Agosta, Kansas State University; Kathleen Shine Cain, Merrimack College; Randolph Chilton, College of St. Francis; David A. Jolliffe, University of Illinois at Chicago; James Kinney, Virginia Commonwealth University; Judith Stanford, Rivier College; Paula P. Yow, Kennesaw College. Finally, we wish to acknowledge the painstaking work of our typists: Joanne Brunette, Betty Uphaus, Valarie Kelly, and Judy Easterbrook. We extend special thanks to Barbara Chernow.

M.M.C.
P.E.G.

"*Do you know what this book makes me want to do? Write.*"

To the Student

Writing for Life reflects our conviction that each individual has a potential to write well. Researchers and professional writers tell us that the development of this potential hinges on two absolute essentials: motivation and practice. As the first step to improved writing, then, writers must realize that writing is important to their personal growth and achievement as well as to their success later in life.

Writing Is Liberation.   Because of our belief in the close relationship between writing, motivation, and personal growth, in our first unit we focus on the experience of eight self-taught writers. For these people, learning informally on their own to write was an all-important means of liberation. Powerfully motivated by the need and desire to learn to write, these writers became obsessed with reading and writing. In the course of mastering these skills, they succeeded in completely turning their lives around. Reading and writing enabled them to break the bonds that were holding them back.

Writing Enlarges our World.   The second unit stresses reading and writing as a lifelong process that deepens and enriches our understanding of ourselves, of our relationships with others, and of the world around us. Through reading and especially in writing we continually enlarge our worlds. For it is in writing that we discipline our thinking and reinforce what we have learned.

Writing Marks the Professional.   Unit III illustrates the importance of reading and writing skills as a vital aspect of life after college — in one's professional life. The first six authors — professionals in medicine, science, economics, and the arts — discuss writing in their respective fields. In the remaining selections, you observe professionals engaged in the kinds of writing that may be required in your careers.

These three units are designed to motivate you to write. To write well, experts agree, you must write often. Philosophers and psychologists as well as professional writers, stress that students *learn by doing: by writing often, by submitting their work to professorial and peer editing, and, above all, by rewriting.* Your own logic tells you that no one becomes an accomplished pianist, a dancer, or an athlete by reading a rule book, taking a lesson now and then, or making a guest appearance at game time. Any skill takes practice. So, too, does writing.

The selections that make up the core of the text have been chosen to stimulate your thinking and writing about subjects that affect your personal lives and your lives as citizens in a democratic society. These articles also serve as models. Just as you learn to speak by imitating your parents and older siblings, you learn to write through reading and imitating good writing. This imitation, of course, as one expert has written, does not mean "cloning" a selection. We have machines to do that. Instead it means learning your craft the way most successful writers have learned theirs: by reading what other writers have written, by observing the way they wrote, and then by adapting those strategies to their own writing. To facilitate this transfer of techniques from seasoned writers to your own writing, we have provided a unique collection of both traditional and popular models that we hope you will agree are both interesting and challenging.

Each unit begins with an introduction and a discussion of some of the techniques used by the writers in the unit. The headnotes preceding each selection gloss the writer's main themes and suggest ideas and techniques to look for in the writing itself. Following each selection are questions about the content, the strategies and structure of the selections, and topics for discussion and writing. At the end of each of the three units are suggestions for experimenting with some of the techniques in short journal entries or in longer essays that combine ideas from several selections. (We suggest that you read Roy Hoffman's "On Keeping a Journal," Unit II, before beginning your journals.)

The format and selections in this text are designed to motivate you to write often and effectively. To this end, we have included a "Survey of the Writing Process," incorporating references to specific selections. It may be used as a review or as a resource. Following it are two student essays that trace the journey of two writers through the writing process. "A Brief Note on Research" offers suggestions for researching and documenting your work.

Our purpose in this book is to help you augment your natural writing talents, develop greater self-confidence, and cultivate the skills necessary for success in your professional life. All these are the rich rewards of good writing.

M.M.C.
P.E.G.

Contents

UNIT ONE

The Writer's Motivation:
Reading the Self-Taught Writer

UNIT TWO

The Writer's Consciousness: Enlarging Our World Through Reading and Writing

UNIT THREE

Writing in the World of Work: Reading and Writing across the Professions

Supplemental Readings

Appendices

The Writer's Motivation: Reading the Self-Taught Writer

_____ I _____

The writings in this opening unit have been deliberately chosen, first of all, to demonstrate that the ability to write is not some rare, esoteric talent inherited from one's ancestors. These eight, *self-taught*, published writers, we believe, should convince you.

To be sure, good writing is a skill, but one that can be acquired by almost anyone willing to put forth the effort. Many prominent writers — both past and present, and not only these eight — have had little formal schooling but have nevertheless been able to teach themselves to write. The first of these writers even had to teach himself to read. Many learned to write while serving in the armed forces, working in shipyards, stealing moments in between household chores, and even while serving time in prison. Their "colleges" or "schools" were newspapers, libraries, and literary models.

Although these writers came from radically different backgrounds and developed their talents in different ways, they are alike in that all possessed a strong *desire* to write. *All of these writers were powerfully motivated to learn to write because they wished to express themselves, literally to change their lives.* Somehow, intuitively, they came to the realization on their own that, as Neil Postman writes in *Teaching As A Conserving Activity,* "language education involves the transformation of personality":

To speak new words in new ways . . . is a way of becoming a new person. It involves learning new things and seeing the world in new ways. . . . Language serves not only to express thought but to make possible thoughts which could not exist without it.

Even though the prospect of teaching yourself to write may seem staggering at first, it is not an impossible task; for experience demonstrates that in the end you are your own best teacher. Handbooks, teachers, and editors can provide guidelines, but you, the writer, must experience and cultivate the elements of good writing: first through reading (and the more extensive and critical the better), and then through practicing and rewriting. As you read these eight writers and study the methods that brought them success, be alert for techniques, hints, or suggestions which you might adapt to improve your own writing.

All of the writers in this unit began where all writers must begin — with their own experiences, which include, of course, knowledge acquired through daily living, in addition to experience acquired vicariously, through reading. Some of these writers had more experience than others, but as all demonstrate, reading can greatly expand one's experience. All formal education, in fact, is based on this simple fact. What is important to remember, however, is that your own experience is your primary resource. Spend some time thinking about it and then augment it by discriminating reading.

To emphasize that writing is a process we have grouped the writers in this unit. First, Douglass and Cleaver illustrate the importance of motivation, though that, of course, is a factor basic to all good writing. Without motivation all the writing courses and formulas in the world will avail little. Motivation for these two writers was special because their goals were special: both were seeking liberation. And in a certain less urgent sense you too may be seeking "liberation" from a narrow, confining past or perhaps a slightly tongue-tied present.

For all eight writers the initial spark of interest eventually fired an all-consuming passion for reading and a subsequent desire to share their ideas through writing. In reading they discovered concepts that intrigued, confused, angered, and challenged them. They found in books opportunities to explore new lands and new frontiers, a chance to overcome past mistakes, and a route to intellectual and social achievement. More importantly, these reading experiences changed their lives.

For Jack London, Malcolm X, and Maya Angelou this preoccupation with reading became an obsession. In Maya Angelou's case, it meant accumulating a wide range of literary allusions upon which she draws for her descriptions of persons and places. Struggling to understand what they read, London and Malcolm X quickly recognized the poverty of their vocabularies, and both labored to enrich them. In acquiring the tools of understanding, they also acquired the indispensable tools of the writer. Both men even copied pages from dictionaries and memorized columns of words in their effort to augment their meager vocabularies. Through reading, these writers built up a storehouse of words and images to facilitate their reading and eventually to launch their writing careers. This emphasis on vocabulary building should have special appeal for you as students, inasmuch as vocabulary and critical reading ability vitally affect your success in college — and in life. And as Jack London's fictional hero — Martin Eden — demonstrates, vocabulary building is easily accomplished.

In the next two selections, Benjamin Franklin and Eric Hoffer tell us something about the need to develop a sense of *style*. It is easy to string words together, but style and grace — which lend distinction to writing — require cultivation and practice. Both Franklin and Hoffer suggest sound, time-proven methods of developing style. Actually, probably all good writers first sought to learn style from writers they admired. Just as the artist, beginner or expert, studies the work of other artists, so the reader–writer studies and observes, adapting what is appealing in other writers in an effort to create his or her own writing personality.

The last selection in this unit is an excerpt from the book *Silences,* by Tillie Olsen, whose "college" was the greatest tuition-free university in the world — the public library. The earlier articles are more or less descriptions of or narratives about the reading and writing process, and provide relatively easy reading. The Tillie Olsen selection, however, goes beyond the others and bears more careful scrutiny. For Olsen writes not about learning to write or developing style *but* instead writes with considerable style about women who write. The selection pulls together ideas on motivation, vocabulary, and reading, while exemplifying good style.

This first section, then, is designed to demonstrate (1) that all of us can learn to write no matter what our background; (2) that motivation and persistence are fundamental to all reading, writing, learning; (3) that we all have unique storehouses of experiences to write about — our own and those gained through reading; and (4) that studying and imitating established writers can be one of the surest means for developing an individual, personal style. The selections, therefore, focus on the fundamentals of writing: the writer's motivation, the writer's experience, the writer's tools (words), and the writer's style.

II

These selections illustrate the importance of motivation, reading, and style. They also contain other elements of good writing. Notice, for example, that each of these authors has a thesis, a controlling idea arrived at after thoughtful consideration of subject, audience, and purpose. Although Douglass and Malcolm X have perhaps the most clearly defined theses, each of the other writers develops ideas that are challenging and significant. Even the titles of the Cleaver, Hoffer, and Olsen selections help the reader identify the thesis, while at the same time they contribute to the unity of the selection.

In supporting their theses, all of these authors utilize narration, one of the simplest, easiest methods of development (see Rhetorical Index). When wisely used, narration (storytelling) lends a certain "naturalness" or "ease" to the writing. When misused, it can lead to aimless, egocentric rambling. (Such rambling is acceptable in journal writing.) All of these writers, however, have marshalled their experiences to make a definite point: demonstrating how their experiences changed their lives. Combining other modes — process, description, example, cause and effect — these authors trace the evolution of their writing abilities and simultaneously guide their readers to deeper insights into the evils of slavery, the joys of learning, or the extent of discrimination against women.

Because all of these selections are personal narratives of one sort or another, they tend to be informal and conversational. These authors have achieved their informality not only through their use of narration but also through the prevalent use of: (1) first and second person (I and you); (2) contractions (I'd, it's, don't); (3) colloquial word choice ("funny thing," "straighten up and fly right," "boola-boola"); (4) an easily understood vocabulary ("slow, painstaking, ragged hand-writing"); and (5) sentence fragments (incomplete sentences such as "Bliss of movement," "Almost impossible for a girl, a woman"). Your own writing can also be informal upon occasion when it is appropriate to your subject, your audience, and your purpose. A more formal tone, of course, was dictated by the solemnity of the subject, occasion, and purpose of the Jefferson, Lincoln, and Kennedy selections in Unit III. In all instances the authors were consistent in maintaining the same tone throughout their writing.

These are but a few examples of things to look for as you read the articles. Questions at the beginning and end of each selection are designed to help in this analysis.

These readings should serve to convince you that you too can become an effective writer. The success stories of these self-taught writers provide encouragement for all writers. With renewed confidence you can now go on to explore the more challenging readings in the ensuing selections, readings selected to nourish your growing talents in reading and writing.

HOW I LEARNED
TO READ AND WRITE
Frederick Douglass

The first two readings were written by blacks, both former "prisoners" of ignorance, one as a consequence of slavery and the other as a consequence of his own misplaced values and society's indifference. Frederick Douglass, as a slave in Maryland, recognized early the importance of education, taught himself (in part, with the inadvertent help of his white playmates) to read and write, and in 1837 escaped to freedom in the North. There he soon achieved prominence as a speaker, writer, and editor, championing the causes of abolition and the rights of women and blacks. In fact, so skilled had Douglass become in his use of the language and so powerful was his oratory that in 1845 he was forced to write his autobiography — Narrative of the Life of Frederick Douglass — in an effort to convince people that he truly was a self-educated, runaway slave. The following selection is taken from his work. Later, Douglass served as Marshal of the District of Columbia, Minister to Haiti, and Secretary of the Santo Domingo Commission.

This excerpt and the one following illustrate the single most important prerequisite for learning to read and write well: self-motivation. Just as motivation is essential in acquiring any skill — be it learning to play the piano, becoming an Olympic sprinter, or developing a powerful backhand — motivation is vital in learning to read and write well. For Douglass this commitment involved painful effort, constant practice, persistence in the face of frustration, and eventual success, a process that should cause you to examine your own motives and goals. Douglass's effort paid off in the achievement of his human potential.

Douglass's Narrative was written some time after the events described, and this excerpt is a fairly straightforward account, confined to the most important details about the actual process of learning to read and write. You may find a first reading very easy. But do not be deceived, for there is more substance here than appears on the surface. Douglass attached great meaning to these events. He has, as Ralph Waldo Emerson would explain, "turned experience into truth." The questions following the essay that relate to "content" are, therefore, designed to enable you not only to understand the passage but also to comprehend Douglass's greater meaning. Questions relating to writing structure and strategy are aimed at emphasizing the way Douglass achieves his purpose. Note the supporting material he selects, and observe the techniques he utilizes for unity.

Very soon after I went to live with Mr. and Mrs. Auld, she very kindly commenced to teach me the A, B, C. After I had learned this, she assisted me in learning to spell words of three or four letters. Just at this point of my progress, Mr. Auld found out what was going on, and at once forbade Mrs. Auld to instruct me further, telling her, among other things, that it was unlawful as well as unsafe, to teach a slave to read. To use his own words, further, he said, "If you give a nigger an inch, he will take an ell. A nigger should know nothing but to obey his master — to do as he is told to do. Learning would *spoil* the best nigger in the world. Now," said he, "if you teach that nigger (speaking of myself) how to read, there would be no keeping him. It would forever unfit him to be a slave. He would at once become unmanageable, and of no value to his master. As to himself, it could do him no good, but a great deal of harm. It would make him discontented and unhappy." These words sank deep into my heart, stirred up sentiments within that lay slumbering, and called into existence an entirely new train of thought. It was a new and special revelation, explaining dark and mysterious things, with which my youthful understanding had struggled, but struggled in vain. I now understood what had been to me a most perplexing difficulty — to wit, the white man's power to enslave the black man. It was a grand achievement, and I prized it highly. From that moment, I understood the pathway from slavery to freedom. It was just what I wanted, and I got it at a time when I the least expected it. Whilst I was saddened by the thought of losing the aid of my kind mistress, I was gladdened by the invaluable instruction which, by the merest accident, I had gained from my master. Though conscious of the difficulty of learning without a teacher, I set out with high hope, and a fixed purpose, at whatever cost of trouble, to learn how to read. The very decided manner with which he spoke, and strove to impress his wife with the evil consequences of giving me instruction, served to convince me that he was deeply sensible of the truths he was uttering. It gave me the best assurance that I might rely with the utmost confidence on the results which, he said, would flow from teaching me to read. What he most dreaded, that I most desired. What he most loved, that I most hated. That which to him was a great evil, to be carefully shunned, was to me a great good, to be diligently sought; and the argument which he so warmly urged, against my learning to read, only served to inspire me with a desire and determination to learn. In learning to read, I owe almost as much to the bitter opposition of my master, as to the kindly aid of my mistress. I acknowledge the benefit of both. . . .

1

Chapter VII

I lived in Master Hugh's family about seven years. During this time, I succeeded 2 in learning to read and write. In accomplishing this, I was compelled to resort to various stratagems. I had no regular teacher. My mistress, who had kindly commenced to instruct me, had, in compliance with the advice and direction of her husband, not only ceased to instruct, but had set her face against my being instructed by any one else. It is due, however, to my mistress to say of her, that she did not adopt this course of treatment immediately. She at first lacked the depravity indispensable to shutting me up in mental darkness. It was at least necessary for her to have some training in the exercise of irresponsible power, to make her equal to the task of treating me as though I were a brute.

My mistress was, as I have said, a kind and tender-hearted woman; and in 3 the simplicity of her soul she commenced, when I first went to live with her, to treat me as she supposed one human being ought to treat another. In entering upon the duties of a slaveholder, she did not seem to perceive that I sustained to her the relation of a mere chattel, and that for her to treat me as a human being was not only wrong, but dangerously so. Slavery proved as injurious to her as it did to me. When I went there, she was a pious, warm, and tender-hearted woman. There was no sorrow or suffering for which she had not a tear. She had bread for the hungry, clothes for the naked, and comfort for every mourner that came within her reach. Slavery soon proved its ability to divest her of these heavenly qualities. Under its influence, the tender heart became stone, and the lamblike disposition gave way to one of tiger-like fierceness. The first step in her downward course was in her ceasing to instruct me. She now commenced to practise her husband's precepts. She finally became even more violent in her opposition than her husband himself. She was not satisfied with simply doing as well as he had commanded; she seemed anxious to do better. Nothing seemed to make her more angry than to see me with a newspaper. She seemed to think that here lay the danger. I have had her rush at me with a face made all up of fury, and snatch from me a newspaper, in a manner that fully revealed her apprehension. She was an apt woman; and a little experience soon demonstrated, to her satisfaction, that education and slavery were incompatible with each other.

From this time I was most narrowly watched. If I was in a separate room 4 any considerable length of time, I was sure to be suspected of having a book, and was at once called to give an account of myself. All this, however, was too late. The first step had been taken. Mistress, in teaching me the alphabet, had given me the *inch,* and no precaution could prevent me from taking the *ell.*

The plan which I adopted, and the one by which I was most successful, 5 was that of making friends of all the little white boys whom I met in the street. As many of these as I could, I converted into teachers. With their kindly aid, obtained at different times and in different places, I finally succeeded in learning to read. When I was sent on errands, I always took my book with me, and by going one part of my errand quickly, I found time to get a lesson before my return. I used also to carry bread with me, enough of which was always in the house, and to which I was always welcome; for I was much better off in this regard than many of the poor white children in our neighborhood. This bread I used to bestow upon the hungry little urchins, who, in return, would give me that more valuable bread of knowledge. I am strongly tempted to give the names of two or three of those little boys, as a testimonial of the gratitude and affection I bear them; but prudence forbids; — not that it would injure me, but it might embarrass them; for it is almost an unpardonable offence to teach slaves to read in this Christian country. It is enough to say of the dear little fellows, that they lived on Philpot Street, very near Durgin and Bailey's ship-yard. I used to talk this matter of slavery over with them. I would sometimes say to them, I wished I could be as free as they would be when they got to be men. "You will be free as soon as you are twenty-one, *but I am a slave for life!* Have not I as good a right to be free as you have?" These words used to trouble them; they would express for me the liveliest sympathy, and console me with the hope that something would occur by which I might be free.

I was now about twelve years old, and the thought of being *a slave for life*   6 began to bear heavily upon my heart. Just about this time, I got hold of a book entitled "The Columbian Orator." Every opportunity I got, I used to read this book. Among much of other interesting matter, I found in it a dialogue between a master and his slave. The slave was represented as having run away from his master three times. The dialogue represented the conversation which took place between them, when the slave was retaken the third time. In this dialogue, the whole argument in behalf of slavery was brought forward by the master, all of which was disposed of by the slave. The slave was made to say some very smart as well as impressive things in reply to his master — things which had the desired though unexpected effect; for the conversation resulted in the voluntary emanicipation of the slave on the part of the master.

In the same book, I met with one of Sheridan's mighty speeches on and in   7 behalf of Catholic emancipation. These were choice documents to me. I read them over and over again with unabated interest. They gave tongue to interesting thoughts of my own soul, which had frequently flashed through my mind, and died away for want of utterance. The moral which I gained from the dialogue was the power of truth over the conscience of even a slaveholder. What I got from Sheridan was a bold denunciation of slavery, and a powerful vindication of human rights. The reading of these documents enabled me to

utter my thoughts, and to meet the arguments brought forward to sustain
slavery; but while they relieved me of one difficulty, they brought on another
even more painful than the one of which I was relieved. The more I read, the
more I was led to abhor and detest my enslavers. I could regard them in no
other light than a band of successful robbers, who had left their homes, and
gone to Africa, and stolen us from our homes, and in a strange land reduced us
to slavery. I loathed them as being the meanest as well as the most wicked of
men. As I read and contemplated the subject, behold! that very discontentment
which Master Hugh had predicted would follow my learning to read had
already come, to torment and sting my soul to unutterable anguish. As I writhed
under it, I would at times feel that learning to read had been a curse rather
than a blessing. It had given me a view of my wretched condition, without the
remedy. It opened my eyes to the horrible pit, but to no ladder upon which to
get out. In moments of agony, I envied my fellow-slaves for their stupidity. I
have often wished myself a beast. I preferred the condition of the meanest
reptile to my own. Any thing, no matter what, to get rid of thinking! It was this
everlasting thinking of my condition that tormented me. There was no getting
rid of it. It was pressed upon me by every object within sight or hearing,
animate or inanimate. The silver trump of freedom had roused my soul to
eternal wakefulness. Freedom now appeared, to disappear no more forever. It
was heard in every sound, and seen in every thing. It was ever present to
torment me with a sense of my wretched condition. I saw nothing without
seeing it, I heard nothing without hearing it, and felt nothing without feeling it.
It looked from every star, it smiled in every calm, breathed in every wind, and
moved in every storm.

I often found myself regretting my own existence, and wishing myself
dead; and but for the hope of being free, I have no doubt but that I should have
killed myself, or done something for which I should have been killed. While in
this state of mind, I was eager to hear any one speak of slavery. I was a ready
listener. Every little while, I could hear something about the abolitionists. It
was some time before I found what the word meant. It was always used in
such connections as to make it an interesting word to me. If a slave ran away
and succeeded in getting clear, or if a slave killed his master, set fire to a barn,
or did any thing very wrong in the mind of a slaveholder, it was spoken of as
the fruit of *abolition.* Hearing the word in this connection very often, I set
about learning what it meant. The dictionary afforded me little or no help. I
found it was "the act of abolishing;" but then I did not know what was to be
abolished. Here I was perplexed. I did not dare to ask any one about its
meaning, for I was satisfied that it was something they wanted me to know
very little about. After a patient waiting, I got one of our city papers, containing
an account of the number of petitions from the north, praying for the abolition

8

of slavery in the District of Columbia, and of the slave trade between the States. From this time I understood the words *abolition* and *abolitionist,* and always drew near when that word was spoken, expecting to hear something of importance to myself and fellow-slaves. The light broke in upon me by degrees. I went one day down on the wharf of Mr. Waters; and seeing two Irishmen unloading a scow of stone, I went, unasked, and helped them. When we had finished, one of them came to me and asked me if I were a slave. I told him I was. He asked, "Are ye a slave for life?" I told him that I was. The good Irishman seemed to be deeply affected by the statement. He said to the other that it was a pity so fine a little fellow as myself should be a slave for life. He said it was a shame to hold me. They both advised me to run away to the north; that I should find friends there, and that I should be free. I pretended not to be interested in what they said, and treated them as if I did not understand them; for I feared they might be treacherous. White men have been known to encourage slaves to escape, and then, to get the reward, catch them and return them to their masters. I was afraid that these seemingly good men might use me so; but I nevertheless remembered their advice, and from that time I resolved to run away. I looked forward to a time at which it would be safe for me to escape. I was too young to think of doing so immediately; besides, I wished to learn how to write, as I might have occasion to write my own pass. I consoled myself with the hope that I should one day find a good chance. Meanwhile, I would learn to write.

The idea as to how I might learn to write was suggested to me by being in Durgin and Bailey's ship-yard, and frequently seeing the ship carpenters, after hewing, and getting a piece of timber ready for use, write on the timber the name of that part of the ship for which it was intended. When a piece of timber was intended for the larboard side, it would be marked thus — "L." When a piece was for the starboard side, it would be marked thus — "S." A piece for the larboard side forward, would be marked thus — "L.F." When a piece was for starboard side forward, it would be marked thus — "S.F." For larboard aft, it would be marked thus — "L.A." For starboard aft, it would be marked thus — "S.A." I soon learned the names of these letters, and for what they were intended when placed upon a piece of timber in the ship-yard. I immediately commenced copying them, and in a short time was able to make the four letters named. After that, when I met with any boy who I knew could write, I would tell him I could write as well as he. The next word would be, "I don't believe you. Let me see you try it." I would then make the letters which I had been so fortunate as to learn, and ask him to beat that. In this way I got a good many lessons in writing, which it is quite possible I should never have gotten in any other way. During this time, my copy-book was the board fence, brick wall, and pavement; my pen and ink was a lump of chalk. With these, I learned mainly how to write. I then commenced and continued copying the Italics in Webster's Spelling Book, until I could make them all without looking on the book. By this time, my little Master Thomas had gone to school, and learned how to write, and had written over a number of copy-books. These had been brought home, and shown to some of our near neighbors, and then laid aside. My mistress used to go to class meeting at the Wilk Street meeting-house every Monday afternoon, and leave me to take care of the house. When left thus, I used to spend the time in writing in the spaces left in Master Thomas's copy-book, copying what he had written. I continued to do this until I could write a hand very similar to that of Master Thomas. Thus, after a long, tedious effort for years, I finally succeeded in learning how to write.

QUESTIONS ON CONTENT:

1. What single idea unifies these nine paragraphs? Can you state the idea in a single sentence?
2. What great truth about the white person's ability to maintain slavery did Douglass learn, and how did he respond to it?
3. What great moral does Douglass glean from his reading of *The Columbian Orator*?
4. Why did Douglass at one time feel that learning to read had been a curse rather than a blessing? (Douglass is pointing up a *paradox*. See Glossary.)
5. In paragraph five, Douglass relates his experience with his little white friends. Why are the children more sympathetic with Douglass's plight than his mistress?

QUESTIONS ON WRITING STRUCTURE AND STRATEGY:

1. What specific words, phrases, transitions does Douglass utilize to secure coherence (see Glossary) between paragraphs? Note his use of very striking metaphors in paragraph three.
2. Paragraph four ends with a reference to a proverb. What is it?
3. In the last part of the first paragraph, Douglass uses *antithesis* (see Glossary) to point up a paradox. What is the effect of this technique on you as the reader? Is it effective? Why or why not?

QUESTIONS FOR DISCUSSION AND WRITING:.

1. How are people today deliberately kept in ignorance? By individuals? By governments? By institutions? Why is it done? Write a short paper in which you explain your answers.
2. In what ways do people ever keep themselves in ignorance? By rationalizing?

11

By finding scapegoats? By thinking in stereotypes? Write a short paper and explain your answer.

3. Have there been parallels in your life to the paradox that Douglass experienced, namely that learning (or education) can become "a curse rather than a blessing"? In applying for a job? In relations with family, friends? In acquiring new beliefs? Concentrate on a single area and write a paper on your experience.

4. What learning experiences have served to "liberate" you? How? Write a paper in which you describe the experience and explain how it affected you.

ON BECOMING
Eldridge Cleaver

Eldridge Cleaver spent much of his youth in California reform schools before being sentenced to the California State Prison at Soledad for possession of marijuana. There, convinced of the need for an education, he began reading extensively and completed the requirements for his high school diploma. While serving an eight-year sentence in yet another prison, he succeeded in perfecting his writing ability sufficiently to have his essays published in Ramparts magazine and later collected in his best-selling book, Soul on Ice.

In this essay, based on his Folsom Prison reflections, Cleaver explains that he had lost his self-respect and had become a stranger to himself. By writing he was able to save himself, sort out who he was, and determine where he was going. You may find it interesting to compare Cleaver's motives for learning to read and write with those of Douglass. Unlike Douglass, Cleaver had some formal education and did not have to undergo Douglass's ordeal of learning on his own how to read and write. Although their original goals differed somewhat, both eventually put their acquired talents to work helping their fellow human beings.

By society's standards, Cleaver was a social misfit. But alone in his cell with his books, he began in earnest to develop his writing skills and gradually to regain his self-respect.

After I returned to prison, I took a long look at myself and, for the first time in my life, admitted that I was wrong, that I had gone astray — astray not so much from the white man's law as from being human, civilized — for I could not approve the act of rape. Even though I had some insight into my own motivations, I did not feel justified. I lost my self-respect. My pride as a man dissolved and my whole fragile moral structure seemed to collapse, completely shattered. 1

That is why I started to write. To save myself. 2

I realized that no one could save me but myself. The prison authorities were both uninterested and unable to help me. I had to seek out the truth and unravel the snarled web of my motivations. I had to find out who I am and what I want to be, what type of man I should be, and what I could do to become the best of which I was capable. I understood that what had happened to me had also happened to countless other blacks and it would happen to many, many more. 3

I learned that I had been taking the easy way out, running away from problems. I also learned that it is easier to do evil than it is to do good. And I have been terribly impressed by the youth of America, black and white. I am 4

13

proud of them because they have reaffirmed my faith in humanity. I have come to feel what must be love for the young people of America and I want to be part of the good and greatness that they want for all people. From my prison cell, I have watched America slowly coming awake. It is not fully awake yet, but there is soul in the air and everywhere I see beauty. I have watched the sit-ins, the freedom raids, the Mississippi Blood Summers, demonstrations all over the country, the FSM movement, the teach-ins, and the mounting protest over Lyndon Strangelove's foreign policy — all of this, the thousands of little details, show me it is time to straighten up and fly right. That is why I decided to concentrate on my writings and efforts in this area. We are a very sick country — I, perhaps, am sicker than most. But I accept that. I told you in the beginning that I am extremist by nature — so it is only right that I should be extremely sick.

I was very familiar with the Eldridge who came to prison, but that Eldridge   5
no longer exists. And the one I am now is in some ways a stranger to me. You may find this difficult to understand but it is very easy for one in prison to lose his sense of self. And if he has been undergoing all kinds of extreme, involved, and unregulated changes, then he ends up not knowing who he is. Take the point of being attractive to women. You can easily see how a man can lose his arrogance or certainty on that point while in prison! When he's in the free world, he gets constant feedback on how he looks from the number of female heads he turns when he walks down the street. In prison he gets only hate-stares and sour frowns. Years and years of bitter looks. Individuality is not nourished in prison, neither by the officials nor by the convicts. It is a deep hole out of which to climb.

What must be done, I believe, is that all these problems — particularly the   6
sickness between the white woman and the black man — must be brought out into the open, dealt with and resolved. I know that the black man's sick attitude toward the white woman is a revolutionary sickness: it keeps him perpetually out of harmony with the system that is oppressing him. Many whites flatter themselves with the idea that the Negro male's lust and desire for the white dream girl is purely an esthetic attraction, but nothing could be farther from the truth. His motivation is often of such a bloody, hateful, bitter, and malignant nature that whites would really be hard pressed to find it flattering. I have discussed these points with prisoners who were convicted of rape, and their motivations are very plain. But they are very reluctant to discuss these things with white men who, by and large, make up the prison staffs. I believe that in the experience of these men lies the knowledge and wisdom that must be utilized to help other youngsters who are heading in the same direction. I think all of us, the entire nation, will be better off if we bring

it all out front. A lot of people's feelings will be hurt, but that is the price that must be paid.

It may be that I can harm myself by speaking frankly and directly, but I do not care about that at all. Of course I want to get out of prison, badly, but I shall get out some day. I am more concerned with what I am going to be after I get out. I know that by following the course which I have charted I will find my salvation. If I had followed the path laid down for me by the officials, I'd undoubtedly have long since been out of prison—but I'd be less of a man. I'd be weaker and less certain of where I want to go, what I want to do, and how to go about it.

7

The price of hating other human beings is loving oneself less.

QUESTIONS ON CONTENT:

1. Although this selection consists of the seven concluding paragraphs of a longer essay, what is the central, unifying theme or thesis? What kind of detail does Cleaver use to connect his ideas?
2. How do Cleaver's motives for writing compare/contrast with those of Douglass?
3. How does Cleaver explain the loss of one's "sense of self" in prison?
4. What is Cleaver's method of curing his "sickness"?

QUESTIONS ON WRITING STRUCTURE AND STRATEGY:

1. Do the title and the concluding remark hold the essay together? How do other techniques contribute to coherence, such as the use of the first person?
2. What purpose does the ten-word second paragraph serve?
3. What rhetorical devices does Cleaver use? Allusions? Parentheticals? Figurative language? What is their effect? (See Glossary.)
4. Although this selection was originally a part of Cleaver's journals, which passages indicate that Cleaver had an audience other than himself in mind when he rewrote these essays for publication?

QUESTIONS FOR DISCUSSION AND WRITING:

1. Are the motives of Douglass and Cleaver similar to your own motivation? That is to say, are you seeking a kind of "liberation"? Finding yourself? Write a paper and explain.
2. How do the reactions of other people—peers, parents, fellow workers, professors—contribute to your "sense of self"? Reflect on your sense of self

and write a paper in which you explain how the reactions of others have shaped this sense of self.

3. Can you apply Cleaver's cure to what you may consider your own inadequacies? Would keeping a journal help? (See Hoffman, Unit II.)

4. Do a little research in the library and prepare a paper on what you discover about Cleaver's postprison activities.

5. How does this selection reflect the time in which it was written (1965)? (See William L. O'Neill, *Coming Apart,* Chapter 6, "From Civil Rights to Black Power.")

MARTIN EDEN
Jack London

Martin Eden is fiction, but much of the novel is based on Jack London's own experiences. In fact, at one time London remarked, "I was Martin Eden." Although autobiographical novels are never wholly literal translations of a person's life into fiction, the following excerpt dealing with Martin's early reading and decision to write closely parallels London's experience. The illegitimate son of an astrologist mother and a spiritualist father, young London struggled through his early years in the depths of poverty, drifting from one menial job to another as a seaman, a factory worker, and an oyster pirate. As a consequence, his schooling was sporadic, but his reading was voracious.

In the novel, Martin Eden's motivations differ from those of Cleaver, Hoffer, and Malcolm X, yet probably in the end love is the greatest prime mover. In this case love for a beautiful woman is coupled with an attempt to improve himself and to rise socially. Once hooked on books, Martin is a slave to the same reading compulsion experienced by the other writers in this section. Frustrated by the lack of "the thought tools with which to think," he zeroes in on the dictionary, eager — as was Malcolm X — to develop his vocabulary. The reader will quickly observe that Martin's ineptness with language is matched by his awkwardness in the social graces, two drawbacks which Martin Eden is determined to overcome.

Because the possibility of formal schooling is out of the question for Martin, he eagerly sets about educating himself. Championing a thorough education, Ruth urges him first to master the fundamentals of grammar, and immediately points out several errors common even to present-day speakers and writers.

London's primary purpose in fiction is to entertain and his secondary one is to teach. To accomplish his primary purpose, he must employ suspense, compose believable dialogue, and convince us that Martin's education is real by challenging us with his own vocabulary and Martin's expanding one.

Chapter VII

A week of heavy reading had passed since the evening he first met Ruth   1
Morse, and still he dared not call. Time and again he nerved himself up to call,
but under the doubts that assailed him his determination died away. He did not

know the proper time to call, nor was there anyone to tell him, and he was afraid of committing himself to an irretrievable blunder. Having shaken himself free from his old companions and old ways of life, and having no new companions, nothing remained for him but to read, and the long hours he devoted to it would have ruined a dozen pairs of ordinary eyes. But his eyes were strong, and they were backed by a body superbly strong. Furthermore, his mind was fallow. It had lain fallow all his life, so far as the abstract thought of the books was concerned, and it was ripe for the sowing. It had never been jaded by study, and it bit hold of the knowledge in the books with sharp teeth that would not let go.

It seemed to him, by the end of the week, that he had lived centuries, so far behind were the old life and outlook. But he was baffled by lack of preparation. He attempted to read books that required years of preliminary specialization. One day he would read a book of antiquated philosophy, and the next day one that was ultra-modern, so that his head would be whirling with the conflict and contradiction of ideas. It was the same with the economists. On the one shelf at the library he found Karl Marx, Ricardo, Adam Smith, and Mill, and the abstruse formulas of the one gave no clue that the ideas of another were obsolete. He was bewildered, and yet he wanted to know. He had become interested, in a day, in economics, industry, and politics. Passing through the City Hall Park, he had noticed a group of men, in the centre of which were half a dozen, with flushed faces and raised voices, earnestly carrying on a discussion. He joined the listeners, and heard a new alien tongue in the mouths of the philosophers of the people. One was a tramp, another was a labour agitator, a third was a law-school student, and the remainder was composed of wordy working-men. For the first time he heard of Socialism, anarchism, and single tax, and learned that there were warring social philosophies. He heard hundreds of technical words that were new to him, belonging to fields of thought that his meagre reading had never touched upon. Because of this he could not follow the arguments closely, and he could only guess at and surmise the ideas wrapped up in such strange expressions. Then there was a black-eyed restaurant waiter, who was a theosophist, a union baker who was an agnostic, an old man who baffled all of them with the strange philosophy that *what is, is right,* and another old man who discoursed interminably about the cosmos, and the father-atom, and the mother-atom.

Martin Eden's head was in a state of addlement when he went away after several hours, and he hurried to the library to look up the definitions of a dozen unusual words. And when he left the library he carried under his arm four volumes: Madame Blavatsky's 'Secret Doctrine', 'Progress and Poverty', 'The Quintessence of Socialism', and 'Warfare of Religion and Science'. Unfortunately, he began on the 'Secret Doctrine'. Every line bristled with

2

3

18

many-syllabled words he did not understand. He sat up in bed, and the dictionary was in front of him more often than the book. He looked up so many new words that, when they recurred, he had forgotten their meaning, and had to look them up again. He devised the plan of writing the definitions in a notebook, and filled page after page with them. And still he could not understand. He read until three in the morning, and his brain was in a turmoil, but not one essential thought in the text had he grasped. He looked up, and it seemed that the room was lifting, heeling, and plunging like a ship upon the sea. Then he hurled the 'Secret Doctrine' and many curses across the room, turned off the gas, and composed himself to sleep. Nor did he have much better luck with the other three books. It was not that his brain was weak or incapable; it could think these thoughts were it not for the lack of training in thinking and lack of the thought-tools with which to think. He guessed this, and for a while entertained the idea of reading nothing but the dictionary, until he had mastered every word of it.

Poetry, however, was his solace, and he read much of it, finding his greatest joy in the simpler poets, who were more understandable. He loved beauty, and there he found beauty. Poetry, like music, stirred him profoundly; and though he did not know it, he was preparing his mind for the heavier work that was to come. The pages of his mind were blank, and, without effort, much he read and liked, stanza by stanza, was impressed upon those pages, so that he was soon able to extract great joy from chanting aloud or under his breath the music and the beauty of the printed words he had read. Then he stumbled upon Gayley's 'Classic Myths' and Bullfinch's 'Age of Fable' side by side on a library shelf. It was illumination, a great light in the darkness of his ignorance, and he read poetry more avidly than ever.

The man at the desk in the library had seen Martin there so often, that he had become quite pleasant, always greeting him with a smile and a nod when he entered. It was because of this that Martin did a daring thing. Drawing some books at the desk, and while the man was stamping the cards, Martin blurted out:

'Say, there's something I'd like to ask you.'

The man smiled and paid attention.

'When you meet a young lady an' she asks you to call, how soon can you call?'

Martin felt his shirt press and cling to his shoulders what of the sweat of the effort.

'Why, I'd say any time,' the man answered.

'Yes, but this is different,' Martin objected. 'She . . . I . . . well, you see, it's this way: maybe she won't be there. She goes to the University.'

'Then call again.'

'What I said ain't what I meant,' Martin confessed falteringly, whilst he made up his mind to throw himself wholly upon the other's mercy. 'I'm just a rough sort of a fellow, an' I ain't never seen anything of society. This girl is all that I ain't, an' I ain't anything that she is. You don't think I'm playin' the fool, do you?' he demanded abruptly.

'No, no; not at all, I assure you,' the other protested. 'Your request is not exactly in the scope of the reference department, but I shall be only too pleased to assist you.'

Martin looked at him admiringly.

'If I could tear it off that way, I'd be all right,' he said.

'I beg pardon?'

'I mean, if I could talk easy that way, an' polite, an' all the rest.'

'Oh!' said the other with comprehension.

'What is the best time to call? The afternoon—not too close to meal-time? Or the evening? Or Sunday?'

'I'll tell you,' the librarian said, with a brightening face. 'You call her up on the telephone and find out.'

'I'll do it,' he said, picking up his books and starting away. He turned back and asked: 'When you're speakin' to a young lady—say, for instance, Miss Lizzie Smith—do you say "Miss Lizzie", or "Miss Smith"?'

'Say "Miss Smith",' the librarian stated authoritatively. 'Say—"Miss Smith" always—until you come to know her better.'

So it was that Martin Eden solved the problem.

'Come down any time; I'll be at home all afternoon,' was Ruth's reply over the telephone to his stammered request as to when he could return the borrowed books.

She met him at the door herself, and her woman's eye took in immediately the creased trousers, and the certain, slight, but indefinable, change in him for the better. . . .

Once they were seated in the living-room, he began to get on easily—more easily by far than he had expected. She made it easy for him, and the gracious spirit with which she did it made him love her more madly than ever. They talked first of the borrowed books, of the Swinburne he was devoted to, and of the Browning he did not understand; and she led the conversation on from subject to subject, while she pondered the problem of how she could be of help to him. She had thought of this often since their first meeting. She wanted to help him. He made a call upon her pity and tenderness that no one had ever made before, and the pity was not so much derogatory of him as maternal in her. Her pity could not be of the common sort, when the man who drew it was so much man as to shock her with maidenly fears, and set her mind and pulse thrilling with strange thoughts and feelings. The old fascination of his neck was there, and there was sweetness in the thought of laying her hands upon it. It seemed still a wanton impulse, but she had grown more used to it. She did not dream that in such guise new-born love would epitomize itself. Nor did she dream that the feeling he excited in her was love. She thought she was merely interested in him as an unusual type possessing various potential excellences, and she even felt philanthropic about it.

She did not know she desired him; but with him it was different. He knew   9
that he loved her, and he desired her as he had never before desired anything in his life. He had loved poetry for beauty's sake; but since he met her the gates to the vast field of love-poetry had been opened wide. She had given him understanding even more than Bullfinch and Gayley. There was a line that a week before he would not have favoured with a second thought — 'God's own mad lover dying on a kiss'; but now it was ever insistent in his mind. He marvelled at the wonder of it and the truth; and as he gazed upon her he knew that he could die gladly upon a kiss. He felt himself God's own mad lover, and no accolade of knighthood could have given him greater pride. And at last he knew the meaning of life, and why he had been born. . . .

The problem in the background of her consciousness was how to help   10
him, and she turned the conversation in that direction; but it was Martin who came to the point first.

'I wonder if I can get some advice from you,' he began, and received an acquiescence   11
of willingness that made his heart bound. 'You remember the other time I was here I said I couldn't talk about books and things because I didn't know how? Well, I've ben doin' a lot of thinkin' ever since. I've ben to the library a whole lot, but most of the books I've tackled have ben over my head. Mebbe I'd better begin at the beginnin'. I ain't never had no advantages. I've worked pretty hard ever since I was a kid, an' since I've ben to the library, lookin' with new eyes at books — an' lookin' at new books, too — I've just about concluded that I ain't ben reading the right kind. You know the books you find in cattle-camps an' fo'c's'ls ain't the same you've got in this house, for instance. Well, that's the sort of readin' matter I've ben accustomed to. And yet — an' I ain't just makin' a brag of it — I've ben different from the people I've herded with. Not that I'm any better than the sailors an' cow-punchers I travelled with — I was cow-punchin' for a short time, you know — but I always liked books, read everything I could lay my hands on, an' . . . well, I guess I think differently from most of 'em.

'Now, to come to what I'm drivin' at. I was never inside a house like this. When I come a week ago, an' saw all this, an' you, an' your mother, an' brothers, an' everything — well, I liked it. I'd heard about such things, an' read about such things in some of the books, an' when I looked around at your house — why, the books come true. But the thing I'm after is I liked it. I wanted it. I want it now. I want to breathe air like you get in this house — air that is filled with books, and pictures, and beautiful things, where people talk in low voices, an' are clean, an' their thoughts are clean. The air I always breathed was mixed up with grub, an' house-rent, an' scrappin', an' booze, an' that's all they talked about, too. Why, when you was crossin' the room to kiss your mother I thought it was the most beautiful thing I ever seen. I've seen a whole lot of life, an' somehow I've seen a whole lot more of it than most of them that was with me. I like to see, an' I want to see more, an' I want to see it different.

'But I ain't got to the point yet. Here it is: I want to make my way to the kind of life you have in this house. There's more in life than booze, an' hard work, an' knockin' about. Now, how am I goin' to get it? Where do I take hold an' begin? I'm willin' to work my passage, you know, an' I can make most men sick when it comes to hard work. Once I get started, I'll work night an' day. Mebbe you think it's funny, me askin' you about all this. I know you're the last person in the world I ought to ask, but I don't know anybody else I could ask . . . unless it's Arthur. Mebbe I ought to ask him. If I was . . . '

His voice died away. His firmly planned intention had come to a halt on the verge of the horrible probability that he should have asked Arthur, and that he had made a fool of himself. Ruth did not speak immediately. She was too absorbed in striving to reconcile the stumbling, uncouth speech and its simplicity of thought with what she saw in his face. She had never looked in eyes that expressed greater power. Here was a man who could do anything, was the message she read there, and it accorded ill with the weakness of his spoken thought. And, for that matter, so complex and quick was her own mind that she did not have a just appreciation of simplicity. And yet she had caught an impression of power in the very groping of this mind. It had seemed to her like a giant writhing and straining at the bonds that held him down. Her face was all sympathy when she did speak.

'What you need you realize yourself, and it is education. You should go back and finish grammar-school, and then go through the high-school and University.'

'But that takes money,' he interrupted.

'Oh!' she cried, 'I had not thought of that. But, then, you have relatives — somebody who could assist you?'

He shook his head.

'My father and mother are dead. I've two sisters — one married, an' the other'll get married soon, I suppose. Then I've a string of brothers — I'm the youngest — but they never helped nobody. They've just knocked around over the world, lookin' out for number one. The oldest died in India. Two are in South Africa now, an' another's on a whaling voyage, an' one's travelin' with a circus — he does trapeze work. An' I guess I'm just like them. I've taken care myself since I was eleven — that's when my mother died. I've got to study by myself I guess, an' what I want to know is where to begin.'

'I should say the first thing of all would be to get a grammar. Your grammar is . . . ' She intended saying 'awful', but she amended it to, 'is not particularly good.'

He flushed and sweated.

'I know I must talk a lot of slang an' words you don't understand. But, then, they're the only words I know . . . how to speak. I've got other words in my mind—picked 'em up from books—but I can't pronounce 'em, so I don't use 'em.'

'It isn't what you say so much as how you say it. You don't mind my being frank, do you? I don't want to hurt you.'

'No, no!' he cried; while he secretly blessed her for her kindness. 'Fire away. I've got to know, an' I'd sooner know from you than anybody else.'

'Well, then, you say "You was"; it should be "You were". You say "I seen" for "I saw". You use the double negative_____'

'What's the double negative?' he demanded, then added humbly: 'You see, I don't even understand your explanations.'

'I'm afraid I didn't explain that,' she smiled. 'A double negative is . . . let me see . . . well, you say, "Never helped nobody". "Never" is a negative. "Nobody" is another negative. It is a rule that two negatives make a positive. "Never helped nobody" means that, not helping nobody, they must have helped somebody.'

'That's pretty clear,' he said. 'I never thought of it before. But it don't mean they *must* have helped somebody, does it? Seems to me that "never helped nobody" just naturally fails to say whether or not they helped somebody. I never thought of it before, and I'll never say it again.'

She was pleased and surprised with the quickness and surety of his mind. As soon as he had got the clue, he not only understood, but corrected her error.

'You'll find it all in the grammar,' she went on. 'There's something else I noticed in your speech. You say "don't" when you shouldn't. "Don't" is a contraction, and stands for two words. Do you know them?'

He thought a moment, then answered: '"Do not".'

She nodded her head, and said: 'And you use "don't" when you mean "does not".'

He was puzzled over this, and did not get it so quickly.

'Give me an illustration,' he asked.

'Well. . . .' She puckered her brows and pursed up her mouth as she thought, while he looked on, and decided that her expression was most adorable. '"It don't do to be hasty." Change "don't" to "do not", and it reads, "It do not do to be hasty", which is perfectly absurd.'

He turned it over in his mind and considered.

'Doesn't it jar on your ear?' she suggested.

'Can't say that it does,' he replied judicially.

'Why didn't you say, "Can't say that it do"?' she queried.

'That sounds wrong,' he said slowly. 'As for the other, I can't make up my mind. I guess my ear ain't had the trainin' yours has.'

23

'There is no such word as "ain't",' she said, prettily emphatic.

Martin flushed again.

'And you say "ben" for "been",' she continued; '"I come" for "I came"; and the way you chop your endings is something dreadful.'

'How do you mean?' He leaned forward, feeling that he ought to get down on his knees before so marvellous a mind. 'How do I chop?'

'You don't complete the endings. "A-n-d" spells "and." You pronounce it "an".'
"I-n-g" spells "ing". Sometimes you pronounce it "ing", and sometimes you leave off the "g". And then you slur by dropping initial letters and diphthongs. "T-h-e-m" spells "them". You pronounce it—oh, well, it is not necessary to go over all of them. What you need is the grammar. I'll get one and show you how to begin.'

As she arose, there shot through his mind something that he had read in the etiquette books, and he stood up awkwardly, worrying as to whether he was doing the right thing, and fearing that she might take it as a sign that he was about to go.

'By the way, Mr. Eden,' she called back, as she was leaving the room, 'what is *booze?* You used it several times, you know.'

'Oh, booze,' he laughed. 'It's slang. It means whiskey and beer—anything that will make you drunk.'

'And another thing,' she laughed back. 'Don't use "you" when you are impersonal. "You" is very personal, and your use of it just now was not precisely what you meant.'

'I don't just see that.'

'Why, you just now said to me, "whiskey and beer—anything that will make you drunk"—make *me* drunk, don't you see?'

'Well, it would, wouldn't it?'

'Yes, of course,' she smiled. 'But it would be nicer not to bring me into it. Substitute "one" for "you", and see how much better it sounds.'

When she returned with the grammar, she drew a chair near his—he wondered if he should have helped her with the chair—and sat down beside him. She turned the pages of the grammar, and their heads were inclined towards each other. He could hardly follow her outlining of the work he must do, so amazed was he by her delightful propinquity. But when she began to lay down the importance of conjugation, he forgot all about her. He had never heard of conjugation, and was fascinated by the glimpse he was catching into the tie-ribs of language. He leaned closer to the page, and her hair touched his cheek. He had fainted but once in his life, and he thought he was going to faint then. He could scarcely breathe, and his heart was pounding the blood up into his throat and suffocating him. Never had she seemed so accessible as now. For the moment the great gulf that separated them was bridged. But there was no

24

diminution in the loftiness of his feeling for her. She had not descended to him. It was he who had been caught up into the clouds and carried to her. His reverence for her in that moment was of the same order as religious awe and fervour. It seemed to him that he had intruded upon the holy of holies, and slowly and carefully he moved his head aside from the contact which thrilled him like an electric shock, and of which she had not been aware.

Chapter IX

Back from sea Martin Eden came, homing for California with a lover's desire. 18
His store of money exhausted, he had shipped before the mast on the treasure-hunting schooner; and Solomon Islands, after eight months of failure to find treasure, had witnessed the breaking up of the expedition. The men had been paid off in Australia and Martin had immediately shipped on a deep-water vessel for San Francisco. Not alone had those eight months earned him enough money to stay on land for many weeks, but they had enabled him to do a great deal of studying and reading.

His was the student's mind, and behind his ability to learn was the 19
indomitability of his nature and his love for Ruth. The grammar he had taken along he went through again and again, until his unjaded brain had mastered it. He noticed the bad grammar used by his shipmates, and made a point of mentally correcting and reconstructing their crudities of speech. To his great joy he discovered that his ear was becoming sensitive, and that he was developing grammatical nerves. A double negative jarred him like a discord, and often, from lack of practice, it was from his own lips that the jar came. His tongue refused to learn new tricks in a day.

After he had been through the grammar repeatedly, he took up the 20
dictionary, and added twenty words a day to his vocabulary. He found that this was no light task, and at wheel or lookout he steadily went over and over his lengthening list of pronunciations and definitions while he invariably memorized himself to sleep. 'Never did anything', 'if I were', and 'those things', were phrases, with many variations, that he repeated under his breath, in order to accustom his tongue to the language spoken by Ruth. 'And' and 'ing', with the 'd' and 'g' pronounced emphatically, he went over thousands of times, and, to his surprise, he noticed that he was beginning to speak cleaner and correcter English than the officers themselves and the gentlemen-adventurers in the cabin who had financed the expedition.

The captain was a fishy-eyed Norwegian, who somehow had fallen into 21
possession of a complete Shakespeare, which he never read, and Martin had washed his clothes for him, and in return had been permitted access to the precious volumes. For a time, so steeped was he in the plays and in the many

favourite passages that impressed themselves almost without effort on his brain, that all the world seemed to shape itself into forms of Elizabethan tragedy or comedy, and his very thoughts were in blank verse. It trained his ear, and gave him a fine appreciation for noble English; withal it introduced into his mind much that was archaic and obsolete.

The eight months had been well spent, and, in addition to what he had learned of right speaking and high thinking, he had learned much of himself. Along with his humbleness, because he knew so little, there arose a conviction of power. He felt a sharp gradation between himself and his shipmates, and was wise enough to realize that the difference lay in potentiality rather than achievement. What he could do, they could do; but within him he felt a confused ferment working that told him there was more in him than he had done. He was tortured by the exquisite beauty of the world, and wished that Ruth were there to share it with him. He decided that he would describe to her many of the bits of South Sea beauty. The creative spirit in him flamed up at the thought, and urged that he re-create this beauty for a wider audience than Ruth. And then, in splendour and glory, came the great idea. He would write. He would be one of the eyes through which the world saw, one of the ears through which it heard, one of the hearts through which it felt. He would write — everything — poetry and prose, fiction and description, and plays like Shakespeare. There was career and the way to win to Ruth. The men of literature were the world's giants, and he conceived them to be far finer than the Mr. Butlers who earned thirty thousand a year, and could be Supreme Court justices if they wanted to.

Once the idea had germinated, it mastered him, and the return voyage to San Francisco was like a dream. He was drunken with unguessed power, and felt that he could do anything. In the midst of the great and lonely sea he gained perspective. Clearly, and for the first time, he saw Ruth and her world. It was all visualized in his mind as a concrete thing, which he could take up in his two hands and turn around and about and examine. There was much that was dim and nebulous in that world, but he saw it as a whole, and not in detail, and he saw, also, the way to master it. To write! The thought was fire in him. He would begin as soon as he got back. The first thing he would do would be to describe the voyage of the treasure-hunters. He would sell it to some San Francisco newspaper. He would not tell Ruth anything about it, and she would be surprised and pleased when she saw his name in print. While he wrote he could go on studying. There were twenty-four hours in each day. He was invincible. He knew how to work, and the citadels would go down before him. He would not have to go to sea again — as a sailor; and for the instant he caught a vision of a steam yacht. There were other writers who possessed steam yachts. Of course, he cautioned himself, it would be slow succeeding at first, and for a time he would be content to earn enough money by his writing to enable him to go on studying. And then, after some time—a very indeterminate time—when he had learned and prepared himself, he would write the great things, and his name would be on all men's lips. But, greater than that—infinitely greater and greatest of all—he would have proved himself worthy of Ruth. Fame was all very well, but it was for Ruth that his splendid dream arose. He was not a fame-monger, but merely one of God's mad lovers.

Arrived in Oakland, with his snug pay-day in his pocket, he took up his old room at Bernard Higginbotham's and set to work. He did not even let Ruth know he was back. He would go and see her when he finished the article on the treasure-hunters. It was not so difficult to abstain from seeing her, because of the violent heat of creative fever that burned in him. Besides, the very article he was writing would bring her nearer to him. He did not know how long an article he should write, but he counted the words in a double-page article in the Sunday supplement of the *San Francisco Examiner,* and guided himself by that. Three days, at white heat, completed his narrative; but when he had copied it carefully, in a large scrawl that was easy to read, he learned from a rhetoric he picked up in the library that there were such things as paragraphs and quotation marks. He had never thought of such things before, and he promptly set to work writing the article over, referring continually to the pages of the rhetoric, and learning more in a day about composition than the average schoolboy in a year. When he had copied the article a second time and rolled it up carefully, he read in a newspaper an item on hints to beginners, and discovered the iron law that manuscripts should never be rolled, and that they should be written on one side of the paper. He had violated the law on both counts. Also, he learned from the item that first-class papers paid a minimum of ten dollars a column. So, while he copied the manuscript a third time, he consoled himself by multiplying ten columns by ten dollars. The product was always the same—one hundred dollars—and he decided that that was better than seafaring. If it hadn't been for his blunders, he would have finished the article in three days. One hundred dollars in three days! It would have taken him three months and longer on the sea to earn a similar amount. A man was a fool to go to sea when he could write, he concluded, though the money in itself meant nothing to him. Its value was in the liberty it would get him, the presentable garments it would buy him, all of which would bring him nearer—swiftly nearer—to the slender, pale girl who had turned his life back upon itself and given him inspiration.

He mailed the manuscript in a flat envelope, and addressed it to the editor of the *San Francisco Examiner.* He had an idea that anything accepted by a paper was published immediately, and as he had sent the manuscript in on Friday he expected it to come out on the following Sunday. He conceived that

27

it would be fine to let that event apprise Ruth of his return. Then, Sunday afternoon, he would call and see her. In the meantime he was occupied by another idea, which he prided himself upon as being a particularly sane, careful, and modest idea. He would write an adventure story for the boys, and sell it to the *Youth's Companion*. He went to the free reading-room and looked through the files of the *Youth's Companion*. Serial stores, he found, were usually published in that weekly in five installments of about three thousand words each. He discovered several serials that ran to seven installments, and decided to write one of that length.

He had been on a whaling voyage in the Arctic once — a voyage that was to have been for three years and which had terminated in shipwreck at the end of six months. While his imagination was fanciful, even fantastic at times, he had a basic love of reality that compelled him to write about the things he knew. He knew whaling, and out of the real materials of his knowledge he proceeded to manufacture the fictitious adventures of the two boys he intended to use as joint-heroes. It was easy work, he decided on Saturday evening. He had completed on that day the first installment of three thousand words — much to the amusement of Jim, and to the open derision of Mr Higginbotham, who sneered throughout meal-time at the 'litery' person they had discovered in the family.   26

Martin contented himself by picturing his brother-in-law's surprise on Sunday morning when he opened his *Examiner* and saw the article on the treasure-hunters. Early that morning he was out himself to the front-door, nervously racing through the many-sheeted newspaper. He went through it a second time very carefully, then folded it up and left it where he had found it. He was glad he had not told anyone about his article. On second thoughts, he concluded that he had been wrong about the speed with which things found their way into newspaper columns. Besides, there had not been any news value in his article, and most likely the editor would write to him about it first.   27

After breakfast he went on with his serial. The words flowed from his pen, though he broke off from the writing frequently to look up definitions in the dictionary or to refer to the rhetoric. He often read or re-read a chapter at a time during such pauses; and he consoled himself that while he was not writing the great things he felt to be in him, he was learning composition, at any rate, and training himself to shape up and express his thoughts. He toiled on till dark, when he went out to the reading-room and explored magazines and weeklies until the place closed at ten o'clock. This was his programme for a week. Each day he did three thousand words, and each evening he puzzled his way through the magazines, taking note of the stories, articles, and poems that editors saw fit to publish. One thing was certain. What these multitudinous writers did he could do, and only give him time, and he would do what they   28 could not do. He was cheered to read in *Book News,* in a paragraph on the payment of magazine writers, not that Rudyard Kipling receive a dollar a word, but that the minimum rate paid by first-class magazines was two cents a word. The *Youth's Companion* was certainly first-class, and at that rate the three thousand words he had written that day would bring him sixty dollars—two months' wages on the sea!

On Friday night he finished the serial—twenty-one thousand words long. At two cents a word, he calculated, that would bring him four hundred and twenty dollars—not a bad week's work. It was more money than he had ever possessed at one time. He did not know how he could spend it all. He had tapped a goldmine. Where this came from he could always get more. He planned to buy some more clothes, to subscribe to many magazines, and to buy dozens of reference-books that at present he was compelled to go to the library to consult. And still there was a large portion of the four hundred and twenty dollars unspent. This worried him until the thought came to him of hiring a servant for Gertrude and of buying a bicycle for Marian. 29

He mailed the bulky manuscript to the *Youth's Companion,* and on Saturday afternoon, after having planned an article on pearl-diving, he went to see Ruth. He had telephoned, and she went herself to greet him at the door. The old familiar blaze of health rushed out from him and struck her like a blow. It seemed to enter into her body and course through her veins in a liquid glow, and to set her quivering with its imparted strength. He flushed warmly as he took her hand and looked into her blue eyes, but the fresh bronze of eight months of sun hid the flush, though it did not protect the neck from the gnawing chafe of the stiff collar. She noted the red line of it with amusement, which quickly vanished as she glanced at his clothes. They really fitted him—it was his first made-to-order suit—and he seemed slimmer and better modelled. In addition, his cloth cap had been replaced by a soft hat, which she commanded him to put on, and then complimented him on his appearance. She did not remember when she had felt so happy. This change in him was her handiwork, and she was proud of it, and fired with ambition further to help him. 30

But the most radical change of all, and the one that pleased her most, was the change in his speech. Not only did he speak more correctly, but he spoke more easily, and there were many new words in his vocabulary. When he grew excited or enthusiastic, however, he dropped back into the old slurring and the dropping of final consonants. Also, there was an awkward hesitancy at times, as he essayed the new words he had learned. On the other hand, along with his ease of expression, he displayed a lightness and facetiousness of thought that delighted her. It was his old spirit of humour and badinage that had made him a favourite in his own class, but which he had hitherto been unable to use in her presence through lack of words and training. He was just beginning to 31 orientate himself, and to feel that he was not wholly an intruder. But he was very tentative — fastidiously so — letting Ruth set the pace of sprightliness and fancy, keeping up with her, but never daring to go beyond her.

He told her of what he had been doing, and of his plan to write for a livelihood, and of going on with his studies. But he was disappointed at her lack of approval. She did not think much of his plan.

32

'You see,' she said frankly, 'writing must be a trade, like anything else. Not that I know anything about it, of course. I only bring common judgment to bear. You couldn't hope to be a blacksmith without spending three years at learning the trade — or is it five years? Now, writers are so much better paid than blacksmiths that there must be ever so many more men who would like to write, who . . . try to write.'

'But, then, may not I be peculiarly constituted to write?' he queried, secretly exulting at the language he had used, his swift imagination throwing the whole scene and atmosphere upon a vast screen along with a thousand other scenes from his life — scenes that were rough and raw, gross and bestial. . . .

'But no matter how peculiarly constituted a man may be for blacksmithing,' she was laughing, 'I never heard of one becoming a blacksmith without first serving his apprenticeship.'

'What would you advise?' he asked. 'And don't forget that I feel in me this capacity to write — I can't explain it; I just know that it is in me.'

'You must get a thorough education,' was the answer, 'whether or not you ultimately become a writer. This education is indispensable for whatever career you select, and it must not be slipshod or sketchy. You should go to high-school.'

'Yes —' he began; but she interrupted with an after-thought:

'Of course, you could go on with your writing, too.'

'I would have to,' he said grimly.

'Why?' She looked at him, prettily puzzled, for she did not quite like the persistence with which he clung to his notion.

'Because, without writing there wouldn't be any high-school. I must live and buy books and clothes, you know.'

'I'd forgotten that,' she laughed. 'Why weren't you born with an income?'

'I'd rather have good health and imagination,' he answered. 'I can make good on the income, but the other things have to be made good for —' He almost said 'you', then amended his sentence to 'have to be made good for one'.

'Don't say "make good,"' she cried, sweetly petulant. 'It's slang, and it's horrid.'

He flushed, and stammered: 'That's right, and I only wish you'd correct me every time.'

'I . . . I'd like to,' she said haltingly. 'You have so much in you that is good that I want to see you perfect.'

33

He was clay in her hands immediately, as passionately desirous of being   34
moulded by her as she was desirous of shaping him into the image of her ideal
of man. And when she pointed out the opportuneness of the time, that the
entrance examinations to high-school began on the following Monday, he
promptly volunteered that he would take them.

Then she played and sang to him, while he gazed with hungry yearning at   35
her, drinking in her loveliness, and marvelling that there should not be a
hundred suitors listening there, and longing for her as he listened and longed.

QUESTIONS ON CONTENT:

1. How do the "philosophers of the people" motivate Martin Eden to read? What
    problems does he encounter when he begins to read about the philosophies he
    has heard discussed, and what is he forced to do?
2. At what point does Martin Eden's obsession with reading evolve into the
    desire to write? What does he seek to gain through his writing?
3. What part does the library play in Martin's social and academic education?

QUESTIONS ON WRITING STRUCTURE AND STRATEGY:

1. Chapter VII is told largely through dialogue, and Chapter IX is largely narra-
    tion. Which method is easier to apprehend? Why?
2. In Chapter VII London contrasts Martin's speech against Ruth's to show
    social distance. What does London intend to convey by Martin's speech in
    Chapter IX? How does he succeed?
3. In the first paragraph of Chapter VII, London employs a series of metaphors to
    comment on Martin's mind. What is London alternately comparing Martin's
    mind to? Do you think London is effective? Why?

QUESTIONS FOR DISCUSSION AND WRITING:

1. London's account of Martin's first few meetings with Ruth are passionate, an
    attempt to render in prose that first intense feeling of a young man for a young
    woman. Try a journal entry in which you "fictionalize," including authentic
    dialogue, your own similar experience.
2. Start a section in your journal where you enter the new words you encounter
    in your reading. Enter the definitions, the sentences in which they appear, and
    several sentences of your own composition using the new words.

3. How is the fictional Martin Eden's expanded vocabulary reflected in London's own writing? Compare the two Martins revealed in Chapters VII and IX.

4. Try a prewriting exercise (timed writing, brainstorming, listing) in which you examine your experience to find possible areas of expertise: cooking, athletics, fishing, hunting, music, collecting, and so on. Develop a short paper from your experiment.

5. Contrast Martin's courtship of Ruth with contemporary courtship examples —from your own experience, from television, or from the movies.

WORDS, WORDS, WORDS
Malcolm X

Malcolm X was the most charismatic of the black nationalist leaders during the turbulent 1960s. As the leading spokesman for the Black Muslims, he preached a doctrine of rigid racial separation and reparation, a program diametrically opposed to that advanced by the Reverend Martin Luther King, Jr. (Unit III). In time, however, Malcolm X broke with the Black Muslims. A pilgrimage to Mecca followed, at which time Malcolm X underwent a religious conversion revealing to him the spiritual unit of all mankind. He returned to America and founded his own organization to further the aims of racial brotherhood. It was during this period that he dictated his Autobiography *to Alex Haley (of* Roots *fame). Shortly thereafter he was assassinated in New York City.*

The excerpt from his Autobiography *that follows serves to underscore the importance of motivation to learning, a relationship illustrated in the two preceding selections. Recognizing the inadequacies of his eighth-grade education and his jive, street lingo, Malcolm X resolved in prison to overcome his background by pursuing "some kind of homemade education." What began so inauspiciously as a chore quickly became a challenge and finally a lifetime fascination with reading and learning: "I could spend the rest of my life reading, just satisfying my curiosity." Books not only opened up a whole new world to Malcolm X but eventually altered the course of his life.*

In tracing Malcom X's struggle to gain an education, some of you may identify with his desperate need to be able to express himself, with his admiration for well-read acquaintances, and with his efforts to acquire an extensive vocabulary. So greatly convinced was he of the importance of an extensive vocabulary that he went to the extraordinary lengths described here to acquire one. You may also be struck by Malcolm X's indomitable persistence and his burgeoning curiosity.

It was because of my letters that I happened to stumble upon starting to   1
acquire some kind of homemade education.

I became increasingly frustrated at not being able to express what I   2
wanted to convey in letters that I wrote, especially those to Mr. Elijah
Muhammad. In the street, I had been the most articulate hustler out there — I
had commanded attention when I said something. But now, trying to write
simple English, I not only wasn't articulate, I wasn't even functional. How
would I sound writing in slang, the way I would *say* it, something such as,
"Look, daddy, let me pull your coat about a cat, Elijah Muhammad —"

Many who today hear me somewhere in person, or on television, or those   3
who read something I've said, will think I went to school far beyond the eighth
grade. This impression is due entirely to my prison studies.

It had really begun back in the Charlestown Prison, when Bimbi first made   4
me feel envy of his stock of knowledge. Bimbi had always taken charge of any
conversations he was in, and I had tried to emulate him. But every book I
picked up had few sentences which didn't contain anywhere from one to
nearly all of the words that might as well have been in Chinese. When I just
skipped those words, of course, I really ended up with little idea of what the
book said. So I had come to the Norfolk Prison Colony still going through only
book-reading motions. Pretty soon, I would have quit even these motions,
unless I had received the motivation that I did.

I saw that the best thing I could do was to get hold of a dictionary — to   5
study, to learn some words. I was lucky enough to reason also that I should try
to improve my penmanship. It was sad. I couldn't even write in a straight line.
It was both ideas together that moved me to request a dictionary along with
some tablets and pencils from the Norfolk Prison Colony school.

I spent two days just riffling uncertainly through the dictionary's pages. I'd 6
never realized so many words existed! I didn't know *which* words I needed to
learn. Finally, just to start some kind of action, I began copying.

In my slow, painstaking, ragged handwriting, I copied into my tablet   7
everything printed on that first page, down to the punctuation marks.

I believe it took me a day. Then, aloud, I read back, to myself, everything   8
I'd written on the tablet. Over and over, aloud, to myself, I read my own
handwriting.

I woke up the next morning, thinking about those words — immensely   9
proud to realize that not only had I written so much at one time, but I'd
written words that I never knew were in the world. Moreover, with a little
effort, I also could remember what many of these words meant. I reviewed the
words whose meanings I didn't remember. Funny thing, from the dictionary
first page right now, that "aardvark" springs to my mind. The dictionary had
a picture of it, a long-tailed, long-eared, burrowing African mammal, which
lives off termites caught by sticking out its tongue as an anteater does for ants.

I was so fascinated that I went on — I copied the dictionary's next page.   10
And the same experience came when I studied that. With every succeeding
page, I also learned of people and places and events from history. Actually the
dictionary is like a miniature encyclopedia. Finally the dictionary's A section
had filled a whole table — and I went on into the B's. That was the way I
started copying what eventually became the entire dictionary. It went a lot
faster after so much practice helped me to pick up handwriting speed. Between

what I wrote in my tablet, and writing letters, during the rest of my time in prison I would guess I wrote a million words.

I suppose it was inevitable that as my word-base broadened, I could for the first time pick up a book and read and now begin to understand what the book was saying. Anyone who has read a great deal can imagine the new world that opened. Let me tell you something: from then until I left that prison, in every free moment I had, if I was not reading in the library, I was reading on my bunk. You couldn't have gotten me out of books with a wedge. . . . 11

The Norfolk Prison Colony's library was in the school building. A variety of classes was taught there by instructors who came from such places as Harvard and Boston universities. The weekly debates between inmate teams were also held in the school building. You would be astonished to know how worked up convict debaters and audiences would get over subjects like "Should Babies Be Fed Milk?" 12

Available on the prison library's shelves were books on just about every general subject. Much of the big private collection that Parkhurst had willed to the prison was still in crates and boxes in the back of the library — thousands of old books. Some of them looked ancient: covers faded, old-time parchment-looking binding. Parkhurst, I've mentioned, seemed to have been principally interested in history and religion. He had the money and the special interest to have a lot of books that you wouldn't have in general circulation. Any college library would have been lucky to get that collection. 13

As you can imagine, especially in a prison where there was heavy emphasis on rehabilitation, an inmate was smiled upon if he demonstrated an unusually intense interest in books. There was a sizable number of well-read inmates, especially the popular debaters. Some were said by many to be practically walking encyclopedias. They were almost celebrities. No university would ask any student to devour literature as I did when this new world opened to me, of being able to read and *understand*. 14

I read more in my room than in the library itself. An inmate who was known to read a lot could check out more than the permitted maximum number of books. I preferred reading in the total isolation of my own room. 15

When I had progressed to really serious reading, every night at about ten P.M. I would be outraged with the "lights out." It always seemed to catch me right in the middle of something engrossing. 16

Fortunately, right outside my door was a corridor light that cast a glow into my room. The glow was enough to read by, once my eyes adjusted to it. So when "lights out" came, I would sit on the floor where I could continue reading in that glow. 17

At one-hour intervals the night guards paced past every room. Each time I 18 heard the approaching footsteps, I jumped into bed and feigned sleep. And as soon as the guard passed, I got back out of bed onto the floor area of that light-glow, where I would read for another fifty-eight minutes — until the guard approached again. That went on until three or four every morning. Three or four hours of sleep a night was enough for me. Often in the years in the streets I had slept less than that. . . .

I can remember accurately the very first set of books that really impressed me. I have since bought that set of books and I have it at home for my children to read as they grow up. It's called *Wonders of the World*. It's full of pictures of archeological finds, statues that depict, usually, non-European people.

I found books like Will Durant's *Story of Civilization*. I read H. G. Wells' *Outline of History*. *Souls Of Black Folk* by W. E. B. Du Bois gave me a glimpse into the black people's history before they came to this country. Carter G. Woodson's *Negro History* opened my eyes about black empires before the black slave was brought to the United States, and the early Negro struggles for freedom.

J. A. Rogers' three volumes of *Sex and Race* told about race-mixing before Christ's time; about Aesop being a black man who told fables; about Egypt's Pharaohs; about the great Coptic Christian Empires; about Ethiopia, the earth's oldest continuous black civilization, as China is the oldest continuous civilization. . . .

Parkhurst's collection also contained some bound pamphlets of the Abolitionist Anti-Slavery Society of New England. I read descriptions of atrocities, saw those illustrations of black slave women tied up and flogged with whips; of black mothers watching their babies being dragged off, never to be seen by their mothers again; of dogs after slaves, and of the fugitive slave catchers, evil white men with whips and clubs and chains and guns. I read about the slave preacher Nat Turner, who put the fear of God into the white slavemaster. Nat Turner wasn't going around preaching pie-in-the-sky and "non-violent" freedom for the black man. There in Virginia one night in 1831, Nat and seven other slaves started out at his master's home and through the night they went from one plantation "big house" to the next, killing, until by the next morning 57 white people were dead and Nat had about 70 slaves following him. White people, terrified for their lives, fled from their homes, locked themselves up in public buildings, hid in the woods, and some even left the state. A small army of soldiers took two months to catch and hang Nat Turner. Somewhere I have read where Nat Turner's example is said to have inspired John Brown to invade Virginia and attack Harper's Ferry nearly thirty years later, with thirteen white men and five Negroes. . . .

When I discovered philosophy, I tried to touch all the landmarks of philosophical development. Gradually, I read most of the old philosophers,

19

20

21

22

23

36

Occidental and Oriental. The Oriental philosophers were the ones I came to prefer; finally, my impression was that most Occidental philosophy had largely been borrowed from the Oriental thinkers. Socrates, for instance, traveled in Egypt. Some sources even say that Socrates was initiated into some of the Egyptian mysteries. Obviously Socrates got some of his wisdom among the East's wise men.

I have often reflected upon the new vistas that reading opened to me. I knew right there in prison that reading had changed forever the course of my life. As I see it today, the ability to read awoke inside me some long dormant craving to be mentally alive. I certainly wasn't seeking any degree, the way a college confers a status symbol upon its students. My homemade education gave me, with every additional book that I read, a little bit more sensitivity to the deafness, dumbness, and blindness that was afflicting the black race in America. Not long ago, an English writer telephoned me from London, asking questions. One was, "What's your alma mater?" I told him, "Books." You will never catch me with a free fifteen minutes in which I'm not studying something I feel might be able to help the black man. . . . 24

But I'm digressing. I told the Englishman that my alma mater was books, a good library. Every time I catch a plane, I have with me a book that I want to read — and that's a lot of books these days. If I weren't out here every day battling the white man, I could spend the rest of my life reading, just satisfying my curiosity — because you can hardly mention anything I'm not curious about. I don't think anybody ever got more out of going to prison than I did. In fact, prison enabled me to study far more intensively than I would have if my life had gone differently and I had attended some college. I imagine that one of the biggest troubles with colleges is there are too many distractions, too much panty-raiding, fraternities, and boola-boola and all of that. Where else but in a prison could I have attacked my ignorance by being able to study intensely sometimes as much as fifteen hours a day? 25

QUESTIONS ON CONTENT:

1. Although Malcolm X had only an elementary education and possessed some street wisdom, he quickly realized that he was at a loss to understand what he read. What does he immediately sense will solve his problem, and what does he do about it? What does he discover in the process?

2. What appears to be the unifying theme of this excerpt from Malcolm X's book?

3. How did Malcolm X go about reading in prison? Why does he italicize the word *understand* in paragraph fourteen?

4.   What does Malcolm X mean when he says he had a craving to be "mentally alive"? What additional insights did he gain from his reading?

QUESTIONS ON WRITING STRUCTURE AND STRATEGY:

1.   This narrative account deals with one aspect of Malcolm X's stay in prison. Which details serve to convince you that he really was in prison?

2.   How do his supporting details compare with those employed by Douglass and Cleaver? Do you find Malcolm X's account more vivid than the others? Explain.

3.   Malcolm X occasionally uses topic sentences. Pinpoint those paragraphs with topic sentences. Can you find any with topic sentences that serve more than one paragraph?

QUESTIONS FOR DISCUSSION AND WRITING:

1.   There appeared to be universal respect for the well-read, articulate inmates in the Norfolk Prison Colony. What is the comparable situation like in high school and/or college today? Do you believe "brains" and "jocks" are stereotyped (i.e. are these valid or fair designations)? How do the movies and television confirm or negate these stereotypes?

2.   Many readers face the same problem Malcolm X faced, an inability to express themselves and the need for an extensive vocabulary. What do most people do about it? What do you do about it?

3.   Malcolm X, who called "books" his *alma mater*, draws some devastating comparisons between his education in prison and education in college. How valid do you think his observations are? Consider that in prison distractions are limited and that the hermetic life prompts one to seek freedom vicariously through books.

MY EARLY BEGINNINGS AS A WRITER
Benjamin Franklin

Benjamin Franklin was the quintessential American self-made man. Consumed by a curiosity similar to the one that fired Malcolm X, Franklin put the knowledge he gathered from books, observation, and experience to practical purpose in inventing the lightning rod, bifocal glasses, and the Franklin stove. He was nothing if not practical, and what more practical way to learn writing than the exercises he describes in the following selection taken from his Autobiography?

Franklin's candlemaker father had originally planned to "tithe" him to the ministry, but because of his "bookish inclination," as Franklin relates, his father apprenticed him to his brother James, a printer. In this capacity Franklin was initiated not only into the printing business but into the whole writing process, pursuing his reading and seeking to improve his writing style by imitating Spectator[1] *models. Franklin's method of self-improvement suggests a very logical way of developing an effective writing style. (Developing writers will also do well to emulate Franklin's effort to master "logical development" and "organization," two of the writer's most exacting tasks.) (See the Writing Process.) A sense of style is of paramount importance, for in the end you must be able to recognize when writing is smooth, idiomatic, effective, and a genuine reflection of your personality. Style proclaims the writer's uniqueness.*

*F*rom my infancy I was passionately fond of reading, and all the little money that came into my hands was laid out in the purchasing of books. I was very fond of voyages. My first acquisition was Bunyan's works in separate little volumes. I afterwards sold them to enable me to buy R. Burton's historical collections; they were small chapmen's books and cheap, forty or fifty in all. My father's little library consisted chiefly of books in polemic divinity, most of which I read. I have since often regretted that at a time when I had such a thirst for knowledge, more proper books had not fallen in my way, since it was now resolved I should not be bred to divinity. There was among them Plutarch's *Lives*, in which I read abundantly, and I still think that time spent to great advantage. There was also a book of Defoe's called an *Essay on Projects* and another of Dr. Mather's called *Essays to do Good*, which perhaps gave me a turn of thinking that had an influence on some of the principal future events of my life.

This bookish inclination at length determined my father to make me a

1

2

---

[1]The *Spectator*, an English publication whose essays by Joseph Addison and Richard Steele aimed to "enliven morality with wit and to temper wit with morality."

printer, though he had already one son (James) of that profession. In 1717 my brother, James, returned from England with a press and letters to set up his business in Boston. I liked it much better than that of my father, but still had a hankering for the sea. To prevent the apprehended effect of such an inclination, my father was impatient to have me bound to my brother. I stood out some time, but at last was persuaded and signed the indenture, when I was yet but twelve years old. I was to serve as apprentice till I was twenty-one years of age, only I was to be allowed journeyman's wages during the last year. In a little time I made a great progress in the business and became a useful hand to my brother. I now had access to better books. An acquaintance with the apprentices of booksellers enabled me sometimes to borrow a small one, which I was careful to return soon and clean. Often I sat up in my room reading the greatest part of the night, when the book was borrowed in the evening and to be returned early in the morning, lest it should be found missing or wanted.

After some time a merchant, an ingenious, sensible man, Mr. Matthew   3
Adams, who had a pretty collection of books and who frequented our printing house, took notice of me, invited me to see his library, and very kindly proposed to lend me such books as I chose to read. I now took a fancy to poetry and made some little pieces. My brother, supposing it might turn to account, encouraged me and induced me to compose two occasional ballads. One was called the "Lighthouse Tragedy," and contained an account of the shipwreck of Capt. Worthilake with his two daughters; the other was a "Sailor's Song on the Taking of the Famous *Teach*, or Blackbeard, the Pirate." They were wretched stuff, in street ballad style; and when they were printed, he sent me about the town to sell them. The first sold prodigiously, the event being recent and having made a great noise. This success flattered my vanity, but my father discouraged me by ridiculing my performances and telling me verse-makers were generally beggars. Thus I escaped being a poet and probably a very bad one. But as prose writing has been of great use to me in the course of my life and was a principal means of my advancement, I shall tell you how in such a situation I acquired what little ability I may be supposed to have in that way.

There was another bookish lad in the town, John Collins by name, with   4
whom I was intimately acquainted. We sometimes disputed, and very fond we were of argument, and very desirous of confuting one another — which disputatious turn, by the way, is apt to become a very bad habit, making people often extremely disagreeable in company, by the contradiction that is necessary to bring it into practice; and thence besides souring and spoiling the conversation, it is productive of disgusts and perhaps enmities where you may have occasion for friendship. I had caught it by reading my father's books of dispute on religion. Persons of good sense, I have since observed, seldom fall

into it, except lawyers, university men, and men of all sorts who have been bred at Edinburgh. A question was once somehow or other started between Collins and me on the propriety of educating the female sex in learning and their abilities for study. He was of opinion that it was improper and that they were naturally unequal to it. I took the contrary side, perhaps a little for dispute's sake. He was naturally more eloquent, having a greater plenty of words, and sometimes, as I thought, I was vanquished more by his fluency than by the strength of his reasons. As we parted without settling the point and were not to see one another again for some time, I sat down to put my arguments in writing, which I copied fair and sent to him. He answered and I replied. Three or four letters on a side had passed, when my father happened to find my papers and read them. Without entering into the subject in dispute, he took occasion to talk with me about my manner of writing, observed that though I had the advantage of my antagonist in correct spelling and pointing (which I owed to the printing house), I fell far short in elegance of expression, in method, and in perspicuity — of which he convinced me by several instances. I saw the justice of his remarks and thence grew more attentive to my manner of writing, and determined to endeavor to improve my style.

About this time I met with an odd volume of the *Spectator*. It was the 5 third. I had never before seen any of them. I bought it, read it over and over, and was much delighted with it. I thought the writing excellent and wished if possible to imitate it. With that view, I took some of the papers, and making short hints of the sentiment in each sentence, laid them by a few days, and then without looking at the book, tried to complete the papers again by expressing each hinted sentiment at length and as fully as it had been expressed before, in any suitable words that should occur to me. Then I compared my *Spectator* with the original, discovered some of my faults, and corrected them. But I found I wanted a stock of words or a readiness in recollecting and using them, which I thought I should have acquired before that time if I had gone on making verses; since the continual search for words of the same import but of different length to suit the measure, or of different sound for the rhyme would have laid me under a constant necessity of searching for variety, and also have tended to fix that variety in my mind, and make me master of it. Therefore I took some of the tales in the *Spectator* and turned them into verse, and after a time, when I had pretty well forgotten the prose, turned them back again. I also sometimes jumbled my collections of hints into confusion, and after some weeks endeavored to reduce them into the best order before I began to form the full sentences and complete the paper. This was to teach me method in the arrangement of the thoughts. By comparing my work afterwards with the original, I discovered many faults and corrected them; but I sometimes had the pleasure of fancying that in certain particulars of small import I had been lucky enough to improve the method or the language, and this encouraged me to think that I might possibly in time come to be a tolerable English writer, of which I was extremely ambitious.

The times I allotted for these exercises and for reading was at night after work, or before it began in the morning, or on Sundays, when I contrived to be in the printing house alone, avoiding as much as I could the common attendance of public worship which my father used to exact of me when I was under his care — and which, indeed, I still thought a duty, though I could not, as it seemed to me, afford the time to practice it.

When about sixteen years of age I happened to meet with a book written by one Tryon, recommending a vegetable diet. I determined to go into it. My brother, being yet unmarried, did not keep house but boarded himself and his apprentices in another family. My refusing to eat flesh occasioned an inconvenience, and I was frequently chid for my singularity. I made myself acquainted with Tryon's manner of preparing some of his dishes, such as boiling potatoes or rice, making hasty pudding, and a few others; and then proposed to my brother that if he would give me weekly half the money he paid for my board, I would board myself. He instantly agreed to it, and I presently found that I could save half what he paid me. This was an additional fund for buying of books. But I had another advantage in it. My brother and the rest going from the printing house to their meals, I remained there alone, and dispatching presently my light repast (which often was no more than a biscuit or a slice of bread, a handful of raisins or a tart from the pastry cook's, and a glass of water) had the rest of the time till their return for study, in which I made the greater progress from that greater clearness of head and quicker apprehension which generally attend temperance in eating and drinking. Now it was that being on some occasion made ashamed of my ignorance in figures, which I had twice failed in learning when at school, I took Cocker's book of arithmetic and went through the whole by myself with the greatest ease. I also read Seller's and Sturmy's book on navigation and became acquainted with the little geometry it contains, but I never proceeded far in that science. I read about this time Locke, *On Human Understanding*, and *The Art of Thinking* by Messrs. du Port Royal.

While I was intent on improving my language, I met with an English grammar (I think it was Greenwood's) at the end of which there were two little sketches on the arts of rhetoric and logic, the latter finishing with a dispute in the Socratic method. And soon after I procured Xenophon's *Memorable Things of Socrates*, wherein there are many examples of the same method. I was charmed with it, adopted it, dropped my abrupt contradiction and positive argumentation, and put on the humble inquirer. And being then, from reading Shaftesbury and Collins, made a doubter, as I already was in many points of our religious doctrines, I found this method the safest for myself and very embarrassing to those against whom I used it; therefore, I took a delight in it, practiced it continually, and grew very artful and expert in drawing people, even of superior knowledge, into concessions the consequences of which they did not foresee, entangling them in difficulties out of which they could not extricate themselves, and so obtaining victories that neither myself nor my cause always deserved. I continued this method some few years but gradually left it, retaining only the habit of expressing myself in terms of modest diffidence, never using when I advance anything that may possibly be disputed the words "certainly," "undoubtedly," or any others that give the air of positiveness to an opinion; but rather say, "I conceive or apprehend a thing to be so or so," "It appears to me," or "I should think it so or so, for such and such reasons," or "I imagine it to be so," or "It is so if I am not mistaken." This habit, I believe, has been of great advantage to me when I have had occasion to inculcate my opinions and persuade men into measures that I have been from time to time engaged in promoting. And as the chief ends of conversation are to *inform*, or to *be informed*, to *please* or to *persuade*, I wish well-meaning and sensible men would not lessen their power of doing good by a positive, assuming manner that seldom fails to disgust, tends to create opposition, and to defeat every one of those purposes for which speech was given to us. In fact, if you wish to instruct others, a positive, dogmatical manner in advancing your sentiments may provoke contradiction and prevent a candid attention. If you desire instruction and improvement from the knowledge of others, you should not at the same time express yourself as firmly fixed in your present opinions; modest and sensible men, who do not love disputation, will probably leave you undisturbed in the possession of your error. In adopting such a manner you can seldom expect to please your hearers, or to persuade those whose concurrence you desire.

QUESTIONS ON CONTENT:

1. Why was Franklin turned away from a career as a poet? What did he later discover about the value of writing poetry? What value did he place on his prose writings?

2. How did Franklin acquire his disputatious manner, and why did he abandon it?

3. What did Franklin learn from Xenophon's *Memorable Things of Socrates*? How did Franklin adapt the Socratic method?

4. Although the thesis of this excerpt from Franklin's *Autobiography* is broadly similar to those of the preceding writers, in what specific ways does Franklin differ from them? Does the last paragraph seem to digress or does it reinforce Franklin's earlier remarks? Explain.

QUESTIONS ON WRITING STRUCTURE AND STRATEGY:

1. Franklin originally composed his *Autobiography* as a long discourse of fatherly advice for the edification of his son. Does this excerpt read like a letter? A sermon? A lecture? Compare its tone with the tone of the Douglass and the more informal Malcolm X selection.

2. Franklin varies the length of his sentences, which, of course, adds interest; however, many of his sentences are long, several of them over eighty words. How would these be changed today? What purposes would be served by the change?

3. Which words or phrases in Franklin's writing seem dated? Which have withstood the passage of time and still strike a contemporary note? How would you alter his words or phrases?

QUESTIONS FOR DISCUSSION AND WRITING:

1. Try Franklin's method for teaching himself to write: Take a passage from a writer you admire and make a few notes on the content; then, after setting it aside for a few days, attempt to recapture the original expression. Experiment with turning some prose into verse and vice versa. Try to improve your abilities to organize by jumbling some of your notes and reconstructing the original argument a week later.

2. Franklin's *Autobiography* is probably the most popular autobiography published in America. It is also popular in Third World countries. How do you account for this great popularity?

3. In Franklin's account of his dispute with his friend, he observed that his opponent's articulateness appeared to win out over Franklin's superior reasoning. From your experience has it generally been true that the very articulate person prevails over those who carefully reason? Is it possible for the carefully reasoning person to be articulate? (For example: are you intimidated by the person who speaks up in class most often? Might not the speaker also be a reasoning person?) Can you think of any very articulate national figures who are at base shallow thinkers? Any who are carefully reasoning persons? What does this tell you about the success of demagogues in public life? Write a paper setting forth your conclusions. (Note: If articulateness always wins out over reason, of what use is reason?)

4. In your journal copy words, phrases, sentences, excerpts you have read that have style, that are well written, memorable. Reviewing these from time to time eventually will help you cultivate a sense of style.

WRITING—NOT A RARE TALENT
Eric Hoffer

Despite Eric Hoffer's lack of schooling and his having spent the major portion of his adult life as a migratory worker or as a longshoreman, he read and studied on his own. In time, he became a popular, respected writer and philosopher with numerous books to his credit. So impressive were his accomplishments that he was invited to lecture at the University of California, later becoming something of a TV personality and occasional advisor to President Lyndon Johnson. His best-selling first book, The True Believer, became a favorite of President Dwight D. Eisenhower.

As Hoffer tells us, "the Hitler decade" nudged his thinking and turned him to writing. Like Franklin, however, he realized he needed to develop a sense of style. Through his reading and rereading of Montaigne, almost to the point of memorization, he cultivated an appreciation for style and writing. Hoffer's conclusion should serve as encouragement for all student writers.

We are often told that the invention of writing in the Middle East about 3000 B.C. marked an epoch in man's knowledge and ideas. Actually, for many centuries after its invention writing was used solely to keep track of the intake and outgo of treasuries and warehouses. Writing was invented not to write books but to keep books. The earliest examples we have of writing are invoices and lists of articles. The scribe who practiced the craft of writing was a civil servant—a clerk and bookkeeper. Literature was the domain of bards and storytellers who no more thought of writing down their stock in trade than other craftsmen would the secrets of their trade. Century after century the scribe went on keeping records. He felt smug in his bureaucratic niche, had no grievances and dreamed no dreams. Then, in every civilization, at some point, the scribe makes his appearance as a "writer." When you try to find out what it was that started the scribe "writing," the answer in every case is the same: the scribe began to write when he became unemployed.

A loss of a sense of usefulness and a passionate desire for impressive action may release a creative flow in all sorts of people—in sheepherders, farmers, officials, generals, politicians, aristocrats, and run-of-the mill clerks. It goes without saying that in addition to a thwarted desire for action there must be talent and a degree of expertise. People who have nothing to say or have no idea how to say it when they have something to say will not start writing no matter how optimal the conditions. La Rochefoucauld obviously had talent and, what is equally important, a taste for a good sentence. The reign of Louis XIV has been called "a despotism tempered by epigram," and La Rochefoucauld also had the salons in which expression was practiced as a fine art. We can,

therefore, expect unemployment to release a creative flow in the masses only if
we assume that the masses in America are not less endowed with genius than
other segments of the population, and that it is possible to bring about a
diffusion of expertise in literature, art, science, etc., comparable to the existing
wide diffusion of expertise in mechanics and sports. I have always had the
feeling that the people I live and work with are lumpy with talent. The cliché
that talent is rare is not founded on fact. All that we know is that there are
short periods in history when genius springs up all over the landscape, and long
periods of mediocrity and inertness. . . .

Where the development of talent is concerned we are still in the food-
gathering stage. We do not know how to grow it. Up to now in this country
when one of the masses starts to write, paint, etc., it is because he happens to
bump into the right accident. In my case the right accident happened in the
1930s. I had the habit of reading from childhood, but very little schooling. I
spent half of my adult life as a migratory worker and the other half as a
longshoreman. The Hitler decade started me thinking, but there is an enormous
distance between thinking and the act of writing. I had to acquire a taste for a
good sentence — taste it the way a child tastes candy — before I stumbled into
writing. Here is how it happened. Late in 1936 I was on my way to do some
placer mining near Nevada City, and I had a hunch that I would get
snowbound. I had to get me something to read, something that would last me
for a long time. So I stopped over in San Francisco to get a thick book. I did
not really care what the book was about — history, theology, mathematics,
farming, anything, so long as it was thick, had small print and no pictures.
There was at that time a large secondhand bookstore on Market Street called
Lieberman's and I went there to buy my book. I soon found one. It had about a
thousand pages of small print and no pictures. The price was one dollar. The
title page said these were *The Essays of Michel de Montaigne*. I knew what
essays were but I did not know Montaigne from Adam. I put the book in my
knapsack and caught the ferry to Sausalito.

Sure enough, I got snowbound. I read the book three times until I knew it
almost by heart. When I got back to the San Joaquin Valley I could not open
my mouth without quoting Montaigne, and the fellows liked it. It got so
whenever there was an argument about anything — women, money, animals,
food, death — they would ask: "What does Montaigne say?" Out came the
book and I would find the right passage. I am quite sure that even now there
must be a number of migratory workers up and down the San Joaquin Valley
still quoting Montaigne. I ought to add that the Montaigne edition I had was
the John Florio translation. The spelling was modern, but the style seventeenth
century — the style of the King James Bible and of Bacon's Essays. The
sentences have hooks in them which stick in the mind; they make platitudes

3

4

sound as if they were new. Montaigne was not above anyone's head. Once in a workers' barrack near Stockton, the man in the next bunk picked up my Montaigne and read it for an hour or so. When he returned it he said: "Anyone can write a book like this."

QUESTIONS ON CONTENT:

1. What does Hoffer mean when he writes that "the scribe began to write when he became unemployed"?
2. Why does Hoffer believe that today's masses possess creative potential? How does he qualify his assertion?
3. How does Hoffer explain the role "accident" plays in shaping the writer? What evidence does he offer to support his theory? Is it convincing?
4. Although Hoffer does tell us how he developed a writing style, what more complex thesis does he develop? What subordinate ideas does he present?

QUESTIONS ON WRITING STRUCTURE AND STRATEGY:

1. Compare Hoffer's style with Franklin's. Which seems more lively? Why? Can you pinpoint specific features that account for your answer?
2. Hoffer speaks about Montaigne's sentences having "hooks" in them. Do you find any such sentences in Hoffer's writing? In any of the other selections?

QUESTIONS FOR DISCUSSION AND WRITING:

1. How may Hoffer's remarks in the first three sentences of paragraph two apply to prison inmates? Show how the writings of Cleaver and Malcolm X illustrate what Hoffer says.
2. In paragraph two, Hoffer expresses a high opinion of the creative possibilities of the American masses. Assess the applicability of his remarks to yourself. How has your education thus far furthered your expertise in literature, art, and science? In the thinking process? In improved reading ability? How does your new expertise compare with your nonacademic abilities (mechanics, sports, hunting, hobbies)?
3. What relevance does Hoffer's remark that he works with people who are "lumpy with talent" have for the belief that every child is educable?
4. Hoffer wrote about the role of accident in his life. Write a paper in which you explore the role of accident in determining your own life or some episode in your life.
5. What people have provided role models for you to further your creative potential (parents, teachers, coaches, political figures, religious figures, celebrities, etc.)? Write a paper about why you have come to admire/emulate a particular person or group of people.

LIFE LINE

Maya Angelou

*As young children, Maya Angelou (the Marguerite in this excerpt) and
her brother Bailey lived several years with their grandmother in
Stamps, Arkansas. "Momma," as they called her, ran a general store
in the black section of town. Because, as Angelou tells us, there was
little for black children to do, she became an avid reader (William
Shakespeare, she writes, was her first "white love"). Later, at age
eight, when she went to live with her mother in St. Louis, she took out
her first library card. She read widely, and though she "enjoyed and
respected" many white writers (Poe, Kipling, Butler, Thackery,
Henley), she relates that she saved her "young and loyal passion for
Paul Lawrence Dunbar, Langston Hughes, James Weldon Johnson,
and W. E. B. Dubois. . . ." Upon her return to Stamps, she met the
black woman whom she said threw her her first "life line." Mrs.
Bertha Flowers, she later wrote, gave her "the secret word" which
called forth a "djinn" who was to serve her all her life: books. In the
following excerpt from her autobiography,* I Know Why the Caged
Bird Sings, *Angelou describes her meeting with this remarkable
woman. Although this is a brief account, Angelou describes Mrs.
Flowers with loving care. Observe how her liberal use of figurative
language, vivid action verbs, and literary allusions give life and lend
felicity to her writing.*

For nearly a year, I sopped around the house, the Store, the school and
the church, like an old biscuit, dirty and inedible. Then I met, or rather got to
know, the lady who threw me my first life line.

Mrs. Bertha Flowers was the aristocrat of Black Stamps. She had the grace
of control to appear warm in the coldest weather, and on the Arkansas summer
days it seemed she had a private breeze which swirled around, cooling her. She
was thin without the taut look of wiry people, and her printed voile dresses
and flowered hats were as right for her as denim overalls for a farmer. She was
our side's answer to the richest white woman in town.

Her skin was a rich black that would have peeled like a plum if snagged,
but then no one would have thought of getting close enough to Mrs. Flowers to
ruffle her dress, let along snag her skin. She didn't encourage familiarity. She
wore gloves too.

I don't think I ever saw Mrs. Flowers laugh, but she smiled often. A slow
widening of her thin black lips to show even, small white teeth, then the slow
effortless closing. When she chose to smile on me, I always wanted to thank
her. The action was so graceful and inclusively benign.

She was one of the few gentlewomen I have ever known, and has remained
throughout my life the measure of what a human being can be.

Momma had a strange relationship with her. Most often when she passed on the road in front of the Store, she spoke to Momma in that soft yet carrying voice, "Good day, Mrs. Henderson." Momma responded with "How you, Sister Flowers?" 6

Mrs. Flowers didn't belong to our church, nor was she Momma's familiar. Why on earth did she insist on calling her Sister Flowers? Shame made me want to hide my face. Mrs. Flowers deserved better than to be called Sister. Then, Momma left out the verb. Why not ask, "How *are* you, *Mrs.* Flowers?" With the unbalanced passion of the young, I hated her for showing her ignorance to Mrs. Flowers. It didn't occur to me for many years that they were as alike as sisters, separated only by formal education. 7

Although I was upset, neither of the women was in the least shaken by what I thought an unceremonious greeting. Mrs. Flowers would continue her easy gait up the hill to her little bungalow, and Momma kept on shelling peas or doing whatever had brought her to the front porch. 8

Occasionally, though, Mrs. Flowers would drift off the road and down to the Store and Momma would say to me, "Sister, you go on and play." As I left I would hear the beginning of an intimate conversation. Momma persistently using the wrong verb, or none at all. 9

"Brother and Sister Wilcox is sho'ly the meanest—" "Is," Momma? "Is"? Oh, please, not "is," Momma, for two or more. But they talked, and from the side of the building where I waited for the ground to open up and swallow me, I heard the soft-voiced Mrs. Flowers and the textured voice of my grandmother merging and melting. They were interrupted from time to time by giggles that must have come from Mrs. Flowers (Momma never giggled in her life). Then she was gone. 10

She appealed to me because she was like people I had never met personally. Like women in English novels who walked the moors (whatever they were) with their loyal dogs racing at a respectful distance. Like the women who sat in front of roaring fireplaces, drinking tea incessantly from silver trays full of scones and crumpets. Women who walked over the "heath" and read morocco-bound books and had two last names divided by a hyphen. It would be safe to say that she made me proud to be Negro, just by being herself. 11

She acted just as refined as whitefolks in the movies and books and she was more beautiful, for none of them could have come near that warm color without looking gray by comparison. 12

It was fortunate that I never saw her in the company of powhitefolks. For since they tend to think of their whiteness as an evenizer, I'm certain that I would have had to hear her spoken to commonly as Bertha, and my image of her would have been shattered like the unmendable Humpty-Dumpty. 13

One summer afternoon, sweet-milk fresh in my memory, she stopped at 14

the Store to buy provisions. Another Negro woman of her health and age
would have been expected to carry the paper sacks home in one hand, but
Momma said, "Sister Flowers, I'll send Bailey up to your house with these things."

She smiled that slow dragging smile, "Thank you, Mrs. Henderson. I'd   15
prefer Marguerite, though." My name was beautiful when she said it. "I've been
meaning to talk to her, anyway." They gave each other age-group looks.

Momma said, "Well, that's all right then. Sister, go and change your dress.   16
You going to Sister Flowers's."

The chifforobe was a maze. What on earth did one put on to go to Mrs.   17
Flowers' house? I knew I shouldn't put on a Sunday dress. It might be
sacrilegious. Certainly not a house dress, since I was already wearing a fresh
one. I chose a school dress, naturally. It was formal without suggesting that
going to Mrs. Flowers' house was equivalent to attending church.

I trusted myself back into the Store.   18

"Now, don't you look nice." I had chosen the right thing, for once.   19

"Mrs. Henderson, you make most of the children's clothes, don't you?"   20

"Yes, ma'am. Sure do. Store-bought clothes ain't hardly worth the thread   21
it take to stitch them."

"I'll say you do a lovely job, though, so neat. That dress looks professional."   22

Momma was enjoying the seldom-received compliments. Since everyone   23
we knew (except Mrs. Flowers, of course) could sew competently, praise was
rarely handed out for the commonly practiced craft.

"I try, with the help of the Lord, Sister Flowers, to finish the inside just   24
like I does the outside. Come here, Sister."

I had buttoned up the collar and tied the belt, apronlike, in back. Momma   25
told me to turn around. With one hand she pulled the strings and the belt fell
free at both sides of my waist. Then her large hands were at my neck, opening
the button loops. I was terrified. What was happening?

"Take it off, Sister." She had her hands on the hem of the dress.   26

"I don't need to see the inside, Mrs. Henderson, I can tell . . ." But the   27
dress was over my head and my arms were stuck in the sleeves. Momma said,
"That'll do. See here, Sister Flowers, I French-seams around the armholes."
Through the cloth film, I saw the shadow approach. "That makes it last longer.
Children these days would bust out of sheet-metal clothes. They so rough."

"That is a very good job, Mrs. Henderson. You should be proud. You can   28
put your dress back on, Marguerite."

"No ma'am. Pride is a sin. And 'cording to the Good Book, it goeth before   29
a fall."

"That's right. So the Bible says. It's a good thing to keep in mind."   30

I wouldn't look at either of them. Momma hadn't thought that taking off   31
my dress in front of Mrs. Flowers would kill me stone dead. If I had refused,

she would have thought I was trying to be "womanish" and might have remembered St. Louis. Mrs. Flowers had known that I would be embarrassed and that was even worse. I picked up the groceries and went out to wait in the hot sunshine. It would be fitting if I got a sunstroke and died before they came outside. Just dropped dead on the slanting porch.

There was a little path beside the rocky road, and Mrs. Flowers walked in front swinging her arms and picking her way over the stones. 32

She said, without turning her head, to me, "I hear you're doing very good school work, Marguerite, but that it's all written. The teachers report that they have trouble getting you to talk in class." We passed the triangular farm on our left and the path widened to allow us to walk together. I hung back in the separate unasked and unanswerable questions. 33

"Come and walk along with me, Marguerite." I couldn't have refused even if I wanted to. She pronounced my name so nicely. Or more correctly, she spoke each word with such clarity that I was certain a foreigner who didn't understand English could have understood her. 34

"Now no one is going to make you talk — possibly no one can. But bear in mind, language is man's way of communicating with his fellow man and it is language alone which separates him from the lower animals." That was a totally new idea to me, and I would need time to think about it. 35

"Your grandmother says you read a lot. Every chance you get. That's good, but not good enough. Words mean more than what is set down on paper. It takes the human voice to infuse them with the shades of deeper meaning." 36

I memorized the part about the human voice infusing words. It seemed so valid and poetic. 37

She said she was going to give me some books and that I not only must read them, I must read them aloud. She suggested that I try to make a sentence sound in as many different ways as possible. 38

"I'll accept no excuse if you return a book to me that has been badly handled." My imagination boggled at the punishment I would deserve if in fact I did abuse a book of Mrs. Flowers'. Death would be too kind and brief. 39

The odors in the house surprised me. Somehow I had never connected Mrs. Flowers with food or eating or any other common experience of common people. There must have been an outhouse, too, but my mind never recorded it. 40

The sweet scent of vanilla had met us as she opened the door. 41

"I made tea cookies this morning. You see, I had planned to invite you for cookies and lemonade so we could have this little chat. The lemonade is in the icebox." 42

It followed that Mrs. Flowers would have ice on an ordinary day, when most families in our town bought ice late on Saturdays only a few times during the summer to be used in the wooden ice-cream freezers. 43

She took the bags from me and disappeared through the kitchen door. I looked around the room that I had never in my wildest fantasies imagined I would see. Browned photographs leered or threatened from the walls and the white, freshly done curtains pushed against themselves and against the wind. I wanted to gobble up the room entire and take it to Bailey, who would help me analyze and enjoy it.

"Have a seat, Marguerite. Over there by the table." She carried a platter covered with a tea towel. Although she warned that she hadn't tried her hand at baking sweets for some time, I was certain that like everything else about her the cookies would be perfect.

They were flat round wafers, slightly browned on the edges and butter-yellow in the center. With the cold lemonade they were sufficient for childhood's lifelong diet. Remembering my manners, I took nice little lady-like bites off the edges. She said she had made them expressly for me and that she had a few in the kitchen that I could take home to my brother. So I jammed one whole cake in my mouth and the rough crumbs scratched the insides of my jaws, and if I hadn't had to swallow, it would have been a dream come true.

As I ate she began the first of what we later called "my lessons in living." She said that I must always be intolerant of ignorance but understanding of illiteracy. That some people, unable to go to school, were more educated and even more intelligent than college professors. She encouraged me to listen carefully to what country people called mother wit. That in those homely sayings was couched the collective wisdom of generations.

When I finished the cookies she brushed off the table and brought a thick, small book from the bookcase. I had read *A Tale of Two Cities* and found it up to my standards as a romantic novel. She opened the first page and I heard poetry for the first time in my life.

"It was the best of times and the worst of times . . ." Her voice slid in and curved down through and over the words. She was nearly singing. I wanted to look at the pages. Were they the same that I had read? Or were there notes, music, lined on the pages, as in a hymn book? Her sounds began cascading gently. I knew from listening to a thousand preachers that she was nearing the end of her reading, and I hadn't really heard, heard to understand, a single word.

"How do you like that?"

It occurred to me that she expected a response. The sweet vanilla flavor was still on my tongue and her reading was a wonder in my ears. I had to speak.

I said, "Yes, ma'am." It was the least I could do, but it was the most also.

"There's one more thing. Take this book of poems and memorize one for me. Next time you pay me a visit, I want you to recite."

52

I have tried often to search behind the sophistication of years for the   54
enchantment I so easily found in those gifts. The essence escapes but its aura
remains. To be allowed, no, invited, into the private lives of strangers, and to
share their joys and fears, was a chance to exchange the Southern bitter
wormwood for a cup of mead with Beowulf or a hot cup of tea and milk with
Oliver Twist. When I said aloud, "It is a far, far better thing that I do, than I
have ever done . . ." tears of love filled my eyes at my selflessness.

On that first day, I ran down the hill and into the road (few cars ever   55
came along it) and had the good sense to stop running before I reached the Store.

I was liked, and what a difference it made. I was respected not as Mrs.   56
Henderson's grandchild or Bailey's sister but for just being Marguerite Johnson.

Childhood's logic never asks to be proved (all conclusions are absolute). I   57
didn't question why Mrs. Flowers had singled me out for attention, nor did it
occur to me that Momma might have asked her to give me a little talking to.
All I cared about was that she had made tea cookies for *me* and read to *me*
from her favorite book. It was enough to prove that she liked me.

Momma and Bailey were waiting inside the Store. He said, "My, what did   58
she give you?" He had seen the books, but I held the paper sack with his
cookies in my arms shielded by the poems.

Momma said, "Sister, I know you acted like a little lady. That do my heart   59
good to see settled people take to you all. I'm trying my best, the Lord knows,
but these days . . ." Her voice trailed off. "Go on in and change your dress."

In the bedroom it was going to be a joy to see Bailey receive his cookies. I   60
said, "By the way, Bailey, Mrs. Flowers sent you some tea cookies — "

Momma shouted, "What did you say, Sister? You, Sister, what did you   61
say?" Hot anger was crackling in her voice.

Bailey said, "She said Mrs. Flowers sent me some — "   62

"I ain't talking to you, Ju." I heard the heavy feet walk across the floor   63
toward our bedroom. "Sister, you heard me. What's that you said?" She
swelled to fill the doorway.

Bailey said, "Momma." His pacifying voice — "Momma, she — "   64

"You shut up, Ju. I'm talking to your sister."   65

I didn't know what sacred cow I had bumped, but it was better to find out   66
than to hang like a thread over an open fire. I repeated, "I said, 'Bailey, by the
way, Mrs. Flowers sent you — '"

"That's what I thought you said. Go on and take off your dress. I'm going   67
to get a switch."

At first I thought she was playing. Maybe some heavy joke that would end   68
with "You sure she didn't send me something?" but in a minute she was back
in the room with a long, ropy, peach-tree switch, the juice smelling bitter at

having been torn loose. She said, "Get down on your knees. Bailey, Junior, you come on, too."

The three of us knelt as she began, "Our Father, you know the tribulations of your humble servant. I have with your help raised two grown boys. Many's the day I thought I wouldn't be able to go on, but you gave me the strength to see my way clear. Now, Lord, look down on this heavy heart today. I'm trying to raise my son's children in the way they should go, but, oh, Lord, the Devil try to hinder me on every hand. I never thought I'd live to hear cursing under this roof, what I try to keep dedicated to the glorification of God. And cursing out of the mouths of babes. But you said, in the last days brother would turn against brother, and children against their parents. That there would be a gnashing of teeth and a rendering of flesh. Father, forgive this child, I beg you, on bended knee."

I was crying loudly now. Momma's voice had risen to a shouting pitch, and I knew that whatever wrong I had committed was extremely serious. She had even left the Store untended to take up my case with God. When she finished we were all crying. She pulled me to her with one hand and hit me only a few times with the switch. The shock of my sin and the emotional release of her prayer had exhausted her.

Momma wouldn't talk right then, but later in the evening I found that my violation lay in using the phrase "by the way." Momma explained that "Jesus was the Way, the Truth and the Light," and anyone who says "by the way" is really saying, "by Jesus," or "by God" and the Lord's name would not be taken in vain in her house.

When Bailey tried to interpret the words with: "Whitefolks use 'by the way' to mean while we're on the subject," Momma reminded us that "whitefolks' mouths were most in general loose and their words were an abomination before Christ."

QUESTIONS ON CONTENT:

1. What specific things about Mrs. Flowers distinguish her as a memorable character?
2. How does Angelou reveal the differences in the educational/social level of Momma and Mrs. Flowers?
3. What clues do you find that tell you when the story takes place?
4. What passages tell you that Marguerite was a reader?

QUESTIONS ON WRITING STRUCTURE AND STRATEGY:

1. Angelou uses figurative language (similes and metaphors — see Glossary).

What do they add to the narrative? Note also her strong action verbs. How do they color and give life to her account? What do her allusions add?

2. Although Angelou employs narration, what other mode (see the Writing Process) does she use to develop her piece? Why does she use it and is it effective?

3. Why does Angelou not end this account with her departure from Mrs. Flowers (i.e., why does she continue and record the confrontation with Momma)?

QUESTIONS ON WRITING AND DISCUSSION:

1. Mrs. Flowers made a great impact on Maya Angelou. She became for Angelou "the measure of what a human being can be." Try your hand at describing a person who is your measure of what a human being can be.

2. In a well-constructed paper in which you maintain a consistent point of view (see Glossary), describe someone (a coach, a neighbor, a teacher, or an employer) who expressed a special interest in you. Explain how that person's interest or advice changed you in some way. Try to focus on one or two specific episodes that demonstrate the person's influence on you. Experiment with figurative language and vivid action verbs as Angelou does in this excerpt.

SILENCES

Tillie Olsen

This excerpt has been intentionally placed last in this section because it is the most difficult and requires the most careful reading. As she explains, Tillie Olsen (whose college was "libraries") wrote during precious moments stolen from household and child-rearing responsibilities, publishing her first book when she was fifty years old.

Although the thesis of Silences *is implied in the title and in the first paragraph of this selection, elsewhere in her book she expands her discussion to include not only women writers but a wide range of creative people of both sexes. In the first part, she sees her own experience as a microcosm of the experience of all would-be women writers whose primary concerns have been their children and homes. In the second part she goes on to explore the causes — social, familial, educational — for the silencing of potential "artists."*

Whereas the other writers in this section have been fairly straightforward and concise, Tillie Olsen's style is complex and subtle. Her writing demands critical study, not only to fathom the nuances of her thesis but also to catch the innumerable allusions (see Glossary) she sprinkles throughout her writing. What Tillie Olsen says is thoughtful and provocative, even polemical; however, the way she says it, her colorful, elliptical style, is equally important. (You will recall it was a "sense of style" that both Franklin and Hoffer were pursuing.) Tillie Olsen's word choice, sentence variety, her use of parallelism and figurative language (see Glossary) constitute a catalogue of stylistic techniques that you as writers can apply to your own writing.

When H. H. Richardson, who wrote the Australian classic *Ultima Thule*, was asked why she — whose children, like all her people, were so profoundly written — did not herself have children, she answered: "There are enough women to do the childbearing and childrearing. I know of none who can write my books." I remember thinking rebelliously, yes, and I know of none who can bear and rear my children either. But literary history is on her side. Almost no mothers — as almost no part-time, part-self persons — have created enduring literature . . . so far.

If I talk now quickly of my own silences — almost presumptuous after what has been told here — it is that the individual experience may add.

In the twenty years I bore and reared my children, usually had to work on a paid job as well, the simplest circumstances for creation did not exist. Nevertheless writing, the hope of it, was "the air I breathed, so long as I shall breathe at all." In that hope, there was conscious storing, snatched reading, beginnings of writing, and always "the secret rootlets of reconnaissance."

When the youngest of our four was in school, the beginnings struggled 4
toward endings. This was a time, in Kafka's words, "like a squirrel in a cage:
bliss of movement, desperation about constriction, craziness of endurance."

Bliss of movement. A full extended family life; the world of my job 5
(transcriber in a dairy-equipment company); and the writing, which I was
somehow able to carry around within me through work, through home. Time
on the bus, even when I had to stand, was enough; the stolen moments at
work, enough; the deep night hours for as long as I could stay awake, after the
kids were in bed, after the household tasks were done, sometimes during. It is
no accident that the first work I considered publishable began: "I stand here
ironing, and what you asked me moves tormented back and forth with the iron."

In such snatches of time I wrote what I did in those years, but there came 6
a time when this triple life was no longer possible. The fifteen hours of daily
realities became too much distraction for the writing. I lost craziness of
endurance. What might have been, I don't know; but I applied for, and was
given, eight months' writing time. There was still full family life, all the
household responsibilities, but I did not have to hold an eight-hour job. I had
continuity, three full days, sometimes more — and it was in those months I
made the mysterious turn and became a writing writer.

Then had to return to the world of work, someone else's work, nine hours, 7
five days a week.

This was the time of festering and congestion. For a few months I was able 8
to shield the writing with which I was so full, against the demands of jobs on
which I had to be competent, through the joys and responsibilities and trials of
family. For a few months. Always roused by the writing, always denied. "I
could not go to write it down. It convulsed and died in me. I will pay."

My work died. What demanded to be written, did not. It seethed, bubbled, 9
clamored, peopled me. At last moved into the hours meant for sleeping. I
worked now full time on temporary jobs, a Kelly, a Western Agency girl (girl!),
wandering from office to office, always hoping to manage two, three writing
months ahead. Eventually there was time.

I had said: always roused by the writing, always denied. Now, like a 10
woman made frigid, I had to learn response, to trust this possibility for fruition
that had not been before. Any interruption dazed and silenced me. It took a
long while of surrendering to what I was trying to write, of invoking Henry
James's "passion, piety, patience," before I was able to re-establish work.

When again I had to leave the writing, I lost consciousness. A time of 11
anesthesia. There was still an automatic noting that did not stop, but it was as
if writing had never been. No fever, no congestion, no festering. I ceased being
peopled, slept well and dreamlessly, took a "permanent" job. The few pieces
that had been published seemed to have vanished like the not-yet-written. I

wrote someone, unsent: "So long they fed each other—my life, the writing—; —the writing or hope of it, my life—; but now they begin to destroy." I knew, but did not feel the destruction.

A Ford grant in literature, awarded me on nomination by others, came almost too late. Time granted does not necessarily coincide with time that can be most fully used, as the congested time of fullness would have been. Still, it was two years.   12

Drowning is not so pitiful as the attempt to rise, says Emily Dickinson. I do not agree, but I know whereof she speaks. For a long time I was that emaciated survivor trembling on the beach, unable to rise and walk. Said differently, I could manage only the feeblest, shallowest growth on that devastated soil. Weeds, to be burned like weeds, or used as compost. When the habits of creation were at last rewon, one book went to the publisher, and I dared to begin my present work. It became my center, engraved on it: "Evil is whatever distracts." (By now had begun a cost to our family life, to my own participation in life as a human being.) I shall not tell the "rest, residue, and remainder" of what I was "leased, demised, and let unto" when once again I had to leave work at the flood to return to the Time-Master, to business-ese and legalese. This most harmful of all my silences has ended, but I am not yet recovered; may still be a one-book silence.   13

However that will be, we are in a time of more and more hidden and foreground silences, women *and* men. Denied full writing life, more may try to "nurse through night" (that part-time, part-self night) "the ethereal spark," but it seems to me there would almost have had to be "flame on flame" first; and time as needed, afterwards; and enough of the self, the capacities, undamaged for the rebeginnings on the frightful task. I would like to believe this for what has not yet been written into literature. But it cannot reconcile for what is lost by unnatural silences. . . .   14

How much it takes to become a writer. Bent (far more common than we assume), circumstances, time, development of craft—but beyond that: how much conviction as to the importance of what one has to say, one's right to say it. And the will, the measureless store of belief in oneself to be able to come to, cleave to, find the form for one's own life comprehensions. Difficult for any male not born into a class that breeds such confidence. Almost impossible for a girl, a woman.   15

The leeching of belief, of will, the damaging of capacity begin so early. Sparse indeed is the literature on the way of denial to small girl children of the development of their endowment as born human: active, vigorous bodies; exercise of the power to do, to make, to investigate, to invent, to conquer obstacles, to resist violations of the self; to think, create, choose; to attain   16

58

community, confidence in self. Little has been written on the harms of instilling constant concern with appearance; the need to please, to support; the training in acceptance, deferring. Little has been added in our century to George Eliot's *The Mill on the Floss* on the effect of the differing treatment — "climate of expectation" — for boys and for girls.

But it is there if one knows how to read for it, and indelibly there in the resulting damage. One — out of twelve. **17**

In the vulnerable girl years, unlike their sisters in the previous century, women writers go to college. The kind of experience it may be for them is stunningly documented in Elaine Showalter's pioneering "Women and the Literary Curriculum." Freshman texts in which women have little place, if at all; language itself, all achievement, anything to do with the human in male terms — *Man in Crises, The Individual and His World.* Three hundred thirteen male writers taught; seventeen women writers: That classic of adolescent rebellion, *A Portrait of the Artist as a Young Man*; and sagas (male) of the quest for identity (but then Erikson, the father of the concept, propounds that identity concerns girls only insofar as making themselves into attractive beings for the right kind of man). Most, *not all*, of the predominantly male literature studied, written by men whose understandings are not universal, but restrictively male (as Mary Ellmann, Kate Millett, and Dolores Schmidt have pointed out); in our time more and more surface, hostile, one-dimensional in portraying women. **18**

In a writer's young years, susceptibility to the vision and style of the great is extreme. Add the aspiration-denying implication, consciously felt or not (although reinforced daily by one's professors and reading) that (as Virginia Woolf noted years ago) women writers, women's experience, and literature written by women are by definition minor. (Mailer will not grant even the minor: "the one thing a writer has to have is balls.") No wonder that Showalter observes: **19**

> Women [students] are estranged from their own experience and unable to perceive its shape and authenticity, in part because they do not see it mirrored and given resonance in literature. . . . They are expected to identify with masculine experience, which is presented as the human one, and have no faith in the validity of their own perceptions and experiences, rarely seeing them confirmed in literature, or accepted in criticism . . . [They] notoriously lack the happy confidence, the exuberant sense of the value of their individual observations which enables young men to risk making fools of themselves for the sake of an idea.

Harms difficult to work through. Nevertheless, some young women **20**

(others are already lost) maintain their ardent intention to write — fed indeed
by the very glories of some of this literature that puts them down.

But other invisible worms are finding out the bed of crimson joy. Self-   21
doubt; seriousness, also questioned by the hours agonizing over appearance;
concentration shredded into attracting, being attractive; the absorbing real need
and love for working with words felt as hypocritical self-delusion ("I'm not
truly dedicated"), for what seems (and is) esteemed is being attractive to men.
High aim, and accomplishment toward it, discounted by the prevalent attitude
that, as girls will probably marry (attitudes not applied to boys who will
probably marry), writing is no more than an attainment of a dowry to be spent
later according to the needs and circumstances within the true vocation:
husband and family. The growing acceptance that going on will threaten other
needs, to love and be loved; ("a woman has to sacrifice all claims to femininity
and family to be a writer").

And the agony — peculiarly mid-century, escaped by their sisters of   22
pre-Freudian, pre-Jungian times — that "creation and femininity are
incompatible." Anaïs Nin's words:

> The aggressive act of creation; the guilt for creating. I did not want to rival man; to steal
> man's creation, his thunder. I must protect them, not outshine them.

The acceptance — against one's experienced reality — of the sexist notion that
the act of creation is not as inherently natural to a woman as to a man, but
rooted instead in unnatural aggression, rivalry, envy, or thwarted sexuality.

And in all the usual college teaching — the English, history, psychology,   23
sociology courses — little to help that young woman understand the source or
nature of this inexplicable draining self-doubt, loss of aspiration, of confidence.

It is all there in the extreme in Plath's *Bell Jar* — that (inadequate) portrait   24
of the artist as young woman (significantly, one of the few that we have) —
from the precarious sense of vocation to the paralyzing conviction that (in a
sense different from what she wrote years later)

> Perfection is terrible. It cannot have children.
> It tamps the womb.

And indeed, in our century as in the last, until very recently almost all   25
distinguished achievement has come from childless women: Willa Cather, Ellen
Glasgow, Gertrude Stein, Edith Wharton, Virginia Woolf, Elizabeth Bowen,
Katherine Mansfield, Isak Dinesen, Katherine Anne Porter, Dorothy Richardson,

Henry Handel Richardson, Susan Glaspell, Dorothy Parker, Lillian Hellman, Eudora Welty, Djuna Barnes, Anaïs Nin, Ivy Compton-Burnett, Zora Neale Hurston, Elizabeth Madox Roberts, Christina Stead, Carson McCullers, Flannery O'Connor, Jean Stafford, May Sarton, Josephine Herbst, Jessamyn West, Janet Frame, Lillian Smith, Iris Murdoch, Joyce Carol Oates, Hannah Green, Lorraine Hansberry.

Most never questioned, or at least accepted (a few sanctified) this different   26
condition for achievement, not imposed on men writers. Few asked the fundamental human equality question regarding it that Elizabeth Mann Borghese, Thomas Mann's daughter, asked when she was eighteen and sent to a psychiatrist for help in getting over an unhappy love affair (revealing also a working ambition to become a great musician although "women cannot be great musicians").

> "You must choose between your art and fulfillment as a woman," the analyst told her, "between music and family life."
>
> "Why?" she asked. "Why must I choose? No one said to Toscanini or to Bach or my father that they must choose between their art and personal, family life; fulfillment as a man. . . . Injustice everywhere."

Not where it is free choice. But where it is forced because of the circumstances for the sex into which one is born—a choice men of the same class do not have to make in order to do their work—that is not choice, that is a coercive working of sexist oppression.

What possible difference, you may ask, does it make to literature whether   27
or not a woman writer remains childless—free choice or not—especially in view of the marvels these childless women have created.

Might there not have been other marvels as well, or other dimensions to   28
these marvels? Might there not have been present profound aspects and understandings of human life as yet largely absent in literature?

More and more women writers in our century, primarily in the last two   29
decades, are assuming as their right fullness of work *and* family life. Their emergence is evidence of changing circumstances making possible for them what (with rarest exception) was not possible in the generations of women before. I hope and I fear for what will result. I hope (and believe) that complex new richness will come into literature; I fear because almost certainly their work will be impeded, lessened, partial. For the fundamental situation remains unchanged. Unlike men writers who marry, most will not have the societal equivalent of a wife—nor (in a society hostile to growing life) anyone but themselves to mother their children. Even those who can afford help, good schools, summer camps, may (*may*) suffer what seventy years ago W. E. B. Du

Bois called "The Damnation of Women": "that only at the sacrifice of the chance to do their best work can women bear and rear children."

> *Substantial creative achievement demands time . . . and with rare exceptions only full-time workers have created it.*

I am quoting myself from "Silences," a talk nine years ago. In motherhood, as it is structured,

> *circumstances for sustained creation are almost impossible. Not because the capacities to create no longer exist, or the need (though for a while as in any fullness of life the need may be obscured), but . . . the need cannot be first. It can have at best only part self, part time . . . Motherhood means being instantly interruptible, responsive, responsible. Children need one* now *(and remember, in our society, the family must often try to be the center for love and health the outside world is not). The very fact that these are needs of love, not duty, that one feels them as one's self; that there is no one else to be responsible for these needs,* gives them primacy. It is distraction, not meditation, that becomes habitual; interruption, not continuity; spasmodic, not constant, toil. Work interrupted, deferred, postponed makes blockage — at best, lesser accomplishment. Unused capacities atrophy, cease to be. . . .*

Yes, the loss in quality, the minor work, the hidden silences, are there in woman after woman writer in our century. We will never have the body of work that we were capable of producing. Blight, said Blake, never does good to a tree:

> *And if a blight kill not a tree but it still bear fruit, let none say that the fruit was in consequence of the blight.*

As for myself, who did not publish a book until I was fifty, who raised children without household help or the help of the "technological sublime" (the atom bomb was in manufacture before the first automatic washing machine); who worked outside the house on everyday jobs as well (as nearly half of all women do now, though a woman with a paid job, except as a maid or prostitute, is still rarest of any in literature); who could not kill the essential angel (there was no one else to do her work); would not — if I could — have killed the caring part of the Woolf angel, as distant from the world of literature most of my life as literature is distant (in content too) from my world:

The years when I should have been writing, my hands and being were at other (inescapable) tasks. Now, lightened as they are, when I must do those tasks into which most of my life went, like the old mother, grandmother in my *Tell Me a Riddle* who could not make herself touch a baby, I pay a psychic cost: "the sweat beads, the long shudder begins." The habits of a lifetime when everything else had to come before writing are not easily broken, even when circumstances now often make it possible for writing to be first; habits of years — response to others, distractibility, responsibility for daily matters — stay with you, mark you, become you. The cost of "discontinuity (that pattern still imposed on women) is such a weight of things unsaid, an accumulation of material so great, that everything starts up something else in me; what should take weeks, takes me sometimes months to write; what should take months, takes years.

I speak of myself to bring here the sense of those others to whom this is in 33 the process of happening (unnecessarily happening, for it need not, must not continue to be) and to remind us of those (I so nearly was one) who never come to writing at all.

We must not speak of women writers in our century (as we cannot speak 34 of women in any area of recognized human achievement) without speaking also of the invisible, the as-innately-capable: the born to the wrong circumstances — diminished, excluded, foundered, silenced.

We who write are survivors, *"only's."* One-out-of-twelve. . . .   35

QUESTIONS ON CONTENT:

1. What is Olsen's thesis?
2. How do you know that Tillie Olsen's remarks are not aimed solely at women writers? What is she saying about creativity, femininity, and men?
3. What does Olsen say about the put-downs of women she finds entrenched in American education? What area does she find most offensive? How does she illustrate this discrimination?
4. What "harms" does she find inculcated in young girls? Precisely how does Olsen characterize the loss to society resulting from what she sees as sexist oppression?

QUESTIONS ON WRITING STRUCTURE AND STRATEGY:

1. What does Olsen mean by her title *Silences*, and where does she first explain it? Where do you find her returning to this theme in other parts of the selection?
2. Olsen achieves balance and rhythm in some sentences by using parallelism (see Glossary). Aside from being grammatically and rhetorically correct, such a technique also contributes to *clarity, euphony, coherence,* and, most impor-

tantly, *emphasis* (see Glossary). Find several examples of parallelism and explain their effect.

3. How is her elliptical style (omitting words without destroying the meaning or sense) similar to conversational speech? What words does she most often omit? Explain the effect of such a technique. Is this what is sometimes meant by the assertion that the reader must bring something of himself or herself to the reading? Is this a good way to avoid wordiness? Explain.

4. Olsen employs a great many parentheticals, using either parentheses or paired dashes. (Note: parenthetical material can be removed without disturbing the grammatical structure of the sentence. In other words, the sentence will still make sense.) What specific kinds of information does Olsen insert parenthetically?

5. Olsen expands her sentences by using subordinate clauses and by inserting modifiers. She achieves sentence variety and power by varying sentence length, using strong verbs instead of forms of the verb "to be," and using precise adjectives. Study her sentences for examples of each of these techniques.

6. Olsen's vocabulary is impressive. How do you think she gained such a vocabulary? Is there internal evidence in the selection directing you to an answer?
   a. Olsen also employs figurative language. Find examples of *simile, metaphor, irony, sarcasm,* and *paradox* (see Glossary).
   b. Note her many allusions. What does she assume about her audience by using so many allusions? How do these allusions underscore the importance of extensive reading? Does she perhaps use too many allusions? Explain.
   c. Olsen's language has a strong emotional appeal. Cite some examples. But her writing also has a strong intellectual appeal. Cite some examples. Does one outweigh the other, or are they gracefully blended into a coherent whole? Explain.

QUESTIONS FOR DISCUSSION AND WRITING:

1. How do Olsen's remarks about the loss to society by sexist oppression relate to racial oppression? In fact, to any kind of discrimination? Write a short paper in which you describe some discrimination you have observed: Against old people, handicapped persons, minorities. (Or perhaps you have experienced or have observed discrimination because of occupation. For instance, you may have worked as a dishwasher or a cashier and found that people made certain assumptions about you because of the job you held.)

2. Olsen asserts in 1965 that college reading is overwhelmingly concerned with male achievement. To what extent is this still true today? Was your high school program similarly tilted in favor of male achievement? For example: what names come most quickly to mind in the arts? In sports? In history? In literature? In other areas?

3. Olsen speaks of what she terms "a climate of expectations." Is there a different climate of expectations in your home for boys and girls? On the job, is there a different climate of expectations for men and women? Write a paper in which you explain.

4. Compare movies and television shows that still seem to stereotype female roles. Which ones reflect the growing independence of women? Can the "independent woman" be a stereotype, too?

SUGGESTIONS FOR JOURNAL ENTRIES

These are essentially suggestions for paragraphs or short journal entries, some of which could serve as prewriting for later fully developed papers, depending on your interests or directions from your instructor. It might be helpful to refer to the Glossary, the Writing Process, and the Rhetorical Index.

1. These eight writers were deeply committed to improving *themselves* through improving their abilities. They had goals, an essential for success in any endeavor. In your efforts to improve your writing, what are your goals? Begin with an assessment of your current writing skills. Which areas are pluses; which need work? Conduct this evaluation over several days if you wish. Be honest and specific in your appraisal. (a) What kinds of writing do you foresee after college in your profession? (b) How confident are you about your writing? (c) Discuss your early writing experiences, your classes and teachers in high school, your work on the school paper, yearbook, or debate squads. (d) Describe your personal writing process. (e) Do you have any problems in organization, development, style, or mechanics? (f) Finally, in specific and realistic terms describe those aspects of your writing that you are seeking to improve. Hereafter, devote at least one paragraph per week (perhaps at the end of your journal—be sure to date each entry) to examining exactly what you did that week to improve your writing.

2. A frequent complaint among business executives is the inability of their employees to summarize material. In anticipation of the demands of later on-the-job writing, take time to summarize each of the assigned text selections in your journals. Keep in mind that summaries should (a) identify the main points and maintain the tone of the original; and (b) retain the order of ideas in the original. This practice will also help you avoid wordiness in your own writing.

3. Write a paragraph on why you intend to keep a journal (in addition to the fact that you are assigned to keep one). What do you foresee as advantages?

FOCUS — ORGANIZATION — DEVELOPMENT

4. These eight authors have successfully employed narration (see Rhetorical Index) in their writing. Review some experiences from your childhood, and, as these authors have done, organize your ideas around some significant point. Try to recall an experience that involved:

   a. A new perspective on society.

   b. A new discovery in nature.

   c. An insight about yourself.

   d. The discovery of a new friend.

   e. Renewed trust or distrust of someone or something.

   Keeping in mind the essential considerations of theses (subject, audience, and purpose), compose a journal entry consisting of (a) an introductory paragraph that includes your thesis; and (b) topic sentences (see Glossary) for each of three or more paragraphs of development. If time warrants, complete your paragraphs using narration, description, and cause and effect (see Rhetorical Index).

5. Practice summarizing in outline form the important lessons a writer might gain from the London selection. Now turn the outline into a straightforward prose journal entry.

6. You may or may not have experienced an identity crisis like Eldridge Cleaver underwent in prison, but have you ever been gravely disappointed in yourself? In your behavior? Your lack of direction? Your action, reaction, or response to a person or situation? Have you ever been tempted to cheat on an exam, to hurt or let down a friend, to turn in less than your best performance in school, in athletics, or on the job? Using specific detail, describe the circumstances and your ultimate decision to remedy the situation.

7. Your preceding journal entry was probably a personal entry with a personal voice and a conversational tone. Now assume a more formal tone appropriate to a more general audience, and using third person and a more challenging vocabulary write a paragraph or two about a disappointment in your government, your president, a sports figure on drugs, a coworker, or an employer.

8. Tillie Olsen describes the plight of a woman who was told that she had to choose between "art and fulfillment as a woman . . . between music and family life." Have you ever been forced to make a choice between two desirable alternatives? Write a journal entry using comparison/contrast or cause/effect (see Rhetorical Index) on the dilemma of having to choose between two equally attractive options.

9. Tillie Olsen describes how she "salvaged" moments of time away from duties to work and family in order to devote herself to her writing. Have you "salvaged" time away from your obligations in order to pursue some person-

66

ally satisfying activity? Hunting? Athletics? Meditation? Hobbies? Practice using description by writing a journal entry describing your experiences.

10. Most of these authors consistently maintained one point of view: they were adults looking back at earlier times in their lives. Try to emulate this consistent point of view by writing a page in your journal on a subject about which you have had several different points of view: a job you once held (or hold), a former friend, a car you once owned, a goal you once strove for. On another day write about that subject from a changed point of view. Avoid being wishy-washy or ambiguous by being consistent in person (I, you, he, she), tense (present or past), and tone (ironic, sympathetic, angry) in each writing situation.

11. All of these authors, as do all people, experience stress. Currently you are probably most familiar with the stresses on college students, especially those trying to manage families, jobs, and studies all at the same time. Keeping in mind the writer's concerns with audience and purpose, write journal entries on three successive days about the stresses college students experience. Address your remarks on one day to parents in general, on the second day to *your* parents, on the third to a son or daughter or a younger sibling. To a certain extent your specific purpose will vary in each case; your method of development, word choice, and examples will surely differ.

12. Malcolm X and London build strong cases for increasing one's vocabulary. As an exercise in discovering strong verbs and adjectives, team up with a friend and photocopy passages from a well-written magazine article. Then white out many of the verbs and adjectives. Exchange paragraphs, fill in the blank spaces, and check with the original.

13. As you read Franklin, you no doubt observed the variety in the number of words in each sentence and in the construction of his sentences. It is tempting, when writing about one's self (especially in letters of application) to begin every sentence "I . . . . " However, not only is it boring for the reader but it also gives the impression of egotism. Note the variety of transitional and introductory phrases Franklin employs: "After some time . . ." "About this time. . . . " "Then . . ." "By comparing my work afterwards with the original . . ." "As we parted without settling the point . . ." Let transitions, introductory phrases, and dependent clauses help you to achieve variety and interest in your writing. Photocopy an earlier journal entry or a passage from one of your class papers and after stapling it in your journal, revise some of the sentences to relieve the repetitive subject, verb, object order: "I . . . . " or "He . . . . "

STYLE

14. All of these writers use description, as well as narration, to develop their theses. In addition, each selection in this unit evidences a distinct personality.

Using description, compose a journal entry on four successive days in which you clearly evidence a personal voice.

a. Tell an imaginary reader about your personality—party-goer, loner, devoted friend, flake, grind, or . . . .

b. Compose another paragraph in which you describe your physical appearance clearly and exactly.

c. Write another paragraph in which you describe yourself humorously. You may resort to sarcasm or irony.

d. Describe your "crowd" or one of your friends.

Loosen up and have fun with your writing. Allow a personal voice to surface. Let the reader see you in four different aspects.

15. Franklin wrote his *Autobiography* for the edification of his son. Try rewriting paragraph four and address it to today's students (i.e., switch the audience from Franklin's son to your peers, and change the eighteenth-century prose style and vocabulary to reflect the twentieth century). Alternately, try rewriting it for a younger sibling. Try inserting your own personal voice into the account.

16. In the London selection, you read several passages of dialogue. Practice writing a little dialogue in your journal. Start with something easy. For example:

a. Someone attempts to persuade you to go to the movies when you have an exam the next morning in your eight o'clock class.

b. You need the family car for an awesome date.

c. You try to talk your roommate into going out on a blind date.

d. You make plans to go to Florida for Spring break.

e. You try to persuade yourself or a friend to quit smoking, to stop procrastinating, or to start dieting.

Read your entries aloud to make sure they sound like genuine conversations.

17. Douglass used antithesis to gain emphasis and euphony. Try your hand at some antithetical sentences. Start using Douglass as a pattern and then take off on your own.

What my roommate _____, I _____.

What my parents _____, I _____.

What my brother _____, I _____.

or

I owed as much to _____, as to _____.

I became as much of a ——————, as a ——————.

I grew to be more of a ——————, than a ——————.

Now go on to invent several examples of antithesis on your own.

SUGGESTED WRITING TOPICS

1. Having read how a half dozen writers taught themselves to write, what conclusions can you draw about them? In your prewriting you may arrive at a topic by composing a series of different lists: consider (a) the writers' meager beginnings; (b) their motivations; (c) their persistence; (d) their later successes; (e) their differences. Organize a few of your insights into a thesis which you support with allusions (as does Tillie Olsen) to specific writers. Develop your paper by adding details from your own personal experience. Although these readings are rather "straight" narratives, your paper could add some colorful touches: humor, tenderness, sadness. Try several versions to see which one best serves your purposes.

2. Many of these writers discuss their reading and describe its impact upon them. Some, like Tillie Olsen, reveal their reading in their writing. All are convinced, however, of the practical and liberating effects of reading. Try a prewriting, brainstorming session in which you concentrate, for example, on Malcolm X and Martin Eden's enthusiasm for reading and fascination with words, on reading as a means of Douglass's enlightenment, on reading as an influence on Franklin's diplomatic skills, or perhaps on your own reading experiences. From this exercise develop a theme on the value of reading for the student-writer, alluding to the experiences of these writers or your own to illustrate and/or buttress your generalizations.

3. Autobiographies are especially popular these days, probably because of people's innate curiosity about other people, although Clare Booth Luce has referred to autobiographies as "alibiographies." But assume you are writing your autobiography and wish to pass on the lessons gained from your experience to a younger, college-bound brother, sister, or friend. Sift through your own experiences — humorous or serious — and shape them into a mini-autobiography (or alibiography). Limit your writing to one segment of your life or focus on one or two lessons.

4. Martin Eden was inspired to read and write because of his love for Ruth. Men and women throughout the ages have been inspired to great, hitherto impossible achievements because of inspiration of one kind or another. Have you, or someone you know, ever been "inspired" to do something that was considered almost impossible? In a clear, well-organized paper, share your recollections of one such achievement and the inspiration that sparked it.

5. The title of Eldridge Cleaver's selection, "On Becoming," relates to the "en-

lightenment process" he underwent in prison. Has some episode or incident, the reading of some book, poem, or play, ever precipitated such a process in your life? At home? At work? In school? Try to isolate those factors making for your "enlightenment" and organize them in a clear, well-organized essay.

6. Eldridge Cleaver says that he had to write in order "to save himself." The writers of the other selections also explicitly or implicitly state their reasons for writing. You should not conclude, however, that people write *only* because they have a problem. Writing — like thinking and the thousand other things we do — is something we do because we are human. It was not simply writing and communicating with which these writers were concerned. Learning to read and building a vocabulary expanded their knowledge and gave them the tools with which to *think*. Now, after some reflection on the readings in this unit, can you write a theme on what is gained by becoming a more effective writer? Are you, for example, a more careful *thinker*? A more discerning reader? Using some of the appropriate prewriting techniques, narrow your subject down to a single, important idea and illustrate with examples from this or other classes.

7. If you have faithfully consulted the dictionary during your reading of these several writers, you will have added a number of new words to your vocabulary. On the basis of your experience, prepare a short essay in which you examine whether or not the following quotation is in any way applicable to that experience: "The limits of my language [words, ideas] mark the limits of my world." Or apply your experience to the following quotation from Ralph Waldo Emerson: "Life [including reading as vicarious living] is our dictionary." That is, you participate in life through reading. (Emerson also says, "I learn immediately from any speaker how much he has already lived through the poverty or splendor of his speech.") Discuss new vocabulary you have acquired in computer class or on a new job that has enlarged your world.

8. While Tillie Olsen's style may be appropriate to her subject and audience, it would be inappropriate for Eric Hoffer, who may perhaps share her audience but whose style is "plainer" and whose personality and experiences are different. Imagine that you are Eric Hoffer and try "translating" several of Olsen's paragraphs into Hoffer's style. Or, try rewriting several of Olsen's paragraphs in your own style. Be careful not to omit any of her ideas. Your object is to rewrite in a plainer style some material that has been presented in a complicated style.

9. Try another experiment with style by taking a paragraph from Malcolm X or Eric Hoffer and attempting to rewrite it in the style of Tillie Olsen. This will require some inventiveness on your part to convert straightforward accounts into Olsen's elliptical style with its parenthetical interrupters and numerous allusions.

10. Eric Hoffer says that during his search for a suitable style he first had to acquire the "taste for a good sentence." He liked Montaigne's sentences,

describing them as "sentences with hooks in them." Go back through these seven selections and find some examples of such sentences. Or examine some of your other textbooks — or newspapers or magazines — for such examples. Prepare a short essay in which you explain how your examples work to accomplish what Hoffer calls for: something to stick in your mind. In your paper, try to include several such sentences of your own composition.

11. If it is possible to secure statistics for male and female registration in your degree-granting departments or colleges, determine how the sexes are distributed. If statistics are unavailable, interview counselors or professors. Do you find the ratio of men to women disproportionate? Do you find the proportions in engineering, nursing, veterinary medicine, human ecology, business administration, and law changing over the past ten years or so? What do these changes say about "the climate of expectations" for young women?

12. Discuss your high school counselors with some of your classmates for any evidence of possible sexism. Were women counseled into less creative roles? Were women apprised of their special advantages in certain fields? Were there outside influences on your choice of a major? Write a paper on your findings.

The Writer's Consciousness: Enlarging Our World Through Reading and Writing

_____ *I* _____

Not only can reading and writing serve as liberation from a limited past — as the authors in Unit I have illustrated — but language can also enrich and expand our worlds. It is fundamental to our understanding of ourselves, our values, and our personal relationships. As a creative outlet, reading and writing can stimulate our imaginations.

Self-Awareness

As a means of self-discovery, writing is of paramount importance, for in committing our innermost thoughts to writing and subjecting them to critical examination, we can take a careful look at who we are, what we're doing, and where we're going. All too often harried lives — complicated by our multiple roles as parents, sons, daughters, siblings, roommates, students, friends, and employees — prevent us from truly getting to know ourselves. Keeping a journal may help, for according to many of the world's great writers, daily writing provides an ideal way to initiate what Henry David Thoreau would call an exploration of the world within us. For the journal keeper the first reading in this section, by Roy Hoffman, points out the rich benefits for the whole person. In addition to improving writing skills through consistent, daily practice, keeping a journal develops our powers of observation, heightens our sensitivity, and provides a valuable emotional release.

Letter writing accomplishes many of the same purposes as journal keeping. In writing letters we are often forced to sort out our ideas and to firm up our stand on personal as well as public issues. Writing letters can initiate, build, and cement relationships as well as provide a permanent record of our feelings. Letters also can serve as a diary, or, when collected, letters may become involuntary autobiography. In "The Mail of the Species," William Swanson humorously enumerates some of the qualities of good letters, all the while deploring the fact that letter writing is becoming a lost art, antiquated by the speed and convenience of "direct dialing."

Self-discovery naturally involves an assessment of values, and here again reading and writing play a vital role. Alan Alda's "You Have to Know What Your Values Are" prods us into taking a good, long look at the values that really control our lives. In examining the causes and consequences of bulimia, an eating disorder prevalent particularly among young women, Jane Brody points out its correlation to the victim's low self-esteem.

Personal Relationships

Reading and writing about our personal relationships enables us to examine our feelings about people, problems, and ideas. One writer's query, "How can I know what I think, 'til I see what I say" carries with it more truth than jest. Many times we are unsure of how we stand on a subject or of the exact dimensions of our views until we put them down on paper (see Swift, Unit III). The next several readings may provide some answers, for they challenge us to look at some very basic personal relationships and emotions: marriage, the family, death, and anger. Arlene Skolnick and Graham Spanier, for example, discuss the once traditional but now seemingly transitional relationships involved in marriage and the family. Family relationships, of course, involve that very special love for one's parents. In a very personal reflection, Ann Bayer lets us share for a moment the heartache and ardor of her love for her mother. In contrast Jane Brody's article reveals some new attitudes toward the expression of anger. Reading these selections and writing about the relationships not only help us to discover what we really believe but also enable us ultimately to communicate those discoveries with grace, clarity, and conviction.

Individual Achievement

Reading and writing can also lead to individual achievement and, as the writers in Unit I demonstrate, can transform our lives. Without an education and the continuing development of reading and writing skills many individuals wind up leading dead-end, unfulfilled lives. In the concluding lines of his autobiographical reminiscence, black novelist Richard Wright testifies to the distance his newly acquired appetite for reading has created "between me and the world in which I lived and tried to make a living." In Wright's case his reading provided the impetus that eventually catapulted him from a tedious job to the enviable position of one of America's most successful authors.

Individual and Society

As our personal concerns broaden and extend outward, we become caught up in the public concerns of the world around us. Our self-awareness now expands into a public awareness as we develop a growing sensitivity to and understanding of some of the concerns of the society in which we live. In "What is the Point of Working?" Lance Morrow examines the changing attitudes about work and its role in our lives. Following that, Arthur Ashe laments the disproportionate time some youngsters spend on the playing field instead of in the library. In "Iliterasee att Wurk," William McGowan points out that despite our seeming emphasis on education, 25 million Americans are functionally illiterate. These growing numbers of Americans (coupled with millions of aliterates who simply don't read) are becoming economic liabilities to themselves and are working a serious toll on the country's industrial productivity.

-------------------- *II* --------------------

What can be learned from the *way* the authors in this section write? Just as individuals perfecting a skill (actors, dancers, golfers, artists, craftsmen) hone their talents by studying the techniques of more experienced individuals, so, too, writers learn by emulating the skills of successful authors—a practice endorsed by Franklin (Unit I) and Medawar (Unit III), who may speak for all writers.

Each of these writings—representing different purposes and directed to a variety of audiences—is characterized by a highly individualistic style, the writer's own particular hallmark. Unfortunately, developing style is not an overnight accomplishment. Reading with an eye to how successful writers achieve

75

their distinctive writing "personality," however, can pay dividends in improved stylistic techniques for most student writers. The selections in this unit provide excellent examples of the effective use of *sentence variety, concrete expression,* and *figurative language,* important components of style.

You will gain greater clarity, interest value, and emphasis by varying the lengths, syntax, and word order of sentences. First, flip back to the Glossary for a brief identification of *sentence variety* and then observe, for example, Lance Morrow's variant sentence lengths: some sentences of more than fifty words are skillfully interspersed with short, five-word sentences. Notice how George Will, typical of many of these authors, writes sentences that vary in (a) purpose, (b) length, (c) syntax (simple, compound, complex, and compound-complex constructions are all represented), (d) word order, and (e) form (both loose and periodic — see Glossary). The frequent use of *subordination* (see Glossary) promotes the ease and smoothness of oral communication and in addition emphasizes the more important ideas in a sentence. Notice in other selections how those writers avoid the routine subject-verb-object/complement order by introducing sentences with modifiers, infinitives, or inverted word order.

Writing that is colorless, uninteresting, and vague is often the result of an author's tendency to generalize or to rely too heavily on abstractions. Therefore, to enliven dull passages, use specific detail, strong verbs, and precise word choice. Jane Brody, for example, avoids vague descriptions about the consequences of bulimia by citing a dozen of the real hazards involved. In "After Death, Mementos Mean a Life" Ann Bayer does not simply generalize about "things" and "objects" that remind her of her mother. Instead she singles out specifics: the flower on the bodice of her nightgown, her mother's hairbrush — "its bristles still laced with her hairs" — an old Christmas list, a hypodermic syringe — telling details, reminders of the good times and the bad.

As you read, look for the strong verbs these authors use to energize their writing: "erupts," "inflame," "binges," "scream . . . carp . . . holler," "jeopardize," and "growls."

Study the writers' precise use of words, words that connote a whole idea, that call up complete pictures in the reader's mind: "post war dinosaurs," "consumer sovereignty argument," "gas guzzlers," "masterminded its own collapse." Note William Swanson's well-chosen words that convey humor and a certain disdain as he describes letters "crackling with esoterica," and junk mail written by "the condominium hustler," or by "presidential hopefuls groveling for your quadrennial support."

Notice how the authors combine and pyramid well-chosen words to help readers visualize situations and ideas. Morrow writes that "all life must be worked at, protected, planted, replanted, fashioned, cooked for, coaxed, diapered, formed, sustained."

The use of *figurative language* as a possible avenue to creative expression is demonstrated in each unit. Review, if necessary, the simile, metaphor, and analogy descriptions in the Glossary, and then check George Will's selection on Ray Kroc

76

as a kaleidoscopic study in comparisons. Will writes about hamburgers that are "alike as Model T's were." He notes that "Kroc's book like his life is as ingenious as an American primitive painting."

These selections offer a smorgasbord of other stylistic devices: parallel construction, irony, rhythm, alliteration, and euphony. And yet these are just a few of the techniques used by successful writers to make their writing come alive, devices that you too can easily employ in your own writing.

In this unit we invite you to read, ponder, write, rewrite, revise, and write again about the ideas these writers have expressed, about what you believe, about where you think they score, and where you think they miss. We hope these selections will stimulate your thinking to take off on a subject suggested by these writers, or better yet on a bright new idea of your own. In your own writing, try to incorporate some of the techniques employed by these successful men and women.

ON KEEPING A JOURNAL

Roy Hoffman

Throughout history diaries and journals have been important avenues of self-expression and self-exploration for people from all walks of life. Writers (Henry David Thoreau, Gustave Flaubert, Virginia Woolf, Samuel Pepys, Anaïs Nin), church leaders (John Wesley, Pope John XXIII, Cotton Mather), statesmen (George Washington, John Adams, John Quincy Adams), in addition to a host of the infamous as well as the famous and nonfamous, have kept journals as a storehouse of significant insights and impressions (or a storehouse of life's most precious and enlightened moments).

In this first selection, which appeared in Newsweek's "On Campus," novelist Roy Hoffman — bemused by the intimate glimpses of a "moodier, more inquisitive, more fun-loving" younger Hoffman — chronicles the evolution of his journal-keeping regimen. From the vantage point of age, the author urges all college students to keep journals, pointing out their unique potential for private expression and self-analysis.

Hoffman's article demonstrates the writer's need to focus on a specific audience. Notice how he develops his thesis and selects examples with those particular readers in mind, in this case, clearly, college students. Notable also is Hoffman's effective use of quotes, similes, and metaphors to add color and vitality to his writing.

As a writer, let journal keeping work for you as a way to cultivate your writing talents. Even when you don't feel like writing, the discipline of making daily entries in a journal is good preparation for postcollege, on-the-job writing. When you do feel like writing, seize the opportunity to experiment, try out new vocabulary, different styles in your notebooks. You can make great strides in articulateness simply by summarizing the articles in this text. Journal writing can serve very useful purposes for your other classes as well. You just may find yourself earning a four point on tomorrow's essay test in history or psychology if you take time now to frame some possible questions and answers in your journal.

Journal keeping can make a difference for you and your writing. Let Hoffman persuade you to start a journal. You might find you like it — now and in the future — when you look back over it and "remember when."

Wherever I go I carry a small notebook in my coat or back pocket for thoughts, observations and impressions. As a writer I use this notebook as an artist would a sketch pad, for stories and essays, and as a sporadic journal of my comings and goings. When I first started keeping notebooks, though, I was not yet a professional writer. I was still in college.

I made my first notebook entries in the summer of 1972, just after my freshman year, in what was actually a travel log. A buddy and I were setting out to trek from our Alabama hometown to the distant tundra of Alaska. With unbounded enthusiasm I began: "Wild, crazy ecstasy wants to wrench my head from my body." The log, written in a university composition book, goes on to chronicle our adventures in the land where the sun never sets, the bars never close and the prepipeline employment prospects were so bleak we ended up taking jobs as night janitors.

When I returned to college that fall I had a small revelation: the world around me of libraries, quadrangles, Frisbees and professors was as rich with material for my journals and notebooks as galumphing moose and garrulous fishermen.

These college notebooks, which built to a pitch my senior year, are gold mines to me now. Classrooms, girlfriends, cups of coffee and lines of poetry — from mine to John Keat's — float by like clouds. As I lie beneath these clouds again, they take on familiar and distinctive shapes.

Though I can remember the campus's main quadrangle, I see it more vividly when I read my description of school on a visit during summer break: "the muggy, lassitudinal air . . . the bird noises that can not be pointed to, the summer emptiness that grows emptier with a few students squeaking by the library on poorly oiled bicycles." An economics professor I fondly remember returns with less fondness in my notebooks, "staring down at the class with his equine face." And a girl I had a crush on senior year, whom I now recall mistily, reappears with far more vitality as "the ample, slightly-gawky, whole-wheat, fractured object of my want gangling down the hall in spring heat today."

When, in reading over my notebooks, I am not peering out at quadrangles, midterm exams, professors or girlfriends, I see a portrait of my parents and hometown during holidays and occasional weekend breaks. Like a wheel, home revolves, each turn regarded differently depending on the novel or political essay I'd been most influenced by the previous semester.

Mostly, though, in wandering back through my notebooks, I meet someone who could be my younger brother: the younger version of myself. The younger me seems moodier, more inquisitive, more fun-loving and surprisingly eager to stay up all night partying or figuring out electron orbitals for a 9 A.M. exam. The younger me wanders through a hall of mirrors of the self, writes of "seeing two or three of myself on every corner," and pens long meditations on God and society before scribbling in the margin, "what a child I am." The younger

79

me also finds humor in trying to keep track of this hall of mirrors, commenting in ragged verse: "I hope that one day/Some grandson or cousin/Will read these books,/And know that I was/Once a youth/Sitting in drugstores with/ Anguished looks,/And poring over coffee,/And should have poured/The coffee/ Over these lines."

I believe that every college student should attempt to keep some form of notebook, journal or diary. A notebook is a secret garden in which to dance, sing, muse, wander, perform handstands, even cry. In the privacy of this little book, you can make faces, curse, turn somersaults and ask yourself if you're *really* in love. A notebook or journal is one of the few places you can call just your own.

Spring of my senior year I wrote: "This notebook shall be/A continuing-inner sanctum,/Where my closest confidante/Will seem like a stranger." It's hard, but necessary, to sustain that conviction. Journal writing suffers when you let someone, in your mind, look over your shoulder. Honesty wilts when a parent, teacher or friend looms up in your imagination to discourage you from putting your *true* thoughts on the page. Journal writing also runs a related hazard: the dizzying suspicion that one day your private thoughts, like those of Samuel Pepys or Virginia Woolf, will be published in several volumes and land up required reading for English 401. How can you write comfortably when the eyes of all future readers are upon you? Keep your notebooks with the abandon of one who knows his words will go up in smoke. Then you might really strike fire a hundred years or so from now if anyone cares to pry.

By keeping notebooks, you improve your writing ability, increasing your capacity to communicate both with yourself and others. By keeping notebooks, you discover patterns in yourself, whether lazy ones that need to be broken or healthy ones that can use some nurturing. By keeping notebooks, you heighten some moments and give substance to others: even a journey to the washateria offers potential for some offbeat journal observations. And by keeping notebooks while still in college, you chart a terrain that, for many, is more dynamically charged with ideas and discussions than the practical, workaday world just beyond. Notebooks, I believe, not only help us remember this dynamic charge, but also help us sustain it.

Not long ago, while traveling with a friend in Yorktown, Va., I passed by a time capsule buried in the ground in 1976, intended to be dug up in 2076. Keeping notebooks and journals is rather like burying time capsules into one's own life. There's no telling what old rock song, love note, philosophical complaint or rosy Saturday morning you'll unearth when you dig up these personal time capsules. You'll be able to piece together a remarkable picture of where you've come from, and may well get some important glimmers about where you're going.

QUESTIONS ON CONTENT:

1. What is Hoffman's revelation upon returning to college after his trip to Alaska?
2. Why have his college notebooks become "gold mines" to him now?
3. How does he define a notebook? What can you *do* in a notebook?
4. What does Hoffman say are the most important advantages of a notebook?
5. What factors does Hoffman say inhibit a journal keeper? What does he urge readers to do to avoid these inhibiting factors?
6. According to Hoffman, how does keeping a notebook help you to improve your writing ability?
7. According to Hoffman, what are the four benefits of keeping a journal?

QUESTIONS ON WRITING STRUCTURE AND STRATEGY:

1. What examples of figurative language do you find in this selection? How do they make his writing more interesting, appealing?
2. In what specific ways has Hoffman geared his writing to appeal to college students? What techniques lead you to think that Hoffman might have designed this article for college students (vocabulary, person, examples)?
3. What purpose might Hoffman have intended with his last sentence?

QUESTIONS FOR DISCUSSION AND WRITING:

1. If you are not already doing so, keep a journal for the next two weeks. Avoid merely keeping a diary of your activities; instead, try to make it a collection of impressions and ideas, as Hoffman has described (new insights from your classes, observations about society, perhaps a bit of poetry).
2. See the Rhetorical Index on "Description" and compose a short paper in which you describe a familiar building on campus, your dormitory room, a landmark, a popular recreational sport or hangout. Seek to make your description colorful and yet sensitive, an impression that will be meaningful when you read it in later years.
3. Write a short paper in which you describe the typical college student on your campus (or whom you encounter in your classes, cafeterias, libraries, or study lounges). You may prefer to describe a person or persons at work — employers, associates, customers. Review Hoffman's extensive use of examples and specific detail (as in paragraph three: "libraries, quadrangles, Frisbee and professors"); then make your writing come alive through carefully chosen words and details that will help you to clearly visualize this person (or a composite picture) at some later time.
4. Write a paper in which you describe several fads on your campus or "trends" in contemporary society. Let Hoffman's strong verbs ("wants to wrench," "suffers," "make faces, curse, turn somersaults") and his precise adjectives

("muggy, lassitudinal," "garrulous," "ragged") inspire you to search for the exact words that convey a whole image.

5.   Write a paper in which you give a sort of "end of the year" evaluation of what you see as the most significant events, developments, trends in one of the following areas: sports, movies, education, economics, the arts (dance, or theater, or writing, or painting, or sculpture). Do not merely catalogue events. The events should lead to some generalization or overview. Here is a chance to pursue an interest or discover an interest. You may want to do a little research before writing.

THE MAIL OF THE SPECIES
William Swanson

The golden age of letter writing, when missives were cherished treasures often committed to memory from repeated readings and then secreted away in beribboned boxes for safekeeping, has come and gone, leaving in its wake monstrous monthly telephone bills and the ubiquitous card shop. In this article William Swanson humorously specifies the qualities of good letters, bemoans their demise, and calls for a revival of letter writing. With tongue-in-cheek sarcasm he puts down the elaborate Christmas letter "extravaganzas," Hallmark "uncaring," and cutesy notepaper.

Despite the ease of picking up the telephone, now and then we all must write letters. Letter writing obviously increases our fluency and articulateness and puts our powers of narration, description, and clarity to the test.

Swanson's article, which appeared in an airline magazine, shows us how a ho-hum subject can come alive through the subtle use of humor and specific detail. Because startlingly new ideas are rare, most interesting and informative writing is a product of the skillful use of language. Although Swanson's article is not earthshaking, his style makes the subject enjoyable and perhaps even memorable.

In many respects this could be considered a how-to or definition paper about letter writing. But notice what this author does to make interesting and palatable reading. Observe Swanson's clear organization, his thesis, his use of topic sentences, his colorful, precise word choice, and his challenging literary allusions.

A gentleman from the Midwest writes: 1

Dear Sir,
What must a fellow do in this day and age to receive a good letter? Time was when it was quite enough to have a handful of literate friends scattered here and there, and to maintain a permanent address. The rest came more or less naturally.
Lamentably,
Waiting for the Post

Dear Waiting, 2
    I know what you mean. I recently received a letter written by—not 3
merely on—a computer. The letter began "Dear Bill" and then attempted to
sell me on timesharing in a Colorado ski-slope condominium. Anybody or
anything familiar enough to address me "Dear Bill" would have known not

83

only that I do not ski, but that I dislike hills. The correspondent was clearly an imposter, the correspondence an imposition. If the truth be told, I can't remember when I last received a really good letter.

How would I define a "good" letter? Well, like sex and the backstroke, it is considerably easier to demonstrate than to explain. Suffice it to say that the "good" refers not to the news a letter contains, but to the quality of the letter itself. Some of the best letters I've ever received were full of bad news — news of broken hearts and shattered hips, of wasted lives and squandered fortunes. Some of the best letters I've ever *read*, for that matter, were written by such anguished souls as Wolfgang Amadeus Mozart and included lines like: "Great God! I would not wish my worst enemy to be in my present position," and "Whereas I felt tolerably well yesterday, I am absolutely wretched today."

I would say further that a good letter possesses at least the following attributes (perhaps a great many more), which I'll list not necessarily in the order of their importance:

PERSONALITY. A good letter is addressed to you as a person, by another person, *not* to you as a consumer, customer, subscriber, patron, draftee, by a computer or some other device. The writer should know, if not love, you, and should ask you for money only if he is a blood relative.

INDIVIDUALITY. A good letter does not begin with "Dear Member of the Class of '63," or "Dear Buick Owner," or even, God knows, "Dear Friend."

"Dear Friend," of course, is the classic salutation of the dreaded Christmas letter. As such, it is acceptable only when posted from the mission fields of Tanzania or Upper Volta. Years ago, the dreaded Christmas letter was easily spotted and consigned to the Yuletime fire, owing to the inferior quality of the copy — a watery and all-but-illegible blue, often still damp from the abysmal mimeograph machine whence it came. Nowadays, though, the wordprocessing personal computer makes each dreaded Christmas letter so fresh and sharp and original-looking that the hapless recipient must peruse the first few sentences before he can determine just what it is. The tip-off is the use of the broadest common denominator of news ("Well, it sure seems quiet around here what with the kids off to college . . ."), the repetition of the kids' and pets' names and ages, and the frequent reminders of Dad's and Mom's occupations and health status.

A good letter, by vivid contrast, is a one-on-one proposition. It is rife with gossip, sly reference, and double-entendre intelligible, at best, only to the sender and recipient. A good letter, or series of good letters, produces what John Updike has called "involuntary autobiography." A good letter shares precious secrets and awful truths — and sometimes, for both parties' sake, should be torched immediately upon reading.

IMPERISHABILITY. A good letter, though crackling with esoterica, is

84

terrific to read years, even decades, later. That is why, against all better judgment, good letters are in fact so rarely torched. A good letter is, indeed, literature of a sort, with all the color and spunk of, say, one of Mark Twain's sketches.

It helps, of course, if the letter's author is Mark Twain, and it is certainly   11
no accident that some of the greatest letters we read today were written by the likes of James, Flaubert, Joyce, and Waugh. Talk about imperishable! Consider this tantalizing introduction, lifted from a letter written by peripatetic Henry James, in Paris, in 1876:

> *Dear Father,*
> *. . . The slender thread of my few personal relations hangs on, without snapping, but it doesn't grow very stout. You crave chiefly news, I suppose, about Ivan Sergeitch [Turgenev!] whom I have lately seen several times. . . .*

Literacy is, of course, a basic requirement of the good-letter writer, which   12
may explain, at least in part, why you, dear Waiting, are waiting. But a person does not have to know a Henry James or an E. B. White to receive a good letter. A person needn't even know a Mozart or a Churchill or a Groucho Marx — although I'd be the first to agree that it would significantly improve one's chances.

FREQUENCY. More often than not, the good letter will come from   13
someone with whom you correspond fairly often. This tends to rule out the condominium hustler seeking your "once-in-a-lifetime" investment dollar and the fund-raising presidential hopeful groveling for your quadrennial support. It should also rule out the dreaded-Christmas-letter writer, who tends to hoard his epistolary non-news for his year-end extravaganza. On the positive side, frequency encourages intimacy, and intimacy is the well of truth, which is of course indispensable to a good letter and most other good things.

LENGTH. It is a rare good letter whose contents can be confined to the   14
few square inches of a postcard or a holiday Hallmark. I have nothing against either one of those formats — or, for that matter, against an occasional telegram — but they simply do not allow sufficient room for the detail and development required of a good letter.

There is not, to my knowledge, any strict requirement as to the number of   15
words in a good letter. But there is, in a good letter, a sense of the heft and volume one finds in a good novel — a heft and volume not found even in the best short stories, much less on a post- or greeting card or in the currently very popular "note." Alas, in the past few years the "cute note" has pretty much taken the place of the good letter. YOU, DEAR WAITING, undoubtedly receive

your share of these "notes." They are usually personal, individual, and all-too-frequent, but they invariably fall far short of the mark in terms of length and imperishability.

The typical note comes written on smallish, pastel-colored paper that suggests nothing more imperishable than a Kleenex tissue. Sometimes there is a little flower or happy face in an upper corner, or a cute saying ("Help! Send chocolate!") along the upper margin where the name and address of the sender is usually embossed on legitimate stationery. And, though intended for a specific individual, notes are generally begun with the commonplace "Hi! Just thought I'd drop you a note . . ." and displayed, envelopeless, under a strawberry-shaped magnet on a refrigerator door.

People jot notes nowadays because they're "too busy" to write letters. And there is indeed an urgent, stenographic quality to most such notes that bespeaks the mad dash of our times. Furthermore, we have so damn many people to keep in touch with today that we should perhaps be forgiven our shortcomings in matters of length and imperishability. Given the demands on our time and attention, perhaps even a note is a minor miracle — a daisy sprouting from a crack in the parking-lot pavement. We could perhaps take care of *all* of our business over the phone.

A friend of mine (via the phone, as it happens) provides an additional thought on the subject. Perhaps, he suggests, we have grown fearful of expressing ourselves imperishably, on paper, lest we literally stamp ourselves something we ought not be: unfashionable, unhip, unwithit. Perhaps, as far as that goes, we've grown fearful of getting people angry at us. It's one thing, my friend reminds me, to call someone a duplicitous cretin on the telephone, by which medium a hasty qualification or even abject apology can be made, if deemed prudent, right on the spot. It's quite another thing to commit your disparagement to letter, a rather more tangible and permanent medium by which the duplicitous cretin may justify his coming to look for you with a chain saw.

I remain unconvinced. Henry James somehow managed to dash off literally thousands of mostly personal, individual, imperishable, frequent, and lengthy letters in a 50-year span otherwise occupied by the writing of some two dozen novels, more than a hundred "tales," a dozen-odd plays, plus countless travel sketches, literary critiques, and more, not to mention his frequent jaunts about the continent and dinner parties with Turgenev, Flaubert, et al. Ernest Hemingway, to use a more recent example, fought Spanish bulls, chased German submarines, and wrote at least a dozen volumes of undying prose, even as he knocked out between 6,000 and 7,000 letters during the 45 years of his writing life. Hemingway was not afraid to speak his mind in his letters either — and there were plenty of duplicitous cretins and chain saws in his day, too. The truth is, I can't imagine a good letter coming from someone who *isn't* up to his eyeballs in the business of a busy life. What on earth would such a person write about?

I don't think it's time or fortitude or literacy that we're lacking nowadays. 20 What we're lacking, I think, is the will and generosity required to shape our thoughts, feelings, and news into a coherent message every once in a while, and to share that message with another person in the world. A good letter, let's face it, is no longer required of us when we wish or need to communicate — even if our communicant lives an ocean away. Thus, a good letter, in this era of telecommunications satellites and quick, quipping note paper, is something akin to a hand-crocheted afghan or a jar of homemade currant preserves: a small act of grace, a hand-wrought little gift from one human being to another.

But I'm afraid I digress, dear Waiting. In answer to your question, I can 21 only reply with what must by now be obvious. In order to *get* a good letter in this day and age, you're probably first going to have to sit down and *write* one.

QUESTIONS ON CONTENT:

1. What, according to Swanson, are the five attributes of a good letter?

2. In his analysis of the "individuality" that should characterize a good letter, Swanson first dismisses the dismal Christmas letter and then contrasts it with a good letter. What qualities does he think help to give a letter "individuality"?

3. What are Swanson's objections to "notes"? With what metaphor does he conclude his discussion of "notes"?

4. In what ways might the "permanence" of a letter prove troublesome to the writer?

5. Why does Swanson think being busy is no excuse for not writing letters?

6. According to Swanson, what three things do letter writers not lack today? What does he believe is lacking? Where has he described these aspects? With what comparison does he conclude his next to last paragraph?

QUESTIONS ON WRITING STRUCTURE AND STRATEGY:

1. How does Swanson provide an emotional tone to his writing? What words does he coin?

2. Instead of continuously repeating the word "letter," what humorous and serious synonyms does Swanson use? What is the effect, other than variety?

3. Cite some examples of Swanson's use of specific details that help the reader to visualize his point.

4. Do you find Swanson's conclusion convincing? How does he move toward it from the original question by "Waiting for the Post"?

QUESTIONS FOR DISCUSSION AND WRITING:

1. Write a letter home or to a friend in another town in which you describe a typical day at college or at work, your relationship with fellow students and professors, or your impressions of college life or college students. Remember Swanson's requirements for a good letter as you write. Try to employ some colorful language.

2. Write a paper in which you compare/contrast some of the letters you have written or received. Which ones simply record happenings, and which ones are "involuntary autobiographies"?

3. Monitor your telephone calls home and to your friends in your journal. Keep track of whom you call and what you talked about. At the end of a week, analyze your conversations and try to determine if in some cases writing a letter would have more accurately communicated your feelings.

YOU HAVE TO KNOW
WHAT YOUR VALUES ARE!
Alan Alda

*No doubt you are already well acquainted with Alan Alda, Captain
Benjamin Franklin Pierce of M*A*S*H fame. Actually, Alda's intended
career in real life was that of his fictional TV character — medicine;
but after flunking a chemistry final he quickly switched majors at
Fordham University to English literature. Following graduation, he
served in the U.S. Army Reserve and then received a Ford Foundation
grant to study at the Cleveland Playhouse. As with most success
stories, Alda's skyrocketing popularity as "Hawkeye" was preceded by
fifteen years of relative obscurity while he polished his skills
performing in episodes of popular TV shows and on Broadway. In
addition to acting, Alda is an accomplished screenwriter, having
written several of the M*A*S*H scripts as well as other TV shows and
movies.*

*Although this excerpt is from his 1979 commencement address (see
Glossary for Speaking-Writing differences) at Drew University, Alda's
penetrating look at values has continuing relevance to American life.
Asking his listeners, both students and parents, to rank their values, he
then urges them to determine whether or not they are living in the
light of those priorities. As you read his concluding paragraphs,
compare your values with his. Then carry your analysis one step
further by reviewing some of the values esteemed by Thomas, Carson,
Owens, and Eiseley from Unit III, as well as those ideas expressed by
other authors in this section. Although this speech is on a serious
subject, determine if the wit and charm you associate with Captain
Benjamin Pierce comes through in Alda's personal voice.*

Someday it's very possible that you will look up from your work and   1
wonder what the point of it all is. You'll wonder how much you are getting
accomplished and how much it all means.

The sentence "What's the purpose of all this?" is written in large letters   2
over the mid-life-crisis butcher shop. You can't miss it as you lug the carcass of
your worldly success through the door to have it dressed and trimmed and
placed in little plastic packages for people to admire. *"What's the purpose of all
this?"* You may be asking yourself that question now or next year or in twenty
years. When you do, consider this: Your life will have meaning when you can
give meaning to it — and only then. No one else is going to give meaning to
your life. There isn't a job or a title or a degree that has meaning in itself. The
world can always go stumbling on without you no matter how high your office.
There isn't a liquor that will give meaning to your life or a drug, or any type of
sexual congress either.

I would like to suggest to you, just in case you haven't done it lately, that   3
it's a good idea to find out what your values in life really are, and then to figure
out how you are going to live by them. It seems to me that knowing what you
care about and then devoting yourself to it is just about the only way you can
have a sense of purpose in life, and it's probably the only way you can go
through the minefield of existence and get out in one piece.

It can be a startling experience when you try to rank your values. Just ask   4
yourself for a second what you feel is the most important thing in the world to
you. Your family, your work, your money, your country, getting to heaven,
sex, dope, alcohol? When you get the answer to that, ask yourself how much
time you actually spend on your number-one value and how much time you
spend on what you thought was number five, or number ten. What *in fact* is the
thing you value most? This may not be so easy to decide, because we live in a
time that seems to be split about its values, it seems almost schizophrenic. For
instance, if you should pick up a magazine that specializes in psychology and
social issues, you might see an article titled something like "White Collar
Crime: It's More Widespread Than You Think," and then turn to the back of
the magazine and find an ad that reads, "We'll Write Your Doctoral Thesis for
Twenty-Five Dollars." (You see how our values are eroding? A doctoral thesis
ought to go for at least a C-note!) Now, who is writing these institutionalized
crib notes? Scholars? I'd love to send away for an article on the ethics of
scholarship and see what they send back. The question is, Where are their
values? *What* do they value?

Unfortunately, the people we look to for leadership seem to be providing   5
it by negative example. All across the country, commencement speakers say to
graduating classes, "We look to you for tomorrow's leaders." That's because
today's leaders are all in jail. I don't mean to be too hard on politicians. Politics
is a very useful, very old profession — in some ways it is the oldest profession.
I may have become somewhat disillusioned about politicians in the past couple
of years because of a few I've met while campaigning for the Equal Rights
Amendment. I've crossed the paths of some very strange legislators.

One assemblyman in a Midwestern state where I campaigned told a   6
woman who was lobbying for the Equal Rights Amendment that he would give
her his vote, he would vote yes for the Equal Rights Amendment, if she showed
up in his hotel room that night. Can you imagine a more inappropriate offer?
That's like saying you will vote yes for emancipation in exchange for a couple
of good slaves.

I was in the Washington office of a United States senator one day when he   7
was trying to get a legislator back in his home state to vote yes on the
amendment, and the guy he was talking to was absolutely opposed to it in
principle. He just didn't believe in it. However, he would change his vote, he

said, if the senator would pay his way to Washington and arrange for his son's high school band to march in the inaugural parade. Now, the question is, Where were these men's values? What did they hold as important? Anything? All that these men seemed to care about was sex, money and power.

There are people influencing our lives who seem to be operating according 8 to no principle whatsoever. And you find them in every field, in every business, in our country. When you sell a product that you know will fall apart in a few months, when you sell the sizzle and you know there's no steak, when you take the money and run, when you write an article or a political speech or a television show that excites and titillates but doesn't lead to understanding and insight, when you are all style and no substance, you might as well be tossing poison into the reservoir we all drink from.

Think about that. Suppose somebody came up to you and offered you $50 9 to throw a little poison into the reservoir. He says, "Look, it's just a little poison, how much harm can it do? What would you take to throw just a little poison into the reservoir? Would you take $50? Would you take $100? How about $10,000? Would you take $500,000 a year, with stock options and a Christmas bonus? The problem is that everyone who's throwing in a little bit of poison combines with everyone else who is doing it, and together we are tampering dangerously with our moral ecology.

No matter what our work is, we all have to face that choice — in my field 10 no less than in others. There may not be a more important field for the dissemination of values in our country than the entire communications industry — most strikingly, television. Networks are very sensitive to that fact, and they employ dozens of censors to prevent all of us from using language on television that an eight year old might have to explain to his parents. But the point that censors miss, I think, is that it is not so much what we *say* that teaches as what we *don't* say. Even programs that attempt to make a moral point don't always make the point that they intended to, because when we sense we are being sold something, we automatically defend ourselves against it. I think it may be the unspoken assumptions that mold an audience.

Look at the way, for instance, that violence is treated on television. It is 11 not only the quantity that offends. There probably is no more violence on television than there is in a Shakespearean tragedy. But on television you find *unfelt* violence and in Shakespeare you tend to find *felt* violence. In Shakespeare the characters react with a human response: They fear, they hurt, they mourn. Most of the time on television, violence is dealt with by sweeping it under the rug as fast as possible and by having people go on about their business as if nothing had happened. (If I can't have less violence, I want at least a better grade of violence.) One of the unspoken assumptions is that violence can be tolerated as long as you ignore it and have no reaction to it. But that seems to me to be dangerously close to psychopathic behavior. I wonder if there is any connection between the long acceptance by our people of the Vietnam war and the thousands and thousands of deaths that we have seen on television over the years that were never mourned, never even paused for except to sell shampoo for sixty seconds.

Maybe our greatest problem is that we have two separate sets of value systems that we use — the one we talk about and the one we live by. We seem to place a very high value on fairness and on human concerns. And yet we still have widespread discrimination based on race, sex and religion. You still don't find Jews, blacks or other minorities in any significant numbers in decision-making positions in the banking industry, for instance. You think that's an accident? I think somebody put a value on that. And you don't find women in any significant numbers in decision-making capacities in *any* industry. Why? Because we place a higher value on appeasing the fragile male ego than we do on fairness and decency? Maybe what we need is a declaration of interdependence.

Maybe we simply need to know what we care about.

If we put a high value on decency, if we put a high value on excellence and on family, if we love the people we share our lives with — our wives and our husbands, our children — and if we don't shortchange them for a few bucks, if we can love the work we do and learn the skill of it, the art of it, if we can give full measure to the people who pay us for our work, if we try not to lie, try not to cheat, try to do good just by doing well whatever we do . . . then we will have made a revolution.

QUESTIONS ON CONTENT:

1. When does Alda believe your life will have meaning, a sense of purpose?
2. According to Alda, what kind of example is being set by our country's leaders? In politics? In business? In the mass media?
3. What is the contradiction he finds in American life? What do we usually call this contradiction?
4. Paraphrase and summarize Alda's criticisms in paragraph eight. Do you agree with them? How are they consistent with what he says in the concluding paragraph? (Or are they inconsistent with his conclusions?)
5. Summarize as best you can what Alda's explicit and implicit values are in this piece.

QUESTIONS ON WRITING STRUCTURE AND STRATEGY:

1. How would you characterize the tone of this selection? Select those elements that convey tone. How is the tone appropriate to the audience, the subject, the occasion?

2. In paragraph nine, Alda uses an analogy to make a point and sums it up with a metaphor. Why is the analogy apt, and how is the metaphor appropriate?
3. Paragraph thirteen is a single ten-word sentence. What is its function, and why is it effective?
4. The concluding paragraph is a periodic sentence (see Glossary) composed of a series of parallel subordinate clauses and a single independent clause. Why is it effective? How does it serve to promote coherence? Has he answered the question posed at the beginning?

QUESTIONS FOR DISCUSSION AND WRITING:

1. Television is an important instrument for the dissemination of values. Write a paper in which you examine several similar television shows and determine what values, implicit or explicit, they appear to be promoting.
2. Rank your values in life and the time you proportionally spend with each. In a short paper explain your findings.
3. Write a short paper in which you discuss occasions in which you have observed two contradictory sets of values at work in the same person (perhaps a self-analysis). Attempt to emulate Alda's variety of sentence lengths and constructions.
4. Write a paper in which you explain how your values differ from those of your parents, roommates, siblings, fellow workers, or children. Do you differ on money, goals, social mores, education, work? Are these differing values the result of the generation gap, the economics of the times, one's early training or environment, or. . . ? Use specific examples (and possibly an analogy) as does Alda.

BULIMIA: BINGE-EATING CYCLES
———— FOLLOWED BY PURGES AND GUILT ————
Jane E. Brody

Eating for most of us is one of life's great pleasures, but for thousands of young women, known as bulimics, the delight has turned into a nightmarish binge–purge compulsion with serious, sometimes deadly consequences. The victim usually gorges on as many as 50,000 calories a day and then, overcome by guilt, quickly induces vomiting to maintain "normal" body weight. Bulimia, akin to the much-publicized anorexia nervosa, and possibly even more common, has recently surfaced as an emotional illness afflicting primarily attractive, successful, perfectionist women suffering from low self-esteem.

In this article, Jane Brody, science and health writer for many years for the New York Times, *identifies and explains the problem of bulimia, profiles the potential bulimic, and describes bulimia's effects in gruesome detail. Her last paragraphs point to the increasing success rate in treating bulimics. Known as the "closet illness" because of the reluctance of victims to come forward to seek treatment, bulimia is a relatively new, complex subject that the author has attempted to analyze within the restrictions of her newspaper column. In doing so she has utilized almost every mode of development in an effort to make her subject clear and dramatic. Notice the impact of her scores of examples, her myriad uses of parallel construction, and the upbeat conclusion subtly admonishing bulimics to get help immediately; no longer must they suffer in isolation.*

SUZANNE: *I have a problem with food I eat. I mean I eat disgusting amounts of food. You can't imagine how much I eat. I go on binges. Then I start thinking about all those calories — and I make myself throw up. I can't stop myself. I hate myself, and I don't believe I'm telling you this.*   1

The slender, attractive 19-year-old speaking to the therapist at her   2
university's health service was describing an increasingly common phenomenon known as bulimia or bulimarexis, an out-of-control cycle of binge-eating followed by purges to get rid of the thousands of calories that may have been consumed in just half an hour.

Suzanne had been voted "most likely to succeed" at her small-town high   3
school. Now at college her high school A's had dwindled to C's and she was riddled with guilt about spending so much of her parents' money on food. At the time of her confession Suzanne had been bingeing and purging three or four times a day for six years, careful to keep her behavior a secret from family and friends and her previous therapist. Now she was desperate for help.

According to her new therapist, Dr. Marlene Boskind-White, Suzanne was   4 the first of hundreds of bulimics to seek help at Cornell University's health service in recent years. Dr. Boskind-White, along with her husband, Dr. William C. White, Jr., are authors of an illuminating book, "Bulimarexia: The Binge/Purge Cycle." The book, both realistic and hopeful, is designed to counter many bulimics' fear of disclosure and resistance to treatment.

Doctors often do not take these patients' problem seriously or sympathetically. Family and friends may try to ignore it, if they know about it at all. Strangers usually react with disbelief and disgust. But to bulimics, most of whom feel horribly guilty and frighteningly out of control, the vicious cycle of binges and purges in which they are caught is very serious, very disabling and very much in need of treatment — the sooner the better.   5

The extent of the problem is unknown. Some estimates say 15 to 30 percent of young women occasionally binge and purge while 1 to 4 percent do it all the time, ostensibly to maintain a normal body weight. About 5 percent of bulimics are male. Most are white and come from middle and upper-class families. Their ages range from 8 to 72 years, with the vast majority in their teens and 20's. Some have been bulimic for more than 10 years and may be suffering serious health consequences yet cannot stop their abnormal behavior. For many, the bulimia takes over their lives and they have time for nothing but working, sleeping, bingeing and purging.   6

Bulimics may consume 10,000 to 20,000 calories at one time, then make themselves vomit, or take hundreds of laxatives and diuretics, or do an abusive amount of exercise to unload the excess before it turns to body fat. A typical binge may begin with two packages of cookies, a loaf of bread, a gallon of milk and half a gallon of ice cream, followed by a basket of fried chicken and fistfuls of candy and pastries. The emphasis is on "forbidden foods" high in calories, fats and simple carbohydrates.   7

A few bulimics ingest as many as 50,000 calories a day and support their habit by taking second jobs, stealing or even becoming prostitutes. To disguise their abnormal food purchases, they may shop at a different store each day, pretend they are buying for a party, order food from catalogues or charge it on credit cards.   8

Experts debate how to characterize the problem. Some (the Drs. White among them) call it a habit or learned behavior; others consider it an addiction, compulsion or form of substance abuse; still others think of it as an emotional disorder or illness. But there is little disagreement about how bulimia usually begins, what perpetuates it and what must be done to overcome it. There is also general agreement that bulimia is often hidden behind a facade of normalcy and that it is more difficult to treat than its more obvious sister problem, anorexia nervosa (self-induced starvation).   9

Most cases of bulimia that have been studied have started with strenuous   10 dieting, perhaps coupled with some precipitating event, such as loss of a loved person, rejection by a sweetheart or leaving home to go to college. After a period of deprivation and hunger, the dieter may lose control and go on a binge.

Terrified of the consequences, the dieter may then seek a way to undo the damage. The purge is seen as the perfect dieting technique, a means, as bulimics put it, of "eating your cake without having to pay the price." 11

Some victims say they first got the idea to purge from an article or television program about bulimia. But many thousands discovered it on their own or took a cue from friends or relatives long before there was any publicity about bulimia. At first, purges may be done only occasionally, but they may soon become increasingly frequent. 12

Most bulimics also share a number of psychological and social characteristics that seem to predispose them to bingeing and purging. They are usually perfectionists with high expectations who present an impressive image. Yet they feel ineffective, lack self-esteem and have a very strong need for approval from other people. 13

They become "bewildered when their perfect presentation does not result in the acceptance or care they are looking for," said Dr. Ellen Schor, a New York bulimia therapist. "They then turn to food as a means of nurturing themselves, turning from the outer world in anger or disappointment." 14

Though initially the binge may be a source of pleasure or comfort, it soon becomes associated with fear, shame, guilt, remorse and a feeling of lost control. The purge restores their sense of self-control and represents a renewed drive for perfection. Dr. Craig Johnson, who studies and treats bulimics at the Michael Reese Hospital in Chicago, examined the feelings of bulimics before, during and after binges and purges. He found that during binges, the women felt less in control, more inadequate, angrier and guiltier than usual. The purge, however, re-established a sense of control and adequacy, dissipated the anger and enhanced alertness. 15

"We must suspect, then, that the purge is the most important, most gratifying part of the sequence," Dr. Johnson concluded. "Clearly, it's some kind of cathartic, reinforcing experience that restores their sense of reality orientation and allows them to feel in control." 16

Janice M. Cauwels, author of the new book "Bulimia: The Binge-Purge Compulsion," says about 90 percent of bulimics who purge do so by vomiting, although many use more than one method. Dr. Johnson says, "Through some transformation, the bingeing becomes only a means to the vomiting, which is more important to them. We've had women tell us that they binge beyond their satiation points to make it easier to vomit and that they select foods that are easiest to bring up." 17

The medical consequences of frequent purges can be severe. Bulimics may 18 suffer terrible damage to teeth and gums from the repeated exposure to acidic vomit. Other hazards of bingeing and purging include esophageal irritation, persistent sore throat, dangerous stretching of the stomach, infection of the salivary glands, hiatal hernia, dehydration, electrolyte imbalance (which can result in abnormal heart rhythm and possible sudden death), loss of normal intestinal muscle action from laxative abuse, intestinal inflammation, loss of menstrual periods, urinary difficulties and kidney failure.

Group therapy has been cited as the most effective means of changing bulimic behavior. It helps victims realize they are not alone, it gives them access to supportive friends, and it counters their isolation. In many groups, a "buddy" system is established and a "contract" of goals is signed to help members control their bulimia. [19]

The first step in treatment, most therapists believe, is to stop purging, since the purges seem to intensify the binges. At the University of Vermont, Dr. James Rosen helps bulimics learn to live through the anxiety induced by a binge by preventing them from purging. He says patients learn to eat large amounts of food without precipitating a desire to purge. As the fear of eating diminishes, the normalcy of eating habits increases, he reports. And, interestingly, few victims gain much weight after treatment. [20]

With bingeing and purging under control, it becomes possible to begin work on underlying problems in individual or group therapy. Victims must learn more effective ways of relieving stress, how to say "no," how to express anger without losing control, how to face pain. Perfectionist notions must be abandoned, and normal means of enhancing self-esteem appreciated. [21]

Many bulimics have trouble with intimate relationships. Bulimic women often depend too much on men for affirmation of their femininity and self-worth, going to abnormal lengths to please men who may treat them badly. Thus, assertiveness training is often a crucial aspect of effective treatment. As bulimics learn to trust themselves and others more, self-esteem increases and they come to realize that they have a *choice* about eating habits. [22]

QUESTIONS ON CONTENT:

1. What is Brody's thesis?
2. What aspects of bulimia do the experts disagree about, and in what areas is there agreement?
3. How does bulimia get started, and what fears perpetuate it?
4. What psychological factors operate in the binge-purge cycle?
5. What types of people are most likely to become bulimics?
6. What kinds of treatment are proving most successful?

QUESTIONS ON WRITING STRUCTURE AND STRATEGY:

1. How does Brody attempt to capture her reader's initial interest?

2. Not surprisingly, journalist Brody employs the traditional approach of her trade. Which paragraphs orient the reader as to the "who," "what," "when," "why," and "how" of the subject?

3. In attempting to cover such a complex subject in so few words, because of space limitations, Brody is trying to pack each sentence with as much information as possible. What widely used sentence structure does she employ a dozen times or more? Pinpoint its use.

QUESTIONS FOR DISCUSSION AND WRITING:

1. Thinness and dieting seem to be two of the major concerns of American women these days. Write a paper in which you explore how society dictates what is beautiful. Consider the images of American women in TV and the movies, advertising, fashion magazines, and so on.

2. Many Americans are on special diets these days — low sodium, high fiber, low cholesterol, vegetarian, high protein. Others are "into" body building, health spas, aerobics, jogging, and so on. These sometimes can become compulsive. In a short paper, discuss your experience or those of your acquaintants with any of these eating or exercising plans. Are they solely concerned with health or are they manifestations of narcissism?

3. Try exploring images of beauty from past eras. Examine magazine illustrations and pictures, art reproductions, etc. Select an era and contrast its concept of beauty with today's.

THE PARADOX OF PERFECTION

Arlene Skolnick

Arlene Skolnick is a research psychologist at the Institute of Human Development at the University of California at Berkeley. In her discussion of the American family, she attempts to account for its current problems by attributing them to an unattainable ideal traceable to the post-Civil War industrial revolution. Skolnick is on solid ground in isolating the perfectionist strain in American culture as the culprit, for other scholars have also commented on this exceptional feature of American civilization. Skolnick's method of development is essentially comparison/contrast, the past with the present. In this effort she relies on the work of other scholars for data and statistics on the evolving American family. Skolnick's article appeared in The Wilson Quarterly, *a semischolarly journal. Consequently, her formal style is tailored to a slightly different audience than that for whom Jane Brody writes in the* New York Times. *In her execution, Skolnick carefully uses transitional words, phrases, and ideas, allowing the reader to pass easily from one paragraph to another. Note paragraph nine, which she uses as a transitional device, taking the reader from the present into the past.*

The American Family, as even readers of *Popular Mechanics* must know by now, is in what Sean O'Casey would have called "a terrible state of chassis." Yet, there are certain ironies about the much-publicized crisis that give one pause.

True, the statistics seem alarming. The U.S. divorce rate, though it has reached something of a plateau in recent years, remains the highest in American history. The number of births out-of-wedlock among all races and ethnic groups continues to climb. The plight of many elderly Americans subsisting on low fixed incomes is well known.

What puzzles me is an ambiguity, not in the facts, but in what we are asked to make of them. A series of opinion polls conducted in 1978 by Yankelovich, Skelley, and White, for example, found that 38 percent of those surveyed had recently witnessed one or more "destructive activities" (e.g., a divorce, a separation, a custody battle) within their own families or those of their parents or siblings. At the same time, 92 percent of the respondents said the family was highly important to them as a "personal value."

Can the family be at once a cherished "value" and a troubled institution? I am inclined to think, in fact, that they go hand in hand. A recent "Talk of the Town" report in *The New Yorker* illustrates what I mean:

A few months ago word was heard from Billy Gray, who used to play brother Bud in "Father Knows Best," the 1950s television show about the nice Anderson family who lived in the white frame house on a side street in some mythical Springfield—the house at which the father arrived each night swinging open the front door and singing out "Margaret, I'm home!" Gray said he felt "ashamed" that he had ever had anything to do with the show. It was all "totally false," he said, and had caused many Americans to feel inadequate, because they thought that was the way life was supposed to be and that their own lives failed to measure up.

As Susan Sontag has noted in *On Photography*, mass-produced images have   5
"extraordinary powers to determine our demands upon reality." The family is especially vulnerable to confusion between truth and illusion. What, after all, is "normal"? All of us have a backstairs view of our own families, but we know The Family, in the aggregate, only vicariously.

Like politics or athletics, the family has become a media event. Television   6
offers nightly portrayals of lump-in-the-throat family "normalcy" ("The Waltons," "Little House on the Prairie") and, nowadays, even humorous "deviance" ("One Day at a Time," "The Odd Couple"). Family advisers sally forth in syndicated newspaper columns to uphold standards, mend relationships, suggest counseling, and otherwise lead their readers back to the True Path. For commercial purposes, advertisers spend millions of dollars to create stirring vignettes of glamorous-but-ordinary families, the kind of family most 11-year-olds wish they had.

All Americans do not, of course, live in such a family, but most share an   7
intuitive sense of what the "ideal" family should be—reflected in the precepts of religion, the conventions of etiquette, and the assumptions of law. And, characteristically, Americans tend to project the ideal back into the past, the time when virtues of all sorts are thought to have flourished.

We do not come off well by comparison with that golden age, nor could   8
we, for it is as elusive and mythical as Brigadoon. If Billy Gray shames too easily, he has a valid point: While Americans view the family as the proper context for their own lives—9 out of 10 people live in one—they have no realistic context in which to view the family. Family history, until recently, was as neglected in academe as it still is in the press. This summer's White House Conference on Families is "policy-oriented," which means present-minded. The familiar, depressing charts of "leading family indicators"—marriage, divorce, illegitimacy—in newspapers and newsmagazines rarely survey the trends before World War II. The discussion, in short, lacks ballast.

Let us go back to before the American Revolution.   9

Perhaps what distinguishes the modern family most from its colonial   10
counterpart is its newfound privacy. Throughout the 17th and 18th centuries, well over 90 percent of the American population lived in small rural

communities. Unusual behavior rarely went unnoticed, and neighbors often intervened directly in a family's affairs, to help or to chastise.

The most dramatic example was the rural "charivari," prevalent in both   11
Europe and the United States until the early 19th century. The purpose of these noisy gatherings was to censure community members for familial transgressions — unusual sexual behavior, marriages between persons of grossly discrepant ages, or "household disorder," to name but a few. As historian Edward Shorter describes it in *The Making of the Modern Family*:

> Sometimes the demonstration would consist of masked individuals circling somebody's house at night, screaming, beating on pans, and blowing cow horns. . . . on other occasions, the offender would be seized and marched through the streets, seated perhaps backwards on a donkey or forced to wear a placard describing his sins.

The state itself had no qualms about intruding into a family's affairs by   12
statute, if necessary. Consider 17th-century New England's "stubborn child" laws that, though never actually enforced, sanctioned the death penalty for chronic disobedience to one's parents.

If the boundaries between home and society seem blurred during the   13
colonial era, it is because they were. People were neither very emotional nor very self-conscious about family life, and, as historian John Demos points out, family and community were "joined in a relation of profound reciprocity." In his *Of Domesticall Duties*, William Gouge, a 17th-century Puritan preacher, called the family "a little community." The home, like the larger community, was as much an economic as a social unit; all members of the family worked, be it on the farm, or in a shop, or in the home.

There was not much to idealize. Love was not considered the basis for   14
marriage but one possible result of it. According to historian Carl Degler, it was easier to obtain a divorce in colonial New England than anywhere else in the Western world, and the divorce rate climbed steadily throughout the 18th century, though it remained low by contemporary standards. Romantic images to the contrary, it was rare for more than two generations (parents and children) to share a household, for the simple reason that very few people lived beyond the age of 60. It is ironic that our nostalgia for the extended family — including grandparents and grandchildren — comes at a time when, thanks to improvements in health care, its existence is less threatened than ever before.

Infant mortality was high in colonial days, though not as high as we are   15
accustomed to believe, since food was plentiful and epidemics, owing to generally low population density, were few. In the mid-1700s, the average age of marriage was about 24 for men, 21 for women — not much different from

what it is now. Households, on average, were larger, but not startlingly so: A typical household in 1790 included about 5.6 members, versus about 3.5 today. Illegitimacy was widespread. Premarital pregnancies reached a high in 18th-century America (10 percent of all first births) that was not equalled until the 1950s.

Form Follows Function

In simple demographic terms, then, the differences between the American family in colonial times and today are not all that stark; the similarities are sometimes striking.   16

The chief contrast is psychological. While Western societies have always   17
idealized the family to some degree, the *most vivid* literary portrayals of family life before the 19th century were negative or, at best, ambivalent. In what might be called the "high tragic" tradition — including Sophocles, Shakespeare, and the Bible, as well as fairy tales and novels — the family was portrayed as a high-voltage emotional setting, laden with dark passions, sibling rivalries, and violence. There was also the "low comic" tradition — the world of hen-pecked husbands and tyrannical mothers-in-law.

It is unlikely that our 18th-century ancestors ever left the Book of Genesis   18
or *Tom Jones* with the feeling that their own family lives were seriously flawed.

By the time of the Civil War, however, American attitudes toward the   19
family had changed profoundly. The early decades of the 19th century marked the beginnings of America's gradual transformation into an urban, industrial society. In 1820, less than 8 percent of the U.S. population lived in cities; by 1860, the urban concentration approached 20 percent, and by 1900 that proportion had doubled.

Structurally, the American family did not immediately undergo a   20
comparable transformation. Despite the large families of many immigrants and farmers, the size of the *average* family declined — slowly but steadily — as it had been doing since the 17th century. Infant mortality remained about the same, and may even have increased somewhat, owing to poor sanitation in crowded cities. Legal divorces were easier to obtain than they had been in colonial times. Indeed, the rise in the divorce rate was a matter of some concern during the 19th century, though death, not divorce, was the prime cause of one-parent families, as it was up to 1965.

Functionally, however, America's industrial revolution has a lasting effect   21
on the family. No longer was the household typically a group of interdependent workers. Now, men went to offices and factories and became breadwinners;

wives stayed home to mind the hearth; children went off to the new public schools. The home was set apart from the dog-eat-dog arena of economic life; it came to be viewed as a utopian retreat or, in historian Christopher Lasch's phrase, a "haven in a heartless world." Marriage was now valued primarily for its emotional attractions. Above all, the family became something to worry about.

The earliest and most saccharine "sentimental model" of the family appeared in the new mass media that proliferated during the second quarter of the 19th century. Novels, tracts, newspaper articles, and ladies' magazines — there were variations for each class of society — elaborated a "Cult of True Womanhood" in which piety, submissiveness, and domesticity dominated the pantheon of desirable feminine qualities. This quotation from *The Ladies Book* (1830) is typical: 22

> *See, she sits, she walks, she speaks, she looks — unutterable things! Inspiration springs up in her very paths — it follows her footsteps. A halo of glory encircles her, and illuminates her whole orbit. With her, man not only feels safe, but actually renovated.*

In the late 1800s, science came into the picture. The "professionalization" of the housewife took two different forms. One involved motherhood and childrearing, according to the latest scientific understanding of children's special physical and emotional needs. (It is no accident that the publishing of children's books became a major industry during this period.) The other was the domestic science movement — "home economics," basically — which focused on the woman as full-time homemaker, applying "scientific" and "industrial" rationality to shopping, making meals, and housework.   23

The new ideal of the family prompted a cultural split that has endured, one that Tocqueville had glimpsed (and rather liked) in 1835. Society was divided more sharply into man's sphere and woman's sphere. Toughness, competition, and practicality were the masculine values that ruled the outside world. The softer values — affection, tranquility, piety — were worshiped in the home and the church. In contrast to the colonial view, the ideology of the "modern" family implied a critique of everything beyond the front door.   24

What is striking as one looks at the writings of the 19th-century "experts" — the physicians, clergymen, phrenologists, and "scribbling ladies" — is how little their essential message differs from that of the sociologists, psychiatrists, pediatricians, and women's magazine writers of the 20th century, particularly since World War II.   25

Instead of men's and women's spheres, of course, sociologists speak of "instrumental" and "expressive" roles. The notion of the family as a retreat from the harsh realities of the outside world crops up as "functional   26 differentiation." And, like the 19th-century utopians who believed society could be regenerated through the perfection of family life, 20th-century social scientists have looked at the failed family as the source of most American social problems.

None of those who promoted the sentimental model of the family — neither the popular writers nor the academics — considered the paradox of perfectionism: the ironic possibility that it would lead to trouble. Yet it has. The image of the perfect, happy family makes ordinary families seem like failures. Small problems loom as big problems if the "normal" family is thought to be one where there are no real problems at all.

One sees this phenomenon at work on the generation of Americans born and reared during the late 19th century, the first generation reared on the mother's milk of sentimental imagery. Between 1900 and 1920, the U.S. divorce rate doubled, from four to eight divorces annually per 1,000 married couples. The jump — comparable to the 100 percent increase in the divorce rate between 1960 and 1980 — is not attributable to changes in divorce laws, which were not greatly liberalized. Rather, it would appear that, as historian Thomas O'Neill believes, Americans were simply more willing to dissolve marriages that did not conform to their ideal of domestic bliss — and perhaps try again.

A "Fun" Morality

If anything, family standards became even more demanding as the 20th century progressed. The new fields of psychology and sociology opened up whole new definitions of familial perfection. "Feelings" — fun, love, warmth, good orgasm — acquired heightened popular significance as the invisible glue of successful families.

Psychologist Martha Wolfenstein, in an analysis of several decades of government-sponsored infant care manuals, has documented the emergence of a "fun morality." In former days, being a good parent meant carrying out certain tasks with punctilio; if your child was clean and reasonably obedient, you had no cause to probe his psyche. Now, we are told, parents must commune with their own feelings and those of their children — an edict which has seeped into the ethos of education as well. The distinction is rather like that between religions of deed and religions of faith. It is one thing to make your child brush his teeth; it is quite another to transform the whole process into a joyous "learning experience."

The task of 20th-century parents has been further complicated by the

104

advice offered them. The experts disagree with each other and often contradict themselves. The kindly Dr. Benjamin Spock, for example, is full of contradictions. In a detailed analysis of *Baby and Child Care*, historian Michael Zuckerman observes that Spock tells mothers to relax ("trust yourself") yet warns them that they have an "ominous power" to destroy their children's innocence and make them discontented "for years" or even "forever."

As we enter the 1980s, both family images and family realities are in a state of transition. After a century and a half, the web of attitudes and nostrums comprising the "sentimental model" is beginning to unravel. Since the mid-1960s, there has been a youth rebellion of sorts, a new "sexual revolution," a revival of feminism, and the emergence of the two-worker family. The huge postwar Baby-Boom generation is pairing off, accounting in part for the upsurge in the divorce rate (half of all divorces occur within seven years of a first marriage). Media images of the family have become more "realistic," reflecting new patterns of family life that are emerging (and old patterns that are re-emerging).   32

Among social scientists, "realism" is becoming something of an ideal in itself. For some of them, realism translates as pluralism: All forms of the family, by virtue of the fact that they happen to exist, are equally acceptable — from communes and cohabitation to one-parent households, homosexual marriages, and, come to think of it, the nuclear family. What was once labeled "deviant" is now merely "variant." In some college texts, "the family" has been replaced by "family systems." Yet, this new approach does not seem to have squelched perfectionist standards. Indeed, a palpable strain of perfectionism runs through the pop literature on "alternative" family lifestyles.   33

For the majority of scholars, realism means a more down-to-earth view of the American household. Rather than seeing the family as a haven of peace and tranquility, they have begun to recognize that even "normal" families are less than ideal, that intimate relations of any sort inevitably involve antagonism as well as love. Conflict and change are inherent in social life. If the family is now in a state of flux, such is the nature of resilient institutions; if it is beset by problems, so is life. The family will survive.   34

QUESTIONS ON CONTENT:

1. What is Skolnick's thesis?
2. According to Skolnick, why are Americans confused about the "truth" and "illusion" of the family?
3. How have the social sciences contributed to the evolution of what she terms the "fun morality"?
4. What is the new "realism" about the American family?

QUESTIONS ON WRITING STRUCTURE AND STRATEGY:

1. How does Skolnick use irony (paradox: see Glossary) to unify the essay?

2. What kinds of evidence does she use to support her thesis? Is she narrowly selective in her use of historical data? For example, does she cite colonial families other than those in New England?

3. Where and how does Skolnick employ topic sentences to achieve clarity? Which serve more than a single paragraph?

4. What is her purpose in the first eight paragraphs, and why is paragraph nine a single sentence?

5. Does Skolnick introduce any unsupported statements in her last paragraph? Is support needed? In what ways is her conclusion effective or ineffective?

QUESTIONS FOR DISCUSSION AND WRITING:

1. How are family images reflected in TV and in the movies of the 1980s, and how do they compare with your own experience of family life? Is your family a "haven in a heartless world"? Write a short paper in which you compare and contrast image and reality.

2. Do you find the concept of perfectionism manifested in your family life? Explain. In your college work? On the job? In relationships? Explain.

3. Check the *Readers' Guide* and the *Social Science Index* for articles on such topics as single-parent families, extended families, and teenage marriages (children having children). If there is a documents section in your library, ask the librarian to help you compile some statistics on the evolving American family. Write a short research paper on your findings.

OUTSIDERS LOOKING IN
Graham B. Spanier

What the world really needs is a litmus paper pretest to guarantee successful marriages. With statistics indicating that marriages of young adults these days have slightly better than a fifty-fifty chance of surviving, research in the field of marriage and the family is commanding even greater interest — and funding. All too often, however, in an area complicated by physical, psychological, emotional, and economic problems, studies produce evidence that is conflicting or inconclusive. In the following excerpt, Graham B. Spanier, coauthor of Adolescent Development: A Life-Span Perspective *(1980), admits that researchers can record* what *is happening to the family but can often only hypothesize about* why *it is happening. In "Outsiders Looking In," Spanier corrals statistics, refers to studies, and gingerly tenders predictions about the impermanence of marriage, cohabitation, and communes in today's society. Although Spanier is a professional and this article appeared in a special issue of* The Wilson Quarterly, *his language is less formal than Skolnick's in the preceding article. Spanier has apparently deliberately keyed his writing to the general reader. Note also his smooth transitions from paragraph to paragraph, desirable features in all writing.*

Today, virtually every U.S. college and university has family specialists on its faculty. There are dozens of scholarly journals and newsletters devoted to the family — from *Demography* to the *Journal of Marriage and the Family*. Professional associations of family researchers such as the National Council on Family Relations have a collective membership in the tens of thousands. . . . 1

For all their uncertainty, the best family researchers can offer some insights into *what* is happening, if not always into *why* it is happening or what it all means for America as a whole. 2

Let us begin with unwed cohabitation (or "living together," née, "living in sin"), a development fostered, so it is said, by the cultural revolution of the 1960s. Data from the Census Bureau's Current Population Survey point to a steady increase in the number of persons living together. The figure more than doubled between 1970 and 1978, to more than 1.1 million couples. Between 1977 and 1978 alone, there was a 19 percent increase.

Such living arrangements are popularly thought to be a lasting alternative to marriage, one more bit of evidence that the nuclear family is in a state of decay. In fact, cohabitation is rarely permanent. About two-fifths of those who now live together are never-married young adults, most of whom will eventually marry someone — if not necessarily the person they currently live with. Another 55 percent are divorced individuals, most of whom will 3 eventually remarry. A few are elderly. Of all never-married persons living together outside of marriage, about 85 percent are under age 35, 8 percent are between 35 and 54 years of age, and 7 percent are 55 or older.

Paul Glick of the Census Bureau and I have recently published data showing that cohabiting couples generally live in large suburbs or cities. They have, on average, relatively low incomes and experience high unemployment, although the women among them are more likely to be employed than are married women. Couples living together who are young and have never been married also tend to be better educated than either their married or previously married counterparts. Blacks account for a disproportionate share of the number of couples living together, but the vast majority of all cohabiting couples are, in fact, white.

What most of these people have in common — perhaps the only thing — is that they have chosen this lifestyle as a temporary convenience, one made possible by effective birth-control techniques and perpetuated to a great extent both by changing mores and, especially among the young, by an increase in the number of career-minded women. "Living together" rarely constitutes an *ideological* rejection of marriage. Indeed, one of the greatest problems for such couples comes when one of them is ready to marry and the other is not.

Marriage is still the norm in our society, and, I suspect, it will remain so. In 1979 alone, more than 4.5 million persons got married; 9 out of 10 Americans eventually march down the aisle. Today's young adults seem to be as committed to the idea of marriage as were previous generations, but there is one difference: They are not in as much of a hurry. The median age at first marriage is now 24 for men and about 22 for women — an increase of nearly two full years each since the 1950s. Among women aged 25 to 29, one in five has never been married, versus one out of ten in 1960.

Why the delay? Demographer Kingsley Davis has cited, among other reasons, the lackluster state of the U.S. economy. Some young couples, he suggests, lack the financial security to launch a family, as happened during the Depression when the average age of first marriage was roughly as high as it is today. Unfortunately, the role of economics is one variable that family researchers have trouble documenting. Even when common sense points to it as a factor, it is difficult to "disaggregate" economics from other underlying variables, such as race, class, and education.

More persuasive explanations of the rising age of first marriage center around changing social values. Most men and women are now sexually experienced before the conclusion of adolescence; they don't need to get married simply to enjoy sex. Effective contraception, if employed, virtually eliminates the chance of an unwanted pregnancy, a fear (or reality) which in the past encouraged (or forced) some early marriages. For some youths, living together may make marriage seem less urgent, at least for a while. Moreover, a higher average age of marriage has historically been associated with higher educational levels, and the U.S. population, in particular the young population, is more educated than ever before. Finally, as I have already noted, the increasing number of ambitious young women looking first to their careers may also help shift the average age of marriage upwards.

Despite the impression often left by the media, the proportion of teen-age 9 marriages has *declined* over the past decade. Those who do marry in their teens, however, are most likely to get divorced. Women who marry at ages 14 to 17 are twice as likely to get divorced as women who marry at ages 18 or 19, who in turn are one and one-half times as likely to get divorced as women who marry in their early twenties, for whom divorce rates are high to begin with. Men who marry in their teens are about twice as likely to get divorced as men who marry in their twenties. Interrupted education, poor job prospects, lack of money, basic immaturity, parental opposition, early (if not premarital) pregnancy — the factors behind the failure rate are clear to everyone except, perhaps, the teen-agers involved.

Teen-age married couples may be especially divorce-prone, but divorce, of 10 course, is not just a teen-age phenomenon. There are now more than 1 million divorces in America each year, involving more than 2 million adults and 1 million children. (There are some 48 million married couples in the United States.) While the upsurge in divorce during the past two decades is finally slowing — the rate had more than doubled since 1960 from about 9 to more than 20 divorces annually per 1,000 married couples — there is nothing to suggest that the rate will actually decline. At best it will level off.

Divorce hits all social groups, but not equally. Divorce rates are 11 considerably higher for blacks than for whites. Although divorce can strike couples of any age and circumstance, those who get a divorce tend to do so relatively early in their marriages. (Paradoxically, many couples who remain married say that their happiest years were those statistically vulnerable early ones.) Generally speaking, the lower the educational level, the higher the divorce rate.

What weight to assign various economic factors — e.g., job stability, 12 income level, welfare availability — is still a matter of dispute. Consider the controversial proposition that "welfare breaks up marriages" — a seemingly plausible hypothesis given that welfare benefits for an intact family are lower than they are for a female-headed family. Dozens of researchers have tested this notion. They have variously found that: the proposition is true; is false; is true for blacks but not whites; is true for whites but not blacks. Some contend that welfare has no effect on divorce rates but *does* delay remarriage; others suggest that some ineffable "third variable" may account for going on welfare *and* getting divorced.

Who Stays Married?

What is the profile of the couple *least* likely to divorce? The wife would have married in her late twenties and would have a B.A. degree, but no more. (Women with graduate degrees have a disproportionately high divorce rate, perhaps owing to a greater sense of economic security and social independence.) The husband would also have a B.A. and would likewise have married in his late twenties. Both would be white and upper-middle-class, and would eventually become the parents of two boys or a boy and a girl (not two girls), with the eldest child born a couple of years after the wedding. Their chances of divorce would be lessened further if they lived in the countryside, were of the same religion, and went to church regularly.

Whatever the roots of marital success or failure, if one assumes that the divorce rate will remain relatively constant over the next couple of decades, then between one-third and two-fifths of all *first* marriages formed during the late 1970s are destined to end in divorce. Considering the whole potential cycle of divorce, remarriage, and redivorce, it is probable that between 40 and 50 percent of *all* marriages formed by today's young adults will not remain intact.

If there is a silver lining, it is that approximately half of those who get divorced do so relatively early in their marriages, often before they have children. The spouses, moreover, are rejecting an *unsuccessful relationship*; they are usually not rejecting the *idea of marriage or family per se*. Many of them, in fact, look forward to a "traditional" family life the next time around. The data on remarriage speak volumes. Approximately 25 percent of divorced persons remarry within a year following termination of a first marriage; 50 percent do so within three years; 80 percent of them do so ultimately. Samuel Johnson once called second marriages "the triumph of hope over experience." It would appear that many Americans are more hopeful about the family than some of the experts.

In any event, divorce may not be the worst of evils, at least for the adults involved. We do not have much hard data on the subject, but a reading of Brontë's *Jane Eyre* or James's *Ambassadors* recalls the tragedy of some 19th-century marriages that obdurately remained intact. There is no evidence that the quality of U.S. marriages has declined (or improved) during the past century—only that Americans have become more willing and able to seek a divorce if a marriage fails to meet expectations.

QUESTIONS ON CONTENT:

1. What is the profile of the average cohabitating couple? What do the partners have in common?
2. What reasons does Spanier advance for young people's delaying marriage?
3. What do the statistics show about the probability of divorce for those marrying young? What factors contribute to these statistics?
4. What are the general characteristics of those couples who stay married?

QUESTIONS ON WRITING STRUCTURE AND STRATEGY:

1. Generally, Spanier employs conventional topic sentences. How does he occasionally vary them? What is the effect?
2. Spanier's writing is free of jargon. What does that tell you about the audience for whom he is writing?
3. How would you characterize the tone of this selection? Does the wealth of statistics contribute to the tone?

QUESTIONS FOR DISCUSSION AND WRITING:

1. From what you have read and what you have observed, how do you account for the failure of so many early marriages?
2. From your own observations about alternative family arrangements — extended families, foster homes, single-parent families — what can you say about their failures, successes, pervasiveness, future? Concentrate on one or two.
3. Survey your classmates or fellow workers about their realistic or unrealistic expectations for a successful marriage: the qualities they most look (or looked) for in a future spouse; the factors in a marriage they could forgive and forget; those that would warrant divorce. For married students: what qualities are most important in the first year(s) of marriage/now? Write a paper on your findings. Be careful not to make sweeping generalizations on such a limited sample.

AFTER DEATH,
MEMENTOS THAT MEAN A LIFE
Ann Bayer

*A native of Cleveland, Ohio, Ann Bayer was graduated from Sarah
Lawrence College in 1963 and has since then been a frequent
contributor to the* New York Times, Cosmopolitan, Saturday Evening
Post, *and* Life. *In 1976, "Department Store" won her distinction by
being included in that year's volume of the O. Henry Memorial Award
stories.*

*Bayer's tribute to her mother (screenwriter and novelist Eleanor
Perry), published in the* New York Times, *may have meaning for you
if you have ever lost anyone close. Bayer loved her mother dearly.
Every phrase, every sentence radiates the deep affection, admiration,
and perhaps even more important, the genuine friendship that existed
between mother and daughter. From Bayer's description of her last
days with her mother we learn little of her mother's physical features
— yet we know that she was warm, gentle, intelligent, well read,
strong-willed, a woman with dignity and charm. Closing our eyes, we
can visualize her perfectly. What makes this tribute so softly eloquent?
The words Bayer uses are common words, nothing very special, but
they contribute to a certain naturalness that tugs at the heart. She
employs similes, metaphors, and symbols. Yet the true poignancy is
found in the intimate, endearing vignettes: "She and I gossiped as
cozily as a manicurist and a favorite customer," "the anemones from
Pansy and Tola," and the final realization "that I can take her with
me into the future."*

After my mother died last March I thought: Something bad has happened   1
and that means that now something good will happen. She died on a Saturday
at home, and it was still early in the morning when I left her apartment. I had
waited until everyone else went — the police, the undertakers, the nurse and
the housekeeper — and when I finally emerged from the elevator in the lobby,
the first person I saw was the doorman, who formalized the occasion by
shaking my hand. That handshake seemed like a dividing line between my past
and my future.

I lived only a block away, and I noticed as I walked home how solid and   2
boastful the buildings along the Avenue of the Americas looked, as if they had
just been subjected to a neutron-bomb blast and wanted to show they had
come through unscathed.

My mother, Time and Newsweek said later, died in New York City, but to   3
me her dying seemed to have nothing to do with the pizzazz of New York.
During the last months of her life the city had become irrelevant, something I

never thought about except, perhaps, when a persistently honking horn 11
floors below her apartment brought it to my attention. My forays into the city
were brief, usually three-way excursions to the corner drugstore, the candy
store and the newsstand. Later, when my mother stopped wanting ice cream
and stopped reading Variety and The Village Voice, I would simply go back
and forth to the drugstore. My small dog, emerging from under my mother's
bed, always accompanied me.

Death altered our route. My dog and I became regular visitors to the
offices of the two executors of my mother's estate. She came along when I
returned some gifts — a terra cotta angel, a small gold cross on a chain — that
my mother had refused to open at Christmas. I even took the dog to the
funeral chapel when I picked up new death certificates to replace those lost in
the mail. She sat in the crook of my arm when I crossed the hall from the
bookkeeper's office into what was euphemistically called the Gramercy Room,
now empty, where, a few weeks before, I "viewed" my mother for the last time.

When my mother walked into her penthouse apartment after a monthlong
stay in the hospital, she wanted to take a tour before going to bed. She held my
arm and we wandered slowly from room to room while she admired the
pictures, the books, the shining mirrors and gleaming floors, the carved angel's
head on the mantelpiece and the welcome-home anemones from Pansy and
Tola, our two dogs. I helped her climb the step to the terrace so she could
observe the newly planted geraniums and the blossoming wisteria. She said: "It
looks as if a fascinating woman lives here." She was pleased with herself for
having survived and for having such a wonderful-looking place to live in and for
having a future.

Ten months later she was dead, and as I wandered alone from room to
room, I thought how it no longer looked as if a fascinating woman or even a
boring woman lived there. Her possessions had the leftover appearance of
things that have exceeded their lifetime guarantee. Even an everyday utilitarian
machine like her typewriter had gone from being a typewriter to being a
memento, something tangible to remember her by.

Occasionally even now I will come upon an object like my mother's
hairbrush, its bristles still laced with her hairs, and even before my brain has
time to think, my tears inform me that I'm never, ever going to see her again.
Then there is the stabbing pain I feel when I open a drawer and test the
sharpness of the half-dozen unused hypodermic syringes I took from my
mother's bathroom. I've kept them as a reminder, a symbol, of all she went
through.

Not that the pain for either of us was incessant. Even as my mother's life
was ending, I felt at times oddly exhilarated. Those moments stand out in
grotesque relief, like the flower embroidered on the bodice of the nightgown

113

she died in. The evening, for example, when her mood suddenly turned gregarious; I sat on her bed and, at her instruction, dialed three friends in a row, catching them all in the middle of dinner. In every case my announcement, "Mom wants to talk to you," elicited an explosion of surprised delight. Or the afternoon I performed the unexpectedly intimate act of applying polish remover to her nails while she and I gossiped as cozily as a manicurist and a favorite customer. Or the time when, thinking she was asleep, I leaned over her and whispered: "I love you. I'll be right back," and was about to tiptoe out when she said: "And I love *you* right back."

Going through my mother's books I came across a copy of Flannery O'Connor's "Complete Stories," in which I had inserted three strips of paper marked "Good," "Better," "Best." I know she never opened that book. Usually our tastes coincided, but for some reason my mother could never, as she put it, "dig" Flannery O'Connor. I pointed out that this was because she had never read O'Connor, and she agreed. My mother was an avid reader of Thomas Merton; I explained that this was all the more reason why she would like O'Connor since Merton considered her right up there with Sophocles. Even that argument did not persuade her.

It was just as hopeless trying to get my mother to sample Jane Austen. When I gave her a boxed set of the complete works, she opened it, burst out laughing, hugged it to her and said that now she was going to find out what the Austen mystique was all about. A year went by, and in the fall of 1980 she asked me which Austen novel I thought she should take with her to Montecatini. I suggested "Emma"; it is not my favorite but I thought it was probably the most accessible. She took it along, but she had a relapse and had to come straight back to New York. She took "Emma" with her to the hospital but never got to it. Then when she came home she kept it beside her bed. She said she had a great idea: She and I would read it aloud to each other, each taking alternate chapters, while she recovered from radiation. We never did.

Not long after she died I read through a notebook that my mother had written in while lying in bed. It was filled with ideas for the murder mystery — a funny one — she was writing. Right in the middle of her notes she wrote the name "Annie" (me) and underneath put:

New Yorker subs.
bath oil
wine
angel

It was obviously a list of things she intended to get me for Christmas before she knew she would be spending Christmas back in the hospital, too ill to give presents and too miserable to open any.

Eventually my mother's death stopped being a current event and started being past history. Other events, public and private, took its place. There was the shooting of Reagan and the Pope and Sadat, and interspersed between the gunshots, a novel my mother wrote went out of print, her apartment was emptied, her will was contested. The "something good" I had been waiting for has yet to materialize. I still believe it might. At times I cannot stand it that my mother will not be here to share my impending happiness. Then I realize that the doorman's handshake was not a dividing line after all and that I can take her with me into the future.

I think sometimes that I may try to finish the mystery novel. The heroine was to have a daughter named Francesca — my mother's favorite name — whose lugubrious disposition was based on my own. At least that character should not be too difficult to write.

And I think I will perpetuate our mutual habit of giving angels — guardian angels — to people who are ailing or who simply need to be watched over, like my mother's doctor. She gave him a smiling guardian angel made of cloth and wearing a bright red dress, and he kept it in his office where it would do him and my mother the most good. She hung several of the angels I gave her from the ceiling over her desk to serve as muses. When she died there was a flute-playing silver cherub on the wall above her bed; from its foot hung a little white-robed pig, from me, wearing a halo and wings. Now as I look at them poised above my own bed, I am convinced that both those angels know, as I do, that she was on their side.

QUESTIONS ON CONTENT:

1. In paragraph one, Bayer writes that she anticipates something good following something bad. Death is the "bad." What is the "good"?
2. What does Bayer originally see as the significance of the doorman's handshake? What does it finally mean to her?
3. What are some of the mementos that Bayer finds mean a life?
4. What is the significance of the angels? Why are angels over her mother's desk? What is the meaning of the last line?

QUESTIONS ON WRITING STRUCTURE AND STRATEGY:

1. How would you characterize the tone of this piece? Is it mournful? Maudlin? Self-pitying? Elegiac? Is the effect of reading this depressing? Explain.
2. What audience is Bayer aiming at? (Note where published.)

115

3. What is the author attempting to convey in contrasting paragraphs three and four? In the penthouse scenes in paragraphs five and six? And in the painful memories and the happy ones in paragraphs seven and eight?

4. What does the author show by noting in paragraph three that she gradually eliminated one excursion after the other?

QUESTIONS FOR DISCUSSION AND WRITING:

1. Very often when someone we know or love dies, seemingly insignificant objects, words, songs, places, or activities evoke memories of those now dead. If you have ever experienced such a loss — of a parent, a relative, a friend, or have been affected by the death of a much-beloved public figure — reflect on what you associate with them and write a journal entry about the "mementos that mean a life." Try to list in a prewriting warm-up the objects, reflections, or activities and then see if there may be something that takes on significance for you as a symbol.

2. Sometimes we find ourselves engaged in a great many activities over a relatively short period of time: graduation activities, the marriage of a sister or brother, a family or high school reunion. These are often happy occasions, sometimes even tinged with sadness. Try a prewriting exercise preparatory to writing a paper in which you try to recall as many details, impressions, and feelings of such an event as you can. Ask yourself why you felt the way you did, why it was such a memorable event. Try to reconstruct your day or days, the things that went right, the things that went wrong, your dominant impression of the whole event. Sort out your notes and write a short account.

3. After intense emotional experiences, people often remember details so vividly that they become inextricably associated with the event. Emily Dickinson wrote a very famous poem about a "certain slant of light" that evoked a previous, intense emotional experience. Search your experience for such a detail or details. Perhaps a sound, a smell, or a taste may trigger your memory. Write a paper describing the experience and the emotion it evokes. It can be happy or sad, funny or absurd.

VENTING ANGER MAY DO
MORE HARM THAN GOOD
Jane E. Brody

*So you think you have nothing to write about. Consider Jane E.
Brody's article on anger, published in the* New York Times. *Not only
is it a fit subject for a newspaper column but it is also the topic for a
number of popular books, such as the controversial one that inspired
this article:* Anger: The Misunderstood Emotion, *by Carol Tavris.
Take a look at what the experts are now saying about anger, its
origins, its expression, its repression, and its suppression, and see how
these new views apply to you. In her prewriting, Brody obviously
undertook extensive research, gathering facts, quotations, examples
from various authorities, even from a novel, to support and illustrate
her analysis. To enhance or support her ideas, she frequently employs a
variety of modes: comparisons of both old and new views and the
slightly differing attitudes of various authorities, cause and effect, and
analysis. Note also Brody's language. By using the language of the
experts, she enables the reader to see the problem of anger as the
experts see it, thereby extending the boundaries of the reader's
knowledge. Brody starts by quoting the popular wisdom, then
introduces a scientific challenge to the wisdom of venting anger. As
she reports the findings of various experts, notice how the challenge is
qualified and refined by other experts. The result of this refining
process makes possible the suggestions with which she concludes. Note
that Brody uses the same general approach in this article as she does
in the earlier one on bulimia.*

For years the popular wisdom has been that strong feelings of anger 1
ought to be expressed. It was healthier, people were frequently advised, to let
loose the reins of anger, to "let it all hang out" like so much laundry.

Anger was described by many psychotherapists as an explosive feeling 2
that, if unexpressed, turned inward to cause such disorders as ulcers, heart
attacks, headaches, overeating and colitis, not to mention the havoc that
festering anger could wreak on human relationships. Women in particular,
many of whom had grown up believing it "not ladylike" to get angry, were
urged to express their anger without hesitation, guilt or tears.

A number of modern treatment techniques, epitomized by Primal Scream 3
therapy (in which the client "regresses" to the moment of birth and rages
against having to leave the warm safety of the womb), have been based on the
notion that people must unearth and release their hidden anger to get rid of
joy-robbing emotional ghosts.

Now, however, some experts are taking a hard new look at this powerful 4
emotion and questioning basic assumptions about its significance to physical

and mental health. Sparked in part by a controversial new book, "Anger: The Misunderstood Emotion," by Carol Tavris (Simon & Schuster), the new view sees anger as often more destructive when expressed than when suppressed. This view prescribes a far more limited role for the ventilation of anger than is now popularly pursued.

A growing body of evidence suggests that exactly how anger is handled   5
may be less important than the fact that anger is so frequently felt in the first place. While venting anger may help to head off some forms of illness, studies suggest it may actually contribute to others. More important, the effect of venting anger on social interactions is often devastating.

"Talking out an emotion doesn't reduce it, *it rehearses it*," wrote Dr.   6
Tavris, a social psychologist who has gathered hundreds of research references to support her views. "People who are most prone to give vent to their rage get angrier, not less angry."

For example, she cited a study among laid-off engineers in San Diego,   7
which showed that the men who were invited to ventilate their anger actually became more hostile toward the company or their supervisors than those who were asked to criticize themselves. In another study, third-grade children who were encouraged to express their anger toward a child who had frustrated them ended up liking that child less than children did who were not permitted to express anger.

In marital arguments as well, an angry outburst frequently erupts into a   8
full-scale battle, Dr. Tavris noted, because one person's anger is threatening to another and can provoke its target to respond in kind. "Few people know how to express anger without attacking and belittling the other person," she remarked.

According to Dr. Leo Madow, a psychoanalyst at the Institute of the   9
Pennsylvania Hospital in Philadelphia, the "get-the-anger-out, be-honest-with-each-other" approach, inspired by the self-awareness movement of the 1970's, can be very destructive. He said, for example, that the 'T groups' held in many companies, "where employees sat around and told each other how they felt about one another, nearly destroyed some companies."

Dr. Madow added: "Freud was one of the first to recognize that catharsis   10
doesn't work. Anger is really a symptom. To deal with it, you have to get back into the unconscious and find out why anger is there."

Dr. Willard Gaylin, a New York psychiatrist, who is president of the   11
Hastings Center in Hastings-on-Hudson, N.Y., calls the ventilation of anger "a form of public littering." He explained in an interview: "Even if ventilation did relieve everything, which it does not, it would still not be justified."

Dr. Gaylin said not enough attention had been paid to the societal aspects   12
of anger. "The real problem is not so much the articulation of anger but the generation of it," he said. "Many people are angry all the time, they have an

inordinate capacity to generate anger." The source of all this anger, he believes, is our technological society in which people are alienated from the rewards of their activities at the same time that happiness is held up as the main goal in life.

Anger is a normal emotional response that occurs in all people from birth to death, regardless of their culture. But what provokes anger and how it is expressed, Dr. Tavris says, varies widely throughout the world. Some people express anger through the use of ritual curses (as in the Yiddish, "May all your teeth fall out but one, and that one have a cavity"); the Kapauku Papuans of West New Guinea hold a culturally circumscribed "mad dance," and the Mbuti hunter-gatherers of Zaire use humor and ridicule when reason fails to end an argument.   13

Physiologically, angry feelings are associated with the release of the same hormones, epinephrine and norepinephrine, that are produced under stress. These hormones stimulate the heart, raise the blood pressure, pour sugar into the blood, constrict the blood vessels to the digestive tract and generally create feelings of excitement and arousal. This has fed the theory that unexpressed anger can produce a host of psychosomatic reactions, ranging from hives and headaches to cancer and heart disease.   14

"Anger is a form of energy and you can't destroy it," Dr. Madow said. "When it's not dealt with it can lead to such problems as headaches and depression." The analyst, who wrote a book called "Anger: How to Recognize and Cope with It" (Scribners), said that while the relationship between anger and illness was difficult to demonstrate in a test-tube investigation, "the consequences of repressed anger are seen clinically every day."   15

Dr. Madow distinguishes between "suppressed" and "repressed" anger. Suppressing anger, he said, is "perfectly fine if you do it consciously and for good reason. But repression leads to trouble because the person has no awareness of the anger." For example, he said, a man may knowingly suppress his anger at his boss for the sake of his job without untoward consequences, but repressed anger at being abandoned by parents early in life can lead to chronic depression.   16

According to Dr. Theodore I. Rubin, a New York psychoanalyst and author of "The Angry Book" (Collier Books), repressed anger is the primary cause of anxiety. "Ninety percent of anxiety attacks represent a surfacing of vehemently repressed anger," he said in an interview. "I'm not against suppression of anger; it's repression—not knowing that a person is angry—when the damage is done. When anger is repressed, it leads to somatic complaints: migraine headaches, colitis, overeating, smoking addiction, and it aggravates psychiatric disorders."   17

Dr. Harvey Rich, a psychoanalyst in Washington, said: "A woman who's been taught that she must bear the burdens of abuse may become a quiet   18 alcoholic, or have an extramarital affair. She's always rationalizing that she is suffering. Her suffering stems from the lack of an avenue for expressing anger."

Still, Dr. Rich agrees with Dr. Tavris that "the gross ventilation of anger — mouthing off — is of no value. Anger is an inappropriate response in many cases. The problem some people have with anger is that it seems to come from nowhere."   19

Dr. Tavris says studies have failed to show a direct link between suppressed anger and illness. "The popular belief that suppressed anger can wreak havoc on the body and bloodstream has been inflated out of realistic proportions," she wrote. "It does not, in any predictable or consistent way, make us depressed, produce ulcers or hypertension, set us off on food binges, or give us heart attacks."   20

In fact, the newest studies of the relationship between anger and heart disease indicate that an excessively hostile attitude, regardless of whether that anger is expressed, increases the risk of disease. Dr. Redford Williams, an internist and psychiatrist at the Duke University Medical Center, studied 255 physicians who had taken a standard personality test 25 years earlier. Those who had scored in the top half of the hostility scale had suffered five to six times more heart attacks and a death rate from heart attack five times as high as those in the lower half.   21

Dr. Williams said the next step will be to examine the consequences of expression and suppression of conscious angry feelings. Although there is as yet no direct evidence, there is the strong suspicion, he said, that those who let their anger out may be more prone to heart disease and those who keep anger in face greater risk of high blood pressure and possibly cancer.   22

Dr. Williams believes excessive hostility is rooted in feelings of being unloved. "These people grow up feeling that they can't trust people to treat them right," he said. "People with this attitude are more likely to experience the emotion of anger more often and to experience it more intensely."   23

Dr. Rich, the Washington psychoanalyst, believes that people who are quick to anger have a "basic sense of badness that stems from the time they felt responsible for everything that happened. Whatever went wrong, it must be their fault. This defensive character organization creates an intense primitive anger just below the surface. When something goes wrong, like the car doesn't start, they experience an infantile rage. It comes from the fantasy that you should be good and if you were good, this wouldn't have happened."   24

Under normal circumstances, Dr. Tavris says, the likelihood of an angry response is often determined by the pre-existing level of physiological arousal. She notes, for example, that noise, crowds, frustration or aggressive sports events do not by themselves generate anger, but they increase the general level   25 of arousal and make it more likely that a minor provocation will trigger an angry response.

Thus, she says, aggression, aggressive feelings and other heightened emotional states can inflame anger as well as the other way around. Encouraging youngsters to play aggressive games as a "healthful" means of venting angry feelings is likely to backfire, she suggests.

26

Dr. Tavris does not believe anger should never be expressed. Rather, she limits the circumstances to those that satisfy three conditions: when anger represents a legitimate plea for justice, when it is directed at someone who is the cause of the anger and when it would result in a correction of the offense or, at the very least, would not cause retaliation. Otherwise, she suggests counting to 10.

27

QUESTIONS ON CONTENT:

1. What is Brody's thesis, and where do you find it?
2. What is the new attitude toward expressing anger these days, and how does it differ from the attitudes of recent years?
3. Why are the distinctions between suppressed and repressed anger important?
4. When does Dr. Tavris believe anger should be expressed?

QUESTIONS ON WRITING STRUCTURE AND STRATEGY:

1. To what audience is Brody directing her remarks? What is her purpose? What is her tone?
2. What does Brody achieve by citing so many authorities?
3. Why is the final section a good conclusion?

QUESTIONS FOR DISCUSSION AND WRITING:

1. Although Brody's article was precipitated by a "controversial" book on anger, once she presented the thesis of the book, she developed her article with expert opinions gained by reading and interviewing. Interview your fellow students on the subject of anger. Is it better to suppress anger or to let it "all hang out"? Get a wide, representative sampling of opinion from all levels, sexes, ages, perhaps even from some of your professors. Take notes and try to get short, telling quotes to use in your paper. (Use separate note cards for each interviewee; this will make it easier to separate your responses in groups.) Now go over your material and see if you have at least two decided points of view. Develop your paper by comparing and contrasting the different viewpoints and see if you can end your paper with some common views on the subject as Brody has done. In your writing, try to use the terms you have acquired from the reading.

121

2. Have you ever been a participant in a gathering when the discussion turned into a "help session" in which you all agreed "constructively" to help each other by pointing out annoying habits or faults? How did the session turn out? How well did the members interact the next day, the next week? Did friendships remain unscathed? How did you feel afterwards about what you did say and what you did not say? Where appropriate, use some of the new vocabulary you have acquired.

3. Analyze an argument with your parents, a roommate, a fellow worker, a friend. What was gained? What was lost?

4. From a spin-off of ideas generated by this article, write a short paper on frustration, retaliation, revenge, hostility, or sulking. You may allude to literary and film models such as Arthur Miller's *The Crucible, The Godfather*, the Rambo films.

IN SEARCH OF
OUR MOTHERS' GARDENS

Alice Walker

Alice Walker is a poet, novelist, and essayist. Her last novel — The
Color Purple — in 1983 won both the National Book Award and the
Pulitzer Prize. In 1986 it was made into a highly successful, albeit
controversial, movie, winning many Academy Award nominations. She
has published several collections of short stories and poetry and a
collection of essays, from which the following is taken. Walker was
born in Georgia and educated at Spelman College, and in New York
City at Sarah Lawrence College. She has taught at several colleges and
currently teaches at the University of California, Berkeley. In her
essay, excerpted from a longer one, she discusses the creativity of black
women. Starting with a series of questions, Walker probes the black
past and her own mother's past for answers. The result of her probing
is a ringing salute to her mother and to all those unknown black
women who died unrecognized as creative beings. Note Walker's
narrative skill and her language, her word choice and imagery. Her
essay brilliantly illustrates how the techniques of the creative artist can
be effectively used by the prose writer.

I described her own nature and temperament. Told how they needed a larger life for their
expression. . . . . I pointed out that in lieu of proper channels, her emotions had
overflowed into paths that dissipated them. I talked, beautifully I thought, about an art
that would be born, an art that would open the way for women the likes of her. I asked her
to hope, and build up an inner life against the coming of that day. . . . . I sang, with a
strange quiver in my voice, a promise song.

—Jean Toomer, *"Avey."*
CANE

The poet speaking to a prostitute who falls asleep while he's talking — 1
When the poet Jean Toomer walked through the South in the early twenties, he
discovered a curious thing: black women whose spirituality was so intense, so
deep, so *unconscious*, that they were themselves unaware of the richness they
held. They stumbled blindly through their lives: creatures so abused and
mutilated in body, so dimmed and confused by pain, that they considered
themselves unworthy even of hope. In the selfless abstractions their bodies
became to the men who used them, they became more than "sexual objects,"
more even than mere women: they became "Saints." Instead of being perceived
as whole persons, their bodies became shrines: what was thought to be their
minds became temples suitable for worship. These crazy Saints stared out at the
world, wildly, like lunatics — or quietly, like suicides; and the "God" that was
in their gaze was as mute as a great stone.

Who were these Saints? These crazy, loony, pitiful women?   2

Some of them, without a doubt, were our mothers and grandmothers.   3

In the still heat of the post-Reconstruction South, this is how they seemed   4
to Jean Toomer: exquisite butterflies trapped in an evil honey, toiling away
their lives in an era, a century, that did not acknowledge them, except as "the
mule of the world." They dreamed dreams that no one knew—not even
themselves, in any coherent fashion—and saw visions no one could
understand. They wandered or sat about the countryside crooning lullabies to
ghosts, and drawing the mother of Christ in charcoal on courthouse walls.

They forced their minds to desert their bodies and their striving spirits   5
sought to rise, like frail whirlwinds from the hard red clay. And when those frail
whirlwinds fell, in scattered particles, upon the ground, no one mourned.
Instead, men lit candles to celebrate the emptiness that remained, as people do
who enter a beautiful but vacant space to resurrect a God.

Our mothers and grandmothers, some of them: moving to music not yet   6
written. And they waited.

They waited for a day when the unknown thing that was in them would   7
be made known; but guessed, somehow in their darkness, that on the day of
their revelation they would be long dead. Therefore to Toomer they walked, and
even ran, in slow motion. For they were going nowhere immediate, and the
future was not yet within their grasp. And men took our mothers and
grandmothers, "but got no pleasure from it." So complex was their passion and
their calm.

To Toomer, they lay vacant and fallow as autumn fields, with harvest time   8
never in sight: and he saw them enter loveless marriages, without joy; and
become prostitutes, without resistance; and become mothers of children,
without fulfillment.

For these grandmothers and mothers of ours were not Saints, but Artists;   9
driven to a numb and bleeding madness by the springs of creativity in them for
which there was no release. They were Creators, who lived lives of spiritual
waste, because they were so rich in spirituality—which is the basis of Art—
that the strain of enduring their unused and unwanted talent drove them
insane. Throwing away this spirituality was their pathetic attempt to lighten
the soul to a weight their work-worn, sexually abused bodies could bear.

What did it mean for a black woman to be an artist in our grandmothers'   10
time? In our great-grandmothers' day? It is a question with an answer cruel
enough to stop the blood.

Did you have a genius of a great-great-grandmother who died under some   11
ignorant and depraved white overseer's lash? Or was she required to bake
biscuits for a lazy backwater tramp, when she cried out in her soul to paint
watercolors of sunsets, or the rain falling on the green and peaceful

pasturelands? Or was her body broken and forced to bear children (who were more often than not sold away from her) — eight, ten, fifteen, twenty children —when her one joy was the thought of modeling heroic figures of rebellion, in stone or clay?

How was the creativity of the black woman kept alive, year after year and   12
century after century, when for most of the years black people have been in America, it was a punishable crime for a black person to read or write? And the freedom to paint, to sculpt, to expand the mind with action did not exist. Consider, if you can bear to imagine it, what might have been the result if singing, too, had been forbidden by law. Listen to the voices of Bessie Smith, Billie Holiday, Nina Simone, Roberta Flack, and Aretha Franklin, among others, and imagine those voices muzzled for life. Then you may begin to comprehend the lives of our "crazy," "Sainted" mothers and grandmothers. The agony of the lives of women who might have been Poets, Novelists, Essayists, and Short-Story Writers (over a period of centuries), who died with their real gifts stifled within them.

And, if this were the end of the story, we would have cause to cry out in   13
my paraphrase of Okot p'Bitek's great poem:

> *O, my clanswomen*
> *Let us all cry together!*
> *Come,*
> *Let us mourn the death of our mother,*
> *The death of a Queen*
> *The ash that was produced*
> *By a great fire!*
> *O, this homestead is utterly dead*
> *Close the gates*
> *With* lacari *thorns,*
> *For our mother*
> *The creator of the Stool is lost!*
> *And all the young women*
> *Have perished in the wilderness!*

But this is not the end of the story, for all the young women — our   14
mothers and grandmothers, *ourselves* — have not perished in the wilderness. And if we ask ourselves why, and search for and find the answer, we will know beyond all efforts to erase it from our minds, just exactly who, and of what, we black American women are.

One example, perhaps the most pathetic, most misunderstood one, can   15 provide a backdrop for our mothers' work: Phillis Wheatley, a slave in the 1700s.

Virginia Woolf, in her book *A Room of One's Own*, wrote that in order for   16
a woman to write fiction she must have two things, certainly: a room of her
own (with key and lock) and enough money to support herself.

What then are we to make of Phillis Wheatley, a slave, who owned not   17
even herself? This sickly, frail black girl who required a servant of her own at
times — her health was so precarious — and who, had she been white, would
have been easily considered the intellectual superior of all the women and most
of the men in the society of her day.

Virginia Woolf wrote further, speaking of course not of our Phillis, that   18
"any woman born with a great gift in the sixteenth century [insert "eighteenth
century," insert "black woman," insert "born or made a slave"] would
certainly have gone crazed, shot herself, or ended her days in some lonely
cottage outside the village, half witch, half wizard [insert "Saint"], feared and
mocked at. For it needs little skill and psychology to be sure that a highly
gifted girl who had tried to use her gift for poetry would have been so thwarted
and hindered by contrary instincts [add "chains, guns, the lash, the ownership
of one's body by someone else, submission to an alien religion"], that she must
have lost her health and sanity to a certainty."

The key words, as they relate to Phillis, are "contrary instincts." For when   19
we read the poetry of Phillis Wheatley — as when we read the novels of Nella
Larsen or the oddly false-sounding autobiography of that freest of all black
women writers, Zora Hurston — evidence of "contrary instincts" is everywhere.
Her loyalties were completely divided, as was, without question, her mind.

But how could this be otherwise? Captured at seven, a slave of wealthy,   20
doting whites who instilled in her the "savagery" of the Africa they "rescued"
her from . . . one wonders if she was even able to remember her homeland as
she had known it, or as it really was.

Yet, because she did try to use her gift for poetry in a world that made her   21
a slave, she was "so thwarted and hindered by . . . contrary instincts, that
she . . . lost her health . . ." In the last years of her brief life, burdened not
only with the need to express her gift but also with a penniless, friendless
"freedom" and several small children for whom she was forced to do strenuous
work to feed, she lost her health, certainly. Suffering from malnutrition and
neglect and who knows what mental agonies, Phillis Wheatley died.

So torn by "contrary instincts" was black, kidnapped, enslaved Phillis that   22
her description of "the Goddess" — as she poetically called the Liberty she did
not have — is ironically, cruelly humorous. And, in fact, has held Phillis up to
ridicule for more than a century. It is usually read prior to hanging Phillis's
memory as that of a fool. She wrote:

The Goddess comes, she moves divinely fair,
Olive and laurel binds her golden hair.
Wherever shines this native of the skies,
Unnumber'd charms and recent graces rise. [My italics]

It is obvious that Phillis, the slave, combed the "Goddess's" hair every   23
morning; prior, perhaps, to bringing in the milk, or fixing her mistress's lunch.
She took her imagery from the one thing she saw elevated above all others.

With the benefit of hindsight we ask, "How could she?"   24

But at last, Phillis, we understand. No more snickering when your stiff,   25
struggling, ambivalent lines are forced on us. We know now that you were not
an idiot or a traitor; only a sickly little black girl, snatched from your home and
country and made a slave; a woman who still struggled to sing the song that
was your gift, although in a land of barbarians who praised you for your
bewildered tongue. It is not so much what you sang, as that you kept alive, in
so many of our ancestors, *the notion of song.*

Black women are called, in the folklore that so aptly identifies one's status   26
in society, "the *mule* of the world," because we have been handed the burdens
that everyone else — *everyone* else — refused to carry. We have also been called
"Matriarchs," "Superwomen," and "Mean and Evil Bitches." Not to mention
"Castraters" and "Sapphire's Mama." When we have pleaded for
understanding, our character has been distorted; when we have asked for
simple caring, we have been handed empty inspirational appellations, then
stuck in the farthest corner. When we asked for love, we have been given
children. In short, even our plainer gifts, our labors of fidelity and love, have
been knocked down our throats. To be an artist and a black woman, even
today, lowers our status in many respects, rather than raises it: and yet, artists
we will be.

Therefore we must fearlessly pull out of ourselves and look at and identify   27
with our lives the living creativity some of our great-grandmothers were not
allowed to know. I stress *some* of them because it is well known that the
majority of our great-grandmothers knew, even without "knowing" it, the
reality of their spirituality, even if they didn't recognize it beyond what
happened in the singing at church — and they never had any intention of giving
it up.

How they did it — those millions of black women who were not Phillis   28
Wheatley, or Lucy Terry or Frances Harper or Zora Hurston or Nella Larsen or
Bessie Smith; or Elizabeth Catlett, or Katherine Dunham, either — brings me to
the title of this essay, "In Search of Our Mothers' Gardens," which is a
personal account that is yet shared, in its theme and its meaning, by all of us. I
found, while thinking about the far-reaching world of the creative black

woman, that often the truest answer to a question that really matters can be found very close.

In the late 1920s my mother ran away from home to marry my father. Marriage, if not running away, was expected of seventeen-year-old girls. By the time she was twenty, she had two children and was pregnant with a third. Five children later, I was born. And this is how I came to know my mother: she seemed a large, soft, loving-eyed woman who was rarely impatient in our home. Her quick, violent temper was on view only a few times a year, when she battled with the white landlord who had the misfortune to suggest to her that her children did not need to go to school.   29

She made all the clothes we wore, even my brothers' overalls. She made all the towels and sheets we used. She spent the summers canning vegetables and fruits. She spent the winter evenings making quilts enough to cover all our beds.   30

During the "working" day, she labored beside — not behind — my father in the fields. Her day began before sunup, and did not end until late at night. There was never a moment for her to sit down, undisturbed, to unravel her own private thoughts; never a time free from interruption — by work or the noisy inquiries of her many children. And yet, it is to my mother — and all our mothers who were not famous — that I went in search of the secret of what has fed that muzzled and often mutilated, but vibrant, creative spirit that the black woman has inherited, and that pops out in wild and unlikely places to this day.   31

But when, you will ask, did my overworked mother have time to know or care about feeding the creative spirit?   32

The answer is so simple that many of us have spent years discovering it. We have constantly looked high, when we should have looked high — and low.   33

For example: in the Smithsonian Institution in Washington, D.C., there hangs a quilt unlike any other in the world. In fanciful, inspired, and yet simple and identifiable figures, it portrays the story of the Crucifixion. It is considered rare, beyond price. Though it follows no known pattern of quilt-making, and though it is made of bits and pieces of worthless rags, it is obviously the work of a person of powerful imagination and deep spiritual feeling. Below this quilt I saw a note that says it was made by "an anonymous Black woman in Alabama, a hundred years ago."   34

If we could locate this "anonymous" black woman from Alabama, she would turn out to be one of our grandmothers — an artist who left her mark in the only materials she could afford, and in the only medium her position in society allowed her to use.   35

As Virginia Woolf wrote further, in *A Room of One's Own:*   36

Yet genius of a sort must have existed among women as it must have existed among the

128

working class. [Change this to "slaves" and "the wives and daughters of sharecroppers."]
Now and again an Emily Brontë or a Robert Burns [change this to "a Zora Hurston or a
Richard Wright"] blazes out and proves its presence. But certainly it never got itself on to
paper. When, however, one reads of a witch being ducked, of a woman possessed by devils
[or "Sainthood"], of a wise woman selling herbs [or root workers], or even a very
remarkable man who had a mother, then I think we are on the track of a lost novelist, a
suppressed poet, of some mute and inglorious Jane Austen. . . . . Indeed, I would venture
to guess that Anon, who wrote so many poems without signing them, was often a
woman. . . .

And so our mothers and grandmothers have, more often than not anonymously,
handed on the creative spark, the seed of the flower they themselves never
hoped to see: or like a sealed letter they could not plainly read.

And so it is, certainly, with my own mother. Unlike "Ma" Rainey's songs,　37
which retained their creator's name even while blasting forth from Bessie
Smith's mouth, no song or poem will bear my mother's name. Yet so many of
the stories that I write, that we all write, are my mother's stories. Only
recently did I fully realize this: that through years of listening to my mother's
stories of her life, I have absorbed not only the stories themselves, but
something of the manner in which she spoke, something of the urgency that
involves the knowledge that her stories — like her life — must be recorded. It is
probably for this reason that so much of what I have written is about
characters whose counterparts in real life are so much older than I am.

But the telling of these stories, which came from my mother's lips as　38
naturally as breathing, was not the only way my mother showed herself as an
artist. For stories, too, were subject to being distracted, to dying without
conclusion. Dinners must be started, and cotton must be gathered before the
big rains. The artist that was and is my mother showed itself to me only after
many years. This is what I finally noticed:

Like Mem, a character in *The Third Life of Grange Copeland*, my mother　39
adorned with flowers whatever shabby house we were forced to live in. And not
just your typical straggly country stand of zinnias, either. She planted ambitious
gardens — and still does — with over fifty different varieties of plants that
bloom profusely from early March until late November. Before she left home
for the fields, she watered her flowers, chopped up the grass, and laid out new
beds. When she returned from the fields she might divide clumps of bulbs, dig
a cold pit, uproot and replant roses, or prune branches from her taller bushes
or trees — until night came and it was too dark to see.

Whatever she planted grew as if by magic, and her fame as a grower of　40
flowers spread over three counties. Because of her creativity with her flowers,
even my memories of poverty are seen through a screen of blooms —

sunflowers, petunias, roses, dahlias, forsythia, spirea, delphiniums, verbena . . . and on and on.

And I remember people coming to my mother's yard to be given cuttings   41
from her flowers; I hear again the praise showered on her because whatever rocky soil she landed on, she turned into a garden. A garden so brilliant with colors, so original in its design, so magnificent with life and creativity, that to this day people drive by our house in Georgia — perfect strangers and imperfect strangers — and ask to stand or walk among my mother's art.

I notice that it is only when my mother is working in her flowers that she   42
is radiant, almost to the point of being invisible — except as Creator: hand and eye. She is involved in work her soul must have. Ordering the universe in the image of her personal conception of Beauty.

Her face, as she prepares the Art that is her gift, is a legacy of respect she   43
leaves to me, for all that illuminates and cherishes life. She has handed down respect for the possibilities — and the will to grasp them.

For her, so hindered and intruded upon in so many ways, being an artist   44
has still been a daily part of her life. This ability to hold on, even in very simple ways, is work black women have done for a very long time.

This poem is not enough, but it is something, for the woman who literally   45
covered the holes in our walls with sunflowers:

> *They were women then*
> *My mama's generation*
> *Husky of voice — Stout of*
> *Step*
> *With fists as well as*
> *Hands*
> *How they battered down*
> *Doors*
> *And ironed*
> *Starched white*
> *Shirts*
> *How they led*
> *Armies*
> *Headragged Generals*
> *Across mined*
> *Fields*
> *Booby-trapped*
> *Kitchens*
> *To discover books*

130

> *Desks*
> *A place for us*
> *How they knew what we*
> Must *know*
> *Without knowing a page*
> *Of it*
> *Themselves*

Guided by my heritage of a love of beauty and a respect for strength — in   46
search of my mother's garden, I found my own.

And perhaps in Africa over two hundred years ago, there was just such a   47
mother; perhaps she painted vivid and daring decorations in oranges and
yellows and greens on the walls of her hut; perhaps she sang — in a voice like
Roberta Flack's — *sweetly* over the compounds of her village; perhaps she wove
the most stunning mats or told the most ingenious stories of all the village
storytellers. Perhaps she was herself a poet — though only her daughter's name
is signed to the poems that we know.

Perhaps Phillis Wheatley's mother was also an artist.   48

Perhaps in more than Phillis Wheatley's biological life is her mother's   49
signature made clear.

QUESTIONS ON CONTENT:

1. What is Walker's thesis? Is it stated or implied? Where do you find it?
2. What is the meaning of Walker's title? Why is it appropriate? Reference to more than her own mother's garden suggests that she uses "gardens" not only in its literal sense. Explain.
3. What avenues for creativity did some black women find in life?
4. How does Walker account for the lack of conventional artistic products (novels, sculpture, painting) in earlier generations of black women?
5. What is the legacy Walker's mother leaves to her daughter?
6. What does Walker say about today's reception of the artistic efforts by black women?

QUESTIONS ON WRITING STRUCTURE AND STRATEGY:

1. Where does Walker employ rhetorical questions? What do they force the reader to do?
2. Aside from the inclusion of one of her poems, what specific sentences or phrases lead you to believe that Walker is an accomplished poet as well as a novelist?
3. Walker frequently uses incomplete sentences. In which instances are they effective or ineffective?

QUESTIONS FOR WRITING AND DISCUSSION:

1. Both Tillie Olsen and Alice Walker write of the stifling of women's creativity. In a clear, well-organized paper compare Olsen's and Walker's different points of view and their conclusions.

2. How is Walker's essay a search for her own creativity? Write a paper in which you explain.

3. Examine the talents and creativity of your own parents or grandparents. Develop a paper about the mirroring of those abilities in you. If you are a parent, which of your creative characteristics do you find in your offspring? What role has environment played in the development of those characteristics?

GENESIS OF A WRITER
Richard Wright

Richard Wright was born near Natchez, Mississippi, the son of a mill worker and a country schoolteacher. His distaste for school prompted him to leave home at fifteen to take a job in Memphis, Tennessee. Memphis provides the setting for the following account from his autobiography, Black Boy, *written in 1937.*

It was, as he relates, Mencken's Book of Prefaces *that not only spurred his desire to read but also excited him with the prospect of writing, even though his family and the conventions of Negro society were against it. For years Wright roamed the country, but so strong was his determination to achieve that he accepted any work that would enable him to continue writing. Finally, a Guggenheim Fellowship made it possible for him to complete his novel* Native Son *(1940), which soon became a best-seller. It was followed by* The Outsider *(1953),* The Long Dream *(1958), and* American Hunger, *a continuation of* Black Boy, *published posthumously. In this selection the reader can expect to find the motivation for Wright's reading and desire to become a writer. Note the resemblance to Martin Eden's experience. Employing first-person narrative, Wright tells a straightforward tale. Observe how he builds suspense in the scene with the librarian. Today's students may find it hard to believe that there was a time in America — not too long ago — when black people in some parts of the country were not allowed to use the public library.*

One morning I arrived early at work and went into the bank lobby where the Negro porter was mopping. I stood at a counter and picked up the Memphis *Commercial Appeal* and began my free reading of the press. I came finally to the editorial page and saw an article dealing with one H. L. Mencken. I knew by hearsay that he was the editor of the *American Mercury*, but aside from that I knew nothing about him. The article was a furious denunciation of Mencken, concluding with one, hot, short sentence: Mencken is a fool. 1

I wondered what on earth this Mencken had done to call down upon him the scorn of the South. The only people I had ever heard denounced in the South were Negroes, and this man was not a Negro. Then what ideas did Mencken hold that made a newspaper like the *Commercial Appeal* castigate him publicly? Undoubtedly he must be advocating ideas that the South did not like. Were there, then, people other than Negroes who criticized the South? I knew that during the Civil War the South had hated northern whites, but I had not encountered such hate during my life. Knowing no more of Mencken than I did at that moment, I felt a vague sympathy for him. Had not the South, which had assigned me the role of a non-man, cast at him its hardest words? 2

Now, how could I find out about this Mencken? There was a huge library   3
near the riverfront, but I knew that Negroes were not allowed to patronize its
shelves any more than they were the parks and playgrounds of the city. I had
gone into the library several times to get books for the white men on the job.
Which of them would now help me to get books? And how could I read them
without causing concern to the white men with whom I worked? I had so far
been successful in hiding my thoughts and feelings from them, but I knew that
I would create hostility if I went about this business of reading in a clumsy way.

I weighed the personalities of the men on the job. There was Don, a Jew;   4
but I distrusted him. His position was not much better than mine and I knew
that he was uneasy and insecure; he had always treated me in an offhand,
bantering way that barely concealed his contempt. I was afraid to ask him to
help me to get books; his frantic desire to demonstrate a racial solidarity with
the whites against Negroes might make him betray me.

Then how about the boss? No, he was a Baptist and I had the suspicion   5
that he would not be quite able to comprehend why a black boy would want to
read Mencken. There were other white men on the job whose attitudes showed
clearly that they were Kluxers or sympathizers, and they were out of the question.

There remained only one man whose attitude did not fit into an anti-Negro   6
category, for I had heard the white men refer to him as a "Pope lover." He was
an Irish Catholic and was hated by the white Southerners. I knew that he read
books, because I had got him volumes from the library several times. Since he,
too, was an object of hatred, I felt that he might refuse me but would hardly
betray me. I hesitated, weighing and balancing the imponderable realities.

One morning I paused before the Catholic fellow's desk.

"I want to ask you a favor," I whispered to him.

"What is it?"

"I want to read. I can't get books from the library. I wonder if you'd let me use your
card?"

He looked at me suspiciously.

"My card is full most of the time," he said.

"I see," I said and waited, posing my question silently.

"You're not trying to get me into trouble, are you, boy?" he asked, staring at me.

"Oh, no, sir."

"What book do you want?"

"A book by H. L. Mencken."

"Which one?"

"I don't know. Has he written more than one?"

"He has written several."

"I didn't know that."

"What makes you want to read Mencken?"

"Oh, I just saw his name in the newspaper," I said.

"It's good of you to want to read," he said. "But you ought to read the right things."

I said nothing. Would he want to supervise my reading?

"Let me think," he said. "I'll figure out something."

I turned from him and he called me back. He stared at me quizzically.

"Richard, don't mention this to the other white men," he said.

"I understand," I said. "I won't say a word."

A few days later he called me to him.

"I've got a card in my wife's name," he said. "Here's mine."

"Thank you, sir."

"Do you think you can manage it?"

"I'll manage fine," I said.

"If they suspect you, you'll get in trouble," he said.

"I'll write the same kind of notes to the library that you wrote when you sent me for books," I told him. "I'll sign your name."

He laughed.

"Go ahead. Let me see what you get," he said.

That afternoon I addressed myself to forging a note. Now, what were the names of books written by H. L. Mencken? I did not know any of them. I finally wrote what I thought would be a foolproof note: *Dear Madam: Will you please let this nigger boy*—I used the word "nigger" to make the librarian feel that I could not possibly be the author of the note—*have some books by H. L. Mencken?* I forged the white man's name. 8

I entered the library as I had always done when on errands for whites, but I felt that I would somehow slip up and betray myself. I doffed my hat, stood a respectful distance from the desk, looked as unbookish as possible, and waited for the white patrons to be taken care of. When the desk was clear of people, I still waited. The white librarian looked at me. 9

"What do you want, boy?" 10

As though I did not possess the power of speech, I stepped forward and simply handed her the forged note, not parting my lips.

"What books by Mencken does he want?" she asked.

"I don't know, ma'am," I said, avoiding her eyes.

"Who gave you this card?"

"Mr. Falk," I said.

"Where is he?"

"He's at work, at the M— — Optical Company," I said. "I've been in here for him before."

"I remember," the woman said. "But he never wrote notes like this."

Oh, God, she's suspicious. Perhaps she would not let me have the books? If she had turned her back at that moment, I would have ducked out the door and never gone back. Then I thought of a bold idea.   11

"You can call him up, ma'am," I said, my heart pounding.   12

"You're not using these books, are you?" she asked pointedly.

"Oh, no, ma'am. I can't read."

"I don't know what he wants by Mencken," she said under her breath.

I knew now that I had won; she was thinking of other things and the race question had gone out of her mind. She went to the shelves. Once or twice she looked over her shoulder at me, as though she was still doubtful. Finally she came forward with two books in her hand.   13

"I'm sending him two books," she said. "But tell Mr. Falk to come in next time, or send me the names of the books he wants. I don't know what he wants to read."   14

I said nothing. She stamped the card and handed me the books. Not daring to glance at them, I went out of the library, fearing that the woman would call me back for further questioning. A block away from the library I opened one of the books and read a title: *A Book of Prefaces*. I was nearing my nineteenth birthday and I did not know how to pronounce the word "preface." I thumbed the pages and saw strange words and strange names. I shook my head, disappointed. I looked at the other book; it was called *Prejudices*. I knew what that word meant; I had heard it all my life. And right off I was on guard against Mencken's books. Why would a man want to call a book *Prejudices*? The word was so stained with all my memories of racial hate that I could not conceive of anybody using it for a title. Perhaps I had made a mistake about Mencken? A man who had prejudices must be wrong.   15

When I showed the books to Mr. Falk, he looked at me and frowned.   16

"That librarian might telephone you," I warned him.   17

"That's all right," he said. "But when you're through reading those books, I want you to tell me what you get out of them."

That night in my rented room, while letting the hot water run over my can of pork and beans in the sink, I opened *A Book of Prefaces* and began to read. I was jarred and shocked by the style, the clear, clean, sweeping sentences. Why   18 did he write like that? And how did one write like that? I pictured the man as a raging demon, slashing with his pen, consumed with hate, denouncing everything American, extolling everything European or German, laughing at the weaknesses of people, mocking God, authority. What was this? I stood up, trying to realize what reality lay behind the meaning of the words . . . Yes, this man was fighting, fighting with words. He was using words as a weapon, using them as one would use a club. Could words be weapons? Well, yes, for here they were. Then, maybe, perhaps, I could use them as a weapon? No. It frightened me. I read on and what amazed me was not what he said, but how on earth anybody had the courage to say it.

Occasionally I glanced up to reassure myself that I was alone in the room. Who were these men about whom Mencken was talking so passionately? Who was Anatole France? Joseph Conrad? Sinclair Lewis, Sherwood Anderson, Dostoevski, George Moore, Gustave Flaubert, Maupassant, Tolstoy, Frank Harris, Mark Twain, Thomas Hardy, Arnold Bennett, Stephen Crane, Zola, Norris, Gorky, Bergson, Ibsen, Balzac, Bernard Shaw, Dumas, Poe, Thomas Mann, O. Henry, Dreiser, H. G. Wells, Gogol, T. S. Eliot, Gide, Baudelaire, Edgar Lee Masters, Stendhal, Turgenev, Huneker, Nietzsche, and scores of others? Where these men real? Did they exist or had they existed? And how did one pronounce their names? 19

I ran across many words whose meanings I did not know, and I either looked them up in a dictionary or, before I had a chance to do that, encountered the word in a context that made its meaning clear. But what strange world was this? I concluded the book with the conviction that I had somehow overlooked something terribly important in life. I had once tried to write, had once reveled in feeling, had let my crude imagination roam, but the impulse to dream had been slowly beaten out of me by experience. Now it surged up again and I hungered for books, new ways of looking and seeing. It was not a matter of believing or disbelieving what I read, but of feeling something new, of being affected by something that made the look of the world different. 20

As dawn broke I ate my pork and beans, feeling dopey, sleepy. I went to work, but the mood of the book would not die; it lingered, coloring everything I saw, heard, did. I now felt that I knew what the white men were feeling. Merely because I had read a book that had spoken of how they lived and thought, I identified myself with that book. I felt vaguely guilty. Would I, filled with bookish notions, act in a manner that would make the whites dislike me? 21

I forged more notes and my trips to the library became frequent. Reading grew into a passion. My first serious novel was Sinclair Lewis's *Main Street*. It made me see my boss, Mr. Gerald, and identify him as an American type. I would smile when I saw him lugging his golf bags into the office. I had always felt a vast distance separating me from the boss, and now I felt closer to him, 22 though still distant. I felt now that I knew him, that I could feel the very limits of his narrow life. And this had happened because I had read a novel about a mythical man called George F. Babbitt.

The plots and stories in the novels did not interest me so much as the point of view revealed. I gave myself over to each novel without reserve, without trying to criticize it; it was enough for me to see and feel something different. And for me, everything was something different. Reading was like a drug, a dope. The novels created moods in which I lived for days. But I could not conquer my sense of guilt, my feeling that the white men around me knew that I was changing, that I had begun to regard them differently. 23

Whenever I brought a book to the job, I wrapped it in newspaper — a habit that was to persist for years in other cities and under other circumstances. But some of the white men pried into my packages when I was absent and they questioned me. 24

"Boy, what are you reading those books for?" 25
"Oh, I don't know, sir."
"That's deep stuff you're reading, boy."
"I'm just killing time, sir."
"You'll addle your brains if you don't watch out."

I read Dreiser's *Jennie Gerhardt* and *Sister Carrie* and they revived in me a vivid sense of my mother's suffering; I was overwhelmed. I grew silent, wondering about the life around me. It would have been impossible for me to have told anyone what I derived from these novels, for it was nothing less than a sense of life itself. All my life had shaped me for the realism, the naturalism of the modern novel, and I could not read enough of them. 26

Steeped in new moods and ideas, I bought a ream of paper and tried to write; but nothing would come, or what did come was flat beyond telling. I discovered that more than desire and feeling were necessary to write and I dropped the idea. Yet I still wondered how it was possible to know people sufficiently to write about them? Could I ever learn about life and people? To me, with my vast ignorance, my Jim Crow station in life, it seemed a task impossible of achievement. I now knew what being a Negro meant. I could endure the hunger. I had learned to live with hate. But to feel that there were feelings denied me, that the very breath of life itself was beyond my reach, that more than anything else hurt, wounded me. I had a new hunger. 27

In buoying me up, reading also cast me down, made me see what was possible, what I had missed. My tension returned, new, terrible, bitter, surging, almost too great to be contained. I no longer *felt* that the world about me was hostile, killing; I *knew* it. A million times I asked myself what I could do to save 28 myself, and there were no answers. I seemed forever condemned, ringed by walls.

I did not discuss my reading with Mr. Falk, who had lent me his library   29
card; it would have meant talking about myself and that would have been too
painful. I smiled each day, fighting desperately to maintain my old behavior, to
keep my disposition seemingly sunny. But some of the white men discerned
that I had begun to brood.

"Wake up there, boy!" Mr. Olin said one day.   30
"Sir!" I answered for the lack of a better word.
"You act like you've stolen something," he said.

I laughed in the way I knew he expected me to laugh, but I resolved to be   31
more conscious of myself, to watch my every act, to guard and hide the new
knowledge that was dawning within me.

If I went north, would it be possible for me to build a new life then? But   32
how could a man build a life upon vague, unformed yearnings? I wanted to
write and I did not even know the English language. I bought English grammars
and found them dull. I felt that I was getting a better sense of the language
from novels than from grammars. I read hard, discarding a writer as soon as I
felt that I had grasped his point of view. At night the printed page stood before
my eyes in sleep.

Mrs. Moss, my landlady, asked me one Sunday morning: 33

"Son, what is this you keep on reading?"   34
"Oh, nothing. Just novels."
"What you get out of 'em?"
"I'm just killing time," I said.
"I hope you know your own mind," she said in a tone which implied that she
doubted if I had a mind.

I knew of no Negroes who read the books I liked and I wondered if any   35
Negroes ever thought of them. I knew that there were Negro doctors, lawyers,
newspapermen, but I never saw any of them. When I read a Negro newspaper
I never caught the faintest echo of my preoccupation in its pages. I felt trapped
and occasionally, for a few days, I would stop reading. But a vague hunger
would come over me for books, books that opened up new avenues of feeling
and seeing, and again I would forge another note to the white librarian. Again I
would read and wonder as only the naïve and unlettered can read and wonder,
feeling that I carried a secret, criminal burden about with me each day.

That winter my mother and brother came and we set up housekeeping,   36
buying furniture on the installment plan, being cheated and yet knowing no

way to avoid it. I began to eat warm food and to my surprise found that regular meals enabled me to read faster. I may have lived through many illnesses and survived them, never suspecting that I was ill. My brother obtained a job and we began to save toward the trip north, plotting our time, setting tentative dates for departure. I told none of the white men on the job that I was planning to go north; I knew that the moment they felt I was thinking of the North they would change toward me. It would have made them feel that I did not like the life I was living, and because my life was completely conditioned by what they said or did, it would have been tantamount to challenging them.

I could calculate my chances for life in the South as a Negro fairly clearly now.   37

I could fight the southern whites by organizing with other Negroes, as my   38
grandfather had done. But I knew that I could never win that way; there were many whites and there were but few blacks. They were strong and we were weak. Outright black rebellion could never win. If I fought openly I would die and I did not want to die. News of lynchings were frequent.

I could submit and live the life of a genial slave, but that was impossible.   39
All of my life had shaped me to live by my own feelings and thoughts. I could make up to Bess and marry her and inherit the house. But that, too, would be the life of a slave; if I did that, I would crush to death something within me, and I would hate myself as much as I knew the whites already hated those who had submitted. Neither could I ever willingly present myself to be kicked, as Shorty had done. I would rather have died than do that.

I could drain off my restlessness by fighting with Shorty and Harrison. I   40
had seen many Negroes solve the problem of being black by transferring their hatred of themselves to others with a black skin and fighting them. I would have to be cold to do that, and I was not cold and I could never be.

I could, of course, forget what I had read, thrust the whites out of my   41
mind, forget them; and find release from anxiety and longing in sex and alcohol. But the memory of how my father had conducted himself made that course repugnant. If I did not want others to violate my life, how could I voluntarily violate it myself?

I had no hope whatever of being a professional man. Not only had I been   42
so conditioned that I did not desire it, but the fulfillment of such an ambition was beyond my capabilities. Well-to-do Negroes lived in a world that was almost as alien to me as the world inhabited by whites.

What, then, was there? I held my life in my mind, in my consciousness   43
each day, feeling at times that I would stumble and drop it, spill it forever. My reading had created a vast sense of distance between me and the world in which I lived and tried to make a living, and that sense of distance was increasing each day. My days and nights were one long, quiet, continuously

contained dream of terror, tension, and anxiety. I wondered how long I could bear it.

QUESTIONS ON CONTENT:

1. What does Wright mean when he writes that he at last awoke to what being a Negro meant? What is this new hunger he feels?
2. What effect does reading have on Richard Wright? How does it affect his feelings for others?
3. Why does he feel an especially strong affinity for H. L. Mencken?
4. Why does Wright abandon his grammar text? What important writing lessons does he learn from his reading? How does his experience with a grammar text compare with Martin Eden's experience?

QUESTIONS ON WRITING STRUCTURE AND STRATEGY:

1. How does Wright's narrative technique work to maintain the reader's interest?
2. What is the effect on the reader of reproducing dialogue instead of merely reporting it?
3. How does Wright infuse his writing with tension, and how does this affect the reader?

QUESTIONS FOR DISCUSSION AND WRITING:

1. Wright becomes aware of style when he reads Mencken. Though he does not tell us how he acquired his, style is evident in this selection. How does his style differ from Mencken's, and why do you think it would have been inappropriate for him to imitate Mencken's style?
2. Write a paper in which you compare the similarities between Wright's reading experience and those of other writers—Malcolm X, Eldridge Cleaver, Jack London (Martin Eden), Frederick Douglass.
3. From his reading of Mencken, Wright concludes that he is using words as weapons. In what way is this account of Wright's early life an illustration of words used as weapons? Write a paper in which you explain. Consider some of the other writers you have read, Tillie Olsen, for example.

REFLECTIONS OF A BLACK SON
Horace Porter

What was it like to be a black student from Georgia on the Amherst College campus during the height of student unrest in the late 1960s and early 1970s? Not only was there student protest against an unpopular war, there was also black student unrest and militancy over what was believed to be "cultural imperialism," the attempt to submerge black culture in a white sea. Horace Porter deals sensitively with these issues as he reflects on the conflicts he felt and on his frustration in trying to resolve them. In addition to relating his personal history, Porter has some very interesting things to say about reading, writing, and education. Notice the many allusions drawn from his reading and the mode of development he uses to tell his story. As you read, compare Porter's recollections to Richard Rodriguez's educational odyssey.

There comes a time when every young man leaves his father's house. I left my home in Columbus, Georgia, on the second of September in 1968. It was a day marked by three extraordinary events in my life: I boarded a plane for my first flight; I left the South for the first time; and that afternoon I walked across the campus of Amherst College.

Late in the day I met my roommate from Grosse Pointe, Michigan. After the usual introductions and small talk, Brian asked me about my religious views. I told him I was a Baptist, a Christian. He stated emphatically that he was an atheist. We assured each other we would not allow the difference to lead to conflict. That night, however, in a scene reminiscent of Queequeg and Ishmael at the Spouter Inn, I got down on my knees to say my prayers. Brian asked if something were wrong. I told him that I was saying my prayers. He nodded, amazed. That was the first and the last night I said my prayers on my knees at Amherst. I reasoned it was time to bring to an end that particular practice of my southern boyhood.

Yet I pondered the events of the day for several hours after my prayers. I thought of my parents. Like many southern blacks born during World War I, neither had made it through high school. Neither had, of course, gone north to college. And neither had heard of Amherst until I spoke about it. At boarding time that morning, they had assured me that they would pray for me, and they asked me to pray and trust in the Lord. As I lay awake, I wondered why my parents had found it necessary to pray. I had expected them to be as ecstatic as I was. I was not, after all, like many of my unfortunate friends, on the way to the battlefields of Vietnam. I was going to college.

It took me a few years and many wakeful nights to understand that my parents had few assurances of my safety and success. They had only a belief in my capacity for perseverance and an inviolable faith in the benevolence of God. As the years passed, I came to understand the reasons why my parents prayed for me. Having heard numerous accounts of handsome Johnnies who went away to college and were led astray — into the world of drugs, wild sex, political militance, or any of the confusions of that raucous decade — they prayed that I would continue to serve God and remain a loyal member of the family. For they also had heard tales of black Johnnies who eventually discovered reasons to stare at their own birth certificates with contempt.

My parents prayed that after the novels and the teacups, I would still be their loyal, humble, and God-fearing son. A remembrance of my parents' reactions surely stirred my emotions, my intuitions, something inscrutable within me. And I prayed silently and alone from time to time.   5

I needed my prayers. Amherst was like a foreign country those first few months. The college itself was undergoing significant transition. Compulsory attendance at chapel had been terminated the year before. The faculty had voted to change the old curriculum (in which certain core courses in mathematics, physics, and English were required) to a system marked by the glorious freedom of distribution requirements in the three major divisions. But Amherst of old still asserted itself. We had to declare ourselves "independent" to avoid fraternity rushing. We were expected to escort young ladies home to Smith and Mount Holyoke at the stroke of 12. And, of course, Marge and Isabelle came to make our beds each morning.   6

The students all appeared wealthy, articulate, and atheistic. Clad in faded bell-bottom jeans and wire-framed glasses, they discussed the war and the coming election with what seemed to me expertise. Everyone, or so it appeared, discussed books I had not read. No one discussed the books I had read. I had spent nights, dawns, and hot summer days reading the Bible, Shakespeare, Austen, Melville, and Twain. Richard Wright, James Baldwin, and Norman Mailer had aided me in effecting a truce with the barren and brutal reality of my last three years in Columbus. But their styles were not as influential as those of the nineteenth-century writers. Therefore, my vocabulary and diction manifested many vestiges of nineteenth-century rhetoric.   7

Moreover, with many words I had merely lexicon acquaintance. I had never heard them come alive in speech. That curious state of verbal affairs occasioned one of the memorable joys of Amherst: During those first weeks words I had known for years via the page emerged in my world of sound. I soon became comfortable enough to pull out a few of my own stops. I used my favorite words without feeling embarrassed and without baffling those with whom I spoke.   8

However, I still had not read Hesse, Kazantzakis, and Beckett. Everyone, it seemed, had already met Godot. I had read some Sartre, but God knows I   9 had not heard of Marcuse. Menaced by my sense of intellectual insecurity, I read books and examined journals and periodicals with a diligence I have not since been able to surpass. It was during that unforgettable season of intellectual passion that I read Ralph Ellison's *Invisible Man*, a novel that shook me with the force of an earthquake. Given the temper of the times, I readily identified with the nameless protagonist who proclaims: "I was my experiences and my experiences were me. . . . " I was driven to explore my own hidden name, my own complex fate.

I read W. E. B. DeBois, James Weldon Johnson, Carter G. Woodson, Jean Toomer, and numerous other Afro-American scholars and writers. Theirs was a valuable legacy for me. In times more trying than my own, they had worked and thought well. Some, like DuBois and Woodson, lived and wrote during the heyday of what came to be known as "scientific racism." The notion of the innate inferiority of the black race suffused the air they breathed. But by dint of their indefatigable wills and their discipline, they wrote novels and histories that spoke eloquently of the souls of black folk — long before my time, even before the time of my parents.

Ironically, those black writers and thinkers helped to bring about the first long, snowy winter of my discontent at Amherst. Only a few Amherst professors had even heard of them when I arrived. No one on the faculty was primarily committed to a study of the Afro-American experience. The one black member of the faculty was a mathematician. That greatly disturbed me. After those initial months of awe and a trip home at Christmas, I began to consider the social and political dimensions of my love for books, words, and ideas. What, I wondered, was in store for me if I decided to make my love my profession? What peculiar problems would I encounter as an Afro-American intellectual? I asked myself what was the real beast in the Afro-American intellectual jungle. My attempt to answer those questions led me to the realization that I owed my soul to the Bible, the Constitution, and the Declaration of Independence, to Shakespeare and Melville, to Freud and Marx, and to the English language in which I thought, spoke, and wrote.

This awareness proved very troubling at the time because of the obsession among black students with all that was unique to the Afro-American experience. Black pride was regarded as inextricably bound with a black consciousness, a black aesthetic, and black English. Intellectually, the assumption was, of course, highly problematic. But discussion was rarely dispassionate during those years. In fact, if one were black and did not use the black vernacular from time to time, one ran the risk of being labelled a "Negro." That was one of the most pejorative epithets a black student could use to describe another brother or sister, an elegant variation of the "oreo" of a decade later. On a deeper level, the question was whether Afro-Americans were

being forced to learn what—in many cases—amounted to an alien tongue. It
was frequently pointed out to me that many Afro-Americans speak a variant of
American English. I knew, of course, that my family's English was very
different from the English of Amherst, that each time I boarded a plane to
return home for a short spell, I had to weed out of my vocabulary much of the
verbal flora I had cultivated. I did not want to sound like a guest in a strange
house. I had to get down, as it were, into the black vernacular. I had to tune
my ears to a different subjunctive and accept, once again, the fact that
inflections really can be marvelous adverbs.

The two languages were indicative of two vastly different worlds. And the 13
trips, over the years, back to the world from which I came, made me bitter and
frustrated. I occasionally encountered high school friends back from Vietnam.
A few had been wounded and they held me spellbound with their stories of the
war. Other classmates had been bruised and disfigured on the streets of
America. One friend—peace to his adventuresome spirit—was murdered. And
I saw friends, relatives, and neighbors—some of the most responsible,
hardworking, and patriotic people I know—who were getting on, although
facing daily, to use Mailer's phrase, "the dirt and dark deliveries of the necessary."

I flew back to Amherst after those trips, back to a room of my own, back 14
to the quiet and comfort of the Robert Frost Library. I felt somewhat guilty
because there was no black community in which to work or play in the town
of Amherst. I began to take perhaps too seriously the charges of militant black
nationalists and other critics of the American society who argued that black
students at prestigious colleges and universities were being bought, that our
loyalties were being subtly besieged by the "system," that life in ivory towers
was a luxury we could not afford at such a late hour, that it was the
responsibility of my generation to destroy "Faulkner, Dick, Jane, and other
perpetuators of evil."

Those arguments, along with the fact that the faculty and administration 15
approached Afro-American and black studies with the same reserve and
circumspection they brought to all important matters, shook my confidence in
the scholarly process. To be sure, I had learned the value of reasoned
discourse. I knew how precious the goals of academic freedom and objectivity
were to the academy. But I also realized that courses concerning Afro-
Americans were no different from others; any course could become partisan or
ideological depending on the teacher and the students. I recognized too that
some scholarly and artistic work necessitates years of contemplation, but I
reasoned that a commitment to the black struggle was not necessarily
incompatible with such endeavor. I wanted the Afro-American presence
asserted at Amherst. I wanted the Afro-American voice heard immediately.

I became a victim of the rhetoric of the time. The charges of certain 16 glaring deficiencies in the Amherst curriculum were valid enough. But I started to associate too many of the ills of American society with what took place at Amherst. Since I assumed that we were some of the most intelligent and promising men of my generation, it seemed to me that Amherst was failing. It was not teaching its students, who would some day wield significant power, the duty of making a new America. The failure of white students and minority students to interact significantly was a salient example. In this matter of race, I frequently asked, why is there so much of the society and so little of the mind at work here at Amherst?

American society at large was as much a cause of my malaise as Amherst College. There were so many palpable evils to be eradicated. To speak out and rebel seemed, at the time, the only right thing to do. I became one of the more prominent members of the Amherst Afro-American Society. I petitioned and protested. I signed angry letters addressed to the Amherst administration and the world. I encouraged the rebellious imperatives of my newly politicized self: I went on strike, I sat in, I fasted, I wept, I prayed.

In many ways, my situation was hardly unique. Professors frequently boasted that they were teaching students to forget the parental world of unexamined obedience and programmed cant. We were urged by Dean of Students Robert Ward to "be your own man." And with the odd combination of insanity and perspicacity that marked the rhetoric of our time, we tried to do exactly that. We asked our teachers, our mentors, our distinguished visitors, how could we be our own men in a system that was racially and politically rigged? How could we be our own men when we were expected and could be called upon almost any day to throw away our lives foolishly defending a rice paddy in Vietnam? How could we be our own men when the courses we took were basically the same ones taken by the men who sat in our nation's highest councils of power?

Every year the student body faced a series of crises and rallying causes. One after another they came, in lockstep: Kent State, Jackson State, Mylai, Calley, Carswell, Angela Davis, George Jackson, Attica. And the war that went on and on led along with the other crises to numerous expressions of moral outrage. We had two moratoria my first year and a major "takeover" by black students and a general strike my second. We sat in at Westover Air Force Base during the spring of my last year. Moreover, the state of things, the times, forced a number of my classmates and other students away from the college. Some did not return. Others tripped on drugs and never really came back. I, too, was frustrated and tired. I longed for a nonpolitical space for myself.

I grew nostalgic at times. Columbus, Georgia, had been a world of black and white (though sometimes unpleasant) certainties. I missed the communal warmth and encouragement of relatives, friends, and neighbors. I missed

Sunday mornings in Columbus—New Providence Baptist Church and the hours of praying, singing, and shouting. Those Sunday mornings had shaped my sense of myself and the world. Yet I now had to admit grudgingly that Sunday morning had been robbed of its hallowed traditions. My singular compulsion had become the Sunday issue of the *New York Times*. I communed quietly with Russell Baker, and the whole galaxy of New York literary personages. Thus, my Sundays became a symbolic critique of my religious past. I now looked at the world with new inner eyes. Furthermore, I was forced to admit that my parents' Christian vision was limited, that it had been impaired by history, circumstances, and time.

But as Faulkner reminds us, our pasts are never really past. In spite of my 21 intellectual attempts to become something other, Christianity was in my blood. My father and grandfather are Baptist deacons. So when I communed with my own heart each Sunday morning at Amherst, I sometimes felt like a sinner—or worse, a backslider. Something deep within told me that it was neither right nor sound to turn my back on the traditions of my forebears, that I was not only being a prodigal son but also a foolish one. I was reminded, too, to use my grandfather's oft-quoted expression, that my arms were too short to box with God.

My teachers, fellow students, and occasional guest lecturers helped me 22 through those days of nostalgia and frustration. . . . One morning [Leo] Marx lectured on Mailer's *Why Are We in Vietnam?* It was the best lecture I ever heard as an undergraduate, a sermon of sorts. That lecture forced me to see that, in many ways, I was as American as DJ and Tex. Sometimes while listening to Marx lecture, I wondered whether his teachers, Perry Miller and F. O. Matthiessen, had been as inspiring.

There were other professors I shall never forget. Theodore P. Greene 23 taught me to avoid long quotations, insisting that what mattered were my own thoughts. When I was a sophomore, Tillie Olsen was our writer in residence. She read my stories with care. She encouraged me to keep a journal and to continue writing. Allen Guttmann, my advisor, became my friend and my guide to clear thinking. He suggested works by black writers of whom I had no knowledge. He taught me how to read novels critically. He was never too busy or too indifferent to read assorted essays that I stuck in his mailbox. He made no secret of the fact that he disagreed with my politics, but on many occasions he invited me home for dinner.

If a student grew bored with the Amherst faculty, many visitors and 24 lecturers—kooks and false prophets as well as eminent scholars and writers— served to dispel his ennui. I shall always remember the day during my freshman year when Ralph Ellison came to Amherst. I had read his novel a few months before and was eager to talk to him. I did not want to appear uninformed in the presence of the man whose novel had changed the way I viewed myself in relation to the world. Consequently, I asked him several questions. "Who is your favorite writer?" I inquired. He assured me that he admired many authors. However, I wanted to know his favorite. He finally answered, "Dostoevsky." I asked him why he had chosen to end the novel in the manner that he did; he responded at length, shrewdly forgetting the name of one of his characters. I promptly provided it and he continued. He was generous and kind. A few other students and I talked with him until dinner time. I had brought my paperback edition of *Invisible Man* along, but I lacked sufficient courage to ask for an autograph. John William Ward, detecting my shyness, called the writer back. Without hesitation Ellison inscribed that tattered paperback, now the most precious of all my volumes. After dinner he lectured to a crowd in Johnson Chapel, discussing race and American literature without notes for well over an hour. Calvin Coolidge stared, seeming to hear all, from a portrait above his shoulder.

That was one of many great days at Amherst. But I was unhappy much of the time too. For I had come as one of the last black delegates of the Civil Rights Era, an era brought symbolically and dramatically to a close by the assassination of Martin Luther King, Jr., a few months before. I had come, that is, with a definite sense of personal and historical purpose. Thus, I readily internalized and was willing to act upon Amherst's motto: *Terras irradient*. The behavior of my peers was at times disheartening. They will do nothing to change America, I often thought and said. Yet I remained because I saw that in its own groping way Amherst was about changing our collective mind and heart. I saw, too, something of the possible beauty and glory of life there. I learned the value of critical and dispassionate discussion. I came to treasure most forms of artistic expression. I experienced the pleasure of leisure time. Many sunny afternoons I leaned and loafed with my friends on the grass of Memorial Hill. Many snowy nights, I danced until dawn. Yet my love for Amherst was tortured by an inarticulate hate, my hate by an undeniable love.

My feelings were similarly contradictory on commencement day. The months of my senior year passed in a flash, and before I knew it I was marching along with my classmates to our seats facing the Robert Frost Library. Faculty members, deans, and various dignitaries stared down at us from the platform that had been constructed on the Library's patio. I had spent most of my 21 years frantically preparing for that day of graduation. Perhaps I was dazed by the bright magic of the occasion. I still do now know; but something happened. My mind's ear closed itself to the speeches, the names, the applause. And I watched my classmates, one after another, accept their diplomas.

Amherst College was sending forth another class of its sons to "illumine the land." And those purple-ribboned diplomas had great significance. They meant that one's sensibilities had been caressed by some of the finest minds in America. They meant that one had been taught some of the best that had been thought and said. They meant that one had experienced profound sweetness and light. But they did not mean that one had an understanding of those brutal truths taught by the university of adversity. They did not mean that one had intimate knowledge of the "fires of human cruelty" or that one had gained an acute awareness of what it means to be disadvantaged, both by law and custom. Perhaps Amherst could never teach that. Perhaps no liberal arts college could. I did not know. But the world of my father's house had taught me much about those particular facts of life. That knowledge distinguished me from most of my classmates. And my mind seized the moment to make it clear.

Then it was my time to stand. I stood and turned, catching my mother's eye. And as I walked toward the platform a poem by Langston Hughes I had memorized years before mysteriously came to mind. I heard a voice, a sweet southern voice, saying:

> Well, son, I'll tell you.
> Life for me ain't been no crystal stair.
> It's had tacks in it,
> And splinters. . . .

I walked across the platform. I accepted my diploma. I started walking back. But I still heard that voice:

> So boy, don't you turn back.
> Don't you set down on the steps
> 'Cause you find it's kinder hard.
> Don't you fall now—
> For I'se still goin', honey,
> I'se still climbin',
> And life for me ain't been no crystal stair.

QUESTIONS ON CONTENT:

1. How did Porter's reading change once he began his studies at Amherst? How did his reading affect his thinking, his behavior?
2. What does Porter mean when he says he became a "victim of the rhetoric of the time," and how did he overcome it?
3. What is the difference between what he learned at Amherst and what he learned in his father and mother's house?

QUESTIONS ON WRITING STRUCTURE AND STRATEGY:

1.   Although Porter uses a narrative form, what method of development does he use to flesh out his story? How does it affect the narrative focus?

2.   Porter's reading is reflected in the many allusions he makes. Isolate some of these and identify them. What do they add?

3.   The title of this selection is "Reflections of a Black Son." To whom might it be addressed? Why? How appropriate is it?

QUESTIONS FOR DISCUSSION AND WRITING:

1.   Porter is aware that his background sets him apart from his classmates at Amherst. Write a paper about what separates you from your classmates. It may lie in your family circumstances, your past education, your special abilities or achievements, your talents, or some unique experiences.

2.   This piece could very well be titled "The Education of Horace Porter" or "The Journey from One World to Another." Write a paper using one of these titles to tell your own story.

3.   "Leaving his father's house" can be understood in this essay both literally and symbolically. Porter is explicit about the literal meaning. Write a paper on the symbolic leave-taking. How is it revealed in this essay?

4.   Write a paper in which you compare Porter's homecoming with that of Richard Rodriguez in "Aria."

A FEMINIST'S JOURNEY
Jean Bethke Elshtain

*Jean Bethke Elshtain is a professor of political science at the University
of Massachusetts, Amherst, where she teaches feminist psychology and
political theory. The following selection is a talk delivered at the
Putney School, Putney, Vermont. As her title indicates, she discusses
one woman's journey through "the dilemma haunting the women's
movement," going on to explain how she solved it for herself. As a
mother of four, she found a place for herself as a professional that did
not alienate her from other human beings. Her concluding remarks to
dream your own dreams, though addressed to young women, are
equally applicable to young men, in fact, to anyone. Note how she
quickly states her purpose in her opening paragraph (one sentence),
defines the dilemma, and, combining narration with analysis,
concludes with an exhortation.*

*Ask yourself as you read how a woman raised in an urban environment
might react to her remarks.*

I have been asked to discuss what the women's movement has been and   1
is and to tie that in with some autobiographical fragments that might help you
to make sense of how the women's movement has affected, in my own case,
the life of a woman born just as this country was entering the Second World
War, a woman about to turn forty just as it seems we are being primed, by the
Reaganites and the military-industrial complex, for another.

That my life is framed by one war and what seems to be the military and   2
psychological build-up for another, despite Vietnam and the trauma of the '60s,
is important for it indicates that the contemporary women's movement, just
like its nineteenth century predecessor, has thus far, despite the efforts of
many noble women, been unable to significantly influence public policy and
the direction of political events away from war. Indeed, at this point we are
even told by some women that, in the name of feminism, they should be *free* to
enter combat duty just like any man because, as one senior woman in the
Pentagon, who calls herself a feminist, put it, "Women need a chance to prove
themselves. You can't become a member of the Joint Chiefs of Staff unless
you've earned your stripes in battle."

Is this what we've come to? Well, it is part of what we've come to and it   3
makes it all the more imperative to think through what feminism is, what it
stands for — or ought to stand for — if the new woman is not to be just a clone
of the old man. Does, or ought, feminism to represent some alternative to
politics as usual, and war, and restless, rootless ambition and striving after
material success, all the costly and damaging dimensions of a particular sort of
upwardly mobile American male ethos?

The truth is: the women's movement has never known, from its inception,   4
whether to join 'em or oppose 'em. Roughly, whether one wished, within the
frame of one feminist perspective, to enter the extant hierarchy of status,
power, and privilege, or whether, from a different feminist perspective, one
questioned hierarchical arrangements and promoted an alternative vision of
society, turned, first, on one's notions of the political community and second,
on one's theories of how men and women got to be the sorts of beings they are,
and were.

Some feminists held to a strict environmentalist thesis: we get to be the   5
way we are because the environment shapes and molds us into certain forms,
including particular ways of looking at the world depending upon whether we
are males or females. This means, by implication, that as women forsake the
world of family and domesticity, with its ideal imperatives of compassion,
nurturance, protection of the weak and the vulnerable and long-range affective
ties and responsibilities for the harder-edged, more driven world of business
and politics, they, too, can and will acquire the characteristics necessary for
success in that world. For many feminists this is unacceptable. They not only
want to retain the virtues and moral imperatives tied to mothering, to kin ties,
to emotional and intimate familial values, they want the public world to be
infused with these qualities and virtues as well.

This bind — this dilemma — has never been resolved. It haunts the   6
feminist movement and the women who identify with it. It helps to explain the
ambivalence many women feel about success on the world's terms. It is
simplistic to label women's reluctance to be whole-heartedly ambitious strivers
their "fear of success." That is a vacuous assumption based on a distorted
psychology. Instead something much more complicated is going on. Women
sense, deep in their bones, that the smaller world, the world of children and
neighbors and simple, necessary tasks has its own virtues and blessings, as well
as real pain in being immersed and tied to the realm within which maternal
thinking and action occur. To forsake that world entirely, to lose its life-
forgiving values when it is at its best, is to lose a great deal and to further
deprive the world of principles that counter the machine of megadeaths we
construct with such energy with each passing month and year.

I can speak of this ambivalence because I feel and have felt it. Deep down.   7
It isn't a superficial conflict I can readily eliminate. It isn't a conflict of
competing statuses, or roles, or all the other thin notions sociologists use a lot.
It isn't "cognitive dissonance" as some psychologist might claim. It is the
competing imperatives of two different ways of being a human being, of
making one's way in the world, or striving to be somebody, to have a clear
self- and social identity, to have, in a world increasingly stripped of it, honor.

My own journey as a feminist began even before I knew the term, before   8 there was such a thing as a women's movement. I grew up, in the rural Colorado West, where people were still judged, in those days at any rate, more by the quality of their character and by their capacities for hard work, duty, and perseverance than by their sex. As far back as I can remember I saw women running the whole show in the house, baking, making homemade catsup and sausage, sewing dresses for my sisters, my cousins, and me out of one-hundred-pound flour sacks. I saw women taking care of the chickens, working in the fields, shoveling silage, driving tractors, milking cows, and, in my grandmother's case, building fences and cupboards and even houses. Farm life was roughly egalitarian — on the family farm there was no clear-cut division of labor. Everyone worked. Everyone contributed. Nobody was idle, or was allowed to remain idle for long.

It came as some surprise to me, when I left this environment, that was 9 both sheltered yet a source of enormous strength of character, to learn that women were supposed to spend their time ironing doilies, playing bridge, or going off to the local beauty salon in order to keep themselves attractive for their husbands. Of course I had no desire to be (this is harsh but then the Lutheran pietism I grew up in is no easy religion) a parasite, a plaything, a decorative do-nothing. We were put on this earth to make a difference, to make a contribution, to leave the world a better place than what we had found it.

How, then, to make that contribution in a rapidly changing epoch that 10 would forever break up and dissolve that rural way of life of my grandmother and my mother and myself as a little girl? I was too restless, I cast my net too wide, to be content to make my contribution within a small compass. I had romantic dreams of adventure — of being a female war correspondent (there's one dimension of the feminist image, for it required a war to be realized) or a compassionate, nurturant leader, a mother to her people (there's another). Along the way I just assumed — I didn't think about choices here — that I would get married and have children. I did — I had three children and a master's degree by the time I was twenty-four. I figured you could do everything.

When I began my prolific adventures there *were* those who said it 11 "couldn't be done," but there was no feminist movement around to tell me the same thing — that it was impossible to be married, have babies, and go to school. I assumed you could do it and I did, although my family pretty much thought I was overdoing it and they tried to get me to slow down. This experience and my study of history have taught me that those within the contemporary feminist movement who specialize in wallowing in self-pity and portraying women as nothing but helpless victims, do women an enormous disservice.

To the extent that you see yourself as nothing but a victim, you will 12 internalize that victimization, come to define yourself under its terms and act just like a victim — you will become the living evidence of your own pathetic view of yourself. It is one thing to point out instances of outrageous brutalization and victimization of women. It is quite something else again to label women nothing but victims. It is false. It is wrong. It is demeaning. It denies women self-respect.

My fourth child was born just nine months after I started work on my Ph.D. in political theory at Brandeis University. That was back in 1966. Now certain academic, or intellectual, problems began. Life had long been hectic, even frenzied. But now it became troubled. I had gone through a lot, personally and politically. But I was now, as a graduate student in a political science department, brought up against those binds (join 'em or fight 'em) I talked about earlier. I was a woman in an epoch when there was, once again, an official feminist movement, a married woman with children at that, hence a "deviant" within the hallowed halls of academe. Let me explain the nature and meaning of this conflict.

Graduate school isn't about learning things — facts and theories and one's specific discipline. It also involves learning *how to think in particular ways* — or at least graduate schools attempt to force their students within a certain mainstream mold. To buck the tide is difficult. It helps, of course, to have a sympathetic professor or two who may be outside the mainstream themselves. I found one who would tolerate what were seen as my eccentricities — in my own case a concern with how political theorists from the Great Tradition, Plato to the present, understood the relationship between women and politics and the categories they used to explore that issue. That became for me a focus on the public and the private — on the distinctions made between public or political notions, activities, relations, purposes and those that were deemed private, for a variety of reasons.

Much hinges on this debate, of course, including a particular theorist's views on whether women were or were not, could or could not be political beings. What also turns on this issue is one's ideal of politics: is it, finally, to do with *Who gets what when where how?* With power, force, violence, and compulsion? Or does politics have something to do with certain ideals of the common good and of public ends and purposes, of the capacity of human beings to transcend narrow self-interest and think and work for the good of others? That was my passion, my concern, and it was, of course, directly related to my life, to my own conflicts over public and private.

But I learned something interesting in graduate school, or at least my teachers attempted to teach me this, and that was that neither my life nor anybody else's had much of anything to do with political science as a particular, abstract, academically organized and structured inquiry. I recall vividly a paper

I wrote for a Political Sociology course. It was a paper about the '60s, the decade we were then in. We were supposed to do something on the student rebellion, civil rights, and so on, and I did. I wrote about the impact of the life and death of John F. Kennedy on my generation — the way he energized us in political ways. I wrote about the vital coming together of politics and culture, the way the music of the '60s, especially Bob Dylan and the Beatles, was not so much 'in the background' as itself constitutive of the activities we were engaged in. The music was *in* the politics; politics was *in* the music. I wrote about hippies and the repudiation of war and violence, particularly as a definition of masculine identity. And my professor said to me, "Well, this is another interesting Jean Elshtain paper. But of course it has nothing to do with the scientific study of politics."

I thought: well to hell with the study of politics then. If politics doesn't   17
have to do with people's lives, what does it have to do with? But in reality I was devastated. I thought: I can't do this. I've got the wrong kind of mind. I don't think the way I'm supposed to think. Somehow I survived and managed to keep on keeping on and at least part of what prevented me from becoming a political science clone was the messy reality of my private life. Of husband and kids and friends and pets and Beatle music and Bob Dylan and the competing loyalties and standards and commitments and the features of human reality they involve.

I have long hated all those book dedications academics write to their   18
wives and children for being quiet and out of sight and patient while they hid away in splendid isolation doing their dry tomes. Well, in the dedication to my book which the Princeton University Press will bring out later this year I thank my children for being always within earshot and eyeshot because that helped me to stay in touch with what counts: with real, concrete, particular human beings. Don't let anyone tell you feminism or a feminist commitment requires certain rigid either/or choices. Either marriage or career/Either children or none. Don't let anyone make you half a human being by fiat, for if you let others make those choices for you, that is precisely what you will become.

What I am trying to convey to you is that, finally, every one of us has the   19
choice to make our own destinies. This doesn't make us individualists, or at least it need not; rather it makes us responsible, choosing, willing human beings rather than patsies, pawns, and blobs. Each of us must struggle to attain and maintain an identity. You cannot allow feminism to create some ready-made identity for you, or you should not, any more than women who rebelled against it allowed the old femininity to create their identities out of whole cloth for them. It is always difficult for social rebels, people who have in some way swum against the tide (and I include myself here as a woman in a profession

with few women who is also part of a minority of that profession, a political theorist, and, further, a minority of that minority, a critical theorist) to accept the fact that others may not wish to follow them in the terms they set up for their own rebellion. It's as if we wish to say, "You don't have to go through all that. I did it for you. I fought that battle, you don't have to." 20

Nobody can do it for you. And if they claim they can—that they only wish to spare you—please be patient and understanding that, most of the time, they mean well. Then go on to live your own life, understanding that it isn't just the visions of life promoted by the "status quo" you need to question but those promoted by the social rebels and revolutionaries as well. In whose behalf is their dream being dreamt? If feminism means anything, it means we can and must dream our own dreams and that these dreams, in the final analysis, must unite us, in peace and fellowship, with other human beings rather than divide us, one from another.

QUESTIONS ON CONTENT:

1. What is the dilemma that "haunts" the women's movement? What does "bind" or "dilemma" in paragraph six refer to?
2. Beginning in paragraph eight, the author recounts her growing-up experience. What truths does she garner from these experiences? Contrast paragraph eight with paragraph nine.
3. What is her view of politics, and how does it contrast with the "scientific" view?
4. In attacking the either/or dilemma, what advice does she offer, especially to young women?

QUESTIONS ON WRITING STRUCTURE AND STRATEGY:

1. What is the purpose of the writer's first sentence? Does she follow through in all particulars?
2. How does the image of the "journey" serve to promote coherence? Do you find other elements contributing to coherence?
3. Elshtain has few short sentences in her paper. What does this suggest about the writer's attitude toward her subject? (Note audience for whom her speech is intended.)

QUESTIONS FOR DISCUSSION AND WRITING:

1. Do you agree with the editors that Elshtain's conclusions about identity and dreams are valid for men as well as women? Why or why not?
2. In President Kennedy's speech (Unit III), he speaks of Frost as one who goes

"against the grain." Write a paper in which you describe Elshtain as one of those persons who goes "against the grain."

3. In the last sentence of paragraph nine, the author summarizes her concept of purpose in life. In a short paper evaluate what she says. How do her remarks relate to your own ideas about life's purpose?

4. As a future wife or husband, what do you perceive are the implications of Elshtain's remarks for your choice of a mate? Or: If already married, how can you relate her remarks to your choice of a mate?

ARIA

Richard Rodriguez

Richard Rodriguez's autobiography, Hunger of Memory *(1982), from which the following excerpt is taken, was widely hailed by critics for its sensitive account of one Mexican-American family's painful assimilation. It was also hailed for showing "more insight and understanding into the familiar problems of contemporary American education than a roomful of studies and reports by scientists." Rodriguez is a graduate of Stanford and Columbia Universities and did graduate work in London and at the University of California. He is a writer and lecturer whose work has appeared in a number of American publications.*

Though born in America, Rodriguez in this account of his early childhood tells us something of what it must have been like for millions of immigrants who came to America. In giving up what he perceived as a "private intimacy," Spanish spoken at home, he gained his "public identity"; he became assimilated. And he discovered in the process that intimacy is not limited by language. Rodriguez's story is a tribute to the socializing and nationalizing function of education. Like Horace Porter ("Reflections of a Black Son"), he experienced the pull of the language of home, the language of his people. And like Porter, he overcame.

Though "Aria" is written as a first-person narrative, note how Rodriguez weaves a variety of modes into a poignant story of what it meant growing up Mexican-American in the world of los gringos. Because this essay is excerpted from a longer account, its organization may appear loose. Rodriguez starts with an anecdote about his past and then turns to the contemporary issue of bilingualism. The balance of the essay shifts back and forth in time as he brings his experience to bear on the supposed benefits of bilingualism in the schools.

1

I remember to start with that day in Sacramento — a California now nearly thirty years past — when I first entered a classroom, able to understand some fifty stray English words.

The third of four children, I had been preceded to a neighborhood Roman Catholic school by an older brother and sister. But neither of them had revealed very much about their classroom experiences. Each afternoon they returned, as they left in the morning, always together, speaking in Spanish as

1

2

they climbed the five steps of the porch. And their mysterious books, wrapped in shopping-bag paper, remained on the table next to the door, closed firmly behind them.

An accident of geography sent me to a school where all my classmates   3
were white, many the children of doctors and lawyers and business executives. All my classmates certainly must have been uneasy on that first day of school —as most children are uneasy—to find themselves apart from their families in the first institution of their lives. But I was astonished.

The nun said, in a friendly but oddly impersonal voice, 'Boys and girls,   4
this is Richard Rodriguez.' (I heard her sound out: *Rich-heard Road-ree-guess*.) It was the first time I had heard anyone name me in English. 'Richard,' the nun repeated more slowly, writing my name down in her black leather book. Quickly I turned to see my mother's face dissolve in a watery blur behind the pebbled glass door.

Many years later there is something called bilingual education—a scheme proposed in the late 1960s by Hispanic-American social activists, later endorsed by a congressional vote. It is a program that seeks to permit non-English-speaking children, many from lower-class homes, to use their family language as the language of school. (Such is the goal its supporters announce.) I hear them and am forced to say no: It is not possible for a child—any child—ever to use his family's language in school. Not to understand this is to misunderstand the public uses of schooling and to trivialize the nature of intimate life—a family's 'language.'

Memory teaches me what I know of these matters; the boy reminds the   5
adult. I was a bilingual child, a certain kind—socially disadvantaged—the son of working-class parents, both Mexican immigrants.

In the early years of my boyhood, my parents coped very well in America.   6
My father had steady work. My mother managed at home. They were nobody's victims. Optimism and ambition led them to a house (our home) many blocks from the Mexican south side of town. We lived among *gringos* and only a block from the biggest, whitest houses. It never occurred to my parents that they couldn't live wherever they chose. Nor was the Sacramento of the fifties bent on teaching them a contrary lesson. . . .

In public, my father and mother spoke a hesitant, accented, not always   7
grammatical English. And they would have to strain—their bodies tense—to catch the sense of what was rapidly said by *los gringos*. At home they spoke Spanish. The language of their Mexican past sounded in counterpoint to the English of public society. The words would come quickly, with ease. Conveyed through those sounds was the pleasing, soothing, consoling reminder of being at home.

During those years when I was first conscious of hearing, my mother and father addressed me only in Spanish; in Spanish I learned to reply. By contrast, English (*inglés*), rarely heard in the house, was the language I came to associate with *gringos*. I learned my first words of English overhearing my parents speak to strangers. At five years of age, I knew just enough English for my mother to trust me on errands to stores one block away. No more.   8

I was a listening child, careful to hear the very different sounds of Spanish and English. Wide-eyed with hearing, I'd listen to sounds more than words. First, there were English (*gringo*) sounds. So many words were still unknown that when the butcher or the lady at the drugstore said something to me, exotic polysyllabic sounds would bloom in the midst of their sentences. Often, the speech of people in public seemed to me very loud, booming with confidence. The man behind the counter would literally ask, 'What can I do for you?' But by being so firm and so clear, the sound of his voice said that he was a *gringo*; he belonged in public society. . . .   9

For me there were none of the gradations between public and private society so normal to a maturing child. Outside the house was public society; inside the house was private. Just opening or closing the screen door behind me was an important experience. I'd rarely leave home all alone or without reluctance. Walking down the sidewalk, under the canopy of tall trees, I'd warily notice the — suddenly — silent neighborhood kids who stood warily watching me. Nervously, I'd arrive at the grocery store to hear there the sounds of the *gringo* — foreign to me — reminding me that in this world so big, I was a foreigner. But then I'd return. Walking back toward our house, climbing the steps from the sidewalk, when the front door was open in summer, I'd hear voices beyond the screen door talking in Spanish. For a second or two, I'd stay, linger there, listening. Smiling, I'd hear my mother call out, saying in Spanish (words): 'Is that you, Richard?' All the while her sounds would assure me: *You are home now; come closer; inside. With us.*   10

'*Sí*,' I'd reply. . . .   11

Plainly, it is not healthy to hear such sounds so often. It is not healthy to distinguish public words from private sounds so easily. I remained cloistered by sounds, timid and shy in public, too dependent on voices at home. And yet it needs to be emphasized: I was an extremely happy child at home. . . .   12

2

Supporters of bilingual education today imply that students like me miss a great deal by not being taught in their family's language. What they seem not   13 to recognize is that, as a socially disadvantaged child, I considered Spanish to be a private language. What I needed to learn in school was that I had the right—and the obligation—to speak the public language of *los gringos*. The odd truth is that my first-grade classmates could have become bilingual, in the conventional sense of that word, more easily than I. Had they been taught (as upper-middle-class children are often taught early) a second language like Spanish or French, they could have regarded it simply as that: another public language. In my case such bilingualism could not have been so quickly achieved. What I did not believe was that I could speak a single public language.

Without question, it would have pleased me to hear my teachers address me in Spanish when I entered the classroom. I would have felt much less afraid. I would have trusted them and responded with ease. But I would have delayed—for how long postponed?—having to learn the language of public society. I would have evaded—and for how long could I have afforded to delay?—learning the great lesson of school, that I had a public identity.   14

Fortunately, my teachers were unsentimental about their responsibility. What they understood was that I needed to speak a public language. So their voices would search me out, asking me questions. Each time I'd hear them, I'd look up in surprise to see a nun's face frowning at me. I'd mumble, not really meaning to answer. The nun would persist, 'Richard, stand up. Don't look at the floor. Speak up. Speak to the entire class, not just to me!' But I couldn't believe that the English language was mine to use. (In part, I did not want to believe it.) I continued to mumble. I resisted the teacher's demands. (Did I somehow suspect that once I learned public language my pleasing family life would be changed?) Silent, waiting for the bell to sound, I remained dazed, diffident, afraid.   15

Because I wrongly imagined that English was intrinsically a public language and Spanish an intrinsically private one, I easily noted the difference between classroom language and the language of home. At school, words were directed to a general audience of listeners. ('Boys and girls.') Words were meaningfully ordered. And the point was not self-expression alone but to make oneself understood by many others. The teacher quizzed: 'Boys and girls, why do we use that word in this sentence? Could we think of a better word to use there? Would the sentence change its meaning if the words were differently arranged? And wasn't there a better way of saying much the same thing?' (I couldn't say. I wouldn't try to say.)   16

Three months. Five. Half a year passed. Unsmiling, ever watchful, my teachers noted my silence. They began to connect my behavior with the difficult progress my older sister and brother were making. Until one Saturday morning three nuns arrived at the house to talk to our parents. Stiffly, they sat on the blue living room sofa. From the doorway of another room, spying the visitors, I noted the incongruity—the clash of two worlds, the faces and voices   17

161

of school intruding upon the familiar setting of home. I overheard one voice
gently wondering, 'Do your children speak only Spanish at home, Mrs.
Rodriguez?' While another voice added, 'That Richard especially seems so
timid and shy.'

That Rich-heard!   18

With great tact the visitors continued, 'Is it possible for you and your   19
husband to encourage your children to practice their English when they are
home?' Of course, my parents complied. What would they not do for their
children's well-being? And how could they have questioned the Church's
authority which those women represented? In an instant, they agreed to give
up the language (the sounds) that had revealed and accentuated our family's
closeness. The moment after the visitors left, the change was observed. '*Ahora*,
speak to us *en inglés*,' my father and mother united to tell us.

At first, it seemed a kind of game. After dinner each night, the family   20
gathered to practice 'our' English. (It was still then *inglés*, a language foreign to
us, so we felt drawn as strangers to it.) Laughing, we would try to define words
we could not pronounce. We played with strange English sounds, often
overanglicizing our pronunciations. And we filled the smiling gaps of our
sentences with familiar Spanish sounds. But that was cheating, somebody
shouted. Everyone laughed. In school, meanwhile, like my brother and sister, I
was required to attend a daily tutoring session. I needed a full year of special
attention. I also needed my teachers to keep my attention from straying in
class by calling out, *Rich-heard* — their English voices slowly prying loose my
ties to my other name, its three notes, *Ri-car-do*. Most of all I needed to hear
my mother and father speak to me in a moment of seriousness in broken —
suddenly heartbreaking — English. The scene was inevitable: One Saturday
morning I entered the kitchen where my parents were talking in Spanish. I did
not realize that they were talking in Spanish however until, at the moment
they saw me, I heard their voices change to speak English. Those *gringo*
sounds they uttered startled me. Pushed me away. In that moment of trivial
misunderstanding and profound insight, I felt my throat twisted by unsounded
grief. I turned quickly and left the room. But I had no place to escape to with
Spanish. (The spell was broken.) My brother and sisters were speaking English
in another part of the house.

Again and again in the days following, increasingly angry, I was obliged to   21
hear my mother and father: 'Speak to us *en inglés*.' (*Speak.*) Only then did I
determine to learn classroom English. Weeks after, it happened: One day in
school I raised my hand to volunteer an answer. I spoke out in a loud voice. And
I did not think it remarkable when the entire class understood. That day, I
moved very far from the disadvantaged child I had been only days earlier. The
belief, the calming assurance that I belonged in public, had at last taken
hold. . . .

At last, seven years old, I came to believe what had been technically true   22
since my birth: I was an American citizen.

But the special feeling of closeness at home was diminished by then. Gone   23
was the desperate, urgent, intense feeling of being at home; rare was the
experience of feeling myself individualized by family intimates. We remained a
loving family, but one greatly changed. No longer so close; no longer bound
tight by the pleasing and troubling knowledge of our public separateness.
Neither my older brother nor sister rushed home after school anymore. Nor did
I. When I arrived home there would often be neighborhood kids in the house.
Or the house would be empty of sounds.

Following the dramatic Americanization of their children, even my parents   24
grew more publicly confident. Especially my mother. She learned the names of
all the people on our block. And she decided we needed to have a telephone
installed in the house. My father continued to use the word *gringo*. But it was
no longer charged with the old bitterness or distrust. (Stripped of any emotional
content, the word simply became a name for those Americans not of Hispanic
descent.) Hearing him, sometimes, I wasn't sure if he was pronouncing the
Spanish word *gringo* or saying gringo in English. . . .

Today I hear bilingual educators say that children lose a degree of   25
'individuality' by becoming assimilated into public society. (Bilingual schooling
was popularized in the seventies, that decade when middle-class ethnics began
to resist the process of assimilation — the American melting pot.) But the
bilingualists simplistically scorn the value and necessity of assimilation. They
do not seem to realize that there are *two* ways a person is individualized. So
they do not realize that while one suffers a diminished sense of *private*
individuality by becoming assimilated into public society, such assimilation
makes possible the achievement of *public* individuality.

The bilingualists insist that a student should be reminded of his difference   26
from others in mass society, his heritage. But they equate mere separateness
with individuality. The fact is that only in private — with intimates — is
separateness from the crowd a prerequisite for individuality. (An intimate
draws me apart, tells me that I am unique, unlike all others.) In public, by
contrast, full individuality is achieved, paradoxically, by those who are able to
consider themselves members of the crowd. Thus it happened for me: Only
when I was able to think of myself as an American, no longer an alien in *gringo*
society, could I seek the rights and opportunities necessary for full public
individuality. The social and political advantages I enjoy as a man result from
the day that I came to believe that my name, indeed, is *Rich-heard Road-ree-
guess*. It is true that my public society today is often impersonal. (My public
society is usually mass society.) Yet despite the anonymity of the crowd and
despite the fact that the individuality I achieve in public is often tenuous —
because it depends on my being one in a crowd — I celebrate the day I acquired

my new name. Those middle-class ethnics who scorn assimilation seem to me filled with decadent self-pity, obsessed by the burden of public life. Dangerously, they romanticize public separateness and they trivialize the dilemma of the socially disadvantaged.

My awkward childhood does not prove the necessity of bilingual education. My story discloses instead an essential myth of childhood—inevitable pain. If I rehearse here the changes in my private life after my Americanization, it is finally to emphasize the public gain. The loss implies the gain: The house I returned to each afternoon was quiet. Intimate sounds no longer rushed to the door to greet me. There were other noises inside. The telephone rang. Neighborhood kids ran past the door of the bedroom where I was reading my schoolbooks—covered with shopping-bag paper. Once I learned public language, it would never again be easy for me to hear intimate family voices. More and more of my day was spent hearing words. But that may only be a way of saying that the day I raised my hand in class and spoke loudly to an entire roomful of faces, my childhood started to end. . . .

This insight unfolded in time. Making more and more friends outside my house, I began to distinguish intimate voices speaking through *English*. I'd listen at times to a close friend's confidential tone or secretive whisper. Even more remarkable were those instances when, for no special reason apparently, I'd become conscious of the fact that my companion was speaking only to me. I'd marvel just hearing his voice. It was a stunning event: to be able to break through his words, to be able to hear this voice of the other, to realize that it was directed only to me. After such moments of intimacy outside the house, I began to trust hearing intimacy conveyed through my family's English. Voices at home at last punctured sad confusion. I'd hear myself addressed as an intimate at home once again. Such moments were never as raucous with sound as past times had been when we had had 'private' Spanish to use. (Our English-sounding house was never to be as noisy as our Spanish-speaking house had been.) Intimate moments were usually soft moments of sound. My mother was in the dining room while I did my homework nearby. And she looked over at me. Smiled. Said something—her words said nothing very important. But her voice sounded to tell me (*We are together*) I was her son.

(*Richard!*)

Intimacy thus continued at home; intimacy was not stilled by English. It is true that I would never forget the great change of my life, the diminished occasions of intimacy. But there would also be times when I sensed the deepest truth about language and intimacy: *Intimacy is not created by a particular language; it is created by intimates.* The great change in my life was not linguistic but social. If, after becoming a successful student, I no longer heard intimate voices as often as I had earlier, it was not because I spoke English rather than

27

28

29

30

Spanish. It was because I used public language for most of the day. I moved easily at last, a citizen in a crowded city of words. . . .

My city seems silent until some ghetto black teenagers board the bus I am   31
on. Because I do not take their presence for granted, I listen to the sounds of their voices. Of all the accented versions of English I hear in a day, I hear theirs most intently. They are *the* sounds of the outsider. They annoy me for being loud—so self-sufficient and unconcerned by my presence. Yet for the same reason they seem to me glamorous. (A romantic gesture against public acceptance.) Listening to their shouted laughter, I realize my own quiet. Their voices enclose my isolation. I feel envious, envious of their brazen intimacy.

I warn myself away from such envy, however. I remember the black   32
political activists who have argued in favor of using black English in schools. (Their argument varies only slightly from that made by foreign-language bilingualists.) I have heard 'radical' linguists make the point that black English is a complex and intricate version of English. And I do not doubt it. But neither do I think that black English should be a language of public instruction. What makes black English inappropriate in classrooms is not something *in* the language. It is rather what lower-class speakers make of it. Just as Spanish would have been a dangerous language for me to have used at the start of my education, so black English would be a dangerous language to use in the schooling of teenagers for whom it reenforces feelings of public separateness.

This seems to me an obvious point. But one that needs to be made. In   33
recent years there have been attempts to make the language of the alien public language. 'Bilingual education, two ways to understand . . . ,' television and radio commercials glibly announce. Proponents of bilingual education are careful to say that they want students to acquire good schooling. Their argument goes something like this: Children permitted to use their family language in school will not be so alienated and will be better able to match the progress of English-speaking children in the crucial first months of instruction. (Increasingly confident of their abilities, such children will be more inclined to apply themselves to their studies in the future.) But then the bilingualists claim another, very different goal. They say that children who use their family language in school will retain a sense of their individuality—their ethnic heritage and cultural ties. Supporters of bilingual education thus want it both ways. They propose bilingual schooling as a way of helping students acquire the skills of the classroom crucial for public success. But they likewise insist that bilingual instruction will give students a sense of their identity apart from the public.

Behind this screen there gleams an astonishing promise: One can become   34
a public person while still remaining a private person. At the very same time one can be both! There need be no tension between the self in the crowd and

the self apart from the crowd! Who would not want to believe such an idea? Who can be surprised that the scheme has won the support of many middle-class Americans? If the barrio or ghetto child can retain his separateness even while being publicly educated, then it is almost possible to believe that there is no private cost to be paid for public success. Such is the consolation offered by any of the current bilingual schemes. Consider, for example, the bilingual voters' ballot. In some American cities one can cast a ballot printed in several languages. Such a document implies that a person can exercise that most public of rights — the right to vote — while still keeping apart, unassimilated from public life.

It is not enough to say that these schemes are foolish and certainly doomed. Middle-class supporters of public bilingualism toy with the confusion of those Americans who cannot speak standard English as well as they can. Bilingual enthusiasts, moreover, sin against intimacy. An Hispanic-American writer tells me, 'I will never give up my family language; I would as soon give up my soul.' Thus he holds to his chest a skein of words, as though it were the source of his family ties. He credits to language what he should credit to family members. A convenient mistake. For as long as he holds on to words, he can ignore how much else has changed in his life.

It has happened before. In earlier decades, persons newly successful and ambitious for social mobility similarly seized upon certain 'family words.' Working-class men attempting political power took to calling one another 'brother.' By so doing they escaped oppressive public isolation and were able to unite with many others like themselves. But they paid a price for this union. It was a public union they forged. The word they coined to address one another could never be the sound (*brother*) exchanged by two in intimate greeting. In the union hall the word 'brother' became a vague metaphor; with repetition a weak echo of the intimate sound. Context forced the change. Context could not be overruled. Context will always guard the realm of the intimate from public misuse.

Today nonwhite Americans call 'brother' to strangers. And white feminists refer to their mass union of 'sisters.' And white middle-class teenagers continue to prove the importance of context as they try to ignore it. They seize upon the idioms of the black ghetto. But their attempt to appropriate such expressions invariably changes the words. As it becomes a public expression, the ghetto idiom loses its sound — its message of public separateness and strident intimacy. It becomes with public repetition a series of words, increasingly lifeless.

The mystery remains: intimate utterance. The communication of intimacy passes through the word to enliven its sound. But it cannot be held by the word. Cannot be clutched or ever quoted. It is too fluid. It depends not on word but on person. . . .

166

QUESTIONS ON CONTENT:

1. What is Rodriguez's thesis?
2. What does he mean when he says, "I remained cloistered by sounds"?
3. Why does Rodriguez attach such great importance to the differences between "public" and "private" language?
4. How did the nuns precipitate the family's Americanization (for example, what was the effect on the parents' public life; how did their relations with their children change)?
5. What does Rodriguez see as the fallacies of the bilingualists' arguments? How is this related to "Black English"?

QUESTIONS ON WRITING STRUCTURE AND STRATEGY:

1. How does Rodriguez's organization—fluctuations between then and now, flashbacks—contribute to clarity and meaning or lack of it?
2. How would you characterize the tone of this essay? Why does he adopt this tone?
3. What is the significance of the title?

QUESTIONS FOR DISCUSSION AND WRITING:

1. In this selection Rodriguez poignantly describes his growing maturity, his gradual weaning away from the bosom of his family. Can you find in your own life events, decisions, experiences that marked your "growing up"? Using Rodriguez's style, write a paper or a journal entry.
2. Check the *Readers' Guide, Humanities Index, Social Science Index, Education Index* for articles favoring bilingualism. Study what the writers have to say. Then in a paper assess the validity of Rodriguez's argument against bilingualism.
3. When you return home from school for the holidays, or when you return to your job or to school after a holiday break, do you find that you are speaking a "language" that differs from your friends, relatives, or coworkers? In a short paper describe the situation and explain your answer.
4. Aside from linguistic groups, what other groups communicate in an "intimate" language? Write a short essay or journal entry.

RAY KROC: ARTIST
OF THE HAMBURGER

George Will

*In this selection George Will, a popular American journalist, has
written about a fabulously successful American — Ray Kroc, the
founder of McDonald's hamburger chain. In some respects this is an
essay, while in other respects it could be considered a book review of
Kroc's autobiography,* Grinding It Out. *Will seeks to impress his
readers with Kroc's genius (or luck? see last sentence) in catapulting
the lowly hamburger into a multi-million dollar industry.*

*Read the selection first as an astounding success story, and then go
back through to study how Will achieves his overall impact. Employing
narration, comparison and contrast, cause and effect, and analysis,
Will explains Kroc's success by looking to the changed American scene
and the success stories of immortals of American business enterprise.
Note Will's skillful use of the "Journalist's Five W's and How" (see
Glossary) (a good technique for any writer). Observe his introductory
paragraph in which he appeals to his reader through the use of the
familiar, the arresting, the coincidental. Look for Will's lavish use of
natural, comfortable, unstrained similes and his frequent use of
statistics and allusions to famous American entrepreneurs.*

Ray Kroc is a small, energetic 75-year-old, as unpretentious as hamburger, 1
as salty as French-fries, as American as frozen apple pie. He is worth upwards
of half a billion dollars, which is not bad for a man who started his business
when he was 52, who paid his secretary stock in lieu of salary (stock now
worth many millions) and whose most expensive product costs less than a
dollar. Born in Chicago, he joined the Army when he was 16 and trained with a
Chicagoan named Disney. So Company A contained two prodigies of mass
marketing, one who would create the Big Mac and one who would create
Mickey Mouse.

Kroc was a cheerful Willy Loman, a salesman with a heavy sample case 2
and boundless enthusiasm for his products, especially the Multimixer, a
machine for mixing five milkshakes simultaneously. Selling had taken him into
a zillion restaurant kitchens by the time, in 1954, he heard that two brothers
were using *eight* Multimixers at their quick-service restaurant in San
Bernardino, California. He went west to investigate and, like Keats's Cortez
staring at the Pacific, looked on with a wild surmise. He got the right to
franchise what he saw, including the brothers' name and the golden arches. In
1955, he opened his first McDonald's in Des Plaines, Illinois, and began
grinding it out.

Today, McDonald's ranks first among retailing companies in terms of net   3
income as a percentage of sales. When McDonald's went public in 1965, one
hundred shares cost $2,250. On December 31, 1975, that investment, adjusted
for splits and dividends, was worth $107,176. McDonald's U.S. stores average
gross sales of $857,000 a year. Some gross more than $2 million. This year
McDonald's will probably open its five thousandth store. It has sold twenty-five
billion hamburgers, and is selling a billion every three months. Twenty-five
billion hamburgers would make twenty piles the size of the world's tallest
building, Chicago's Sears Tower, a monument to another retailing genius. The
flour for twenty-five billion buns would make five feet of powder on the ski
slopes of Aspen and Vail. McDonald's has sold enough shakes to fill every gas
tank in America.

The earth must slope before a river can flow, and the public must be   4
predisposed before a success on the scale of McDonald's can happen. The
Second World War got many American palates accustomed to standardized
fare, from C rations and from factory canteens. Europeans linger over meals;
Americans regard food as fuel to be taken on the way steam locomotives took
on water, scooping it at full speed from troughs between the rails. This vast
and polyglot nation has never pretended to have a national cuisine. Americans
generally want food that is hygienic, copious and fast.

What Isaac Singer's machine did for clothing; what Charles Walgreen did   5
for drugs; what Aaron Montgomery Ward, Richard Sears, Alvah Roebuck and
F. W. Woolworth did for "dry goods"; what Gail Borden did for condensed
food; what Philip Armour and Gustavus Swift did for fresh meat; what George
Gilman and George Huntington Hartford and their Great Atlantic & Pacific Tea
Co. did for produce, Kroc has done for fast food. He did not just launch a
company, he energized an industry. The fast-food industry — $14 billion a
year — is one reason that one of every three American meals is eaten out. Kroc
has been called "the service sector's equivalent of Henry Ford." Consider Peter
Drucker's description of Ford:

There is no machine, no tool, no new product, no process that bears his name, was
invented by him, or could have been patented by him. Everything he used was known.
There were plenty of automobiles on the market before he brought out his first one. And
yet Henry Ford was a true innovator. What he contributed were mass production, the
mass market, the profitability of the very cheap . . .

At McDonald's hamburger university, students earn degrees in hamburgerology   6
by mastering computerized French-fries and other technology that enables

unskilled teen-agers in Tokyo or Trenton to produce hamburgers as alike as Model T's were. This uniformity is especially remarkable because McDonald's is primarily a confederation of small-business men, the franchise owners who buy all materials from independent suppliers. Franchising is a solution to the problem of distributing goods in a continental nation. Automobiles, gasoline, motels, fast food: many franchised products are for mobile people who value familiarity because they want to feel at home away from home. Franchised products are part of the homogenizing of experience that a nation of travelers finds more reassuring than boring.

Kroc has a nineteenth-century feeling for the romance of enterprise. Like the English industrialist who cut down a grove of trees so that he could gaze from his parlor at smoke from his factory, Kroc cherished his first California home because it was on a hill from which he could watch, through binoculars, a McDonald's. His autobiography, *Grinding It Out*, recalls a popular nineteenth-century literary genre, the entrepreneur's lyric. "It requires a certain kind of mind," he writes, "to see beauty in a hamburger bun. Yet, is it any more unusual to find grace in the texture and softly curved silhouette of a bun than to reflect lovingly on . . . the arrangement of textures and colors in a butterfly's wing?" Warming to his theme, he praises buns and Fred Turner, his aide, for studying them:

> *At first they were cluster buns, meaning that the buns were attached to each other in clusters of four to six, and they were only partially sliced. Fred pointed out that it would be easier and faster for a griddle man if we had individual buns instead of clusters and if they were sliced all the way through. The baker could afford to do it our way because of the quantities of buns we were ordering. Fred also worked . . . on the design of a sturdy, reusable box for our buns. Handling these boxes instead of the customary packages of twelve reduced the baker's packaging cost, so he was able to give us a better price . . . It also . . . streamlined our operations. With the old packages, it didn't take long for a busy griddle man to find himself buried in paper. Then there was the time spent opening packages, pulling buns from the cluster, and halving them. These fractions of seconds added up to wasted minutes.*

Kroc's book, like his life, is as ingenuous as an American primitive painting. His prose, like his enterprise, expresses the prosaic idea on which American prosperity rests: *things add up*. Enough billions of fractions of anything (seconds, pennies) add up to a lot of something. Obsessive attention to detail — to boxes of buns, to time-and-motion studies — pays because America is the realm of mass effects: throughout American life you see astounding cumulative consequences of minute increments. Kroc's genius, like that of many

170

entrepreneurs, is for acting on the obvious — or what seems obvious after he
has acted on it.

QUESTIONS ON CONTENT:

1. Does Will present an explicit thesis, or is it implicit? Can you state his thesis?
2. How does Will account for Ray Kroc's success?
3. What characteristics of Americans and the American way of life made Kroc's success possible?
4. How are Henry Ford and Ray Kroc alike?
5. Why did Will call Kroc the "artist of the hamburger"?

QUESTION ON WRITING STRUCTURE AND STRATEGY:

1. Why is the picture of Kroc in the first paragraph such an appealing one to Americans?
2. What is the effect of the statistics quoted in paragraph three?
3. What is Will's purpose in turning his statistics into concrete images?
4. How do the "Journalist's Five W's and How" furnish Will with his basic organization? Do you find any deviation?

QUESTIONS FOR DISCUSSION AND WRITING:

1. The success of McDonald's has opened the door to work for many young people. Is working there or at other fast-food outlets a valid introduction to the world of work? In a short paper discuss this question in terms of management, coworkers, customers, sanitary conditions.
2. From your own observations and reading discuss the validity of Will's explanation for the popularity of fast foods. Can you think of any other significant social phenomenon he has left out?
3. McDonald's and other fast-food firms are now engaged in stiff competition for the public's favor. What are some of the new features various fast-food outlets have added to attract customers? (Question local managers of McDonald's, Burger King, Taco Bell, and so on.) What do these changes say about American lifestyles? Tastes? Is it just an attempt to be different or is it responding to a need? Write a paper in which you assess these changes.

WHAT IS THE POINT
OF WORKING?

Lance Morrow

Lance Morrow, poet, playwright, was a reporter on the Washington
Star *before becoming a contributing editor to* Time *magazine and a
frequent author of the* Time *"Essays." In the following essay, Morrow
uses a wide variety of writing methods to deal with a much-debated
subject: the American work ethic. After setting the historical
background, he traverses the history of American attitudes toward
work up to the present day and explains the reasons for what he sees
as the weakening of traditional attitudes. You might quarrel with his
argument: does he really come back to the issue of productivity
mentioned in paragraph three? Does he have anything to say about
quality? Notice his "Timestyle" writing: striking nouns and strong
verbs, processions of adjectives, and a liberal use of figurative
language. It makes for lively, diverting reading. As you read, look for
clues indicating his intended audience (see his allusions). At the same
time, reexamine your own attitude toward work. What do you expect
from it beyond the necessities of life?*

When God foreclosed on Eden, he condemned Adam and Eve to go to   1
work. Work has never recovered from that humiliation. From the beginning,
the Lord's word said that work was something bad: a punishment, the great
stone of mortality and toil laid upon a human spirit that might otherwise soar
in the infinite, weightless playfulness of grace.

A perfectly understandable prejudice against work has prevailed ever   2
since. Most work in the life of the world has been hard, but since it was
grindingly inevitable, it hardly seemed worth complaining about very much.
Work was simply the business of life, as matter-of-fact as sex and breathing. In
recent years, however, the ancient discontent has grown elaborately articulate.
The worker's usual old bitching has gone to college. Grim tribes of sociologists
have reported back from office and factory that most workers find their labor
mechanical, boring, imprisoning, stultifying, repetitive, dreary, heartbreaking.
In his 1972 book *Working*, Studs Terkel began: "This book, being about work,
is, by its very nature, about violence — to the spirit as well as to the body."
The historical horrors of industrialization (child labor, Dickensian squalor, the
dark satanic mills) translate into the 20th century's robotic busywork on the
line, tightening the same damned screw on the Camaro's fire-wall assembly,
going nuts to the banging, jangling Chaplinesque whirr of modern materialism
in labor, bringing forth issue, disgorging itself upon the market.

The lamentations about how awful work is prompt an answering wail   3
from the management side of the chasm: nobody wants to work any more. As

American productivity, once the exuberant engine of national wealth, has dipped to an embarrassingly uncompetitive low, Americans have shaken their heads: the country's old work ethic is dead. About the only good words for it now emanate from Ronald Reagan and certain beer commercials. Those ads are splendidly mythic playlets, romantic idealizations of men in groups who blast through mountains or pour plumingly molten steel in factories, the work all grit and grin. Then they retire to flip around iced cans of sacramental beer and debrief one another in a warm sundown glow of accomplishment. As for Reagan, in his presidential campaign he enshrined work in his rhetorical "community of values," along with family, neighborhood, peace and freedom. He won by a landslide.

Has the American work ethic really expired? Is some old native eagerness   4
to level wilderness and dig and build and invent now collapsing toward a decadence of dope, narcissism, income transfers and aerobic self-actualization?

The idea of work—work as an ethic, an abstraction—arrived rather late   5
in the history of toil. Whatever edifying and pietistic things may have been said about work over the centuries (Kahlil Gibran called work "love made visible," and the Benedictines say, "To work is to pray"), humankind has always tried to avoid it whenever possible. The philosophical swells of ancient Greece thought work was degrading; they kept an underclass to see to the laundry and other details of basic social maintenance. That prejudice against work persisted down the centuries in other aristocracies. It is supposed, however, to be inherently un-American. Edward Kennedy likes to tell the story of how, during his first campaign for the Senate, his opponent said scornfully in a debate: "This man has never worked a day in his life!" Kennedy says that the next morning as he was shaking hands at a factory gate, one worker leaned toward him and confided, "You ain't missed a goddamned thing."

The Protestant work ethic, which sanctified work and turned it into   6
vocation, arrived only a few centuries ago in the formulations of Martin Luther and John Calvin. In that scheme, the worker collaborates with God to do the work of the universe, the great design. One scholar, Leland Ryken of Illinois' Wheaton College, has pointed out that American politicians and corporate leaders who preach about the work ethic do not understand the Puritans' original, crucial linkage between human labor and God's will.

During the 19th century industrialization of America, the idea of work's   7
inherent virtue may have seemed temporarily implausible to generations who labored in the mines and mills and sweatshops. The century's huge machinery of production punished and stunned those who ran it.

And yet for generations of immigrants, work *was* ultimately availing; the   8
numb toil of an illiterate grandfather got the father a foothold and a high school education, and the son wound up in college or even law school. A

woman who died in the Triangle Shirtwaist Co. fire in lower Manhattan had a niece who made it to the halcyon Bronx, and another generation on, the family went to Westchester County. So for millions of Americans, as they labored through the complexities of generations, work worked, and the immigrant work ethic came at last to merge with the Protestant work ethic.

The motive of work was all. To work for mere survival is desperate. To work for a better life for one's children and grandchildren lends the labor a fierce dignity. That dignity, an unconquerably hopeful energy and aspiration — driving, persisting like a life force — is the American quality that many find missing now.

The work ethic is not dead, but it is weaker now. The psychology of work is much changed in America. The acute, painful memory of the Great Depression used to enforce a disciplined and occasionally docile approach to work — in much the way that older citizens in the Soviet Union do not complain about scarce food and overpopulated apartments, because they remember how much more horrible everything was during the war. But the generation of the Depression is retiring and dying off, and today's younger workers, though sometimes laid off and kicked around by recessions and inflation, still do not keep in dark storage that residual apocalyptic memory of Hoovervilles and the Dust Bowl and banks capsizing.

Today elaborate financial cushions — unemployment insurance, union benefits, welfare payments, food stamps and so on — have made it less catastrophic to be out of a job for a while. Work is still a profoundly respectable thing in America. Most Americans suffer a sense of loss, of diminution, even of worthlessness, if they are thrown out on the street. But the blow seldom carries the life-and-death implications it once had, the sense of personal ruin. Besides, the wild and notorious behavior of the economy takes a certain amount of personal shame out of joblessness; if Ford closes down a plant in New Jersey and throws 3,700 workers into the unemployment lines, the guilt falls less on individuals than on Japanese imports or American car design or an extortionate OPEC.

Because today's workers are better educated than those in the past, their expectations are higher. Many younger Americans have rearranged their ideas about what they want to get out of life. While their fathers and grandfathers and great-grandfathers concentrated hard upon plow and drill press and pressure gauge and tort, some younger workers now ask previously unimaginable questions about the point of knocking themselves out. For the first time in the history of the world, masses of people in industrially advanced countries no longer have to focus their minds upon work as the central concern of their existence.

In the formulation of Psychologist Abraham Maslow, work functions in a hierarchy of needs: first, work provides food and shelter, basic human maintenance. After that, it can address the need for security and then for friendship and "belongingness." Next, the demands of the ego arise, the need for respect. Finally, men and women assert a larger desire for "self-actualization." That seems a harmless and even worthy enterprise but sometimes degenerates into self-infatuation, a vaporously selfish discontent that dead-ends in isolation, the empty face that gazes back from the mirror.

Of course in patchwork, pluralistic America, different classes and ethnic groups are perched at different stages in the work hierarchy. The immigrants — legal and illegal — who still flock densely to America are fighting for the foothold that the jogging tribes of self-actualizers achieved three generations ago. The zealously ambitious Koreans who run New York City's best vegetable markets, or boat people trying to open a restaurant, or chicanos who struggle to start a small business in the *barrio* are still years away from est and the Sierra Club. Working women, to the extent that they are new at it, now form a powerful source of ambition and energy. Feminism — and financial need — have made them, in effect, a sophisticated-immigrant wave upon the economy. 14

Having to work to stay alive, to build a future, gives one's exertions a tough moral simplicity. The point of work in that case is so obvious that it need not be discussed. But apart from the sheer necessity of sustaining life, is there some inherent worth in work? Carlyle believed that "all work, even cotton spinning, is noble; work is alone noble." Was he right? 15

It is seigneurial cant to romanticize work that is truly detestable and destructive to workers. But misery and drudgery are always comparative. Despite the sometimes nostalgic haze around their images, the pre-industrial peasant and the 19th century American farmer did brutish work far harder than the assembly line. The untouchable who sweeps excrement in the streets of Bombay would react with blank incomprehension to the malaise of some $17-an-hour workers on a Chrysler assembly line. The Indian, after all, has passed from "alienation" into a degradation that is almost mystical. In Nicaragua, the average 19-year-old peasant has worked longer and harder than most Americans of middle age. Americans prone to restlessness about the spiritual disappointments of work should consult unemployed young men and women in their own ghettos: they know with painful clarity the importance of the personal dignity that a job brings. 16

Americans often fall into fallacies of misplaced sympathy. Psychologist Maslow, for example, once wrote that he found it difficult "to conceive of feeling proud of myself, self-loving and self-respecting, if I were working, for example, in some chewing-gum factory . . ." Well, two weeks ago, Warner-Lambert announced that it would close down its gum-manufacturing American Chicle factory in Long Island City, N.Y.; the workers who had spent years 17 there making Dentyne and Chiclets were distraught. "It's a beautiful place to work," one feeder-catcher-packer of chewing gum said sadly. "It's just like home." There is a peculiar elitist arrogance in those who discourse on the brutalizations of work simply because they cannot imagine themselves performing the job. Certainly workers often feel abstracted out, reduced sometimes to dreary robotic functions. But almost everyone commands endlessly subtle systems of adaptation; people can make the work their own and even cherish it against all academic expectations. Such adaptations are often more important than the famous but theoretical alienation from the process and product of labor.

Work is still the complicated and crucial core of most lives, the occupation melded inseparably to the identity; Freud said that the successful psyche is one capable of love and of work. Work is the most thorough and profound organizing principle in American life. If mobility has weakened old blood ties, our co-workers often form our new family, our tribe, our social world; we become almost citizens of our companies, living under the protection of salaries, pensions and health insurance. Sociologist Robert Schrank believes that people like jobs mainly because they need other people; they need to gossip with them, hang out with them, to schmooze. Says Schrank: "The workplace performs the function of community."

Unless it is dishonest or destructive — the labor of a pimp or a hit man, say — all work is intrinsically honorable in ways that are rarely understood as they once were. Only the fortunate toil in ways that express them directly. There is a Renaissance splendor in Leonardo's effusion: "The works that the eye orders the hands to make are infinite." But most of us labor closer to the ground. Even there, all work expresses the laborer in a deeper sense: all life must be worked at, protected, planted, replanted, fashioned, cooked for, coaxed, diapered, formed, sustained. Work is the way that we tend the world, the way that people connect. It is the most vigorous, vivid sign of life — in individuals and in civilizations.

QUESTIONS ON CONTENT:

1. Morrow's thesis is implicit. Can you state it in a single sentence? (Note that his title asks a question. Do you get an answer?)

2. Over the years, how has the American work ethic changed, and what specific factors have caused the change? How does this changed work ethic contrast with the work ethic of the most recent immigrants? Contrast your observations with Morrow's.

3. Though attitudes toward work have changed, what important needs are served by work?

QUESTIONS ON WRITING STRUCTURE AND STRATEGY:

1. Morrow's order of development is primarily chronological, and he employs a variety of modes. Pinpoint his use of comparison and contrast, description, cause and effect, classification, definition, and examples. Which do you find most effective?

2. Morrow's writing is an excellent example of what has been called "*Time*style":

    a. imaginative nouns: "*tribes* of sociologists," "philosophical *swells* of ancient Greece"

    b. strong verbs: "God *foreclosed* on Eden," "*disgorging* itself upon the market"

    c. powerful, sometimes ironic, often multiple adjectives: "*banging, jangling, Chaplinesque* whirr," "*sacramental* beer"

    d. intensifying adverbs: "has grown *elaborately* articulate," "*embarrassingly* uncompetitive low?"

    e. figurative language: "ethic groups are *perched* . . . still *flock*," "[women] a sophisticated *immigrant wave* upon the economy"

    Pinpoint other examples of "*Time*style" that you find. What is the effect of such style on the reader? Though you may not wish to copy the style, you can learn the value of precise word choice to convey your meaning and add color and liveliness to otherwise bland writing.

3. Though Morrow's essay may appear choppy with its paragraphs of varying lengths, what elements do you find that promote coherence? Look at his transitions, connectives, repetition, rhetorical questions.

QUESTIONS FOR DISCUSSION AND WRITING:

1. In paragraph seventeen, Morrow contrasts psychologist Maslow's disdain for work in a chewing gum factory with the attitude of the worker who found herself out of work. Work provides "community" that people no longer find in American life outside work. Have you ever experienced a sense of community on a job? Write a paper in which you describe and comment on this sense of community.

2. Write a journal entry in which you discuss a job you have held that you liked or hated, including an analysis of its dignity, worth, purpose, or lack of them.

3. In a short paper, discuss your "philosophy of work" and its influence on your choice of a vocation.

SEND YOUR CHILDREN
TO THE LIBRARIES
Arthur Ashe

*Arthur Ashe, Davis Cup Winner, Wimbledon tennis champion, issues
a direct appeal to black students to spend more time in libraries and
less time on the athletic field, for the odds against a career in
professional sports are a thousand to one. Ashe's advice reflects a
growing concern for athletes who are used as "superjocks" in college
and end up without an education or a hope of being picked up by the
pros, the "Play now, pay later" syndrome. Though his remarks are
brief, the force of what he has to say lies in his realistic analysis of the
statistics of professional sports (the odds at the library being better)
and his generous use of familiar examples. This article appeared in the
New York Times and is aimed at the general reader. Note, however,
how Ashe very early identifies with his black readers. He continues this
identification through the main body of the article. Finally, note the
very personal — yet familiar — way in which he ends the article.*

Since my sophomore year at University of California, Los Angeles, I have   1
become convinced that we blacks spend too much time on the playing fields
and too little time in the libraries.

Please don't think of this attitude as being pretentious just because I am a   2
black, single, professional athlete.

I don't have children, but I can make observations. I strongly believe the   3
black culture expends too much time, energy and effort raising, praising and
teasing our black children as to the dubious glories of professional sport.

All children need models to emulate — parents, relatives or friends. But   4
when the child starts school, the influence of the parent is shared by teachers
and classmates, by the lure of books, movies, ministers and newspapers, but
most of all by television.

Which televised events have the greatest number of viewers? — Sports —   5
The Olympics, Super Bowl, Masters, World Series, pro basketball playoffs,
Forest Hills. ABC-TV even has sports on Monday night prime time from April
to December.

So your child gets a massive dose of O. J. Simpson, Kareem Abdul-Jabbar,   6
Muhammad Ali, Reggie Jackson, Dr. J. and Lee Elder and other pro athletes.
And it is only natural that your child will dream of being a pro athlete himself.

But consider these facts: For the major professional sports of hockey,   7
football, basketball, baseball, golf, tennis and boxing, there are roughly only
3,170 major league positions available (attributing 200 positions to golf, 200 to
tennis and 100 to boxing). And the annual turnover is small.

8

178

We blacks are a subculture of about 28 million. Of the 13½ million men, 5 to 6 million are under 20 years of age, so your son has less than one chance in 1,000 of becoming a pro. Less than one in a thousand. Would you bet your son's future on something with odds of 999 to 1 against you? I wouldn't.   9

Unless a child is exceptionally gifted, you should know by the time he enters high school whether he has a future as an athlete. But what is more important is what happens if he doesn't graduate or doesn't land a college scholarship and doesn't have a viable alternative job career. Our high school dropout rate is several times the national average, which contributes to our unemployment rate of roughly twice the national average.   10

And how do you fight the figures in the newspapers every day. Ali has earned more than $30 million boxing, O. J. just signed for $2½ million, Dr. J. for almost $3 million, Reggie Jackson for $2.8 million, Nate Archibald for $400,000 a year. All that money, recognition, attention, free cars, girls, jobs in the offseason—no wonder there is Pop Warner football, Little League baseball, National Junior Tennis League tennis, hockey practice at 5 A.M. and pickup basketball games in any center city at any hour.   11

There must be some way to assure that the 999 who try but don't make it to pro sports don't wind up on the street corners or in the unemployment lines. Unfortunately, our most widely recognized role models are athletes and entertainers—"runnin'" and "jumpin'" and "singin'" and "dancin.'" While we are 60 percent of the National Basketball Association, we are less than 4 percent of the doctors and lawyers. While we are about 35 percent of major league baseball we are less than 2 percent of the engineers. While we are about 40 percent of the National Football League, we are less than 11 percent of construction workers such as carpenters and bricklayers.   12

Our greatest heroes of the century have been athletes—Jack Johnson, Joe Louis and Muhammad Ali. Racial and economic discrimination forced us to channel our energies into athletics and entertainment. These were the ways out of the ghetto, the ways to get that Cadillac, those alligator shoes, that cashmere sport coat.   13

Somehow, parents must instill a desire for learning alongside the desire to be Walt Frazier. Why not start by sending black professional athletes into high schools to explain the facts of life.   14

I have often addressed high school audiences and my message is always the same. For every hour you spend on the athletic field, spend two in the library. Even if you make it as a pro athlete, your career will be over by the time you are 35. So you will need that diploma.   15

Have these pro athletes explain what happens if you break a leg, get a sore arm, have one bad year or don't make the cut for five or six tournaments.

Explain to them the star system, wherein for every O. J. earning millions there are six or seven others making $15,000 or $20,000 or $30,000 a year.

But don't just have Walt Frazier or O. J. or Abdul-Jabbar address your class. Invite a benchwarmer or a guy who didn't make it. Ask him if he sleeps every night. Ask him whether he was graduated. Ask him what he would do if he became disabled tomorrow. Ask him where his old high school athletic buddies are.

We have been on the same roads—sports and entertainment—too long. We need to pull over, fill up at the library and speed away to Congress and the Supreme Court, the unions and the business world. We need more Barbara Jordans, Andrew Youngs, union card-holders, Nikki Giovannis and Earl Graveses. Don't worry: we will still be able to sing and dance and run and jump better than anybody else.

I'll never forget how proud my grandmother was when I graduated from U.C.L.A. in 1966. Never mind the Davis Cup in 1968, 1969 and 1970. Never mind the Wimbledon title, Forest Hills, etc. To this day, she still doesn't know what those names mean.

What mattered to her was that of her more than 30 children and grandchildren, I was the first to be graduated from college, and a famous college at that. Somehow, that made up for all those floors she scrubbed all those years.

QUESTIONS ON CONTENT:

1. What is Ashe's thesis?
2. How does he account for the fact that earlier blacks had to excel in athletics and entertainment?
3. What does he suggest be done to overcome the unrealistic expectations of high school athletes?
4. Although Ashe became a tennis champion, which of his accomplishments mattered most to his grandmother?

QUESTIONS ON WRITING STRUCTURE AND STRATEGY:

1. To what audience is Ashe addressing his remarks? How do you know? Given the facts, is this the most appropriate forum? (See when published.)
2. Why is Ashe's analysis of statistics probably the most effective supporting detail?
3. "Playing fields" and "libraries" are figures of speech (see "Metonymy" in Glossary). What larger entities do they stand for? Why is this a particularly arresting opening sentence?

QUESTIONS FOR DISCUSSION AND WRITING:

1. Are professional sports in America overpraised and overpublicized to the detriment of academic pursuits? How do you account for this? Discuss your conclusions in a paper.
2. Critics decry Little League (and other such organized sports), citing physical injuries and psychological damage to immature youngsters. What are the advantages? What alternatives are there to such organized activities for young people?
3. How will the "no pass, no play" requirements affect academic commitment on the part of the athlete? Write a paper in which you explain what other implications such requirements might have. You may do some library re-search to see what the effect has been in Texas.

THE COSTS OF DRINKING
John S. Hoppock

John S. Hoppock is an emergency physician at Providence Medical Center in Portland, Oregon. His wide experience with emergencies resulting from drinking has furnished him with the necessary data to reach the widest possible audience, both drinkers and nondrinkers, since, as he emphasizes, the "real problem" is not alcoholism but "death and destruction," and "we all pay." Hoppock's short essay has an impact not only because of his grim litany of facts but also because of the clipped, staccato method of presentation and his powerful paragraph openers and closers. Note his ironic tone (appropriate to one who obviously disapproves of a "slap on the wrist" for offenders); his use of parallelism to amass facts; alliteration to underscore; short sentences — sentence fragments — to suggest urgency; and rhetorical questions to engage the reader. All of these elements contribute to his tone.

Portland, Ore. — Weekend and holiday shifts, especially, they keep me awake all night — the ones who don't make it home, and those who aren't safe even there. 1

The worst come by ambulance — the critical trauma cases, for which we have to get everyone out of bed. Others are brought by family or friends, horns blaring at the entrance. Many simply walk, or limp, or stagger in. 2

We bet on the blood-alcohol levels. It takes some practice. A level of .300 can kill some people; it may mean relative sobriety for others. Histories are irrelevant. "Only three or four beers" probably means that number of sixpacks. 3

The extent to which alcohol contributes to accidents is estimated variously. I would put it at about 80 percent. It's a biased view — I only deal with the ones who get hurt. Most are from M.V.A.'s — multiple-car, -motorcycle, or auto-pedestrian acccidents. The drunk may be at the wheel or walking the street. Neither of two drivers may be legally intoxicated, but added together they equal one drunk. 4

Conscious or comatose, the patients are difficult to manage. Is it the ethanol or the injury that has altered their mental state? They can't tell us accurately where they hurt, what parts aren't working right. Too many might have broken necks. While they thrash about, it may take six of us to hold them still for an X-ray, and there are never that many lead shields for our own protection. 5

The police are practical about it. They frequently wait until we know the full extent of the injury, only wanting blood-alcohol results if someone else has been killed or if we might be sending the patient home. They like to look at X-rays. If we can show them a crushed skull or pelvis, they don't bother issuing a traffic citation. 6

Most of my patients are survivors. But that can be misleading—the 7
quadriplegic who will die years later of complications, the young woman who
will see her face forever scarred in the mirror.

Streets and highways are not the only places where accidents happen. 8
Cafe coronaries are almost always preceded by a few drinks, as are many of
the falls that break hips and shoulders, the lacerations from plate-glass
windows, the hand fractures from poorly placed punches. And the resulting
infections, dysfunctions, and disabilities.

Trauma isn't the only thing that brings them in. Unconscious. Needing 9
their stomachs pumped. Choking, with vomit clogging the trachea. Doubled
over in pain with a pancreas that has started to digest itself. Or, after many
years' drinking, atherosclerotic and hypertensive, cirrhotic and jaundiced.
Wondering why.

Sometimes they show up just wanting help with the problem. At 3 A.M., 10
while I am trying to deal with everything else, someone has decided that the
drinking has become an emergency. What do you want me to do about it? Give
us the cure, doctor.

Is there one? Is the fault with the individual, or society? The answers 11
won't be found in my emergency department, only the problems. My own
specialty deals with effects, not causes. Self-destructive behavior is rarely a
private matter.

The real victims are those who were stone-cold sober but in the wrong 12
place at the wrong time. When it comes to fault, legislatures and courts
determine degrees of responsibility. But when I "pronounce" someone, dead is
dead.

We all pay, of course—through higher insurance rates, taxes, hospital 13
bills. Yet we tolerate so much with a slap on the wrist, a fine, a suspended
sentence. Or simply put it down to chance. We encourage brinksmanship—the
driver's manual tells you how much you can consume and still pass the
breathalizer test.

Who are we kidding? The problem with drinking isn't so much 14
"alcoholism." The probelm is death and destruction—of lives, property,
relationships. Warped personalities and blunted perceptions may be annoying,
but that is inconsequential when weighed against the protection of life—yet
there is a parking lot next to every cocktail lounge.

I am at an age when I stand a better chance of being killed by a drinking 15
driver than of dying from any other kind of homicide or accident, or cancer, or
cardiovascular disease. They are a greater threat to my life than any mugger or
terrorist. What would I do without them? Feel safer at places other than work,
certainly. Make less money, probably. And, of course, get more sleep at night.

QUESTIONS ON CONTENT:

1. Does the author's short essay answer the question implied in the title?

2. What does the author mean when he says that destructive behavior is rarely a private matter?

3. What does Hoppock say is the *real* problem with drinking?

4. Although most alcohol-related accidents are MVA's, what are the full ramifications of drinking?

QUESTIONS ON WRITING STRUCTURE AND STRATEGY:

1. Why is the opening sentence arresting? What is omitted?

2. What purpose is served by the author's catalog of injuries and otherwise damaged bodies and minds?

3. How does Hoppock engage the interest of the reader who is not a "drinking driver"?

4. Paragraph nine begins with a sentence and is followed by six incomplete sentences. Do you find this effective? Why or why not? Is it consistent with the author's style?

5. What are the costs of drinking and who pays? How does the answer serve to give the essay coherence?

QUESTIONS FOR DISCUSSION AND WRITING:

1. Do an informal survey and determine the extent of drinking on your own campus. Who among those surveyed has had a friend killed or maimed as a result of drinking? (You might consult your own Department of Public Safety — that is, campus police — and local hospital emergency room.) Determine your own costs of drinking.
   OR:
   If you have had a friend killed as the result of a drunk driving accident, or if you know of someone who died as a result of a drunk driving accident, write a paper on how either instance affected your subsequent behavior or the behavior of your friends.

2. Examine your school's regulations concerning drinking and write a short essay in which you discuss a responsible student code respecting drinking. Consider the effectiveness of your school's code.

3. Analyze in a short paper some of your observations about the drinking habits of high school students versus college students. Evaluate the influence of peer pressure.
   OR:
   Analyze the differences in drinking habits of men and women.

4. Examine the laws in your state governing drunken driving. Are they strong? Effective?

SNARLING CARS
Paul Blumberg

In the selection that follows — written by a professor of sociology — we have a scornful indictment of American automobile manufacturers. Beginning with an ironic news story, Blumberg adopts a devastatingly critical tone. He lashes out at Detroit (a metonymy: something associated with an idea stands for the idea) for what he sees as its cynical pursuit of profits at the expense of quality, American lives, and, ultimately, American jobs. Blumberg's vigorous writing is attributable to his use of emotional and highly connotative language, through which he conveys much of his meaning and feeling. This is not to say that his argument lacks convincing supporting detail — chiefly statistical — though he is selective in his choice of such detail. Note, then, especially, his diction and how much of his message is carried by it. (See Glossary, "Coherence/Connectives" for an analysis of Blumberg's paragraph coherence.)

LINCOLN-MERCURY COUGAR SLAIN

PITTSBURGH (UPI) — *The cougar that served as the Lincoln-Mercury advertising trademark was shot and killed today after it attacked a 9-year-old boy at an automobile show.* — News item.

In this macabre incident, the cougar seized the boy by the neck, pinned him to the ground, resisted all efforts by the trainer to pull him from his prey, and was finally shot to death by an off-duty policeman. The boy, suffering severe neck wounds, was rushed to the hospital in serious condition. He has since recovered. The health of the American automobile industry, however, still hangs in the balance. 1

For decades, one of Detroit's major advertising ploys was to market its products as instruments of violence. During the entire postwar period, in fact, Detroit's marketing strategy was not to sell automobiles as sensible family transportation, as one might expect in a reasonably civilized society, but as vehicles of mayhem and destruction. 2

What's in a name? In Detroit's case, plenty. Because over the years, as an auto writer once observed, the very names Detroit managers gave to their cars reveal quite plainly the industry's appeal to motives of violence and aggression. Consider the Oldsmobile *Cutlass*, the Buick *Le Sabre*, the Plymouth *Fury*, the Plymouth *Barracuda*, the Chevrolet Corvette *Stingray*, the Ford Mustang *Cobra*, the American Motors *Matador*, the Mercury *Lynx*, Mercury *Bobcat*, and Mercury *Cougar* — killers all, the last one, this time, almost literally. The theme 3 of violence in these names has a cunning economic logic behind it. As we now know, Detroit management's guiding theology during the postwar era was: big car, big profit; small car, small profit. And what better way to sell big, powerful cars than to link them in the public's mind with the libidinal release of destructive impulses?

In the postwar auto industry, as the horsepower race heated up, the managers of each company dropped ever-larger and hungrier engines into ever-bigger, heavier, and more option-laden automobiles. As late as 1970, 85 percent of U.S. cars were sold with V-8 engines. Consequently, as one sage assessed the peculiar logic of the American automobile industry, Detroit sold a 5,000-pound car to a 100-pound woman so she could drive one block to buy a one-pound loaf of bread. When Marx wrote of the anarchy of production under capitalism, he knew whereof he spoke, though he lived before Detroit management had honed the principle to perfection.

Of all the gadgets on the Road Locomotives (as Consumers Union called these American behemoths thirty years ago), none so clearly opens a window into the mind of the Detroit executive as the design of the speedometer. In keeping with management's appeal to raw power rather than sensible transportation, the speedometer had to show speeds of 120, 140, or 150 miles per hour — far faster, of course, than was safe, legal, or even possible for most cars. But when you scale up a small guage with speeds to 150 m.p.h., the numbers must all be crammed so close together that it's difficult to read any of them. Here in a nutshell (or a dial) were management's values: style and libido over engineering logic. And while Detroit managers were busy refining these priorities with tail fins and sleek but dangerous hardtop convertibles (whose roofs, lacking a center pillar, might collapse if the car rolled over), foreign manufacturers were making disc brakes and radial tires.

When Detroit's managers are accused of foisting the Road Locomotives on the American public and thus being unprepared for the small-car revolution, they neatly shift the blame to the public. The postwar dinosaurs weren't their idea, they protest, they were simply giving their customers what they wanted. This, the consumer sovereignty argument, overlooks the fact that consumer taste does not develop in a vacuum but is shaped by manufacturers through massive advertising. In one recent year, the auto industry spent $700 million on TV ads, $340 million more on newspaper ads, and $225 million for magazine advertising — well over $1 billion in just one year (not counting the money spent on radio, billboards, and other forms of advertising). Throughout the postwar years Detroit spent comparable billions fashioning public taste for the gas guzzlers, and then proceeded to satisfy that taste.

Of course, public taste cannot be totally programmed by advertising. Ford failed to generate much interest in the Edsel, and some new and highly

4

5

6

7

promoted products do occasionally fail. Nonetheless, though massive advertising cannot guarantee demand for individual products, there is no question that the billions Detroit spent after World War II pushing the big, heavy, powerful V-8s did in fact create the taste and habit for these cars. Because of postwar affluence, which allowed an ethic of conspicuous waste, and because of the underlying macho element in American culture, there was a basic public receptivity to the marketing strategy of selling murder on wheels. But if the ground was fertile, Detroit management sowed the seeds and carefully tended the fields.

In 1949 The U.A.W.'s research and engineering people published an article, "A Motor Car Named Desire," that called on Detroit to build a small, light, affordable car, suitable for postwar urban America. They cited a contemporary opinion survey taken by the Society of Automotive Engineers, which showed that 60 percent of Americans wanted the U.S. auto industry to produce a small car. Specifically, the U.A.W. proposed a car about 170 inches in length, weighing about 2,000 pounds, with a small six- or four-cylinder engine that would get more than 25 miles to the gallon. In other words, the U.A.W. proposed a car almost identical in conception to the Datsuns, Toyotas, and Hondas now inundating America. Had Detroit heeded the U.A.W.'s advice then, it would now have the experience to meet and beat the small-car competition from abroad, rather than belatedly struggling to catch up. But it ignored the suggestion; in fact, it responded to Walter Reuther's presumption with a bold assertion of executive power meant to keep the union in its place and to protect the principle of managerial prerogative. In its contract with the U.A.W. in 1950, and in every contract thereafter, G.M. inserted a clause stipulating the "Rights of Management." It provided that "the products to be manufactured, the location of plants, the schedules of production, the methods, processes and means of manufacturing are solely and exclusively the responsibility of the Corporation."

When sensible, small-car transportation became necessary after the 1973 OPEC oil embargo, Detroit was unprepared. By hooking the American consumer on far bigger and more powerful cars than were rational or necessary, Detroit became the victim of its own shortsightedness and masterminded its own collapse. Until 1955 Detroit had the U.S. auto market all to itself; foreign imports comprised less than 1 percent of sales. But in the late 1950s the U.S. was invaded by a horde of insects—the Volkswagen beetles. And between 1955 and 1960, foreign auto imports rose to nearly 7 percent of sales. Though opposed in principle to building small, inexpensive cars, Detroit management realized that it had to offer the American public something to offset the growing popularity of the Volkswagen, the other small European cars, and the initial flow of Japanese cars. So at the end of the 1950s Detroit introduced its own compact cars—the Plymouth Valiant, Ford Falcon, Chevrolet Corvair, and the like.

These practical American compacts sold well, and the foreign car tide began to recede. By 1965 imports accounted for a smaller share of the U.S. market than they had in 1960. But Detroit executives were so hooked on the big-is-beautiful formula that they said, in effect, "Well, we'll build these compacts if we have to, but they're going to be the biggest, widest, heaviest, most powerful, most expensive compacts the world has even seen." Each year U.S. compacts got bigger, more powerful, more loaded with options, and more costly. The U.S. auto industry was so successful in building the world's biggest compacts that it eventually abandoned the small-car field altogether. Into this vacuum came the European cars again, and with them the Japanese—this time for keeps. Foreign imports rose from just 5.5 percent of sales in 1965 to 23 percent in 1970. With that kind of a foothold the imports now could not be dislodged. But if Detroit management had stayed with the compacts in the 1960s and redirected its advertising to wean Americans from the gospel of speed, power, and mayhem, the U.S. industry could have overcome or at least minimized the foreign car challenge, perhaps forstalled the protectionist tide, and might even have started exporting significant numbers of cars itself.

Friends of the U.S. auto industry like to argue that protectionism would never have become an issue if the working men and women who build the cars weren't so greedy. Detroit cannot compete with the Japanese, it is alleged, because American workers earn $8 an hour more than Japanese workers. Most objective observers agree, however, that the presumed $8-an-hour wage difference has been exaggerated and omits such things as the substantial housing subsidies Japanese companies provide for their workers. Although U.S. workers are more highly paid, wage differences between the U.S. and Japan probably amount to less than $500 per car, which is virtually offset by duty and cost of shipping from Japan to the U.S.

Moreover, low price is not the reason foreign cars are selling here. In fact, foreign cars sold in the U.S., which years ago were cheaper than American cars, are now on the average more expensive than American cars. Commerce Department figures show that in the last quarter of 1981 the average selling price of an American car was $9,012, and the average selling price of a foreign car sold here was $9,318. Japanese companies are selling cars in this country primarily because they have the product, and they have the product because they've had long experience making it. American companies don't.

The lesson of Detroit's decline is clear: just as war is too important to leave to the generals, business is too important to leave to the managers. Detroit management has failed; their marketing strategy has been cynical and antisocial for at least a generation; their world view is obsolete. Until recently the idea of economic democracy — the participation of workers, consumers, and the public in corporate decisionmaking — was a radical, utopian dream. Today it may be an economic necessity.

The paradox of all this is that Detroit management's prime concern with the bottom line by selling big cars for big profits proved in the long run to be extremely unprofitable. Had saner voices among workers, consumers, and the public prevailed, a sensible automobile for urban America would probably have been produced decades ago, which might have saved the U.S. auto industry from its present debacle. Ironically, production for use would have been more profitable than production for profit. 14

A final note: recently Dodge management introduced a new small truck. They call it the Dodge *Rampage*. These guys will never change. 15

QUESTIONS ON CONTENT:

1. To what human motives did Detroit appeal in the postwar period? How did Detroit manipulate the appeal to maximize profits?
2. What is Blumberg's thesis, and where does he locate it?
3. Why did the automobile industry turn down the United Auto Workers' proposal for a compact car?
4. What happened to the early concept of the American compact car?

QUESTIONS ON WRITING STRUCTURE AND STRATEGY:

1. To avoid the tiresome repetition of the same word, authors often employ synonyms — which are not always easy to come by. Underline the various synonyms Blumberg uses for "big cars," and determine if they reinforce his argument and contribute to his tone.
2. Note the connotation of the terms Blumberg applies to the auto industry and to auto executives. Are any complimentary? How does his use of these terms fit into his thesis and contribute to his tone?
3. How does Blumberg capture the reader's interest in the introduction?
4. What device does Blumberg use in paragraph four to ridicule the reigning ethos in the auto industry?

QUESTIONS FOR DISCUSSION AND WRITING:

1. Survey some of the current advertising for cars — in magazines, newspapers, radio ads, and TV ads. Determine the kind of appeal being made. Do the ads reflect any concern for conservation? For patriotism? Do they appeal to economy? Size? Safety? Is there a difference between ads for American cars and foreign cars? Write a report on your findings.
2. What are the advantages and disadvantages to the automaker of a policy of protectionsim? What are the advantages and disadvantages to auto workers

of a policy of protection? What are the advantages and disadvantages to the consumer of a policy of protectionism? Write a paper on how a policy of protectionism affects the consumer. Try to come up with some strongly connotative language as Blumberg does.

3.   Compare the names of American cars with those of Japan, France, Italy, Sweden, Germany, and Great Britain. What do you deduce from your comparative study? How are the foreign names different? Are names an important selling point for American buyers of foreign cars, or are there other considerations? Write a paper in which you explore some of these questions.

ILITERASEE ATT WURK
William McGowan

William McGowan served as a corporate public relations officer, and the following tightly constructed essay provides evidence of his ability to order facts, statistics, and testimony into forceful, persuasive prose. His title carries a double meaning—both announcing and illustrating the subject of his essay. In this remarkably clear, concise, well-organized essay, you find a startling introduction designed to "hook" the reader. Next, observe how he achieves clarity and coherence by making the first sentence of each paragraph the topic sentence, each relating to his thesis and each containing the word "illiteracy" or a synonym, and by employing the journalist's Five W's. Though his paragraphs are short, they are packed with all the alarming supporting details needed to convey his warning. His concluding paragraph is particularly effective. Alluding to a popular star in a well-known movie, he rekindles interest and finally drives home admonitions about the consequences of illiteracy.

According to a 1979 Ford Foundation report, 25 million Americans can't read at all and 35 million more could be considered functionally illiterate. The inability of 60 million native-born Americans to cope with the routine paperwork of life—a classified job ad, an instructional manual—is a problem with far-reaching consequences. 1

The illiteracy crisis is particularly sharp in business and industry, especially in banking, telecommunications and data processing, where huge labor pools having competent reading skills are most in demand. Unless the private sector addresses the problem by promoting mass-literacy programs, corporate profits will slip and the vitality of American industry will eventually pale before stiffened competition from countries such as West Germany and Japan, where higher rates of literacy and productivity march hand-in-hand. 2

The impact of illiteracy on the corporate bottom line is hard to calculate, but it's generally agreed that productivity and profits suffer significantly. Mutual of New York estimates that 70 percent of its dictated correspondence has to be redone at least once because of errors. In 1975, a herd of prime beef cattle was killed accidentally when a Chicago feed-lot laborer misread a package label and gave the cattle poison instead of food. 3

Every day, sales orders are botched, bank transactions bungled, messages scrambled and things by the million misfiled—all, to some extent, because of substandard reading skills. Just how vital will the much vaunted "information age" be if people simply can't read? A General Electric computer executive said, "We must remember that computers process error at the same bewildering speed at which they process truth." 4

An estimated 800,000 adult illiterates live in the New York area. 5
"Educational mismatching" — the situation in which jobs exist but qualified
manpower does not — was cited by the Regional Planning Association of New
York as the area's chief industrial problem for the next two decades. One
corporate executive asks, "Where will the workers come from to operate
complicated gear if they already make mistakes with a drill press?"

If left unarrested, rampant illiteracy will intensify the disjunction between 6
available jobs and qualified manpower and will create an unlettered underclass
that will be locked out of tomorrow's predominantly high-technology economy.
It will deepen existing social inequities, perhaps with explosive repercussions.
Black women, the only breadwinners in many inner-city households, are more
illiterate as a group than any other in the nation. As the work place grows
more reliant on sophisticated technologies such as robots with artificial
intelligence, they will grow more unemployable, especially in the service and
clerical positions where they now cluster. Their joblessness is bound to spur
further urban troubles.

Several decades of Federal efforts to eradicate illiteracy have largely 7
lacked funding and commitment. The Reagan Administration wants to cut the
$100 million now pledged to illiteracy programs down to $86 million, a figure
far short of the $5 billion to $25 billion demanded by some literacy activists
like Jonathan Kozol, the author of a penetrating study on illiteracy, "Prisoners
of Silence." Mr. Kozol and others in his camp have given up on Government
programs in favor of remedies that the private sector may propose in the new
spirit of "voluntarism." Their hopes are now pinned on corporations seeing
that they have a stake — or as an International Paper Company executive put
it, a "commercial motivation" — in developing a labor force able to read at
minimum standards.

While the private sector hasn't yet mounted any coordinated assault on 8
illiteracy, Dow Chemical, General Motors and Philip Morris are among two
dozen major companies that are sponsoring reading improvement programs for
employees or for students in public schools who might someday be on their
payroll. The National Coalition for Literacy and the National Advertising
Council plan a joint publicity campaign in 1983, hoping to draw energy and
initiatives from a broad spectrum of affected businesses. But so far, not enough
leading corporations have recognized that they have a vested interest in ridding
the country of a specter that is darkening future economic prospects.

When asked how he managed all his life without being able to read, 9
Johnny Cash, playing an illiterate man in a film called "The Pride of Jesse
Hallam," answered, "You lie a lot, you get cheated some and you fake it." As
foreign competition grows stronger, and as the economy vaults into the 21st
century, American industry will no longer be able to fake it, and unchecked

illiteracy will surely take its toll on social stability and industrial productivity. It will grab a share of corporate profit, too.

QUESTIONS ON CONTENT:

1. How is the illiteracy crisis manifested in the corporate sector? What are the consequences of the illiteracy crisis to the economy and to worker productivity?
2. What is meant by "educational mismatching"? How serious is this problem?
3. What are the social consequences of illiteracy? According to McGowan? Do you see literacy as giving power to people?
4. What is being done about the illiteracy crisis? Why has the problem shifted to the corporations?
5. Unless checked, what does McGowan say the consequences are for America in the twenty-first century?

QUESTIONS ON WRITING STRUCTURE AND STRATEGY:

1. Who are McGowan's potential audiences, and which one is best served by language?
2. What examples and statistics does McGowan use to illustrate his point? Why do these add authority to his remarks?
3. McGowan's tone is an urgent one (in the early paragraphs we find "far-reaching consequences," "crisis," "botched," "bungled," "scrambled," "misfiled," "rampant illiteracy"). Go through the rest of the article and pinpoint additional words that connote urgency.

QUESTIONS FOR DISCUSSION AND WRITING:

1. McGowan does not attempt to account for this growing illiteracy. What are some of the possible causes?
2. Have the aural and visual media contributed to or helped to eliminate the problem? (Refer to the Postman selection.)
3. If you have trouble organizing what you have to say, McGowan has good news for you. This is an extremely well organized essay.
   a. Take the second sentence of paragraph one as your thesis sentence.
   b. Under it list each of the paragraph topic sentences in order.
   c. You now have an outline. Using the method Benjamin Franklin describes, try to rewrite the essay in your own words without references to the original.

CONFESSIONS OF A
FEMALE CHAUVINIST SOW
Anne Roiphe

*Novelist and essayist Anne Roiphe was educated in New York, at
Sarah Lawrence College, and in Munich, Germany. In 1968 she
published the first of her novels,* Digging Out. *Subsequently she
published two more,* Up the Sandbox *(1971) and* Torch Song *(1977).
She has worked as a public relations specialist and written articles for*
Vogue *and the* New York Times Magazine. *The following article
appeared in* New York Magazine, *which enjoys a rather sophisticated
readership, and her remarks are tailored to that audience. She is at
times ironic, sometimes hyperbolic, always amusing. She uses striking
figures of speech and makes many contemporary and historical
allusions, with which she assumes her readers are familiar. Part of her
strategy for getting at female prejudice is to balance the most
outrageous female beliefs about men with examples of insensitive male
behavior toward women. In this way she disarms her potential female
critics. The result is at once amusing and charming. Appropriately,
her tone is good-humored. Apparently she sees no need to engage in
polemics for a sophisticated audience. As you read, make a mental
note when you find her confirming what may be your own prejudice.*

I once married a man I thought was totally unlike my father and I
imagined a whole new world of freedom emerging. Five years later it was clear
even to me — floating face down in a wash of despair — that I had simply
chosen a replica of my handsome daddy-true. The updated version spoke
English like an angel but — good God! — underneath he was my father exactly:
wonderful, but not the right man for me.

Most people I know have at one time or another been fouled up by their
childhood experiences. Patterns tend to sink into the unconscious only to
reappear, disguised, unseen, like marionette strings, pulling us this way or that.
Whatever ails people — keeps them up at night, tossing and turning — also ails
movements no matter how historically huge or politically important. The
women's movement cannot remake consciousness, or reshape the future,
without acknowledging and shedding all the unnecessary and ugly baggage of
the past. It's easy enough now to see where men have kept us out of clubs,
baseball games, graduate schools; its easy enough to recognize the hidden
directions that limit Sis to cake-baking and Junior to bridge-building; it's now
possible for even Miss America herself to identify what *they* have done to us,
and, of course, *they* have and *they* did and *they* are. . . . But along the way we
also developed our own hidden prejudices, class assumptions and an anti-male
humor and collection of expectations that gave us, like all oppressed groups, a

secret sense of superiority (co-existing with a poor self-image — it's not news that people can believe two contradictory things at once).

Listen to any group that suffers materially and socially. They have a lexicon with which they tease the enemy: ofay, goy, honky, gringo. "Poor pale devils," said Malcolm X loud enough for us to hear, although blacks had joked about that to each other for years. Behind some of the women's liberation thinking lurk the rumors, the prejudices, the defense systems of generations of oppressed women whispering in the kitchen together, presenting one face to their menfolk and another to their card clubs, their mothers and sisters. All this is natural enough but potentially dangerous in a revolutionary situation in which you hope to create a future that does not mirror the past. The hidden anti-male feelings, a result of the old system, will foul us up if they are allowed to persist.

During my teen years I never left the house on my Saturday night dates without my mother slipping me a few extra dollars — mad money, it was called. I'll explain what it was for the benefit of the new generation in which people just sleep with each other: the fellow was supposed to bring me home, lead me safely through the asphalt jungle, protect me from slithering snakes, rapists and the like. But my mother and I knew young men were apt to drink too much, to slosh down so many rye-and-gingers that some hero might well lead me in front of an oncoming bus, smash his daddy's car into Tiffany's window or, less gallantly, throw up on my new dress. Mad money was for getting home on your own, no matter what form of insanity your date happened to evidence. Mad money was also a wallflower's rope ladder; if the guy you came with suddenly fancied someone else, well, you didn't have to stay there and suffer, you could go home. Boys were fickle and likely to be unkind; my mother and I knew that, as surely as we knew they tried to make you do things in the dark they wouldn't respect you for afterwards, and in fact would spread the word and spoil your rep. Boys liked to be flattered; if you made them feel important they would eat out of your hand. So talk to them about their interests, don't alarm them with displays of intelligence — we all knew that, we groups of girls talking into the wee hours of the night in a kind of easy companionship we thought impossible with boys. Boys were prone to have a good time, get you pregnant, and then pretend they didn't know your name when you came knocking on their door for finances or comfort. In short, we believed boys were less moral than we were. They appeared to be hypocritical, self-seeking, exploitative, untrustworthy and very likely to be showing off their precious masculinity. I never had a girl friend I thought would be unkind or embarrass me in public. I never expected a girl to lie to me about her marks or sports skill or how good she was in bed. Altogether — without anyone's directly coming out and saying so — I gathered that men were sexy, powerful, very

3

4

interesting, but not very nice, not very moral, humane and tender, like us. Girls played fairly while men, unfortunately, reserved their honor for the battlefield.

Why are there laws insisting on alimony and child support? Well, everyone knows that men don't have an instinct to protect their young and, given half a chance, with the moon in the right phase, they will run off and disappear. Everyone assumes a mother will not let her child starve, yet it is necessary to legislate that a father must not do so. We are taught to accept the idea that men are less than decent; their charms may be manifold but their characters are riddled with faults. To this day I never blink if I hear that a man has gone to find his fortune in South America, having left his pregnant wife, his blind mother and taken the family car. I still gasp in horror when I hear of a woman leaving her asthmatic infant for a rock group in Taos because I can't seem to avoid the assumption that men are naturally heels and women the ordained carriers of what little is moral in our dubious civilization.

My mother never gave me mad money thinking I would ditch a fellow for some other guy or that I would pass out drunk on the floor. She knew I would be considerate of my companion because, after all, I was more mature than the boys that gathered about. Why was I more mature? Women just are people-oriented; they learn to be empathetic at an early age. Most English students (students interested in humanity, not artifacts) are women. Men and boys — so the myth goes — conceal their feelings and lose interest in anybody else's. Everyone knows that even little boys can tell the difference between one kind of car and another — proof that their souls are mechanical, their attention directed to the nonhuman.

I remember shivering in the cold vestibule of a famous men's athletic club. Women and girls are not permitted inside the club's door. What are they doing in there, I asked? They're naked, said my mother, they're sweating, jumping up and down a lot, telling each other dirty jokes and bragging about their stock market exploits. Why can't we go in? I asked. Well, my mother told me, they're afraid we'd laugh at them.

The prejudices of childhood are hard to outgrow. I confess that every time my business takes me past that club, I shudder. Images of large bellies resting on massage tables and flaccid penises rising and falling with the Dow Jones average flash through my head. There it is, chauvinism waving its cancerous tentacles from the depths of my psyche.

Minorities automatically feel superior to the oppressor because, after all, they are not hurting anybody. In fact, they feel morally better. The old canard that women need love, men need sex — believed for too long by both sexes — attributes moral and spiritual superiority to women and makes of men beasts whose urges send them prowling into the night. This false division of good and bad, placing deforming pressures on everyone, doesn't have to contaminate the future. We know that the assumptions we make about each other become a part of the cultural air we breathe and, in fact, become social truths. Women who want equality must be prepared to give it and to believe in it, and in order to do that is not enough to state that you are as good as any man, but also it must be stated that he is as good as you and both will be humans together. If we want men to share in the care of the family in a new way, we must assume them as capable of consistent loving tenderness as we.

I rummage about and find in my thinking all kinds of anti-male prejudices.   10
Some are just jokes and others I will have a hard time abandoning. First, I share an emotional conviction with many sisters that women given power would not create wars. Intellectually I know that's ridiculous; great queens have waged war before; the likes of Lurleen Wallace, Pat Nixon and Mrs. General Lavelle can be depended upon in the future to guiltlessly condemn to death other people's children in the name of some ideal of their own. Little girls, of course, don't take toy guns out of their hip pockets and say "Pow, pow" to all their neighbors and friends like the average well-adjusted little boy. However, if we gave little girls the six-shooters, we would soon have double the pretend body count.

Aggression is not, as I secretly think, a male-sex-linked characteristic: 11
brutality is masculine only by virtue of opportunity. True, there are 1,000 Jack the Rippers for every Lizzie Borden, but that surely is the result of social forms. Women as a group are indeed more masochistic than men. The practical result of this division is that women seem nicer and kinder, but when the world changes, women will have a fuller opportunity to be just as rotten as men and there will be fewer claims of female moral superiority.

Now that I am entering early middle age, I hear many women complaining   12
of husbands and ex-husbands who are attracted to younger females. This strikes the older woman as unfair, of course. But I remember a time when I thought all boys around my age and grade were creeps and bores. I wanted to go out with an older man: a senior or, miraculously, a college man. I had a certain contempt for my coevals, not realizing that the freshman in college I thought so desirable, was some older girl's creep. Some women never lose that contempt for men of their own age. That isn't fair either and may be one reason why some sensible men of middle years find solace in young women.

I remember coming home from school one day to find my mother's card   13
game dissolved in hysterical laughter. The cards were floating in black rivers of running mascara. What was so funny? A woman named Helen was lying on a couch pretending to be her husband with a cold. She was issuing demands for orange juice, aspirin, suggesting a call to a specialist, complaining of neglect, of

fate's cruel finger, of heat, of cold, of sharp pains on the bridge of the nose that might indicate brain involvement. What was so funny? The ladies explained to me that all men behave just like that with colds, they are reduced to temper tantrums by simple nasal congestion, men cannot stand any little physical discomfort—on and on the laughter went.

The point of this vignette is the nature of the laughter—us laughing at them, us feeling superior to them, us ridiculing them behind their backs. If they were doing it to us we'd call it male chauvinist pigness; if we do it to them, it is inescapably female chauvinist sowness and, whatever its roots, it leads to the same isolation. Boys are messy, boys are mean, boys are rough, boys are stupid and have sloppy handwriting. A cacophony of childhood memories rushes through my head, balanced, of course, by all the well-documented feelings of inferiority and envy. But the important thing, the hard thing, is to wipe the slate clean, to start again without the meanness of the past. That's why it's so important that the women's movement not become anti-male and allow its most prejudiced spokesmen total leadership. The much-chewed-over abortion issue illustrates this. The women's-liberation position, insisting on a woman's right to determine her own body's destiny, leads in fanatical extreme to a kind of emotional immaculate conception in which the father is not judged even half-responsible—he has no rights, and no consideration is to be given to his concern for either the woman or the fetus.

Woman, who once was abandoned and disgraced by an unwanted pregnancy, has recently arrived at a new pride of ownership or disposal. She has traveled in a straight line that still excludes her sexual partner from an equal share in the wanted or unwanted pregnancy. A better style of life may develop from an assumption that men are as human as we. Why not ask the child's father if he would like to bring up the child? Why not share decisions, when possible, with the male? If we cut them out, assuming an old-style indifference on their part, we perpetrate the ugly divisiveness that has characterized relations between the sexes so far.

Hard as it is for many of us to believe, women are not really superior to men in intelligence or humanity—they are only equal.

QUESTIONS ON CONTENT:

1. Pinpoint Roiphe's thesis. Does she repeat it? Where?
2. What are some of the female prejudices against men?
3. In seeking male participation in family care, what assumptions must women make about men?
4. Why does the author believe that female prejudices against men must be abandoned?

QUESTIONS ON WRITING STRUCTURE AND STRATEGY:

1. How does Roiphe attempt to capture and maintain the reader's interest?

2. What devices does Roiphe employ to maintain coherence?

3. Why has the author chosen this title? In what way does the title reveal the author's tone?

4. Point out Roiphe's use of parallel construction, paradox, analogy, allusion, hyperbole. (See Glossary.) Explain how these elements contribute to the writer's purpose.

QUESTIONS FOR DISCUSSION AND WRITING:

1. If you are familiar with the varying currents in today's women's movement, how would you classify Roiphe's position? Is her position presently dominant?

2. It is said "girls" marry their fathers and "boys" marry their mothers. This observation about the conscious or subconscious tendency of young people to marry a person who evidences characteristics common to their opposite-sex parent proved true but very wrong for her, according to Roiphe's introductory paragraph. Take a long look at your boyfriend/girlfriend or your husband/wife or your fantasy, ideal marriage partner. Then write a paper, in a serious or humorous vein, in which you examine the myth or reality of the statement. Or write a paper in which you discuss the traits of both parents that you desire or wish to avoid in a future mate.

3. Female readers: Examine your own views about men—in school or on the job—and determine to what extent those views are confirmed by what Roiphe writes. Male readers: Write a paper in which you discuss your own prejudices toward women.
OR:
Interview your female friends (or survey a representative sample of females) for their antimale prejudices. Write a paper on your findings.
OR:
Interview your male friends (or survey males) for their antifemale prejudices. Write a paper on your findings.

4. Write a paper in which you discuss any of your ideas that were changed as a result of reading Roiphe's essay.

5. It's a truism, as Roiphe explains, that our early, childhood experiences condition our ideas and behavior in later life. Search your storehouse of memories and write a paper about a saying, a parental admonition, a family conditioning, a school experience, a prejudice, an ingrained attitude that has tended to mold your behavior so far in life. Or choose an experience, an idea, an attitude that has, as Roiphe says, at one time or another "fouled up" your life.

199

SUGGESTIONS FOR JOURNAL ENTRIES

These are essentially suggestions for paragraphs or short journal entries, some of which you could develop further, depending on your interests or directions from your instructor. Perhaps do some prewriting for some part of these entries. It might be helpful to refer to the Glossary, The Writing Process, and the Rhetorical Index.

FOCUS — ORGANIZATION — DEVELOPMENT

1. Compose a paragraph in which you compare or contrast a letter with a phone call, or a letter with a greeting card. You could describe waiting for the mail, the size and shape of the envelope, the handwriting, and so on. You might carry on a conversation with yourself about the choice you have made: phone call, letter, or greeting card.

2. Write a paragraph in which you describe waiting for a very important letter and your elation or disappointment with the result of your wait. Build up suspense.

3. Hoffman, Alda, and Ashe, for example, illustrate a writer's primary concerns about subject, audience, and purpose and the need to tailor one's tone, word choice, focus, and examples for particular readers. On several successive days explain your preference for a certain type of music (classical, rock, soul, or _____) to (1) your parents or grandparents, (2) a classmate or coworker, (3) a fellow musician or devotee, or (4) a son or daughter or younger sibling. Let your audience help determine your tone, definitions, examples, and development.

4. Alan Alda addresses values and priorities in his article. Imagine yourself forced by a move to get rid of many of your "collectibles." If you are a traditional student, what things from high school will you toss out — dance programs, class notes, diaries, textbooks, clothes, or pennants? Which things will you save? Write a page in your journal about the specific things you would relinquish or keep. Then on another page, on another day, describe the less tangible things, such as high school jargon, habits, myths, friendships, or priorities, that you would cast out or save. Older students might consider the things you would save from the early years of marriage, from a former marriage, from your children's younger days, or from your own childhood. Use specific detail in describing your "treasures." Try to make some worthwhile point in your writing (a growing maturity, a reliving of bygone days, a delight in the here and now).

5. Horace Porter found his education changed his attitudes toward himself, his family, and the world. Turn this idea around and describe a time in life when your parents, friends, or siblings looked at you in a different light: perhaps

when you left for college, obtained a job, won an award, made a team, brought a super date to a party, or got dressed up. Make clear their surprise or newly acquired admiration.

6. Just as Porter's attitudes changed with time and knowledge, so, too, do our concepts alter over the years. Using comparison and contrast write a paragraph about an attitude you changed toward
   1. your career
   2. alcohol
   3. divorce
   4. religion
   5. a product
   6. a person

7. After reading Skolnick and Spanier, list the qualities you are looking for in a husband/wife/boyfriend/girlfriend. Compare your specifications with what your parents seem to have looked for/found in each other.

8. Skolnick and Spanier employ classification as one of their methods of development. As practice in classification observe and then classify:
   1. guys "watching the girls go by"
   2. dancers at the local hangout
   3. types of coworkers
   4. shoppers at the local mall
   5. spectators at a sporting event
   6. people in line at the cafeteria
   7. children at play or at the dinner table
   8. people around the Thanksgiving table
   9. types of popular music
   10. types of teachers.

9. After reading Skolnick and Spanier, use specific examples to develop a journal entry about the things that make your family unique or average.

10. Ann Bayer used the symbol of the guardian angel to give unity and dimension to her writing. Try to think of an article, a memento, maybe even a saying that has symbolic meaning for you — perhaps an object or an "in family joke" deriving from your family life or peer relationships. Experiment with a journal entry that you introduce and conclude with some reference to your "symbol."

11. People have been using the term "scofflaws" to refer to people who ignore "laws" — the speed limits, seat belt restrictions, drinking laws. After reading Alan Alda's speech on values, compose the first paragraph of an essay in which you define the term "scofflaws." Then continue with a second paragraph in which you illustrate your definition with examples.

12. Experiment with possible introductory paragraphs for a paper on the plight of

the homeless in our large cities, on the problems of world hunger, on the increasing number of teenage runaways, on the growing numbers of children having children, or on the dilemma presented by illegal immigrants. Attempt to "hook" the reader by using startling statistics (McGowan); a confession (Brody, "Bulimia"); a shocking incident (Blumberg); a popular "myth" (Brody, "Anger"); a line of philosophy (Bayer).

13. For six successive pages of your journal tape in photocopies of introductions and conclusions from your out-of-class reading that seem particularly effective. Paste the photocopy on the right-hand page, and on the left-hand page comment on why you like the ones you have chosen.

14. Using colorful and imaginative language as do Swanson, Will, Hoppock, and virtually every writer in this text, describe items at a garage sale and seek to find some hint in the array of merchandise that tells you about the sellers.

STYLE

15. Alan Alda makes effective use of parallel construction in the conclusion of his commencement address: "If we put . . . if we put . . . if we love. . . ." Imagine you are preparing a paper on procrastination, on dieting, or on a subject of your own choosing. Try building up two possible introductory paragraphs, one humorous and one serious, in which you use a similar repetition of construction to enumerate your resolutions. (Note Lewis Thomas in Unit III concludes with a similar construction.)

16. In suggestion 7 you classified people or things. Often such classifications stir up mental pictures of other groupings or images. To add color and clarity to your writing try making your classifications come alive by using similes and metaphors (see Glossary).

17. Try your hand at using highly unfavorable connotative language (as Paul Blumberg does) in order to express your disapproval of something.

18. Emphasis in writing is achieved through rhetorical as well as mechanical means. Double-check the Glossary for suggestions and write a journal entry about a change you believe is needed in costs of textbooks, increases in tuition, distribution of football tickets, extension of quiet hours, or procedures on the job. Emphasize important words or ideas by using appropriate techniques from the Glossary list. Examples of emphasis are evidenced in all of the readings.

19. George Will's article makes effective use of similes, metaphors, and analogies. Check the explanation of analogy in the Rhetorical Index and compose a paragraph in which you use an analogy based on the similarities between your place of work and . . . ; between a campus cafeteria at lunch time and . . . ; between your dorm room or home at 7 A.M. and . . . ; or between your economics exam and. . . . Remember, the more points of similarity, the more convincing and shrewd your analogy.

20. Fast-food restaurants have had a marked influence not only on America but on the world. Keeping in mind the vital concerns of audience and point of view, compose a journal entry in which you discuss the importance of fast-food chains in terms of (1) the teenage worker, (2) the traveler, (3) the community, (4) the two-career family, (5) the nation's nutritional problems, or in terms of any other issue.

Suggested Writing Topics

1. Alan Alda speaks of the double standard Americans employ in observing values. Without getting moralistic, write a paper in which you single out one particular value Americans profess to believe in but do not faithfully observe.

2. On the basis of what you have read and observed, write a paper in which you argue for or against the continuation of bilingual education. (See especially Rodriguez, and Bettelheim and Zelan.)

3. The rising divorce rate in America does not speak well for our society and its future. Aside from the tragedy to the divorced couple, the tragedy visited upon the children is perhaps even greater. On the basis of what you have read and observed (perhaps supplemented by library research): (a) Write a paper suggesting some ways in which the high divorce rate can be diminished; (b) write a paper discussing the tragedy of divorce from the child's point of view. What are the problems of the children? (c) write a paper explaining a possible positive side to divorce.

4. How are Rodriquez and Porter alike in what they reveal about the educational process they underwent? Has any one of them communicated to you what you consider a valuable insight into yourself?

5. Has any one of the readings in this unit caused you to change your mind about a particular subject or issue? Write a paper in which you describe your belief and explain how it was changed.
   OR:
   Has any one or several of the readings in this unit confirmed you in any one of your beliefs? Write a paper in which you describe your belief and explain how it was confirmed.

6. The Blumberg selection deals with automobiles. For many Americans cars serve as status symbols, outward expressions of some inner psychic need. The inner needs of other Americans may find expression in different material objects or sometimes in patterns of behavior, the desire for thinness that Brody writes about, for example. Consider some of the phenomena you have observed or read about, narrow your subject down, and write an essay in

which you describe and then explain the significance of one such phenomenon.

7. The pace of change in 1980s America is so accelerated that young people are often baffled by the wide range of options open to them. Some muddle through and learn how to cope painfully by trial and error. Others may succumb and fall by the wayside. Several of the writers in this unit deal with some of the specific problems facing young people: youthful marriages, abuses of one's health, work, and interpersonal relationships. Consider what the writers in this unit have to say about some of these problems. Do you feel similarly baffled? Select a single subject suggested by these writers and write a paper.

8. Select a movie, book, short play, or TV program, and show how it reflects at least two values of contemporary society.

9. Write a paper based on any of the following quotations, all taken from Elshtain's "A Feminist's Journey."

   a. "To the extent that you see yourself as nothing but a victim, you will internalize that victimization, come to define yourself under its terms and act just like a victim — you will become the living evidence of your own pathetic view of yourself."

   b. ". . . everyone of us has the choice to make our own destinies."

   c. "Each of us must struggle to attain and maintain an identity."

   d. "Nobody can do it for you. . . . Then go on to live your own life, understanding that it isn't just the vision of life promoted by the 'status quo' you need to question but those promoted by the social rebels and revolutionaries as well."

   e. ". . . we can and must dream our own dreams. . . . these dreams, in the final analysis, must unite us, in peace and fellowship, with other human beings rather than divide us, one from another."

   f. "We were put on this earth to make a difference, to make a contribution, to leave the world a better place than what we had found it."

   g. "What also turns on this issue is one's ideal of politics: is it, finally, to do with *Who gets what when where how*? With power, force, violence, and compulsion? Or does politics have something to do with certain ideals of the common good and of public ends and purposes, of the capacity of human beings to transcend narrow self-interest and think and work for the good of others?"

10. The title of one of Richard Wright's novels is *The Outsider*. American society contains many "outsiders," but American blacks probably constitute the single largest group. Consider the black writers you have read so far — Douglass, Cleaver, Malcolm X, Owens, Wright, Porter, Walker, Angelou, and Ashe as representative American blacks. Discuss how any one or several of

these figures view reading and writing as a means of becoming an "insider." You may jog your thinking by examining what other writers have said about reading and nonreading.

11. Or, think of yourself as an "outsider." As a college student think of your education as your attempt to get further "inside" the culture, the system, the society, the mainstream of American life. Write an essay about reading as the vehicle that will carry you from the "outside" to the "inside." Consider all that is implied by the word *reading*. It means learning to "think," acquiring skills, learning about your American culture and identity, gaining self-knowledge. Use specific examples from this text, from your reading in other classes, and from whatever reading you have done on your own related to the goal of getting "inside."

12. Several of the selections in this unit are process or "how to" papers. Devise clear, well-organized directions on any of the following: "How to Study," "How to Survive Registration," "How to Get Through College Without Even Studying," "How to Get Along with Roommates," "How to Teach a Younger Sibling to Drive," "How to Pick Stereo Equipment," "How to Ask for a Salary Raise," "How to Say No," "How to Get a Promotion," "How to Handle a Job, A Family, and 12 Credit Hours of College."

13. In the light of your experience and what you have read in this text, if you had your life to live over again (that is, your school and work experience), how would you do things differently? Concentrate on reading, writing, and studying habits. Be specific about the changes and the causes for the changes.
OR:
Given the same conditions, how would you change the present elementary or high school curriculum? Be specific and cite your reasons for the changes you would make.

14. In working to improve writing, you, in the final analysis, must be your own "boss," especially on the job when you are without a teacher overseeing your work. If you have not done so already, you individually or the class in a joint effort should attempt to set up criteria for good writing, a list of attributes that can serve as a touchstone before, while, and after you write and edit. In this section and elsewhere in this text you have been given some very concrete ideas about what constitutes effective writing. Organize these suggestions and add to them specifics from your previous English classes or from a rhetoric or handbook, and outline the specific qualities that constitute good writing. Consider organization, style, voice, tone, mechanics, and so on.

15. Friendships are an important part of our personal relationships. Can you categorize friendships — acquaintances, social friends, office or business friends, family friends? With some friends do you discuss trivial subjects; with others do you confide your innermost feelings? Do you have what psychologists call "foul weather" friends — friends who commiserate with you when

you're down and then later become jealous of your successes? Do you have some friends who are more concerned with the color coordination of their clothes than with your problems at home or school? What are the *obligations* of friendship — loyalty, compassion, honesty (if so, how much honesty?), sacrifice, or . . .? Consider some in-depth aspects of friendships and write a paper in which you arrive at a thesis that makes a perceptive statement about types of friendships or the obligations of friendships. Classify friendships or qualities, if you wish, but avoid simply listing. Use challenging descriptions and examples to support your ideas, as do Swanson and Nilsen.

Writing in the World of Work: Reading and Writing Across the Professions

I.

Academic success in college is to a large extent determined by your performance on essay tests and by your ability to write clear, accurate lab reports, research papers, take-home finals, and critiques. (For some of you, writing skills will take on even greater importance as you go on to graduate school and undertake advanced degrees, bar, medical, or MBA exams.) Later, throughout the course of your working and professional life, memos, letters of recommendation, project reports, annual reports, conference reports, proposals for research grants, position papers, speeches, and hundreds of other assignments will further test your writing abilities.

In recent years the amount of writing in business, industry, and government has increased rather than diminished. As a consequence, today, more than ever, the ability to write well is a decided asset in the job market.[1] Not only can it help in

---

[1]Richard D. McCormick, President for Northwestern Bell, reports that the standard employee appraisal form at his company "lists only five categories for evaluation. But one is 'written and oral communication'!" He frankly admits that promotions are often based on the candidate's memos, letters, and general communication skills. Judging from the testimony from hundreds of other executives, it would appear McCormick speaks for the vast number of business leaders throughout the country.

getting a job, but it can also catapult you from the regional office to the executive suite. In fact, the higher up the corporate ladder you go, the more you have to write.

The readings in this section, representing a cross section of literate, professional people writing on a variety of subjects, illustrate the professional as writer. In the first six selections, professionals write about writing; in the remaining selections, professionals write in their special fields for the common reader. As this latter group demonstrates, no matter what your field, you often find yourself writing to a general audience.

These selections should provide convincing evidence that physicians, scientists, engineers, nurses, and sports figures *all* write — and are conscious of the importance of being able to write well. (Various authors, introduced in other sections — Ashe, Alda, Hoppock, Skolnick, Spanier, and all the journalists — had they not been included elsewhere, could serve equally well to exemplify the professional as writer.) These readings, therefore, not only point up the importance of writing skills in the professions but also serve to enlighten and stimulate our thinking about the many issues that daily confront us as citizens.

The first five authors address the subject of writing, pointing out that effective writing derives from *reading, practicing,* and *rewriting.* In stressing that the only way to learn how to write is "above all else to read, to study good models and to practice," Nobel Prize – winner Sir Peter Medawar sums up the precise philosophy advocated in this text. Swift and Galbraith reiterate the need to *reread, rethink,* and *revise* what we write. Through a series of memos,[2] Swift demonstrates that in the process of revising our work we are at the same time shaping, refining, and clarifying our thinking; in effect, we discover what we want to say as we write. Thus writing becomes a learning process, as Swift says, providing "feedback" and a way to discover ourselves. In "Poetry? For Engineers?" Sousa underscores the importance of a strong vocabulary, a fact already discovered by Malcolm X and Jack London. (Actor Tony Randall, who serves on the *American Heritage Dictionary* panel, asserts that the better command you have of words "the better chance you have . . . of getting what you want in the world.") Medawar, Sweetnam, Galbraith, and Swift all emphasize the need for *clarity* and *conciseness,* the former two authors enlivening their own writing with imagery and deft touches of humor.

II

Now, what can these professionals teach us about writing? Each author, of course, exhibits special techniques of composition, development, and style, which the

---

[2]Jack D. Erdlen, executive director of the Employment Management Association, an organization of corporate placement directors, says that today's graduates are much brighter than they used to be in terms of book learning. But, he says, "the trouble comes with written and verbal skills. . . . More managers are complaining about the fact that their younger people don't have the writing skills to compose a memo. In job interviews, they are finding college students have inadequate vocabularies."

questions at the end of each selection will help you to ferret out. Overall, however, several selections in this unit warrant study as excellent examples of writers who have carefully considered the *interrelationships between their subject, their purpose, and their intended audience,* and have tailored their writing accordingly. As experienced writers these authors have obviously analyzed their potential readers and directed their *focus, vocabulary, tone,* and *psychological appeals* to the interests and needs of a particular audience.

In this unit, five authors (six if we include Faulkner) discuss language and writing, yet each writer has a different *purpose*: (a) Medawar to help young scientists write for publication in learned journals; (b) Swift to demonstrate the relationship between clear writing and clear thinking; (c) Sweetnam to help businesspeople communicate more effectively; (d) Galbraith to reminisce about advice for people learning to write; and (e) Sousa to inspire engineers to be more imaginative. (Both Medawar and Galbraith may *also* have sought to entertain and persuade as well as to inform.)

In addition, each of these five selections has been shaped for a different *audience.* Medawar's remarks, for example, about the practices in American scientific writing introduced from Germany would have little application to Swift's office manager. Notice also that Sousa's vocabulary would certainly be inappropriate for Galbraith's readers. The statesmen, Jefferson, Lincoln, and Kennedy, have chosen their words not only to fit a special audience but also to fit a special occasion.

As you study these writings note the attention given to *organization.* Most of these writers support their theses or controlling ideas with paragraphs introduced by topic sentences. (This is not to say that all paragraphs must have a topic sentence; however, topic sentences can provide a framework for organization, making for clear, speedy, reading.)

As Franklin and Hoffer point out in Section I, style is an important element in all good writing. The styles exhibited by several of the authors in this section are worthy of special attention. Notice, for example, Galbraith's *precise* and economical *use of words.* Following Mark Twain's admonition that "the difference between the right adjective and the next best adjective is the difference between lightning and a lightning bug," Galbraith uses one precise word instead of five or ten vague words. Look for the *imagery,* the *figures of speech* (similies, metaphors, analogies) in the Eiseley, Medawar, and Carson pieces, for example. Jefferson's Declaration of Independence is replete with *parallel constructions* that provide *clarity, emphasis,* and *euphony,* for which the document is famous. In the official pronouncements of the three statesmen — Jefferson, Lincoln, and Kennedy — we have superb examples of statemen-writers addressing their fellow citizens with a grace and eloquence that appeals both to our minds and to our hearts.

Notice also that in a unique way each of the selections reveals something of the writer's personality, hints at a human being behind the scene. There's a certain winsome quality, for example, about Eiseley's writing, a warmth and charm reflected in Thomas's celebration of the nursing profession, a refreshing humor in

Medawar's and Galbraith's prose, a genuineness in Jesse Owens' writing. This humanness, this subtle emergence of personality, is exactly what we mean when we urge you to allow a *personal voice* to show through. These professionals seems to know instinctively that impersonal, clinical writing is often just that — cold and uninteresting. They bear witness to the fact that often there can be a touch of the writer's personality in even the most serious writing.

These selections, then, are obviously not technical, scientific treatises. Although the writers in this unit are experts in their fields, they are expressing themselves here as professionals who care: people who write in their field of necessity but also out of a compassionate spirit, out of a commitment to their fellow human beings.

Sir Peter Medawar

Who could possibly be better qualified to offer Advice to a Young Scientist than Sir Peter Medawar, 1960 Nobel Prize winner? In his book, the author addresses such perplexing questions as: "How Can I Tell If I Am Cut Out to Be a Scientific Research Worker?" "How Can I Equip Myself to Be a Scientist or a Better One?" "What Shall I Do Research On?" In his chapter "Presentations," from which the following selection is excerpted, Medawar sets forth specific instructions on how to write a scientific paper for publication in a learned journal. Although you may not be quite ready to submit a manuscript to a scholarly magazine at present, Medawar gives sound, practical advice, applicable to scientific writing in particular and to almost all forms of report writing in general. These suggestions are especially pertinent to your junior and senior years of specialization and later on in graduate work. Medawar's writing is British English laced with a touch of good humor. Not only is his advice corroborated by other scientific writers, but it is also proof positive that a scientist can be warm and humane without being pedantic. He reinforces the idea that all scientists must write, that scientific research is neither complete nor definitive until it has been published. Note especially his advice in paragraph three about how to learn to write, advice upon which his book is predicated.

No number of lectures, seminars or other verbal communications can take the place of a contribution to a learned journal. It is well known, though, that the prospect of writing a paper fills scientists with dismay and brings on a flurry of displacement activities: uselessly uninformative experiments, the building of functionless or unnecessary apparatus, or even, *in extremis*, attendance at committees ("If I don't occasionally attend the security committee, everyone will think that I'm the thief"). The traditional reason given for a scientist's reluctance to write a paper is that it takes time away from research; but the real explanation is that writing a paper — writing anything, indeed, even the begging letters that are necessary if a laboratory is to remain solvent — is something most scientists know they are bad at: it is a skill they have not acquired.   1

Scientists are supposed to have an intuitive ability to write papers because they have consulted so many, just as young teachers are supposed to be able to give lectures because they have so often listened to them.   2

I feel disloyal but dauntlessly truthful in saying that most scientists do *not* know how to write, for insofar as style does betray *l'homme même*, they write as if they hated writing and wanted above all else to have done with it. The only way to learn how to write is above all else to read, to study good models,   3 and to practice. I do not mean to practice in the sense in which young pianists practice "The Merry Peasant," but practice by writing whenever writing is called for, instead of making excuses for not doing so, and writing, if necessary, over and over again, until clarity has been achieved and the style, if not graceful, is at least not raw and angular. A good writer never makes one feel as if one were wading through mud or picking one's way with bare feet through broken glass. Further, writing should be as far as possible natural — that is, not worn like a Sunday suit and not too far removed from ordinary speech, but rather as if one were addressing one's departmental chairman or other high-up who was asking about one's progress.

No number of "don'ts" will make a "do," but certain practices should certainly be shunned. One such was introduced into American English from Germany — that of using nouns attributively (as if they were adjectives), sometimes stringing them all together to make one huge nounlike monster in constant danger of falling apart. A skillful linguist but habitual liar once told me of a single word in German standing for "the window of the man who issued tickets at reduced prices for admission on Sundays to the zoo." This is untrue, of course, but it illustrates the principle, and if I myself have not read about "vegetable oil polyunsaturated fatty acid guinea pig skin delayed type hypersensitivity reaction properties," I have read some equally daunting nounal phrases. An incentive to write like this is that most editors restrict the length of a paper, so that a scientist who makes one word do the work of ten may feel he is one up on the editor.

Another little rule (for medical scientists especially) is that mice, rats, and other laboratory animals should never be injected. Few hypodermic needles are large enough for even the smallest mouse to pass through, especially if it is injected with something. ("Mice were injected with rabbit serum albumin mixed with Freund's adjuvant," we read. "Ah, but what into?" the cry goes up.) Mice should receive injections, or substances should be injected into them. Preciosity? Considered in isolation, yes, but it is the accumulation of such errors of taste that disfigures what could otherwise be a straightforward and readable paper. Avoid, too, such weary tropes as "the role of (or the part played by) adrenocortical hormones in immunity." Why not write instead "the contribution of adrenal cortical hormones to . . ." and so on. Give thought to prepositions, too: the regulation of electrolytes in the body is mediated not *by* but *through* the adrenal gland. Again, we are (or are not) tolerant *of*, not tolerant *to*, errors of literary judgment, and so on.

Another thought to bear in mind is that good writing upon a subject is almost always shorter than bad writing on the same subject. It is often much more memorable, too. Who but Winston Churchill could have said so much in so few words as my Lord Bacon's comment on an ambitious political rival: "He doth like the ape, that the higher he clymbes the more he shows his ars [*sic*]."

But if a young scientist is to study models, which are they to be? Any 7
technically skillful writer will do, especially if it is a writer the reader admires
and would like to read anyway. Fiction and other nonexpository writing will
do very well; Bernard Shaw wrote a very good sentence, and some of
Congreve's writing is miraculously skillful, but I especially recommend the
writing of those who are expounding difficult subjects and are determined to
make themselves understood. Although not all philosophers satisfy this
requirement, they are in the main an excellent choice, particularly, I believe,
those who have been professors of philosophy in University College London;
A. J. Ayer, Stuart Hampshire, Bernard Williams, and Richard Wollheim are
among them. Essayists are often good models; Bacon's essays are superlative,
and some of Bertrand Russell's essays (for example, his *Sceptical Essays*) are
brilliantly well written. So are many of J. B. S. Haldane's, now mostly out of
print. Gravity, wit and a strong understanding have never been more effectively
combined than in Dr. Johnson's *Lives of the Poets*.

In the English-speaking world (people think differently about these things 8
in France), scientific and philosophic writing is never now allowed to be an
exercise in the high rhetoric style. . . .

In writing a paper, a young scientist should make up his mind about 9
whom he is addressing. The easy way out is to address one's professional
colleagues only — and of them, only those who work in a field cognate with
one's own. This is not at all the way to go about it. A scientist should reflect
that his more intelligent peers probably browse in the literature for intellectual
recreation and might like to find out what he is up to. The time will come,
moreover, when a young scientist will be judged upon his written work by
referees and adjudicators. They are entitled to feel annoyed — and often
do — when they can't make out what the paper is about or why the author
undertook the investigation, anyway. A formal paper should therefore begin
with a paragraph of explanation that describes the problem under investigation
and the main lines of the way the author feels he has been able to contribute to
its solution.

Great pains should be taken over the paper's summary, which should 10
make use of the whole of the journal's ration of space (one-fifth or one-sixth of
the length of the text, as the case may be), and its composition is the severest
test of an author's literary skill, particularly in days when "précis writing" has
been dropped from the syllabus in most schools for fear of stifling the scholars'
creative afflatus. The writing of a summary tests the author's powers of
apprehension and sense of proportion — the feeling for what is really important
and what can be left out. A summary must be complete in its own limits. It
may well start with a statement of the hypothesis under investigation and end

with its evaluation. Nothing is more abjectly feeble than to write some such sentence as "The relevance of these findings to the etiology of Bright's disease is discussed." If it *has* been discussed, the discussion should be summarized, too. If not, say nothing. The preparation of abstracts is a public service a young scientist should sometimes volunteer to do. Even if his work is overseen by an experienced editor before it goes to press, abstracting can be good practice in writing.

The number of references cited in the literature list (be always scrupulously careful to observe the house style) should be that which is sufficient and necessary; it may be a symptom of scientmanship to quote references from journals published so long ago that librarians desperate for space have long since had them stashed away in the galleries of disused mines. Due homage and justice to one's predecessors are criteria to keep in mind, although some names are so great and some ideas so familiar that omission is homage greater than citation. Nice judgment is needed, though; one man's compliment may be another's source of grievance. 11

Papers embodying good work may be rejected by an editor for a variety of reasons. Publishers of scientific journals like it to be known that they are being beggared by the prolixity of their contributors, and a length disproportionate to content is indeed the most common cause of rejection. Another is citation in the literature list of papers not referred to in the text or vice versa. In such a case, rejection is condign. Whatever the reason given for it, rejection of a paper is always damaging to the pride, but it is usually better to try to find another home for it than to wrangle with referees. There are times when referees are inimical for personal reasons and enjoy causing the discomfiture that rejection brings with it; too strenuous an attempt to convince an editor that this is so may, however, convince him only that the author has paranoid tendencies. 12

Of the internal structure of a paper I have said only that one should have a first explanatory paragraph describing in effect the problem that is preying on the author's mind. The layout of the text that has come to be regarded as conventional is that which perpetuates the illusion that scientific research is conducted by the inductive process. In this conventional style, a section called "Methods" describes in sometimes needless detail the technical procedures and reagents the author has used in his research. Sometimes a separate section headed "Previous Work" may concede that others have dimly groped their way toward the truths the author is now proposing to expound. Worst of all, a paper in the conventional layout may contain a section called "Results" — a voluble pouring forth of factual information, usually with no connecting narrative to explain why one observation is made or one experiment done rather than another. Then follows a passage called "Discussion" in which the author plays out the little charade that he is now going to collect and sort out all 13

214

the information he has gathered by wholly objective observation with the purpose of finding out what, if anything, it means. This is the reductio ad absurdum of inductivism — a faithful embodiment of the belief that scientific inquiry is a compilation of facts by the contemplation or logical manipulation of which an enlargement of the understanding must inevitably follow. This division of "Results" from "Discussion" may be thought to have its parallel in the praiseworthy editorial policy of those reputable newspapers which divide news from editorial comment upon it, but the two cases are in no way parallel; the reasoning that is called "Discussion" in a scientific paper is in real life integral with the process of securing information and having the incentive to do so. The separation of "Results" from "Discussion" is a quite arbitrary subdivision of what is in effect a single process of thought. Nothing of the kind applies to the dissociation of news of events or legislative action from editorial comment upon them, for these two can vary independently.

A scientist who completes writing — or, as people unaccountably say, "writing up" a paper (by which, of course, they mean "writing down") — should feel proud of it, should feel, indeed, "this will make people sit up." It shows either a poor spirit or perhaps good judgment if no such thought enters the author's head.   14

When I was director of the National Institute for Medical Research, a young colleague of mine completed a brief letter to *Nature* — the traditional vehicle of important scientific news — that was so important, he felt, and so eagerly awaited by the world that it should not be entrusted to the post but must be delivered by hand. So it was. But then, unfortunately, it was lost and had to be resubmitted. This time, it went by post. We all felt that on the previous occasion it had been pushed under the door and therefore probably ended up under the welcome mat. *Moral:* use the recognized channels of communication.   15

QUESTIONS ON CONTENT:

1. What recommendations does Medawar make to the young scientist about learning how to write good scientific papers? What are some typical models of good writing he recommends?
2. What recommendations does Medawar make about assessing one's audience?
3. What should characterize a scientific paper's introduction and conclusion?
4. What advice does Medawar give about documentation?

QUESTIONS ON WRITING STRUCTURE AND STRATEGY:

1. What elements in Medawar's writing contribute to its distinctive tone and style? Notice especially his figures of speech.

2. Examine Medawar's paragraphs. Some begin with a topic sentence and some with a rhetorical question. What is the effect of each?

3. Analyze Medawar's vocabulary in relationship to his possible audience.

QUESTIONS FOR DISCUSSION AND WRITING:

1. Compare Medawar's remarks about writing scientific papers with some other writers in the text who address the subject of writing (Galbraith and Swift). How are they alike? Does your comparison reveal that there are some universal rules applicable to all good writing?

2. Find a short scientific article, or a passage from a scientific or sociological textbook, and subject it to the criteria Medawar presents here. Write a paper or journal entry on your analysis.

3. As a switch, take a short scientific article and rewrite it in Medawar's style to make it more accessible to the common reader. Insofar as possible, try to emulate Medawar's charm, humor, grace. Spend some time on revision to capture at least some of the essence of his style.

CLEAR WRITING MEANS
CLEAR THINKING MEANS . . .
Marvin H. Swift

*Though Professor Swift is not a business executive but a teacher whose
specialty is teaching business executives, his reconstruction of a
writing task facing a business executive is typical of such problems.
Swift clearly illustrates two very important aspects of writing
applicable to all who wish to write well: (a) the necessity of narrowing
down the subject to its essentials, eliminating all irrelevancies and
redundancies, and (b) the necessity of refining thinking through
writing, revision, and rewriting. Describing his own process, Swift
takes the reader through the various stages of preparing a typical
memo, analyzing as he moves from stage to stage. In the process the
business executive gradually eliminates unnecessary words, substitutes
more appropriate words, modifies the tone, and in the end discovers
for the first time what he actually wants to say. The writing and
rewriting, in other words, have stimulated the writer to think and
gradually, in the process, to uncover his true intention. Note Swift's
clarity and directness of approach, but most of all, carefully observe his
analysis of the process of writing, revising, rewriting. Something of the
same process can be observed in Jeffrey Potter's "Finals Are Not the
Finale" (see the Writing Process).*

If you are a manager, you constantly face the problem of putting words on 1
paper. If you are like most managers, this is not the sort of problem you enjoy.
It is hard to do, and time consuming; and the task is doubly difficult when, as
is usually the case, your words must be designed to change the behavior of
others in the organization.

But the chore is there and must be done. How? Let's take a specific case. 2

Let's suppose that everyone at X Corporation, from the janitor on up to 3
the chairman of the board, is using the office copiers for personal matters;
income tax forms, church programs, children's term papers, and God knows
what else are being duplicated by the gross. This minor piracy costs the
company a pretty penny, both directly and in employee time, and the general
manager—let's call him Sam Edwards—decides the time has come to lower
the boom.

Sam lets fly by dictating the following memo to his secretary: 4

TO: All Employees
FROM: Samuel Edwards, General Manager
SUBJECT: Abuse of Copiers

It has recently been brought to my attention that many of the people who are employed
by this company have taken advantage of their positions by availing themselves of the

copiers. More specifically, these machines are being used for other than company business.

Obviously, such practice is contrary to company policy and must cease and desist immediately. I wish therefore to inform all concerned — those who have abused policy or will be abusing it — that their behavior cannot and will not be tolerated. Accordingly, anyone in the future who is unable to control himself will have his employment terminated.

If there are any questions about company policy, please feel free to contact this office.

Now the memo is on his desk for his signature. He looks it over; and the more he looks, the worse it reads. In fact, it's lousy. So he revises it three times, until it finally is in the form that follows:

TO: All Employees
FROM: Samuel Edwards, General Manager
SUBJECT: Use of Copiers

We are revamping our policy on the use of copiers for personal matters. In the past we have not encouraged personnel to use them for such purposes because of the costs involved. But we also recognize, perhaps belatedly, that we can solve the problem if each of us pays for what he takes.

We are therefore putting these copiers on a pay-as-you-go basis. The details are simple enough . . . .

Samuel Edwards

This time Sam thinks the memo looks good, and it *is* good. Not only is the writing much improved, but the problem should now be solved. He therefore signs the memo, turns it over to his secretary for distribution, and goes back to other things.

From Verbiage to Intent

I can only speculate on what occurs in a writer's mind as he moves from a poor   5
draft to a good revision, but it is clear that Sam went through several specific
steps, mentally as well as physically, before he had created his end product:

- He eliminated wordiness.
- He modulated the tone of the memo.
- He revised the policy it stated.

218

Let's retrace his thinking through each of these processes.

Eliminating Wordiness

Sam's basic message is that employees are not to use the copiers for their own 6
affairs at company expense. As he looks over his first draft, however, it seems
so long that this simple message has become diffused. With the idea of
trimming the memo down, he takes another look at his first paragraph:

It has recently been brought to my attention that many of the people who are employed
by this company have taken advantage of their positions by availing themselves of the
copiers. More specifically, these machines are being used for other than company business.

He edits it like this:

> *Item:* "recently"
> *Comment to himself*: Of course; else why write about the problem? So delete
>   the word.
> *Item:* "It has been brought to my attention"
> *Comment:* Naturally. Delete it.
> *Item:* "the people who are employed by this company"
> *Comment:* Assumed. Why not just "employees"?
> *Item:* "by availing themselves" and "for other than company business"
> *Comment:* Since the second sentence repeats the first, why not coalesce?

And he comes up with this:

Employees have been using the copiers for personal matters.

He proceeds to the second paragraph. More confident of himself, he moves in
broader swoops, so that the deletion process looks like this:

Obviously, such practice is contrary to company policy and ~~must cease and desist
immediately. I wish therefore to inform all concerned—those who have abused policy or
will be abusing it—that their behavior cannot and will not be tolerated. Accordingly,
anyone in the future who is unable to control himself will have his employment terminated.~~
will result in dismissal.

219

The final paragraph, apart from "company policy" and "feel free," looks all right, so the total memo now reads as follows:

TO: All Employees
FROM: Samuel Edwards, General Manager
SUBJECT: Abuse of Copiers

Employees have been using the copiers for personal matters. Obviously, such practice is contrary to company policy and will result in dismissal.

If there are any questions, please contact this office.

Sam now examines his efforts by putting these questions to himself:

Question: Is the memo free of deadwood?
Answer: Very much so. In fact, it's good, tight prose.
Question: Is the policy stated?
Answer: Yes — sharp and clear.
Question: Will the memo achieve its intended purpose?
Answer: Yes. But it sounds foolish.
Question: Why?
Answer: The wording is too harsh; I'm not going to fire anybody over this.
Question: How should I tone the thing down?

To answer this last question, Sam takes another look at the memo.

Correcting the Tone

What strikes his eye as he looks it over? Perhaps these three words:

- Abuse . . .
- Obviously . . .
- . . . dismissal . . .

The first one is easy enough to correct: he substitutes "use" for "abuse." But "obviously" poses a problem and calls for reflection. If the policy is obvious, why are the copiers being used? Is it that people are outrightly dishonest? Probably not. But that implies the policy isn't obvious; and whose fault is this? Who neglected to clarify policy? And why "dismissal" for something never publicized?

These questions impel him to revise the memo once again: 8

TO: All Employees
FROM: Samuel Edwards, General Manager
SUBJECT: Use of Copiers

Copiers are not to be used for personal matters. If there are any questions, please contact this office.

Revising the Policy Itself

The memo now seems courteous enough — at least it is not discourteous — but 9
it is just a blank, perhaps overly simple, statement of policy. Has he really
thought through the policy itself?

Reflecting on this, Sam realizes that some people will continue to use the 10
copiers for personal business anyhow. If he seriously intends to enforce the
basic policy (first sentence), he will have to police the equipment, and that
raises the question of costs all over again.

Also, the memo states that he will maintain an open-door policy (second 11
sentence) — and surely there will be some, probably a good many, who will
stroll in and offer to pay for what they use. His secretary has enough to do
without keeping track of affairs of that kind.

Finally, the first and second sentences are at odds with each other. The 12
first says that personal copying is out, and the second implies that it can be
arranged.

The facts of organizational life thus force Sam to clarify in his own mind 13
exactly what his position on the use of copiers is going to be. As he sees the
problem now, what he really wants to do is put the copiers on a pay-as-you-go
basis. After making that decision, he begins anew:

TO: All Employees
FROM: Samuel Edwards, General Manager
SUBJECT: Use of copiers

We are revamping our policy on the use of copiers. . . . .

This is the draft that goes into distribution and now allows him to turn his
attention to other problems.

The Chicken or the Egg?

What are we to make of all this? It seems a rather lengthy and tedious report of   14
what, after all, is a routine writing task created by a problem of minor
importance. In making this kind of analysis, have I simply labored the obvious?

To answer this question, let's drop back to the original draft. If you read it   15
over, you will see that Sam began with this kind of thinking:

- "The employees are taking advantage of the company."
- "I'm a nice guy, but now I'm going to play Dutch uncle."
- ∴ "I'll write them a memo that tells them to shape up or ship out."

In his final version, however, his thinking is quite different:

- "Actually, the employees are pretty mature, responsible people. They're capable of understanding a problem."
- "Company policy itself has never been crystallized. In fact, this is the first memo on the subject."
- "I don't want to overdo this thing—any employee can make an error in judgment."
- ∴ "I'll set a reasonable policy and write a memo that explains how it ought to operate."

Sam obviously gained a lot of ground between the first draft and the final   16
version, and this implies two things. First, if a manager is to write effectively,
he needs to isolate and define, as fully as possible, all the critical variables in
the writing process and scrutinize what he writes for its clarity, simplicity,
tone, and the rest. Second, after he has clarified his thoughts on paper, he may
find that what he has written is not what has to be said. In this sense, writing
is feedback and a way for the manager to discover himself. What are his real
attitudes toward that amorphous, undifferentiated gray mass of employees "out
there"? Writing is a way of finding out. By objectifying his thoughts in the
medium of language, he gets a chance to see what is going on in his mind.

In other words, *if the manager writes well, he will think well.* Equally, the   17
more clearly he has thought out his message before he starts to dictate, the
more likely he is to get it right on paper the first time round. In other words, *if
he thinks well, he will write well.*

Hence we have a chicken-and-the-egg situation: writing and thinking go   18
hand in hand; and when one is good, the other is likely to be good.

Revision Sharpens Thinking

More particularly, rewriting is the key to improved thinking. It demands a real   19
openmindedness and objectivity. It demands a willingness to cull verbiage so
that ideas stand out clearly. And it demands a willingness to meet logical
contradictions head on and trace them to the premises that have created them.
In short, it forces a writer to get up his courage and expose his thinking
process to his own intelligence.

   Obviously, revising is hard work. It demands that you put yourself   20
through the wringer, intellectually and emotionally, to squeeze out the best you
can offer. Is it worth the effort? Yes, it is—if you believe you have a
responsibility to think and communicate effectively.

QUESTIONS ON CONTENT:

1. What does the author mean when he says that the writing problem presented
    at the beginning of the essay is "doubly difficult"?
2. In what specific ways is the final memo different from the original in tone,
    wordiness, and consequences?
3. What does Swift have to say about writing and thinking?
4. What are Swift's two important injunctions to manager-writers?

QUESTIONS ON WRITING STRUCTURE AND STRATEGY:

1. For what audience is Swift writing? Is his language appropriate for his audi-
    ence? Defend your answer.
2. In his development, has Swift skipped any important steps or included any
    unnecessary ones, failed to define any important terms?
3. In his process technique, why is Swift's reproduction of the memo writer's
    thinking effective?
4. How does the personal voice of the writer come through in this analysis? Are
    you more likely to believe the writer because of it? Explain.

QUESTIONS FOR WRITING AND DISCUSSION:

1. Consider the author's title and what it means. Write a journal entry in which
    you explore the idea that writing, rewriting, revising, and editing *clarify
    thinking*, help you to discover what you in fact *do* think.
2. Imagine yourself an administrator and set yourself a problem in memo writing
    to bring about a change in behavior. Consider such problems as food waste in
    the cafeteria, excessive noise in the dorms, vandalism. Try several drafts to

clarify your thinking. Ask yourself the kinds of questions Swift imagines his executive must have asked himself.

OR:

Imagine that you are the manager of a fast-food operation. Address a memo to your employees about a problem, real or imagined: punctuality, cleanliness, esprit de corps, courtesy, or pilferage.

3.   Write a letter of complaint in which you seek replacement of, or a refund for, a defective product. As you revise your letter, consider tone, possible wordiness, clarity. Because you want satisfaction, consider your psychological approach. Are you merely venting your anger? Do the rewriting and revising reveal to you what you really want?

HOW TO ORGANIZE YOUR THOUGHTS
FOR BETTER COMMUNICATION
Sherry Sweetnam

*Sherry Sweetnam, president of Sweetnam Communications, is a
communications consultant for many Fortune 500 companies. She
conducts "communications and persuasion workshops," specializing
in written communications skills. Under the Fulbright-Hays
Commission she has conducted international workshops and trained
personnel in Asia. Her book,* The Executive Memo: A Guide to
Persuasive Business Communications, *was published in 1986. In the
following article, appearing in* Personnel *(1986), Sweetnam explains
the principle of frontloading, emphasizing reader-oriented
communication. Note the various devices Sweetnam uses to attract and
hold the reader's attention. Some of these include an inviting title,
short paragraphs, italics and subheads. What else?*

Do you want to analyze the way you communicate and the way you think   1
and organize your thoughts? Study your writing. It will tell you whether you
are reader-sensitive or whether you are communicating strictly from your own
point of view.

This example shows communication strictly from the writer's point of view: 2

The Personnel Department
is pleased to announce that
MARY R. NAKOVEY
formerly special assistant to the director
executive director of human resources
and associate executive director
Department of Manpower Planning
has joined the firm
as manager of personnel.

What's the problem with this business announcement? *It wastes time.* The   3
big news is the new personnel manager; so why not say it up front? Instead,
the writer forces you to wade through 30 words to get to the main point.
Stalling the main point causes frustration, annoyance, and tension in the reader
and creates negative feelings toward the writer and the information.

Many of us fail to get to the point when we communicate — both orally   4
and in writing. There are logical explanations as to why we organize our
thoughts like this. They are:

1. *We're trying to impress.* Often, we're so concerned about building our credibil-

225

ity and establishing our importance that we show off when we write. But showing off turns most people off. Readers don't care how great a person, department, or unit is. The readers' business concerns are: What's new? How is this going to affect me?

2. *We're trying to figure out what we think.* Writing helps us clarify thought. It is an excellent tool for moving through the thinking process itself. However, writers need to edit their work so that their key information is not buried in the maze of the process itself.

3. *We're not clear about what is important to our readers.* In writing sheerly from our own point of view, we lose sight of the reader's concerns and interests. It's fine to write this way in the initial drafts, but the final draft should be reshaped with the reader's interests in mind.

4. *We tend to organize information chronologically rather than psychologically.* Most of us are natural storytellers. ("Guess what happened on the subway today!" "Let me tell you what happened in yesterday's marketing meeting.") As storytellers, we naturally slip into a system of ordering information chronologically. There's nothing wrong with using the story format in the appropriate environment. The "right" organization to use always depends on who is reading the report and what their needs are.

5. *We were trained to write that way in school.* We learned to put the summary, conclusion, the last word, the bottom line, at the end of our school compositions and reports. We memorized and religiously followed the academic formula: (1) introduction, (2) body, (3) conclusion. And we continue to use it.

There's nothing wrong with organizing our communications that way *if*   5
we have a captive audience, *if* we are so interesting no one can put our writing
down, and *if* people have a lot of time. But that is rarely true in business. Most
people are very busy with their own agendas and don't have time to wade
through a lot of words to get to the point. When we bury our key points we
lose credibility because we are not being sensitive to our reader's interests and
time constraints.

Positioning Your Thoughts

Effective business communication organizes thought in the opposite way. The   6
rule is to get to your point up front; then give the background and details. That
is why executive summaries are so popular. After getting the nuggets up front,
the reader can decide whether he or she wants to continue reading.

    The most critical ideas should be in the most powerful of the three   7
positions on the page — the beginning, middle, or end.

    The beginning. The most powerful position is the first 50 words of a memo,   8

226

letter, report, or proposal. Since the opening paragraph is key, that's where you want to load your most important ideas.

The middle. This is no-man's land — the weakest position on a page. It may or may not get read, depending on whether you've been able to hold your reader's interest up front.

The end. This is the second strongest position (assuming the reader gets to it). Why? Because it is the last thing that the reader will read. Therefore, it has greater impact than what was in no-man's land.

How to Frontload Writing

Frontloading means placing your key idea first. To do this, first go through your writing with a pencil and underline the key ideas in sentences and paragraphs. Then rearrange those key phrases and ideas so that they appear at the beginning of the memo, paragraph, or sentence.

Consider, for example, the difference in impact between these titles:

Subject: Statistical Data Due Dates

vs.

Subject: Due Dates for Statistical Data

The phrase *statistical data* is not the critical information in the title. It doesn't hook the reader because it doesn't answer such critical questions as: What do I have to do? Why is it important that I read this? The phrase *due date* is urgent; therefore, it needs to be frontloaded.

Frontloading Letters

Here is an example of how writers backload key information in a letter. The key information is italicized and appears at the end of the letter.

Due to a processing error, your June payroll deduction, credited to your account on January 24, 1986, was inadvertently priced at $33.15145. The correct price for this transaction should have been $36.4214. *We have corrected this problem and adjusted your account accordingly.*

The last sentence should be repositioned so that it becomes the first

227

sentence. The result could possibly read, "We have adjusted your account because we made an error in our calculations."

Why does this work? Because it is written from the reader's point of view. When it comes to problems and solutions, what most readers and customers want to know is: Have you solved the problem? If the news is good, then don't bury it! As a rule, give your reader the good news first instead of striking a negative note at the outset.

Frontloading Action Requests

The following is an example of a request for action. Notice that the request is buried in the second paragraph:

> *Steve, I have been searching the lower Minneapolis area for over three months for qualified candidates with a strong knowledge of AVS to support the chemical data system. I have been unsuccessful. As a result, the project is in jeopardy.*
>
> *Therefore, I am requesting your support to obtain the necessary approvals required to begin reviewing candidates from outside the lower Minneapolis area.*

By repositioning the request at the beginning of the piece, it would become a far more powerful communication.

Why don't we state requests up front? Because we don't want to appear too bold or too aggressive. In fact, however, stating your request up front is considered by many to be direct, forthright, and nonmanipulative. It is also good business because it gets to the point quickly. Again, there's no waste of time.

Frontloading to Persuade

Writing to persuade someone about an idea, service, or product is trickier than writing to inform or request action. You must decide how interested your reader is in what you're trying to persuade him of. If your reader is interested, then state your idea up front. For example, you might start out by writing: "I recommend that we buy XYZ computer."

However, if your reader isn't so interested, backload your recommendation and frontload the benefits of your idea or product so the reader will be sold.

Tough Messages: The Three Exceptions to Frontloading

There are three situations in which frontloading your key idea doesn't work: 21

1. *When you have to say "no."* When you have to tell someone "no," it makes much more sense to begin with a positive tone or a kiss. Then you can ease into the bad news or the kick in the second paragraph. In this way, the *no* isn't such a blow.
2. *When your reader is not interested in buying your new idea, service, or product.* When you have to convince someone of your ideas, then it makes sense to frontload the benefits and advantages and conclude with your recommendations.
3. *When you know your reader doesn't want to comply with your request.* The best thing to do in this instance is to ease into your request or suggestions.

Why Rethink?

One of the best ways to achieve force and interest in your writing is to frontload 22
ideas. This means frontloading in all your writing—your titles; all types of memos, letters and reports; and at the sentence and paragraph level.
Frontloading will grab your reader's interest and get your memos read. The inner voice of your reader will be saying, "Here's a writer who knows what's important and doesn't waste my time."

A fringe benefit of reorganizing your written communications is that you 23
will find yourself getting to the point more often when you're speaking to people. Frontloading is a mental exercise that trains you to get to the point in all of your communications.

QUESTIONS ON CONTENT:

1. What is the psychology behind Sweetnam's instructions to frontload important information?
2. What is the psychology behind Sweetnam's three exceptions to frontloading?
3. What does Sweetnam mean by saying some business writers are not reader-sensitive? What causes them to be insensitive to their readers?
4. What decisions must you make about your audience before you backload or frontload your communication?

QUESTIONS ON WRITING STRUCTURE AND STRATEGY:

1. Is Sweetnam's title a good one or a bad one? Explain.
2. In what ways does Sweetnam seek to engage the reader's interest?

3. Single out Sweetnam's use of parallelism. For what purposes does she use it?

4. Sweetnam practices what she preaches by making her writing direct and to the point. What factors contribute to her directness?

QUESTIONS FOR DISCUSSION AND WRITING:

1. Writing memos seems simple enough; however, they are usually read quickly and easily misinterpreted. With Sweetnam's suggestions in mind, write a memo to a roommate, a colleague at work, your family, or committee members about observing quiet hours, assuming a specific job responsibility, giving advance notice for typing requests, and so on.

2. Short memos ad magazine and newspaper advertisements are alike in that both are designed to affect human behavior. Select a number of magazine advertisements and determine if the copywriter has "frontloaded" the copy. Write a paper on your analysis.

3. If you have ever received advertising and/or sales letters in the mail, examine one or several to see how the writer has pitched the message. Has the writer frontloaded the copy or adopted some other strategy? Analyze the letter for its relative effectiveness.

WRITING, TYPING & ECONOMIC$
John Kenneth Galbraith

Although he is noted as an economist, John Kenneth Galbraith has worn many hats over the years as educator, author, political adviser, ambassador, TV script writer, philosopher, administrator. A professor at Harvard University for many years, Galbraith has written over twenty books, including the international best-seller The Affluent Society, *and in the 1950s and early 1960s served as political adviser and speech writer for Adlai E. Stevenson and John F. Kennedy. Following Kennedy's inauguration as President in 1961 (Galbraith, incidentally, wrote the first draft of his address), he was appointed Ambassador to India, where he continued his writing in addition to his diplomatic duties. Some of his recent work includes the TV series "The Age of Uncertainty" for the BBC. Now retired, Galbraith still devotes his mornings to writing.*

In this selection, typical of most of his work, Galbraith weaves wit (and sarcasm) with shrewd insights to enliven what sometimes might seem dull and complex. Examine his sentences closely to see just how he goes about achieving this "light touch" with serious subjects. Study his epigrammatical style, his use of understatement, precise word choice, contrast, varying sentence lengths, anecdotes, and allusions. Galbraith clearly demonstrates how serious subjects can be made much more palatable and even understandable when given a touch of humor.

Six or seven years ago, when I was spending a couple of terms at Trinity   1
College, Cambridge, I received a proposal of more than usual interest from the University of California. It was that I resign from Harvard and accept a chair there in English. More precisely, it was to be a chair in rhetoric; they assured me that rhetoric was a traditional and not, as one would naturally suppose, a pejorative title. My task would be to hold seminars with the young on what I had learned about writing in general and on technical matters in particular.

I was attracted by the idea. I had spent several decades attempting to   2
teach the young about economics. And the practical consequences were not reassuring. When I entered the field in the early 1930s, it was generally known that the modern economy could suffer a serious depression, and that it could have a serious inflation. In the ensuing forty years my teaching had principally advanced to the point of telling that it was possible to have both at once. This was soon to be associated with the belief of William Simon and Alan Greenspan, the gifts of Richard Nixon and Gerald Ford to our science, that progress in this subject is measured by the speed of the return to the ideas of the eighteenth century. A subject where it can be believed that you go ahead by

going back has many problems for a teacher. Things are better now. Mr. Carter's economists do not believe in going back. But they are caught in a delicate balance between their fear of inflation and unemployment and their fear of doing anything about them. It is hard to conclude that economics is a productive intellectual and pedagogical investment.

Then I began to consider what I could tell about writing. My experience   3
was certainly ample. I had been initiated by two inspired professors in Canada, O. J. Stevenson and E. C. McLean. They were men who deeply loved their craft and who were willing to spend endless hours with a student, however obscure his talent. I had been an editor of *Fortune*, which in my day meant mostly being a writer. Editor was thought a more distinguished title and justified more pay. Both as an editor proper and as a writer, I had had the close attention of Henry Robinson Luce. Harry Luce is in danger of being remembered for his political judgments, which left much to be desired; he found unblemished merit in John Foster Dulles, Robert A. Taft, and Chiang Kai-shek. But more important, he was an acute businessman and a truly brilliant editor. One proof is that while Time, Inc., publications have become politically more predictable since he departed, they have become infinitely less amusing.

Finally, as I reflected, among my qualifications was the amount of my life   4
that I have spent at a typewriter. Nominally I have been a teacher. In practice I have been a writer — as generations of Harvard students have suspected. Faced with the choice of spending time on the unpublished scholarship of a graduate student or the unpublished work of Galbraith, I have rarely hesitated. Superficially, at least, I was well qualified for that California chair.

There was, however, a major difficulty. It was that I could tell everything I   5
knew about writing in approximately half an hour. For the rest of the term I would have nothing to say except as I could invite discussion, this being the last resort of the empty academic mind. I could use up a few hours telling how a writer should deal with publishers. This is a field of study in which I especially rejoice. All authors should seek to establish a relationship of warmth, affection, and mutual mistrust with their publishers. This is in the hope that the uncertainty will add, however marginally, to compensation. But instruction on how to deal with publishers and how to bear up under the inevitable defeat would be for a very advanced course. It is not the sort of thing that the average beginning writer at Berkeley would find immediately practical.

So I returned to the few things that I could teach. The first lesson would   6
have to do with the all-important issue of inspiration. All writers know that on some golden mornings they are touched by the wand — are on intimate terms with poetry and cosmic truth. I have experienced those moments myself. Their lesson is simple: It's a total illusion. And the danger in the illusion is that you will wait for those moments. Such is the horror of having to face the typewriter

232

that you will spend all your time waiting. I am persuaded that most writers, like most shoemakers, are about as good one day as the next (a point which Trollope made), hangovers apart. The difference is the result of euphoria, alcohol, or imagination. The meaning is that one had better go to his or her typewriter every morning and stay there regardless of the seeming result. It will be much the same.

All professions have their own ways of justifying laziness. Harvard professors are deeply impressed by the jeweled fragility of their minds. More than the thinnest metal, these are subject terribly to fatigue. More than six hours teaching a week is fatal—and an impairment of academic freedom. So, at any given moment, they are resting their minds in preparation for the next orgiastic act of insight or revelation. Writers, in contrast, do nothing because they are waiting for inspiration.

In my own case there are days when the result is so bad that no fewer than five revisions are required. However, when I'm greatly inspired, only four revisions are needed before, as I've often said, I put in that note of spontaneity which even my meanest critics concede. My advice to those eager students in California would be, "Do not wait for the golden moment. It may well be worse." I would also warn against the flocking tendency of writers and its use as a cover for idleness. It helps greatly in the avoidance of work to be in the company of others who are also waiting for the golden moment. The best place to write is by yourself, because writing becomes an escape from the terrible boredom of your own personality. It's the reason that for years I've favored Switzerland, where I look at the telephone and yearn to hear it ring.

The question of revision is closely allied with that of inspiration. There may be inspired writers for whom the first draft is just right. But anyone who is not certifiably a Milton had better assume that the first draft is a very primitive thing. The reason is simple: Writing is difficult work. Ralph Paine, who managed *Fortune* in my time, used to say that anyone who said writing was easy was either a bad writer or an unregenerate liar. Thinking, as Voltaire avowed, is also a very tedious thing which men—or women—will do anything to avoid. So all first drafts are deeply flawed by the need to combine composition with thought. Each later draft is less demanding in this regard. Hence the writing can be better. There does come a time when revision is for the sake of change—when one has become so bored with the words that anything that is different looks better. But even then it may be better.

For months in 1955–1956, when I was working on *The Affluent Society,* my title was "The Opulent Society." Eventually I could stand it no longer: the word opulent had a nasty, greasy sound. One day, before starting work, I looked up the synonyms in the dictionary. First to meet my eye was the word "affluent." I had only one worry; that was whether I could possibly sell it to

233

the publisher. All publishers wish to have books called *The Crisis in American Democracy*. My title, to my surprise, was acceptable. Mark Twain once said that the difference between the right adjective and the next-best adjective is the difference between lighting and a lightning bug.

Next, I would stress a rather old-fashioned idea to those students. It was above all the lesson of Harry Luce. No one who worked for him ever again escaped the feeling that he was there looking over one's shoulder. In his hand was a pencil; down on each page one could expect, any moment, a long swishing wiggle accompanied by the comment: "This can go." Invariably it could. It was written to please the author and not the reader. Or to fill in the space. The gains from brevity are obvious; in most efforts to achieve brevity, it is the worst and dullest that goes. It is the worst and dullest that spoils the rest.

I know that brevity is now out of favor. *The New York Review of Books* prides itself on giving its authors as much space as they want and sometimes twice as much as they need. Even those who have read only Joyce must find their thoughts wandering before the end of the fortnightly article. Writing for television, I've learned in the last year or two, is an exercise in relentless condensation. It has left me with the feeling that even brevity can be carried to extremes. But the danger, as I look at some of the newer fashions in writing, is not great.

The next of my injunctions, which I would impart with even less hope of success, would concern alcohol. Nothing is so pleasant. Nothing is so important for giving the writer a sense of confidence in himself. And nothing so impairs the product. Again there are exceptions: I remember a brilliant writer at *Fortune* for whom I was responsible, who could work only with his hat on and after consuming a bottle of Scotch. There were major crises in the years immediately after World War II, when Scotch was difficult to find. But it is, quite literally, very sobering to reflect upon how many good American writers have been destroyed by this solace — by the sauce. Scott Fitzgerald, Sinclair Lewis, Thomas Wolfe, Ernest Hemingway, William Faulkner — the list goes on and on. Hamish Hamilton, once my English publisher, put the question to James Thurber: "Jim, why is it so many of your great writers have ruined themselves with drink?" Thurber thought long and carefully and finally replied: "It's this way, Jamie. They wrote these novels, and they sold very well. They made a lot of money and so they could buy whiskey by the case."

Their reputation was universal. A few years before his death, John Steinbeck, an appreciative but not a compulsive drinker, went to Moscow. It was a triumphal tour; and in a letter that he sent me about his hosts, he said: "I found I enjoyed the Soviet hustlers pretty much. There was a kind of youthful honesty about their illicit intentions that was not without charm. And their lives are difficult under their four-party system [a reference that escapes me]. It takes a fairly deft or very lucky man to make his way upward in the worker's paradise." I later heard that one night, after a particularly effusive celebration, he decided to make his way back to the hotel on foot. On the way he was overcome by fatigue and the hospitality he had received and sat down on a bench in a small park to rest. A policeman, called a militiaman in Moscow, came along and informed John, who was now asleep, and his companion, who spoke Russian, that the benches could not be occupied at that hour. His companion explained, rightly, that John was a very great American writer and that an exception should be made. The militiaman insisted. The companion explained again, insisted more strongly. Presently a transcendental light came over the policeman's face. He looked at Steinbeck asleep on the bench, inspected his condition more closely, recoiled slightly from the fumes, and said, "Oh, oh, Gemingway." Then he took off his cap and tiptoed carefully away.

We are all desperately afraid of sounding like Carry Nation. I must take the   15
risk. Any writer who wants to do his best against a deadline should stick to Coca-Cola. If he doesn't have a deadline, he can risk Seven-Up.

Next, I would want to tell my students of a point strongly pressed, if my   16
memory serves, by Shaw. He once said that as he grew older, he became less and less interested in theory, more and more interested in information. The temptation in writing is just the reverse. Nothing is so hard to come by as a new and interesting fact. Nothing is so easy on the feet as a generalization. I now pick up magazines and leaf through them looking for articles that are rich with facts; I do not care much what they are. Richly evocative and deeply percipient theory I avoid. It leaves me cold unless I am the author of it. My advice to all young writers is to stick to research and reporting with only a minimum of interpretation. And especially this is my advice to all older writers, particularly to columnists. As the feet give out, they seek to have the mind take their place.

Reluctantly, but from a long and terrible experience, I would urge my   17
young writers to avoid all attempts at humor. It does greatly lighten one's task. I've often wondered who made it impolite to laugh at one's own jokes; it is one of the major enjoyments of life. And that is the point. Humor is an intensely personal, largely internal thing. What pleases some, including the source, does not please others. One laughs; another says, "Well, I certainly see nothing funny about that." And the second opinion has just as much standing as the first, maybe more. Where humor is concerned, there are no standards—no one can say what is good or bad, although you can be sure that everyone will. Only a very foolish man will use a form of language that is wholly uncertain in its effect. That is the nature of humor.

There are other reasons for avoiding humor. In our society the solemn   18
person inspires far more trust than the one who laughs. The politician allows himself one joke at the beginning of his speech. A ritual. Then he changes his

expression, affects an aspect of morbid solemnity signaling that, after all, he is a totally serious man. Nothing so undermines a point as its association with a wisecrack—the very word is pejorative.

Also, as Art Buchwald has pointed out, we live in an age when it is hard to invent anything that is as funny as everyday life. How could one improve, for example, on the efforts of the great men of television to attribute cosmic significance to the offhand and hilarious way Bert Lance combined professed fiscal conservatism with an unparalleled personal commitment to the deficit financing of John Maynard Keynes? And because the real world is so funny, there is almost nothing you can do, short of labeling a joke a joke, to keep people from taking it seriously. A few years ago in *Harper's* I invented the theory that socialism in our time was the result of our dangerous addiction to team sports. The ethic of the team is all wrong for free enterprise. The code words are cooperation; team spirit; accept leadership; the coach is always right. Authoritarianism is sanctified; the individualist is a poor team player, a menace. All this our vulnerable adolescents learn. I announced the formation of an organization to combat this deadly trend and to promote boxing and track instead. I called it the C.I.A.—Congress for Individualist Athletics. Hundreds wrote in to *Harper's* asking to join. Or demanding that baseball be exempted. A batter is on his own. I presented the letters to the Kennedy Library. 19

Finally, I would come to a matter of much personal interest, intensely self-serving. It concerns the peculiar pitfalls of the writer who is dealing with presumptively difficult or technical matters. Economics is an example, and within the field of economics the subject of money, with the history of which I have been much concerned, is an especially good case. Any specialist who ventures to write on money with a view to making himself intelligible works under a grave moral hazard. He will be accused of oversimplification. The charge will be made by his fellow professionals, however obtuse or incompetent. They will have a sympathetic hearing from the layman. That is because no layman really expects to understand about money, inflation, or the International Monetary Fund. If he does, he suspects that he is being fooled. One can have respect only for someone who is decently confusing. 20

In the case of economics there are no important propositions that cannot be stated in plain language. Qualifications and refinements are numerous and of great technical complexity. These are important for separating the good students from the dolts. But in economics the refinements rarely, if ever, modify the essential and practical point. The writer who seeks to be intelligible needs to be right; he must be challenged if his argument leads to an erroneous conclusion and especially if it leads to the wrong action. But he can safely dismiss the charge that he has made the subject too easy. The truth is not difficult. 21

Complexity and obscurity have professional value; they are the academic 22

236

equivalents of apprenticeship rules in the building trades. They exclude the outsiders, keep down the competition, preserve the image of a privileged or priestly class. The man who makes things clear is a scab. He is criticized less for his clarity than for his treachery.

Additionally, and especially in the social sciences, much unclear writing is   23
based on unclear or incomplete thought. It is possible with safety to be technically obscure about something you haven't thought out. It is impossible to be wholly clear on something you do not understand. Clarity thus exposes flaws in the thought. The person who undertakes to make difficult matters clear is infringing on the sovereign right of numerous economists, sociologists, and political scientists to make bad writing the disguise for sloppy, imprecise or incomplete thought. One can understand the resulting anger. Adam Smith, John Stuart Mill, John Maynard Keynes were writers of crystalline clarity most of the time. Marx had great moments, as in *The Communist Manifesto*. Economics owes very little, if anything, to the practitioners of scholarly obscurity. If any of my California students should come to me from the learned professions, I would counsel them in all their writing to keep the confidence of their colleagues. This they should do by being always complex, always obscure, invariably a trifle vague.

You might say that all this constitutes a meager yield for a lifetime of writing. Or that writing on economics, as someone once said of Kerouac's prose, is not writing but typing. True.

QUESTIONS ON CONTENT:

1. What are Galbraith's seven suggestions for writers? Where have you seen the same ideas expressed by other writers on writing?
2. How does Galbraith evaluate his qualifications for a Professorship of Rhetoric at the University of California? What does he see as his problems or difficulties?

QUESTIONS ON WRITING STRUCTURE AND STRATEGY:

1. What do you think is Galbraith's purpose in using humor? Does it occasionally cause you to doubt his seriousness? Or does it cause you to read more carefully, more critically?
2. Is the ending appropriate? How does it relate to the title?
3. How does Galbraith's subject matter dictate his organization?
4. In paragraph ten, Galbraith quotes Mark Twain on the importance of exact word choice. Look for Galbraith's use of the right word. For example, in paragraph one, ". . . rhetoric was a traditional . . . not . . . a pejorative title"; paragraph fourteen, ". . . John Steinbeck, an appreciative but not a compulsive drinker . . .", paragraph ten, "The Opulent Society" versus

"The Affluent Society." (This may require use of the dictionary if you find some unfamiliar words in the essay.)

5. How do his anecdotes and allusions clarify his points and at the same time provide humor?

6. Do you find any apt or memorable phrases, "hooks" à la Hoffer, that speak volumes? For example, "flocking tendencies." Find others.

QUESTIONS FOR DISCUSSION AND WRITING:

1. Galbraith warns the writer against procrastination—putting off writing. Some writers, he says, insist they are waiting for inspiration. Others betray what he calls "flocking tendencies," seeking out other procrastinating writers to engage in time-wasting bull sessions. Both, Galbraith says, are covers for idleness. Writers are not the only ones who procrastinate. Reflect on your own experience or on your observations of others. Write a paper on the human tendency to procrastinate. Narrow your subject down and concentrate on a few observations and on the reasons people most often give to justify their behavior.

2. Based on your experience, how valid are Galbraith's remarks about professors, especially sociologists, economists, and political scientists?

3. In urging clarity in writing, Galbraith says that obscurity and complexity are "the academic equivalent of apprenticeship rules in building trades." They serve to exclude the outsider. Survey some of your textbooks, articles in mass circulation magazines and in professional journals. Does the writing seem to exclude? Select a short sample and try rewriting it in your journal. Try to clarify the obscurity/complexity.

4. Try rewriting a paragraph on a serious topic, even taken from one of your textbooks, giving it a light touch without making it slapstick.

POETRY? FOR ENGINEERS?
PART 1—THE BEST WORD
Anthony J. Sousa

*Should engineers study poetry? That's what Anthony J. Sousa asks in
this article. As a consulting engineer and a sometime teacher at
Cooper Union in New York City, Sousa aims to improve the quality of
writing by engineers, many of whom, he claims, are pedestrian writers
at best. Such limitations, Sousa insists, often translate into a denial of
promotion or raises. For strictly utilitarian reasons, Sousa strongly
suggests that engineers take up writing poetry in order to develop what
he calls "the inner you." He points out a number of ways in which
writing poetry will improve one's writing and enhance one's
professional standing. While we may think of engineering as an
entirely rational enterprise, Sousa demonstrates that there is room for
feeling, and this is where the realms of poetry and engineering
somehow blend. Sousa employs a variety of methods to communicate
his obvious enthusiasm for his subject. His liberal use of illustrations
clarifies and breaks up his exposition with bright and often
inspirational moments. All these elements serve powerfully to convince
the reader of the validity of Sousa's thesis. Both at the beginning and
at the end of his essay Sousa makes clear that his intended audience is
male, pointing up the fact that writers must always consider their
audience. He needs to reassess his audience in terms of today's
growing number of women engineers.*

I believe that men enter engineering because they seek an environment   1
that is not subject to human vagaries; where they are judged for their true
worth. So, it is a letdown when the engineer finds human politics determining
his future growth despite the hopes that all those beautifully exact courses in
math, physics and chemistry offered.

When an engineer has a problem, his usual answer is to learn more, to   2
brush up on his science and technology. Will that help?

No, the problem isn't technical. Then what is it? It's summed up by that   3
TV comic, Rodney Dangerfield, who turns to the audience with his popping
eyes and clownlike face and says, "You know my trouble, I don't get no respect."

You know what I mean: like when they moved your desk into a room with   4
four other engineers and gave you one-eighth of a secretary; or when they left
you out of a meeting with the client on your research results; or when the
electrician came to the pilot plant and boasted that he was making more than
you and he never went to school; or when they brought in that new man at
your level and you had to train him, and now they bypass you. Yes, engineers
don't get much respect, and although they take it as a joke, they don't think
it's funny.

Like it or not, your real problem is that you are missing an inner something that is preventing you from winning friends and influencing money — and reading technical journals this summer is not going to find it for you. Then what will? Anything that will develop the inner you, like Yoga meditation, painting, philosophy, music, turning hippie, or practicing any art that will help you to find yourself.

But I have a specific recommendation that I'll tell you about if you promise not to laugh too loudly — engineers, spend some summer writing poetry! What?, you say. Suppose somebody catches me? Then deny everything and say it's a plot to discredit you. What if you don't write anything worthwhile? I guarantee that you will not write anything worthwhile; but attempting to achieve such a goal will start you on a path of inner development that will produce real changes in the years to come.

In case you didn't notice, I said *write* poetry, not read poetry; of course, you'll have to read it as a minimum to accomplish the almost impossible task of writing it. I recommend it over other arts because when one practices poetry, one is writing — and few will argue with me when I state that engineers are very weak in writing. Poetry will definitely strengthen you in this art and your increased sensitivity to words will decrease spelling errors and grammatical mistakes, and in short diminish any hangups that interfere with successful communication through writing. This alone is sufficient reason for studying poetry.

Poetry will do more. It could bridge the generation gap, since it is now so often used in rock and roll music. Poetry can sensitize one, and provide the image that a man is educated and not merely someone with a degree. Poetry can only be dug out of one's self and is therefore self-educational (and in the words of the poet Robert Frost, "The only worthwhile education is self-education").

But even after finding yourself, you may still remain one of the seduced instead of the seducer; there is just so much room at the top. And, if you were destined to fail in this world — then create an inner world where you win. If this is not sufficiently satisfying to you, then you'll require a personality transplant; develop the arrogance of a flamenco dancer, the voice of a trial lawyer, and the presence of a Shakesperean actor — anything that will assist you in getting your own way.

But even with all this, you may still miss "making it," since in the words of Peter's Principle, one rises by pull from above rather than by push from below. Or, as the poet Emily Dickinson put it:

We never know how high we are
Till we are asked to rise

ANTHONY J. SOUSA

And then if we are true to plan
Our statures touch the skies.

Poetry as a Key to Writing

The poet Coleridge of *Ancient Mariner* fame, wrote: "Prose — words in their   11
best order; poetry — the best words in their best order."

    Obviously, poetry has fewer degrees of freedom and is the more difficult   12
to write. I like to think of poetry as the calculus of writing, and prose as the
algebra of the art. Engineers all have experienced the improvement in their
grasp of algebra after calculus. I propose a similar improvement in their
(engineering) prose from a study of the higher art of poetry. It is analogous to
taking graduate courses to do routine engineering, or jogging just to occasionally
catch a train, or as Robert Browning put it:

> "Ah, but a man's reach should exceed his grasp,
> Or what's a heaven for?"

After the proper development, we may find engineers making entries in their   13
lab notebooks in a manner similar to Coleridge:

> *My hands are scarred with scratches from a cat, whose back I was rubbing in the dark in*
> *order to see whether the sparks from it were refrangible by a prism.*

The entry is clear as written and has the added feature of some artistic beauty.   14
Would it have been easier to read a shortened version of the entry written in
the third person to conform with modern engineering report writing? I think not.

    Poetry is very much "first person," with lots of I's, and very much in   15
conflict with the accepted third-person method of reporting. But why should
there not be I's in engineering reports. The work of an engineer is very personal
and possesses distinctive character for each individual, and should not be lost
in that infinite gray heat sink "it."

What Do I Mean by Poetry?

Poetry is a difficult thing to define in words; one must feel how it differs from   16
other writing. Poetry need not rhyme — it can, but there is the danger that it
will deteriorate into verse. Verse is easy to write. For example, if I begin,

241

"There once was a man named Fred" (which is a line that already lacks poetry),
I know that the next line must rhyme with Fred, and could be dead or lead.
Then, I merely put words in between that have about the same rhythm, and I
have a second line. Take the following poem, which was an attempt to visualize
the kind of poem a young engineer might write to his secretary:

> *Your eyes are like offsites*
> *Your teeth equimolar*
> *Your hair is cold reflux*
> *On my shoulder.*
>
> *O what's the reaction*
> *Improved entropy?*
> *In a fixed or a fluid*
> *Bed down by the sea.*

   Most engineers like this verse because it uses engineering words, all the
lines rhyme, and the meaning is clear. But this is *not* what I mean by poetry.
(Please don't get the idea that I mean that poetry isn't fun.)
   Poetry is magical—a memorable grouping of words that put forth a whole
mood, express a truth with great impact. It need not be complete as in most
poems. It could be a single line, or as little as a few words. Poetry is produced
almost accidentally, and results in ordinary words that mathematically model
magical, mysterious, joyous, and always interesting and moving, thoughts.
Great poems are seldom achieved and one must search hard among the
greatest writing to find them. Unlike engineering, there is hardly agreement on
the merits of a given work. You must decide on the poetry that is yours! What
pleases others is of little interest.
   Consider these lines of Emily Dickinson:

> *Hope is the thing with feathers*
> *That perches in the soul,*
> *And sings the tune without the words,*
> *And never stops at all.*

   Could you begin to describe the human feeling "hope" better. Poetry
dares to communicate feelings, the most elusive of things, yet not unimportant
—even in engineering. For example, what is your answer when the V.P. asks
you whether you feel the catalyst will have as long a life in the commercial
reactor as it did in the bench-scale unit. He is not asking for facts, he is asking

for the feelings you have. The exact answer is that you really don't know because no one can predict what exposure the catalyst will receive in the real plant; and as it is, you are not even sure what the catalyst life is in the bench-scale unit. But you may feel that it will hold up, or can be easily regenerated if it doesn't.

But what has poetry to do with engineering? You may be aware of the 21 Mond process for purifying nickel, which consists of passing CO gas over a crude nickel to form gaseous $Ni(CO)_4$, which is then decomposed into pure nickel. Feel more on home grounds again? Lord Kelvin hailed this process as "one which gives wings to a heavy metal." I would say that he described it poetically without loss of scientific accuracy, and was a rounder and more interesting man for it. The scientist Sir Humphrey Davy dabbled in poetry, and Coleridge is said to have remarked of him, "If Davy had not been the first chemist, he would have been the first poet of his Age."

Writing Poetry

How does one go about writing poetry? They say a poem starts with a lump in 22 the throat. I say it is a joy or a depression that fills the mind to capacity, then supersaturates the brain until something insignificant occurs, a word, some small event, and the solution precipitates in a shower of crystals that show up as words with excitement and tension. One must experience it to understand.

What's in a Word?

What's in a name? That which we call a rose
By any other name would smell as sweet.

The above lines from *Romeo and Juliet* must be favorites for engineers. If 23 the rose were renamed "sludge flower," most would sense little loss of beauty and would be quite satisfied with the change, after having made the proper correction in their dictionaries.

Engineers are notoriously uninterested in words. Take the engineer who 24 just returned from an exciting four-month startup near the Tibetan border:

"How was the trip, Jim?"
"All right."
"Understand you stayed with the Dalai Lama."

"Yep."

"What's he like?"

"He's O.K."

To most engineers, one word is as good as another, as long as it gets the job
done. Does the new product have an odor? a smell? a scent? an aroma? Will any
word do?

Engineers need a great deal of work in the area of developing an inner
sense for the feel of words irrespective of their dictionary meanings. Words are
notorious liars; they are all two-faced at best, and while they stand conveying
their dictionary meaning on the one hand, they are sticking their tongues out on
the other hand and conveying secondary meanings and feelings. It is these
subtle secondary perturbations that allow the poet to achieve heights of
compact meaning from ordinary words. Control of this secondary feature is the
key to the art of writing, and this control can be developed only through
feeling, which ultimately culminates in a "taste" or sense for good writing.

The Art in Words

I suggest that you play with words in order to sense their feeling, their inherent
rhythm, their aesthetic poetry and their beauty; that which is independent of
their proper or dictionary meanings. But let me explain what is not readily
explainable in words, but readily understood by feeling.

Cathode is a word that senses smooth, mysterious; while its ever-present
companion, anode, is short, stifled and uninteresting. I prefer cracking to
pyrolysis. Pyrolysis reminds me too much of paralysis. I prefer HTU to HETP
as a combination of letters, whatever they mean. I prefer catsup to ketchup—
the k is too strong.

Take the periodic table. The latest element discovered is eka-hafnium. Can
you think of an uglier name? Compare it to beryllium. Listen to the music,
sense the brightness, the brilliance. And selenium—say it slowly, feel its
smoothness, its slipperiness. Sense the heat in hydrogen. Helium feels not only
light but giddy to me. Germanium is rhythmical and has the sense of
germination, which gives it a kind of earthiness. Don't you think so? Yes, I
want your opinion. Don't give me that "whatever you say is O.K. with me"
jazz. And stop fingering "Perry's" and looking in your old English notes. There
are no teachers around—this is an exam where you correct your own paper.
I'm asking you to look inside yourself. Take your time. Take a week. Sense the
word, feel it. Clank it against other words and ask yourself, "What is it about
the word that appeals to me?"

A List of Random Engineering Words Based on Their Feeling and in My Opinion

---

POETICAL

melamine	cascade	risers
enthalpy	modulus	poromeric
ilmenite	polyisoprene	ethanolamine
selectivity	fuller's earth	Elgin Tower
tie lines	tunnel caps	liquid seal
Teflon	cathode	cooling curve
downspouts	Murphree	capillary
colloidal	electrolyte	flights
laminar		

NON-POETICAL

leaching	blowdown	eddy
batch	equimolar	thickener
sieve	osmosis	raffinate
berl saddles	entrainment eliminators	sliding vane
coagulator	sludge digester	slurry valve
chelating	pesticides	fungicides
coking	mother liquor	flocculator
wetted wall	hysteresis	reflux
Fenske	cash flow	crud

Some words have been perfectly named. Acetylene is both incendiary in reality and in feeling. One poet wrote, "The sky was bright acetylene," which says nothing but conveys the feeling of a brightly heightened and active sky. Here, acetylene was used not for its proper meaning but for its feeling.   30

Engineering is filled with beautiful and not so beautiful words. A partial list is shown in the box that, in my opinion, can be divided into two categories: poetical and nonpoetical. As an example, imagine the pretty girl next door whose name is Polyisoprene; or sense the elegance of the Elgin Tower, or the richness in fuller's earth.   31

On the other hand, visualize this typical outcry emanating from the plant disposal group, "Cut off the slurry to the sludge digester before the crud coagulates in the thickener." An entrainment eliminator may be important to efficient plant operation, but it sounds more like some kind of laxative. Heap leaching is a little-used unit operation, thank heavens, and mother liquor has many secondary meanings.   32

245

The Best Word

If one has the time, the genius, or the luck to find the best word, it can greatly   33
strengthen one's writing. Engineers should develop the patience to wait for
inspiration to provide them with the best word. Suppose you wish to express
the feeling that brain-storming sessions are useful because one man's idea
stimulates another man to create a new idea, and so on. We might say in our
report that ideas tend to breed new ideas, but a better statement might be,
"ideas tend to germinate," which says it all.

In his poem *The Hollow Men*, T. S. Eliot wrote,   34

> *This is the way the world ends*
> *Not with a bang but with a whimper.*

How did Eliot ever find "whimper"? The choice was truly inspired and adds   35
greatly to the interest and activity in these lines.

The Smothers Brothers have a routine in which they sing about a man   36
who falls into a vat of chocolate; when asked what he did, he replies "I
shouted Fire. What should I have shouted? Chocolate?" In this case, the best
word was "fire," since it produced the desired result of his being rescued.

A famous World War II novel was originally named *Catch 17*. For weeks   37
the publisher looked for a new title that would be more appealing, and finally
arrived at *Catch 22*. The difference is significant. The word seventeen has a
downturning pessimism in it, while the word twenty-two has a lift at the end
that peaks* one's interest.

The choosing of a name can be an important event in the engineering   38
field, especially since the return on a huge research project may depend on the
final appeal of the product's name. Du Pont pioneered fluorocarbon
refrigerants, using the name Freon, and was later followed by Allied with its
Genetron flurocarbons. Which name do you prefer? Teflon is an excellent name
for a plastic; it is neuter and yet pleasing. Corfam is not quite so pleasing.
Qiana, Du Pont's latest fiber, is not appealing — even if it was chosen by
computer to avoid conflict with other tradenames. And it is also often
misspelled by people who insist on putting a u after the Q.

I feel fortunate in finding a poem by a great poet that exemplifies the art   39
of using the best words. It is a sonnet by Elinor Wylie.

---

*Poets can be a problem. I can't figure out if this is an imaginative use of a word, or a misspelling of
"piques." — Ed.

ANTHONY J. SOUSA

Pretty Words
Poets make pets of pretty docile words:
I love smooth words, like gold-enamelled fish
Which circle slowly with a silken swish,
And tender ones, like downy-feathered birds:
Words shy and dappled, deep-eyed deer in herds,
Come to my hand and playful if I wish
Or purring softly at a silver dish,
Blue Persian kittens, fed on cream and curds.

I love bright words, words up and singing early;
Words that are luminous in the dark, and sing;
Warm lazy words, white cattle under trees;
I love words opalescent, cool, and pearly,
Like midsummer moths, and honied word like bees,
Gilded and sticky, with a little sting.

The reason for all this discussion on words is to make us well aware of the   40
tricky devils we are dealing with; to loosen up the viselike grip of using words
only for their meanings; and to call up words more on feeling than on meaning,
since they come quicker by that route.

Try letting your wife read this article. I find women, by nature, have a   41
deeper sense for the feeling of words than men do.

QUESTIONS ON CONTENT:

1. Sousa speaks of developing the "inner you." For what specific reasons does
    he recommend that engineers try writing poetry? What are the practical
    reasons and what are the aesthetic reasons?
2. What does he say about the dictionary meanings of words (denotation) and
    the "two-faced" meanings of words (connotation)?
3. How does Sousa define poetry? How is poetry different from the writing
    engineers normally do?

QUESTIONS ON WRITING STRUCTURE AND STRATEGY:

1. Why does Sousa frame his title as a question? Is it provocative? Where else
    and for what purpose does he use rhetorical questions?
2. Sousa uses a variety of modes to achieve his purpose. Identify his use of
    analogy, definition, cause and effect, comparison and contrast, classification,
    example, persuasion. Does he use humor at all?
3. How do his quotations serve to make his ideas clear? How would your

understanding be affected if these were eliminated? What does the use of these quotations tell you about Sousa? (And sexist language?)

QUESTIONS FOR DISCUSSION AND WRITING:

1. Select a particularly abstract paragraph from one of your textbooks — preferably a technical one — and rewrite it according to Sousa's directions: select the best word. Find the best word by examining connotation, or by fashioning metaphors and similes. Like Lord Kelvin, describe something poetically without distorting meaning or accuracy. (Do not go overboard and lapse into purple prose.)

2. In "Art in Words" and "The Best Word" Sousa is talking about *euphony* and "feeling," the beauty of words and their connotations. Imagine that you are a copywriter in an advertising agency and have to come up with a name for a new product and perhaps a slogan to accompany it. Try your hand at one of the following and write a paper in which you explain how you went about your task and justify what you have come up with.

    a. a new self-fading jean
    b. a new hair shampoo
    c. a new soft drink
    d. a new candy bar

    e. a new sneaker
    f. a new deodorant
    g. a new mouthwash
    h. a new sports car (see "Snarling Cars," Unit II)

THE WRITER'S DUTY
William Faulkner

William Faulkner was one of America's greatest twentieth-century authors. Born and raised in Mississippi, he set most of his fiction in the American South, much of it concerned with violence, depravity, and inhumanity. Faulkner's ringing affirmation of the individual's nobility in this Nobel prize address, therefore, came as something of a surprise to those who had followed his career. But there was also another reason for surprise. To understand this it is necessary to know something of the historical context. Faulkner was speaking to a distinguished audience, the monarchs of Sweden and Norway and a glittering assemblage of notables. As he spoke of the young writer's fear of being "blown up," Faulkner knew that his audience was aware that the USSR had perfected its first atomic bomb the year before and that just two weeks prior the Chinese Communists had counterattacked the United Nations forces then fighting in Korea. The times were fearful, and today's fear of nuclear war began with the knowledge that the Russians now possessed what had heretofore been an American monopoly. Faulkner's stirring closing remarks, in spite of these new dangers, were therefore doubly significant, raising the speech to its high level of eloquence.

In enumerating the duties of the writer, Faulkner necessarily spoke in abstractions. But note their similarity to those President John F. Kennedy mentions in his tribute to Robert Frost.

I feel that this award was not made to me as a man but to my work—a 1
life's work in the agony and sweat of the human spirit, not for glory and least of all for profit, but to create out of the materials of the human spirit something which did not exist before. So this award is only mine in trust. It will not be difficult to find a dedication for the money part of it commensurate with the purpose and significance of its origin. But I would like to do the same with the acclaim too, by using this moment as a pinnacle from which I might be listened to by the young men and women already dedicated to the same anguish and travail, among whom is already that one who will someday stand here where I am standing.

Our tragedy today is a general and universal physical fear so long sustained 2
by now that we can even bear it. There are no longer problems of the spirit. There is only the question: When will I be blown up? Because of this, the young man or woman writing today has forgotten the problems of the human heart in conflict with itself which alone can make good writing because only that is worth writing about, worth the agony and the sweat.

He must learn them again. He must teach himself that the basest of all 3
things is to be afraid; and, teaching himself that, forget it forever, leaving no

room in his workshop for anything but the old verities and truths of the heart, the old universal truths lacking which any story is ephemeral and doomed — love and honor and pity and pride and compassion and sacrifice. Until he does so he labors under a curse. He writes not of love but of lust, of defeats in which nobody loses anything of value, of victories without hope and worst of all without pity or compassion. His griefs grieve on no universal bones, leaving no scars. He writes not of the heart but of the glands.

Until he relearns these things he will write as though he stood among and   4
watched the end of man. I decline to accept the end of man. It is easy enough to say that man is immortal simply because he will endure; that when the last ding-dong of doom has clanged and faded from the last worthless rock hanging tideless in the last red and dying evening, that even then there will still be one more sound: that of his puny inexhaustible voice, still talking. I refuse to accept this. I believe that man will not merely endure: he will prevail. He is immortal, not because he alone among creatures has an inexhaustible voice, but because he has a soul, a spirit capable of compassion and sacrifice and endurance. The poet's, the writer's, duty is to write about these things. It is his privilege to help man endure by lifting his heart, by reminding him of the courage and honor and hope and pride and compassion and pity and sacrifice which have been the glory of his past. The poet's voice need not merely be the record of man, it can be one of the props, the pillars to help him endure and prevail.

QUESTIONS ON CONTENT:

1.   What is Faulkner's thesis? How does he support it? With facts or assertions?
2.   Why were the writers of Faulkner's day not fulfilling their duties as writers according to Faulkner? What were they writing about?
3.   What does he believe writers should concern themselves with and why?

QUESTIONS ON WRITING STRUCTURE AND STRATEGY:

1.   Faulkner may be said to be speaking to several audiences. Which one is the most important?
2.   In paragraph three Faulkner uses a series of abstractions. What technique does he use in order to help clarify his ideas? Does the brevity of the speech force you to concentrate more keenly on these abstractions?
3.   How would you characterize the tone of Faulkner's speech? Can you isolate some of the elements — words, phrases, ideas, word order — that contribute to the tone?

QUESTIONS FOR DISCUSSION AND WRITING:

1.   Compare Faulkner's address with President John F. Kennedy's speech on

Frost. Both speeches are ultimately addressed to young people. Why?

2. How will writing about the "old verities and truths of the heart" enable people to endure and prevail? Does Faulkner make a good case? Reflect on these questions and write a paper.

3. What have you read that reflects these truths? What have you read that reinforces what Faulkner rejects, the physical, the ephemeral, the doomed? Write a paper in which you explore your reading.

4. Apply Faulkner's exhortations to the writer to the TV script writer. Review some popular television programs—dramas, soap operas, situation comedies—and determine which attempt to deal with some of Faulkner's "eternal verities." Write a paper on your findings.

NURSES

Lewis Thomas

Dr. Lewis Thomas, biologist, researcher, and chancellor of the Memorial Sloan-Kettering Cancer Center in New York, is one of America's most popular scientist-essayists. However, Thomas's early career as a writer was not so auspicious. In fact, the editor of the New England Journal of Medicine *used one of Thomas's early writing efforts to illustrate the execrable quality of writing in the medical sciences. By 1970, however, that same editor asked Thomas to contribute a column to his journal. The transformation of Thomas's prose from hideous to elegant culminated in the publication four years later of his award-winning collection of these column essays—The* Lives of a Cell, *which sold over one million copies. Five years later he published* The Medusa and the Snail. *Because Thomas successfully bridges the world of science and the humanities, his philosophical, highly informative, and gracefully written essays have found a wide lay audience. The following essay—taken from* The Youngest Science: Notes of a Medicine-Watcher *(1983)—pays homage to nurses from the vantage point of a physician as well as a patient. In doing so, he points up the problems resulting from changes in society, in medicine, and in the education of nurses. Using comparison/contrast and cause/effect, he reasons inductively to his conclusion. As you read, note the factors that promote clear, smooth, logical, easy reading/writing, techniques one would expect from a physician-scientist: the introductory topic sentence for each paragraph, specific examples in detailing his comparison of the changing role of nurses, effective parallelism, varied sentence structure and length, and variations in the use of subject-verb-object order.*

When my mother became a registered nurse at Roosevelt Hospital, in 1903, there was no question in anyone's mind about what nurses did as professionals. They did what the doctors ordered. The attending physician would arrive for his ward rounds in the early morning, and when he arrived at the ward office the head nurse would be waiting for him, ready to take his hat and coat, and his cane, and she would stand while he had his cup of tea before starting. Entering the ward, she would hold the door for him to go first, then his entourage of interns and medical students, then she followed. At each bedside, after he had conducted his examination and reviewed the patient's progress, he would tell the nurse what needed doing that day, and she would write it down on the part of the chart reserved for nursing notes. An hour or two later he would be gone from the ward, and the work of the rest of the day and the night to follow was the nurse's frenetic occupation. In addition to the stipulated orders, she had an endless list of routine things to do, all learned in

1

her two years of nursing school: the beds had to be changed and made up with fresh sheets by an exact geometric design of folding and tucking impossible for anyone but a trained nurse; the patients had to be washed head to foot; bedpans had to be brought, used, emptied, and washed; temperatures had to be taken every four hours and meticulously recorded on the chart; enemas were to be given; urine and stool samples collected, labeled, and sent off to the laboratory; throughout the day and night, medications of all sorts, usually pills and various vegetable extracts and tinctures, had to be carried on trays from bed to bed. At most times of the year about half of the forty or so patients on the ward had typhoid fever, which meant that the nurse couldn't simply move from bed to bed in the performance of her duties; each typhoid case was screened from the other patients, and the nurse was required to put on a new gown and wash her hands in disinfectant before approaching the bedside. Patients with high fevers were sponged with cold alcohol at frequent intervals. The late-evening back rub was the rite of passage into sleep.

In addition to the routine, workaday schedule, the nurse was responsible   2
for responding to all calls from the patients, and it was expected that she would do so on the run. Her rounds, scheduled as methodical progressions around the ward, were continually interrupted by these calls. It was up to her to evaluate each situation quickly: a sudden abdominal pain in a typhoid patient might signify intestinal perforation; the abrupt onset of weakness, thirst, and pallor meant intestinal hemorrhage; the coughing up of gross blood by a tuberculous patient was an emergency. Some of the calls came from neighboring patients on the way to recovery; patients on open wards always kept a close eye on each other: the man in the next bed might slip into coma or seem to be dying, or be indeed dead. For such emergencies the nurse had to get word immediately to the doctor on call, usually the intern assigned to the ward, who might be off in the outpatient department or working in the diagnostic laboratory (interns of that day did all the laboratory work themselves; technicians had not yet been invented) or in his room. Nurses were not allowed to give injections or to do such emergency procedures as spinal punctures or chest taps, but they were expected to know when such maneuvers were indicated and to be ready with appropriate trays of instruments when the intern arrived on the ward.

It was an exhausting business, but by my mother's accounts it was the   3
most satisfying and rewarding kind of work. As a nurse she was a low person in the professional hierarchy, always running from place to place on orders from the doctors, subject as well to strict discipline from her own administrative superiors on the nursing staff, but none of this came through in her recollections. What she remembered was her usefulness.

Whenever my father talked to me about nurses and their work, he spoke   4 with high regard for them as professionals. Although it was clear in his view that the task of the nurses was to do what the doctor told them to, it was also clear that he admired them for being able to do a lot of things he couldn't possibly do, had never been trained to do. On his own rounds later on, when he became an attending physician himself, he consulted the ward nurse for her opinion about problem cases and paid careful attention to her observations and chart notes. In his own days of intern training (perhaps partly under my mother's strong influence, I don't know) he developed a deep and lasting respect for the whole nursing profession.

I have spent all of my professional career in close association with, and close dependency on, nurses, and like many of my faculty colleagues, I've done a lot of worrying about the relationship between medicine and nursing. During most of this century the nursing profession has been having a hard time of it. It has been largely, although not entirely, an occupation for women and sensitive issues of professional status, complicated by the special issue of the changing role of women in modern society, have led to a standoffish, often adversarial relationship between nurses and doctors. Already swamped by an increasing load of routine duties, nurses have been obliged to take on more and more purely administrative tasks: keeping the records in order; making sure the supplies are on hand for every sort of ward emergency; supervising the activities of the new paraprofessional group called LPNs (licensed practical nurses), who now perform much of the bedside work once done by RNs (registered nurses); overseeing ward maids, porters, and cleaners; seeing to it that patients scheduled for X rays are on their way to the X-ray department on time. Therefore, they have to spend more of their time at desks in the ward office and less time at the bedsides. Too late maybe, the nurses have begun to realize that they are gradually being excluded from the one duty which had previously been their most important reward but which had been so taken for granted that nobody mentioned it in listing the duties of a nurse: close personal contact with patients. Along with everything else nurses did in the long day's work, making up for all the tough and sometimes demeaning jobs assigned to them, they had the matchless opportunity to be useful friends to great numbers of human beings in trouble. They listened to their patients all day long and through the night, they gave comfort and reassurance to the patients and their families, they got to know them as friends, they were depended on. To contemplate the loss of this part of their work has been the deepest worry for nurses at large, and for the faculties responsible for the curricula of the nation's new and expanding nursing schools. The issue lies at the center of the running argument between medical school and nursing school administrators, but it is never clearly stated. Nursing education has been upgraded in recent years.

5

Almost all the former hospital schools, which took in high school graduates and provided an RN certificate after two or three years, have been replaced by schools attached to colleges and universities, with a four-year curriculum leading simultaneously to a bachelor's degree and an RN certificate.

The doctors worry that nurses are trying to move away from their historical responsibilities to medicine (meaning, really, to the doctors' orders). The nurses assert that they are their own profession, responsible for their own standards, coequal colleagues with physicians, and they do not wish to become mere ward administrators or technicians (although some of them, carrying the new and prestigious title of "nurse practitioner," are being trained within nursing schools to perform some of the most complex technological responsibilities in hospital emergency rooms and intensive care units). The doctors claim that what the nurses really want is to become substitute psychiatrists. The nurses reply that they have unavoidable responsibilities for the mental health and well-being of their patients, and that these are different from the doctors' tasks. Eventually the arguments will work themselves out, and some sort of agreement will be reached, but if it is to be settled intelligently, some way will have to be found to preserve and strengthen the traditional and highly personal nurse-patient relationship.

I have had a fair amount of firsthand experience with the issue, having been an apprehensive patient myself off and on over a three-year period on the wards of the hospital for which I work. I am one up on most of my physician friends because of this experience. I know some things they do not know about what nurses do.

One thing the nurses do is to hold the place together. It is an astonishment, which every patient feels from time to time, observing the affairs of a large, complex hospital from the vantage point of his bed, that the whole institution doesn't fly to pieces. A hospital operates by the constant interplay of powerful forces pulling away at each other in different directions, each force essential for getting necessary things done, but always at odds with each other. The intern staff is an almost irresistible force in itself, learning medicine by doing medicine, assuming all the responsibility within reach, pushing against an immovable attending and administrative staff, and frequently at odds with the nurses. The attending physicians are individual entrepreneurs trying to run small cottage industries at each bedside. The diagnostic laboratories are feudal fiefdoms, prospering from the insatiable demands for their services from the interns and residents. The medical students are all over the place, learning as best they can and complaining that they are not, as they believe they should be, at the epicenter of everyone's concern. Each individual worker in the place, from the chiefs of surgery to the dieticians to the ward maids, porters, and elevator operators, lives and works in the conviction that the whole apparatus would come to a standstill without his or her individual contribution, and in one sense or another each of them is right.

My discovery, as a patient first on the medical service and later in surgery, is that the institution is held together, *glued* together, enabled to function as an organism, by the nurses and by nobody else.   9

The nurses, the good ones anyway (and all the ones on my floor were good), make it their business to know everything that is going on. They spot errors before errors can be launched. They know everything written on the chart. Most important of all, they know their patients as unique human beings, and they soon get to know the close relatives and friends. Because of this knowledge, they are quick to sense apprehensions and act on them. The average sick person in a large hospital feels at risk of getting lost, with no identity left beyond a name and a string of numbers on a plastic wristband, in danger always of being whisked off on a litter to the wrong place to have the wrong procedure done, or worse still, *not* being whisked off at the right time. The attending physician or the house officer, on rounds and usually in a hurry, can murmur a few reassuring words on his way out the door, but it takes a confident, competent, and cheerful nurse, there all day long and in and out of the room on one chore or another through the night, to bolster one's confidence that the situation is indeed manageable and not about to get out of hand.   10

Knowing what I know, I am all for the nurses. If they are to continue their professional feud with the doctors, if they want their professional status enhanced and their pay increased, if they infuriate the doctors by their claims to be equal professionals, if they ask for the moon, I am on their side.   1

QUESTIONS ON CONTENT:

1. What did Thomas's mother feel was the greatest reward of her job?
2. Specifically how have nurses' duties, attitudes, status, and education changed during this century? What factors have led to this change, and what have nurses lost as a consequence? What have they gained?
3. In paragraph eight, Thomas describes the highly individualistic activities of various hospital professionals. What kind of picture emerges from his description? How does this whole operation become a community of patient-serving professionals?
4. What is Thomas's thesis?

QUESTIONS ON WRITING STRUCTURE AND STRATEGY:

1. Thomas's organization is typical of the scientific mind. Note his subject in

paragraphs one through three; a new subject in paragraph four; and the insertion of himself in remaining paragraphs. How does this lead logically to his thesis in the last paragraph?

2. In three sections of the essay, Thomas presents long lists of specific details. In fact, one sentence in the first paragraph is over 130 words long and employs 18 marks of punctuation. Identify these sections. What single rhetorical device does he employ, and why?

3. Assuming that Thomas wishes to attract maximum readership, what is the advantage of placing his thesis last?

4. What purpose is served by Thomas's use of parallelism in his conclusion?

QUESTIONS FOR DISCUSSION AND WRITING:

1. If you have ever had to spend time in a hospital, worked as a hospital volunteer, or had an experience with a campus health center or a public health agency, list those things you observed nurses doing. Assess the quality of the work they did and, if a patient, the personal attention you did or did not get. After you have assembled your facts and sorted them out, prepare a paper either supporting or taking issue with Thomas's account.

2. If you have ever had dealings over a period of time with other specialists (auto mechanics, for example) or other professionals, prepare two lists — "plus" and "minus" — and record all the facts you can remember, entering them in the appropriate column. On the basis of your lists, prepare an assessment of the way the person performed his/her duties.

THE OBLIGATION TO ENDURE

Rachel Carson

In Silent Spring, *Rachel Carson, a brilliant marine biologist and author of several highly acclaimed books (*The Sea Around Us, The Edge of the Sea, *and* Under the Sea Wind) *fired the first salvo in the war against the growing contamination of the environment through the indiscriminate use of chemical pesticides. Although her book, published some twenty-five years ago, drew immediate fire from the chemical industry, it also shocked many scientists and the public into taking a careful look at our destruction of the natural ecosystem. Carson's book spawned the modern environmentalist movement, which resulted in the establishment of the Environmental Protection Agency, the banning of DDT, and the restriction of aldrin and clordane. Today, however, the use of hundreds of new, although significantly modified, insecticides and herbicides has become merely one aspect of the world's increasing concern over the nuclear and chemical pollution of our land, air, and water.*

This selection, Chapter II, the essence of her book, is a classic example of lucid, well-organized, graceful prose, praised by both her admirers and detractors alike. For a valuable crash course in organization and style take extra time to study Carson's writing: note her use of topic sentences for maximum clarity, her transitional words for unity and coherence, and her deliberate choice of ominous words for their persuasive and dramatic impact.

The history of life on earth has been a history of interaction between living things and their surroundings. To a large extent, the physical form and the habits of the earth's vegetation and its animal life have been molded by the environment. Considering the whole span of earthly time, the opposite effect, in which life actually modifies its surroundings, has been relatively slight. Only within the moment of time represented by the present century has one species — man — acquired significant power to alter the nature of his world.

During the past quarter century this power has not only increased to one of disturbing magnitude but it has changed in character. The most alarming of all man's assaults upon the environment is the contamination of air, earth, rivers, and sea with dangerous and even lethal materials. This pollution is for the most part irrecoverable; the chain of evil it initiates not only in the world that must support life but in living tissues is for the most part irreversible. In this now universal contamination of the environment, chemicals are the sinister and little recognized partners of radiation in changing the very nature of the world — the very nature of its life. Strontium 90, released through nuclear explosions into the air, comes to earth in rain or drifts down as fallout, lodges in soil, enters the grass or corn or wheat grown there, and in time takes up its abode in the bones of a human being, there to remain until his death. Similarly, chemicals sprayed on croplands or forests or garden lie long in soil, entering into living organisms, passing from one to another in a chain of poisoning and death. Or they pass mysteriously by underground streams until they emerge and through the alchemy of air and sunlight, combine into new forms that kill vegetation, sicken cattle, and work unknown harm on those who drink from once pure wells. As Albert Schweitzer has said, "Man can hardly even recognize the devils of his own creation."

It took hundreds of millions of years to produce the life that now inhabits the earth—eons of time in which that developing and evolving and diversifying life reached a state of adjustment and balance with its surroundings. The environment, rigorously shaping and directing the life it supported, contained elements that were hostile as well as supporting. Certain rocks gave out dangerous radiation; even within the light of the sun, from which all life draws its energy, there were short-wave radiations with power to injure. Given time—time not in years but in millennia—life adjusts, and a balance has been reached. For time is the essential ingredient; but in the modern world there is no time.   3

The rapidity of change and the speed with which new situations are created follow the impetuous and heedless pace of man rather than the deliberate pace of nature. Radiation is no longer merely the background radiation of rocks, the bombardment of cosmic rays, the ultraviolet of the sun that have existed before there was any life on earth; radiation is now the unnatural creation of man's tampering with the atom. The chemicals to which life is asked to make its adjustment are no longer merely the calcium and silica and copper and all the rest of the minerals washed out of the rocks and carried in rivers to the sea; they are the synthetic creations of man's inventive mind, brewed in his laboratories, and having no counterparts in nature.   4

To adjust to these chemicals would require time on the scale that is nature's; it would require not merely the years of a man's life but the life of generations. And even this, were it by some miracle possible, would be futile, for the new chemicals come from our laboratories in an endless stream; almost five hundred annually find their way into actual use in the United States alone. The figure is staggering and its implications are not easily grasped—500 new chemicals to which the bodies of men and animals are required somehow to adapt each year, chemicals totally outside the limits of biologic experience.   5

Among them are many that are used in man's war against nature. Since the mid-1940's over 200 basic chemicals have been created for use in killing insects, weeds, rodents, and other organisms described in the modern   6 vernacular as "pests"; and they are sold under several thousand different brand names.

These sprays, dusts, and aerosols are now applied almost universally to farms, gardens, forests, and homes—nonselective chemicals that have the power to kill every insect, the "good" and the "bad," to still the song of birds and the leaping of fish in the streams, to coat the leaves with a deadly film, and to linger on in soil—all this though the intended target may be only a few weeds or insects. Can anyone believe it is possible to lay down such a barrage of poisons on the surface of the earth without making it unfit for all life? They should not be called "insecticides," but "biocides."

The whole process of spraying seems caught up in an endless spiral. Since DDT was released for civilian use, a process of escalation has been going on in which ever more toxic materials must be found. This has happened because insects, in a triumphant vindication of Darwin's principle of the survival of the fittest, have evolved super races immune to the particular insecticide used, hence a deadlier one has always to be developed—and then a deadlier one than that. It has happened also because destructive insects often undergo a "flareback," or resurgence, after spraying, in numbers greater than before. Thus the chemical war is never won, and all life is caught in its violent crossfire.

Along with the possibility of the extinction of mankind by nuclear war, the central problem of our age has therefore become the contamination of man's total environment with such substances of incredible potential for harm—substances that accumulate in the tissues of plants and animals and even penetrate the germ cells to shatter or alter the very material of heredity upon which the shape of the future depends.

Some would-be architects of our future look toward a time when it will be possible to alter the human germ plasm by design. But we may easily be doing so now by inadvertence for many chemicals, like radiation, bring about gene mutations. It is ironic to think that man might determine his own future by something so seemingly trivial as the choice of an insect spray.

All this has been risked—for what? Future historians may well be amazed by our distorted sense of proportion. How could intelligent beings seek to control a few unwanted species by a method that contaminated the entire environment and brought the threat of disease and death even to their own kind? Yet this is precisely what we have done. We have done it, moreover, for reasons that collapse the moment we examine them. We are told that the enormous and expanding use of pesticides is necessary to maintain farm production. Yet is our real problem not one of *overproduction*? Our farms, despite measures to remove acreages from production and to pay farmers *not* to produce, have yielded such a staggering excess of crops that the American taxpayer in 1962 is paying out more than one billion dollars a year as the total carrying cost of the surplus-food storage program. And is the situation helped when one branch of the Agriculture Department tries to reduce production while another states, as it did in 1958, "It is believed generally that reduction of crop acreages under provisions of the Soil Bank will stimulate interest in use of chemicals to obtain maximum production on the land retained in crops."

All this is not to say there is no insect problem and no need of control. I am saying, rather, that control must be geared to realities, not to mythical situations, and that the methods employed must be such that they do not destroy us along with the insects.   12

The problem whose attempted solution has brought such a train of disaster in its wake is an accompaniment of our modern way of life. Long before the age of man, insects inhabited the earth — a group of extraordinarily varied and adaptable beings. Over the course of time since man's advent, a small percentage of the more than half a million species of insects have come into conflict with human welfare in two principal ways: as competitors for the food supply and as carriers of human disease.   13

Disease-carrying insects become important where human beings are crowded together, especially under conditions where sanitation is poor, as in time of natural disaster or war or in situations of extreme poverty and deprivation. Then control of some sort becomes necessary. It is a sobering fact, however, that the method of massive chemical control has had only limited success, and also threatens to worsen the very conditions it is intended to curb.   14

Under primitive agricultural conditions the farmer had few insect problems. These arose with the intensification of agriculture — the devotion of immense acreages to a single crop. Such a system set the stage for explosive increases in specific insect populations. Single-crop farming does not take advantage of the principles by which nature works; it is agriculture as an engineer might conceive it to be. Nature has introduced great variety into the landscape, but man has displayed a passion for simplifying it. Thus he undoes the built-in checks and balances by which nature holds the species within bounds. One important natural check is a limit on the amount of suitable habitat for each species. Obviously then, an insect that lives on wheat can build up its population to much higher levels on a farm devoted to wheat than on one in which wheat is intermingled with other crops to which the insect is not adapted.   15

The same thing happens in other situations. A generation or more ago, the towns of large areas of the United States lined their streets with the noble elm tree. Now the beauty they hopefully created is threatened with complete destruction as disease sweeps through the elms, carried by a beetle that would have only limited chance to build up large populations and to spread from tree to tree if the elms were only occasional trees in a richly diversified planting.   16

261

Another factor in the modern insect problem is one that must be viewed against a background of geologic and human history: the spreading of thousands of different kinds of organisms from their native homes to invade new territories. This worldwide migration has been studied and graphically described by the British ecologist Charles Elton in his recent book *The Ecology of Invasions*. During the Cretaceous Period, some hundred million years ago, flooding seas cut many land bridges between continents and living things found themselves confined in what Elton calls "colossal separate nature reserves." There, isolated from others of their kind, they developed many new species. When some of the land masses were joined again, about 15 million years ago, these species began to move out into new territories — a movement that is not only still in progress but is now receiving considerable assistance from man.

The importation of plants is the primary agent in the modern spread of species, for animals have almost invariably gone along with the plants, quarantine being a comparatively recent and not completely effective innovation. The United States Office of Plant Introduction alone has introduced almost 200,000 species and varieties of plants from all over the world. Nearly half of the 180 or so major insect enemies of plants in the United States are accidental imports from abroad, and most of them have come as hitchhikers on plants.

In new territory, out of reach of the restraining hand of the natural enemies that kept down its numbers in its native land, an invading plant or animal is able to become enormously abundant. Thus it is no accident that our most troublesome insects are introduced species.

These invasions, both the naturally occurring and those dependent on human assistance, are likely to continue indefinitely. Quarantine and massive chemical campaigns are only extremely expensive ways of buying time. We are faced, according to Dr. Elton, "with a life-and-death need not just to find new technological means of suppressing this plant or that animal"; instead we need the basic knowledge of animal populations and their relations to their surroundings that will "promote an even balance and damp down the explosive power of outbreaks and new invasions."

Much of the necessary knowledge is now available but we do not use it. We train ecologists in our universities and even employ them in our government agencies but we seldom take their advice. We allow the chemical death rain to fall as though there were no alternative, whereas in fact there are many, and our ingenuity could soon discover many more if given opportunity.

Have we fallen into a mesmerized state that makes us accept as inevitable that which is inferior or detrimental, as though having lost the will or the vision to demand that which is good? Such thinking, in the words of the ecologist Paul Shepard, "idealizes life with only its head out of the water, inches above the limits of toleration of the corruption of its own environment. . . . Why should we tolerate a diet of weak poisons, a home in insipid surroundings, a circle of acquaintances who are not quite our enemies, the noise of motors with just enough relief to prevent insanity? Who would want to live in a world which is just not quite fatal?"

Yet such a world is pressed upon us. The crusade to create a chemically sterile, insect-free world seems to have engendered a fanatic zeal on the part of many specialists and most of the so-called control agencies. On every hand there is evidence that those engaged in spraying operations excercise a ruthless power. "The regulatory entomologists . . . function as prosecutor, judge and jury, tax assessor and collector and sheriff to enforce their own orders," said Connecticut entomologist Neely Turner. The most flagrant abuses go unchecked in both state and federal agencies.   23

It is not my contention that chemical insecticides must never be used. I do contend that we have put poisonous and biologically potent chemicals indiscriminately into the hands of persons largely or wholly ignorant of their potentials for harm. We have subjected enormous numbers of people to contact with these poisons, without their consent and often without their knowledge. If the Bill of Rights contains no guarantee that a citizen shall be secure against lethal poisons distributed either by private individuals or by public officials, it is surely only because our forefathers, despite their considerable wisdom and foresight, could conceive of no such problem.   24

I contend, furthermore, that we have allowed these chemicals to be used with little or no advance investigation of their effect on soil, water, wildlife, and man himself. Future generations are unlikely to condone our lack of prudent concern for the integrity of the natural world that supports all life.   25

There is still very limited awareness of the nature of the threat. This is an era of specialists, each of whom sees his own problem and is unaware of or intolerant of the larger frame into which it fits. It is also an era dominated by industry, in which the right to make a dollar at whatever cost is seldom challenged. When the public protests, confronted with some obvious evidence of damaging results of pesticide applications, it is fed little tranquilizing pills of half truth. We urgently need an end to these false assurances, to the sugar coating of unpalatable facts. It is the public that is being asked to assume the risks that the insect controllers calculate. The public must decide whether it wishes to continue on the present road, and it can do so only when in full possession of the facts. In the words of Jean Rostand, "The obligation to endure gives us the right to know."   26

QUESTIONS ON CONTENT:

1. What is Carson's thesis, and where is it located?
2. What is the difference between the way nature changes the environment and

the way humans change it? What is the advantage of one over the other?

3. What has been the role of human beings in increasing insect invasions?

QUESTIONS ON WRITING STRUCTURE AND STRATEGY:

1. To whom is Carson addressing her remarks? How do you know?

2. How does she seek to convince her readers? Does she use a logical or an emotional approach — or both? How does her choice of language reinforce her arguments?

3. What specific words and phrases provide the transitions that unify her writing?

4. What types of support does she use?

QUESTIONS FOR DISCUSSION AND WRITING:

1. Outlining can pay big dividends in comprehending (and remembering) what you read as well as in helping to organize ideas prior to writing. The ability to outline is also an important talent in preparing reports (in college and later on the job), in taking notes, or in writing up minutes in a meeting. This selection is surprisingly easy to outline. Try summarizing in one sentence each of the paragraphs, and you have an excellent outline of the whole chapter that will remain meaningful years from now. (Check your handbook for the particular outlining format in your class.)

2. Précis writing (see Medawar) is a relatively simple way to master conciseness and focus. Write a 200 to 400 word summary of the chapter, covering the thesis and major supporting points.

3. This selection offers an opportunity to get further acquainted with the library. See what the critics had to say about *Silent Spring* by looking in *Book Review Digest*. Check *Readers' Guide*, the *New York Times Index* for 1962 and 1963, and more recently for articles applauding or condemning her stance. Write a paper in which you persuasively argue your conclusions of the controversy. (Incidentally, Carson devoted six years to researching her subject and included fifty-five pages of documentation. You may wish to include several "sources" to give weight and credibility to your statements.)

4. As another possible research project: investigate the use of defoliants in Vietnam and the continuing claims of veterans that they have suffered irreparable damage from "Agent Orange," a defoliant.

5. Inventory your own home and determine how many chemicals or chemical products are used against insects, weeds, ants, moles, and other pests. Do they contain harmful ingredients? What is their "life span"? Are they biodegradable (examine labels on containers)? Can they be dispensed with? Write an account of your experience in your journal or compose a short paper.

AMERICA'S MANAGEMENT CRISIS
David Vogel

*Today everyone from the assembly-line worker to the corporation
president has a ready answer for the problems of business and
industry. David Vogel, business consultant, author, and educator,
analyzes management's current crisis in the following selection.
Although he begins by praising America's unique talent for innovation
and application in improving the nation's industrial output, he warns
that America is fast losing out to foreign competition. Instead of
concerning itself with long-range improvements in quality and
increased productivity, it is shortsightedly concerning itself with
immediate profits. Vogel's article, appearing in* The New Republic, *a
weekly journal of opinion, is aimed not only at management and
students of management but at the common reader.*

*In his analysis, observe Vogel's effective use of topic sentences for
clarity, of cogent examples and statistics for support, and of cause and
effect reasoning for persuasion. Compare and contrast this selection
with Blumberg's article on the problems in the automobile industry.*

The creativity of American management has been one of the historic   1
strengths of the American business system. Most of the technological
innovations underlying the industrial revolution were developed in England,
but it was the United States that pioneered new organizational techniques for
improving productivity. Innovations such as standardized parts, introduced by
Eli Whitney, the moving assembly line, conceived by Henry Ford, and the
principles of scientific management developed by Frederick Taylor were
responsible for much of the dramatic gains in America's industrial output
during the 19th and early 20th centuries. The modern form of corporate
organization now in use throughout the world was developed by railroad
executives in the United States before the Civil War. The United States still has
the world's most extensive and prestigious system of professional management
education.

But American business managers, traditionally an important source of   2
competitive strength, now have become a cause of national decline, even
though business executives continue to blame governmental policies for the
poor performance of the American economy. A widely quoted recent article in
the *Harvard Business Review* asserted that much of the "competitive
listlessness" of the US economy is due to the "attitudes, preoccupations, and
practices of American managers." The article charged that preoccupation with
"short-term results" and quantitative measurements of performance has led
American managers to neglect the kinds of investments and innovations
necessary to increase the nation's capacity to generate wealth. The authors,

two Harvard Business School professors, conclude that many American managers "have effectively forsworn long-term technological superiority as a competitive weapon." *Business Week*'s special issue on reindustrialization a few months ago featured a similar indictment, specifically criticizing American managers for their lack of technical skills and for their nonentrepreneurial mentality.

Even many corporate executives have become self-critical on this score. In 3
a recent poll, three out of four US executives criticized corporate incentive plans for rewarding short-term performance and thus discouraging risky long-term projects. One out of three believed that senior managers didn't know enough about technology and underemphasized innovation.

There is some hard evidence to support these perceptions. Industry 4
spending for basic research declined 12 percent in real terms between 1966 and 1976. A 1969 survey of manufacturing companies revealed that 20 percent had a policy requiring all capital expenditures for modernization and replacement to pay for themselves within three years. A decade later this policy had been adopted by 25 percent of the companies polled. The change is small, but the trend is significant.

Senior managers have been spending more energy trying to increase their 5
companies' short-term profits through financial manipulation. In 1979 companies spent more than $40 billion in cash on acquiring other companies. This is far more than they spent on research and development. Some of these mergers may have led to improved efficiency, but most of them were little more than private sector transfer payments—money passing from one set of balance sheets to another without producing any net increase in actual wealth. The most striking (though admittedly least interesting) aspect of the recent Agee-Cunningham flap at Bendix Corporation was what it revealed about the way many senior executives are spending their time. Evidently William Agee, the head of one of America's largest industrial corporations, spent most of his life running around the country buying and selling various parts of Bendix, rather than improving the productivity of operators the company already owned. These escapades may ultimately benefit Bendix's shareholders, or may not, but they add nothing to America's ability to compete with the Japanese.

More and more chief executive officers have only the most casual 6
familiarity with what their companies actually make and how. They are more likely than ever before to have been hired away from another company, often in a completely unrelated line of business. And they are less likely than before to have had any operating or line experience. Since the mid-1950s, the proportion of American chief executives trained in either law or finance has increased by nearly half while the proportion with technical backgrounds has declined by nearly 15 percent. *Business Week* writes: "Just as the general practitioner who

made house calls is a dim memory, so is the hands-on corporate leader who rose through the ranks, learning every aspect of the business before managing it." In a survey of 1,700 American corporate vice presidents, 47 percent began their careers in either marketing or finance. American executives are far more likely to possess an MBA than their foreign counterparts, but German, French, Swiss, and Swedish top executives are far more likely to have had technical training. The only nation where executives have less technical education than the United States is the United Kingdom.

Critical business decisions too often are made not on the basis of a true understanding of the technology but on elegant formulas learned in business school. Increasingly, executives manage their companies in the detached way that investors manage that portfolios.   7

The typical chief executive officer now holds office for an average of five years, compared to 10 years a generation ago. Since CEOs tend to be judged and judge themselves by the profits reported while they are in charge, they are understandably reluctant to pursue long-term projects that depress current earnings and won't pay off until after they retire. Executives frequently criticize politicians for making decisions on the basis of short-term considerations in order to ensure their reelection. But the same indictment applies even more to managers in the private sector. Elected officials have a time horizon of at least two years, but executive promotions within companies often are based on earnings calculated on an annual basis. Akio Morita, the chairman of Sony, recently observed: "The annual bonus some American executives receive depends on annual profit, and the executive who knows his firm's production facilities should be modernized isn't likely to make a decision to invest in new equipment if his own income and managerial ability are judged based only on annual profit. . . . I have heard many American managers say, 'Why should I sacrifice my profit for my successor?' "   8

For many years, a powerful piece of evidence against British management has been that American owned and managed companies in Great Britain have higher productivity than other firms in the British economy. A similar unflattering comparison now may be made between the productivity of native-run and foreign-run companies in the United States. The best known example is a television plant in Illinois. When it was run by Motorola, inspectors found 140 defects for every 100 television sets. Since the plant was bought by Matsushita Electric Industrial Company in 1974, the number of defects declined to less than six per 100 sets. The number of warranty claims dropped by seven-eighths. American managers frequently attribute Japanese efficiency to values peculiar to Japanaese culture; but one assembly line at Sony's San Diego plant holds the company's worldwide record for production: 200 days without a serious defect.   9

The contrast in quality between American and Japanese products has become increasingly obvious over the last decade. American consumers continue to prefer Japanese products (often as not made in Taiwan and South Korea) even as the Japanese price advantage has all but disappeared. According to a recent article in *Fortune*, a new American car is almost twice as likely to have a problem as a Japanese model, and American-made computer chips are three times more likely to fail than Japanese ones.

Both our slow productivity growth and the relatively poor quality of many American goods are connected to the training and incentives of American managers. It is difficult for MBAs — trained to measure discounted cash flow and capital asset pricing models — to work closely with employees in search of ways to improve procedures and equipment. The incentives for managers to make productivity improvements actually declined during the 1970s, as many companies switched from a strategy of expanding sales to one emphasizing immediate return of assets. According to the *Wall Street Journal*, the consequence of rewarding executives by this second measure encouraged them to make small investments that paid off quickly, rather than larger outlays that might greatly improve productivity eventually, but that were riskier and would take longer to show results.

Many large corporations have made the transition from founder-entrepreneur to professional management without suffering any decline of entrepreneurial vigor. Firms such as IBM, Dupont, Boeing, Texas Instruments, and Minnesota Mining and Manufacturing have demonstrated both a willingness to make investments in risky new technologies and patience in waiting for the pay-off. A company run by a scientist is not guaranteed continued success, as Polaroid's recent experiences indicate. Nor, as the history of the steel industry reveals, does a policy of promoting from within the ranks ensure informed management decisions. Various companies and plants throughout the United States have demonstrated impressive increases in productivity by involving workers in the decision-making process at the plant level. But the overall picture remains discouraging.

Managers are not completely at fault, of course. Just one special problem they face is that American industry is far more dependent on the stock market as a source of capital than our foreign competitors are. Japanese and German firms are financed mostly by borrowing, not selling shares. This frees them to make long-term investments without Wall Street money-managers scrutinizing each quarterly earnings report. It is impossible to determine the precise role played by any one factor in America's economic difficulties. But it is important that public discussion of the economy's poor performance not focus exclusively on the need for changes in government policy.

Under President Reagan the business community may get many of the   14
changes in tax and regulatory policies that it claims it needs. But unless the
private sector's own pattern of incentives and training is reformed, US-managed
companies are likely to continue to lose market shares to foregin competitors.
Instead of hiring more lobbyists, American companies should promote more
engineers. We need to reexamine the kind of education that those to whom we
entrust our economic future are getting. Has the notion of a professional
manager—an individual who learns a set of general analytical, abstract,
decision-making skills that can be applied equally well to the problems faced
by any institution—become as irrelevant as the British classical Oxbridge
education became several generations ago? Why are the nations with the most
developed systems of professional management education, the United States
and Great Britain, performing so poorly, when two nations that provide almost
no professional management training, Germany and Japan, have been the
outstanding successes of the postwar period? Virtually none of the nation's
major business schools require courses in production or offer adequate training
in the management of human resources. Business schools ignore foreign
language training and place little emphasis on teaching students to understand
foreign cultures. The popularity of finance courses at business schools probably
has contributed to the preoccupation of recently graduated MBAs with short-
term time horizons.

Corporate critics also need to redirect their thinking. Except in cases of   15
particularly gross blunders, like the recent bloopers of the automobile and steel
industries, critics of business tend to take the competence of US management
for granted. They most often criticize companies for being *too* successful in
their pursuit of profits, and thereby neglecting other legitimate social needs.
But Milton Friedman is right in saying that the most important social
responsibility of business is in fact to produce wealth. We need to be as critical
about the inability of companies to grow and innovate as we are about their
failures of social responsibility.

QUESTIONS ON CONTENT:

1. In citing the achievements of American industrialism in the late nineteenth
   and early twentieth century, what specific contributions does Vogel mention?
2. In what specific ways does Vogel fault most American management and their
   training?
3. How is the increasingly poor quality of American-made goods and declining
   productivity a manifestation of the management crisis?
4. What reforms does Vogel advocate?

QUESTIONS ON WRITING STRUCTURE AND STRATEGY:

1. How does Vogel employ illustrations/examples to buttress his argument?

2. How do his comparisons with past American success and with industries in other countries help to support his thesis?

3. Examine Vogel's analysis for its emotional appeal and for its rational appeal. Which seems to predominate? Is this appeal appropriate to the subject? Why?

QUESTIONS FOR DISCUSSION AND WRITING:

1. Write a short paper on your experiences and/or those of your friends who have purchased foreign cars, electronic equipment, and so on, in which you discuss reasons for preferring these products over American counterparts. Explain fully.

2. Examine your college catalog and analyze the courses offered in the business college. Then interview business students and determine the extent to which they are aware of the problems cited in Vogel's essay. Should they be aware of the problems? Are there any courses that deal specifically with these problems?

3. For a short research project, familiarize yourself with *Harvard Business Review, Business Week, Forbes, Barron's Weekly, Wall Street Journal,* and *Fortune,* all concerned with business and the economy. Choose one or several of these publications and survey their stories about American management, its successes and failures. Do you find any stories that confirm Vogel's arguments? Or do you find any that challenge his conclusions? Write short summaries of these articles.

4. Do a short exercise on Vogel's diction. What is there to indicate that this article is meant for the general lay reader?
   OR:
   Examine several of the business/management publications and survey the kind of material they publish. Write an analysis of the content of one or several of the publications. Are they directed solely to the specialist? Or are they written to appeal to a general audience?

OPEN LETTER
TO A YOUNG NEGRO
Jesse Owens and Paul G. Neimark

His feats were incredible for a black man in his day—for any athlete anywhere ever—tying one world track record and breaking three others, all in forty-five minutes one May afternoon in Ann Arbor, Michigan, and a year later winning four gold medals in the 1936 Olympics in Berlin. He was a superstar in the world's eyes, and yet Hitler, host for the Berlin games, walked out of the stadium rather than watch him in the long jump trials and adamantly refused to present him with his medals. In 1936, for Jesse Owens, there was no Presidential phone call, no invitation to visit the White House. There were no lucrative jobs doing TV commercials or endorsing cereals and sports equipment. Instead, the famous Olympic hero accepted the best offer he received, that of a playground janitor, supplementing his earnings racing against cars and animals. President Carter probably best described Jesse Owens, upon his death in 1980: "Perhaps no athlete better symbolized the human struggle against tyranny, poverty, and racial bigotry."

Born in 1913 in Danville, Alabama, Jesse Owens went on to become one of the greatest athletes of all time. Despite his impressive high school track record, Owens earned his tuition at Ohio State University by running an elevator because there were no athletic scholarships. Virtually nothing daunted Owens in his pursuit of excellence, not even a painful back injury that prevented him from warming up or even stretching before the 1935 Ann Arbor Big Ten Meet.

Years later, in recalling Hitler's snub, Owens good-naturedly commented: "It was all right with me. I didn't go to Berlin to shake hands with him, anyway. All I know is that I'm here now, and Hitler isn't." But with considerably less geniality he pointed out, "When I came back after all those stories about Hitler and his snub, I came back to my native country, and I couldn't ride in the front of the bus. I had to go to the back door. I couldn't live where I wanted. Now, what's the difference?"

Eventually, perseverance paid off for Owens, and he founded a very successful public relations and marketing firm, and authored two books, Blackthink and I Have Changed. For many years he was a popular public speaker, traveling some 200,000 miles per year. Although his records have gradually been surpassed (some not until the late 1960s), the charisma surrounding his name can never be eradicated.

271

Observe in this selection how Owens builds up the reader's interest through dialogue and suspense.

"Tell them how the good times between us were."

—LUZ LONG

"All black men are insane. . . . Almost any living thing would quickly go mad under the unrelenting exposure to the climate created and reserved for black men in a white racist society. . . . I am secretly pleased about the riots. Nothing would please the tortured man inside me more than seeing bigger and better riots every day."

Those words were spoken by Bob Teague to his young son in *Letters to a Black Boy.* He wrote these letters to "alert" his son to "reality" so that the boy wouldn't "be caught off guard—unprepared and undone."

Are his words true?

Does a black man have to be just about insane to exist in America?

Do all Negroes feel a deep twinge of pleasure every time we see a white man hurt and a part of white society destroyed?

Is reality something so stinking terrible that it'll grab your heart out of your chest with one hand and your manhood with the other if you don't meet it armed like a Nazi storm trooper?

Bob Teague is no "militant." He's a constructive, accomplished journalist with a wife and child. If he feels hate and fear, can *you* ever avoid feeling it?

Whether it's Uncle Tom or ranting rioter doing the talking today, you're told that you'll have to be afraid and angry. The only difference is that one tells you to hold it in and the other tells you to let it out. Life is going to be torture because you're a Negro, they all say. They only differ on whether you should grin and bear it or take it out on everyone else. But National Urban League official, Black Panther leader or any of the in-betweens all seem to agree on one thing today: "We must organize around our strongest bond—our blackness."

Is that really our strongest bond? Isn't there something deeper, richer, better in this world than the color of one's skin?

Let me tell you the answer to that. Let me prove it to you so strong and deep that you'll taste it for all the days to come. Let me throw my arm around your shoulder and walk you to where so much good is and where the only blackness worth fearing is the black they're trying to color your soul.

Even though you weren't born for ten, maybe twenty years after, you've probably heard the story—the story of the 1936 Olympics and how I managed to come out with four gold medals. A lot of words have been written about those medals and about the one for the broad jump in particular. Because it was during that event that Hitler walked out on me and where, in anger, I supposedly fouled on my first two jumps against his prize athlete, Luz Long. The whole Olympics for me and, symbolically, for my country, seemed to rest on that third jump.

Yes, a lot of words have been written about that day and the days that followed. And they've almost been true, just as it's almost true that sometimes every black man weakens a little and does hate the white man, just as it's almost true that reality is tough at times and does make you want to weaken.   12

Yet, just like *those* "truths," what was written about me was only a half-truth without some other more important words. I want to say them to you now.   13

I *was* up against it, but long before I came to the broad jump. Negroes had gone to the Olympics before, and Negroes had won before. But so much more was expected of me. Because this was the time of the most intense conflict between dictatorship and freedom the world had ever known. Adolf Hitler was arming his country against the entire world, and almost everyone sensed it. It was ironic that these last Olympic Games before World War II was to split the earth were scheduled for Berlin, where he would be the host. From the beginning, Hitler had perverted the games into a test between two forms of government, just as he perverted almost everything else he touched.   14

Almost everything else.   15

The broad jump preliminaries came before the finals of the other three events I was in—the hundred-meter and two-hundred-meter dashes and the relay. How I did in the broad jump would determine how I did in the entire Olympics. For here was where I held a world record that no one had ever approached before except one man: Luz Long, Hitler's best athlete.   16

Long, a tall, sandy-haired, perfectly built fellow (the ideal specimen of Hitler's "Ayran supremacy" idea), had been known to jump over twenty-six feet in preparing for the Games. No one knew for sure what he could really do because Hitler kept him under wraps. But stories had filtered out that he had gone as far as I had, farther than anyone else in the world. I was used to hearing rumors like that and tried not to think too much about it. Yet the first time I laid eyes on Long, I sensed that the stories hadn't been exaggerated. After he took his first jump, I knew they hadn't. This man was something. I'd have to set an Olympic record and by no small margin to beat him.   17

It would be tough. August in Berlin was muggier than May in Ann Arbor or Columbus. Yet the air was cool, and it was hard getting warmed up. The ground on the runway to the broad jump pit wasn't the same consistency as that at home. Long was used to it. I wasn't.   18

His first jump broke the Olympic record. In the trials!   19

Did it worry me a little? More than a little. He was on his home ground   20

273

and didn't seem susceptible to the pressure. In fact, he'd already done one thing I always tried to do in every jumping event and race I ran: discourage the competition by getting off to a better start.

Well, there was only one way to get back the psychological advantage. Right off the bat I'd have to make a better jump than he did. I didn't want to do it that way — it wasn't wise to use up your energy in preliminaries. Long could afford to showboat in the trials. This was his only event, the one he'd been groomed for under Hitler for years. I had to run three races besides, more than any other athlete on either team.

But I felt I had to make a showing right then. I measured off my steps from the takeoff board and got ready. Suddenly an American newspaperman came up to me. "Is it true, Jesse?" he said.

"Is what true?" I answered.

"That Hitler walked out on you? That he wouldn't watch you jump?"

I looked over at where the German ruler had been sitting. No one was in his box. A minute ago he had been there. I could add two and two. Besides, he's already snubbed me once by refusing the Olympic Committee's request to have me sit in that box.

This was too much. I was mad, hate-mad, and it made me feel wild. I was going to show him. He'd hear about this jump, even if he wouldn't see it!

I felt the energy surging into my legs and tingling in the muscles of my stomach as it never had before. I began my run, first almost in slow motion, then picking up speed, and finally faster and faster until I was moving almost as fast as I did during the hundred-yard dash. Suddenly the takeoff board was in front of me. I hit it, went up, up high — so high I knew I was outdoing Long and every man who ever jumped.

But they didn't measure it. I heard the referee shout "Foul!" in my ears before I even came down. I had run too fast, been concentrating too much on a record and not enough on form. I'd gone half a foot over the takeoff board.

All the newspaper stories and books I've ever seen about that Olympic broad jump had me fouling on the next of my three tries, because the writers felt that made the story more dramatic. The truth is I didn't foul at all on my second jump.

I played it safe. Too safe. I was making absolutely sure I didn't foul. All right, I said to myself. Long had won his point. But who would remember the preliminaries tomorrow? It was the finals that counted. I had to make sure I got into those finals. I wasn't going to let him psyche me out of it. I wasn't going to let Hitler anger me into throwing away what I'd worked ten years for.

So I ran slower, didn't try to get up as high during my jump. Hell, I said to myself, if I can do twenty-six feet trying my best, I sure ought to be able to do a foot less without much effort. That would be enough to qualify for the finals, and there I'd have three fresh jumps again. That's where I'd take apart Luz Long.

It's funny how sometimes you can forget the most important things. I forgot that I wasn't the kind of guy who could ever go halfway at anything. More than that, no sprinter or jumper can really take just a little bit off the top. It's like taking a little bit off when you're working a mathematical equation or flying an airplane through a storm. You need the total concentration and total effort from beginning to end. One mistake and you're dead. More than that, my whole style was geared to giving everything I had, to using all my speed and energy every second of what I was doing. Once or twice I'd tried a distance race just for kicks. I was miserable at it. If I couldn't go all out all the time, I was no good.   32

So my second jump was no good.   33

I didn't foul. But I didn't go far enough to qualify, either. It wasn't just Long and Owens in the event anymore. There were dozens of other participants from other countries, and a bunch of them — too many — were now ahead of me.   34

I had one jump left.   35

It wasn't enough.   36

I looked around nervously, panic creeping into every cell of my body. On my right was Hitler's box. Empty. His way of saying I was a member of an inferior race who would give an inferior performance. In back of that box was a stadium containing more than a hundred thousand people, almost all Germans, all wanting to see me fail. On my right was the broad jump official. Was he fair? Yeah. But a Nazi. If it came to a close call, a hairline win-or-lose decision, deep down didn't he, too, want to see me lose? Worst of all, a few feet away was Luz Long, laughing with a German friend of his, unconcerned, confident, *Aryan*.   37

They were against me. Every one of them. I was back in Oakville again. I was a nigger.   38

Did I find some hidden resource deep within me, rise to the occasion and qualify for the finals — as every account of those Olympics says?   39

The hell I did.   40

I found a hidden resource, but it wasn't inside of me. It was in the most unlikely and revealing place possible.   41

Time was growing short. One by one the other jumpers had been called and taken their turns. What must have been twenty minutes or half an hour suddenly seemed like only seconds. I was going to be called next. I wasn't ready. I wanted to shout it — *I wasn't ready!*   42

Then the panic was total. I had to walk in a little circle to keep my legs from shaking, hold my jaw closed tight to stop my teeth from chattering. I   43 didn't know what to do. I was lost, with no Charles Riley* to turn to. If I gave it everything I had, I'd foul again. If I played it safe, I wouldn't go far enough to qualify. *And this is what it all comes down to,* I thought to myself. *Ten years and 4,500 miles to make a nigger of myself and not even reach the finals!*

And then I couldn't even think anymore. I started to feel faint, began to gasp for breath. Instinctively, I turned away from everyone so they couldn't see me. But I couldn't help hearing them. The thousands of different noises of the stadium congealed into one droning hum — *ch-ch-ch-ch ch-ch-ch-ch,* louder and louder in my ears. It was as though they were all chanting it. Hatefully, gleefully. *Ch-ch-ch-ch. Ch-ch-ch-ch. CH-CH-CH-CH.*

Suddenly I felt a firm hand on my arm. I turned and looked into the sky-blue eyes of my worst enemy.

"Hello, Jesse Owens," he said. "I am Luz Long."

I nodded. I couldn't speak.

"Look," he said. "There is no time to waste with manners. What has taken your goat?"

I had to smile a little in spite of myself — hearing his mixed-up American idiom.

"Aww, nothing," I said. "You know how it is."

He was silent for a few seconds. "Yes," he said finally, "I know how it is. But I also know you are a better jumper than this. Now, *what has taken your goat?"*

I laughed out loud this time. But I couldn't tell him, him above all. I glanced over at the broad jump pit. I was about to be called.

Luz didn't waste words, even if he wasn't sure of which ones to use.

"Is it what Reichskenzler Hitler did?" he asked.

I was thunderstruck that he'd say it. "I—" I started to answer. But I didn't know what to say.

"I see," he said. "Look, we talk about that later. Now you must jump. And you must qualify."

"But how?" I shot back.

"I have thought," he said. "You are like I am. You must do it one hundred percent. Correct?" I nodded. "Yet you must be sure not to foul." I nodded again, this time in frustration. And as I did, I heard the loudspeaker call my name.

Luz talked quickly. "Then you do both things, Jesse. You remeasure your steps. You take off six inches behind the foul board. You jump as hard as you can. But you need not fear to foul."

All at once the panic emptied out of me like a cloudburst.

---

*His high school coach who had encouraged his career.

Of course!

I jogged over to the runway. I remeasured my steps again. Then I put a   62
towel parallel to the place half a foot before the takeoff board from where I
wanted to jump.

I walked back to the starting spot. I began my run, hit the place beside the   63
towel, shot up into the air like a bird and qualified by more than a foot.

The next day I went into the finals of the broad jump and waged the most   64
intense competition of my life with Luz Long. He broke his own personal
record and the Olympic record, too, and then I—thanks to him—literally flew
to top that. Hours before I had won the hundred meters in 10.3, and then
afterward the 200 meters in 20.7 and helped our team to another gold medal
and record in the relay.

During the evenings that framed those days, I would sit with Luz in his   65
space or mine in the Olympic village, and we would form an even more intense
friendship. We were sometimes as different inside as we looked on the outside.
But the things that were the *same* were much more important to us.

Luz had a wife and a young child, too. His was a son. We talked about   66
everything from athletics to art, but mostly we talked about the future. He
didn't say it in so many words, but he seemed to know that war was coming
and he would have to be in it. I didn't know then whether the United States
would be involved, but I did realize that this earth was getting to be a
precarious place for a young man trying to make his way. And, like me, even if
war didn't come, Luz wasn't quite sure how he would make the transformation
from athletics to life once the Olympics were over.

We talked, of course, about Hitler and what he was doing. Luz was torn   67
between two feelings. He didn't believe in Aryan supremacy any more than he
believed the moon was made of German cheese, and he was disturbed at the
direction in which Hitler was going. Yet he loved his country and felt a loyalty
to fight for it if it came to that, if only for the sake of his wife and son. I
couldn't understand how he could go along with Hitler under any
circumstances, though, and I told him so.

He wasn't angry when I said it. He just held out his hands and nodded. He   68
didn't explain because he didn't understand completely himself, just as I
couldn't explain to him how the United States tolerated the race situation. So
we sat talking about these things, some nights later than two Olympic
performers should have. We didn't come up with any final answers then, only
with a unique friendship. For we were simply two uncertain young men in an
uncertain world. One day we would learn the truth, but in the meantime, we
would make some mistakes. Luz's mistake would cost him too much.

Yet we didn't make the mistake of not seeing past each other's skin color   69 to what was within. If we couldn't apply that principle to things on a world scale, we still could live it fully in our own way in the few days we had together, the only days together we would ever have.

We made them count. We crammed as much understanding and fun as we could into every hour. We didn't even stop when we got out on the track. Luz was at my side cheering me on for every event, except the broad jump, of course. There he tried to beat me for all he was worth, but nature had put just a little more spring into my body and I went a handful of inches farther.

After he failed in his last attempt to beat me, he leaped out of the pit and raced to my side. To congratulate me. Then he walked toward the stands pulling me with him while Hitler was glaring, held up my hand and shouted to the gigantic crowd, "Jesse Owens! Jesse Owens!"

The stadium picked it up. "Jesse Owens!" they responded — though it sounded more like *Jaz-eee-ooh-wenz*. Each time I went for a gold medal and a record in the next three days, the crowd would greet me with *"Jaz-eee-ooh-wenz! Jaz-eee-ooh-wenz!"*

I'd had people cheering me before, but never like this. Many of those men would end up killing my countrymen, and mine theirs, but the truth was that they didn't want to, and would only do it because they "had" to. Thanks to Luz, I learned that the false leaders and sick movements of this earth must be stopped in the beginning, for they turn humanity against itself.

Luz and I vowed to write to each other after the Games, and we did. For three years we corresponded regularly, though the letters weren't always as happy as our talks at the Olympics had been. Times were hard for me and harder for Luz. He had had to go into the German army, away from his wife and son. His letters began to bear strange postmarks. Each letter expressed more and more doubt about what he was doing. But he felt he had no other choice. He was afraid for his family if he left the army. And how could they leave Germany? It was Luz's world, just as the South had been the only world for so many Negroes.

The last letter I got from him was in 1939. "Things become more difficult," he said, "and I am afraid, Jesse. Not just the thought of dying. It is that I may die for the wrong thing. But whatever might become of me, I hope only that my wife and son will stay alive. I am asking you who are my only friend outside of Germany, to someday visit them if you are able, to tell them about why I had to do this, and how the good times between us were. Luz."

I answered right away, but my letter came back. So did the next, and the one after. I inquired about Luz through a dozen channels. Nothing. A war was on. Finally, when it was over, I was able to get in touch with Luz's wife and find out what had happened to him. He was buried somewhere in the African desert.

Luz Long had been my competition in the Olympics. He was a white man—a Nazi white man who fought to destroy my country. 77

I loved Luz Long, as much as my own brothers. I still love Luz Long. 78

I went back to Berlin a few years ago and met his son, another fine young man. And I told Karl about his father. I told him that, though fate may have thrown us against one another, Luz rose above it, rose so high that I was left with not only four gold medals I would never have had, but with the priceless knowledge that the only bond worth anything between human beings is their humanness. 79

Today there are times when that bond doesn't seem to exist. I know. I felt the same way before my third jump at the 1936 Olympics, as well as a thousand other times. There've been many moments when I did feel like hating the white man, all white men, felt like giving in to fearful reality once and for all. 80

But I've learned those moments aren't the real me. And what's true of me is true of most men I've met. My favorite speech in a movie is the scene in *High Noon* when Gary Cooper, alone and hunted by the four sadistic killers, momentarily weakens and saddles a horse to get out of town. Like everyone else, his deputy wants him to do it and helps him. But Cooper finally won't get up on the horse. 81

"Go on!" his deputy shouts. "Do it!" 82

"I can't do it," Cooper says. 83

"You were going to a minute ago!" 84

"I was tired," Cooper tells him. "A man thinks a lotta things when he's tired. But I can't do it." 85

We all get tired. But know yourself, know your humanness, and you'll know why you can never finally throw in with the bigotry of blackthink. You must not be a Negro. You must be a human being first and last, if not always. 86

Reach back, Harry Edwards. Reach back inside yourself and grapple for that extra ounce of guts, that last cell of manhood even you didn't know you had, that something that lets you stand the pain and beat the ghetto and go on to break the records. Use it now to be totally honest with yourself. 87

For when the chips are really down, you can either put your skin first or you can go with what's inside it. 88

Sure, there'll be times when others try to keep you from being human. But remember that prejudice isn't new. It goes way back, just as slavery goes way 89 back, to before there ever was an America. Men have always had to meet insanity without losing their own minds.

That doesn't mean you should stand still for bigotry. Fight it. Fight it for all you're worth. But fight your *own* prejudice, too. Don't expect perfection in your white brother until there's not an ounce of blackthink left in you. And remember that the hardest thing for all of us isn't to fight, but to stop and think. *Black, think* . . . is the opposite of . . . *blackthink*.

I'm not going to play any Establishment games with you. My way isn't its own reward. Self-knowledge, getting rid of the bitterness, a better life are the rewards.

So be a new kind of "militant," an *immoderate moderate*, one hundred percent involved, but as a man, not a six-foot hunk of brown wrapping paper, be an extremist when it comes to your ideals, a moderate when it comes to the raising of your fist.

Live every day deep and strong. Don't pass up *your* Olympics and *your* Luz Long. Don't let the blackthinkers sell you out for a masquerade rumble where the real you can never take off the mask.

You see, black *isn't* beautiful.

White isn't beautiful.

Skin-deep is *never* beautiful.

QUESTIONS ON CONTENT:

1. Why were the 1936 Olympics important to so many people? Why was Owens especially aware of its importance?

2. For two men so seemingly different, what important thing did Long and Owens hold in common? How does it coincide with the original Olympic ideal, and how did it shape Owens's life?

3. Compare and contrast Long's reluctance to leave Germany and the reluctance of blacks to leave the South or America.

4. What is the difference between "blackthink" and "Black, think"?

QUESTIONS ON WRITING STRUCTURE AND STRATEGY:

1. What is the purpose of the rhetorical question at the beginning of the essay? What is the purpose of the rhetorical questions posed in paragraph nine? How does the last question tie in with the conclusion?

2. Why does Owens use so many short paragraphs and so much dialogue? What do they add to the writing, and what is the total effect on the reader? What do his colloquialisms add?

3. When Owens discusses German Aryan supremacy, what mode of development does he employ? How valid is it?

QUESTIONS FOR DISCUSSION AND WRITING:

1. Write a short paper about some competitive occasion you might have been involved in when humanness surfaced (Long's encouragement of Owens).

2. If you are familiar with the events of the 1984 Olympics, or with the recent Olympic tryouts, compare the prospects today for black athletes with the situation Owens faced in 1936. What is different? You might do a bit of research on the 1936 event.
OR:
Do a bit of research on today's black athlete: in basketball, football, tennis, golf, baseball, or other sports. Write a paper on the results of your survey. What are the implications for American society? For aspiring black athletes? (See Arthur Ashe.) For America's image in the world?

3. Richard Wright and Jesse Owens grew up in an America different from that in which Horace Porter grew up. You may want to tackle a larger paper in which you compare/contrast these two Americas.

SEXISM IN ENGLISH:
A FEMINIST VIEW
Alleen Pace Nilsen

Alleen Pace Nilsen concludes that the English language is sexist. You may, too, after reading her essay, originally published in Female Studies (1972). Beginning with her doctoral dissertation on sexism in children's books, she has pursued her concern with the subject in other areas of American life, collaborating on several books dealing with sexism in language. Though Nilsen is a linguistics professional, she uses language that is easily understood by the nonprofessional. She begins her essay with two questions, answering the first with an impressive mass of detail to support her thesis, and leaving the second to speculation. Especially significant in this essay is the way she has carefully organized her evidence for clear exposition. Grouping data according to common characteristics (classification) is probably the most efficient way to handle a large amount of data to document a thesis. Although what Nilsen writes constitutes a devastating critique of the language, her tone is noteworthy. To characterize it you may wish to compare it with that of other feminists in the text: Olsen, Elshtain, Walker, and Woolf.

Does culture shape language? Or does language shape culture? This is as difficult a question as the old puzzler of which came first, the chicken or the egg, because there's no clear separation between language and culture.

A well-accepted linguistic principle is that as culture changes so will the language. The reverse of this — as a language changes so will the culture — is not so readily accepted. This is why some linguists smile (or even scoff) at feminist attempts to replace *Mrs.* and *Miss* with *Ms.* and to find replacements for those all-inclusive words which specify masculinity, *e.g., chairman, mankind, brotherhood, freshman,* etc.

Perhaps they are amused for the same reason that it is the doctor at a cocktail party who laughs loudest at the joke about the man who couldn't afford an operation so he offered the doctor a little something to touch up the X-ray. A person working constantly with language is likely to be more aware of how really deep-seated sexism is in our communication system.

Last winter I took a standard desk dictionary and gave it a place of honor on my night table. Every night that I didn't have anything more interesting to do, I read myself to sleep making a card for each entry that seemed to tell something about male and female. By spring I had a rather dog-eared dictionary, but I also had a collection of note cards filling two shoe boxes. The cards tell some rather interesting things about American English.

First, in our culture it is a woman's body which is considered important while it is a man's mind or his activities which are valued. A woman is sexy. A man is successful.

I made a card for all the words which came into modern English from   6
somebody's name. I have a two-and-one-half inch stack of cards which are men's names now used as everyday words. The women's stack is less than a half inch high and most of them came from Greek mythology. Words coming from the names of famous American men include *lynch, sousaphone, sideburns, Pullman, rickettsia, Schick test, Winchester rifle, Franklin stove, Bartlett pear, teddy bear,* and *boysenberry.* The only really common words coming from the names of American women are *bloomers* (after Amelia Jenks Bloomer) and *Mae West jacket.* Both of these words are related in some way to a woman's physical anatomy, while the male words (except for *sideburns* after General Burnsides) have nothing to do with the namesake's body.

This reminded me of an earlier observation that my husband and I made   7
about geographical names. A few years ago we became interested in what we called "Topless Topography" when we learned that the Grand Tetons used to be simply called *The Tetons* by French explorers and *The Teats* by American frontiersmen. We wrote letters to several map makers and found the following listings: *Nippletop* and *Little Nipple Top* near Mt. Marcy in the Adirondacks, *Nipple Mountain* in Archuleta County, Colordao, *Nipple Peak* in Coke County, Texas, *Nipple Butte,* in Pennington, South Dakota, *Squaw Peak* in Placer County, California (and many other places), *Maiden's Peak* and *Squaw Tit* (they're the same mountain) in the Cascade Range in Oregon, *Jane Russell Peaks* near Stark, New Hampshire, and *Mary's Nipple* near Salt Lake City, Utah.

We might compare these names to Jackson Hole, Wyoming, or Pikes   8
Peak, Colorado. I'm sure we would get all kinds of protests from the Jackson and Pike descendants if we tried to say that these topographical features were named because they in some way resembled the bodies of Jackson and Pike, respectively.

This preoccupation with women's breasts is neither new nor strictly   9
American. I was amused to read the derivation of the word *Amazon.* According to Greek folk etymology, the *a* means "without" as in *atypical* or *amoral* while *mazon* comes from *mazōs* meaning "breast." According to the legend, these women cut off one breast so that they could better shoot their bows. Perhaps the feeling was that the women had to trade in part of their femininity in exchange for their active or masculine role.

There are certain pairs of words which illustrate the way in which sexual   10
connotations are given to feminine words while the masculine words retain a serious, businesslike aura. For example, being a *callboy* is perfectly respectable. It simply refers to a person who calls actors when it is time for them to go on stage, but being a *call girl* is being a prostitute.

Also we might compare *sir* and *madam*. *Sir* is a term of respect while   1
madam has acquired the meaning of a brothel manager. The same thing has
happened to the formerly cognate terms, *master* and *mistress*. Because of its
acquired sexual connotations, *mistress* is now carefully avoided in certain
contexts. For example, the Boy Scouts have *scoutmasters* but certainly not
scoutmistresses. And in a dog show the female owner of a dog is never referred
to as the *dog's mistress*, but rather as the *dog's master*.

Master appears in such terms as *master plan, concert master, schoolmaster,*   1
mixmaster, master charge, master craftsman, etc. But *mistress* appears in very
few compounds. This is the way it is with dozens of words which have male and
female counterparts. I found two hundred such terms, e.g., *usher – usherette,*
heir – heiress, hero – heroine, etc. In nearly all cases it is the masculine word
which is the base with a feminine suffix being added for the alternate version.
The masculine word also travels into compounds while the feminine word is a
dead end; e.g., *king – queen* comes from *kingdom* but not *queendom*, from
sportsman – sportslady comes *sportsmanship* but not *sportsladyship*, etc. There is
one — and only one — semantic area in which the masculine word is not the
base or more powerful word. This is in the area dealing with sex and marriage.
Here it is the feminine word which is dominant. *Prostitute* is the base word
with *male prostitute* being the derived term. *Bride* appears in *bridal shower,*
bridal gown, bridal attendant, bridesmaid, and even in *bridegroom*, while *groom*
in the sense of *bridegroom* does not appear in any compounds, not even to
name the groom's attendants or his prenuptial party.

At the end of a marriage, this same emphasis is on the female. If it ends in   1
divorce, the woman gets the title of *divorcée* while the man is usually described
with a statement, such as, "He's divorced." When the marriage ends in death,
the woman is a *widow* and the *-er* suffix which seems to connote masculine
(probably because it is an agentive or actor type suffix) is added to make
widower. *Widower* doesn't appear in any compounds (except for *grass widower*,
which is another companion term), but *widow* appears in several compounds
and in addition has some acquired meanings, such as the extra hand dealt to the
table in certain card games and an undesirable leftover line of type in printing.

If I were an anthropological linguist making observations about a strange   1
and primitive tribe, I would duly note on my tape recorder that I had found
linguistic evidence to show that in the area of sex and marriage the female
appears to be more important than the male, but in all other areas of the
culture, it seems that the reverse is true.

But since I am not an anthropological linguist, I will simply go on to my   1
second observation, which is that women are expected to play a passive role
while men play an active one.

One indication of women's passive role is the fact that they are often   1

284

identified as something to eat. What's more passive than a plate of food? Last spring I saw an announcement advertising the Indiana University English Department picnic. It read "Good Food! Delicious Women!" The publicity committee was probably jumped on by local feminists, but it's nothing new to look on women as "delectable morsels." Even women compliment each other with "You look good enough to eat," or "You have a peaches and cream complexion." Modern slang constantly comes up with new terms, but some of the old standbys for women are: *cute tomato, dish, peach, sharp cookie, cheese cake, honey, sugar,* and *sweetie-pie.* A man may occasionally be addressed as *honey* or described as a *hunk of meat,* but certainly men are not laid out on a buffet and labeled as women are.

Women's passivity is also shown in the comparisons made to plants. For example, to *deflower* a woman is to take away her virginity. A girl can be described as a *clinging vine,* a *shrinking violet,* or a *wall flower.* On the other hand, men are too active to be thought of as plants. The only time we make the comparison is when insulting a man we say he is like a woman by calling him a *pansy.* 17

We also see the active-passive contrast in the animal terms used with males and females. Men are referred to as *studs, bucks,* and *wolves,* and they go *tomcatting around.* These are all aggressive roles, but women have such pet names as *kitten, bunny, beaver, bird, chick, lamb,* and *fox.* The idea of being a pet seems much more closely related to females than to males. For instance, little girls grow up wearing *pigtails* and *ponytails* and they dress in *halters* and *dog collars.* 18

The active-passive contrast is also seen in the proper names given to boy babies and girl babies. Girls are much more likely to be given names like *Ivy, Rose, Ruby, Jewel, Pearl, Flora, Joy,* etc., while boys are given names describing active roles such as *Martin* (warlike), *Leo* (lion), *William* (protector), *Ernest* (resolute fighter), and so on. 19

Another way that women play a passive role is that they are defined in relationship to someone else. This is what feminists are protesting when they ask to be identified as *Ms.* rather than as *Mrs.* or *Miss.* It is a constant source of irritation to women's organizations that when they turn in items to newspapers under their own names, that is, Susan Glascoe, Jeanette Jones, and so forth, the editors consistently rewrite the item so that the names read Mrs. John Glascoe, Mrs. Robert E. Jones. 20

In the dictionary I found what appears to be an attitude on the part of the editors that it is almost indecent to let a respectable woman's name march unaccompanied across the pages of a dictionary. A woman's name must somehow be escorted by a male's name regardless of whether or not the male contributed to the woman's reason for being in the dictionary, or in his own 21 right was as famous as the woman. For example, Charlotte Brontë is identified as Mrs. Arthur B. Nicholls, Amelia Earhart is identified as Mrs. George Palmer Putnam, Helen Hayes is identified as Mrs. Charles MacArthur, Zona Gale is identified as Mrs. William Llwelyn Breese, and Jenny Lind is identified as Mme. Otto Goldschmidt.

Although most of the women are identified as Mrs.——— or as the wife of———, other women are listed with brothers, fathers, or lovers. Cornelia Otis Skinner is identified as the daughter of Otis, Harriet Beecher Stowe is identified as the sister of Henry Ward Beecher, Edith Sitwell is identified as the sister of Osbert and Sacheverell, Nell Gwyn is identified as the mistress of Charles II, and Madame Pompadour is identified as the mistress of Louis XV.

The women who did get into the dictionary without the benefit of a masculine escort are a group sort of on the fringes of respectability. They are the rebels and the crusaders: temperance leaders Frances Elizabeth Caroline Willard and Carry Nation, women's rights leaders Carrie Chapman Catt and Elizabeth Cady Stanton, birth control educator Margaret Sanger, religious leader Mary Baker Eddy, and slaves Harriet Tubman and Phillis Wheatley.

I would estimate that far more than fifty percent of the women listed in the dictionary were identified as someone's wife. But of all the men — and there are probably ten times as many men as women — only one was identified as "the husband of. . . . " This was the unusual case of Frederic Joliot who took the last name of Joliot-Curie and was identified as "husband of Irene." Apparently Irene, the daughter of Pierre and Marie Curie, did not want to give up her maiden name when she married and so the couple took the hyphenated last name.

There are several pairs of words which also illustrate the more powerful role of the male and the relational role of the female. For example, a *count* is a high political officer with a *countess* being simply the wife of a count. The same is true for a *duke* and a *duchess* and a *king* and a *queen*. The fact that a king is usually more powerful than a queen might be the reason that Queen Elizabeth's husband is given the title of *prince* rather than *king*. Since *king* is a stronger word than *queen*, it is reserved for a true heir to the throne because if it were given to someone coming into the royal family by marriage, then the subjects might forget where the true power lies. With the weaker word of *queen*, this would not be a problem; so a woman marrying a ruling monarch is given the title without question.

My third observation is that there are many postive connotations connected with the concept of masculine, while there are either trivial or negative connotations connected with the corresponding feminine concept.

Conditioning toward the superiority of the masculine role starts very early in life. Child psychologists point out that the only area in which a girl has more freedom than a boy is in experimenting with an appropriate sex role. She is much freer to be a *tomboy* than is her brother to be a *sissy*. The proper names given to children reflect this same attitude. It's perfectly all right for a girl to have a boy's name, but not the other way around. As girls are given more and more of the boys' names, parents shy away from using boy names that might be mistaken for girl names, so the number of available masculine names is constantly shrinking. Fifty years ago *Hazel, Beverley, Marion, Frances,* and *Shirley* were all perfectly acceptable boys' names. Today few parents give these names to baby boys and adult men who are stuck with them self-consciously go by their initials or by abbreviated forms such as *Haze* or *Shirl.* But parents of little girls keep crowding the masculine set and currently popular girls' names include *Jo, Kelly, Teri, Cris, Pat, Shawn, Toni,* and *Sam.*

When the mother of one of these little girls tells her to *be a lady,* she 28 means for her to sit with her knees together. But when the father of a little boy tells him to *be a man,* he means for him to be noble, strong, and virtuous. The whole concept of manliness has such positive connotations that it is a compliment to call a male a *he-man,* a *manly man,* or a *virile man* (*virile* comes from the Indo-European *vir,* meaning "man"). In each of these three terms, we are implying that someone is doubly good because he is doubly a man.

Compare *chef* with *cook, tailor* and *seamstress,* and *poet* with *poetess.* In 29 each case, the masculine form carries with it an added degree of excellence. In comparing the masculine *governor* with the feminine *governess* and the masculine *major* with the feminine *majorette,* the added feature is power.

The difference between positive male and negative female connotations 30 can be seen in several pairs of words which differ denotatively only in the matter of sex. For instance compare *bachelor* with the terms *spinster* and *old maid. Bachelor* has such positive connotations that modern girls have tried to borrow the feeling in the term *bachelor-girl. Bachelor* appears in glamorous terms such as *bachelor pad, bachelor party,* and *bachelor button.* But *old maid* has such strong negative feelings that it has been adopted into other areas, taking with it the feeling of undesirability. It has the metaphorical meaning of shriveled and unwanted kernels of pop corn, and it's the name of the last unwanted card in a popular game for children.

Patron and *matron* (Middle English for *father* and *mother*) are another set 31 where women have tried to borrow the postive masculine connotations, this time through the word *patroness,* which literally means "female father." Such a peculiar term came about because of the high prestige attached to the word *patron* in such phrases as *"a patron of the arts"* or *"a patron saint." Matron* is more apt to be used in talking about a woman who is in charge of a jail or a public restroom.

Even *lord* and *lady* have different levels of connotations. *Our Lord* is used 32 as a title for deity, while the corresponding *Our Lady* is a relational title for Mary, the mortal mother of Jesus. *Landlord* has more dignity than *landlady* probably because the landlord is more likely to be thought of as the owner while the landlady is the person who collects the rent and enforces the rules. *Lady* is used in many insignificant places where the corresponding *lord* would never be used, for example, *ladies room, ladies sizes, ladies aid society, ladybug,* etc.

This overuse of *lady* might be compared to the overuse of *queen* which is rapidly losing its prestige as compared to *king.* Hundreds of beauty queens are crowned each year and nearly every community in the United States has its *Dairy Queen* or its *Freezer Queen,* etc. Some homosexuals have adopted the term* and advertisers who are constantly on the lookout for euphemisms to make unpleasant sounding products salable have recently dealt what might be a death blow to the prestige of the word *queen.* They have begun to use it as an indication of size. For example, *queen-size* panty hose are panty hose for fat women. The meaning comes through a comparison with *king-size,* meaning big. However, there's a subtle difference in that our culture considers it desirable for males to be big because size is an indication of power, but we prefer that females be small and petite. So using *king-size* as a term to indicate bigness partially enhances the prestige of *king,* but using *queen-size* to indicate bigness brings unpleasant assocations to the word *queen.*

Another set that might be compared are *brave* and *squaw.* The word *brave* carries with it the connotations of youth, vigor, and courage, while *squaw* implies almost opposite characteristics. With the set *wizard* and *witch,* the main difference is that *wizard* implies skill and wisdom combined with magic, while *witch* implies evil intentions combined with magic. Part of the unattractiveness of both *squaw* and *witch* is that they suggest old age, which in women is particularly undesirable. When I lived in Afghanistan (1967–1969), I was horrified to hear a proverb stating that when you see an old man you should sit down and take a lesson, but when you see an old woman you should throw a stone. I was equally startled when I went to compare the connotations of our two phrases *grandfatherly advice* and *old wives' tales.* Certainly it isn't expressed with the same force as in the Afghan proverb, but the implication is similar.

In some of the animal terms used for women the extreme undesirability of female old age is also seen. For instance consider the unattractiveness of *old nag* as compared to *filly,* of *old crow* or *old bat* as compared to *bird,* and of being *catty* as compared to being *kittenish.* The chicken metaphor tells the whole story of a girl's life. In her youth she is a *chick,* then she marries and begins feeling *cooped up,* so she goes to *hen parties* where she *cackles* with her

---

*Changes made in accordance with permission granted from THE FEMINIST PRESS

friends. Then she has her *brood* and begins to *henpeck* her husband. Finally she turns into *an old biddy.*

QUESTIONS ON CONTENT:

1. With what questions does Nilsen open her essay? Why is the answer to the second question important to feminists?
2. What is Nilsen's thesis?
3. What are the three observations Nilsen makes about sexism in the English language?
4. How does Nilsen classify the evidence of women's passivity she finds?

QUESTIONS ON WRITING STRUCTURE AND STRATEGY:

1. To what specific audience does Nilsen's article appear to be directed? What is the evidence for your answer?
2. Although this article reflects informal research, what elements of more scientific research do you observe?
3. What effective transitional devices appear in this article?
4. What modes of development does Nilsen employ? When and why does Nilsen use italics?
5. How is her conclusion different from the standard? Is it effective or ineffective? Why?

QUESTIONS FOR DISCUSSION AND WRITING:

1. With what other authors in this text could you compare and/or contrast Nilsen? In point of view? In tone? In . . .?
2. Nilsen says that culture shapes language. Consider how American cultural racism has shaped our language. How have our attitudes toward the elderly shaped language? Our attitudes toward the handicapped? (I.e., our attitudes toward these various groups have determined the kind of words we use, the kind of language we use to refer to them.) Select one subject and write a paper. (Note: consider the subject both in its negative and positive aspects; that is to say, before we became conscious of our failing with respect to our fellow-citizens, our language was shaped negatively. Since we have become more aware, we have shaped our language more positively.)
3. In a clear, well-unified paper, discuss and classify sexism in one or several of the following: the musical field (lyrics, performers, etc.), athletics, television, literature, textbooks, newspapers, or magazines.
4. The following words are Americanisms: *jumbo, baby-sitter, Mickey Mouse, smog, cloverleaf, snafu, gizmo, caucus, crackerjack.* Check the dictionary for the story of their origins. You will probably have to go to the library and check some of the specialized dictionaries of the American language. Select a few of these words and write a paper demonstrating how culture has shaped our language.

SPARROW HAWKS

Loren Eiseley

*Loren Eiseley was distinguished both as an eminent anthropolugist
and as a talented writer. Throughout his academic career, which
included his many years as chairman of the Department of
Anthropology and Provost of the University of Pennsylvania, he found
time to write numerous books, articles, and essays for scholarly as well
as lay publications. His participation in various anthropological
expeditions in the western and southwestern United States and his
extensive research on Darwin and the theory of evolution resulted in
such award-winning books as* Darwin's Century *(1958),* Francis
Bacon and the Modern Dilemma *(1963), and his collection of essays*
The Immense Journey *(1957), which met with critical acclaim for its
"eloquence and imagination."*

*In this selection Eiseley, while engaged in a routine scientific
expedition, undergoes an experience so profound that it marks him for
life. In turn, Eiseley's poignant descriptions mark his readers. What
could have been an aseptic recounting of a field trip is made
memorable by Eiseley's precise use of detail and his skillful blending
of, for the most part, common, everyday words that build to a
remarkably eloquent conclusion.*

I joined some colleagues heading higher into a remote windy tableland   1
where huge bones were reputed to protrude like boulders from the turf. . . .
There had been talk of birds in connection with my duties. Birds are intense,
fast-living creatures — reptiles, I suppose one might say, that have escaped out
of the heavy sleep of time, transformed fairy creatures dancing over sunlit
meadows. It is a youthful fancy, no doubt, but because of something that
happened up there among the escarpments of that range, it remains with me a
lifelong impression. I can never bear to see a bird imprisoned.

We came into that valley through the trailing mists of a spring night. It   2
was a place that looked as though it might never have known the foot of man,
but our scouts had been ahead of us and we knew all about the abandoned
cabin of stone that lay far up on one hillside. It had been built in the land rush
of the last century and then lost to the cattlemen again as the marginal soils
failed to take to the plow.

There were spots like this all over that country. Lost graves marked by   3
unlettered stones and old corroding rim-fire cartridge cases lying where
somebody had made a stand among the boulders that rimmed the valley. They
are all that remain of the range wars; the men are under the stones now. I
could see our cavalcade winding in and out through the mist below us: torches,
the reflection of the truck lights on our collecting tins, and the far-off bumping

290

of a loose dinosaur thigh bone in the bottom of a trailer. I stood on a rock a moment looking down and thinking what it cost in money and equipment to capture the past.

We had, in addition, instructions to lay hands on the present. The word had come through to get them alive — birds, reptiles, anything. A zoo somewhere abroad needed restocking. It was one of those reciprocal matters in which science involves itself. Maybe our museum needed a stray ostrich egg and this was the payoff. Anyhow, my job was to help capture some birds and that was why I was there before the trucks.

The cabin had not been occupied for years. We intended to clean it out and live in it, but there were holes in the roof and the birds had come in and were roosting in the rafters. You could depend on it in a place like this where everything blew away, and even a bird needed some place out of the weather and away from coyotes. A cabin going back to nature in a wild place draws them till they come in, listening at the eaves, I imagine, pecking softly among the shingles till they find a hole and then suddenly the place is theirs and man is forgotten. . . .

I got the door open softly and I had the spotlight all ready to turn on and blind whatever birds there were so they couldn't see to get out through the roof. I had a short piece of ladder to put against the far wall where there was a shelf on which I expected to make the biggest haul. I had all the information I needed just like any skilled assassin. I pushed the door open, the hinges squeaking only a little. A bird or two stirred — I could hear them — but nothing flew and there was a faint starlight through the holes in the roof.

I padded across the floor, got the ladder up and the light ready, and slithered up the ladder till my head and arms were over the shelf. Everything was dark as pitch except for the starlight at the little place back of the shelf near the eaves. With the light to blind them, they'd never make it. I had them. I reached my arm carefully over in order to be ready to seize whatever was there and I put the flash on the edge of the shelf where it would stand by itself when I turned it on. That way I'd be able to use both hands.

Everything worked perfectly except for one detail — I didn't know what kinds of birds were there. I never thought about it at all, and it wouldn't have mattered if I had. My orders were to get something interesting. I snapped on the flash and sure enough there was a great beating and feathers flying, but instead of my having them, they, or rather he, had me. He had my hand, that is, and for a small hawk not much bigger than my fist he was doing all right. I heard him give one short metallic cry when the light went on and my hand descended on the bird beside him; after that he was busy with his claws and his beak was sunk in my thumb. In the struggle I knocked the lamp over on the shelf, and his mate got her sight back and whisked neatly through the hole

4

5

6

7

8

in the roof and off among the stars outside. It all happened in fifteen seconds and you might think I would have fallen down the ladder, but no, I had a professional assassin's reputation to keep up, and the bird, of course, made the mistake of thinking the hand was the enemy and not the eyes behind it. He chewed my thumb up pretty effectively and lacerated my hand with his claws, but in the end I got him, having two hands to work with.

He was a sparrow hawk and a fine young male in the prime of life. I was 9 sorry not to catch the pair of them, but as I dripped blood and folded his wings carefully, holding him by the back so that he couldn't strike again, I had to admit the two of them might have been more than I could have handled under the circumstances. The little fellow had saved his mate by diverting me, and that was that. He was born to it, and made no outcry now, resting in my hand hopelessly, but peering toward me in the shadows behind the lamp with a fierce, almost indifferent glance. He neither gave nor expected mercy and something out of the high air passed from him to me, stirring a faint embarrassment.

I quit looking into that eye and managed to get my huge carcass with its 10 fist full of prey back down the ladder. I put the bird in a box too small to allow him to injure himself by struggle and walked out to welcome the arriving trucks. It had been a long day, and camp still to make in the darkness. In the morning that bird would be just another episode. He would go back with the bones in the truck to a small cage in a city where he would spend the rest of his life. And a good thing, too. I sucked my aching thumb and spat out some blood. An assassin has to get used to these things. I had a professional reputation to keep up.

In the morning, with the change that comes on suddenly in that high 11 country, the mist that had hovered below us in the valley was gone. The sky was a deep blue, and one could see for miles over the high outcroppings of stone. I was up early and brought the box in which the little hawk was imprisoned out onto the grass where I was building a cage. A wind as cool as a mountain spring ran over the grass and stirred my hair. It was a fine day to be alive. I looked up and all around and at the hole in the cabin roof out of which the other little hawk had fled. There was no sign of her anywhere that I could see.

"Probably in the next county by now," I thought cynically, but before 12 beginning work I decided I'd have a look at my last night's capture.

Secretively, I looked again all around the camp and up and down and 13 opened the box. I got him right out in my hand with his wings folded properly and I was careful not to startle him. He lay limp in my grasp and I could feel his heart pound under the feathers but he only looked beyond me and up.

I saw him look that last look away beyond me into a sky so full of light 14 that I could not follow his gaze. The little breeze flowed over me again, and nearby a mountain aspen shook all its tiny leaves. I suppose I must have had an idea then of what I was going to do, but I never let it come up into consciousness. I just reached over and laid the hawk on the grass.

He lay there a long minute without hope, unmoving, his eyes still fixed on   15
that blue vault above him. It must have been that he was already so far away
in heart that he never felt the release from my hand. He never even stood. He
just lay with his breast against the grass.

In the next second after that long minute he was gone. Like a flicker of   16
light, he had vanished with my eyes full on him, but without actually seeing
even a premonitory wing beat. He was gone straight into that towering
emptiness of light and crystal that my eyes could scarcely bear to penetrate.
For another long moment there was silence. I could not see him. The light was
too intense. Then from far up somewhere a cry came ringing down.

I was young then and had seen little of the world, but when I heard that   17
cry my heart turned over. It was not the cry of the hawk I had captured; for,
by shifting my position against the sun, I was now seeing further up. Straight
out of the sun's eye, where she must have been soaring restlessly above us for
untold hours, hurtled his mate. And from far up, ringing from peak to peak of
the summits over us, came a cry of such unutterable and ecstatic joy that it
sounds down across the years and tingles among the cups on my quiet breakfast
table.

I saw them both now. He was rising fast to meet her. They met in a great   18
soaring gyre that turned to a whirling circle and a dance of wings. Once more,
just once, their two voices, joined in a harsh wild medley of question and
response, struck and echoed against the pinnacles of the valley. Then they
were gone forever somewhere into those upper regions beyond the eyes of men.

QUESTIONS ON CONTENT:

1.   What does Eiseley mean by
     a.   "the costs in money and equipment to capture the past"?
     b.   "one of those reciprocal matters in which science involves itself"?
     c.   "the bird, of course, made the mistake of thinking the hand was the
            enemy and not the eyes behind it"?
2.   Trace the evolution of Eiseley's attitude toward the bird. Why does he let the
     bird go, and what does this tell you about Eiseley?

QUESTIONS ON WRITING STRUCTURE AND STRATEGY:

1.   What is Eiseley's purpose in this excerpt?
2.   Where, how, and why does Eiseley use the analogy of the "assassin"?
3.   To what type of audience is this selection aimed, and how do you know?
4.   What characterizes Eiseley's style? His verbs? His vocabulary? How does he
     employ contrasts?

QUESTIONS FOR DISCUSSION AND WRITING:

1. Ralph Waldo Emerson has written that "there are sermons in sticks and stones." Write about an experience in or with nature that caused you to change an idea/attitude or imparted an idea that became a permanent part of your outlook on life. Take care to avoid excessive sentimentality (see Glossary).

2. Eiseley writes: "I can never bear to see a bird imprisoned." Yet canaries, parakeets, and parrots bring happiness and companionship to many people, old and young. Write a paper on the pros and cons of the issue of caged birds. Would you qualify Eiseley's comment to allow for these exceptions? Explain. (You might do some research on the caging of the California condors in an attempt to save this endangered species.)

3. Early in this excerpt, Eiseley creates a mood by conveying to the reader something of the history of the country he and his companions were moving into. Note especially paragraph three. Artifacts evoke an image of the past. Reflect on your own experience. Perhaps some landscape, some particular place, a building, or an artifact evoked images of people who had gone before. Write a journal entry describing your experience of this historical sense.

LETTER FROM BIRMINGHAM JAIL
Martin Luther King, Jr.

Martin Luther King, Jr., was born in Atlanta, Georgia, and educated at Morehouse College, Atlanta; the Crozier Theological Seminary in Chester, Pennsylvania; and Boston University. In 1955, at the age of 26, he became the pastor of the Dexter Avenue Baptist Church in Montgomery, Alabama. It was his leadership of the bus boycott in that city the same year, initiated by blacks to protest racial segregation, that brought King to national attention. This was the first demonstration of a nonviolent civil rights protest. King's account of it in his book Stride Toward Freedom: The Montgomery Story *(1958) set forth the model for the civil rights revolution of the 1950s and 1960s. Because of his leadership during the boycott and because of his oratorical skills and fearlessness, he was made leader of the Southern Christian Leadership Conference, which was to spearhead civil rights campaigns throughout the South. In 1963, King led a march on Washington to demonstrate a united resolve that racial injustice in America must end. At that gathering, held on the mall facing the Lincoln Memorial, King delivered his famous "I Have a Dream" speech, a blueprint for an America united in brotherhood. King's efforts to gain racial justice in America attracted worldwide attention, and in 1964 the Nobel Prize Committee awarded him the Peace Prize. From then on he was an international figure. In 1968, while supporting a strike of black garbage collectors in Memphis, Tennessee, King was assassinated. The United States Congress, in 1986, established King's birthday — January 15 — as a national holiday.*

"Letter from Birmingham Jail" was written while he was in jail for leading a civil rights march without a permit. The letter is a response to a published statement by a group of Birmingham clergymen who were critical of his action. King writes that he began the letter by writing on the margins of newspapers and scraps of paper. He finished it on a legal pad supplied by his lawyer.

As you read, notice how King's introductory classification of just and unjust laws sets the tone of his whole letter. Observe also how his consistent "you" and "I" focus provides a framework and coherence as well as establishing a very personal relationship between King and his readers.

April 16, 1963

My Dear Fellow Clergymen:

While confined here in the Birmingham city jail, I came across your recent statement calling my present activities "unwise and untimely." Seldom do I pause to answer criticism of my work and ideas. If I sought to answer all the criticisms that cross my desk, my secretaries would have little time for anything

1

other than such correspondence in the course of the day, and I would have no time for constructive work. But since I feel that you are men of genuine good will and that your criticisms are sincerely set forth, I want to try to answer your statement in what I hope will be patient and reasonable terms.

I think I should indicate why I am here in Birmingham, since you have been influenced by the view which argues against "outsiders coming in." I have the honor of serving as president of the Southern Christian Leadership Conference, an organization operating in every southern state, with headquarters in Atlanta, Georgia. We have some eighty-five affiliated organizations across the South, and one of them is the Alabama Christian Movement for Human Rights. Frequently we share staff, educational and financial resources with our affiliates. Several months ago the affiliate here in Birmingham asked us to be on call to engage in a nonviolent direct-action program if such were deemed necessary. We readily consented, and when the hour came we lived up to our promise. So I, along with several members of my staff, am here because I was invited here. I am here because I have organizational ties here.

But more basically, I am in Birmingham because injustice is here. Just as the prophets of the eighth century B.C., left their villages and carried their "thus saith the Lord" far beyond the boundaries of their home towns, and just as the Apostle Paul left his village of Tarsus and carried the gospel of Jesus Christ to the far corners of the Greco-Roman world, so am I compelled to carry the gospel of freedom beyond my own home town. Like Paul, I must constantly respond to the Macedonian call for aid.

Moreover, I am cognizant of the interrelatedness of all communities and states. I cannot sit idly by in Atlanta and not be concerned about what happens in Birmingham. Injustice anywhere is a threat to justice everywhere. We are caught in an inescapable network of mutuality, tied in a single garment of destiny. Whatever affects one directly, affects all indirectly. Never again can we afford to live with the narrow, provincial "outside agitator" idea. Anyone who lives inside the United States can never be considered an outsider anywhere within its bounds.

You deplore the demonstrations taking place in Birmingham. But your statement, I am sorry to say, fails to express a similar concern for the conditions that brought about the demonstrations. I am sure than none of you would want to rest content with the superficial kind of social analysis that deals merely with effects and does not grapple with underlying causes. It is unfortunate that demonstrations are taking place in Birmingham, but it is even more unfortunate that the city's white power structure left the Negro community with no alternative.

In any nonviolent campaign there are four basic steps: collection of the facts to determine whether injustices exist; negotiation; self-purification; and direct action. We have gone through all these steps in Birmingham. There can be no gainsaying the fact that racial injustice engulfs this community. Birmingham is probably the most thoroughly segregated city in the United States. Its ugly record of brutality is widely known. Negroes have experienced grossly unjust treatment in the courts. There have been more unsolved bombings of Negro homes and churches in Birmingham than in any other city in the nation. These are the hard, brutal facts of the case. On the basis of these conditions, Negro leaders sought to negotiate with the city fathers. But the latter consistently refused to engage in good-faith negotiation.

Then, last September, came the opportunity to talk with leaders of Birmingham's economic community. In the course of the negotiations, certain promises were made by the merchants — for example, to remove the stores' humiliating racial signs. On the basis of these promises, the Reverend Fred Shuttlesworth and the leaders of the Alabama Christian Movement for Human Rights agreed to a moratorium on all demonstrations. As the weeks and months went by, we realized that we were the victims of a broken promise. A few signs, briefly removed, returned; the others remained.

As in so many past experiences, our hopes had been blasted, and the shadow of deep disappointment settled upon us. We had no alternative except to prepare for direct action, whereby we would present our very bodies as a means of laying our case before the conscience of the local and the national community. Mindful of the difficulties involved, we decided to undertake a process of self-purification. We began a series of workshops on nonviolence, and we repeatedly asked ourselves: "Are you able to accept blows without retaliating?" "Are you able to endure the ordeal of jail?" We decided to schedule our direct-action program for the Easter season, realizing that except for Christmas, this is the main shopping period of the year. Knowing that a strong economic-withdrawal program would be the by-product of direct action, we felt that this would be the best time to bring pressure to bear on the merchants for the needed change.

Then it occurred to us that Birmingham's mayoral election was coming up in March, and we speedily decided to postpone action until after election day. When we discovered that the Commissioner of Public Safety, Eugene "Bull" Connor, had piled up enough votes to be in the run-off, we decided again to postpone action until the day after the run-off so that the demonstrations could not be used to cloud the issues. Like many others, we waited to see Mr. Connor defeated, and to this end we endured postponement after postponement. Having aided in this community need, we felt that our direct-action program could be delayed no longer.

You may well ask: "Why direct action? Why sit-ins, marches and so forth? Isn't negotiation a better path?" You are quite right in calling for

7

8

9

10

297

negotiation. Indeed, this is the very purpose of direct action. Nonviolent direct action seeks to create such a crisis and foster such a tension that a community which has constantly refused to negotiate is forced to confront the issue. It seeks so to dramatize the issue that it can no longer be ignored. My citing the creation of tension as part of the work of the nonviolent-resister may sound rather shocking. But I must confess that I am not afraid of the word "tension." I have earnestly opposed violent tension, but there is a type of constructive, nonviolent tension which is necessary for growth. Just as Socrates felt that it was necessary to create a tension in the mind so that individuals could rise from the bondage of myths and half-truths to the unfettered realm of creative analysis and objective appraisal, so must we see the need for nonviolent gadflies to create the kind of tension in society that will help men rise from the dark depths of prejudice and racism to the majestic heights of understanding and brotherhood.

The purpose of our direct-action program is to create a situation so crisis-packed that it will inevitably open the door to negotiation. I therefore concur with you in your call for negotiation. Too long has our beloved Southland been bogged down in a tragic effort to live in monologue rather than dialogue.

One of the basic points in your statement is that the action that I and my associates have taken in Birmingham is untimely. Some have asked: "Why didn't you give the new city administration time to act?" The only answer that I can give to this query is that the new Birmingham administration must be prodded about as much as the outgoing one, before it will act. We are sadly mistaken if we feel that the election of Albert Boutwell as mayor will bring the millennium to Birmingham. While Mr. Boutwell is a much more gentle person than Mr. Connor, they are both segregationists, dedicated to maintenance of the status quo. I have hope that Mr. Boutwell will be reasonable enough to see the futility of massive resistance to desegregation. But he will not see this without pressure from devotees of civil rights. My friends, I must say to you that we have not made a single gain in civil rights without determined legal and nonviolent pressure. Lamentably, it is an historical fact that privileged groups seldom give up their privileges voluntarily. Individuals may see the moral light and voluntarily give up their unjust posture; but, as Reinhold Niebuhr has reminded us, groups tend to be more immoral than individuals.

We know through painful experience that freedom is never voluntarily given by the oppressor; it must be demanded by the oppressed. Frankly, I have yet to engage in a direct-action campaign that was "well-timed" in view of those who have not suffered unduly from the disease of segregation. For years now I have heard the word "Wait!" It rings in the ear of every Negro with piercing familiarity. This "Wait" has almost always meant "Never." We must come to see, with one of our distinguished jurists, that "justice too long delayed is justice denied."

We have waited for more than 340 years for our constitutional and   14
God-given rights. The nations of Asia and Africa are moving with jetlike speed toward gaining political independence, but we still creep at horse-and-buggy pace toward gaining a cup of coffee at a lunch counter. Perhaps it is easy for those who have never felt the stinging darts of segregation to say, "Wait." But when you have seen vicious mobs lynch your mothers and fathers at will and drown your sisters and brothers at whim; when you have seen hate-filled policemen curse, kick and even kill your black brothers and sisters; when you see the vast majority of your twenty million Negro brothers smothering in an airtight cage of poverty in the midst of an affluent society; when you suddenly find your tongue twisted and your speech stammering as you seek to explain to your six-year-old daughter why she can't go to the public amusement park that has just been advertised on television, and see tears welling up in her eyes when she is told that Funtown is closed to colored children, and see ominous clouds of inferiority beginning to form in her little mental sky, and see her beginning to distort her personality by developing an unconscious bitterness toward white people; when you have to concoct an answer for a five-year-old son who is asking: "Daddy, why do white people treat colored people so mean?"; when you take a cross-country drive and find it necessary to sleep night after night in the uncomfortable corners of your automobile because no motel will accept you; when you are humiliated day in and day out by nagging signs reading "white" and "colored"; when your first name becomes "nigger," your middle name becomes "boy" (however old you are) and your last name becomes "John," and your wife and mother are never given the respected title "Mrs."; when you are harried by day and haunted by night by the fact that you are a Negro, living constantly at tiptoe stance, never quite knowing what to expect next, and are plagued with inner fears and outer resentments; when you are forever fighting a degenerating sense of nobodiness" — then you will understand why we find it difficult to wait. There comes a time when the cup of endurance runs over, and men are no longer willing to be plunged into the abyss of despair. I hope, sirs, you can understand our legitimate and unavoidable impatience.

You express a great deal of anxiety over our willingness to break laws.   15
This is certainly a legitimate concern. Since we so diligently urge people to obey the Supreme Court's decision of 1954 outlawing segregation in the public schools, at first glance it may seem rather paradoxical for us consciously to break laws. One may well ask: "How can you advocate breaking some laws and obeying others?" The answer lies in the fact that there are two types of laws: just and unjust. I would be the first to advocate obeying just laws. One

has not only a legal but a moral responsibility to obey just laws. Conversely, one has a moral responsibility to disobey unjust laws. I would agree with St. Augustine that "an unjust law is no law at all."

Now, what is the difference between the two? How does one determine whether a law is just or unjust? A just law is a man-made code that squares with the moral law or the law of God. An unjust law is a code that is out of harmony with the moral law. To put it in the terms of St. Thomas Aquinas: An unjust law is a human law that is not rooted in eternal law and natural law. Any law that uplifts human personality is just. Any law that degrades human personality is unjust. All segregation statutes are unjust because segregation distorts the soul and damages the personality. It gives the segregator a false sense of superiority and the segregated a false sense of inferiority. Segregation, to use the terminology of the Jewish philosopher Martin Buber, substitutes an "I-it" relationship for an "I-thou" relationship and ends up relegating persons to the status of things. Hence segregation is not only politically, economically and sociologically unsound, it is morally wrong and sinful. Paul Tillich has said that sin is separation. Is not segregation an existential expression of man's tragic separation, his awful estrangement, his terrible sinfulness? Thus it is that I can urge men to obey the 1954 decision of the Supreme Court, for it is morally right; and I can urge them to disobey segregation ordinances, for they are morally wrong.

Let us consider a more concrete example of just and unjust laws. An unjust law is a code that a numerical or power majority group compels a minority group to obey but does not make binding on itself. This is *difference* made legal. By the same token, a just law is a code that a majority compels a minority to follow and that it is willing to follow itself. This is *sameness* made legal.

Let me give another explanation. A law is unjust if it is inflicted on a minority that, as a result of being denied the right to vote, had no part in enacting or devising the law. Who can say that the legislature of Alabama which set up that state's segregation laws was democratically elected? Throughout Alabama all sorts of devious methods are used to prevent Negroes from becoming registered voters, and there are some counties in which, even though Negroes constitute a majority of the population, not a single Negro is registered. Can any law enacted under such circumstances be considered democratically structured?

Sometimes a law is just on its face and unjust in its application. For instance, I have been arrested on a charge of parading without a permit. Now, there is nothing wrong in having an ordinance which requires a permit for a parade. But such an ordinance becomes unjust when it is used to maintain segregation and to deny citizens the First-Amendment privilege of peaceful assembly and protest.

I hope you are able to see the distinction I am trying to point out. In no [20] sense do I advocate evading or defying the law, as would the rabid segregationist. That would lead to anarchy. One who breaks an unjust law must do so openly, lovingly, and with a willingness to accept the penalty. I submit that an individual who breaks a law that conscience tells him is unjust, and who willingly accepts the penalty of imprisonment in order to arouse the conscience of the community over its injustice, is in reality expressing the highest respect for law.

Of course, there is nothing new about this kind of civil disobedience. It [21] was evidenced sublimely in the refusal of Shadrach, Meshach and Abednego to obey the laws of Nebuchadnezzar, on the ground that a higher moral law was at stake. It was practiced superbly by the early Christians, who were willing to face hungry lions and the excruciating pain of chopping blocks rather than submit to certain unjust laws of the Roman Empire. To a degree, academic freedom is a reality today because Socrates practiced civil disobedience. In our own nation, the Boston Tea Party represented a massive act of civil disobedience.

We should never forget that everything Adolf Hitler did in Germany was [22] "legal" and everything the Hungarian freedom fighters did in Hungary was "illegal." It was "illegal" to aid and comfort a Jew in Hitler's Germany. Even so, I am sure that, had I lived in Germany at the time, I would have aided and comforted my Jewish brothers. If today I lived in a Communist country where certain principles dear to the Christian faith are suppressed, I would openly advocate disobeying that country's antireligious laws.

I must make two honest confessions to you, my Christian and Jewish [23] brothers. First, I must confess that over the past few years I have been gravely disappointed with the white moderate. I have almost reached the regrettable conclusion that the Negro's great stumbling block in his stride toward freedom is not the White Citizen's Counciler or the Ku Klux Klanner, but the white moderate, who is more devoted to "order" than to justice; who prefers a negative peace which is the absence of tension to a positive peace which is the presence of justice; who constantly says: "I agree with you in the goal you seek, but I cannot agree with your methods of direct action"; who paternalistically believes he can set the timetable for another man's freedom; who lives by a mythical concept of time and who constantly advises the Negro to wait for a "more convenient season." Shallow understanding from people of good will is more frustrating than absolute misunderstanding from people of ill will. Lukewarm acceptance is much more bewildering than outright rejection.

I had hoped that the white moderate would understand that law and order [24] exist for the purpose of establishing justice and that when they fail in this purpose they become the dangerously structured dams that block the flow of social progress. I had hoped that the white moderate would understand that the present tension in the South is a necessary phase of the transition from an obnoxious negative peace, in which the Negro passively accepted his unjust plight, to a substantive and positive peace, in which all men will respect the dignity and worth of human personality. Actually, we who engage in nonviolent direct action are not the creators of tension. We merely bring to the surface the hidden tension that is already alive. We bring it out in the open, where it can be seen and dealt with. Like a boil that can never be cured so long as it is covered up but must be opened with all its ugliness to the natural medicines of air and light, injustice must be exposed, with all the tension its exposure creates, to the light of human conscience and the air of national opinion before it can be cured.

In your statement you assert that our actions, even though peaceful, must be condemned because they precipitate violence. But is this a logical assertion? Isn't this like condemning a robbed man because his possession of money precipitated the evil act of robbery? Isn't this like condemning Socrates because his unswerving commitment to truth and his philosophical inquiries precipitated the act by the misguided populace in which they made him drink hemlock? Isn't this like condemning Jesus because his unique God-consciousness and never-creasing devotion to God's will precipitated the evil act of crucifixion? We must come to see that, as the federal courts have consistently affirmed, it is wrong to urge an individual to cease his efforts to gain his basic constitutional rights because the quest may precipitate violence. Society must protect the robbed and punish the robber.

I had also hoped that the white moderate would reject the myth concerning time in relation to the struggle for freedom. I have just received a letter from a white brother in Texas. He writes: "All Christians know that the colored people will receive equal rights eventually, but it is possible that you are in too great a religious hurry. It has taken Christianity almost two thousand years to accomplish what it has. The teachings of Christ take time to come to earth." Such an attitude stems from a tragic misconception of time, from the strangely irrational notion that there is something in the very flow of time that will inevitably cure all ills. Actually, time itself is neutral; it can be used either destructively or constructively. More and more I feel that the people of ill will have used time much more effectively than have the people of good will. We will have to repent in this generation not merely for the hateful words and actions of the bad people but for the appalling silence of the good people. Human progress never rolls in on wheels of inevitability; it comes through the tireless efforts of men willing to be co-workers with God, and without this hard work, time itself becomes an ally of the forces of social stagnation. We must use time creatively, in the knowledge that the time is always ripe to do right. Now is the time to make real the promise of democracy and transform our pending national elegy into a creative psalm of brotherhood. Now is the time to lift our national policy from the quicksand of racial injustice to the solid rock of human dignity.

You speak of our activity in Birmingham as extreme. At first I was rather 27 disappointed that fellow clergymen would see my nonviolent efforts as those of an extremist. I began thinking about the fact that I stand in the middle of two opposing forces in the Negro community. One is a force of complacency, made up in part of Negroes who, as a result of long years of oppression, are so drained of self-respect and a sense of "somebodiness" that they have adjusted to segregation; and in part of a few middle-class Negroes who, because of a degree of academic and economic security and because in some ways they profit by segregation, have become insensitive to the problems of the masses. The other force is one of bitterness and hatred, and it comes perilously close to advocating violence. It is expressed in the various black nationalist groups that are springing up across the nation, the largest and best-known being Elijah Muhammad's Muslim movement. Nourished by the Negro's frustration over the continued existence of racial discrimination, this movement is made up of people who have lost faith in America, who have absolutely repudiated Christianity, and who have concluded that the white man is an incorrigible "devil."

I have tried to stand between these two forces, saying that we need 28 emulate neither the "do-nothingism" of the complacent nor the hatred and despair of the black nationalist. For there is the more excellent way of love and nonviolent protest. I am grateful to God that, through the influence of the Negro church, the way of nonviolence became an integral part of our struggle.

If this philosophy had not emerged, by now many streets of the South 29 would, I am convinced, be flowing with blood. And I am further convinced that if our white brothers dismiss as "rabble-rousers" and "outside agitators" those of us who employ nonviolent direct action, and if they refuse to support our nonviolent efforts, millions of Negroes will, out of frustration and despair, seek solace and security in black-nationalist ideologies — a development that would inevitably lead to a frightening racial nightmare.

Oppressed people cannot remain oppressed forever. The yearning for 30 freedom eventually manifests itself, and that is what has happened to the American Negro. Something within has reminded him of his birthright of freedom, and something without has reminded him that it can be gained. Consciously or unconsciously, he has been caught up by the *Zeitgeist*, and with his black brothers of Africa and his brown and yellow brothers of Asia, South America and the Caribbean, the United States Negro is moving with a sense of great urgency toward the promised land of racial justice. If one recognizes this vital urge that has engulfed the Negro community, one should readily understand why public demonstrations are taking place. The Negro has many pent-up resentments and latent frustrations, and he must release them. So let him march; let him make prayer pilgrimages to the city hall; let him go on freedom rides — and try to understand why he must do so. If his repressed emotions are not released in nonviolent ways, they will seek expression through violence; this is not a threat but a fact of history. So I have not said to my people: "Get rid of your discontent." Rather, I have tried to say that this normal and healthy discontent can be channeled into the creative outlet of nonviolent direct action. And now this approach is being termed extremist.

But though I was initially disappointed at being categorized as an extremist, as I continued to think about the matter I gradually gained a measure of satisfaction from the label. Was not Jesus an extremist for love: "Love your enemies, bless them that curse you, do good to them that hate you, and pray for them which despitefully use you, and persecute you." Was not Amos an extremist for justice: "Let justice roll down like waters and righteousness like an ever-flowing stream." Was not Paul an extremist for the Christian gospel: "I bear in my body the marks of the Lord Jesus." Was not Martin Luther an extremist: "Here I stand; I cannot do otherwise, so help me God." And John Bunyan: "I will stay in jail to the end of my days before I make a butchery of my conscience." And Abraham Lincoln: "This nation cannot survive half slave and half free." And Thomas Jefferson: "We hold these truths to be self-evident, that all men are created equal . . ." So the question is not whether we will be extremists, but what kind of extremists we will be. Will we be extremists for hate or for love? Will we be extremists for the preservation of injustice or for the extension of justice? In that dramatic scene on Calvary's hill three men were crucified. We must never forget that all three were crucified for the same crime — the crime of extremism. Two were extremists for immorality, and thus fell below their environment. The other, Jesus Christ, was an extremist for love, truth, and goodness, and thereby rose above his environment. Perhaps the South, the nation and the world are in dire need of creative extremists.

I had hoped that the white moderate would see this need. Perhaps I was too optimistic; perhaps I expected too much. I suppose I should have realized that few members of the oppressor race can understand the deep groans and passionate yearnings of the oppressed race, and still fewer have the vision to see that injustice must be rooted out by strong, persistent and determined action. I am thankful, however, that some of our white brothers in the South have grasped the meaning of this social revolution and committed themselves to it. They are still all too few in quantity, but they are big in quality. Some — such as Ralph McGill, Lillian Smith, Harry Golden, James McBride Dabbs, Ann Braden and Sarah Patton Boyle — have written about our struggle in eloquent and prophetic terms. Others have marched with us down nameless streets of the South. They have lanquished in filthy, roach-infested jails, suffering the abuse and brutality of policemen who view them as "dirty nigger-lovers." Unlike so many of their moderate brothers and sisters, they have recognized the urgency of the moment and sensed the need for powerful "action" antidotes to combat the disease of segregation.

Let me take note of my other major disappointment. I have been so 33 greatly disappointed with the white church and its leadership. Of course, there are some notable exceptions. I am not unmindful of the fact that each of you has taken some significant stands on this issue. I commend you, Reverend Stallings, for your Christian stand on this past Sunday, in welcoming Negroes to your worship service on a nonsegregated basis. I commend the Catholic leaders of this state for integrating Spring Hill College several years ago.

But despite these notable exceptions, I must honestly reiterate that I have 34 been disappointed with the church. I do not say this as one of those negative critics who can always find something wrong with the church. I say this as a minister of the gospel, who loves the church; who was nurtured in its bosom; who has been sustained by its spiritual blessings and who will remain true to it as long as the cord of life shall lengthen.

When I suddenly catapulted into the leadership of the bus protest in 35 Montgomery, Alabama, a few years ago, I felt we would be supported by the white church. I felt that the white ministers, priests and rabbis of the South would be among our strongest allies. Instead, some have been outright opponents, refusing to understand the freedom movement and misrepresenting its leaders; all too many others have been more cautious than courageous and have remained silent behind the anesthetizing security of stained-glass windows.

In spite of my shattered dreams, I came to Birmingham with the hope that 36 the white religious leadership of this community would see the justice of our cause and, with deep moral concern, would serve as the channel through which our just grievances could reach the power structure. I had hoped that each of you would understand. But again I have been disappointed.

I have heard numerous southern religious leaders admonish their 37 worshipers to comply with a desegregation decision because it is the law, but I have longed to hear white ministers declare: "Follow this decree because integration is morally right and because the Negro is your brother." In the midst of blatant injustices inflicted upon the Negro, I have watched white churchmen stand on the sideline and mouth pious irrelevancies and sanctimonious trivialities. In the midst of a might struggle to rid our nation of racial and economic injustice, I have heard many ministers say: "Those are social issues, with which the gospel has no real concern." And I have watched many churches commit themselves to a completely otherwordly religion which makes a strange, un-Biblical distinction between body and soul, between the sacred and the secular.

I have traveled the length and breadth of Alabama, Mississippi and all the other southern states. On sweltering summer days and crisp autumn mornings I have looked at the South's beautiful churches with their lofty spires pointing heavenward. I have beheld the impressive outlines of her massive religious-education buildings. Over and over I have found myself asking: "What kind of people worship here? Who is their God? Where were their voices when the lips of Governor Barnett dripped with words of interposition and nullification? Where were they when Governor Wallace gave a clarion call for defiance and hatred? Where were their voices of support when bruised and weary Negro men and women decided to rise from the dark dungeons of complacency to the bright hills of creative protest?"

Yes, these questions are still in my mind. In deep disappointment I have wept over the laxity of the church. But be assured that my tears have been tears of love. There can be no deep disappointment where there is not deep love. Yes, I love the church. How could I do otherwise? I am in the rather unique position of being the son, the grandson and the great-grandson of preachers. Yes, I see the church as the body of Christ. But, oh! How we have blemished and scarred that body through social neglect and through fear of being nonconformists.

There was a time when the church was very powerful—in the time when the early Christians rejoiced at being deemed worthy to suffer for what they believed. In those days the church was not merely a thermometer that recorded the ideas and principles of popular opinion; it was a thermostat that transformed the mores of society. Whenever the early Christians entered a town, the people in power became disturbed and immediately sought to convict the Christians for being "disturbers of the peace" and "outside agitators." But the Christians pressed on, in the conviction that they were "a colony of heaven," called to obey God rather than man. Small in number, they were big in commitment. They were too God-intoxicated to be "astronomically intimidated." By their effort and example they brought an end to such ancient evils as infanticide and gladiatorial contests.

Things are different now. So often the contemporary church is a weak, ineffectual voice with an uncertain sound. So often it is an archdefender of the status quo. Far from being disturbed by the presence of the church, the power structure of the average community is consoled by the church's silent—and often even vocal—sanction of things as they are.

But the judgment of God is upon the church as never before. If today's church does not recapture the sacrificial spirit of the early church, it will lose its authenticity, forfeit the loyalty of millions, and be dismissed as an irrelevant social club with no meaning for the twentieth century. Every day I meet young people whose disappointment with the church has turned into outright disgust.

Perhaps I have once again been too optimistic. Is organized religion too   43 inextricably bound to the status quo to save our nation and the world? Perhaps I must turn my faith to the inner spiritual church, the church within the church, as the true *ekklesia* and the hope of the world. But again I am thankful to God that some noble souls from the ranks of organized religion have broken loose from the paralyzing chains of conformity and joined us as active partners in the struggle for freedom. They have left their secure congregations and walked the streets of Albany, Georgia, with us. They have gone down the highways of the South on tortuous rides for freedom. Yes, they have gone to jail with us. Some have been dismissed from their churches, have lost the support of their bishops and fellow ministers. But they have acted in the faith that right defeated is stronger than evil triumphant. Their witness has been the spiritual salt that has preserved the true meaning of the gospel in these troubled times. They have carved a tunnel of hope through the dark mountain of disappointment.

I hope the church as a whole will meet the challenge of this decisive hour.   44 But even if the church does not come to the aid of justice, I have no despair about the future. I have no fear about the outcome of our struggle in Birmingham, even if our motives are at present misunderstood. We will reach the goal of freedom in Birmingham and all over the nation, because the goal of America is freedom. Abused and scorned though we may be, our destiny is tied up with America's destiny. Before the pilgrims landed at Plymouth, we were here. Before the pen of Jefferson etched the majestic words of the Declaration of Independence across the pages of history, we were here. For more than two centuries our forebears labored in this country without wages; they made cotton king; they built the homes of their masters while suffering gross injustice and shameful humiliation—and yet out of a bottomless vitality they continued to thrive and develop. If the inexpressible cruelties of slavery could not stop us, the opposition we now face will surely fail. We will win our freedom because the sacred heritage of our nation and the eternal will of God are embodied in our echoing demands.

Before closing I feel impelled to mention one other point in your statement   45 that has troubled me profoundly. You warmly commended the Birmingham police force for keeping "order" and "preventing violence." I doubt that you would have so warmly commended the police force if you had seen its dogs sinking their teeth into unarmed, nonviolent Negroes. I doubt that you would so quickly commend the policemen if you were to observe their ugly and inhumane treatment of Negroes here in the city jail; if you were to watch them push and curse old Negro women and young Negro girls; if you were to see them slap and kick old Negro men and young boys; if you were to observe them, as they did on two occasions, refuse to give us food because we wanted to sing our grace together. I cannot join you in your praise of the Birmingham police department.

It is true that the police have exercised a degree of discipline in handling the demonstrators. In this sense they have conducted themselves rather "nonviolently" in public. But for what purpose? To preserve the evil system of segregation. Over the past few years I have consistently preached that nonviolence demands that the means we use must be as pure as the ends we seek. I have tried to make clear that it is wrong to use immoral means to attain moral ends. But now I must affirm that it is just as wrong, or perhaps even more so, to use moral means to preserve immoral ends. Perhaps Mr. Connor and his policemen have been rather nonviolent in public, as was Chief Pritchett in Albany, Georgia, but they have used the moral means of nonviolence to maintain the immoral end of racial injustice. As T. S. Eliot has said: "The last temptation is the greatest treason: To do the right deed for the wrong reason."

I wish you had commended the Negro sit-inners and demonstrators of Birmingham for their sublime courage, their willingness to suffer and their amazing discipline in the midst of great provocation. One day the South will recognize its real heroes. They will be the James Merediths, with the noble sense of purpose that enables them to face jeering and hostile mobs, and with the agonizing loneliness that characterizes the life of the pioneer. They will be old, oppressed, battered Negro women, symbolized in a seventy-two-year-old woman in Montgomery, Alabama, who rose up with a sense of dignity and with her people decided not to ride segregated buses, and who responded with ungrammatical profundity to one who inquired about her weariness: "My feets is tired, but my soul is at rest." They will be the young high school and college students, the young ministers of the gospel and a host of their elders, courageously and nonviolently sitting in at lunch counters and willingly going to jail for conscience' sake. One day the South will know that when these disinherited children of God sat down at lunch counters, they were in reality standing up for what is best in the American dream and for the most sacred values in our Judao-Christian heritage, thereby bringing our nation back to those great wells of democracy which were dug deep by the founding fathers in their formulation of the Constitution and the Declaration of Independence.

Never before have I written so long a letter. I'm afraid it is much too long to take your precious time. I can assure you that it would have been much shorter if I had been writing from a comfortable desk, but what else can one do when he is alone in a narrow jail cell, other than write long letters, think long thoughts and pray long prayers?

If I have said anything in this letter that overstates the truth and indicates   49
an unreasonable impatience, I beg you to forgive me. If I have said anything
that understates the truth and indicates my having a patience that allows me to
settle for anything less than brotherhood, I beg God to forgive me.

I hope this letter finds you strong in the faith. I also hope that   50
circumstances will soon make it possible for me to meet each of you, not as an
integrationist or a civil-rights leader but as a fellow clergyman and a Christian
brother. Let us all hope that the dark clouds of racial prejudice will soon pass
away and the deep fog of misunderstanding will be lifted from our fear-
drenched communities, and in some not too distant tomorrow the radiant stars
of love and brotherhood will shine over our great nation with all their
scintillating beauty.

Yours for the cause of Peace and Brotherhood,
MARTIN LUTHER KING, JR.
1963

QUESTIONS ON CONTENT:

1. How does King answer the charge that he is an "outsider"?
2. What are the four steps for a nonviolent campaign? What do they mean?
3. How does King distinguish between "just" and "unjust" laws?
4. Why is King disappointed with the "white moderate"?
5. How does King answer the charge that he is an "extremist"?
6. Why is King disappointed with the leaders of white churches?

QUESTIONS ON WRITING STRUCTURE AND STRATEGY:

1. How does King appeal to authorities to buttress his arguments? Is it effective?
2. King's ostensible audience is the group of clergy who published a reaction to his march. What other audience is King addressing? How do you know?
3. How would you characterize King's tone in this letter? Pinpoint those elements that contribute to its tone.
4. In paragraph fourteen, one of King's sentences contains over 400 words. Examine how King has constructed this sentence so his readers can easily follow his ideas. What devices does he employ? At what point does the reader get the full meaning of the sentence? How does if affect you as the reader? How would you classify this sentence?

QUESTIONS FOR DISCUSSION AND WRITING:

1. King's letter contains a number of aphorisms, short, pithy remarks containing some wisdom. Chose one of the following and explores its implications in a paper:

"Injustice anywhere is a threat to justice everywhere."

"Privileged groups seldom give up their privileges voluntarily."

"Groups tend to be more immoral than individuals."

2. Write a paper in which you discuss the differences between King's letter and the ordinary kind of letter Swanson discusses in "The Mail of the Species."

3. For a research project, check the *Readers' Guide,* the *New York Times Index,* and the *Humanities Index* for stories and articles describing reactions to King's campaign in Birmingham and to his famous "Letter." Summarize some of the reactions to his campaign.
    OR:
    Review *America: History and Life* (a compilation of abstracts) to see how one writes an abstract. Prepare several abstracts on articles about King's Birmingham campaign. Then check your abstracts against those on the same articles appearing in *America: History and Life.*

4. King uses the letter form to justify himself to a group of skeptics. Have you ever felt the need to justify your actions to skeptics? It could be any decision you may have taken against the advice of, or by the consent of, others. Write a paper about the experience.

SELF-EDUCATION
OF A LABOR LEADER[1]

Samuel Gompers

*Samuel Gompers was one of nine children born to Dutch-Jewish
parents in London in 1850. His formal schooling ended at the age of
ten, and at the age of thirteen he emigrated to America with his
family, apprenticed to his father, a cigarmaker. The following year he
joined Local 144 of the Cigarmakers' Union of New York City as a
journeyman. In his Autobiography, he credits Ferdinand Laurrell with
teaching him the value to labor of nonpolitical craft unions and of
working within the capitalist system. For Gompers, the proper aim of
craft unions was to gain workers more pay, more leisure, and more
freedom. Gompers quickly moved up in the labor movement, and when
the American Federation of Labor was organized in 1886, he was
elected its first president. Except for one year, he served in that office
and was American labor's chief spokesman until his death in 1924.
Gompers' self-education follows the pattern of other men and women
who achieved prominence in spite of little formal education. The
reading program of the Cigarmakers' Union, as he describes it, was
unique, aiding greatly in the economic eduation of the workers. Note
his remarks about reading, especially the* New York Sun. *Though he
disagreed with its editorial policy, he learned the essentials of good
writing from that newspaper.*

Anyone who does not know the cigarmaking trade will find it difficult to
appreciate the educational value of the little forum existing in each shop. It
gave education in such a way as to develop personality, for in no other place
were we so wholly natural. The nature of our work developed a camaraderie of
the shop such as few workers enjoy. It was a world in itself — a cosmopolitan
world. Shopmates came from everywhere — some had been nearly everywhere.
When they told us of strange lands and peoples, we listened eagerly. No one
ever questioned another as to his past life, for many were revolutionists who
sought new opportunity and safety by leaving the past blank. . . .

Shop life stimulated my mental development. Another impetus came
through newspapers. Someone has said that newspapers are the characteristic
literature of Americans. Whether that statement is an epigram or a truth, when
as a lad I came to New York, I soon learned what a mine of information
awaited one in the New York papers. I carried newspapers with me from early
morning, reading every chance I got. I read in the morning as I got ready to go
to work and often I walked to the shop — for New York streets in those days
were not the maelstrom of humanity found today. During this period I was

1

2

---

[1]Editor's title.

reading greedily whatever came to hand on general subjects, for I was young and strong and eager to know all things about life. *The New York Sun* under Charles A. Dana was the publication I read most thoroughly and persistently. It was the great daily of the time publishing a wider range of informational matter than the other papers. This sentence, printed on the first page, *The news culled here and there by* The Sun's *ubiquitous reporter*, remains in my memory despite all the intervening years. Every week *The Sun* published able book reviews signed by M. W. H. (Hazeltine). These reviews usually quoted generously from the books. I found in them much information in addition to acquiring familiarity with many volumes I never had the opportunity to read. Both editorial and news columns were edited carefully. From them I absorbed ideas of style, sentence structure, and the use of words. Charles A. Dana's editorials were in themselves a daily stimulus to my mind. Though I more often than not disagreed with the editorial policy of *The Sun* in dealing with local and national affairs, in its treatment of international affairs, I found a large fund of information with which I was in complete accord.

In the shop there was also reading. It was the custom of the cigarmakers to chip in to create a fund for purchasing papers, magazines, and books. Then while the rest worked, one of our members would read to us perhaps for an hour at a time, sometimes longer. In order that the reader might not be the loser financially, each one of the other men in the shop gave him a definite number of cigars. I had a habit of saving any interesting magazine or newspaper articles to read to my shopmates. Others did the same. As my voice was strong and the men could hear me easily whenever I read, they always asked me to read more than my period. In fact, these discussions in the shops were more like public debating societies or what we call these days "labor forums." This practice had a great deal to do with developing the interest of cigarmakers in leading economic questions. . . .

There were at that time many pamphlet publications of interest to labor, and cheap paper-covered editions of books. Henry George's *Progress and Poverty* was first published in pamphlet form. Additional chapters were published from time to time as separate articles until finally the material had grown to book size. If my memory serves me, the George articles read in our shop were published by the *Irish World*. Whatever we read served as the basis for discussion. Sometimes when an individual tried to monopolize the discussion we had a crude but effective defense. A cigarmaker who was bored would twist his blade against his cutting board in such a way as to make a curious whanging sound. When two or three did this together or in succession the long-winded one was forced into silence. I don't wish to convey the idea that our shop was a sort of Donnybrook fair, but we did devise a democratic arrangement for effective discipline. All associated effort must have discipline.

312

QUESTIONS ON CONTENT:

1. Can you frame a thesis for this selection?
2. In what specific ways did newspapers contribute to Gompers' education?
3. What unique self-educating practice did the cigarmakers devise?

QUESTIONS ON WRITING STRUCTURE AND STRATEGY:

1. For what audience do you think Gompers' *Autobiography* is intended? How do you know?
2. Can you detect the influence of good journalistic writing in Gompers' prose? Note his choice of words, his sparing use of subordination, and his tight organization.

QUESTIONS FOR DISCUSSION AND WRITING:

1. In a short paper compare Gompers' education and background with two or three of the following: Franklin, Douglass, Malcolm X, London, Hoffer. How do they differ and how are they alike?
2. Why would it be difficult for contemporary workers to employ the cigarmakers' technique of self-education? Write a paper on possible ways in which workers could get the kind of education that Gompers and his shopmates got. You might engage in some library research on current union educational practices.
3. Discuss the implications of Gompers' last sentence for you. Can you make some contemporary application to activity in which you have been engaged or are now engaged?

THE TEACHINGS OF
THE MEDIA CURRICULUM
Neil Postman

*A professor of media ecology at New York University, Neil Postman in
1969 published* Teaching as a Subversive Activity, *calling for more
electives and more student self-expression. Ten years later, he had
completely changed his mind when he published* Teaching as a
Conserving Activity, *from which the following chapter is taken. Asked
why he had changed his mind, Postman pointed to the unanticipated
rapid growth of a "media curriculum" hostile to the school curriculum.
Calling it the "first curriculum," he finds the "media curriculum"
more powerful and pervasive than the school curriculum, now viewed
as the "alternate curriculum." Because the "media curriculum" is
based on "analogues" (rapid transmission of images), it produces
effects that are antithetical to those produced by "linearity" (lines of
type in books), by which we have been conditioned and upon which all
education in civilization is based. Already he sees deleterious effects on
students, which he attributes to the rising dominance of the "media
curriculum," and he warns against the possible future consequences.*

*Although Postman's remarks are primarily analytical and concerned in
part with abstractions, his comparison and contrast of the two
"curriculums" is nevertheless easy to follow. Observe his easy
transitions between paragraphs. Observe also the evidence he offers to
support his assertions about student behavior: limited attention span,
inarticulateness, and the elevation of feelings over rationality. Though
Postman's intended audience may have been a special one, what he
has to say is important to all who are concerned with the future of
American education and society.*

Since the television curriculum is pervasive and powerful, we can assume
that it will have effects at several levels, including the physiological, the
psychological, and the social. Of the physiological, we can, of course, only
make conjectures. Nothing will really be known for a very long time, and not
by us. But it can reasonably be imagined that excessive immersion in
nonlinguistic, analogic symbols will have the effect of amplifying the functions
of the right hemisphere of the brain while inhibiting the functions of the left.
The left hemisphere is the source of most of our language power (at least for
righthanded people). A left hemisphere lesion will lead to damage to our
capacity to speak, write, count, compute, and reason (but not necessarily to our
capacity to sing, a fact which might have been suspected by Plato had he been
a brain surgeon). The right hemisphere of the brain is largely nonlinguistic and
nonlogical in both its coding and decoding of information. Such language as it

314

is capable of is underdeveloped and lacks both the syntax and semantics required for digital communication. Apparently, the right brain works through pattern recognition, which is to say it apprehends the world holistically rather than through linguistic structures. In recognizing a human face, or a picture of it, or anything that requires an "all at once" perception, such as watching TV, we are largely using the right hemisphere of the brain, the left possibly being something of a burden in the process. Thus, continuous TV watching over centuries could conceivably have the effect of weakening left-brain activity, and producing a population of "right-brained" people.

What this would mean is difficult to say except that we may guess that   2
such people would be strong on intuition and feeling but weak on reflection and analysis. The left hemisphere, being the source of our power to speak and, therefore, to categorize, name, and objectify experience, has apparently been in the ascendancy for several millennia of human development. A good case can be made, along the lines Julian Jaynes has pursued, that the gradual emergence of left-brain dominance has generated our uniquely human capacity for consciousness; that is, our capacity to reconstruct the past and project ourselves into a future. A reversal of this trend is certainly imaginable as the word recedes in importance and the fast-moving, analogic image replaces it. If we imagine such a reverse trend carried to an extreme over many centuries, we might, then, have people who are "in touch with their feelings," who are spontaneous and musical, and who live in an existential world of immediate experience but who, at the same time, cannot "think" in the way we customarily use that word. In other words, people whose state of mind is somewhat analogous to that of a modern-day baboon.

But one does not need to resort to millennia-wide speculation about the   3
modification of brain functions in order to talk about the consequences of an unopposed TV education. There are, even now, observable behaviors in our youth that indicate they are undergoing certain serious psychological changes, at least in part attributable to television. For example, I have already suggested that the highly compressed TV learning modules, especially those of ten- to thirty-second commercials, are affecting attention span. Many teachers have commented on the fact that students, of all ages, "turn off" when some lesson or lecture takes longer than, say, eight to ten minutes. TV conditioning leads to the expectation that there will be a new point of view or focus of interest or even subject matter every few minutes, and it is becoming increasingly difficult for the young to sustain attention in situations where there is a fixed point of view or an extended linear progression.

There is also evidence that youth are exhibiting behaviors — for example,   4
in school — that are appropriate to TV watching but not to situations requiring

group attention. For instance, it is not uncommon for teachers to report that students will openly read newspapers in class or engage in other unconcealed side-involvements which are usually considered to be "rude" in the context of a lesson or lecture. My own investigation of this phenomenon suggests that these behaviors are not "rude" if we mean by that word a deliberate effort to violate the rules of a social situation. Many students are not aware that they have violated any rule at all. In watching television, or listening to records or the radio, they continuously engage in such side-involvements without reproach, and do not always understand why these behaviors are inappropriate when carried over to other communication environments.

It has, of course, also been widely noticed that the linguistic powers of our   5 youth appear to be diminishing. Scores on reading tests are in decline. But even more important, writing, which is the clearest demonstration of the power of analytical and sequential thinking, seems increasingly to be an alien form to many of our young, even to those who may be regarded as extremely intelligent. Moreover, it has been observed that oral expression has not improved as writing skills have fallen off. There are many teachers, for example, who have abandoned giving writing assignments altogether but who have not found their students to be especially organized or even coherent in talking about anything of minimal complexity.

What makes this deficiency especially alarming is that it suggests we are,   6 in fact, not moving back to a pre-Platonic oral culture in which memory, argumentation, and dialectic take command. Astonishingly, the two electronic media which are perfectly suited to the transmission of the human voice — the radio and phonograph — have been given over almost entirely to the transmission of music. Such language as is heard on records is little else but comedy routines, or song lyrics at the level of Neanderthal chanting. On radio, language is largely a commercial message, mostly a parody of human speech — disjointed, semihysterical, almost completely devoid of ideational content.

I believe this development to be only in part a consequence of the   7 economic structure of the broadcasting and record industries. For if we say that these industries only give our youth what they will pay for, the question remains, Why do our youth turn away from civilized speech? The answer, in my opinion, is that the electronic information environment, with television at its center, is fundamentally hostile to conceptual, segmented, linear modes of expression, so that both writing and speech must lose some of their power. Language is, by its nature, slow moving, hierarchical, logical, and continuous. Whether writing or speaking, one must maintain a fixed point of view and a continuity of content; one must move to higher or lower levels of abstraction; one must follow to a greater or lesser degree rules of syntax and logic. Even more, language is inevitably ambiguous. As Chaim Perelman says it, language is filled with confused notions. It is this very ambiguity that gives natural language its conceptual scope and versatility. For every word contains the possibility of multiple meanings and therefore of multiple ideas. And because words do not have closed, invariant meanings, they are our most effective instruments for changing our concepts and making them grow. The word is not just an idea. It is a small universe of ideas. Even further, every spoken sentence contains the seed of an argument, not only because of its ambiguity but because whatever is asserted simultaneously implies its negation or opposite. Every proposition is debatable or at least an impetus to inquiry.

But the television curriculum will have none of this. Or, at least, very little. As I have argued, its imagery is fast moving, concrete, discontinuous, alogical, requiring emotional response, not conceptual processing. Not being propositional in form, its imagery does not provide grounds for argument and contains little ambiguity. There is nothing to debate about. Nothing to refute. Nothing to negate. There are only feelings to be felt. Thus the TV curriculum poses a serious challenge not merely to school performance but to civilization itself. And the challenge is not made only by the TV curriculum, for in considering what we are facing we must take into account the cumulative impact of the entire electronic information environment of which TV is only an element, although a central one. Radio, the LP record, audio-tape, the photograph, and film, each in its own way lends support to the undermining of traditional patterns of thought and response. Taken together, their "hidden curriculum" conspires against almost all of the assumptions on which the slowly disseminated, logically ordered, and cognitively processed work is based. In an environment in which nonlinguistic information is moved at the speed of light, in nonhierarchical patterns, in vast and probably unassimilable quantities, the word and all it stands for must lose prestige, power, and relevance. 8

Our problem, then, is not how to produce higher reading scores or better school compositions but how to close the "generation gap." "Generation gap" means here that on one side there stands the age-old tradition of a language-centered view of the world, and on the other there stands a recently emerged image-centered view. On one side, therefore, there is always an historical presence with its mirror image, the future. On the other there is only an overpowering present. On one side there is the ideal of reason; on the other there is the ideal of authenticity of feeling. 9

Do I overstate the case? I certainly hope so. And yet the effects to which I am alluding can be observed not simply in the fragmented, impatient speech of the young or their illogical, unsyntactical writing but in the rapid emergence of an all-instant society: instant therapy, instant religion, instant food, instant friends, even instant reading. Instancy is one of the main teachings of our present information environment. Constancy is one of the main teachings of civilization. But constancy presupposes the relevance of historical precedence, of continuity, and above all, of complexity and the richness of ambiguity but 10 for the meaning of one's own past. And a person who abandons a five-thousand- or two-thousand-year-old religious tradition to follow a fourteen-year-old messenger from God has somehow learned to value novelty more than continuity.

Where does the seeming plausibility of instancy as a way of life come from? It is at least a reasonable hypothesis that it emerges from the "world view" advanced by our present information environment. Consider this: Every one of the one million commercials — every one — that a youngster will see or hear on TV or the radio presents a problem and a solution. The problem, as I have noted, is rarely trivial but the solution always is. Your anxiety about your sexual appeal gets solved with Scope — in thirty seconds. Your failure to achieve social status gets solved with a bottle of Coke and a song — in sixty seconds. Your fear of nature gets solved with Scott toilet tissue — in twenty seconds. Even the heartbreak of psoriasis can be relieved in a few seconds, not to mention the agony of hemorrhoidal tissues or, through Pan Am, the boredom of your life. These are powerful and incessant teachings, which are not only directed at the young. They present us all with a paradigm of how to think and how to live and what to expect. We become, as Edmund Carpenter says, what we behold. The new media are more than extensions of our senses. They are ultimately metaphors for life itself, directing us to search for time-compressed experience, short-term relationships, present-oriented accomplishment, simple and immediate solutions. Thus, the teaching of the media curriculum must lead inevitably to a disbelief in long-term planning, in deferred gratification, in the relevance of tradition, and in the need for confronting complexity.

But this is far from the end of it. There are many reasonable hypotheses about the teachings of our electronic information environment for which there exists suggestive evidence and against which civilization must prepare itself. For example, the nonlinear, nonsequential nature of electronic information works in powerful ways to create a frame of mind hostile to science. Science depends on linearity of thought, the step-by-step presentation of evidence and argumentation. This method of organizing information is the structural basis of scientific thought. It makes possible the refutation of evidence and argument; it permits translation into other digital forms, such as mathematics; it encourages delayed response and reflective analysis. The growth of science also depends on our ability to create increasingly sophisticated abstractions, particularly in digital modes. What happens, then, if our information environment does not encourage this mode of thinking? It is improbable that scientists will disappear but we shall quite likely have fewer of them, and they are likely to form, even in the short run, an elite class who, like priests of the pictographic age, will be believed to possess mystical powers. The rest of the population may move rapidly toward an increasing fascination with mysticism and superstition; in other words, beliefs which are neither refutable or comprehensible but which are expressed with great feeling. There is already some evidence that this is in fact happening, as we can see in growth of interest and belief in the occult, astrology, Eastern mysticism, levitating gurus, and English-speaking extraterrestrials.

Scientific thinking must also recede in prestige and relevance because of the discontinuity of content that characterizes much of our information environment. The fundamental assumption of science is that there is order and unity in diversity. A scientist must believe that events can be explained by reference to some organizing principle. Above all, he must believe the world *makes sense*. But when one is immersed in a world of disconnected media presentations, it is extremely difficult to internalize this assumption. The young in particular are experiencing an acute inability to make connections, and some have given up trying. The TV curriculum, we must remember, stresses the fragmented and discrete nature of events, and indeed is structually unable to organize them into coherent themes or principles. 13

This fact must inevitably contribute to the undermining of a sense of history, as well. Like science, history requires a belief in connectedness — the assumption that there are explanatory principles which account for social change or human conflict or intellectual growth. In this context, Jacob Bronowski's *The Ascent of Man* offers an instructive case of the nature of our problem, for it is about both history and science. Although the book version of his ideas was, in fact, a television script, it has the power, because it is a book, to explain the principles by which culture and science have developed; that is, the book has a thesis. In the TV version, the thesis disappeared. And so did history. Television is always in the present tense. There is no way to show what happened in the past. Whatever is shown appears as something that *is* happening. This is why we must be told frequently that a videotape we are watching was actually recorded at some earlier date. But even when film is used, as was the case in Bronowski's programs, it must present history as "now." In the "grammar" of both film and TV, there simply is no correlate to a linguistic past tense. So, much of Bronowski's point of view was lost. He was concerned to show historical development but the audience saw only a series of interesting events of equivalent contemporaneousness. Moreover, TV or film cannot reveal a thesis. A thesis, a principle, a theme, a law, a hypothesis — these are all linguistic concepts. Pictures have no theses. They are analogues whose level of abstraction is concrete and invariable, and whose impact is immediate and existential. While Bronowski *talked* his thesis as a supplement to the images, his talk could not compete with his pictures. In the end, what the audience saw was a series of discrete, disconnected images which had no history and suggested no principles. 14

We must also worry about the plausible hypothesis that any decline in linguistic power will tend to increase the extent of personal maladjustment. As I write, there are reports from colleges and universities all over the country 15 about the widespread incidence of suicide and other less definitive but serious symptoms of emotional difficulty among youth. We appear to have an epidemic on our hands. Without meaning to deprecate the usefulness of either art or music therapy, I think it accurate to say that articulate language is our chief weapon against mental disturbance. Through language we are able to formulate in relatively clear terms the origins and nature of our distress, and through language we may chart the route toward resolution and relief. I seriously doubt if you can sing, dance, draw, or scream your way out of an impulse to suicide. But you can talk your way out. Of course, you can talk your way in, as well, which is why knowledge of and competence in language are so essential to helping one achieve and maintain emotional balance. I have already written one book on this subject, *Crazy Talk, Stupid Talk*, and do not intend to rewrite it here. But surely it is no startling thesis to say that any decline in the resources of language is likely to be accompanied by an increase in personal maladjustment or, if you will, crazy talk . . .

We can be sure that a curriculum as powerful as the electronic information environment will have powerful effects, and in suggesting what these might be, I have done nothing more than what educators do every September when they predict effects of a school curriculum. They tell us that certain things will be taught in certain ways, within a certain context, and that there are certain results that can be expected. I am saying the same thing, with this difference: The curriculum I am referring to has more money spent on it, commands greater attention, is more pervasive, and is less carefully monitored than the school curriculum. Moreover, in its competition with the school curriculum for the control of our young, the electronic curriculum is an ungracious — one might even say, merciless — adversary. It makes no concessions whatsoever to the school curriculum, unless you want to count *Sesame Street*, which is, in my opinion, no concession at all but a promiscuous flaunting of everything the TV curriculum represents and the school curriculum does not. The school curriculum, on the other hand, yields at almost every point and in the worst possible way — by trying to mimic the forms of the electronic curriculum and therefore to indulge its biases. School courses are reduced to twenty-minute modules so that children's attention will not wander. Required courses are eliminated and replaced with inconsequential electives. Teachers become entertainers. Programmed machines and other techniques which stress isolated learning are introduced. Audio-visual aids flood the classroom. Relevant — that is, attention-centered — topics are stressed. There even develops a widespread interest in what are called "alternative curriculums." But the school as we normally think of it (or used to think of it) is now, itself, an alternative curriculum, one whose teachings very much need to be preserved in the face of the onslaught of the First Curriculum.

The school curriculum is subject-matter-centered, work-centered, 17 reason-centered, future-centered, hierarchical, secular, socializing, segmented, and coherent. Assuming that these characteristics are maintained, and even strengthened, we may hope that the education of our youth will achieve a healthful balance, and therefore a survival-insuring direction. Marshall McLuhan wrote prophetically more than a decade ago that our education must assume a thermostatic function. He said: "Just as we now try to control atom-bomb fallout, so we will one day try to control media fallout. Education will become recognized as civil defense against media fallout."

QUESTIONS ON CONTENT:

1. What are the physiological effects of the media curriculum on individuals?
2. Postman asserts that the "media curriculum" produces effects at three levels: physiological, psychological and social. What evidence does he offer to support his contention that the psychological effects are already apparent?
3. What are the distinguishing characteristics of the school curriculum? Of the media curriculum? Do you agree with Postman?
4. How does Postman say that the media curriculum will affect the study of science?

QUESTIONS ON STRUCTURE AND WRITING STRATEGY:

1. In his opening sentence Postman says he will deal with the effects of television on three levels. What kind of evidence does he produce to make these divisions clear? Try to pinpoint clear divisions in the text.
2. Admittedly much of what Postman says is speculative. Do you find him qualifying his assertions, or does he proceed mainy as if all were proven fact? Explain.
3. Though speculative, abstract, and philosophical at times, how does Postman achieve concreteness for the common reader?

QUESTIONS FOR DISCUSSION AND WRITING:

1. Analyze Postman's interpretation of the Generation Gap in terms of its language-centered versus its image-centered view, its future versus present perspective, its constancy versus its instancy.
2. Postman assembles a formidable number of charges against the electronic media. Do you find any of these convincing? Why?
3. Postman makes a strong argument against the electronic media and only hints at antidotes or alternatives. Accepting his premise, what would you offer as a solution to this predicament?

WHY CHILDREN
DON'T LIKE TO READ
Bruno Bettelheim and Karen Zelan

*"Why won't Johnny read?" "Why won't Janie read?" To account for
the growing "aliteracy," the refusal to read, Dr. Bruno Bettelheim and
his associate at the Orthogenic School of the University of Chicago,
Dr. Karen Zelan, point the accusing finger at the way many American
children are introduced to reading in the early grades. There is a
"magic to reading," and children, they assert, are naturally fascinated
with meaning. But the materials currently used and the practices
presently employed in many American school systems work against a
young child's natural curiosity. Based on their many years of
experience and research with children and learning — both in Chicago
and Boston — their message is a disturbing one. As you trace the
argument in the following selection, compare your own experiences
with those described. Note how the authors — employing comparison
and contrast, cause and effect — marshal their evidence from actual
classroom studies, analyses of earlier primers, and comparisons with
Swiss schools and methods. Future parents, teachers, or administrators
will find valuable suggestions to employ later on with their own
students and offspring.*

A child's attitude toward reading is of such importance that, more often
than not, it determines his scholastic fate. Moreover, his experiences in learning
to read may decide how he will feel about learning in general, and even about
himself as a person.

Family life has a good deal to do with the development of a child's ability
to understand, to use, and to enjoy language. It strongly influences his
impression of the value of reading, and his confidence in his intelligence and
academic abilities. But regardless of what the child brings from home to school,
the most important influence on his ability to read once he is in class is how
his teacher presents reading and literature. If the teacher can make reading
interesting and enjoyable, then the exertions required to learn how will seem
worthwhile.

A child takes great pleasure in becoming able to read some words. But the
excitement fades when the texts the child must read force him to reread the
same word endlessly. Word recognition — "decoding" is the term used by
educational theorists — deteriorates into empty rote learning when it does not
lead directly to the reading of meaningful content. The longer it takes the child
to advance from decoding to meaningful reading, the more likely it becomes
that his pleasure in books will evaporate. A child's ability to read depends
unquestionably on his learning pertinent skills. But he will not be interested in

learning basic reading skills if he thinks he is expected to master them for their own sake. That is why so much depends on what the teacher, the school, and the textbooks emphasize. From the very beginning, the child must be convinced that skills are only a means to achieve a goal, and that the only goal of importance is that he become literate—that is, come to enjoy literature and benefit from what it has to offer.

A child who is made to read, "Nan had a pad. Nan had a tan pad. Dad ran. Dad ran to the pad," and worse nonsense can have no idea that books are worth the effort of learning to read. His frustration is increased by the fact that such a repetitive exercise is passed off as a story to be enjoyed. The worst effect of such drivel is the impression it makes on a child that sounding out words on a page—decoding—is what reading is all about. If, on the contrary, a child were taught new skills as they became necessary to understand a worthwhile text, the empty achievement "Now I can decode some words" would give way to the much more satisfying recognition "Now I am reading something that adds to my life." From the start, reading lessons should nourish the child's spontaneous desire to read books by himself.   4

Benjamin S. Bloom, professor of education at the University of Chicago, has found that who will do well in school and who will do poorly is largely determined by the end of the third grade. Thus, reading instruction during the first three grades is crucial. Unfortunately, the primers used in most American schools up to and sometimes through the third grade convey no sense that there are rewards in store. And since poor readers continue to be subjected to these primers well past the third grade, their reading can only get worse as their interests and experience diverge further from the content of the books.   5

That rote learning is the wrong way to teach reading was recognized more than seventy years ago. In the first important treatise on the teaching of reading published in this country, *The Psychology and Pedagogy of Reading* (1908), the author, Edmund Burke Huey, urged that drills be kept separate from the activity of reading. He wrote: "The school should cease to make primary reading the fetich [sic] it has long been. The child should never be permitted to read for the sake of reading, as a formal process or end in itself. The reading should always be for the intrinsic interest or value of what is read. . . . Word-pronouncing will therefore always be secondary to getting whole sentence-meanings, and this from the very first. . . . School readers, especially primers, should largely disappear, except as they may be competent editings of the real literature of the mother tongue, presented in literary wholes, or as they may be records of the children's own experiences and thoughts."   6

For many decades, textbooks have been used as the basis for reading   7 instruction by the vast majority of elementary school teachers, and they are much worse today than the ones Huey objected to. According to one study, first readers published in the 1920s contained an average of 645 new words. By the late 1930s, this number had dropped to about 460 words. In the 1940s and 1950s, vocabulary declined further, to about 350 words. The vocabularies of primers in seven textbook series published between 1960 and 1963 ranged from 113 to 173 new words. More recent primers, compared with the 1920s editions, also have small vocabularies. For example, *Let's See the Animals*, published in 1970 by Bowmar/Noble, introduces 108 new words; *May I Come In?*, published in 1973, by Ginn & Company, introduces 219 new words; *Finding Places*, published by the American Book Company, in 1980, introduces 192 new words. Although in the 1920s few children went to kindergarten and little preschool reading instruction was given, by the 1970s, when many children were attending kindergarten and reading was consistently taught there, the first-grade primers contained only a quarter of the vocabulary presented to first-graders fifty years ago.

When they enter school, most children already know and use 4,000 or more words. Nobody has to make a deliberate effort to teach them these words, with the exception of the first few learned in infancy. Children make words their own because they want to, because they find them pleasing and useful. Even the least verbal group of first-graders has mastered well over 2,000 words, thus invalidating the claim that children of culturally deprived families would be unfairly burdened by primers of larger vocabulary. This condescending assumption ignores the richness of daily life in even the poorest households. By encouraging the adoption of less challenging books, it has helped to deprive most children at school just as poverty deprives many children at home.

The Scholastic Aptitude Test (SAT) is a particularly reliable measure of an age group's intellectual accomplishment, because, unlike most of the various achievement tests administered in schools, its standards do not change from one year to the next. The mean score on the verbal SAT (which registers reading comprehension) has been declining for the past ten years. Although it would be difficult to establish a cause-and-effect relationship between the declining verbal ability of college-bound high school juniors and seniors and the decline in vocabulary of primers over the past several decades, there can be no doubt that the scores reflect diminishing regard for the written word.

Research in the teaching of reading, far from justifying the continuous reduction in the number of words used in primers, fails to show any reason for it. It is therefore hard to understand why textbook publishers have pursued this course, and why educators have not rebelled. One possible explanation is that as primers become simpler, children, because they are bored, read them with less and less facility. The publishers, in response, make the books even simpler and, thus, even less effective.

Primers have no authors. Many people help to create the books, and the financial investment required runs into the millions. (The sizable staff of one large publishing house worked for five years to produce a first-grade program alone.) Yet despite such prodigious effort and expense, all basic series are more or less alike. To recoup the large investment in a series, a publishing house must be able to sell it to schools all over the country. It cannot risk controversy.

We can cite two examples from our own experience. One publisher, in an effort to improve a first-grade reader, came up with a story in which children bring a balloon home from a fair, whereupon a cat leaps on it and it bursts. The story would seem harmless enough to most people, but when the book was tested in an Illinois school system, cat-lovers were outraged: the story had maligned their pets, turned children against animals, and so on. The local school superintendent, who was coming up for re-election, decided to withdraw the book, and the publisher, fearing similar setbacks elsewhere, decided to drop the story.

Another publishing house was preparing a new edition of its widely used series. One of us, asked to consult, objected in detail to the blandness of the stories proposed. The company's vice-president in charge of textbooks confessed that he, too, thought the stories would bore young readers, but he was obliged to keep in mind that neither children nor teachers buy textbooks: school boards and superintendents do. And their first concern is that no one mind their choices. Fairy tales, for example, would never do. Some people would complain that the stories insult stepmothers; others would find the punishment of evildoers too cruel.

The result of such constraints is a book full of endlessly repeated words passed off as stories. Many teachers have told us that they don't like such a book, but assume that since a primer has been put together by experts, and approved by experts, it must be appropriate for children even if it is obnoxious to an adult. In the course of our research on the teaching of reading we have talked to children who were not so credulous. Many told us that their teachers must have faked an interest in the stories, or that they must think children are not very smart.

Fourth- and fifth-graders who had left the beginners' books behind described their resentments to us quite clearly. One rather quiet boy, who preferred to read or work by himself and rarely participated in class, spoke up all on his own and with deep feeling. He had felt so ashamed to say the things written in primers that he could not bring himself to do it. And although he now liked reading a lot, he said, he still had a hard time reading aloud.

The first- and second-graders were as unhappy with their books as the older children remembered being. They said they read only because they had to, and that on their own they would never choose such "junk." "It's all impossible," one of them said. When he was asked why, answers came from around the room: "The children aren't real!" "They aren't angry!" When one child exclaimed, "They aren't anything!" all agreed that there was nothing more to be said.

Textbook writers and publishers know that their books are dull, and they have tried to make them more attractive by commissioning many colorful illustrations. For example, the number of pictures in primers of the Scott, Foresman series doubled between 1920 and 1962, from about one picture per one hundred words to nearly two per hundred words. The trouble with pictures is that the printed text becomes even less appealing in comparison. Words seem to be less vivid and to convey less information. Worse, being able to guess from the pictures what the text is about, a child who is reluctant to read has no incentive to learn.

The publisher's advice to teachers reinforces this syndrome. Typically, the elaborate teachers' guides for each book in a series suggest that the class be asked questions about the pictures before reading the story. Yet there is evidence that pictures retard or interfere with learning to read. Consider the following report by a psychologist of reading, Eleanor J. Gibson: "Children in the second term of kindergarten were given practice with three-letter common words ('cat,' 'bed,' 'dog,' etc.) on flash cards. In one group, the word on the card was accompanied by the appropriate picture. In another, it appeared alone. Training trials, in which the experimenter pronounced the word as it was displayed to the child, alternated with test trials [in which] the child was shown the word alone and asked to say what it was. The picture group made significantly more errors and took longer . . . than the group without pictures. The pictorial redundancy appeared to be distracting rather than useful." Yet in most of the preprimers and primers in classrooms today, words are used primarily as labels and captions.

Learning to read is not an entertainment but hard work. Rather than face this directly, publishers seek to distract children with references to play. But allusions to strenuous physical activities make a child want to move, not think. Worse, a first-grader knows from his own experience just how complex a ball game can be. So a weak story about a ball game is most likely to convince the child that reading about a ball game is dull compared with playing in one.

In Harper & Row's "Janet and Mark" series (1966), school makes its first appearance in second grade in *All Through the Year*. The last section of the book is titled "Too Much Is Too Much of Anything," and the first story about the things that are too much, "A Feeling in the Air," is about school. "Everyone was waiting. . . . It was the last day of school. A little while, and it would be all over." The children are "daydreaming . . . of baseball and swimming and bicycle rides." In the last picture of the story, we see them streaming out of the school building, joyful to be released.

Psychoanalytic studies of the so-called "double bind" have shown that nothing is more confusing and disturbing to a child, or has more detrimental effects, than contradictory messages from an adult about important issues. Almost every preprimer and primer bears such contradictory messages. Tacitly, they say that the educational system, which requires the child to go to school and presents him with a book so that he may learn to read, holds that school and learning are serious business. But the explicit message of the text and pictures is that the child should think—that is, read—only about playing. The idea seems to be that a suggestion of what books are really for—to open new worlds of thought and imagination—would have the most undesirable consequences for the child's reading achievement. 21

From a psychoanalytic perspective, the primer's emphasis on play ensures that the books will be addressed solely to the child's pleasure-seeking ego— the earliest, most basic, but also most primitive motivating force in man. But as the child reaches school age, around age five, he should have learned to exchange (at least to some extent) living by the pleasure principle for making choices in accord with the reality principle. The primers, by presenting him almost exclusively with images of fun, throw the child back to the developmental phase he is trying, with difficulty, to outgrow. Such primers insult the child's intelligence and his sense of worth, and the offense goes far to explain why children reject their reading books as empty. The books talk down to children; they do not take children's aspirations seriously. . . . 22

It is not impossible to teach children to read while respecting their intelligence and dignity. The primers used in Europe are generally far more difficult than those in use in this country. We believe their success is proved by the fact that at the end of the first grade, the average European child has a larger reading vocabulary than that of the average American child. Moreover, reading retardation, the curse of so many young Americans, is much less common among European children and, when it occurs, is rarely as severe. 23

The most recent series of basic readers published in Switzerland stands as a notable alternative to the American textbooks that we have complained about. The early reading program consists of three preprimers and one primer. The preprimers are loose-leaf booklets, each page (with a single exception) comprising a few short lines of text and an illustration. Since there are no pictures on the covers of the booklets, the child is encouraged to form his own opinion of what each booklet is about by reading. The first preprimer is entitled *We are all here*, meaning "here to read together." Its first page has 24

only two words: "I am." And on this page there is no picture, no face to rival
the child's own. The Swiss child's reading thus begins with the strongest
statement of self-assertion imaginable. After sixteen more pages, each with a
few words for the child to learn, there follow twenty-eight pages devoted either
to snatches of well-known songs or to a few lines from popular fairy tales. In
this way, the first preprimer leads easily to the next, *Once upon a time*, which
is composed of five fairy tales from Grimm. Though quite simple, these
versions are nonetheless faithful in all essentials to the originals.

The third Swiss preprimer, *Edi*, is about a little boy who might be the peer
of the children reading about him. The first page shows Edi with his school
satchel on his back, standing between his father and mother. The story goes
that Edi, who has eaten something that disagrees with him, gets sick and is
sent to the country to stay with relatives and get well. We follow Edi's
experiences on the farm until the end of the book, when he returns home, his
health fully restored. There he finds that while he was away, his mother had a
baby; Edi has a sister. Edi's story deals with two of the most critical events in a
child's life: sickness and the birth of a sibling.

The primer of the Swiss series, *It's your turn*, meaning "it's your turn to
read," begins with counting rhymes and songs typically sung by children as
accompaniment to their games. Since Swiss children know all these rhymes and
songs, they know how the words they are decoding ought to sound, and so it is
likely that at this more difficult level of reading, their attempts will be error-
free. Thus the children's confidence in their ability to read this new, thicker,
rather scary-looking book is supported, and they are ready for the remaining
sections, which are longer and a little harder.

It's your turn has many colorful pictures that embellish the text without
giving away its meaning; the child *must* read in order to understand. For
example, a poem by Christian Morgenstern, "Winternight," is illustrated by a
picture of a town at night, covered with falling snow; the picture conveys the
spirit of the poem but permits no conclusion about its substance. In addition to
the Morgenstern poem, the book contains a number of other poems and short
stories, many by famous German authors. The selection represents all periods of
German literature: contemporary, Romantic, classical, and medieval, and
legendary folktales, rhymes, and riddles.

This first Swiss reader, like its American counterparts, tries to introduce
children to reading by means of attractive and fairly easy material. The chief
difference is that none of the pieces in the Swiss reader patronize the child;
there is no deviation from ordinary language or ordinary usage. Children have
been reciting the counting rhymes to each other for hundreds of years. No
words are avoided because they might be difficult (as is done constantly in

American primers) — and they prove not to be too hard, because the child who uses them in everyday conversation already knows what they mean, and is thus eager to master whatever technical obstacles they present on the page. In one way or another, all the stories appeal to children of primary age, but in none of them is there even the mention of active play. If anything, the pieces are on the contemplative side, though with a light touch. The most impressive difference between this book and American primers is the literary quality of many of its selections. The Swiss primer manages to introduce the child to literacy at the same time that it teaches him the rudiments of reading.

These primers, used in the German-speaking parts of Switzerland, have a   29
special lesson to teach American educators and publishers. It has been argued that our primers have to employ unnaturally simple words because many minority children speak a different language at home: Spanish, Chinese, "black English," and so on. But the language that *all* children growing up in the German parts of Switzerland speak — a dialect called *Schweizer Deutsch*, or *Swiss German* — is very different from the High German they must speak and read in school. Although during the first few months of school the children are allowed to speak to the teacher in their dialect, from the start they learn to read only the High German in which their primers are published. For some reason, Swiss children do not find this enforced bilingualism such a handicap that they fail to become able readers. We believe that their lack of difficulty is explained to a great extent by the fact that they like what they are given to read.

QUESTIONS ON CONTENT:

1.   What is the relationship of reading to the "scholastic fate" of children? To their learning in general? To their self-images? What is the relationship of family and teachers to the learning of children?
2.   Why are Bettelheim and Zelan critical of contemporary primers?
3.   What has happened to the introduction of new words in primers over the years? Do you believe this is an important issue?

QUESTIONS ON WRITING STRUCTURE AND STRATEGY:

1.   How do the authors "hook" the reader with the first paragraph? What audience are they addressing?
2.   What kind of evidence do the authors bring to support their charge against American primers? Is it convincing?
3.   What is the purpose of the last seven paragraphs and how does the conclusion relate to the thesis?

QUESTIONS FOR DISCUSSION AND WRITING:

1. Write a paper in which you compare the authors' analysis of the role of motivation in learning to read with the experiences of some of the writers in Unit I.

2. In the vicious circle the authors describe — students, teachers, superintendents, parents, special interest groups, publishers — where does the responsibility lie for the inferior quality of American primers? What can be done about it? Compose a paper in which you examine the issue.

3. Based on your own experience, write a paper on what you see as the chief faults and virtues of your early reading experience, your primers, your teachers.

4. Analyze your later reading experiences — in high school, or, so far, in college. Have these experiences helped or hindered you? Do you enjoy reading? Do you see reading primarily as a chore? A tool? An escape?

5. Write a paper in which you compare what Rodriguez ("Aria") has to say about bilingualism and what Bettelheim and Zelan have to say about Swiss students and bilingualism.

SHY RIGHTS:
WHY NOT PRETTY SOON?
Garrison Keillor

*Garrison Keillor is a writer (Lake Wobegon Days, 1986) and the
popular host of the P.B.S. Radio's A Prairie Home Companion, a
unique variety program. In between the musical offerings are sprinkled
Keillor's observations about the residents of Lake Wobegon,
Minnesota, ostensibly his hometown. Invariably Keillor will comment
on the problems of shy people, about whom he is specially concerned
and for whom the program's product sponsor is designed: "Powdermilk
Biscuits in the big blue box give shy persons the strength to get up and
do what needs to be done." The following essay on "shys" is one of his
more popular ones; and although it is designed primarily to entertain,
it also comments on the absurdity of carrying some commendable
ideas to ridiculous extremes. Most devotees of the program will tell you
that you have to hear Keillor to get the full impact of his humor, but
less than the full impact is enough to entertain. This essay is a
splendid example of the use of irony for humorous effect, but its
humor also rides on the back of parody (see Glossary).*

Recently I read about a group of fat people who had organized to fight
discrimination against themselves. They said that society oppresses the
overweight by being thinner than them and that the term "overweight" itself is
oppressive because it implies a "right" weight that the fatso has failed to make.
Only weightists use such terms, they said; they demanded to be called "total"
people and to be thought of in terms of wholeness; and they referred to thin
people as being "not all there."

Don't get me wrong. This is fine with me. If, to quote the article if I may,
"Fat Leaders Demand Expanded Rights Act, Claim Broad Base of Support," I
have no objections to it whatsoever. I feel that it is their right to speak up and I
admire them for doing so, though of course this is only my own opinion. I
could be wrong.

Nevertheless, after reading the article, I wrote a letter to President Jimmy
Carter demanding that his administration take action to end discrimination
against shy persons sometime in the very near future. I pointed out three target
areas — laws, schools, and attitudes — where shy rights maybe could be
safeguarded. I tried not to be pushy but I laid it on the line. "Mr. President," I
concluded, "you'll probably kill me for saying this but compared to what
you've done for other groups, we shys have settled for 'peanuts.' As you may
know, we are not ones to make threats, but it is clear to me that if we don't get
some action on this, it could be a darned quiet summer. It is up to you, Mr.
President. Whatever you decide will be okay by me. Yours very cordially."

331

I never got around to mailing the letter, but evidently word got around in   4
the shy community that I had written it, and I've noticed that most shy persons
are not speaking to me these days. I guess they think the letter went too far.
Probably they feel that making demands is a betrayal of the shy movement (or
"gesture," as many shys call it) and an insult to shy pride and that it risks the
loss of some of the gains we have already made, such as social security and
library cards.

Perhaps they are right. I don't claim to have all the answers. I just feel that   5
we ought to begin, at least, to think about some demands that we *might* make
if, for example, we *had* to someday. That's all. I'm not saying we should make
fools of ourselves, for heaven's sake!

Shut Up (a slogan)

Sometimes I feel that maybe we shy persons have borne our terrible burden for   6
far too long now. Labeled by society as "wimps," "dorks," "creeps," and
"sissies," stereotyped as Milquetoasts and Walter Mittys, and tagged as
potential psychopaths ("He kept pretty much to himself," every psychopath's
landlady is quoted as saying after the arrest, and for weeks thereafter every shy
person is treated like a leper), we shys are desperately misunderstood on every
hand. Because we don't "talk out" our feelings, it is assumed that we haven't
any. It is assumed that we never exclaim, retort, or cry out, though naturally we
do on occasions when it seems called for.

Would anyone dare to say to a woman or a Third World Person, "Oh,   7
don't be a woman! Oh, don't be so Third!"? And yet people make bold with us
whenever they please and put an arm around us and tell us not to be shy.

Hundreds of thousands of our shy brothers and sisters (and "cousins   8
twice-removed," as militant shys refer to each other) are victimized every year
by self-help programs that promise to "cure" shyness through hand-buzzer
treatments, shout training, spicy diets, silence-aversion therapy, and every other
gimmick in the book. Many of them claim to have "overcome" their shyness,
but the sad fact is that they are afraid to say otherwise.

To us in the shy movement, however, shyness is not a disability or disease   9
to be "overcome." It is simply the way we are. And in our own quiet way, we
are secretly proud of it. It isn't something we shout about at public rallies and
marches. It is Shy Pride. And while we don't have a Shy Pride Week, we do
have many private moments when we keep our thoughts to ourselves, such as
"Shy is nice," "Walk short," "Be proud—shut up," and "Shy is beautiful, for
the most part." These are some that I thought up myself. Perhaps other shy
persons have some of their own, I don't know.

GARRISON KEILLOR

A "Number One" Disgrace

Discrimination against the shy is our country's No. 1 disgrace in my own
personal opinion. Millions of men and women are denied equal employment,
educational and recreational opportunities, and rewarding personal
relationships simply because of their shyness. These injustices are nearly
impossible to identify, not only because the shy person will not speak up when
discriminated against, but also because the shy person almost always
anticipates being denied these rights and doesn't ask for them in the first place.
(In fact, most shys will politely decline a right when it is offered to them.)

Most shy lawyers agree that shys can never obtain justice under our
current adversary system of law. The Sixth Amendment, for example, which
gives the accused the right to confront his accusers, is anti-shy on the face of it.
It effectively denies shy persons the right to accuse anyone of anything.

One solution might be to shift the burden of proof to the defendant in case
the plaintiff chooses to remain silent. Or we could create a special second-class
citizenship that would take away some rights, such as free speech, bearing
arms, and running for public office, in exchange for some other rights that we
need more. In any case, we need some sort of fairly totally new concept of law
if we shys are ever going to enjoy equality, if indeed that is the sort of thing we
could ever enjoy.

A Million-Dollar Ripoff

Every year, shy persons lose millions of dollars in the form of overcharges that
aren't questioned, shoddy products never returned to stores, refunds never
asked for, and bad food in restaurants that we eat anyway, not to mention all
the money we lose and are too shy to claim when somebody else finds it.

A few months ago, a shy friend of mine whom I will call Duke Hand (not
his real name) stood at a supermarket checkout counter and watched the
cashier ring up thirty fifteen-cent Peanut Dream candy bars and a $3.75 copy
of *Playhouse* for $18.25. He gave her a twenty-dollar bill and thanked her for
his change, but as he reached for his purchases, she said, "Hold on. There's
something wrong here."

"No, really, it's okay," he said.

"Let me see that cash register slip," she said.

"No, really, thanks anyway," he whispered. Out of the corner of his eye,
he could see that he had attracted attention. Other shoppers in the vicinity had
sensed that something was up, perhaps an attempted price-tag switch or

333

insufficient identification, and were looking his way. "It's not for me," he pleaded. "I'm only buying this for a friend."

Nevertheless, he had to stand there in mute agony while she counted all of the Peanut Dreams and refigured the total and the correct change. (In fairness to her, it should be pointed out that Duke, while eventually passing on each copy of *Playhouse* to a friend, first reads it himself.)

Perhaps one solution might be for clerks and other business personnel to try to be a little bit more careful about this sort of thing in the first place. Okay?

How About Shy History?

To many of us shys, myself included, the worst tragedy is the oppression of shy children in the schools, and while we don't presume to tell educators how to do their work, work that they have been specially trained to do, we do feel that schools must begin immediately to develop programs of shy history, or at the very least to give it a little consideration.

History books are blatantly prejudiced against shyness and shy personhood. They devote chapter after chapter to the accomplishments of famous persons and quote them at great length, and say nothing at all, or very little, about countless others who had very little to say, who never sought fame, and whose names are lost to history.

Where in the history books do we find mention of The Lady in Black, Kilroy, The Unknown Soldier, The Forgotten Man, The Little Guy, not to mention America's many noted recluses?

Where, for example, can we find a single paragraph on America's hundreds of scale models, those brave men of average height whose job it was to pose beside immense objects such as pyramids and dynamos so as to indicate scale in drawings and photographs? The only credit that scale models ever received was a line in the caption—"For an idea of its size, note man (arrow, at left)." And yet, without them, such inventions as the dirigible, the steam shovel, and the swingspan bridge would have looked like mere toys, and natural wonders such as Old Faithful, the Grand Canyon, and the giant sequoia would have been dismissed as hoaxes. It was truly a thankless job.

Shys on "Strike"

The scale models themselves never wanted any thanks. All they wanted was a rope or device of some type to keep them from falling off tall structures, plus a tent to rest in between drawings, and in 1906, after one model was carried away by a tidal wave that he had been hired to pose in front of, they formed a union and went on strike.

Briefly, the scale models were joined by a contingent of shy artists' models who had posed for what they thought was to be a small monument showing the Battle of Bull Run only to discover that it was actually a large bas-relief entitled "The Bathers" and who sat down on the job, bringing the work to a halt. While the artists' models quickly won a new contract and went back to work (on a non-representational basis), the scale models' strike was never settled.

True to their nature, the scale models did not picket the work sites or negotiate with their employers. They simply stood quietly a short distance away and, when asked about their demands, pointed to the next man. A year later, when the union attempted to take a vote on the old contract, it found that most of the scale models had moved away and left no forwarding addresses.

It was the last attempt by shy persons to organize themselves anywhere in the country.

Now is the Time, We Think

Now is probably as good a time as any for this country to face up to its shameful treatment of the shy and to do something, almost anything, about it. On the other hand, maybe it would be better to wait for a while and see what happens. All I know is that it isn't easy trying to write a manifesto for a bunch of people who dare not speak their names. And that the shy movement is being inverted by a tiny handful of shy militants who do not speak for the majority of shy persons, nor even very often for themselves. This secret cadre, whose members are not known even to each other, advocate doing "less than nothing." They believe in tokenism, and the smaller the token the better. They seek only to promote more self-consciousness: that ultimate shyness that shy mystics call "the fear of fear itself." What is even more terrifying is the ultimate goal of this radical wing: They believe that they shall inherit the earth, and they will not stop until they do. Believe me, we moderates have our faces to the wall.

Perhaps you are saying, "What can I do? I share your concern at the plight of the shy and wholeheartedly endorse your two- (or three-) point program for shy equality. I pledge myself to work vigorously for its adoption. My check for ($10 $25 $50 $100 $_____) is enclosed. In addition, I agree to (circulate petitions, hold fund-raising party in my home, write to congressman and senator, serve on local committee, write letters to newspapers, hand out literature door-to-door during National Friends of the Shy Drive)."

Just remember: You said it, not me.

335

QUESTIONS ON CONTENT:

1. In what ways do "shys" suffer discrimination?
2. What measures have been used to cure people of their shyness?
3. What is Keillor parodying here? (i.e., in his prewriting stage, what do you think he was reacting to on the contemporary scene?)

QUESTIONS ON WRITING STRUCTURE AND STRATEGY:

1. At what audience is Keillor aiming? How do you know?
2. What specific techniques does Keillor use to achieve humor? Double meanings? Colloquialisms? Self-deprecation? Understatement? Put-downs? Puns (paranomasia)? Parody? Absurdities? Incongruity?
3. How does he use dialogue to heighten humor and interest?
4. How do his slogans and allusions contribute to his irony and humor?

QUESTIONS FOR DISCUSSION AND WRITING:

1. Is Keillor really distressed about the mistreatment of "shy"? Explain.
2. How much of this essay can you take seriously? Do "shys" suffer *any* discrimination? Some?
3. Using Keillor's essay as a model, try your hand at writing an ironic (and satirical) paper in which you argue for the rights of: dull people, lazy people, bumblers, nonjocks, procrastinators, or average students. (For example: In a prewriting exercise try listing what dull people do, what characterizes them, and contrast that with a listing of what lively, highly animated people do.)
4. Write an essay supporting or attacking the following proposition: Fat people are discriminated against in serious ways. (Keillor's satire pokes fun at an attempt to oppose such discrimination by trivializing it. For this reason we might conclude that Keillor is off-base.)
5. Try a satire of your pet peeve in school or work regulations. Or satirize institutional food—which students always complain about. Remember: the idea is to poke fun, not to give offense.

LARVAL STAGE
OF A BOOKWORM
H. L. Mencken

*Starting out as a newspaperman in Baltimore—without the benefit of
a college education—H. L. Mencken became America's most
influential literary and cultural critic during the Roaring Twenties. As
coeditor with George Jean Nathan of* The American Mercury *(1924–
1933), he made that magazine the most controversial, iconoclastic
publication ever published in America up to that time. Blasting away
at the lingering Victorianism of American life, he encouraged the new
breed of writers who were demanding liberation from all the empty
pieties and platitudes that characterized the Genteel Tradition, the
reigning literary tradition. Mencken's unique style, as well as the
targets of his scorn, gave his writings gusto and wide appeal. (His
continuing interest in language led him to compile his scholarly study
of* The American Language *[1919], later revised and supplemented.)
The famous Mencken style, evident in this autobiographical account of
his early reading, is typical: a mingling of elegant words with slang,
metaphors and foreign words, outrageous juxtapositions of words, all
served up as ironic and understated verbal delicacies. (Mencken's style
is deliberate, since he is attempting to achieve an effect. Obviously, you
would imitate him only when you are attempting to achieve a similar
effect.) As he recounts his discovery of Mark Twain, and especially of*
Huckleberry Finn, *compare his caustic denigration of rejected writers
with his love for Twain. Mencken's early love of reading made possible
his long and fabulous career as a writer, demonstrating that everyone
can profit from reading widely and from a careful attention to and
love of words.*

The first long story I ever read was "The Moose Hunters," a tale of the   1
adventures of four half-grown boys in the woods of Maine, published in
Chatterbox for 1887. *Chatterbox*, which now seems to be pretty well forgotten,
was an English annual that had a large sale, in those days, in the American
colonies, and "The Moose Hunters" seems to have been printed as a sort of sop
or compliment to that trade, just as an English novelist of today lards his
narrative with such cheery native bait as "waal, pardner," "you betcha" and
"geminy-crickets." The rest of the 1887 issue was made up of intensely English
stuff; indeed, it was so English that, reading it and looking at the woodcuts, I
sucked in an immense mass of useless information about English history and the
English scene, so that to this day I know more about Henry VIII and Lincoln
Cathedral than I know about Millard Fillmore or the Mormon Temple at Salt
Lake City.

"The Moose Hunters," which ran to the length of a full-length juvenile,   2 was not printed in one gob, but spread through *Chatterbox* in instalments. This was an excellent device, for literary fans in the youngest brackets do their reading slowly and painfully, and like to come up frequently for air. But writing down to them is something else again, and that error the anonymous author of "The Moose Hunters" avoided diligently. Instead, he wrote in the best journalese of the era, and treated his sixteen-year-old heroes precisely as if they were grown men. So I liked his story very much, and stuck to it until, in a series of perhaps twenty sessions, I had got it down.

This was in the Summer of 1888 and during hot weather, for I remember sitting with the volume on the high marble front steps of our house in Hollins street, in the quiet of approaching dusk, and hearing my mother's warnings that reading by failing light would ruin my eyes. The neighborhood apprentices to gang life went howling up and down the sidewalk, trying to lure me into their games of follow-your-leader and run-sheep-run, but I was not to be lured, for I had discovered a new realm of being and a new and powerful enchantment. What was follow-your-leader to fighting savage Canucks on the Little Magalloway river, and what was chasing imaginary sheep to shooting real meese? I was near the end of the story, with the Canucks all beaten off and two carcasses of gigantic meese hanging to trees, before the author made it clear to me that the word *moose* had no plural, but remained unchanged *ad infinitum.*

Such discoveries give a boy a considerable thrill, and augment his sense of dignity. It is no light matter, at eight, to penetrate suddenly to the difference between *to, two* and *too,* or to that between *run* in baseball and *run* in topographical science, or *cats* and *Katz.* The effect is massive and profound, and at least comparable to that which flows, in later life, out of filling a royal flush or debauching the wife of a major-general of cavalry. I must have made some effort to read *Chatterbox* at the time my Grandmother Mencken gave it to me, which was at Christmas, 1887, but for a while it was no go. I could spell out the shorter pieces at the bottoms of columns, but the longer stories were only jumbles of strange and baffling words. But then, as if by miracle, I found suddenly that I could read them, so I tackled "The Moose Hunters" at once, and stuck to it to the end. There were still, of course, many hard words, but they were no longer insurmountable obstacles. If I staggered and stumbled somewhat, I nevertheless hung on, and by the Fourth of July, 1888, I had blooded my first book. . . .

But before you set me down a prig, let me tell you the rest of it. That rest of it is my discovery of "Huckleberry Finn," probably the most stupendous event of my whole life. The time was the early part of 1889, and I wandered into Paradise by a kind of accident. Itching to exercise my newly acquired art of reading, and with "The Moose Hunters" exhausted and Grimms' Fairy Tales playing me false, I began exploring the house for print. The Baltimore *Sunpaper* and *Evening News*, which came in daily, stumped me sadly, for they were full of political diatribes in the fashion of the time, and I knew no more about politics than a chimpanzee. My mother's long file of *Godey's Lady's Book* and her new but growing file of the *Ladies' Home Journal* were worse, for they dealt gloomily with cooking, etiquette, the policing of children, and the design and construction of millinery, all of them sciences that still baffle me. Nor was there any pabulum for me in the hired girl's dog's-eared files of *Bow Bells* and the *Fireside Companion*, the first with its ghastly woodcuts of English milkmaids in bustles skedaddling from concupiscent baronets in frock-coats and cork-screw mustaches. So I gradually oscillated, almost in despair, toward the old-fashioned secretary in the sitting-room, the upper works of which were full of dismal volumes in the black cloth and gilt stamping of the era. I had often eyed them from afar, wondering how long it would be before I would be ripe enough to explore them. Now I climbed up on a chair, and began to take them down.

They had been assembled by my father, . . . But among them, thumbing   6 round, I found a series of eight or ten volumes cheek by jowl, and it appeared on investigation that the whole lot had been written by a man named Mark Twain. I had heard my father mention this gentleman once or twice in talking to my mother, but I had no idea who he was or what he had done: he might have been, for all I knew, a bartender, a baseball-player, or one of the boozy politicoes my father was always meeting in Washington. But here was evidence that he was a man who wrote books, and I noted at once that the pictures in those books were not of the usual funereal character, but light, loose and lively. So I proceeded with my inquiry, and in a little while I had taken down one of them, a green quarto, sneaked it to my bedroom, and stretched out on my bed to look into it. It was, as smarties will have guessed by now, "Huckleberry Finn."

If I undertook to tell you the effect it had upon me my talk would sound   7 frantic, and even delirious. Its impact was genuinely terrific. I had not gone further than the first incomparable chapter before I realized, child though I was, that I had entered a domain of new and gorgeous wonders, and thereafter I pressed on steadily to the last word. My gait, of course, was still slow, but it became steadily faster as I proceeded. As the blurbs on the slip-covers of murder mysteries say, I simply couldn't put the book down. After dinner that evening, braving a possible uproar, I took it into the family sitting-room, and resumed it while my father searched the *Evening News* hopefully for reports of the arrest, clubbing and hanging of labor leaders. Anon, he noticed what I was at, and demanded to know the name of the book I was reading. When I held up the green volume his comment was "Well, I'll be durned!"

I sensed instantly that there was no reproof in this, but a kind of shy   8 rejoicing. Then he told me that he had once been a great reader of Mark Twain himself—in his younger days. He had got hold of all the volumes as they came out—"The Innocents" in 1869, when he was still a boy himself; "Roughing It" in 1872, "The Gilded Age" in 1873, "Tom Sawyer" in 1876, "A Tramp Abroad" in 1880, the year of my birth, and so on down to date. (All these far from pristine firsts are still in the Biblioteca Menckeniana in Hollins street, minus a few that were lent to neighbor boys and never returned, and had to be replaced.) My father read them in the halcyon days before children, labor troubles and Grover Cleveland had begun to frazzle him, and he still got them down from the shelf on quiet evenings, after the first-named were packed off to bed. But a man of advancing years and cares had to consider also the sorrows of the world, and so he read in Mark less than aforetime.

As for me, I proceeded to take the whole canon at a gulp—and presently gagged distressfully. "Huckleberry Finn," of course, was as transparent to a boy of eight as to a man of eighty, and almost as pungent and exhilarating, but there were passages in "A Tramp Abroad" that baffled me, and many more in "The Innocents," and a whole swarm in "The Gilded Age." I well recall wrestling with the woodcut by W. F. Brown on page 113 of the "Tramp." It shows five little German girls swinging on a heavy chain stretched between two stone posts on a street in Heilbronn, and the legend under it is "Generations of Bare Feet." That legend is silly, for all the girls have shoes on, but what puzzled me about it was something quite different. It was a confusion between the word *generation* and the word *federation*, which latter was often in my father's speech in those days, for the American Federation of Labor had got under way only a few years before, and was just beginning in earnest to harass and alarm employers. Why I didn't consult the dictionary (or my mother, or my father himself) I simply can't tell you. At eight or nine, I suppose, intelligence is no more than a small spot of light on the floor of a large and murky room. So instead of seeking help I passed on, wondering idiotically what possible relation there could be between a gang of little girls in pigtails and the Haymarket anarchists, and it was six or seven years later before the "Tramp" became clear to me, and began to delight me. . . .

"Huck," of course, was my favorite, and I read it over and over. In fact, I read it regularly not less than annually down to my forties, and only a few months ago I hauled it out and read it once more—and found it as magnificent as ever. . . .

The influence of "Huck Finn" was immensely more powerful and durable. It not only reinforced my native aversion to the common run of boys' books; it also set me upon a systematic exploration of all the volumes in the old secretary, and before I finished with them I had looked into every one of them, including even Brother Schultz's sombre history of Freemasonry in Maryland.

How many were actually intelligible to a boy of eight, nine, ten? I should say about a fourth. I managed to get through most of Dickens, but only by dint of hard labor, and it was not until I discovered Thackeray, at fourteen, that the English novel really began to lift me. George Eliot floored me as effectively as a text in Hittite, and to the present day I have never read "Adam Bede" or "Daniel Deronda" or "The Mill on the Floss," or developed any desire to do so. So far as I am concerned, they will remain mere names to the end of the chapter, and as hollow and insignificant as the names of Gog and Magog.

But I plowed through Chambers' Encyclopedia relentlessly, beginning with the shortest articles and gradually working my way into the longer ones. The kitchen-midden of irrelevant and incredible information that still burdens me had its origins in those pages, and I almost wore them out acquiring it. I read, too, the whole of Lossing, nearly all of Charlotte M. Yonge, and even some of Duyckinck, perhaps the dullest historian ever catalogued by faunal naturalists on this or any other earth. My brother Charlie and I enjoyed "Our Living World" chiefly because of the colored pictures, but I also read long stretches of it, and astonished my father by calling off the names of nearly all the wild beasts when the circus visited Baltimore in 1889. Finally, I recall reading both "Life Among the Mormons" and "One Thousand Proofs That the Earth Is Not a Globe." 12

Thus launched upon the career of a bookworm, I presently began to reach out right and left for more fodder. When the Enoch Pratt Free Library of Baltimore opened a branch in Hollins street, in March, 1886, I was still a shade too young to be excited, but I had a card before I was nine, and began an almost daily harrying of the virgins at the delivery desk. In 1888 my father subscribed to *Once-a-Week*, the predecessor of *Collier's*, and a little while later there began to come with it a long series of cheap reprints of contemporary classics, running from Tennyson's poems to Justin M'Carthy's "History of Our Own Times"; and simultaneously there appeared from parts unknown a similar series of cheap reprints of scientific papers, including some of Herbert Spencer. I read them all, sometimes with shivers of puzzlement and sometimes with delight, but always calling for more. I began to inhabit a world that was two-thirds letterpress and only one-third trees, fields, streets and people. I acquired round shoulders, spindly shanks, and a despondent view of humanity. I read everything that I could find in English, taking in some of it but boggling most of it. 13

This madness ran on until I reached adolescence, and began to distinguish between one necktie and another, and to notice the curiously divergent shapes, dispositions and aromas of girls. Then, gradually, I began to let up. 14

But to this day I am still what might be called a reader, and have a high regard for authors. 15

QUESTIONS ON CONTENT:

1. What is Mencken's thesis and where is it explicitly stated?
2. Why did he prefer "The Moose Hunters" over the translations of Grimm's fairy tales?
3. What was "the most stupendous event" in his whole life?

QUESTIONS ON WRITING STRUCTURE AND STRATEGY:

1. Mencken achieves humor and often flaunts his cynicism by his lavish use of ironic hyperbole (a straight-faced overstatement, absurd on its face). Find several examples and explain how they serve to produce humor.
2. How does Mencken's frequent use of humor suggest that reading is fun?
3. How does Mencken's choice of verbs and use of the vernacular contribute to his style?

QUESTIONS FOR DISCUSSION AND WRITING:

1. How does your own early reading experience differ from Mencken's, and how do you account for any difference?
2. The writings of H. L. Mencken inspired Richard Wright to become a writer (See Wright, Unit II). What is evident in Mencken's writing that would prompt a young, Southern black man to want to become a writer?
3. Try your hand in a journal entry about a personal experience in which you imitate Mencken's style. (College or governmental bureaucracy, a professor, a foreman/forelady, a boss, a monotonous job, a dull class, a slow clerk, and so on.)

THE CONSTITUTION
AND THE PEOPLE

Barbara Jordan

*Barbara Jordan was born in Houston, Texas, and educated at Texas
Southern University and Boston University. She came to national
attention when she was elected to the Texas legislature in 1966, the
first black woman ever to win a seat in that body. More attention was
focused on her when in 1972 she was elected to the United States
Congress, the first black woman to be elected from a Southern state.
As a member of the House Judiciary Committee that considered the
possible impeachment of President Richard M. Nixon, she achieved
even greater prominence for her ringing defense of the Constitution,
eliciting what can only be called prideful astonishment from her
Congressional colleagues and praise from one end of the country to the
other. Thereafter, wrote her biographer, she became "public property"
and a "folk-hero." Harvard University honored this new "folk-hero"
in 1978 by conferring upon her an honorary Doctor of Laws and
inviting her to deliver the Commencement Address on a subject of her
own choosing. Appropriately enough, she again took the Constitution
as her theme, addressing herself to a problem she had observed during
government service. In the excerpt below, note her skillful use of
rhetorical questions as a framework for her remarks. Note also how
she turns around a clichéd opening to make it fresh and lively. Jordan
is currently Professor of Political Ethics at the University of Texas,
Austin.*

Mr. President, were I to begin what I am going to say this afternoon by   1
starting out, "I am very pleased to have been invited to speak to the Harvard
community," you would probably discount that as a trite beginning. But if you
did that, you would be in error. I have always held Harvard in high regard. I
have always viewed a Harvard education as an unexcelled badge of intellectual
achievement—if not superiority. I've always felt that way.

My appearance here this afternoon may not honor you very much, but it   2
certainly honors me.

You know, the truth of the matter is, that one of the reasons I attended   3
Boston University Law School was because I wanted to be close to Harvard. But
my earliest brush with Harvard occurred over twenty years ago. I was a junior
at Texas Southern University. Now, I might add that the original name of TSU
was Texas State University for Negroes. It was created to keep blacks out of
the University of Texas. So a Harvard debate team came to TSU—a Harvard
debate team. And I was a debater. And I couldn't understand why this
institution so revered by me would send debaters to TSU. But they came

anyway. And the debate occurred. And the judges said that the debate ended in a tie.

Well, now, it occurs to me today that if Harvard students were so superior —or as superior as we all thought—they should have won. And since the judges said the debate ended in a tie, we must have won. So, Mr. President and all of the alumni, I hereby declare that when that debate was held over twenty years ago, we won. And if you have any surplus trophies around anywhere I'll take one home to the team. And if you should run into two gentlemen—one's name was Jared Diamond and the other, James Sykes—they were the Harvard debaters at that time, I invite you to offer them my condolences.

I received a letter of invitation to make this speech today. And as I read it, it appeared designed either to challenge or intimidate. One or the other. I want to quote to you one unedited paragraph from the letter of invitation I received. Now listen to this:

"We invite you to speak on whatever topic you find suitable. A number of Harvard Commencement speeches have been memorable." That's not the end of the quote. It went on. "Perhaps the most memorable was that of Secretary of State George C. Marshall, who used the occasion to announce the Marshall Plan for Europe."

Well, I read that, and, I can promise you, you're not getting a Jordan Plan today. I don't have a plan to create, ameliorate, eliminate, or anything else at this time, and if I happen to develop one at some time during the remainder of my life, I'll ask you to invite me back.

Now, even though I will not present a plan to you this afternoon which will be celebrated thirty years hence, I will talk about a problem which concerns me greatly. The answers to this problem are not in the back of the book, and they're not at the end of this speech.

Of late many articles have been written, and speeches delivered, about the importance of the input of people into the affairs of government—symbolic gestures have been staged, and populist rhetoric has been translated into law—the point of it all is to make people feel that they really do count. That the government does care what they think. Such actions are said to be the logical extension and proper fulfillment of an amorphous something called The Promise of America.

Question: Do the governors of America sincerely believe that people are a valuable resource of the government? Or do the governors really believe that the people are merely an indispensable nuisance to a democracy?

Let us reflect on our history for a moment and maybe we'll try to answer that question.

The Declaration of Independence, the first sentence: "When it becomes necessary for one people to dissolve the political bonds whenever government

344

becomes destructive of certain unalienable rights, it is the right of the people to alter or abolish it."

And then, when they started to itemize the oppressiveness of George the Third: "He has refused to pass other laws for the accommodation of large districts of people unless those people would relinquish the right of representation in the legislature — "

It continues his invasions on the rights of the people: "He has sent hither swarms of officers to harass our people. He has destroyed the lives of our people."

And then, finally, in the Declaration: "It is made in the name and by the authority of the good people."

People.

People, throughout it.

Subsequently, the Constitution was written. It augmented and implemented the political philosophy espoused in the Declaration of Independence, the *raison d'être* of the new government.

People again.

"The political well-being of the people, the government's source of authority."

The people. Once more and again. The quintessence: "We the People of the United States."

"The House of Representatives chosen every second year by the people . . . the right of the people peaceably to assemble . . . the people to be secure in their persons . . . the enumeration of certain rights retained by the people, and certain powers reserved to the people."

And then as the states began to ratify that Constitution a debate developed wherein a delegate wanted to strip Congress of the power to lay and collect taxes, and Alexander Hamilton, trying to allay the delegate's fear, addressed him, the proponent of the resolution. And what did Hamilton say? "Here, sir, the people govern."

"Here, sir, the people govern"!

Do you believe that?

Do the people govern? Or has there been a mutation from a commitment to people to a commitment to self-interest on the part of the governors?

Is the applause meter paramount, and the welfare of the people, at best, merely tangential? The government has built an elaborate network of illusions. That network is designed to make people believe that their opinions are genuinely wanted and considered, that they do participate, in fact, in making the decisions of government.

We go to great lengths to sustain that illusion.

Prevalent phrases among some of the recent legislation the Congress has passed, phrases which are substitutes for people: Citizen participation, advisory

13

14

15

16

17
18

19

20

21

22

23

24
25
26

27

28

29

council, advisory committee, maximum feasible participation, public
participation, community participation, petition for intervention. The words are
all there. But is citizen intervention encouraged or discouraged?

Petitions to intervene: The citizen wants to intervene in proceedings of the
Atomic Energy Commission and he goes to the rule book and asks: "How do I
intervene before this Atomic Energy Commission?"

The rule is stated this way, it's headed "Intervention":

"Any person whose interests may be affected by a proceeding and who
desires to participate as a party shall file a written petition for leave to
intervene. Any petition shall identify the specific aspect or aspects on which
the subject matter of the proceeding as to which he wishes to intervene. He
must set forth with particularity both the facts pertaining to his interest and the
basis of his contentions with regard to each aspect on which he desires to
intervene."

Now that clear paragraph is followed by seventeen sections and
subsections. There are other regulatory agencies with rules equally as
burdensome.

The people have a right to intervene. Though statutory and regulatory
language may well include provisions for petitions to intervene, the fact is that
proper citizen intervention often requires an attorney or an expert witness.

The citizen is denied the right to intervene.

Getting into federal court, there is a $10,000 requirement that that amount
must be in controversy before you can get in. The Supreme Court has said you
still won't get in unless each member of the class satisfies that jurisdictional
amount. The Court has ruled again that a person bringing a class action suit
must notify all parties at his own expense.

The Supreme Court has said only the Congress may authorize the
payments of such fees, and Congress is very reluctant to do that.

Have the Supreme Court decisions furthered opportunities for citizen
participation? Well, recently the Supreme Court has acted to limit both the
right to sue, and class action litigation. The Court has ruled, for one instance,
that citizens and taxpayers have no standing to challenge an action of the
government unless they can show a concrete injury in fact.

Another ruling: That ghetto residents of Rochester lacked standing to sue
because they could not prove that the alleged wrong hurt them personally.
Another ruling: Plaintiffs must demonstrate that the complaint they offer is not
simply arguable but actual.

People.

The people want in.

How much longer, how much longer will people tolerate a network of
illusions and vacuous rhetoric? How much longer?

What the people want is very simple: They want an America as good as its promise. That's what they want. 43

The people do not want to be outskirters. They want to be insiders on America. 44

We want to be in control of our lives. Whether we are jungle fighters, craftsmen, company men, gamesmen, we want to be in control. And when the government erodes that control, we are not comfortable. We're not comfortable at all. 45

I submit to you that the re-inclusion of the people in their government would be recombinant of predictable and laudable results. It would be a return of a right which we once considered unalienable. 46

The stakes, the stakes are too high for government to be a spectator sport. 47

QUESTIONS ON CONTENT:

1. Why does Jordan say that T.W.U. won its debate with Harvard?
2. What is Jordan's thesis? Where is it located? What evidence does she offer to support it?
3. What does she mean by "The Promise of America"?

QUESTIONS ON WRITING STRUCTURE AND STRATEGY:

1. What might Jordan seek to accomplish with an anecdote at the beginning of her remarks?
2. How and where does Jordan use rhetorical questions? How effective are they?
3. What is gained by the repetition of the word "people"?
4. Writers are often encouraged to develop a personal voice. What evidence of a personal voice do you detect here?

QUESTIONS FOR DISCUSSION AND WRITING:

1. Jordan ends with what might be called an aphorism (a short, pithy saying embodying some wisdom). Using her remark as a cue, write a paper in which you set forth what you see as citizen responsibility to participate in government.
2. The problem Jordan discusses is similar to those one often faces when confronting a bureaucracy. If you have ever experienced some frustration with a bureaucracy, government or otherwise, write out an account. Try to use Jordan's approach employing a series of rhetorical questions.
3. In a clear, well-organized paper, using specific examples since 1978, discuss the ways the government has abridged the rights of citizens to participate in government.

NURSES GET A RAW DEAL

Priscilla Scherer

Priscilla Scherer is a nurse and an assistant editor of the American Journal of Nursing. *She is also a novelist (*Half Life, *1985). A distinguished graduate of Columbia University, she went on to pursue her nursing career at the Missouri Baptist Hospital School of Nursing in St. Louis, after which she joined the staff of the Cornell Medical Center in New York City. In this article — published in the* New York Times — *Scherer speaks for all American nurses, whom she sees as the most "misunderstood and undervalued" of American professionals. Starting with her title — which sets forth her thesis — she builds her case point by point. She carefully contrasts the shallow image of nurses depicted in the popular arts with the living reality. Note her use of topic sentences and her tight paragraph development. Because tone is important in this article, observe her careful choice of words. This selection abounds in parallel constructions. Scherer skillfully uses this device to achieve euphony, economy, and emphasis. What appears to be her primary method of development? What other methods does she use?*

A popular misconception about nurses is that if they were smart enough they would be doctors. Medicine is a fine profession, and there are many admirable physicians around, a few of them former nurses. But most nurses, if you can believe it, would rather be nurses.

True, no one's exactly excited about being a nurse anymore. Sometimes we're even embarrassed to admit to nursing because of the reactions that follow, the lethargy that overtakes anyone within hearing distance. At parties, stockbrokers and editorial assistants are thought to be fascinating, but no one knows what to say to a nurse. We're seen as one-dimensional, possibly intelligent, but not achieving our potential.

Our image of ourselves suffers as a result. We're joked about, leered at and scapegoated. In movies and television, nurses are usually the background business, behind the desk answering phones, while the real action happens up front, with the doctors. Patients are grateful to nurses, but it's the physician who commands their respect.

All this is unfair — and inaccurate. The doctor may be able to describe the patient's basal ganglia in detail, but it's the nurse who really gets to know the patient, who teaches him how to regulate his insulin, helps him walk to the solarium, makes him laugh, explains how his medicines work and what to watch for in case they don't. We help people in fundamental ways, improving their lives and sometimes easing their deaths. We build relationships with patients that could never be achieved by five minutes at the foot of the bed — and these relationships enhance their medical care.

What the patient sees is the nurse pushing and prodding him, waking him 5
to take his blood pressure or his temperature, to shine a light in his eyes or
stick needles in him. When the doctor finally comes, he omnipotently
prescribes treatment and lets the patient go back to sleep.

In fact, the nurse has been gathering clues all along. A good nurse sifts 6
through the facts and figures, discards the extraneous material, and presents
the pertinent information to the doctor. In an ideal world, the two of them
discuss the clues and piece the puzzle together. True, we take orders from
doctors — and spend as much as one-fourth of the day carrying them out. But
the other 75 percent of the time, a nurse is on her own, observing the patient
and helping him.

Admittedly, we may be our own worst enemies. A friend in advertising 7
noticed that the way nurses talk about their work is different from the way
doctors talk about theirs. Doctors are fascinated and proud of the most minute
aspects of medicine, so that even when they are boring you silly with self-
serving anecdotes, you can't help but admire their enthusiasm. Nurses are
rarely so excited about nursing, and we often seem angry.

Sure, nurses see nursing as a profession, parallel to that of doctors. But 8
somehow it isn't quite the same. A profession implies a certain level of
education, responsibility, authority, autonomy, plus a fee charged for services.
We have the responsibility and the education: many of the nurses delivering
care in hospitals have graduate degrees. But our authority is bogged down in
bureaucracy and by physicians blundering onto our territory. Since a hospital
depends on nurses 24 hours a day, we must be counted on to work shifts, and
our time is not our own. So much for autonomy. Nor do we send bills: we're
paid an hourly wage.

Clearly, it's a schizophrenic situation. We're a white-collar sensibility in a 9
blue-collar slot, and we're stuck there by circumstances. We can't stroll in to
work at 11 A.M., we can't take a two-hour lunch. Part of the responsibility is to
be there on time. Perhaps we should send bills, or take a commission from
doctors' fees.

Nursing began as a product of war. The first nurses were camp followers, 10
wives and sweethearts of soldiers, plus a few enterprising prostitutes, who
followed the troops from battle to battle. ("Hooker" was first applied to
women who served Gen. Joseph Hooker's men in the Civil War.) Nursing —
dressing wounds, bathing down a fever, keeping watch over a dying corporal
—was a natural extension of the other services provided by the women. Nurses
were unskilled, and they drew on basic common sense and experience, much
like self-taught doctors who started out as barbers.

In the mid-1800's, when Florence Nightingale was beginning to change 11
the image of nursing, doctors were treating patients with leeches and suction

cups. One accepted therapy for sudden paralysis (a stroke) was to pour boiling water on the affected limbs and beat the strength back into them. Those early medical malpractices have been forgotten, but 19th century stereotypes still haunt nurses. In 1985, it's past time for that to change.

QUESTIONS ON CONTENT:

1. What are some of the misconceptions people have about nurses?
2. What kinds of services do nurses perform that help build important relationships with patients?
3. According to Scherer, what is the real role of a nurse?
4. In what ways are nurses their own worst enemies?
5. In what ways do nurses and physicians differ as professionals? In what ways are they alike?
6. What does Scherer mean when she writes that nurses are "a white-collar sensibility in a blue-collar job?"

QUESTIONS ON WRITING STRUCTURE AND STRATEGY:

1. Which paragraphs have topic sentences? What techniques does Scherer use to support her assertions?
2. How would you characterize the tone of this selection? Explain how the tone of her article is or is not in harmony with her purpose.
3. What purpose does the brief history lesson in the concluding paragraphs serve?

QUESTIONS FOR DISCUSSION AND WRITING:

1. Write a clear, well-organized paper in which you compare/contrast the role of nurses as seen through the eyes of Lewis Thomas and Priscilla Scherer. You may wish to augment your findings in these selections with interviews of nurses in which you examine the pros and cons of the profession. What seem to be the chief problems on the job?
2. Write a well-developed paper in which you analyze your nursing care or that of a friend or family member in a hospital or in an emergency room. How did the roles of the physicians and the nurses differ?
3. If you are interested in nursing or medicine, write a journal entry in which you describe your reasons for embarking on such a career.
4. Check out your library for books dealing with Civil War nursing. You will find the whole field of wartime medicine (including medical care during World War I or II — or any war) provides interesting reading as well as excellent research paper topics. You might examine some of the following: Agatha

Young, *The Women and the Crisis*; Nina Baker, *Cyclone in Calico*; Louisa May Alcott, *Hospital Sketches*; or some of Walt Whitman's journals. You may also investigate the field of Civil War medicine in Stewart Brooks's *Civil War Medicine*, or Paul Eby Steiner's *Disease in the Civil War*, or John Gardiner Perry's *Letters From a Surgeon of the Civil War*. For a sampling of World War I experiences see William L. Hanson, *World War I: I Was There*; Guy Emerson Bowerman, Jr., *The Compensations of War*; Enid Bagnold, *A Diary Without Dates*. For World War II see Morris Fishbein, editor, *Doctors at War*; Robert Collier Page, *Air Commando Doc*; John Maloney, *Let There Be Mercy*.

LITERACY REQUIRES
LEARNING THE CULTURE
Albert Shanker

Albert Shanker was President of the American Federation of Teachers.
Before assuming leadership of the country's second largest teachers'
union, he headed the New York A.F.T. and taught in the New York
City public schools. For a number of years he has written a weekly
column on educational affairs, published by the union as an
"advertisement" in the Sunday edition of the New York Times. *These*
columns have marked Shanker as an authority on public education. In
the column presented here, which appeared in August, 1985, Shanker
discusses "cultural illiteracy" and the public schools. Note his
generous use of examples to illustrate his ideas. Note also how he has
tailored his language to his audience—the lay public.

A few weeks ago I wrote about an important new theory which explains
that millions of American students and adults are illiterate not so much because
they can't sound out or recognize words (though some can't) but because they
don't have the background information they need to understand what they're
reading. The following examples illustrate how not having the appropriate
information makes a difference:

A perfectly literate Englishman may not be able to understand much of the
sports page in an American newspaper, not because he can't read the words
but because he doesn't know enough about baseball, football or basketball.

A recent item in a New York City newspaper reported a conversation
between a Manhattan bus driver and a woman about to board the bus, which,
if I remember correctly, went something like this: She asked the driver if the
bus stopped at 42nd Street. The driver responded, "Didn't you read the sign in
front of the bus which says we go to 8th Street?" The woman said, "I'm from
out of town. Do you stop at 42nd Street?" The driver came back with, "Even
people from out of town can read, lady." But the driver missed the point. Even
though the woman could read, what she read didn't answer her question,
because she didn't know how Manhattan streets were laid out—she didn't
have the required background information.

All writers assume that readers have adequate background knowledge. But
according to E. D. Hirsch, Jr., while today's students may know their alphabet,
"at the present time, our students in the early grades are not getting the ABCs
of knowledge." What is it, then, in addition to phonics, that students need to
know if they're to be able to read? And why aren't they getting it? Hirsch, who
is a professor of English at the University of Virginia, provides some of the
answers in "Cultural Literacy and the Schools," appearing in the Summer 1985
issue of *The American Educator*. One thing needed is what Hirsch calls

352

"extensive knowledge," which he describes as "broad, but superficial." Writers feel free to use certain words, names, concepts, facts without explanation, expecting the general reader to know them. If the reader can pronounce the words but doesn't "know" them, reading can be tough or even impossible. Hirsch gives some examples of what an American reader needs, and a forthcoming book will list thousands of such words and concepts. Here are his brief listings in several categories:

Pre-1965 people — John Adams, Benedict Arnold, Daniel Boone, John 5
Brown, Aaron Burr, John C. Calhoun, Henry Clay, James Fenimore Cooper, Lord Cornwallis, Davy Crockett, Emily Dickinson, Stephen A. Douglas, Frederick Douglass, Jonathan Edwards, Ralph Waldo Emerson, Benjamin Franklin, Robert Fulton, Ulysses S. Grant, Alexander Hamilton, Nathaniel Hawthorne (Hirsch stopped at "H").

Water and mountains — Antarctic Ocean, Arctic Ocean, Atlantic Ocean, 6
Baltic Sea, Black Sea, Caribbean Sea, Gulf of Mexico, North Sea, Pacific Ocean, Red Sea; Alps, Appalachians, Himalayas, Rocky Mountains, Mt. Everest, Mt. Vesuvius, the Matterhorn.

Our "literary and mythic heritage" — Adam and Eve, Cain and Abel, Noah 7
and the Flood, David and Goliath, the 23rd Psalm, Humpty Dumpty, Jack Sprat, Jack and Jill, Little Jack Horner, Cinderella, Jack and the Beanstalk, Mary Had a Little Lamb, The Night Before Christmas, Peter Pan, Pinocchio, The Princess and the Pea.

Patriotic songs — The Battle Hymn of the Republic; Columbia, the Gem of 8
the Ocean; My Country, 'Tis of Thee; America the Beautiful; The Star-Spangled Banner; This Land Is Your Land; Yankee Doodle.

Hirsch points out that while we may know very little about some of these people, places, literature and songs — "that little is of crucial importance because it enables writers to assume a foundation from which they can treat in detail whatever they wish to focus on."

Why don't students learn as much of these as they should? There are a 10
number of reasons. First, there's a strong bias in our schools against "mere memorization." Committing things to memory is considered old-fashioned, a waste of time when you can "always look it up." This bias is probably a healthy reaction to the oldtime heavy emphasis on memorization, but it has been taken to its opposite extreme. Remembering things — and not exclusively through rote memorization but by memorable teaching and example and gentle repetition grade to grade — is essential as a base for literacy.

A second reason is the widely held view that children can learn to read 11
with virtually any subject matter or content — that it's the skill that counts. So why not motivate them with things that are intrinsically interesting to them,

materials on rock stars or sports heroes, for example? But it's just not true that any material will make them literate; there is a body of information which, says Hirsch, "is not arbitrary" and "which is known to be central by every truly literate person in our culture." Kids should begin to have this information as early as possible, so that they can absorb and build upon it. It's a mistake to think that kids cannot be as excited by Daniel Boone or Davy Crockett or John Brown as much as by Bruce Springsteen or Dwight Gooden.

Finally, there's the legitimate need to provide reading materials that enhance the image of groups which have largely been excluded from literature —blacks, Hispanics, women and others. This is worthwhile and necessary— but not as a substitute for what students must know in order to be literate. Future such lists will undoubtedly be less male, Anglo-Saxon and white, but "until we succeed in changing the literate culture," says Hirsch, "we must not misinform our students by pretending that its contents are just what we wish them to be."

Hirsch and others who have engaged in the research are arguing for a permanent traditional curriculum, especially in the early grades, and the evidence is on their side. He writes: "In the early grades, children are fascinated by straightforward information. . . . Young children are eager to master the materials essential for adult life, and if they believe in the materials they will proudly soak them up like sponges and never forget them. . . . Young children have an urge to become acculturated into the adult world by learning the facts of the tribe long before they can make any sense out of them." If we want a truly literate society, the educational community has an obligation to transmit that society's longstanding culture—the sooner the better.

QUESTIONS ON CONTENT:

1. What does Shanker mean when he says that some people are illiterate because they lack "background information"?
2. What is meant by "extensive knowledge," "intensive knowledge"?
3. How does Shanker account for the failure of American students to acquire "cultural literacy"?

QUESTIONS ON WRITING STRUCTURE AND STRATEGY:

1. How does Shanker go about proving the thesis set forth in paragraph one?
2. How does Shanker demonstrate what is meant by "extensive knowledge"?
3. What method of development does Shanker use to support his thesis?
4. What helpful transitional technique does Shanker use to present his reasons for student "cultural illiteracy"?

QUESTIONS FOR DISCUSSION AND WRITING:

1. Survey a representative sample of students on your campus to determine their familiarity with the items listed in paragraphs 5, 6, 7, and 8.

2. OR:
Interview a select group of students on how well their primary and secondary schools educated them on the "extensive knowledge" listed in paragraphs 5, 6, 7, and 8. Write an essay setting forth your findings.

3. Survey some of your professors on the necessity of "background information" to an understanding of their subject (i.e., what assumptions must the professor in a particular subject make about students in order to be sure that they understand?).

4. Comment on Shanker's support of Hirsch's idea that "until we succeed in changing the literate culture," we must not assign so many minorities and women writers. How do Shanker and Hirsch expect the accepted canon to change if professors do not introduce newly "discovered" writers to their students? Does he *really* want the canon to change?

THE DECLARATION OF INDEPENDENCE

Thomas Jefferson

*On April 29, 1962, President John F. Kennedy, at a State Dinner in
the White House honoring the Nobel Prize winners of North America,
46 of whom were Americans, said to his guests: "I want to tell you
how welcome you are to the White House. I think this is the most
extraordinary collection of talent, of human knowledge, that has ever
been gathered together at the White House, with the possible exception
of when Thomas Jefferson dined alone." A tribute justly deserved, for
in addition to being President of the United States, Jefferson was a
scientist, architect, linguist, horticulturist, musician, and philosopher.
And he was, of course, author of the Declaration of Independence. But
even Jefferson's draft of that immortal document had to be revised by
John Adams, Benjamin Franklin, and members of the Continental
Congress. Jefferson and many of the founding fathers were well read
in the classics and familiar with classical rhetoric. And Jefferson used
the classic syllogism — moving deductively from the general to the
specific — to argue the case for independence (see Glossary). Jefferson
has been justly praised for the marked felicity of his writing. That
felicity derives from Jefferson's use of parallelism to produce balanced
sentences, subordination and repetition to gain emphasis, and precise
word choice to achieve clarity. Note his use of periodicity (see
Glossary) in the second paragraph and in the penultimate sentence,
and, in the last sentence, a stirring tricolon (see Highet).*

I will state the form of the declaration as originally
reported. The parts struck out by Congress shall be
distinguished by a black line drawn under them; & those
inserted by them shall be placed in the margin or in a
concurrent column:

A Declaration by the representatives of the United
states of America, in [General] Congress assembled.

When in the course of human events it becomes
necessary for one people to dissolve the political bands
which have connected them with another, and to
assume among the powers of the earth the separate &
equal station to which the laws of nature and of nature's
god entitle them, a decent respect to the opinions of
mankind requires that they should declare the causes
which impel them to the separation.

We hold these truths to be self evident; that all men
are created equal; that they they are endowed by their
creator with ∧ [inherent and] inalienable rights; that   ∧ certain

among these are life, liberty & the pursuit of happiness;
that to secure these rights, governments are instituted
among men, deriving their just powers from the consent
of the governed; that whenever any form of government
becomes destructive of these ends, it is the right of the
people to alter or to abolish it, & to institute new
government, laying its foundation on such principles, &
organising its powers in such form, as to them shall
seem most likely to effect their safety & happiness.
Prudence indeed will dictate that governments long
established should not be changed for light & transient
causes; and accordingly all experience hath shewn that
mankind are more disposed to suffer while evils are
sufferable than to right themselves by abolishing the
forms to which they are accustomed. But when a long
train of abuses & usurpations [begun at a distinguished
period and] pursuing invariably the same object, evinces
a design to reduce them under absolute despotism it is
their right, it is their duty to throw off such government,
& to provide new guards for their future security. Such
has been the patient sufferance of these colonies; &
such is now the necessity which constrains them to ∧   ∧ alter

[expunge] their former systems of government. The
history of the present king of Great Britain is a history
of ∧ [unremitting] injuries & usurpations, [among which   ∧ repeated

appears no solitary fact to contradict the uniform tenor
of the rest but all have] ∧ in direct object the   ∧ all having

establishment of an absolute tyranny over these states.
To prove this let facts be submitted to a candid world
[for the truth of which we pledge a faith yet unsullied by
falsehood.]

He has refused his assent to laws the most   4
wholsome & necessary for the public good.

He has forbidden his governors to pass laws of   5
immediate & pressing importance, unless suspended in
their operation till his assent should be obtained; &

when so suspended, he has utterly neglected to attend to them.

He has refused to pass other laws for the accommodation of large districts of people, unless those people would relinquish the right of representation in the legislature, a right inestimable to them, & formidable to tyrants only.

He has called together legislative bodies at places unusual, uncomfortable, and distant from the depository of their public records, for the sole purpose of fatiguing them into compliance with his measures.

He has dissolved representative houses repeatedly [& continually] for opposing with manly firmness his invasions on the rights of the people.

He has refused for a long time after such dissolutions to cause others to be elected, whereby the legislative powers, incapable of annihilation, have returned to the people at large for their exercise, the state remaining in the mean time exposed to all the dangers of invasion from without & convulsions within.

He has endeavored to prevent the population of these states; for that purpose obstructing the laws for naturalization of foreigners, refusing to pass others to encourage their migrations hither, & raising the conditions of new appropriations of lands.

He has ∧ [suffered] the administration of justice   ∧ obstructed

[totally to cease in some of these states] ∧ refusing his   ∧ by

assent to laws for establishing judiciary powers.

He has made [our] judges dependant on his will alone, for the tenure of their offices, & the amount & paiment of their salaries.

He has erected a multitude of new offices [by a self assumed power] and sent hither swarms of new officers to harrass our people and eat out their substance.

He has kept among us in times of peace standing armies [and ships of war] without the consent of our legislatures.

He has affected to render the military independant of, & superior to the civil power.

He has combined with others to subject us to a

jurisdiction foreign to our constitutions &
unacknowledged by our laws, giving his assent to their
acts of pretended legislation for quartering large bodies
of armed troops among us; for protecting them by a
mock-trial from punishment for any murders which they
should commit on the inhabitants of these states; for
cutting off our trade with all parts of the world; for
imposing taxes on us without our consent; for depriving
us ∧ of the benefits of trial by jury; for transporting us   ∧ in many cases

beyond seas to be tried for pretended offences; for
abolishing the free system of English laws in a
neighboring province, establishing therein an arbitrary
government, and enlarging its boundaries, so as to
render it at once an example and fit instrument for
introducing the same absolute rule into these ∧ [states];   ∧ colonies

for taking away our charters, abolishing our most
valuable laws, and altering fundamentally the forms of
our governments; for suspending our own legislatures, &
declaring themselves invested with power to legislate for
us in all cases whatsoever.

He has abdicated government here ∧ [withdrawing   ∧ by declaring us   17

his governors, and declaring us out of his allegiance &   out of his
protection.]   protection &
    waging war
He has plundered our seas, ravaged our coasts,   against us.   18
burnt our towns, & destroyed the lives of our people.

He is at this time transporting large armies of   19
foreign mercenaries to compleat the works of death,
desolation & tyranny already begun with circumstances
of cruelty and perfidy ∧ unworthy the head of a civilized   ∧ scarcely paralleled
    in the most
nation.   barbarous ages, &
He has constrained our fellow citizens taken   totally   20
captive on the high seas to bear arms against their
country, to become the executioners of their friends &
brethren, or to fall themselves by their hands.

He has ∧ endeavored to bring on the inhabitants of   ∧ excited domestic   21
    insurrections
our frontiers the merciless Indian savages, whose known   amongst us, & has
rule of warfare is an undistinguished destruction of all
ages, sexes, & conditions [of existence.]

[He has incited treasonable insurrections of our
fellow-citizens, with the allurements of forfeiture &
confiscation of our property.

He has waged cruel war against human nature
itself, violating its most sacred rights of life and liberty
in the persons of a distant people who never offended
him, captivating & carrying them into slavery in another
hemisphere or to incur miserable death in their
transportation thither. This piratical warfare, the
opprobrium of *infidel* powers, is the warfare of the
Christian king of Great Britain. Determined to keep
open a market where *Men* should be bought & sold, he
has prostituted his negative for suppressing every
legislative attempt to prohibit or to restrain this
execrable commerce. And that this assemblage of
horrors might want no fact of distinguished die, he is
now exciting those very people to rise in arms among us,
and to purchase that liberty of which he has deprived
them, by murdering the people on whom he also
obtruded them: thus paying off former crimes committed
against the *Liberties* of one people, with crimes which he
urges them to commit against the *lives* of another.]

In every stage of these oppressions we have
petitioned for redress in the most humble terms: our
repeated petitions have been answered only by repeated
injuries. A prince whose character is thus marked by
every act which may define a tyrant in unfit to be the
ruler of a ∧ people [who mean to be free. Future ages]   ∧free

will scarcely believe that the hardiness of one man
adventured, within the short compass of twelve years
only, to lay a foundation so broad & so undisguised for
tyranny over a people fostered & fixed in principles of
freedom.]

Nor have we been wanting in attentions to our
British brethren. We have warned them from time to
time of attempts by their legislature to extend ∧ [a]   ∧an unwarrantable

jurisdiction over ∧ [these our states.] We have reminded   ∧us

them of the circumstances of our emigration &
settlement here, [no one of which could warrant so

strange a pretension: that these were effected at the
expence of our own blood & treasure, unassisted by the
wealth or the strength of Great Britain: that in
constituting indeed our several forms of government, we
had adopted one common king, thereby laying a
foundation for perpetual league & amity with them: but
that submission to their parliament was no part of our
constitution, nor ever in idea, if history may be credited:
and,] we ∧ appealed to their native justice and

∧ have

magnanimity ∧ [as well as to] the ties of our common

∧ and we have
conjured them by

kindred to disavow these usurpations which ∧ [were

∧ would inevitably

likely to] interrupt our connection and correspondence.
They too have been deaf to the voice of justice & of
consanguinity, [and when occasions have been given
them, by the regular course of their laws, of removing
from their councils the disturbers of our harmony, they
have, by their free election, re-established them in
power. At this very time too they are permitting their
chief magistrate to send over not only souldiers of our
common blood, but Scotch & foreign mercenaries to
invade & destroy us. These facts have given the last stab
to agonizing affection, and manly spirit bids us to
renounce for ever these unfeeling brethren. We must
endeavor to forget our former love for them, and to hold
them as we hold the rest of mankind enemies in war, in
peace friends. We might have been a free and a great
people together; but a communication of grandeur & of
freedom it seems is below their dignity. Be it so, since
they will have it. The road to happiness & to glory is
open to us too. We will tread it apart from them, and] ∧

∧ we must therefore

acquiesce in the necessity which denounces our [eternal]
separation ∧!

∧ and hold them as
we hold the rest
of mankind,
enemies in war, in
peace friends.

We therefore the representatives of the United states of America in General Congress assembled, appealing to the supreme judge of the world for the rectitude of our intentions, do in the name, & by the authority of the good people of these colonies, solemnly publish & declare that these United colonies are & of right ought to be free & independant states; that they are absolved from all allegiance to the British crown, and that all political connection between them & the state of Great Britain is, & ought to be, totally dissolved; & that as free & independant states they have full power to levy war, conclude peace, contract alliances, establish commerce & to do all other acts & things which independant states may of right do.

And for the support of this declaration, with a firm reliance on the protection of divine providence we mutually pledge to each other our lives, our fortunes & our sacred honour.

26

27

We therefore the representatives of the United states of America in General Congress assembled do in the name, & by the authority of the good people of these [states reject & renounce all allegiance & subjection to the kings of Great Britain & all others who may hereafter claim by, through or under them: we utterly dissolve all political connection which may heretofore have subsisted between us & the people or parliament of Great Britain: & finally we do assert & declare these colonies to be free & independant states,] & that as free & independant states, they have full power to levy war, conclude peace, contract alliances, establish commerce, & to do all other acts & things which independant states may of right do. And for the support of this declaration we mutually pledge to each other our lives, our fortunes & our sacred honour.

2

QUESTIONS ON CONTENT:

1. Paragraph three sets forth what "The Age of Reason" called "The Natural Rights Doctrine," a body of self-evident truths. What are some of these specific beliefs?

2. Against whom are the grievances — beginning in paragraph four — directed? Who are the ostensible authors of these charges?

QUESTIONS ON WRITING STRUCTURE AND STRATEGY:

1. What is the purpose of paragraph two?

2. Who constitutes the audience for this declaration?

3. The Declaration presents a deductive argument in the form of categorical syllogism (see Glossary). What support does Jefferson offer for his major premise? His minor premise?

4. Jefferson uses parallelism throughout the Declaration. Point out some examples and explain how they function in the document. Where is the use of parallelism particularly effective? Where is his use of repetition especially effective? How and why does he use subordination?

5. G. K. Chesterton has said of the Declaration that it is "perhaps the only piece of practical politics that is alone theoretical politics and also great literature." Examine Jefferson's diction and isolate words, phrases, and sentences that contribute to its literary quality.

QUESTIONS FOR DISCUSSION AND WRITING:

1. For a reseach project: For many years Carl Becker's *The Declaration of Independence* (1922) was a standard work. With the publication in 1979 of Garry Wills' *Inventing America: Jefferson's Declaration of Independence*, controversy has arisen over the origin of Jefferson's ideas and the influence of John Locke. Other key works are: Julian P. Boyd, *The Declaration of Independence, The Evolution of the Text* (1945) and John H. Hazelton, *The Declaration of Independence, Its History* (1906). Check *Book Review Digest* and *Humanities Index* for reviews of the Wills book. Look up the originals, one popular and one scholarly, and write a paper on the book's reception and the issues raised. (For a popular, dramatic version of the proceedings of the Continental Congress and the drafting of the Declaration of Independence, see the play by Stone and Edwards, *1776*.)

2. Choose a topic of popular interest and argue deductively to persuade your readers to your way of thinking. You might argue about the draft, drinking laws, campus or dormitory regulations, or something more worldwide in scope: the nuclear arms freeze, nuclear power plant restriction, protectionism, or the mandatory seat belt law. Here's how you might go about it: frame a thesis with a "because" clause to support it; then turn the "because" clause into a major premise. For example: Dormitory regulations should be abolished *because they infringe upon an individual's freedom*. Major premise becomes: "Any regulation that infringes upon an individual's freedom should be abolished." Question: Is the major premise a universal proposition (i.e., applicable in *every* situation)? Obviously not. Therefore, you have to modify your major premise. It now becomes "Any regulation that *unreasonably* infringes upon an individual's freedom should be abolished." Your argument will now center on the *unreasonableness* of the regulations.

3. Examine the revisions. Do you think the changes represent improvements on the original? Do you find Jefferson wordy? Has he always chosen the best word? What about the unaltered tricolon (the last eight words)? What is the logic of the order? Write a paper on your findings.

ADDRESS AT THE
DEDICATION OF THE
GETTYSBURG NATIONAL CEMETERY
Abraham Lincoln

As students of Lincoln know, Edward Everett, the first speaker that memorable November day in 1863, celebrated as America's finest orator, spoke for two and one half hours. It was only then that Lincoln, invited to speak at the ceremonies almost as an afterthought, rose tall and gaunt, and in his "few words" (266, to be exact) succeeded in transforming the commemoration into a rededication to the hope of life and peace, away from the death and destruction that still permeated the battlefield atmosphere. His speech framed the vision of a whole nation and proved once again, as a famous writer once wrote, "that the pen is not always mightier than the sword but once in a while it can be."

Although it seems almost sacrilegious to analyze the address, it continues to serve as a wellspring of eloquence and imagery for writers, politicians, and speakers of all ages. Why is it "the noblest monument of American prose"? Once again examine its phrasing, considering the occasion, the audience, the purpose. Evaluate its virtues from a practical, moral, literary perspective, and then go to study Gilbert Highet's detailed analysis of its rhetorical structure.

Four score and seven years ago our fathers brought forth on this continent, a new nation, conceived in Liberty, and dedicated to the proposition that all men are created equal.

Now we are engaged in a great civil war; testing whether that nation, or any nation so conceived and so dedicated, can long endure. We are met on a great battlefield of that war. We have come to dedicate a portion of that field as a final resting-place for those who here gave their lives that that nation might live. It is altogether fitting and proper that we should do this.

But, in a larger sense, we cannot dedicate — we cannot consecrate — we cannot hallow — this ground. The brave men, living and dead, who struggled here have consecrated it, far above our poor power to add or detract. The world will little note, nor long remember, what we say here, but it can never forget what they did here. It is for us the living, rather, to be dedicated here to the unfinished work which they who fought here have thus far so nobly advanced. It is rather for us to be here dedicated to the great task remaining before us — that from these honored dead we take increased devotion to that cause for which they gave the last full measure of devotion; that we here highly resolve that these dead shall not have died in vain; that this nation, under God, shall have a new birth of freedom; and that government of the people, by the people, for the people, shall not perish from the earth.

QUESTIONS ON CONTENT:

1. What are Lincoln's ostensible purposes in this address, and what does he also accomplish in the last clause of the last sentence?
2. This speech is only three paragraphs long. What time chronology is apparent as Lincoln proceeds, paragraph by paragraph, in its development?

QUESTIONS ON WRITING STRUCTURE AND STRATEGY:

1. Can you find multiple birth and death imagery? Why is Lincoln's use of the imagery of birth and death appropriate to his purpose here?
2. How would you characterize the tone of this speech? Isolate those elements that contribute to tone.

QUESTIONS FOR DISCUSSION AND WRITING:

1. Would Lincoln's appeal to patriotism have the same impact today? Does the intensity of its impact depend upon the occasion? If so, what appeals would a contemporary public figure use to accomplish some national purpose? Write a paper in which you explore these questions.
2. Consider the recent dedication of the Vietnam Memorial in Washington: would the sentiments in Lincoln's speech be appropriate for the dedication of that memorial? Why or why not? Write a paper in which you explain.

THE GETTYSBURG ADDRESS
Gilbert Highet

*Scholar, educator, poet, and author, Gilbert Highet was known as a
"popularizer" of the classics, a classicist who was "readable as well as
erudite." A popular professor of Greek and Latin at Columbia
University from 1937 until his retirement in 1972, he found time to
write fourteen books (on both scholarly and popular subjects), present
a weekly radio program for seven years during the 1950s, and serve as
literary critic for* Harper's *from 1952 to 1954.*

Here Highet provides us with the background and setting for Lincoln's
Gettysburg Address, *briefly describes the ceremonies and the mixed
reception the speech engendered, and then arrives at the pièce de
résistance — a laudatory analysis of the Address as a work of art. His
examination reveals Lincoln the man and the artist. Pay particular
attention to Highet's discussion of Lincoln's use of antithesis and the
tricolon.*

Fourscore and seven years ago. . . .   1

These five words stand at the entrance to the best-known monument of   2
American prose, one of the finest utterances in the entire language, and surely
one of the greatest speeches in all history. Greatness is like granite; it is
molded in fire, and it lasts for many centuries.

Fourscore and seven years ago. . . . It is strange to think that President   3
Lincoln was looking back to the 4th of July 1776, and that he and his speech are
now further removed from us than he himself was from George Washington
and the Declaration of Independence. Fourscore and seven years before the
Gettysburg Address, a small group of patriots signed the Declaration. Fourscore
and seven years after the Gettysburg Address, it was the year 1950, and that
date is already receding rapidly into our troubled, adventurous, and valiant past.

Inadequately prepared and at first scarcely realized in its full importance,   4
the dedication of the graveyard at Gettysburg was one of the supreme
moments of American history. The battle itself had been a turning point of the
war. On the 4th of July 1863, General Meade repelled Lee's invasion of
Pennsylvania. Although he did not follow up his victory, he had broken one of
the most formidable aggressive enterprises of the Confederate armies. Losses
were heavy on both sides. Thousands of dead were left on the field, and
thousands of wounded died in the hot days following the battle. At first, their
burial was more or less haphazard; but thoughtful men gradually came to feel
that an adequate burying place and memorial were required. These were
established by an interstate commission that autumn, and the finest speaker in
the North was invited to dedicate them. This was the scholar and statesman
Edward Everett of Harvard. He made a good speech — which is still extant: not

at all academic, it is full of close strategic analysis and deep historical understanding.

Lincoln was not invited to speak, at first. Although peopole knew him as   5 an effective debater, they were not sure whether he was capable of making a serious speech on such a solemn occasion. But one of the impressive things about Lincoln's career is that he constantly strove to *grow*. He was anxious to appear on that occasion and to say something worthy of it. (Also, it has been suggested, he was anxious to remove the impression that he did not know how to behave properly—an impression which had been strengthened by a shocking story about his clowning on the battlefield of Antietam the previous year.) Therefore when he was invited he took considerable care with his speech. He drafted rather more than half of it in the White House before leaving, finished it in the hotel at Gettysburg the night before the ceremony (not in the train, as sometimes reported), and wrote a fair copy next morning.

There are many accounts of the day itself, 19 November 1863. There are   6 many descriptions of Lincoln, all showing the same curious blend of grandeur and awkwardness, or lack of dignity, or—it would be best to call it humility. In the procession he rode horseback: a tall lean man in a high plug hat, straddling a short horse, with his feet too near the ground. He arrived before the chief speaker, and had to wait patiently for half an hour or more. His own speech came right at the end of a long and exhausting ceremony, lasted less than three minutes, and made little impression on the audience. In part this was because they were tired, in part because (as eyewitnesses said) he ended almost before they knew he had begun, and in part because he did not speak the Address, but read it, very slowly, in a thin high voice, with a marked Kentucky accent, pronouncing "to" as "toe" and dropping his final R's.

Some people of course were alert enough to be impressed. Everett   7 congratulated him at once. But most of the newspapers paid little attention to the speech, and some sneered at it. The *Patriot and Union* of Harrisburg wrote, "We pass over the silly remarks of the President; for the credit of the nation we are willing . . . that they shall no more be repeated or thought of"; and the London *Times* said, "The ceremony was rendered ludicrous by some of the sallies of that poor President Lincoln," calling his remarks "dull and commonplace." The first commendation of the Address came in a single sentence of the Chicago *Tribune*, and the first discriminating and detailed praise of it appeared in the Springfield *Republican*, the Providence *Journal*, and the Philadelphia *Bulletin*. However, three weeks after the ceremony and then again the following spring, the editor of *Harper's Weekly* published a sincere and thorough eulogy of the Address, and soon it was attaining recognition as a masterpiece.

At the time, Lincoln could not care much about the reception of his words.   8

He was exhausted and ill. In the train back to Washington, he lay down with a
wet towel on his head. He had caught smallpox. At that moment he was
incubating it, and he was stricken down soon after he re-entered the White
House. Fortunately it was a mild attack, and it evoked one of his best jokes: he
told his visitors, "At last I have something I can give to everybody."

He had more than that to give to everybody. He was a unique person, far   9
greater than most people realize until they read his life with care. The wisdom
of his policy, the sources of his statesmanship—these were things too complex
to be discussed in a brief essay. But we can say something about the
Gettysburg Address as work of art.

A work of art. Yes: for Lincoln was a literary artist, trained both by others   10
and by himself. The textbooks he used as a boy were full of difficult exercises
and skillful devices in formal rhetoric, stressing the qualities he practiced in his
own speaking: antithesis, parallelism, and verbal harmony. Then he read and
reread many admirable models of thought and expression: the King James
Bible, the essays of Bacon, the best plays of Shakespeare. His favorites were
Hamlet, Lear, Macbeth, Richard III, and *Henry VIII,* which he had read dozens
of times. He loved reading aloud, too, and spent hours reading poetry to his
friends. (He told his partner Herndon that he preferred getting the sense of any
document by reading it aloud.) Therefore his serious speeches are important
parts of the long and noble classical tradition of oratory which begins in
Greece, runs through Rome to the modern world, and is still capable (if we do
not neglect it) of producing masterpieces.

The first proof of this is that the Gettysburg Address if full of quotations—   11
or rather of adaptations—which give it strength. It is partly religious, partly
(in the highest sense) political: therefore it is interwoven with memories of the
Bible and memories of American history. The first and the last words are
Biblical cadences. Normally Lincoln did not say "fourscore" when he meant
eighty; but on this solemn occasion he recalled the important dates in the
Bible—such as the age of Abraham when his first son was born to him, and he
was "fourscore and six years old." Similarly he did not say there was a chance
that democracy might die out: he recalled the somber phrasing on the Book of
Job—where Bildad speaks of the destruction of one who shall vanish without a
trace, and says that "his branch shall be cut off; his remembrance shall perish
from the earth." Then again, the famous description of our State as
"government of the people, by the people, for the people" was adumbrated by
Daniel Webster in 1830 (he spoke of "the people's government, made for the
people, made by the people, and answerable to the people") and then
elaborated in 1854 by the abolitionist Theodore Parker (as "government of all
the people, by all the people, for all the people"). There is good reason to think
that Lincoln took the important phrase "under God" (which he interpolated at

the last moment) from Weems, the biographer of Washington; and we know
that it had been used at least once by Washington himself.

Analyzing the Address further, we find that it is based on a highly
imaginative theme, or group of themes. The subject is—how can we put it so
as not to disfigure it?—the subject is the kinship of life and death, that
mysterious linkage which we see sometimes as the physical succession of birth
and death in our world, sometimes as the contrast, which is perhaps a unity,
between death and immortality. The first sentence is concerned with birth: 12

Our fathers brought forth a new *nation,* conceived *in liberty.*

The final phrase but one expresses the hope that

this nation, under God, shall have a new birth *of freedom.*

And the last phrase of all speaks of continuing life as the triumph over death.
Again and again throughout the speech, this mystical contrast and kinship
reappear: "those who *gave their lives* that that nation might *live,*" "the brave
men *living* and *dead,*" and so in the central assertion that the dead have
already consecrated their own burial place, while "it is for us, the *living,* rather
to be dedicated . . . to the great task remaining." The Gettysburg Address is a
prose poem; it belongs to the same world as the great elegies, and the adagios
of Beethoven.

Its structure, however, is that of a skillfully contrived speech. The 13
oratorical pattern is perfectly clear. Lincoln describes the occasion, dedicates
the ground, and then draws a larger conclusion by calling on his hearers to
dedicate themselves to the preservation of the Union. But within that, we can
trace his constant use of at least two important rhetorical devices.

The first of these is *antithesis*: opposition, contrast. The speech is full of it. 14
Listen:

The world will little note

    nor long remember   *what* we say *here*

but   *it can never* forget   *what* they did here.

And so in nearly every sentence: "brave men, *living* and *dead*"; "to *add* or
detract." There is the antithesis of the Founding Fathers and men of Lincoln's
own time:

369

Our fathers brought forth *a new nation* . . .
now we are testing whether that nation . . . can *long endure.*

And there is the more terrible antithesis of those who have already died and those who still live to do their duty. Now, antithesis is the figure of contrast and conflict. Lincoln was speaking in the midst of a great civil war.

The other important pattern is different. It is technically called *tricolon* — the division of an idea into three harmonious parts, usually of increasing power. The most famous phrase of the Address is a tricolon:

> *government of the people*
> > *by the people*
> > *for the people.*

The most solemn sentence is a tricolon:

> *we cannot dedicate*
> *we cannot consecrate*
> *we cannot hallow*   *this ground.*

And above all, the last sentence (which has sometimes been criticized as too complex) is essentially two parallel phrases, with a tricolon growing out of the second and then producing another tricolon: a trunk, three branches, and a cluster of flowers. Lincoln says that it is for his hearers to be dedicated to the great task remaining before them. Then he goes on.

> *that from these honored dead*

apparently he means "in such a way that from these honored dead"

> *we take increased devotion to that cause.*

Next, he restates this more briefly:

> *that we here highly resolve. . . .*

And now the actual resolution follows, in three parts of growing intensity:

that these dead shall not have died in vain
that this nation, under God, shall have a new birth
    of freedom

and that (one more tricolon)

government of the people
    by the people
and   for the people
shall not perish from the earth.

Now, the tricolon is the figure which, through division, emphasizes basic harmony and unity. Lincoln used antithesis because he was speaking to a people at war. He used the tricolon because he was hoping, planning, praying for peace.

No one thinks that when he was drafting the Gettysburg Address, Lincoln   16 deliberately looked up these quotations and consciously chose these particular patterns of thought. No, he chose the theme. From its development and from the emotional tone of the entire occasion, all the rest followed, or grew — by that marvelous process of choice and rejection which is essential to artistic creation. It does not spoil such a work of art to analyze it as closely as we have done; it is altogether fitting and proper that we should do this: for it helps us to penetrate more deeply into the rich meaning of the Gettysburg Address, and it allows us the very rare privilege of watching the workings of a great man's mind.

QUESTIONS ON CONTENT:

1. Given the facts Highet provides about the occasion of Lincoln's Gettysburg Address, was the President's speech geared to his immediate audience or to posterity? Explain your answer.
2. How did Abraham Lincoln develop his skill as a writer, and what are some of the sources of Lincoln's literary artistry? How are they reflected in the speech?
3. Highet defines and identifies antithesis and tricolon in Lincoln's speech. What are they and how does Lincoln use them?

QUESTIONS ON WRITING STRUCTURE AND STRATEGY:

1. How does Highet organize his remarks?
   a. How does Highet gain the reader's attention in the first sentence?

b.   What is the effect of Highet's first three paragraphs?

c.   What does the summary in paragraph nine contribute to Highet's analysis?

d.   What important historical background do paragraphs four through eight provide?

e.   Do you find a necessary relationship between paragraphs seven and eight? Explain.

f.   What three aspects of Abraham Lincoln's writing are discussed in paragraphs nine through fifteen?

g.   How does Highet's concluding paragraph relate to paragraph two to secure coherence?

QUESTIONS FOR DISCUSSION AND WRITING:

1.   Too often people conclude that memorable phrases are spontaneous, off-the-cuff utterances. More often, they have evolved over a period of time, being polished and adapted with each expression. Highet provides a cursory history of the famous "of the people, by the people, for the people." Consult the library for a more complete history of this famous definition of democracy.

2.   Eloquence — such as Lincoln's — can be used to serve an ignoble cause as well as a noble one. (Consider one of Adolph Hitler's speeches or some of his exhortations in his *Mein Kampf*.) Aside from an emotional response to oratory, what must we also bring to the evaluation of a particular piece of writing or oratory?

3.   Try using Highet's method of analyzing a famous speech — Lincoln's Second Inaugural, Franklin D. Roosevelt's First Inaugural, or John F. Kennedy's Inaugural. Briefly sketch in the historical perspective (time, place, occasion, audience, purpose) and then analyze the piece for its organization and writing techniques (parallelism, antithesis, figurative language, allusion, word choice, tone, and so on).

REMARKS AT AMHERST COLLEGE
UPON RECEIVING
AN HONORARY DEGREE

John F. Kennedy

President John F. Kennedy was, in Lewis Mumford's words, "the first American President to give art, literature, and music a place of dignity and honor in our national life." He was convinced, says Arthur Schlesinger, "that the health of the arts was vitally related to the health of society." Consequently, beginning with his inauguration — the first in which an American poet, Robert Frost, was invited to participate — President Kennedy led the nation in honoring its artists. Not only were they welcomed at his inauguration — over fifty were on the rostrum when he took the oath — but, during his three years as president, American artists from all fields of endeavor were invited to the White House to meet with and/or perform for visiting chiefs of state. The nation was thus able to display — on its most appropriate platform — the best of its civilization. He also rehabilitated the Presidential Medal of Freedom to give visible evidence of the nation's desire to honor those "whose talent enlarges the public vision of the dignity with which life can be graced and the fullness with which it can be lived."

In this tribute and appeal to altruism and patriotism, observe Kennedy's careful attention to language — evident in both Jefferson and Lincoln — and to his use of all the resources of language: parallelism, antithesis, alliteration, metaphor, and sentence variety, all made memorable with appropriate quotations from Frost's poetry.

. . . The problems which this country now faces are staggering, both at 1
home and abroad. We need the service, in the great sense, of every educated
man or woman to find 10 million jobs in the next 2½ years, to govern our
relations — a country which lived in isolation for 150 years, and is now
suddenly the leader of the free world — to govern our relations with over 100
countries, to govern those relations with success so that the balance of power
remains strong on the side of freedom, to make it possible for Americans of all
different races and creeds to live together in harmony, to make it possible for a
world to exist in diversity and freedom. All this requires the best of all of us.

Therefore, I am proud to come to this college whose graduates have 2
recognized this obligation and to say to those who are now here that the need
is endless, and I am confident that you will respond.

Robert Frost said: 3

> *Two roads diverged in a wood, and I—*
> *I took the one less traveled by,*
> *And that has made all the difference.*

I hope that road will not be the less traveled by, and I hope your   4
commitment to the Great Republic's interest in the years to come will be
worthy of your long inheritance since your beginning.

This day devoted to the memory of Robert Frost offers an opportunity for   5
reflection which is prized by politicians as well as by others, and even by
poets, for Robert Frost was one of the granite figures of our time in America.
He was supremely two things: an artist and an American. A nation reveals itself
not only by the men it produces but also by the men it honors, the men it
remembers.

In America, our heroes have customarily run to men of large   6
accomplishments. But today this college and country honors a man whose
contribution was not to our size but to our spirit, not to our political beliefs but
to our insight, not to our self-esteem, but to our self-comprehension. In
honoring Robert Frost, we therefore can pay honor to the deepest sources of
our national strength. That strength takes many forms, and the most obvious
forms are not always the most significant. The men who create power make an
indispensable contribution to the Nation's greatness, but the men who question
power make a contribution just as indispensable, especially when that
questioning is disinterested, for they determine whether we use power or
power uses us.

Our national strength matters, but the spirit which informs and controls   7
our strength matters just as much. This was the special significance of Robert
Frost. He brought an unsparing instinct for reality to bear on the platitudes and
pieties of society. His sense of the human tragedy fortified him against self-
deception and easy consolation. "I have been," he wrote, "one acquainted with
the night." And because he knew the midnight as well as the high noon,
because he understood the ordeal as well as the triumph of the human spirit,
he gave his age strength with which to overcome despair. At bottom, he held a
deep faith in the spirit of man, and it is hardly an accident that Robert Frost
coupled poetry and power, for he saw poetry as the means of saving power
from itself. When power leads man towards arrogance, poetry reminds him of
his limitations. When power narrows the area of man's concern, poetry

reminds him of the richness and diversity of his existence. When power corrupts, poetry cleanses. For art established the basic human truth which must serve as the touchstone of our judgment.

The artist, however faithful to his personal vision of reality, becomes the   8
last champion of the individual mind and sensibility against an intrusive
society and an officious state. The great artist is thus a solitary figure. He has,
as Frost said, a lover's quarrel with the world. In pursuing his perceptions of
reality, he must often sail against the currents of his time. This is not a popular
role. If Robert Frost was much honored during his lifetime, it was because a
good many preferred to ignore his darker truths. Yet in retrospect, we see how
the artist's fidelity has strengthened the fibre of our national life.

If sometimes our great artists have been the most critical of our society, it   9
is because their sensitivity and their concern for justice, which must motivate
any true artist, makes him aware that our Nation falls short of its highest
potential. I see little of more importance to the future of our country and our
civilization than full recognition of the place of the artist.

If art is to nourish the roots of our culture, society must set the artist free   10
to follow his vision wherever it takes him. We must never forget that art is not a
form of propaganda; it is a form of truth. And as Mr. MacLeish once remarked
of poets, there is nothing worse for our trade than to be in style. In free society
art is not a weapon and its does not belong to the sphere of polemics and
ideology. Artists are not engineers of the soul. It may be different elsewhere.
But democratic society — in it, the highest duty of the writer, the composer, the
artist is to remain true to himself and to let the chips fall where they may. In
serving his vision of the truth, the artist best serves his nation. And the nation
which disdains the mission of art invites the fate of Robert Frost's hired man,
the fate of having "nothing to look backward to with pride, and nothing to
look forward to with hope."

I look forward to a great future for America, a future in which our country   11
will match its military strength with our moral restraint, its wealth with our
wisdom, its power with our purpose. I look forward to an America which will
not be afraid of grace and beauty, which will protect the beauty of our natural
environment, which will preserve the great old American houses and squares
and parks of our national past, and which will build handsome and balanced
cities for our future.

I look forward to an America which will reward achievement in the arts as   12
we reward achievement in business or statecraft. I look forward to an America
which will steadily raise the standards of artistic accomplishment and which
will steadily enlarge cultural opportunities for all of our citizens. And I look
forward to an America which commands respect throughout the world not only

for its strength but for its civilization as well. And I look forward to a world which will be safe not only for democracy and diversity but also for personal distinction. . . .

QUESTIONS ON CONTENT:

1. Specifically for what reasons is Kennedy honoring Robert Frost?
2. Why does Kennedy feel that coupling "poetry and power" is important?
3. Why is the artist invariably a lonely figure?
4. What is the duty of the artist in a democratic society, and what is the purpose of art as Kennedy sees it?
5. What is the composition of Kennedy's specific audience? What road is he calling them to travel by, and what does the road symbolize?

QUESTIONS ON WRITING STRUCTURE AND STRATEGY:

1. Where do you find effective use of parallel construction? Antithesis?
2. What device does the President use to point up the uniqueness of the democratic artist?
3. Examine the sentence structure: Are there too many long sentences? How effective is his use of short sentences? Read some passages aloud and determine their rhythmicity. Is this important for reader appeal?

QUESTIONS FOR DISCUSSION AND WRITING:

1. Write a paper in which you compare Kennedy's definition of the role of the artist with that of William Faulkner. What are the differences? What are the similarities?
2. Consider some contemporary artists who appear to be fulfilling the role Kennedy describes — or some other type of American, someone who goes against the grain. Write a paper in which you show how the person/s fit Kennedy's description.
3. Write a paper on how the role you have chosen for yourself coincides in any way with what Kennedy calls for in this speech.
4. In the past decade or so refugee writers, poets, dancers, and musicians have been flocking to America. For what reasons do they come? Do some library research and write a paper on the reasons these people give for leaving their homelands. Are their reasons relevant to what Kennedy spoke about in his speech? (For example, Joseph Brodsky, poet; Mstislov Rostropovich, cellist and orchestra leader; Lubov Pisarenkova and Yuri Krasnov, circus performers, are all from the Soviet Union.)
5. Consider some not so celebrated contemporary refugees to our shores. Do you know any whom you might interview? Do some research and confine yourself to their reasons for coming. (Perhaps you may have some relative

who has recently come to America, or some friends or neighbors. Interview them and write a paper on what you have learned.)

6. Compare Kennedy as a politician and visionary to some contemporary politicians on the local, state, or national scene. You may have to do some library research.

SUGGESTIONS FOR JOURNAL ENTRIES

These are essentially suggestions for paragraphs or short journal entries, some of which you could develop further, depending on your interests or directions from your instructor. Perhaps do some prewriting for some part of these entries. It might be helpful to refer to the Glossary, the Writing Process, and the Rhetorical Index.

FOCUS — ORGANIZATION — DEVELOPMENT

1. Medawar's article is taken from his book *Advice to a Young Scientist*. In a journal entry use narration or description to explain the best advice you have ever *received* in life. Possibilities might include:
   a. To go to college.
   b. To quit or accept a job.
   c. To steer clear of a particular crowd.
   d. To forgive and forget.
   e. To join or not to join an organization that restricts membership: a sorority or fraternity, country club or athletic club.
   f. To take a risk.

2. Medawar's article contains advice to a young scientist from the viewpoint of a mature scientist. A precise and consistent viewpoint is vital to good writing. In a paragraph or two practice describing "The Perfect Babysitter" from the viewpoint of the baby's parents, the baby's siblings, the babysitter, or the baby itself. Or describe "The Perfect Employer or Employee." You may be serious or humorous.

3. Write a memo to your roommate, suitemates, coworkers, classmates, or fellow volunteers which you sign and in which you ask the culprits to be neater, less neat, less noisy, to cool the borrowing or practical jokes, or. . . . Following Swift's suggestions do some rewriting to make sure you are emphatic yet politic.

4. Sousa supports his ideas by quoting lines from famous poets — T. S. Eliot, Elinor Wylie, Robert Browning. Do a journal entry in which you use an appropriate quotation as your introduction or conclusion.

5. Just for fun decide on a few memorable lines from television, or advertising, or music, or sports that will go down in history as carrying great significance or that will typify the era. Use of of them as an introduction for a proposed paper about the 1980s.

6. David Vogel employs numerous examples as support for his article "America's Management Crisis." Compose a journal entry in which you discuss a general subject, such as conformity, cheating in high school or in college, or white-collar crime, in which you cite specific details and examples to make the abstract concrete.

7. Vogel makes frequent comparisons in his article. Write a journal entry in which you compare and/or contrast styles of music, styles of writing, styles of dress, or styles of walking.

8. Jesse Owens evidenced a change in attitude in "Open Letter to a Young Negro." Using comparison and contrast, discuss your change in attitude toward (a) a fellow worker, (b) a friend, (c) a politician, (d) a teacher, or (e) a TV personality.

9. Practice inductive reasoning by examining one of the generalizations you hold. Now try merely listing — in chronological sequence if possible — those ideas, episodes, observations, conversations, and discoveries that led you to adopt that conclusion/generalization. Then take your list and try writing out a straightforward prose account.

10. Review the graduation requirements at your college in terms of required undergraduate courses. In a journal entry record your approval or disapproval of the requirements. Then write an explanation of your reasoning process and examine those parts that are inductive and those that are deductive.

11. In Garrison Keillor's article, *shy*, of course, is the key word holding the selection together. In addition, you notice other transitional words or phrases: "nevertheless," "perhaps they are right," "however," "a year later," "What is even more terrifying," "And" (it's acceptable as the first word in a sentence. There's no rule against it). Now, photocopy an earlier journal entry or a previously written paper, and revise the transitions in red ink to improve unity and smoothness. Don't forget — you need transitions between sentences as well as between paragraphs.

12. Read the Glossary entry on coherence/connectives and try your hand at the same kind of analysis of several short paragraphs from different articles.

13. In anticipation of genetic engineering's potential, what attributes would you most like to see perpetuated or introduced in the future? This topic should nudge you into some elementary prewriting (listing or mapping) and should expand your experience with classification. (See Sousa, Nilsen, and Shanker.) As an exercise in creativity, do a second entry in a humorous vein in which you fantasize about some future genetic engineering feats.

STYLE

14. After reading Medawar's article, write a paragraph or two in which you offer specific advice to a younger brother or sister about college life. Experiment with *tone* in writing by

    (a) doing one humorous paragraph on advice which you really intend to be taken seriously (recheck Galbraith).

    (b) composing another paragraph in a more serious tone on advice that is enlightening yet not frightening.

15. Write a paragraph or two as part of a *speech* (a) nominating a roommate or a classmate for a dormitory or class office, (b) suggesting your mother for "Mom of the Year," or (c) recommending a friend for a job. Be sure to direct your speech to a *very specific* audience (your classmates, Rotary Club members, office colleagues. See Glossary on Speaking-Writing Differences). With these differences in mind, first, write a paragraph in a somewhat informal manner. (This entry might be more like the Alda speech where he was addressing college graduates.) Then in a second entry rewrite that paragraph in a more formal manner. There will be many occasions in your professional and civic life when you *must* be "formal." It might be well to review William Faulkner's and John F. Kennedy's speeches. Notice the formality Faulkner achieved particularly in paragraph three through: (a) the use of parallel construction, (b) his repetition of words ("He must. . . . He must. . . ."), and his pairing of abstract nouns ("honor and hope," "pride and compassion," and "sacrifice and endurance"). Try to use some of these techniques in your "speeches."

16. Kennedy's speech is replete with parallel construction. Examine particularly the last two paragraphs where each sentence is built on parallel construction. Develop several parallel constructions of your own, perhaps involving your hopes for peace, the cessation of terrorism, the reduction of illiteracy in the United States, an increase in the number of exchange students, improvements in the salaries of women and blacks.

17. Jesse Owens develops a memorable conclusion with three short sentences that emphatically drive home his message. Double-check Owens' final sentences and experiment with a similar conclusion for (a) a paper you have written during the term, (b) an imaginary paper that you are planning to write, or (c) an article in a newspaper or magazine you have been reading.

    _____ isn't _____
    _____ isn't _____
    _____ is never _____

    Try a series in which you use a stronger verb than "is" (such as "forces," "stifles," "demands").

18. Anthony Sousa sprinkles allusions (see Glossary) throughout his writing. Do a journal entry about a favorite book in which you allude (refer) to other books by way of comparison/contrast or example. Notice how such allusions strengthen your content, make you, the writer, appear knowledgeable, and flatter your readers to a certain extent as they recognize the reference.

19. Notice the number of writers who conclude with sentences consisting of ten or fewer words (for example, Medawar, Owens, Gompers, Postman, Skolnick, Wright). Photocopy an article and include it in your journal along with several experimental endings. Try at least one or two endings that are terse and emphatic.

20. Rhetorical questions, when they evoke serious thinking on the part of your reader, can be used as effective introductions (Sweetnam and Nilsen). Within a paper they can help set the stage for an explanation or an analysis (Jordan and Sousa). In a journal entry phrase several provocative rhetorical questions as possible introductions for a paper on overpopulation, surrogate mothers, or nuclear waste disposal. Dull, hackneyed, superficial questions deter readers. Make your questions challenging and thought-provoking. Try using a series of questions for emphasis.

21. In line with Sousa's suggestions, experiment with writing some poetry of your own. Let the lines rhyme or not as the spirit moves you, but do try to capture images that stir your reader's thoughts and emotions.

Suggested Writing Topics

1. Kennedy's speech concludes with a parallel series, each element beginning "I look forward to an America. . . ." What do you look forward to as an American? Write a paper in which you define what you consider to be America's major unfinished task and discuss reasons why you believe it is important to complete this task.

2. This unit encompasses viewpoints of a variety of writers committed to a community of interests. In a well-organized paper, argue for or against any one of the following statements:

    "No man is an island."
    "The things which tie humanity together are greater than the things which pull humanity apart."
    "It is important for young people to have heroes."
    "We come to college to get over our little-mindedness."

3. One fact is clear from these writers: their writing reveals their confidence that they know their subject (i.e., they are masters in their particular fields). All of us are knowledgeable about at least one subject. Maybe it is cars, hunting,

380

photography, selling, sports; perhaps dancing, singing, playing some musical instrument. Write a paper on a subject about which you feel that you are a master of sorts. Explain how something works, what you get out of a particular activity, why it is important to you. Assume you are writing for an audience unfamiliar with the subject.

4. Medawar, Sousa, Swift, Faulkner, Galbraith, Highet, and Kennedy deal with some aspect of the writing process. Our aim in including this selection of writing professionals is to demonstrate to you that writing is a vital part of every educated person's life. Select several ideas from these writers that have struck a responsive chord in you and that you believe will be useful to you in your professional life. Write a paper in which you discuss these ideas and the reasons for your choice.

5. As human beings we respond to language both intellectually and emotionally. And as you can see, in varying degrees all these writers reveal their awareness of this fact. Write a paper in which you discuss those writers who primarily appealed to you intellectually and those who appealed to you emotionally. Or you may discuss one or several who appealed to you because of the way they balanced both approaches. What parts appealed to you intellectually, and how did emotional appeals affect your response to the writing?

6. Write a paper in which you discuss how some of these writers employed humor to make their points. How effective were they? Did humor detract from the seriousness of their subject? Why do we as readers welcome an occasional injection of humor?

7. Both William Faulkner and President John F. Kennedy address themselves to the writer's duty, Faulkner to writers in general and President Kennedy specifically to American writers. Both can be said to make the same kind of appeal—to our humanness—to our duty to our fellow human beings. Discuss how one or several of the writers in this section reveal in their writing that they are aware of such duties outside themselves and in their own way are attempting to help build and sustain the human community.

8. You have samples from three American presidents from three different centuries: Jefferson from the eighteenth, Lincoln from the nineteenth, and Kennedy from the twentieth. Consider their writing, and consider also their ideas. They are writing for three different occasions, but perhaps you may detect some similarities in tone. Is the tone what you would expect of an American statesman? What differences do you find among them? Write a paper in which you analyze your impressions of these three utterances. Avoid trying to cover too much. Narrow your subject down so that you can say something significant about a limited thesis.

9. As the headnote to the Faulkner selection notes, Faulkner spoke at a particularly fearful time and called on writers to return to the old truths of the heart. Many people believe that we are living in fearful times today. Who or what (even an institution) is fulfilling the duties that Faulkner spoke of for Americans today? Where are you learning about the old verities? Write a paper in

which you name a source and discuss some of the values that are being broadcast. Or, your may wish to examine your culture and discuss *what* values are in fact being broadcast. They may be completely antithetical to Faulkner's. Here is an opportunity for you to adopt an ironic tone.

10. After having read Jefferson, Lincoln, and Kennedy, what do you consider the most important qualities necessary for a leader today — in government, in professional life, in the business world, or in campus politics? Narrow your subject down to one area and consider several qualities you consider vital.

11. Several authors in this section use effective figures of speech. As an exercise in creativity, use your imagination to invent new, fresh similes to replace half a dozen of the old, trite similes and half a dozen of the old metaphors. Then invent at least three original similes and three new metaphors of your own.

Trite Similes	Trite Metaphors
a. good as gold	a. dog-tired
b. rich as Croesus	b. bone-dry
c. red as a rose	c. icy glance
d. old as Methuselah	d. snail's pace
e. smooth as silk	e. rat race
f. thirsty as a sponge	f. vicious circle
g. mean as a snake	g. pounding surf
h. tough as nails	h. angry sea
i. clever as a fox	i. threatening clouds
j. slow as molasses	j. raining cats and dogs
k. clean as a whistle	k. tongue-lashing

12. "Life, liberty and the pursuit of happiness" are rights set forth in the Declaration of Independence. In a clear, well-organized essay, discuss your personal definition of the "pursuit of happiness."

Supplemental Readings

POLITICS AND THE
ENGLISH LANGUAGE
George Orwell

*M*ost people who bother with the matter at all would admit that the   1
English language is in a bad way, but it is generally assumed that we cannot by
conscious action do anything about it. Our civilization is decadent and our
language — so the argument runs must inevitably share in the general collapse.
It follows that any struggle against the abuse of language is a sentimental
archaism, like preferring candles to electric light or hansom cabs to aeroplanes.
Underneath this lies the half-conscious belief that language is a natural growth
and not an instrument which we shape for our own purposes.

Now, it is clear that the decline of a language must ultimately have   2
political and economic causes: it is not due simply to the bad influence of this
or that individual writer. But an effect can become a cause, reinforcing the
original cause and producing the same effect in an intensified form, and so on
indefinitely. A man may take to drink because he feels himself to be a failure,
and then fail all the more completely because he drinks. It is rather the same
thing that is happening to the English language. It becomes ugly and inaccurate
because our thoughts are foolish, but the slovenliness of our language makes it
easier for us to have foolish thoughts. The point is that the process is
reversible. Modern English, especially written English, is full of bad habits
which spread by imitation and which can be avoided if one is willing to take
the necessary trouble. If one gets rid of these habits one can think more
clearly, and to think clearly is a necessary first step toward political
regeneration: so that the fight against bad English is not frivolous and is not the
exclusive concern of professional writers. I will come back to this presently,
and I hope that by that time the meaning of what I have said here will have
become clearer. Meanwhile, here are five specimens of the English language as
it is now habitually written.

These five passages have not been picked out because they are especially   3
bad — I could have quoted far worse if I had chosen — but because they
illustrate various of the mental vices from which we now suffer. They are a
little below the average, but are fairly representative samples. I number them so
that I can refer back to them when necessary:

1.   *I am not, indeed, sure whether it is not true to say that the Milton who once
    seemed not unlike a seventeenth-century Shelley had not become, out of an experience even*

more bitter in each year, more alien [sic] *to the founder of that Jesuit sect which nothing could induce him to tolerate.*

PROFESSOR HAROLD LASKI (*Essay in Freedom of Expression*)

2. *Above all, we cannot play ducks and drakes with a native battery of idioms which prescribes such egregious collocations of vocables as the Basic* put up with *for* tolerate *or* put at a loss *for* bewilder.

PROFESSOR LANCELOT HOGBEN (*Interglossa*)

3. *On the one side we have the free personality: by definition it is not neurotic, for it has neither conflict nor dream. Its desires, such as they are, are transparent, for they are just what institutional approval keeps in the forefront of consciousness; another institutional pattern would alter their number and intensity; there is little in them that is natural, irreducible, or culturally dangerous. But on the other side, the social bond itself is nothing but the mutual reflection of these self-secure integrities. Recall the definition of love. Is not this the very picture of a small academic? Where is there a place in this hall of mirrors for either personality or fraternity?*

ESSAY ON PSYCHOLOGY IN POLITICS (*New York*)

4. *All the "best people" from the gentlemen's clubs, and all the frantic fascist captains, united in common hatred of Socialism and bestial horror of the rising tide of the mass revolutionary movement, have turned to acts of provocation, to foul incendiarism, to medieval legends of poisoned wells, to legalize their own destruction of proletarian organizations, and rouse the agitated petty-bourgeoisie to chauvinistic fervor on behalf of the fight against the revolutionary way out of the crisis.*

COMMUNIST PAMPHLET

5. *If a new spirit is to be infused into this old country, there is one thorny and contentious reform which must be tackled, and that is the humanization and galvanization of the B.B.C. Timidity here will bespeak canker and atrophy of the soul. The heart of Britain may be sound and of strong beat, for instance, but the British lion's roar at present is like that of Bottom in Shakespeare's* Midsummer Night's Dream—*as gentle as any sucking dove. A virile new Britain cannot continue indefinitely to be traduced in the eyes or rather ears, of the world by the effete languors of Langham Place, brazenly masquerading as "standard English." When the Voice of Britain is heard at nine o'clock, better far and infinitely less ludicrous to hear aitches honestly dropped than the present priggish, inflated, inhibited, school-ma'amish arch braying of blameless bashful mewing maidens!*

LETTER IN TRIBUNE

Each of these passages has faults of its own, but, quite apart from avoidable ugliness, two qualities are common to all of them. The first is staleness of imagery; the other is lack of precision. The writer either has a meaning and cannot express it, or he inadvertently says something else, or he is almost indifferent as to whether his words mean anything or not. This mixture of vagueness and sheer incompetence is the most marked characteristic of modern English prose, and especially of any kind of political writing. As soon as certain topics are raised, the concrete melts into the abstract and no one seems able to think of turns of speech that are not hackneyed: prose consists less and less of *words* chosen for the sake of their meaning, and more and more of *phrases* tacked together like the sections of a prefabricated henhouse. I list below, with notes and examples, various of the tricks by means of which the work of prose-construction is habitually dodged:

Dying Metaphors

A newly invented metaphor assists thought by evoking a visual image, while on the other hand a metaphor which is technically "dead" (e.g., *iron resolution*) has in effect reverted to being an ordinary word and can generally be used without loss of vividness. But in between these two classes there is a huge dump of worn-out metaphors which have lost all evocative power and are merely used because they save people the trouble of inventing phrases for themselves. Examples are: *Ring the changes on, take up the cudgels for, toe the line, ride roughshod over, stand shoulder to shoulder with, play into the hands of, no axe to grind, grist to the mill, fishing in troubled waters, on the order of the day, Achilles' heel, swan song, hotbed.* Many of these are used without knowledge of their meaning (what is a "rift," for instance?), and incompatible metaphors are frequently mixed, a sure sign that the writer is not interested in what he is saying. Some metaphors now current have been twisted out of their original meaning without those who use them even being aware of the fact. For example, *toe the line* is sometimes written *tow the line.* Another example, is *the hammer and the anvil,* now always used with the implication that the anvil gets the worst of it. In real life it is always the anvil that breaks the hammer, never the other way about: a writer who stopped to think what he was saying would be aware of this, and would avoid perverting the original phrase.

Operators or Verbal False Limbs

These save the trouble of picking out appropriate verbs and nouns, and at the same time pad each sentence with extra syllables which give it an appearance of symmetry. Characteristic phrases are *render inoperative, militate against, make contact with, be subjected to, give rise to, give grounds for, have the effect of, play a leading part (role) in, make itself felt, take effect, exhibit a tendency to, serve the purpose of, etc., etc.* The keynote is the elimination of simple verbs. Instead of being a single word, such as *break, stop, spoil, mend, kill,* a verb becomes a *phrase,* made up of a noun or adjective tacked on to some general-purpose verb

385

such as *prove, serve, form, play, render.* In addition, the passive voice is wherever possible used in preference to the active, and noun constructions are used instead of gerunds *(by examination of* instead of *by examining).* The range of verbs is further cut down by means of the *-ize* and *de-* formations, and the banaĺ statements are given an appearance of profundity by means of the *not un-* formation. Simple conjunctions and prepositions are replaced by such phrases as *with respect to, having regard to, the fact that, by dint of, in view of, in the interests of, on the hypothesis that;* and the ends of sentences are saved from anticlimax by such resounding commonplaces as *greatly to be desired, cannot be left out of account, a development to be expected in the near future, deserving of serious consideration, brought to a satisfactory conclusion,* and so on and so forth.

Pretentious Diction

Words like *phenomenon, element, individual* (as noun), *objective, categorical, effective, virtual, basic, primary, promote, constitute, exhibit, exploit, utilize, eliminate, liquidate,* are used to dress up simple statement and give an air of scientific impartiality to biased judgments. Adjectives like *epoch-making, epic, historic, unforgettable, triumphant, age-old, inevitable, inexorable, veritable,* are used to dignify the sordid processes of international politics, while writing that aims at glorifying war usually takes on an archaic color, its characteristic words being: *realm, throne, chariot, mailed fist, trident, sword, shield, buckler, banner, jackboot, clarion.* Foreign words and expressions such as *cul de sac, ancien régime, deus ex machina, mutatis mutandis, status quo, gleichschaltung, weltanschauung,* are used to give an air of culture and elegance. Except for the useful abbreviations *i.e., e.g., and etc.,* there is no real need for any of the hundreds of foreign phrases now current in English. Bad writers, and especially scientific, political, and sociological writers, are nearly always haunted by the notion that Latin or Greek words are grander than Saxon ones, and unnecessary words like *expedite, ameliorate, predict, extraneous, deracinated, clandestine, subaqueous,* and hundreds of others constantly gain ground from their Anglo-Saxon opposite numbers.[1] The jargon peculiar to Marxist writing (*hyena, hangman, cannibal, petty bourgeois, these gentry, lackey, flunkey, mad dog, White Guard,* etc.) consists largely of words and phrases translated from Russian, German, or French; but the normal way of coining a new word is to use a Latin or Greek root with the appropriate affix and, where necessary, the size

7

---

[1] An interesting illustration of this is the way in which the English flower names which were in use till very recently are being ousted by Greek ones, *snapdragon* becoming *antirrhinum, forget-me-not* becoming *myosotis,* etc. It is hard to see any practical reason for this change of fashion: it is probably due to an instinctive turning away from the more homely word and a vague feeling that the Greek word is scientific. [Orwell's Note]

formation. It is often easier to make up words of this kind (*deregionalize, impermissible, extramarital, nonfragmentary* and so forth) than to think up the English words that will cover one's meaning. The result, in general, is an increase in slovenliness and vagueness.

Meaningless Words

In certain kinds of writing, particularly in art criticism and literary criticism, it is normal to come across long passages which are almost completely lacking in meaning.[2] Words like *romantic, plastic, values, human, dead, sentimental, natural, vitality,* as used in art criticism, are strictly meaningless, in the sense that they not only do not point to any discoverable object, but are hardly ever expected to do so by the reader. When one critic writes, "The outstanding feature of Mr. X's work is its living quality," while another writes, "The immediately striking thing about Mr. X's work is its peculiar deadness," the reader accepts this as a simple difference of opinion. If words like *black* and *white* were involved, instead of the jargon words *dead* and *living,* he would see at once that language was being used in an improper way. Many political words are similarly abused. The word *Facism* has now no meaning except in so far as it signifies "something not desirable." *The words democracy, socialism, freedom, patriotic, realistic, justice,* have each of them several different meanings which cannot be reconciled with one another. In the case of a word like *democracy,* not only is there no agreed definition, but the attempt to make one is resisted from all sides. It is almost universally felt that when we call a country democratic we are praising it: consequently the defenders of every kind of régime claim that it is a democracy, and fear that they might have to stop using the word if it were tied down to any one meaning. Words of this kind are often used in a consciously dishonest way. That is, the person who uses them has his own private definition, but allows his hearer to think he means something quite different. Statements like *Marshal Pétain was a true patriot, The Soviet press is the freest in the world, The Catholic Church is opposed to persecution,* are almost always made with intent to deceive. Other words used in variable meanings, in most cases more or less dishonestly, are: *class, totalitarian, science, progressive, reactionary, bourgeois, equality.*

Now that I have made this catalogue of swindles and perversions, let me give another example of the kind of writing that they lead to. This time it must

8

9

---

[2]Example: "[Alex] Comfort's catholicity of perception and image, strangely Whitmanesque in range, almost the exact opposite in aesthetic compulsion, continues to evoke that trembling atmospheric accumulative hinting at a cruel, an inexorably serene timelessness. . . . Wrey Gardiner scores by aiming at simple bull's-eyes with precision. Only they are not so simple, and through this contented sadness runs more than the surface bittersweet of resignation." (*Poetry Quarterly.*) [Orwell's Note]

of its nature be an imaginary one. I am going to translate a passage of good English into modern English of the worst sort. Here is a well-known verse from *Ecclesiastes*:

> *I returned and saw under the sun, that the race is not to the swift, nor the battle to the strong, neither yet bread to the wise, nor yet riches to men of understanding, not yet favour to men of skill; but time and chance happeneth to them all.*

Here it is in modern English:

> *Objective considerations of contemporary phenomena compels the conclusion that success or failure in competitive activities exhibits no tendency to be commensurate with innate capacity, but that a considerable element of the unpredictable must invariably be taken into account.*

This is a parody, but not a very gross one. Exhibit (3), above, for instance, contains several patches of the same kind of English. It will be seen that I have not made a full translation. The beginning and ending of the sentence follow the original meaning fairly closely, but in the middle the concrete illustrations —race, battle, bread— dissolve into the vague phrase "success or failure in competitive activities." This had to be so, because no modern writer of the kind I am discussing— no one capable of using phrases like "objective consideration of contemporary phenomena" — would ever tabulate his thoughts in that precise and detailed way. The whole tendency of modern prose is away from concreteness. Now analyze these two sentences a little more closely. The first contains forty-nine words but only sixty syllables, and all its words are those of everyday life. The second contains thirty-eight words of ninety syllables: eighteen of its words are from Latin roots, and one from Greek. The first sentence contains six vivid images, and only one phrase ("time and chance") that could be called vague. The second contains not a single fresh, arresting phrase, and in spite of its ninety syllables it gives only a shortened version of the meaning contained in the first. Yet without a doubt it is the second kind of sentence that is gaining ground in modern English. I do not want to exaggerate. This kind of writing is not yet universal, and outcrops of simplicity will occur here and there in the worst-written page. Still, if you or I were told to write a few lines on the uncertainty of human fortunes, we should probably come much nearer to my imaginary sentence than to the one from *Ecclesiastes.*

As I have tried to show, modern writing at its worst does not consist in picking out words for the sake of their meaning and inventing images in order to make the meaning clearer. It consists in gumming together long strips of words which have already been set in order by someone else, and making the results presentable by sheer humbug. The attraction of this way of writing is that it is easy. It is easier—even quicker, once you have the habit—to say *In my opinion it is not an unjustifiable assumption that* than to say *I think*. If you use ready-made phrases, you not only don't have to hunt about for words; you also don't have to bother with the rhythms of your sentences, since these phrases are generally so arranged as to be more or less euphonious. When you are composing in a hurry—when you are dictating to a stenographer, for instance, or making a public speech—it is natural to fall into a pretentious, Latinized style. Tags like *a consideration which we should do well to bear in mind* or *a conclusion to which all of us would readily assent* will save many a sentence from coming down with a bump. By using stale metaphors, similes, and idioms, you save much mental effort, at the cost of leaving your meaning vague, not only for your reader but for yourself. This is the significance of mixed metaphors. The sole aim of a metaphor is to call up a visual image. When these images clash—as in *The Fascist octopus has sung its swan song, the jackboot is thrown into the melting pot*—it can be taken as certain that the writer is not seeing a mental image of the objects he is naming; in other words he is not really thinking. Look again at the examples I gave at the beginning of this essay. Professor Laski (1) uses five negatives in fifty-three words. One of these is superfluous, making nonsense of the whole passage, and in addition there is the slip—*alein* for akin—making further nonsense, and several avoidable pieces of clumsiness which increase the general vagueness. Professor Hogben (2) plays ducks and drakes with a battery which is able to write prescriptions, and, while disapproving of the everyday phrase *put up with*, is unwilling to look *egregious* up in the dictionary and see what it means; (3), if one takes an uncharitable attitude towards it, is simply meaningless: probably one could work out its intended meaning by reading the whole of the article in which it occurs. In (4), the writer knows more or less what he wants to say, but an accumulation of stale phrases chokes him like tea leaves blocking a sink. In (5), words and meaning have almost parted company. People who write in this manner usually have a general emotional meaning—they dislike one thing and want to express solidarity with another—but they are not interested in the detail of what they are saying. A scrupulous writer, in every sentence that he writes, will ask himself at least four questions, thus: What am I trying to say? What words will express it? What image or idiom will make it clearer? Is this image fresh enough to have an effect? And he will probably ask himself two more: Could I put it more shortly? Have I said anything that is avoidably ugly? But you are not obliged to go to all this trouble. You can shirk it by simply throwing your mind open and letting the ready-made phrases come crowding in. They will construct your sentences for your—even think your thoughts for you, to a certain extent—and at need they will perform the important service of partially concealing your meaning even from yourself. It is at this point that the special connection between politics and the debasement of language becomes clear.

In our time it is broadly true that political writing is bad writing. Where it is not true, it will generally be found that the writer is some kind of rebel, expressing his private opinions and not a "party line." Orthodoxy, of whatever color, seems to demand a lifeless, imitative style. The political dialects to be found in pamphlets, leading articles, manifestoes, White Papers and the speeches of undersecretaries do, of course, vary from party to party, but they are all alike in that one almost never finds in them a fresh, vivid, homemade turn of speech. When one watches some tired hack on the platform mechanically repeating the familiar phrases—*bestial atrocities, iron heel, bloodstained tyranny, free peoples of the world, stand shoulder to shoulder*— one often has a curious feeling that one is not watching a live human being but some kind of dummy: a feeling which suddenly becomes stronger at moments when the light catches the speaker's spectacles and turns them into blank discs which seem to have no eyes behind them. And this is not altogether fanciful. A speaker who uses that kind of phraseology has gone some distance toward turning himself into a machine. The appropriate noises are coming out of his larynx, but his brain is not involved as it would be if he were choosing his words for himself. If the speech he is making is one that he is accustomed to make over and over again, he may be almost unconscious of what he is saying, as one is when one utters the responses in church. And this reduced state of consciousness, if not indispensable, is at any rate favorable to political conformity.

In our time, political speech and writing are largely the defense of the indefensible. Things like the continuance of British rule in India, the Russian purges and deportations, the dropping of the atom bombs on Japan, can indeed be defended, but only by arguments which are too brutal for most people to face, and which do not square with the professed aims of political parties. Thus political language has to consist largely of euphemism, question-begging and sheer cloudy vagueness. Defenseless villages are bombarded from the air, the inhabitants driven out into the countryside, the cattle machine-gunned, the huts set on fire with incendiary bullets: this is called *pacification*. Millions of peasants are robbed of their farms and sent trudging along the roads with no more than they can carry: this is called *transfer of population* or *rectification of frontiers*. People are imprisoned for years without trial, or shot in the back of the neck or sent to die of scurvy in Arctic lumber camps: this is called *elimination of unreliable elements*. Such phraseology is needed if one wants to name things without calling up mental pictures of them. Consider for instance some comfortable English professor defending Russian totalitarianism. He cannot say outright, "I believe in killing your opponents when you can get good results by doing so." Probably, therefore, he will say something like this:

"While freely conceding that the Soviet régime exhibits certain features   14
which the humanitarian may be inclined to deplore, we must, I think, agree that a certain curtailment of the right to political opposition is an unavoidable concomitant of transitional periods, and that the rigors which the Russian people have been called upon to undergo have been amply justified in the sphere of concrete achievement."

The inflated style is itself a kind of euphemism. A mass of Latin words   15
falls upon the facts like soft snow, blurring the outlines and covering up all the details. The great enemy of clear language is insincerity. When there is a gap between one's real and one's declared aims, one turns as it were instinctively to long words and exhausted idioms, like a cuttlefish squirting out ink. In our age there is no such thing as "keeping out of politics." All issues are political issues, and politics itself is a mass of lies, evasions, folly, hatred, and schizophrenia. When the general atmosphere is bad, language must suffer. I should expect to find — this is a guess which I have not sufficient knowledge to verify — that the German, Russian and Italian languages have all deteriorated in the last ten or fifteen years, as a result of dictatorship.

But if thought corrupts language, language can also corrupt thought. A bad   16
usage can spread by tradition and imitation, even among people who should and do know better. The debased language that I have been discussing is in some ways very convenient. Phrases like *a not unjustifiable assumption, leaves much to be desired, would serve no good purpose, a consideration which we should do well to bear in mind,* are a continuous temptation, a packet of aspirins always at one's elbow. Look back through this essay, and for certain you will find that I have again and again committed the very faults I am protesting against. By this morning's post I have received a pamphlet dealing with conditions in Germany. The author tells me that he "felt impelled" to write it. I open it at random, and here is almost the first sentence that I see: "[The Allies] have an opportunity not only of achieving a radical transformation of Germany's social and political structure in such a way as to avoid a nationalistic reaction in Germany itself, but at the same time of laying the foundations of a co-operative and unified Europe." You see, he "feels impelled" to write — feels, presumably, that he has something new to say — and yet his words, like calvary horses answering the bugle, group themselves automatically into the familiar dreary pattern. This invasion of one's mind by ready-made phrases (*lay the foundation, achieve a radical transformation*) can only be prevented if one is constantly on guard against them, and every such phrase anaesthetizes a portion of one's brain.

I said earlier that the decadence of our language is probably curable. 17
Those who deny this would argue, if they produced an argument at all, that
language merely reflects existing social conditions, and that we cannot influence
its development by any direct tinkering with words and constructions. So far as
the general tone or spirit of a language goes, this may be true, but it is not true
in detail. Silly words and expressions have often disappeared, not through any
evolutionary process but owing to the conscious action of a minority. Two
recent examples were *explore every avenue* and *leave no stone unturned*, which
were killed by the jeers of a few journalists. There is a long list of flyblown
metaphors which could similarly be got rid of if enough people would interest
themselves in the job; and it should also be possible to laugh the *not un-*
formation out of existence,[3] to reduce the amount of Latin and Greek in the
average sentence, to drive out foreign phrases and strayed scientific words, and,
in general, to make pretentiousness unfashionable. But all these are minor
points. The defense of the English language implies more than this, and
perhaps it is best to start by saying what it does *not* imply.

To begin with it has nothing to do with archaism, with the salvaging of 18
obsolete words and turns of speech, or with the setting up of a "standard
English" which must never be departed from. On the contrary, it is especially
concerned with the scrapping of every word or idiom which has outworn its
usefulness. It has nothing to do with correct grammar and syntax, which are of
no importance so long as one makes one's meaning clear, or with the
avoidance of Americanisms, or with having what is called a "good prose style."
On the other hand it is not concerned with fake simplicity and the attempt to
make written English colloquial. Nor does it even imply in every case preferring
the Saxon word to the Latin one, though it does imply using the fewest and
shortest words that will cover one's meaning. What is above all needed is to let
the meaning choose the word, and not the other way about. In prose, the worst
thing one can do with words is to surrender to them. When you think of a
concrete object, you think wordlessly, and then, if you want to describe the
thing you have been visualizing you probably hunt about till you find the exact
words that seem to fit it. When you think of something abastract you are more
inclined to use words from the start, and unless you make a conscious effort to
prevent it, the existing dialect will come rushing in and do the job for you, at
the expense of blurring or even changing your meaning. Probably it is better to
put off using words as long as possible and get one's meaning as clear as one
can through pictures or sensations. Afterward one can choose — not simply
accept — the phrases that will best cover the meaning, and then switch round

---

[3]One can cure oneself of the *not un-* formation by memorizing this sentence: *A not unblack dog was
chasing a not unsmall rabbit across a not ungreen field.*

and decide what impression one's words are likely to make on another person. This last effort of the mind cuts out all stale or mixed images, all prefabricated phrases, needless repetitions, and humbug and vagueness generally. But one can often be in doubt about the effect of a word or a phrase, and one needs rules that one can rely on when instinct fails. I think the following rules will cover most cases:

(i)   Never use a metaphor, simile, or other figure of speech which you are used to seeing in print.
(ii) Never use a long word where a short one will do.
(iii) If it is possible to cut a word out, always cut it out.
(iv) Never use the passive where you can use the active.
(v)   Never use a foreign phrase, a scientific word, or a jargon word if you can think of an everyday English equivalent.
(vi) Break any of these rules sooner than say anything outright barbarous.

These rules sound elementary, and so they are, but they demand a deep change of attitude in anyone who has grown used to writing in the style now fashionable. One could keep all of them and still write bad English, but one could not write the kind of stuff that I quoted in those five specimens at the beginning of this article.

I have not here been considering the literary use of language, but merely language as an instrument for expressing and not for concealing or preventing thought. Stuart Chase and others have come near to claiming that all abstract words are meaningless, and have used this as a pretext for advocating a kind of political quietism. Since you don't know what Fascism is, how can you struggle against Fascism? One need not swallow such absurdities as this, but one ought to recognize that the present political chaos is connected with the decay of language, and that one can probably bring about some improvement by starting at the verbal end. If you simplify your English, you are freed from the worst follies of orthodoxy. You cannot speak any of the necessary dialects, and when you make a stupid remark its stupidity will be obvious, even to yourself. Political language — and with variations this is true of all political parties, from Conservatives to Anarchists — is designed to make lies sound truthful and murder respectable, and to give an appearance of solidity to pure wind. One cannot change this all in a moment, but one can at least change one's own habits, and from time to time one can even, if one jeers loudly enough, send some worn-out and useless phrases — some *jackboot, Achilles' heel, hotbed, melting pot, acid test, veritable inferno*, or other lump of verbal refuse — into the dustbin where it belongs.

19

THE METHOD
———— OF SCIENTIFIC INVESTIGATION ————
Thomas Henry Huxley

*T*he method of scientific investigation is nothing but the expression of the
necessary mode of working of the human mind. It is simply the mode at which
all phenomena are reasoned about, rendered precise and exact. There is no
more difference, but there is just the same kind of difference, between the
mental operations of a man of science and those of an ordinary person, as there
is between the operations and methods of a baker or of a butcher weighing out
his goods in common scales, and the operations of a chemist in performing a
difficult and complex analysis by means of his balance and finely graduated
weights. It is not that the action of the scales in the one case, and the balance
in the other, differ in the principles of their construction or manner of working;
but the beam of one is set on an infinitely finer axis than the other, and of
course turns by the addition of a much smaller weight.

You will understand this better, perhaps, if I give you some familiar
example. You have all heard it repeated, I dare say, that men of science work
by means of induction and deduction, and that by the help of these operations,
they, in a sort of sense, wring from Nature certain other things, which are
called natural laws, and causes, and that out of these, by some cunning skill of
their own, they build up hypotheses and theories. And it is imagined by many,
that the operations of the common mind can be by no means compared with
these processes, and that they have to be acquired by a sort of special
apprenticeship to the craft. To hear all these large words, you would think that
the mind of a man of science must be constituted differently from that of his
fellow men; but if you will not be frightened by terms, you will discover that
you are quite wrong, and that all these terrible apparatus are being used by
yourselves every day and every hour of your lives.

There is a well-known incident in one of Molière's plays, where the author
makes the hero express unbounded delight on being told that he had been
talking prose during the whole of his life. In the same way, I trust, that you
will take comfort, and be delighted with yourselves, on the discovery that you
have been acting on the principles of inductive and deductive philosophy
during the same period. Probably there is not one here who has not in the
course of the day had occasion to set in motion a complex train of reasoning, of
the very same kind, though differing of course in degree, as that which a
scientific man goes through in tracing the causes of natural phenomena.

A very trivial circumstance will serve to exemplify this. Suppose you go
into a fruiterer's shop, wanting an apple — you take up one, and, on biting it,
you find it is sour; you look at it, and see that that it is hard and green. You
take up another one, and that too is hard, green, and sour. The shopman offers

you a third, but, before biting it, you examine it, and find it is hard and green, and you immediately say that you will not have it, as it must be sour, like those that you have already tried.

Nothing can be more simple than that, you think; but if you will take the trouble to analyse and trace out into its logical elements what has been done by the mind, you will be greatly surprised. In the first place, you have performed the operation of induction. You found that, in two experiences, hardness and greenness in apples went together with sourness. It was so in the first case, and it was confirmed by the second. True, it is a very small basis, but still it is enough to make an induction from; you generalise the facts, and you expect to find sourness in apples where you get hardness and greenness. You found upon that a general law, that all hard and green apples are sour; and that, so far as it goes, is a perfect induction. Well, having got your natural law in this way, when you are offered another apple which you find is hard and green, you say, "All hard and green apples are sour; this apple is hard and green, therefore this apple is sour." That train of reasoning is what logicians call a syllogism, and has all its various parts and terms—its major premiss, its minor premiss, and its conclusion. And, by the help of further reasoning, which, if drawn out, would have to be exhibited in two or three other syllogisms, you arrive at your final determination, "I will not have that apple." So that, you see, you have, in the first place, established a law of induction, and upon that you have founded a deduction, and reasoned out the special conclusion of the particular case. Well now, suppose, having got your law, that at some time afterwards you are discussing the qualities of apples with a friend: you will say to him, "It is a very curious thing, but I find that all hard and green apples are sour!" Your friend says to you, "But how do you know that?" You at once reply, "Oh, because I have tried them over and over again, and have always found them to be so." Well, if we were talking science instead of common sense, we should call that an experimental verification. And, if still opposed, you go further, and say, "I have heard from the people in Somersetshire and Devonshire, where a large number of apples are grown, that they have observed the same thing. It is also found to be the case in Normandy, and in North America. In short, I find it to be the universal experience of mankind wherever attention has been directed to the subject." Whereupon, your friend, unless he is a very unreasonable man, agrees with you, and is convinced that you are quite right in the conclusion you have drawn. He believes, although perhaps he does not know he believes it, that the more extensive verifications are—that the more frequently experiments have been made, and results of the same kind arrived at—that the more varied the conditions under which the same results are attained, the more certain is the ultimate conclusion, and he disputes the question no further. He sees that the

395

experiment has been tried under all sorts of conditions, as to time, place, and people, with the same result; and he says with you, therefore, that the law you have laid down must be a good one, and he must believe it.

In science we do the same thing; the philosopher exercises precisely the same faculties, though in a much more delicate manner. In scientific inquiry it becomes a matter of duty to expose a supposed law to every possible kind of verification, and to take care, moreover, that this is done intentionally, and not left to a mere accident, as in the case of the apples. And in science, as in common life, our confidence in a law is in exact proportion to the absence of variation in the result of our experimental verifications. For instance, if you let go your grasp of an article you may have in your hand, it will immediately fall to the ground. That is a very common verification of one of the best established laws of nature — that of gravitation. The method by which men of science establish the existence of that law is exactly the same as that by which we have established the trivial proposition about the sourness of hard and green apples. But we believe it in such an extensive, thorough, and unhesitating manner because the universal experience of mankind verifies it, and we can verify it ourselves at any time; and that is the strongest possible foundation on which any natural law can rest.

So much, then, by way of proof that the method of establishing laws in science is exactly the same as that pursued in common life. Let us now turn to another matter (though really it is but another phase of the same question), and that is, the method by which, from the relations of certain phenomena, we prove that some stand in the position of causes towards the others.

I want to put the case clearly before you, and I will therefore show you what I mean by another familiar example. I will suppose that one of you, on coming down in the morning to the parlour of your house, finds that a teapot and some spoons which had been left in the room on the previous evening are gone — the window is open, and you observe the mark of a dirty hand on the window frame, and perhaps, in addition to that, you notice the impress of a hobnailed shoe on the gravel outside. All these phenomena have struck your attention instantly, and before two seconds have passed you say, "Oh, somebody has broken open the window, entered the room, and run off with the spoons and the teapot!" That speech is out of your mouth in a moment. And you will probably add, "I know he has; I am quite sure of it!" You mean to say exactly what you know; but in reality you are giving expression to what is, in all essential particulars, an hypothesis. You do not know it at all; it is nothing but an hypothesis rapidly framed in your own mind. And it is an hypothesis founded on a long train of inductions and deductions.

What are those inductions and deductions, and how have you got at this hypothesis? You have observed, in the first place, that the window is open; but

6

7

8

9

by a train of reasoning involving many inductions and deductions, you have probably arrived long before at the general law—and a very good one it is—that windows do not open of themselves; and you therefore conclude that something has opened the window. A second general law that you have arrived at in the same way is, that teapots and spoons do not go out of a window spontaneously, and you are satisfied that, as they are not now where you left them, they have been removed. In the third place, you look at the marks on the window sill, and the shoemarks outside, and you say that in all previous experience the former kind of mark has never been produced by anything else but the hand of a human being; and the same experience shows that no other animal but man at present wears shoes with hobnails in them such as would produce the marks in the gravel. I do not know, even if we could discover any of those "missing links" that are talked about, that they would help us to any other conclusion! At any rate the law which states our present experience is strong enough for my present purpose. You next reach the conclusion that, as these kinds of marks have not been left by any other animal than man, nor are liable to be formed in any other way than by a man's hand and shoe, the marks in question have been formed by a man in that way. You have, further, a general law, founded on observation and experience, and that, too, is, I am sorry to say, a very universal and unimpeachable one—that some men are thieves; and you assume at once from all these premises—and that is what constitutes your hypothesis—that the man who made the marks outside and on the window sill, opened the window, got into the room, and stole your teapot and spoons. You have now arrived at a *vera causa* [real cause]; you have assumed a cause which, it is plain, is competent to produce all the phenomena you have observed. You can explain all these phenomena only by the hypothesis of a thief. But that is a hypothetical conclusion, of the justice of which you have no absolute proof at all; it is only rendered highly probable by a series of inductive and deductive reasonings.

I suppose your first action, assuming that you are a man of ordinary common sense, and that you have established this hypothesis to your own satisfaction, will very likely be to go off for the police, and set them on the track of the burglar, with the view to the recovery of your property. But just as you are starting with this object, some person comes in, and on learning what you are about, says, "My good friend, you are going on a great deal too fast. How do you know that the man who really made the marks took the spoons? It might have been a monkey that took them, and the man may have merely looked in afterwards." You would probably reply, "Well, that is all very well, but you see it is contrary to all experience of the way teapots and spoons are abstracted; so that, at any rate, your hypothesis is less probable than mine." While you are talking the thing over in this way, another friend arrives, one of

10

397

that good kind of people that I was talking of a little while ago. And he might say, "Oh, my dear sir, you are certainly going on a great deal too fast. You are most presumptuous. You admit that all these occurrences took place when you were fast asleep, at a time when you could not possibly have known anything about what was taking place. How do you know that the laws of Nature are not suspended during the night? It may be that there has been some kind of supernatural interference in this case." In point of fact, he declares that your hypothesis is one of which you cannot at all demonstrate the truth, and that you are by no means sure that the laws of Nature are the same when you are asleep as when you are awake.

Well, now, you cannot at the moment answer that kind of reasoning. You feel that your worthy friend has you somewhat at a disadvantage. You will feel perfectly convinced in your own mind, however, that you are quite right, and you say to him, "My good friend, I can only be guided by the natural probabilities of the case, and if you will be kind enough to stand aside and permit me to pass, I will go and fetch the police." Well, we will suppose that your journey is successful, and that by good luck you meet with a policeman; that eventually the burglar is found with your property on his person, and the marks correspond to his hand and to his boots. Probably any jury would consider those facts a very good experimental verification of your hypothesis, touching the cause of the abnormal phenomena observed in your parlour, and would act accordingly.

Now, in this supposititious case, I have taken phenomena of a very common kind, in order that you might see what are the different steps in an ordinary process of reasoning, if you will only take the trouble to analyse it carefully. All the operations I have described, you will see, are involved in the mind of any man of sense in leading him to a conclusion as to the course he should take in order to make good a robbery and punish the offender. I say that you are led, in that case, to your conclusion by exactly the same train of reasoning as that which a man of science pursues when he is endeavouring to discover the origin and laws of the most occult phenomena. The process is, and always must be, the same; and precisely the same mode of reasoning was employed by Newton and Laplace in their endeavours to discover and define the causes of the movements of the heavenly bodies, as you, with your own common sense, would employ to detect a burglar. The only difference is, that the nature of the inquiry being more abstruse, every step has to be most carefully watched, so that there may not be a single crack or flaw in your hypothesis. A flaw or crack in many of the hypotheses of daily life may be of little or no moment as affecting the general correctness of the conclusions at which we may arrive; but, in a scientific inquiry, a fallacy, great or small, is always of importance, and is sure to be in the long run constantly productive of mischievous, if not fatal results.

Do not allow yourselves to be misled by the common notion that an hypothesis is untrustworthy simply because it is an hypothesis. It is often urged, in respect to some scientific conclusion, that, after all, it is only an hypothesis. But what more have we to guide us in nine-tenths of the most important affairs of daily life than hypotheses, and often very ill based ones? So that in science, where the evidence of an hypothesis is subjected to the most rigid examination, we may rightly pursue the same course. You may have hypotheses, and hypotheses. A man may say, if he likes, that the moon is made of green cheese: that is an hypothesis. But another man, who has devoted a great deal of time and attention to the subject, and availed himself of the most powerful telescopes and the results of the observations of others, declares that in his opinion it is probably composed of materials very similar to those of which our own earth is made up: and that is also only an hypothesis. But I need not tell you that there is an enormous difference in the value of the two hypotheses. That one which is based on sound scientific knowledge is sure to have a corresponding value; and that which is a mere hasty random guess is likely to have but little value. Every great step in our progress in discovering causes has been made in exactly the same way as that which I have detailed to you. A person observing the occurrence of certain facts and phenomena asks, naturally enough, what process, what kind of operation known to occur in Nature applied to the particular case, will unravel and explain the mystery? Hence you have the scientific hypothesis; and its value will be proportionate to the care and completeness with which its basis has been tested and verified. It is in these matters as in the commonest affairs of practical life: the guess of the fool will be folly, while the guess of the wise man will contain wisdom. In all cases, you see that the value of the result depends on the patience and faithfulness with which the investigator applied to his hypothesis every possible kind of verification.

A MODEST PROPOSAL

For preventing the children of poor people in Ireland from being a burthen to their parents or country, and for making them beneficial to the public
Jonathan Swift

It is a melancholy object to those who walk through this great town, or travel in the country, when they see the streets, the roads, and cabin doors crowded with beggars of the female sex followed by three, four, or six children, all in rags and importuning every passenger for an alms. These mothers, instead of being able to work for their honest livelihood, are forced to employ all their time in strolling, to beg sustenance for their helpless infants, who, as they grow up, either turn thieves for want of work or leave their dear native country to fight for the Pretender in Spain or sell themselves to the Barbadoes.   1

I think it is agreed by all parties that this prodigious number of children, in the arms or on the backs or at the heels of their mothers and frequently of their fathers, is in the present deplorable state of the kingdom a very great additional grievance, and therefore whoever could find out a fair, cheap, and easy method of making these children sound and useful members of the commonwealth would deserve so well of the public as to have his statue set up for a preserver of the nation.   2

But my intention is very far from being confined to provide only for the children of professed beggars; it is of a much greater extent, and shall take in the whole number of infants at a certain age who are born of parents in effect as little able to support them as those who demand our charity in the streets.   3

As to my own part, having turned my thoughts for many years upon this important subject and maturely weighed the several schemes of other projectors, I have always found them grossly mistaken in their computation. It is true, a child just dropped from its dam may be supported by her milk for a solar year, with little other nourishment, at the most not above the value of two shillings, which the mother may certainly get, or the value in scraps, by her lawful occupation of begging; and it is exactly at one year old that I propose to provide for them in such a manner as, instead of being a charge upon their parents or the parish or wanting food and raiment for the rest of their lives, they shall on the contrary contribute to the feeding, and partly to the clothing, of many thousands.   4

There is likewise another great advantage in my scheme, that it will prevent those voluntary abortions and that horrid practice of women murdering their bastard children, alas! too frequent among us, sacrificing the poor innocent babes, I doubt more to avoid the expense than the shame, which would move tears and pity in the most savage and inhuman breast.   5

The number of souls in this kingdom being usually reckoned one million   6 and a half, of these I calculate there may be about two hundred thousand couple whose wives are breeders, from which number I subtract thirty thousand couple who are able to maintain their own children (although I apprehend there cannot be so many, under the present distresses of the kingdom); but this being granted, there will remain a hundred and seventy thousand breeders. I again subtract fifty thousand for those women who miscarry or whose children die by accident or disease within the year. There only remain a hundred and twenty thousand children of poor parents annually born. The question therefore is how this number shall be reared and provided for, which, as I have already said, under the present situation of affairs is utterly impossible by all the methods hitherto proposed. For we can neither employ them in handicraft or agriculture; we neither build houses (I mean in the country) nor cultivate land; they can very seldom pick up a livelihood by stealing, till they arrive at six years old, except where they are of towardly parts, although I confess they learn the rudiments much earlier, during which time they can, however, be properly looked upon only as probationers; as I have been informed by a principal gentleman in the County of Cavan who protested to me that he never knew above one or two instances under the age of six, even in a part of the kingdom so renowned for the quickest proficiency in that art.

I am assured by our merchants that a boy or a girl before twelve years old 7 is no saleable commodity, and even when they come to this age they will not yield above three pounds or three pounds and half a crown at most on the exchange, which cannot turn to account either to the parents or the kingdom, the charge of nutriment and rags having been at least four times that value.

I shall now, therefore, humbly propose my own thoughts, which I hope 8 will not be liable to the least objection.

I have been assured by a very knowing American of my acquaintance in 9 London that a young, healthy child well nursed is, at a year old, a most delicious, nourishing, and wholesome food, whether stewed, roasted, baked, or boiled; and I make no doubt that it will equally serve in a fricassee or a ragout.

I do therefore humbly offer it to public consideration that of the hundred 10 and twenty thousand children already computed, twenty thousand may be reserved for breed, whereof only one fourth part to be males, which is more than we allow to sheep, black cattle, or swine; and my reason is that these children are seldom the fruits of marriage, a circumstance not much regarded by our savages; therefore one male will be sufficient to serve four females. That the remaining hundred thousand may, at a year old, be offered in sale to the persons of quality and fortune through the kingdom, always advising the mother to let them suck plentifully in the last month, so as to render them plump and fat for a good table. A child will make two dishes at an entertainment for friends; and when the family dines alone, the fore- or hind-quarter will make a reasonable dish, and seasoned with a little pepper or salt, will be very good boiled on the fourth day, especially in winter. I have reckoned, upon a medium, that a child just born will weigh twelve pounds, and in a solar year, if tolerably nursed, will increase to twenty-eight pounds.

I grant this food will be somewhat dear, and therefore very proper for the landlords, who, as they have already devoured most of the parents, seem to have the best title to the children.

Infant's flesh will be in season throughout the year, but more plentifully in March and a little before and after; for we are told by a grave author, an eminent French physician, that fish being a prolific diet, there are more children born in Roman Catholic countries about nine months after Lent than at any other season; therefore, reckoning a year after Lent, the markets will be more glutted than usual, because the number of Popish infants is at least three to one in this kingdom; and therefore it will have one other collateral advantage, by lessening the number of Papists among us. I have already computed the charge of nursing a beggar's child (in which list I reckon all cottagers, laborers, and four fifths of the farmers) to be about two shillings per annum, rags included; and I believe no gentleman would repine to give ten shillings for the carcass of a good fat child, which, as I have said, will make four dishes of excellent nutritive meat, when he has only some particular friend or his own family to dine with him. Thus the squire will learn to be a good landlord and grow popular among his tenants; the mother will have eight shillings net profit and be fit for work till she produces another child.

Those who are more thrifty (as I must confess the times require) may flay the carcass, the skin of which, artificially dressed, will make admirable gloves for ladies and summer boots for fine gentlemen.

As to our city of Dublin, shambles may be appointed for this purpose in the most convenient parts of it; and butchers, we may be assured, will not be wanting, although I rather recommend buying the children alive than dressing them hot from the knife as we do roasting pigs.

A very worthy person, a true lover of his country, and whose virtues I highly esteem, was lately pleased in discoursing on this matter to offer a refinement upon my scheme. He said that many gentlemen of this kingdom having of late destroyed their deer, he conceived that the want of venison might be well supplied by the bodies of young lads and maidens; not exceeding fourteen years of age nor under twelve, so great a number of both sexes in every country being now ready to starve for want of work and service; and these to be disposed of by their parents if alive, or otherwise by their nearest relations. But with due deference to so excellent a friend and so deserving a patriot, I cannot be altogether in his sentiments: for as to the males, my

American acquaintance assured me, from frequent experience, that their flesh was generally tough and lean, like that of our school-boys, by continual exercise, and their taste disagreeable; and to fatten them would not answer the charge. Then as to the females, it would, I think, with humble submission, be a loss to the public, because they would soon become breeders themselves: and besides, it is not improbable that some scrupulous people might be apt to censure such a practice (although indeed very unjustly) as a little bordering upon cruelty, which, I confess, has always been with me the strongest objection against any project, however so well intended.

But in order to justify my friend, he confessed that this expedient was put into his head by the famous Psalmanazar, a native of the island Formosa, who came from thence to London above twenty years ago and in conversation told my friend that in his country, when any young person happened to be put to death, the executioner sold the carcass to persons of quality as a prime dainty and that in his time the body of a plump girl of fifteen, who was crucified for an attempt to poison the emperor, was sold to his Imperial Majesty's prime minister of state and other great mandarins of the court in joints from the gibbet at four hundred crowns. Neither, indeed, can I deny that if the same use were made of several plump young girls in this town who, without one single groat to their fortunes, cannot stir abroad without a chair, and appear at playhouse and assemblies in foreign fineries which they never will pay for, the kingdom would not be the worse. 16

Some persons of a desponding spirit are in great concern about that vast number of poor people who are aged, diseased, or maimed, and I have been desired to employ my thoughts what course may be taken to ease the nation of so grievous an encumbrance. But I am not in the least pain upon the matter, because it is very well known that they are every day dying and rotting by cold, and famine, and filth, and vermin, as fast as can be reasonably expected. And as to the young laborers, they are now in almost as hopeful a condition; they cannot get work and consequently pine away for want of nourishment to a degree that if at any time they are accidentally hired to common labor, they have not strength to perform it; and thus the country and themselves are happily delivered from the evils to come. 17

I have too long digressed and therefore shall return to my subject. I think the advantages by the proposal which I have made are obvious and many, as well as of the highest importance. 18

For first, as I have already observed, it would greatly lessen the number of Papists, with whom we are yearly overrun, being the principal breeders of the nation as well as our most dangerous enemies, and who stay at home on purpose to deliver the kingdom to the Pretender, hoping to take their advantage 19 by the absence of so many good Protestants, who have chosen rather to leave their country than stay at home and pay tithes, against their conscience, to an Episcopal curate.

Secondly, the poorer tenants will have something valuable of their own which by law may be made liable to distress and help to pay their landlord's rent, their corn and cattle being already seized and money a thing unknown.

Thirdly, whereas the maintenance of a hundred thousand children from two years old and upwards cannot be computed at less than ten shillings apiece per annum, the nation's stock will thereby be increased fifty thousand pounds per annum, besides the profit of a new dish introduced to the tables of all gentlemen of fortune in the kingdom who have any refinement in taste. And the money will circulate among ourselves, the goods being entirely of our own growth and manufacture.

Fourthly, the constant breeders, beside the gain of eight shillings sterling per annum by the sale of their children, will be rid of the charge of maintaining them after the first year.

Fifthly, this food would likewise bring great custom to taverns, where the vintners will certainly be so prudent as to procure the best receipts for dressing it to perfection and consequently have their houses frequented by all the fine gentlemen who justly value themselves upon their knowledge in good eating; and a skillful cook who understands how to oblige his guests will contrive to make it as expensive as they please.

Sixthly, this would be a great inducement to marriage, which all wise nations have either encouraged by rewards or enforced by laws and penalties. It would increase the care and tenderness of mothers toward their children when they were sure of a settlement for life to the poor babes, provided in some sort by the public, to their annual profit or expense. We would see an honest emulation among the married women, which of them could bring the fattest child to the market. Men would become as fond of their wives during the time of their pregnancy as they are now of their mares in foal, their cows in calf, or sows when they are ready to farrow, nor offer to beat or kick them (as is too frequent a practice) for fear of a miscarriage.

Many other advantages might be enumerated. For instance, the addition of some thousand carcasses in our exportation of barreled beef; the propagation of swine's flesh and improvement in the art of making good bacon, so much wanted among us by the great destruction of pigs, too frequent at our table, which are no way comparable in taste or magnificence to a well-grown, fat yearling child, which, roasted whole, will make a considerable figure at a lord mayor's feast or any other public entertainment. But this and many others I omit, being studious of brevity.

Supposing that one thousand families in this city would be constant

404

customers for infant's flesh, beside others who might have it at merry-meetings, particularly at weddings and christenings, I compute that Dublin would take off annually about twenty thousand carcasses and the rest of the kingdom (where probably they will be sold somewhat cheaper) the remaining eighty thousand.

I can think of no one objection that will possibly be raised against this 27 proposal unless it should be urged that the number of people will be thereby much lessened in the kingdom. This I freely own, and it was indeed one principal design in offering it to the world. I desire the reader will observe that I calculate my remedy for this one individual kingdom of Ireland and for no other that ever was, is, or I think can ever be, upon earth. Therefore let no man talk to me of other expedients: of taxing our absentees at five shillings a pound; of using neither clothes nor household furniture except what is of our own growth and manufacture; of utterly rejecting the materials and instruments that promote foreign luxury; of curing the expensiveness of pride, vanity, idleness, and gaming in our women; of introducing a vein of parsimony, prudence, and temperance; of learning to love our country, in the want of which we differ even from Laplanders and the inhabitants of Tupinamba; of quitting our animosities and factions, nor acting any longer like the Jews, who were murdering one another at the very moment their city was taken; of being a little cautious not to sell our country and conscience for nothing; of teaching landlords to have at least one degree of mercy toward their tenants; lastly, of putting a spirit of honesty, industry, and skill into our shop-keepers, who, if a resolution could now be taken to buy only our native goods, would immediately unite to cheat and exact upon us in the price, the measure, and the goodness, nor could ever yet be brought to make one fair proposal of just dealing, though often and earnestly invited to it.

Therefore, I repeat, let no man talk to me of these and the like expedients 28 till he has at least some glimpse of hope that there will be ever some hearty and sincere attempt to put them in practice.

But as to myself, having been wearied out for many years with offering 29 vain, idle, visionary thoughts and at length utterly despairing of success, I fortunately fell upon this proposal, which, as it is wholly new, so it has something solid and real, of no expense and little trouble, full in our own power, and whereby we can incur no danger in disobliging England. For this kind of commodity will not bear exportation, the flesh being of too tender a consistence to admit a long continuance in salt, although perhaps I could name a country which would be glad to eat up our whole nation without it.

After all, I am not so violently bent upon my own opinion as to reject any 30 offer proposed by wise men which shall be found equally innocent, cheap, easy, and effectual. But before something of that kind shall be advanced in contradiction to my scheme and offering a better, I desire the author or authors will be pleased maturely to consider two points: first, as things now stand, how they will be able to find food and raiment for a hundred thousand useless mouths and backs; and secondly, there being a round million of creatures in human figure throughout this kingdom whose whole subsistence, put into a common stock, would leave them in debt two millions of pounds sterling, adding those who are beggars by profession to the bulk of farmers, cottagers, and laborers, with the wives and children who are beggars in effect, I desire those politicians who dislike my overture, and may perhaps be so bold as to attempt an answer, that they will first ask the parents of these mortals whether they would not at this day think it a great happiness to have been sold for food at a year old in the manner I prescribe, and thereby have avoided such a perpetual scene of misfortunes as they have since gone through by the oppression of landlords, the impossibility of paying rent without money or trade, the want of common sustenance, with neither house nor clothes to cover them from the inclemencies of the weather, and the most inevitable prospect of entailing the like of greater miseries upon their breed forever.

I profess in the sincerity of my heart that I have not the least personal interest in endeavoring to promote this necessary work, having no other motive than the public good of my country, by advancing our trade, providing for infants, relieving the poor, and giving some pleasure to the rich. I have no children by which I can propose to get a single penny, the youngest being nine years old and my wife past childbearing.

31

CIVIL DISOBEDIENCE
Henry David Thoreau

I heartily accept the motto, "That government is best which governs   1
least;" and I should like to see it acted up to more rapidly and systematically.
Carried out, it finally amounts to this, which also I believe, — "That government
is best which governs not at all;" and when men are prepared for it, that will
be the kind of government which they will have. Government is at best but an
expedient; but most governments are usually, and all governments are
sometimes, inexpedient. The objections which have been brought against a
standing army, and they are many and weighty, and deserve to prevail, may
also at last be brought against a standing government. The standing army is
only an arm of the standing government. The government itself, which is only
the mode which the people have chosen to execute their will, is equally liable to
be abused and perverted before the people can act through it. Witness the
present Mexican war, the work of comparatively a few individuals using the
standing government as their tool; for, in the outset, the people would not have
consented to this measure.

This American government, — what is it but a tradition, though a recent   2
one, endeavoring to transmit itself unimpaired to posterity, but each instant
losing some of its integrity? It has not the vitality and force of a single living
man; for a single man can bend it to his will. It is a sort of wooden gun to the
people themselves. But it is not the less necessary for this; for the people must
have some complicated machinery or other, and hear its din, to satisfy that
idea of government which they have. Governments show thus how successfully
men can be imposed on, even impose on themselves, for their own advantage.
It is excellent, we must all allow. Yet this government never of itself furthered
any enterprise, but by the alacrity with which it got out of its way. *It* does not
keep the country free. *It* does not settle the West. *It* does not educate. The
character inherent in the American people has done all that has been
accomplished; and it would have done somewhat more, if the government had
not sometimes got in its way. For government is an expedient by which men
would fain succeed in letting one another alone; and, as has been said, when it
is most expedient, the governed are most let alone by it. Trade and commerce,
if they were not made of india-rubber, would never manage to bounce over the
obstacles which legislators are continually putting in their way; and, if one
were to judge these men wholly by the effects of their actions and not partly by
their intentions, they would deserve to be classed and punished with those
mischievous persons who put obstructions on the railroads.

But, to speak practically and as a citizen, unlike those who call themselves   3
no-government men, I ask for, not at once no government, but *at once* a better

government. Let every man make known what kind of government would command his respect, and that will be one step toward obtaining it.

After all, the practical reason why, when the power is once in the hands of the people, a majority are permitted, and for a long period continue, to rule is not because they are most likely to be in the right, nor because this seems fairest to the minority, but because they are physically the strongest. But a government in which the majority rule in all cases cannot be based on justice, even as far as men understand it. Can there not be a government in which majorities do not virtually decide right and wrong, but conscience? — in which majorities decide only those questions to which the rule of expediency is applicable? Must the citizen ever for a moment, or in the least degree, resign his conscience to the legislator? Why has every man a conscience, then? I think that we should be men first, and subjects afterward. It is not desirable to cultivate a respect for the law, so much as for the right. The only obligation which I have a right to assume is to do at any time what I think right. It is truly enough said that a corporation has no conscience; but a corporation of conscientous men is a corporation *with* a conscience. Law never made men a whit more just; and, by means of their respect for it, even the well-disposed are daily made the agents of injustice. A common and natural result of an undue respect for law is, that you may see a file of soldiers, colonel, captain, corporal, privates, powder-monkeys, and all, marching in admirable order over hill and dale to the wars, against their wills, ay, against their common sense and consciences, which makes it very steep marching indeed, and produces a palpitation of the heart. They have no doubt that it is a damnable business in which they are concerned; they are all peaceably inclined. Now, what are they? Men at all? or small movable forts and magazines, at the service of some unscrupulous man in power? Visit the Navy-Yard, and behold a marine, such a man as an American government can make, or such as it can make a man with its black arts, — a mere shadow and reminiscence of humanity, a man laid out alive and standing, and already, as one may say, buried under arms with funeral accompaniments, though it may be, —

> "Not a drum was heard, not a funeral note,
> As his corse to the rampart we hurried;
> Not a soldier discharged his farewell shot
> O'er the grave where our hero we buried."

The mass of men serve the state thus, not as men mainly, but as machines, with their bodies. They are the standing army, and the militia, jailers, constables, *posse comitatus*, etc. In most cases there is no free exercise whatever of the judgment or of the moral sense; but they put themselves on a level with wood and earth and stones; and wooden men can perhaps be manufactured that will serve the purpose as well. Such command no more respect than men of straw or a lump of dirt. They have the same sort of worth only as horses and dogs. Yet such as these even are commonly esteemed good citizens. Others — as most legislators, politicians, lawyers, ministers, and office-holders — serve the state chiefly with their heads; and, as they rarely make any moral distinctions, they are as likely to serve the devil, without *intending* it, as God. A very few — as heroes, patriots, martyrs, reformers in the great sense, and *men* — serve the state with their consciences also, and so necessarily resist it for the most part; and they are commonly treated as enemies by it. A wise man will only be useful as a man, and will not submit to be "clay," and "stop a hole to keep the wind away," but leave that office to his dust at least: —

> *"I am too high-born to be propertied,*
> *To be a secondary at control,*
> *Or useful serving-man and instrument*
> *To any sovereign state throughout the world."*

He who gives himself entirely to his fellow-men appears to them useless and selfish; but he who gives himself partially to them is pronounced a benefactor and philanthropist.   6

How does it become a man to behave toward this American government to-day? I answer, that he cannot without disgrace be associated with it. I cannot for an instant recognize that political organization as *my* government which is the *slave's* government also.   7

All men recognize the right of revolution; that is, the right to refuse allegiance to, and to resist, the government, when its tyranny or its inefficiency are great and unendurable. But almost all say that such is not the case now. But such was the case, they think, in the Revolution of '75. If one were to tell me that his was a bad government because it taxed certain foreign commodities brought to its ports, it is most probable that I should not make an ado about it, for I can do without them. All machines have their friction; and possibly this does enough good to counterbalance the evil. At any rate, it is a great evil to make a stir about it. But when the friction comes to have its machine, and oppression and robbery are organized, I say, let us not have such a machine any longer. In other words, when a sixth of the population of a nation which has undertaken to be the refuge of liberty are slaves, and a whole country is unjustly overrun and conquered by a foreign army, and subjected to military law, I think that it is not too soon for honest men to rebel and revolutionize.   8

What makes this duty the more urgent is the fact that the country so overrun is not our own, but ours is the invading army.

Paley, a common authority with many on moral questions, in his chapter on the "Duty of Submission to Civil Government," resolves all civil obligation into expediency; and he proceeds to say that "so long as the interest of the whole society requires it, that is, so long as the established government cannot be resisted or changed without public inconveniency, it is the will of God . . . that the established government be obeyed, — and no longer. This principle being admitted, the justice of every particular case of resistance is reduced to a computation of the quantity of the danger and grievance on the one side, and of the probability and expense of redressing it on the other." Of this, he says, every man shall judge for himself. But Paley appears never to have contemplated those cases to which the rule of expediency does not apply, in which a people, as well as an individual, must do justice, cost what it may. If I have unjustly wrested a plank from a drowning man, I must restore it to him though I drown myself. This, according to Paley, would be inconvenient. But he that would save his life, in such a case, shall lose it. This people must cease to hold slaves, and to make war on Mexico, though it cost them their existence as a people.

In their practice, nations agree with Paley; but does any one think that Massachusetts does exactly what is right at the present crisis?

> *"A drab of state, a cloth-o'-silver slut,*
> *To have her train borne up, and her soul trail in the dirt."*

Practically speaking, the opponents to a reform in Massachusetts are not a hundred thousand politicians at the South, but a hundred thousand merchants and farmers here, who are more interested in commerce and agriculture than they are in humanity, and are not prepared to do justice to the slave and to Mexico, *cost what it may.* I quarrel not with far-off foes, but with those who, near at home, coöperate with, and do the bidding of, those far away, and without whom the latter would be harmless. We are accustomed to say, that the mass of men are unprepared; but improvement is slow, because the few are not materially wiser or better than the many. It is not so important that many should be as good as you, as that there be some absolute goodness somewhere; for that will leaven the whole lump. There are thousands who are *in opinion* opposed to slavery and to the war, who yet in effect do nothing to put an end to them; who, esteeming themselves children of Washington and Franklin, sit down with their hands in their pockets, and say that they know not what to do, and do nothing; who even postpone the question of freedom to the question

410

of free trade, and quietly read the prices-current along with the latest advices from Mexico, after dinner, and, it may be, fall asleep over them both. What is the price-current of an honest man and patriot to-day? They hesitate, and they regret, and sometimes they petition; but they do nothing in earnest and with effect. They will wait, well disposed, for others to remedy the evil, that they may no longer have it to regret. At most, they give only a cheap vote, and a feeble countenance and God-speed, to the right, as it goes by them. There are nine hundred and ninety-nine patrons of virtue to one virtuous man. But it is easier to deal with the real possessor of a thing than with the temporary guardian of it.

All voting is a sort of gaming, like checkers or backgammon, with a slight moral tinge to it, a playing with right and wrong, with moral questions; and betting naturally accompanies it. The character of the voters is not staked. I cast my vote, perchance, as I think right; but I am not vitally concerned that that right should prevail. I am willing to leave it to the majority. Its obligation, therefore, never exceeds that of expediency. Even voting *for the right* is *doing* nothing for it. It is only expressing to men feebly your desire that it should prevail. A wise man will not leave the right to the mercy of chance, nor wish it to prevail through the power of the majority. There is but little virtue in the action of masses of men. When the majority shall at length vote for the abolition of slavery, it will be because they are indifferent to slavery, or because there is but little slavery left to be abolished by their vote. *They* will then be the only slaves. Only *his* vote can hasten the abolition of slavery who asserts his own freedom by his vote.

I hear of a convention to be held at Baltimore, or elsewhere, for the selection of a candidate for the Presidency, made up chiefly of editors, and men who are politicians by profession; but I think, what is it to any independent, intelligent, and respectable man what decision they may come to? Shall we not have the advantage of his wisdom and honesty, nevertheless? Can we not count upon some independent votes? Are there not many individuals in the country who do not attend conventions? But no: I find that respectable man, so called, has immediately drifted from his position, and despairs of his country, when his country has more reason to despair of him. He forthwith adopts one of the candidates thus selected as the only *available* one, thus proving that he is himself *available* for any purposes of the demagogue. His vote is of no more worth than that of any unprincipled foreigner or hireling native, who may have been bought. O for a man who is a *man*, and, as my neighbor says, has a bone in his back which you cannot pass your hand through! Our statistics are at fault: the population has been returned too large. How many *men* are there to a square thousand miles in this country? Hardly one. Does not America offer any inducement for men to settle here? The American has dwindled into an Odd

11

12

Fellow, one who may be known by the development of his organ of gregariousness, and a manifest lack of intellect and cheerful self-reliance; whose first and chief concern, on coming into the world, is to see that the almshouses are in good repair; and, before yet he has lawfully donned the virile garb, to collect a fund for the support of the widows and orphans that may be; who, in short, ventures to live only by the aid of the Mutual Insurance company, which has promised to bury him decently.

It is not a man's duty, as a matter of course, to devote himself to the eradication of any, even the most enormous, wrong; he may still properly have other concerns to engage him; but it is his duty, at least, to wash his hands of it, and, if he gives it no thought longer, not to give it practically his support. If I devote myself to other pursuits and contemplations, I must first see, at least, that I do not pursue them sitting upon another man's shoulders. I must get off him first, that he may pursue his contemplations too. See what gross inconsistency is tolerated. I have heard some of my townsmen say, "I should like to have them order me out to help put down an insurrection of the slaves, or to march to Mexico; — see if I would go;" and yet these very men have each, directly by their allegiance, and so indirectly, at least, by their money, furnished a substitute. The soldier is applauded who refuses to serve in an unjust war by those who do not refuse to sustain the unjust government which makes the war; is applauded by those whose own act and authority he disregards and sets at naught; as if the state were penitent to that degree that it hired one to scourge it while it sinned, but not to that degree that it left off sinning for a moment. Thus, under the name of Order and Civil Government, we are all made at last to pay homage to and support our own meanness. After the first blush of sin comes its indifference; and from immoral it becomes, as it were, unmoral, and not quite unnecessary to that life which we have made.

The broadest and most prevalent error requires the most disinterested virtue to sustain it. The slight reproach to which the virtue of patriotism is commonly liable, the noble are most likely to incur. Those who, while they disapprove of the character and measures of a government, yield to it their allegiance and support are undoubtedly its most conscientious supporters, and so frequently the most serious obstacles to reform. Some are petitioning the State to dissolve the Union, to disregard the requisitions of the President. Why do they not dissolve it themselves, — the union between themselves and the State, — and refuse to pay their quota into its treasury? Do not they stand in the same relation to the State that the State does to the Union? And have not the same reasons prevented the State from resisting the Union which have prevented them from resisting the State?

How can a man be satisfied to entertain an opinion merely, and enjoy *it*? Is there any enjoyment in it, if his opinion is that he is aggrieved? If you are

412

cheated out of a single dollar by your neighbor, you do not rest satisfied with knowing that you are cheated, or with saying that you are cheated, or even with petitioning him to pay you your due; but you take effectual steps at once to obtain the full amount, and see that you are never cheated again. Action from principle, the perception and the performance of right, changes things and relations; it is essentially revolutionary, and does not consist wholly with anything which was. It not only divides States and churches, it divides families; ay, it divides the *individual*, separating the diabolical in him from the divine.

Unjust laws exist: shall we be content to obey them, or shall we endeavor to amend them, and obey them until we have succeeded, or shall we transgress them at once? Men generally, under such a government as this, think that they ought to wait until they have persuaded the majority to alter them. They think that, if they should resist, the remedy would be worse than the evil. But it is the fault of the government itself that the remedy *is* worse than the evil. *It* makes it worse. Why is it not more apt to anticipate and provide for reform? Why does it not cherish its wise minority? Why does it cry and resist before it is hurt? Why does it not encourage its citizens to be on the alert to point out its faults, and *do* better than it would have them? Why does it always crucify Christ, and excommunicate Copernicus and Luther, and pronounce Washington and Franklin rebels? 16

One would think, that a deliberate and practical denial of its authority was the only offence never contemplated by government; else, why has it not assigned its definite, its suitable and proportionate, penalty? If a man who has no property refuses but once to earn nine shillings for the State, he is put in prison for a period unlimited by any law that I know, and determined only by the discretion of those who placed him there; but if he should steal ninety times nine shillings from the State, he is soon permitted to go at large again. 17

If the injustice is part of the necessary friction of the machine of government, let it go, let it go: perchance it will wear smooth, — certainly the machine will wear out. If the injustice has a spring, or a pulley, or a rope, or a crank, exclusively for itself, then perhaps you may consider whether the remedy will not be worse than the evil; but if it is of such a nature that it requires you to be the agent of injustice to another, then, I say, break the law. Let your life be a counter-friction to stop the machine. What I have to do is see, at any rate, that I do not lend myself to the wrong which I condemn. 18

As for adopting the ways which the State has provided for remedying the evil, I know not of such ways. They take too much time, and a man's life will be gone. I have other affairs to attend to. I came into this world, not chiefly to make this a good place to live in, but to live in it, be it good or bad. A man has not everything to do, but something; and because he cannot do *everything*, it is not necessary that he should do *something* wrong. It is not my business to be 19 petitioning the Governor or the Legislature any more than it is theirs to petition me; and if they should not hear my petition, what should I do then? But in this case the State has provided no way: its very Constitution is the evil. This may seem to be harsh and stubborn and unconciliatory; but it is to treat with the utmost kindnes and consideration the only spirit that can appreciate or deserves it. So is all change for the better, like birth and death, which convulse the body.

I do not hesitate to say, that those who call themselves Abolitionists should at once effectually withdraw their support, both in person and property, from the government of Massachusetts, and not wait till they constitute a majority of one, before they suffer the right to prevail through them. I think that it is enough if they have God on their side, without waiting for that other one. Moreover, any man more right than his neighbors constitutes a majority of one already.

I meet this American government, or its representative, the State government, directly, and face to face, once a year — no more — in the person of its tax-gatherer; this is the only mode in which a man situated as I am necessarily meets it; and it then says distinctly, Recognize me; and the simplest, the most effectual, and, in the present posture of affairs, the indispensablest mode of treating with it on this head, of expressing your little satisfaction with and love for it, is to deny it then. My civil neighbor, the tax-gatherer, is the very man I have to deal with, — for it is, after all, with men and not with parchment that I quarrel, — and he has voluntarily chosen to be an agent of the government. How shall he ever know well what he is and does as an officer of the government, or as a man, until he is obliged to consider whether he shall treat me, his neighbor, for whom he has respect, as a neighbor and well-disposed man, or as a maniac and disturber of the peace, and see if he can get over this obstruction to his neighborliness without a ruder and more impetuous thought or speech corresponding with his action. I know this well, that if one thousand, if one hundred, if ten men whom I could name, — if ten *honest* men only, — ay, if *one* HONEST man, in this State of Massachusetts, *ceasing to hold slaves*, were actually to withdraw from this copartnership, and be locked up in the county jail therefor, it would be the abolition of slavery in America. For it matters not how small the beginning may seem to be: what is once well done is done forever. But we love better to talk about it: that we say is our mission. Reform keeps many scores of newspapers in its service, but not one man. If my esteemed neighbor, the State's ambassador, who will devote his days to the settlement of the question of human rights in the Council Chamber, instead of being threatened with the prisons of Carolina, were to sit down the prisoner of Massachusetts, that State which is so anxious to foist the sin of slavery upon her sister, — though at present she can discover only an act of inhospitality to be the ground of a quarrel with her, — the Legislature would not wholly waive the subject the following winter.

Under a government which imprisons any unjustly, the true place for a just man is also a prison. The proper place to-day, the only place which Massachusetts has provided for her freer and less desponding spirits, is in her prisons, to be put out and locked out of the State by her own act, as they have already put themselves out by their principles. It is there that the fugitive slave, and the Mexican prisoner on parole, and the Indian come to plead the wrongs of his race should find them; on that separate, but more free and honorable, ground, where the State places those who are not *with* her, but *against* her, — the only house in a slave State in which a free man can abide with honor. If any think that their influence would be lost there, and their voices no longer afflict the ear of the State, that they would not be as an enemy within its walls, they do not know by how much truth is stronger than error, nor how much more eloquently and effectively he can combat injustice who has experienced a little in his own person. Cast your whole vote, not a strip of paper merely, but your whole influence. A minority is powerless while it conforms to the majority; it is not even a minority then; but it is irresistible when it clogs by its whole weight. If the alternative is to keep all just men in prison, or give up war and slavery, the State will not hesitate which to choose. If a thousand men were not to pay their taxbills this year, that would not be a violent and bloody measure, as it would be to pay them, and enable the State to commit violence and shed innocent blood. This is, in fact, the definition of a peaceable revolution, if any such is possible. If the tax-gatherer, or any other public officer, asks me, as one has done, "But what shall I do?" my answer is, "If you really wish to do anything, resign your office." When the subject has refused allegiance, and the officer has resigned his office, then the revolution is accomplished. But even suppose blood should flow. Is there not a sort of blood shed when the conscience is wounded? Through this wound a man's real manhood and immortality flow out, and he bleeds to an everlasting death. I see this blood flowing now.

I have contemplated the imprisonment of the offender, rather than the seizure of his goods, — though both will serve the same purpose, — because they who assert the purest right, and consequently are most dangerous to a corrupt State, commonly have not spent much time in accumulating property. To such the State renders comparatively small service, and a slight tax is wont to appear exorbitant, particularly if they are obliged to earn it by special labor with their hands. If there were one who lived wholly without the use of money, the State itself would hesitate to demand it of him. But the rich man — not to make any invidious comparison — is always sold to the institution which makes him rich. Absolutely speaking, the more money, the less virtue; for

22

23

415

money comes between a man and his objects, and obtains them for him; and it was certainly no great virtue to obtain it. It puts to rest many questions which he would otherwise be taxed to answer; while the only new question which it puts is the hard but superfluous one, how to spend it. Thus his moral ground is taken from under his feet. The opportunities of living are diminished in proportion as what are called the "means" are increased. The best thing a man can do for his culture when he is rich is to endeavor to carry out those schemes which he entertained when he was poor. Christ answered the Herodians according to their condition. "Show me the tribute-money," said he; — and one took a penny out of his pocket; — if you use money which has the image of Caesar on it, and which he has made current and valuable, that is, *if you are men of the State*, and gladly enjoy the advantages of Caesar's government, then pay him back some of his own when he demands it. "Render therefore to Caesar that which is Caesar's, and to God those things which are God's," — leaving them no wiser than before as to which was which; for they did not wish to know.

When I converse with the freest of my neighbors, I perceive that, whatever they may say about the magnitude and seriousness of the question, and their regard for the public tranquility, the long and the short of the matter is, that they cannot spare the protection of the existing government, and they dread the consequences to their property and families of disobedience to it. For my own part, I should not like to think that I ever rely on the protection of the State. But, if I deny the authority of the State when it presents its tax-bill, it will soon take and waste all my property, and so harass me and my children without end. This is hard. This makes it impossible for a man to live honestly, and at the same time comfortably, in outward respects. It will not be worth the while to accumulate property; that would be sure to go again. You must hire or squat somewhere, and raise but a small crop, and eat that soon. You must live within yourself, and depend upon yourself always tucked up and ready for a start, and not have many affairs. A man may grow rich in Turkey even, if he will be in all respects a good subject of the Turkish government. Confucius said: "If a state is governed by the principles of reason, poverty and misery are subjects of shame; if a state is not governed by the principles of reason, riches and honors are the subjects of shame." No: until I want the protection of Massachusetts to be extended to me in some distant Southern port, where my liberty is endangered, or until I am bent solely on building up an estate at home by peaceful enterprise, I can afford to refuse allegiance to Massachusetts, and her right to my property and life. It costs me less in every sense to incur the penalty of disobedience to the State than it would to obey. I should feel as if I were worth less in that case.

Some years ago, the State met me in behalf of the Church, and commanded me to pay a certain sum toward the support of a clergyman whose preaching my father attended, but never I myself. "Pay," it said, "or be locked up in the jail." I declined to pay. But, unfortunately, another man saw fit to pay it. I did not see why the schoolmaster should be taxed to support the priest, and not the priest the schoolmaster; for I was not the State's schoolmaster, but I supported myself by voluntary subscription. I did not see why the lyceum should not present its tax-bill, and have the State to back its demand, as well as the Church. However, at the request of the selectmen, I condescended to make some such statement as this in writing: — "Know all men by these presents, that I, Henry Thoreau, do not wish to be regarded as a member of any incorporated society which I have not joined." This I gave to the town clerk; and he has it. The State, having thus learned that I did not wish to be regarded as a member of that church, has never made a like demand on me since; though it said that it must adhere to its original presumption that time. If I had known how to name them, I should then have signed off in detail from all the societies which I never signed on to; but I did not know where to find a complete list.

I have paid no poll-tax for six years. I was put into a jail once on this account, for one night; and, as I stood considering the walls of solid stone, two or three feet thick, the door of wood and iron, a foot thick, and the iron grating which strained the light, I could not help being struck with the foolishness of that institution which treated me as if I were mere flesh and blood and bones, to be locked up. I wondered that it should have concluded at length that this was the best use it could put me to, and had never thought to avail itself of my services in some way. I saw that, if there was a wall of stone between me and my townsmen, there was a still more difficult one to climb or break through before they could get to be as free as I was. I did not for a moment feel confined, and the walls seemed a great waste of stone and mortar. I felt as if I alone of all my townsmen had paid my tax. They plainly did not know how to treat me, but behaved like persons who are underbred. In every threat and in every compliment there was a blunder; for they thought that my chief desire was to stand the other side of that stone wall. I could not but smile to see how industriously they locked the door on my meditations, which followed them out again without let or hindrance, and *they* were really all that was dangerous. As they could not reach me, they had resolved to punish my body; just as boys, if they cannot come at some person against whom they have a spite, will abuse his dog. I saw that the State was half-witted, that it was timid as a lone woman with her silver spoons, and that it did not know its friends from its foes, and I lost all my remaining respect for it, and pitied it. 26

Thus the State never intentionally confronts a man's sense, intellectual or moral, but only his body, his senses. It is not armed with superior wit or 27

417

honesty, but with superior physical strength. I was not born to be forced. I will breathe after my own fashion. Let us see who is the strongest. What force has a multitude? They only can force me who obey a higher law than I. They force me to become like themselves. I do not hear of *men* being *forced* to live this way or that by masses of men. What sort of life were that to live? When I meet a government which says to me, "Your money or your life," why should I be in haste to give it my money? It may be in a great strait, and not know what to do: I cannot help that. It must help itself; do as I do. It is not worth the while to snivel about it. I am not responsible for the successful working of the machinery of society. I am not the son of the engineer. I perceive that, when an acorn and a chestnut fall side by side, the one does not remain inert to make way for the other, but both obey their own laws, and spring and grow and flourish as best they can, till one, perchance, overshadows and destroys the other. If a plant cannot live according to its nature, it dies; and so a man.

The night in prison was novel and interesting enough. The prisoners in their short-sleeves were enjoying a chat and the evening air in the doorway, when I entered. But the jailer said, "Come, boys, it is time to lock up;" and so they dispersed, and I heard the sound of their steps returning into the hollow apartments. My roommate was introduced to me by the jailer as "a first-rate fellow and a clever man." When the door was locked, he showed me where to hang my hat, and how he managed matters there. The rooms were whitewashed once a month; and this one, at least, was the whitest, most simply furnished, and probably the neatest apartment in the town. He naturally wanted to know where I came from, and what brought me there; and, when I had told him, I asked him in my turn how he came there, presuming him to be an honest man, of course; and, as the world goes, I believe he was. "Why," said he, "they accuse me of burning a barn; but I never did it." As near as I could discover, he had probably gone to bed in a barn when drunk, and smoked his pipe there; and so a barn was burnt. He had the reputation of being a clever man, had been there some three months waiting for his trial to come on, and would have to wait as much longer; but he was quite domesticated and contented, since he got his board for nothing, and thought that he was well treated.

He occupied one window, and I the other; and I saw that if one stayed there long, his principal business would be to look out the window. I had soon read all the tracts that were left there, and examined where former prisoners had broken out, and where a grate had been sawed off, and heard the history of the various occupants of that room; for I found that even here there was a history and a gossip which never circulated beyond the walls of the jail. Probably this is the only house in the town where verses are composed, which are afterward printed in a circular form, but not published. I was shown quite a long list of verses which were composed by some young men who had been detected in an attempt to escape, who avenged themselves by singing them.

I pumped my fellow-prisoner as dry as I could, for fear I should never see him again; but at length he showed me which was my bed, and left me to blow out the lamp. 30

It was like traveling into a far country, such as I had never expected to behold, to lie there for one night. It seemed to me that I never had heard the town clock strike before, nor the evening sounds of the village; for we slept with the windows open, which were inside the grating. It was to see my native village in the light of the Middle Ages, and our Concord was turned into a Rhine stream, and visions of knights and castles passed before me. They were the voices of old burghers that I heard in the streets. I was an involuntary spectator and auditor of whatever was done and said in the kitchen of the adjacent village inn, — a wholly new and rare experience to me. It was a closer view of my native town. I was fairly inside of it. I never had seen its institutions before. This is one of its peculiar institutions; for it is a shire town. I began to comprehend what its inhabitants were about. 31

In the morning, our breakfasts were put through the hole in the door, in small oblong-square tin pans, made to fit, and holding a pint of chocolate, with brown bread, and an iron spoon. When they called for the vessels again, I was green enough to return what bread I had left; but my comrade seized it, and said that I should lay that up for lunch or dinner. Soon after he was let out to work at haying in a neighboring field, whither he went every day, and would not be back till noon; so he bade me good-day, saying that he doubted if he should see me again. 32

When I came out of prison, — for some one interfered, and paid that tax, — I did not perceive that great changes had taken place on the common, such as he observed who went in a youth and emerged a tottering and gray-headed man; and yet a change had to my eyes come over the scene, — the town, and State, and country, — greater than any that mere time could effect. I saw yet more distinctly the State in which I lived. I saw to what extent the people among whom I lived could be trusted as good neighbors and friends; that their friendship was for summer weather only; that they did not greatly propose to do right; that they were a distinct race from me by their prejudices and superstitions, as the Chinamen and Malays are; that in their sacrifices to humanity they ran no risks, not even to their property; that after all they were not so noble but they treated the thief as he had treated them, and hoped, by a certain outward observance and a few prayers, and by walking in a particular straight though useless path from time to time, to save their souls. This may be to judge my neighbors harshly; for I believe that many of them are not aware that they have such an institution as the jail in their village. 33

It was formerly the custom in our village, when a poor debtor came out of 34 jail, for his acquaintances to salute him, looking through their fingers, which were crossed to represent the grating of a jail window, "How do ye do?" My neighbors did not thus salute me, but first looked at me, and then at one another, as if I had returned from a long journey. I was put into jail as I was going to the shoemaker's to get a shoe which was mended. When I was let out the next morning, I proceeded to finish my errand, and, having put on my mended shoe, joined a huckleberry party, who were impatient to put themselves under my conduct; and in half an hour, — for the horse was soon tackled, — was in the midst of a huckleberry field, on one of our highest hills, two miles off, and then the State was nowhere to be seen.

This is the whole history of "My Prisons."

I have never declined paying the highway tax, because I am as desirous of being a good neighbor as I am of being a bad subject; and as for supporting schools, I am doing my part to educate my fellow-countrymen now. It is for no particular item in the tax-bill that I refuse to pay it. I simply wish to refuse allegiance to the State, to withdraw and stand aloof from its effectually. I do not care to trace the course of my dollar, if I could, till it buys a man or a musket to shoot one with, — the dollar is innocent, — but I am concerned to trace the effects of my allegiance. In fact, I quietly declare war with the State, after my fashion, though I will still make what use and get what advantage of her I can, as is usual in such cases.

If others pay the tax which is demanded of me, from a sympathy with the State, they do but what they have already done in their own case, or rather they abet injustice to a greater extent than the State requires. If they pay the tax from a mistaken interest in the individual taxed, to save his property, or prevent his going to jail, it is because they have not considered wisely how far they let their private feelings interfere with the public good.

This, then, is my position at present. But one cannot be too much on his guard in such a case, lest his action be biased by obstinacy or an undue regard for the opinions of men. Let him see that he does only what belongs to himself and to the hour.

I think sometimes, Why, this people mean well, they are only ignorant; they would do better if they knew how; why give your neighbors this pain to treat you as they are not inclined to? But I think again, This is no reason why I should do as they do, or permit others to suffer much greater pain of a different kind. Again, I sometimes say to myself, When many millions of men, without heat, without ill will, without personal feeling of any kind, demand of you a few shillings only, without the possibility, such is their constitution, of retracting or altering their present demand, and without the possibility, on your side, of appeal to any other millions, why expose yourself to this overwhelming brute force? You do not resist cold and hunger, the winds and

the waves, thus obstinately; you quietly submit to a thousand similar
necessities. You do not put your head into the fire. But just in proportion as I
regard this as not wholly a brute force, but partly a human force, and consider
that I have relations to those millions as to so many millions of men, and not of
mere brute or inanimate things, I see that appeal is possible, first and
instantaneously, from them to the Maker of them, and, secondly, from them to
themselves. But if I put my head deliberately into the fire, there is no appeal to
fire or to the Maker of fire, and I have only myself to blame. If I could convince
myself that I have any right to be satisfied with men as they are, and to treat
them accordingly, and not according, in some respects, to my requisitions and
expectations of what they and I ought to be, then, like a good Mussulman and
fatalist, I should endeavor to be satisfied with things as they are, and say it is
the will of God. And, above all, there is this difference between resisting this
and a purely brute or natural force, that I can resist this with some effect; but I
cannot expect, like Orpheus, to change the nature of the rocks and trees and
beasts.

I do not wish to quarrel with any man or nation. I do not wish to split   40
hairs, to make fine distinctions, or set myself up as better than my neighbors. I
seek rather, I may say, even an excuse for conforming to the laws of the land. I
am but too ready to conform to them. Indeed, I have reason to suspect myself
on this head; and each year, as the tax-gatherer comes round, I find myself
disposed to review the acts and position of the general and State governments,
and the spirit of the people, to discover a pretext for conformity.

> "We must affect our country as our parents,
>   And if at any time we alienate
>   Our love or industry from doing it honor,
>   We must respect effects and teach the soul
>   Matter of conscience and religion,
>   And not desire of rule or benefit."

I believe that the State will soon be able to take all my work of this sort out of
my hands, and then I shall be no better a patriot than my fellow-countrymen.
Seen from a lower point of view, the Constitution, with all its faults, is very
good; the law and the courts are very respectable; even this State and this
American government are, in many respects, very admirable, and rare things,
to be thankful for, such as a great many have described them; but seen from a
point of view a little higher, they are what I have described them; seen from a
higher still, and the highest, who shall say what they are, or that they are
worth looking at or thinking of at all?

However, the government does not concern me much, and I shall bestow the fewest possible thoughts on it. It is not many moments that I live under a government, even in this world. If a man is thought-free, fancy-free, imagination-free, that which *is not* never for a long time appearing *to be* to him, unwise rulers or reformers cannot fatally interrupt him.

I know that most men think differently from myself; but those whose lives are by profession devoted to the study of these or kindred subjects content me as little as any. Statesmen and legislators, standing so completely within the institution, never distinctly and nakedly behold it. They speak of moving society, but have no resting-place without it. They may be men of a certain experience and discrimination, and have no doubt invented ingenious and even useful systems, for which we sincerely thank them; but all their wit and usefulness lie within certain not very wide limits. They are wont to forget that the world is not governed by policy and expediency. Webster never goes behind government, and so cannot speak with authority about it. His words are wisdom to those legislators who contemplate no essential reform in the existing government; but for thinkers, and those who legislate for all time, he never once glances at the subject. I know of those whose serene and wise speculations on this theme would soon reveal the limits of his mind's range and hospitality. Yet, compared with the cheap professions of most reformers, and the still cheaper wisdom and eloquence of politicians in general, his are almost the only sensible and valuable words, and we thank Heaven for him. Comparatively, he is always strong, original, and, above all, practical. Still, his quality is not wisdom, but prudence. The lawyer's truth is not Truth, but consistency or a consistent expediency. Truth is always in harmony with herself, and is not concerned chiefly to reveal the justice that may consist with wrong-doing. He well deserves to be called, as he has been called, the Defender of the Constitution. There are really no blows to be given by him but defensive ones. He is not a leader, but a follower. His leaders are the men of '87. "I have never made an effort," he says, "and never propose to make an effort; I have never countenanced an effort, and never mean to countenance an effort, to disturb the arrangement as originally made, by which the various States came into the Union." Still thinking of the sanction which the Constitution gives to slavery, he says, "Because it was a part of the original compact, — let it stand." Notwithstanding his special acuteness and ability, he is unable to take a fact out of its merely political relations, and behold it as it lies absolutely to be disposed of by the intelligent, — what, for instance, it behooves a man to do here in America to-day with regard to slavery, — but ventures, or is driven, to make some such desperate answer as the following, while professing to speak absolutely, and as a private man, — from which what new and singular code of

422

social duties might be inferred? "The manner," says he, "in which the governments of those States where slavery exists are to regulate it is for their own consideration, under their responsibility to their constituents, to the general laws of propriety, humanity, and justice, and to God. Associations formed elsewhere, springing from a feeling of humanity, or any other cause, have nothing whatever to do with it. They have never received any encouragement from me, and they never will."

They who know of no purer sources of truth, who have traced up its   43
stream no higher, stand, and wisely stand, by the Bible and the Constitution, and drink at it there with reverence and humility; but they who behold where it comes trickling into this lake or that pool, gird up their loins once more, and continue their pilgrimage toward its fountain-head.

No man with a genius for legislation has appeared in America. They are   44
rare in the history of the world. There are orators, politicians, and eloquent men, by the thousand; but the speaker has not yet opened his mouth to speak who is capable of settling the much vexed questions of the day. We love eloquence for its own sake, and not for any truth which it may utter, or any heroism it may inspire. Our legislators have not yet learned the comparative value of free trade and of freedom, of union, and of rectitude, to a nation. They have no genius or talent for comparatively humble questions of taxation and finance, commerce and manufactures and agriculture. If we were left solely to the wordy wit of legislators in Congress for our guidance, uncorrected by the seasonable experience and the effectual complaints of the people, America would not long retain her rank among the nations. For eighteen hundred years, though perchance I have no right to say it, the New Testament has been written; yet where is the legislator who has wisdom and practical talent enough to avail himself of the light which it sheds on the science of legislation?

The authority of government, even such as I am willing to submit to, — for   45
I will cheerfully obey those who know and can do better than I, and in many things even those who neither know nor can do so well, — is still an impure one: to be strictly just, it must have the sanction and consent of the governed. It can have no pure right over my person and property but what I concede to it. The progress from an absolute to a limited monarchy, from a limited monarchy to a democracy, is a progress toward a true respect for the individual. Even the Chinese philosopher was wise enough to regard the individual as the basis of the empire. Is a democracy, such as we know it, the last improvement possible in government? Is it not possible to take a step further towards recognizing and organizing the rights of man? There will never be a really free and enlightened State until the State comes to recognize the individual as a higher and independent power, from which all its own power and authority are

derived, and treats him accordingly. I please myself with imagining a State at last which can afford to be just to all men, and to treat the individual with respect as a neighbor; which even would not think it inconsistent with its own repose if a few were to live aloof from it, not meddling with it, nor embraced by it, who fulfilled all the duties of neighbors and fellow-men. A State which bore this kind of fruit, and suffered it to drop off as fast as it ripened, would prepare the way for a still more perfect and glorious State, which also I have imagined, but not yet anywhere seen.
1847

PROFESSIONS FOR WOMEN
Virginia Woolf

When your secretary invited me to come here, she told me that your Society is concerned with the employment of women and she suggested that I might tell you something about my own professional experiences. It is true I am a woman; it is true I am employed; but what professional experiences have I had? It is difficult to say. My profession is literature; and in that profession there are fewer experiences for women than in any other, with the exception of the stage — fewer, I mean, that are peculiar to women. For the road was cut many years ago — by Fanny Burney, by Aphra Behn, by Harriet Martineau, by Jane Austen, by George Eliot — many famous women, and many more unknown and forgotten, have been before me, making the path smooth, and regulating my steps. Thus, when I came to write, there were very few material obstacles in my way. Writing was a reputable and harmless occupation. The family peace was not broken by the scratching of a pen. No demand was made upon the family purse. For ten and sixpence one can buy paper enough to write all the plays of Shakespeare — if one has a mind that way. Pianos and models, Paris, Vienna and Berlin, masters and mistresses, are not needed by a writer. The cheapness of writing is, of course, the reason why women have succeeded as writers before they have succeeded in the other professions.

But to tell you my story — it is a simple one. You have only got to figure to yourselves a girl in a bedroom with a pen in her hand. She had only to move that pen from left to right — from ten o'clock to one. Then it occurred to her to do what is simple and cheap enough for all — to slip a few of those pages into an envelope, fix a penny stamp in the corner, and drop the envelope into the red box at the corner. It was thus that I became a journalist; and my effort was rewarded on the first day of the following month — a very glorious day it was for me — by a letter from an editor containing a cheque for one pound ten shillings and sixpence. But to show you how little I deserve to be called a professional woman, how little I know of the struggles and difficulties of such lives, I have to admit that instead of spending that sum upon bread and butter, rent, shoes and stockings, or butcher's bills, I went out and bought a cat — a beautiful cat, a Persian cat, which very soon involved me in bitter disputes with my neighbours.

What could be easier than to write articles and to buy Persian cats with the profits? But wait a moment. Articles have to be about something. Mine, I seem to remember, was about a novel by a famous man. And while I was writing this review, I discovered that if I were going to review books I should need to do battle with a certain phantom. And the phantom was a woman, and when I came to know her better I called her after the heroine of a famous poem, The Angel in the House. It was she who used to come between me and

1

2

3

425

my paper when I was writing reviews. It was she who bothered me and wasted my time and so tormented me that at last I killed her. You who come of a younger and happier generation may not have heard of her — you may not know what I mean by the Angel in the House. I will describe her as shortly as I can. She was intensely sympathetic. She was immensely charming. She was utterly unselfish. She excelled in the difficult arts of family life. She sacrificed herself daily. If there was a chicken, she took the leg; if there was a draught she sat in it — in short she was so constituted that she never had a mind or a wish of her own, but preferred to sympathize always with the minds and wishes of others. Above all — I need not say it — she was pure. Her purity was supposed to be her chief beauty — her blushes, her great grace. In those days — the last of Queen Victoria — every house had its Angel. And when I came to write I encountered her with the very first words. The shadow of her wings fell on my page; I heard the rustling of her skirts in the room. Directly, that is to say, I took my pen in hand to review that novel by a famous man, she slipped behind me and whispered: "My dear, you are a young woman. You are writing about a book that has been written by a man. Be sympathetic; be tender; flatter; deceive; use all the arts and wiles of our sex. Never let anybody guess that you have a mind of your own. Above all, be pure." And she made as if to guide my pen. I now record the one act for which I take some credit to myself, though the credit rightly belongs to some excellent ancestors of mine who left me a certain sum of money — shall we say five hundred pounds a year? — so that it was not necessary for me to depend solely on charm for my living. I turned upon her and caught her by the throat. I did my best to kill her. My excuse, if I were to be had up in a court of law, would be that I acted in self-defence. Had I not killed her she would have killed me. She would have plucked the heart out of my writing. For, as I found, directly I put pen to paper, you cannot review even a novel without having a mind of your own, without expressing what you think to be the truth about human relations, morality, sex. And all these questions, according to the Angel in the House, cannot be dealt with freely and openly by women; they must charm, they must conciliate, they must — to put it bluntly — tell lies if they are to succeed. Thus, whenever I felt the shadow of her wing or the radiance of her halo upon my page, I took up the inkpot and flung it at her. She died hard. Her fictitious nature was of great assistance to her. It is far harder to kill a phantom than a reality. She was always creeping back when I thought I had despatched her. Though I flatter myself that I killed her in the end, the struggle was severe; it took much time that had better have been spent upon learning Greek grammar; or in roaming the world in search of adventures. But it was a real experience; it was an experience that was bound to befall all women writers at that time. Killing the Angel in the House was part of the occupation of a woman writer.

But to continue my story. The Angel was dead; what then remained? You   4
may say that what remained was a simple and common object—a young
woman in a bedroom with an inkpot. In other words, now that she had rid
herself of falsehood, that young woman had only to be herself. Ah, but what is
"herself"? I mean, what is a woman? I assure you, I do not know. I do not
believe that you know. I do not believe that anybody can know until she has
expressed herself in all the arts and professions open to human skill. That
indeed is one of the reasons why I have come here—out of respect for you,
who are in process of showing us by your experiments what a woman is, who
are in process of providing us, by your failures and successes, with that
extremely important piece of information.

But to continue the story of my professional experiences. I made one   5
pound ten and six by my first review; and I bought a Persian cat with the
proceeds. Then I grew ambitious. A Persian cat is all very well, I said; but a
Persian cat is not enough. I must have a motor car. And it was thus that I
became a novelist—for it is a very strange thing that people will give you a
motor car if you will tell them a story. It is a still stranger thing that there is
nothing so delightful in the world as telling stories. It is far pleasanter than
writing reviews of famous novels. And yet, if I am to obey your secretary and
tell you my professional experiences as a novelist, I must tell you about a very
strange experience that befell me as a novelist. And to understand it you must
try first to imagine a novelist's state of mind. I hope I am not giving away
professional secrets if I say that a novelist's chief desire is to be as unconscious
as possible. He has to induce in himself a state of perpetual lethargy. He wants
life to proceed with the utmost quiet and regularity. He wants to see the same
faces, to read the same books, to do the same things day after day, month after
month, while he is writing, so that nothing may break the illusion in which he
is living—so that nothing may disturb or disquiet the mysterious nosings
about, feelings round, darts, dashes and sudden discoveries of that very shy
and illusive spirit, the imagination. I suspect that this state is the same both for
men and women. Be that as it may, I want you to imagine me writing a novel
in a state of trance. I want you to figure to youselves a girl sitting with a pen in
her hand, which for minutes, and indeed for hours, she never dips into the
inkpot. The image that comes to my mind when I think of this girl is the image
of a fisherman lying sunk in dreams on the verge of a deep lake with a rod held
out over the water. She was letting her imagination sweep unchecked round
every rock and cranny of the world that lies submerged in the depths of our
unconscious being. Now came the experience, the experience that I believe to
be far commoner with women writers than with men. The line raced through
the girl's fingers. Her imagination had rushed away. It had sought the pools,
the depths, the dark places where the largest fish slumber. And then there was

a smash. There was an explosion. There was foam and confusion. The imagination had dashed itself against something hard. The girl was roused from her dream. She was indeed in a state of the most acute and difficult distress. To speak without figure she had thought of something, something about the body, about the passions which it was unfitting for her as a woman to say. Men, her reason told her, would be shocked. The consciousness of what men will say of a woman who speaks the truth about her passions had roused her from her artist's state of unconsciousness. She could write no more. The trance was over. Her imagination could work no longer. This I believe to be a very common experience with women writers—they are impeded by the extreme conventionality of the other sex. For though men sensibly allow themselves great freedom in these respects, I doubt that they realize or can control the extreme severity with which they condemn such freedom in women.

These then were two very genuine experiences of my own. These were two of the adventures of my professional life. The first—killing the Angel in the House—I think I solved. She died. But the second, telling the truth about my own experiences as a body, I do not think I solved. I doubt that any woman has solved it yet. The obstacles against her are still immensely powerful—and yet they are very difficult to define. Outwardly, what is simpler than to write books? Outwardly, what obstacles are there for a woman rather than for a man? Inwardly, I think, the case is very different; she has still many ghosts to fight, many prejudices to overcome. Indeed it will be a long time still, I think, before a woman can sit down to write a book without finding a phantom to be slain, a rock to be dashed against. And if this is so in literature, the freest of all professions for women, how is it in the new professions which you are now for the first time entering?

Those are the questions that I should like, had I time, to ask you. And indeed, if I have laid stress upon these professional experiences of mine, it is because I believe that they are, though in different forms, yours also. Even when the path is nominally open—when there is nothing to prevent a woman from being a doctor, a lawyer, a civil servant—there are many phantoms and obstacles, as I believe, looming in her way. To discuss and define them is I think of great value and importance; for thus only can the labour be shared, the difficulties be solved. But besides this, it is necessary also to discuss the ends and the aims for which we are fighting, for which we are doing battle with these formidible obstacles. Those aims cannot be taken for granted; they must be perpetually questioned and examined. The whole position, as I see it—here in this hall surrounded by women practising for the first time in history I know not how many different professions—is one of extraordinary interest and importance. You have won rooms of your own in the house hitherto exclusively owned by men. You are able, though not without great labour and effort, to pay the rent. You are earning your five hundred pounds a year. But this freedom is only a beginning; the room is your own, but it is still bare. It has to be furnished; it has to be decorated; it has to be shared. How are you going to furnish it, how are you going to decorate it? With whom are you going to share it, and upon what terms? These, I think are questions of the utmost importance and interest. For the first time in history you are able to ask them; for the first time you are able to decide for yourselves what the answers should be. Willingly would I stay and discuss those questions and answers—but not tonight. My time is up; and I must cease.

Brief Overview of the Writing Process

We wish we could offer you a neat, step-by-step formula for fast, easy composition. Unfortunately, there is no magic formula. Extensive research in composition and the testimony of professional writers provide convincing evidence that most effective writing is the product of a complex process that plays few favorites. It indiscriminately demands effort, patience, and commitment from every writer, novice and veteran alike.

Not only is writing a slow, exacting process for most writers, but even the process itself varies from writer to writer. The following overview of the writing process, therefore, is merely a bare-bones, highly condensed summary of the ways some writers go about writing. It describes a process that you must adapt to your own abilities and sensibilities. For conventional college students, this survey can serve as a review or a resource; for students who are some years removed from previous writing courses, it can function as a refresher course. The suggestions included here are simply choices: ways to get started, to develop theses, or to devise introductions and conclusions. We have deliberately made this review brief so that you will take the time to study the parenthetical references to the Glossary and to specific selections that illustrate ideas in the text. Observing writing techniques and strategies in the context of whole essays, you will find, can be far more helpful than studying isolated examples.

AN OVERVIEW

Let's assume, for example, that you are confronted with a writing assignment: a paper required for a college composition or history class or perhaps a report in connection with your work. Although there are as many different ways to write as there are writers, the composition process generally involves:

PREWRITING: thinking, planning, researching, inventing ideas
WRITING: producing a rough draft
REWRITING: revising, reorganizing, eliminating, polishing, to achieve maximum effect

Actually, there is considerable overlapping of these areas. Throughout the process you are discovering and inventing ideas, experimenting with ideas, words, sentences, and paragraphs, and revising them for effective presentation. Often the assignment, the time limits, or the inspiration of the moment will determine your particular process.

PREWRITING

Where do you begin? What do you write about? Where do you get ideas? If just getting started presents a problem, then try one of the following techniques as a way to warm up and generate ideas. Experiment with several of these activities at different times and under different circumstances.

Freewriting: Devote ten minutes to simply writing anything that comes to mind. Don't stop for punctuation, word choice, or organization. If you are unable to think of anything to say, repeat the same phrases again and again. Simply "run" with words. (For example, see the prewriting in the Potter selection at the end of this section.)

Brainstorming: List all the ideas you can think of associated with a particular topic. No need to worry about order or appropriateness—organization will come later.

Mapping: Write a possible subject in the center of a blank page and then brainstorm or free associate for any ideas, words, or phrases that come to mind. As you work jot down these thoughts at random about the page, and when you have finished, try to "map" or connect any relationships you discover. Use circles and arrows to indicate relationships between your randomly noted words, questions, images, or figures as you attempt to discover a topic and potential supporting material. This procedure can also help you eliminate irrelevant material.

Free Association: Jot down abstract (nonspecific) words about a possible subject such as "love," "duty," "virtue," in one column, and in another column freely associate ideas or antonyms (opposites), perhaps even sight, sound, smell, taste, and touch impressions that these words call to mind. Or try making a specific association or example of each abstract word you have listed.

Questioning: Bombard a possible subject with questions to help focus on a new aspect or a special insight. Use the journalist's Five W's and How (see Glossary) to identify and explore a subject. (This can help later in developing opening paragraphs.)

Other Sources of Ideas:

Reading and Researching: Consult your bookshelves or visit the library for additional material about a subject that interests you. Read the work of good essayists to help get you in the mood to write.

Journal Keeping: Keep a journal (see Glossary for the definitions of journal versus diary) of ideas, experiences, reactions to personal, campus, national, or world events, quotations, new vocabulary words, interesting figures of speech. All these can provide a wealth of ideas to write about.

Sounding Out Friends: Bounce ideas off your roommate or a fellow worker to get their reactions.

Although these techniques do not necessarily guarantee success, they are some of the many methods successful writers employ whenever writer's block sets in.

Discovering A Thesis

Once you have something down on paper, go over it to see if you can associate any ideas. Do any of your listings suggest a possible controlling idea? Is there a pattern in your work? Is there an insight that will make your reader think, react, or perhaps recall a personal experience that emphasizes your point? Can you group ideas to strengthen an observation? Can you put an umbrella over several related ideas?

Underline, cross out, draw arrows, and then proceed to focus, regroup, limit, and you may come up with a working thesis, an idea that can serve as a tentative starting point. Your real thesis (a concise assertion about a topic — see Glossary) may not emerge until you are well along in the writing process itself, for as you write, as you limit and revise, you discover the essence of what you really want to say (see Swift, Unit III).

Determining Audience and Purpose

Two major considerations as you shape your thesis will be your audience and your purpose. Will your potential readers be your classmates, your professor, your employer, the everyday reader? Consider the age, sex, educational level, interests, hobbies or prejudices of your audience. Then gear the tone (see Glossary), word choice, style, and development to that specific audience. A paper on "Drugs," for example, would have an entirely different emphasis for an audience of physicians, pharmacists, chemists, or teenagers. (Contrast the informality of Alda and Hoffman in Unit II, addressing college audiences, with the formality of Lincoln in Unit III, speaking on a most somber occasion.)

At the outset, decide whether your primary purpose is to entertain, inform, or persuade your reader. Eventually you need to determine how you want your readers to react (smile, reminisce, become informed, modify their behavior, change their attitudes, see new dimensions to a subject, consider alternatives, take a certain prescribed action). Only then will your writing take on real direction and focus.

Choosing The Best Thesis

Try to design a challenging thesis: choose a subject that makes your reader think. Give your thesis an "edge," that is, an argumentative slant. Present your material in a slightly different light or from a somewhat different perspective. For example, Morrow, in Unit II, traces historical prejudices toward work and then asks his readers to examine their relationship to their own work. In Unit III, Eiseley, an anthropologist, writes about an unforgettable experience while on a scientific expedition.

Usually it takes considerable time to devise a thesis. Now and then, if you're lucky, you may come up with an idea for a specific thesis in the early stages. More often, however, you probably will not settle on your specific thesis until well into the writing process. If you are like most writers, you will rethink and revise your thesis numerous times.

Imagine for a moment you are writing a paper about the educational aspects of television. As you work you might consider these possible theses:

1. Television can sometimes be educational.
2. Television is unquestionably the most powerful medium for educating students.
3. How can television be educational?
4. Television should supplement rather than supplant classroom education.
5. Although prolonged, indiscriminate television viewing may adversely affect a student's creativity and values, at its best, selective television viewing (of documentaries, news programs, dramatizations of the classics) can add an exciting dimension to classroom education.

In examining these sentences as possible theses, you would no doubt discard the first four statements. The first states an established fact that would leave little to prove. The second is a bit too dogmatic and would be difficult to prove without an extensive comparison of other media and considerable research. The third is a

434

question and not a positive statement about the topic. (The answer to the question, however, might well become part of your thesis.) The fourth is too vague and general. In time, after considering your audience and purpose (and frequently only after several drafts) you might eventually come up with the more workable, specific fifth choice.

Stating and Positioning Theses

Although a sound thesis is vital to good writing, not all writing contains a specifically stated thesis sentence. In some cases the thesis is formally written out, often as the last sentence in the opening paragraph. In other writing, the thesis is only implied. (The McGowan selection, in Unit II, positions the thesis in the opening paragraphs and restates it in the conclusion. Compare this effort with the Hoppock essay, in which the thesis is merely implied.) Here again, there is no single correct way to write. The important consideration, however, is to have some central controlling idea — stated or implied — giving direction and coherence to your writing.

Discovering An Organization

As you become more involved with your writing, one of your primary concerns will be how to organize your material in the clearest, most convincing arrangement. Keep in mind that almost any writer with self-discipline and commitment can produce a well-constructed paper by

1. Capturing the reader's attention in the first few sentences.
2. Presenting a challenging thesis.
3. Continuing with a clear, logical development (in some cases making the first sentence of each new paragraph a topic sentence — a summary of that paragraph and related to the thesis — see Glossary).
4. Concluding by emphasizing the main ideas.

Some instructors suggest that you follow this basic structure; others, however, will allow much greater flexibility in writing as long as you do not sacrifice clarity. As you write more papers, you will undoubtedly be encouraged to try other options. Again, we stress, there is no infallible recipe for writing — only guidelines and suggestions. The one final pragmatic test for writing is: do you effectively communicate?

For some writers organizing a paper means an elaborate sentence outline. For most writers, however, scratch outlines, brief lists of ideas, several key sentences, or five or six comprehensive words representing whole ideas serve the purpose.

Planning Introductions

In preparing to write and as you write, map out some tentative categories for beginning, middle, and end — the introduction, body, and conclusion. Although the introduction and conclusion will not become primary concerns until you are well along in the process, keep looking for possibilities as you work.

Good introductions are designed to entice readers to continue reading and to orient them in time and place (possibly through the Journalist's Five W's and How — see Glossary and McGowan, Unit II). Furthermore, they hint at what is to follow by their tone (see Glossary) and content. Keeping your subject, audience, and purpose in mind, you might consider introducing your subject by

1. Providing *important* background material for the reader.
2. Defining any *necessary* terms.
3. Using a quotation, a question, an anecdote, a metaphor, an analyogy.
4. Citing statistics or authority.
5. Depicting an unusual happening.
6. Referring to a current or an historical event.
7. Using dialogue.
8. Introducing color and vitality with a vivid illustration.
9. Dramatizing the situation.
10. Employing a conciliatory approach.

The writers in this text, you will observe, are as diverse in their introductions as they are in their styles. For example, Arthur Ashe (Unit II) uses his thesis as his opening sentence, while George Will (Unit II) begins by comparing characteristics of his subject (Ray Kroc, the originator of McDonald's) to three of the company's most famous products. Jane Brody starts off with the confession of a distraught bulimic. William Swanson (Unit II), whose subject is letter writing, appropriately opens with a letter, which provides the framework for his article. A startling quotation and shocking statistics are used by Jesse Owens (Unit III) and William McGowan (Unit II) in their attempts to gain the reader's attention.

Developing Conclusions

The drafting of the conclusion will come much later in the process, but sometimes, even in prewriting, you may come upon an idea for the perfect conclusion. Conclusions, of course, should hammer home your message, perhaps even repeating it in different words, in a final attempt to convince or persuade your reader. Effective conclusions tie up loose ends, round out the analysis, give the reader a feeling of completion, and, if possible, provide a sense of climax, thus making your idea memorable. Experienced writers avoid introducing new ideas in the conclusion. If it is a good idea, it should more appropriately be in the body of the paper.

For a sampling of the variety of conclusions offered by the writers in this book, start by examining Lance Morrow's (Unit II) optimistic conclusion in which he moves from the specific to the general, bridging the "work connection" between the individual and the wider world. Both Rachel Carson and Neil Postman

(Unit III) round out their articles with summary quotations. Lewis Thomas caps off his essay on nurses with a clear, direct summary of his attitude toward nurses — an enthusiastic tribute to the entire nursing profession. The subtle touch of humor in John Galbraith's conclusion is very much in keeping with the light tone of his entire article. A conclusion tying in a famous singer and a popular movie is very effective, as demonstrated by William McGowan. Arlene Skolnick concludes with a succinct four-word prediction.

Supporting Ideas

First, as a basic premise, consider all of your writing to be more or less persuasive. That is, approach your writing with the intent of convincing your reader of the truth of your thesis. By recognizing that your reader needs to be persuaded and by marshaling relevant evidence (convincing facts, statistics, examples, testimony) to that end, you prove your thesis. Your writing thus becomes more than just vague ramblings about a subject. For example, instead of merely commenting on values in abstract terms, Alan Alda (Unit II) pyramids examples and specific detail in an effort to *persuade* his listeners to live their lives in the light of their real priorities. Carson (Unit III) employs data from scientific research. Ashe (Unit II) uses statistics, examples, and experience. Both Medawar and Galbraith (Unit III) draw examples from wide personal experience. Martin Luther King's (Unit III) appeals to authority.

Often, supporting materials can come from your own personal experience and prior knowledge about a subject. Other times you need to research a topic by going to the library, interviewing an authority, or visiting an organization's headquarters.

How then do you go about ordering your evidence in the most effective manner? Just as lawyers look over the evidence before determining their strategies — both logical and emotional — they will use to win over the judge or jury to their cause, so you, too, will examine your material and experiment with various techniques to communicate your ideas.

You have dozens of options. You may decide to use one or more of the following: description, narration, examples, definition, classification, comparison or contrast, analogy, cause and effect, process, or argumentation. (Take a minute to review the brief descriptions of these methods of development in the Rhetorical Index.) Rarely, of course, would you ever decide in the early stages of writing to develop your subject by one specific method. Methods of development are not something you arbitrarily impose on your writing. Rather, these methods constitute choices, which grow out of your data and purpose. Only infrequently does one method serve as the basis for a whole essay; most writers use a combination of methods.

Note, for instance, in this text how McGowan (Unit II) uses statistics, specific example, cause and effect, description, argumentation, and testimony to emphasize his concern over the growing problem of illiteracy in America. Hoppock (Unit

II) uses description, statistics, examples, cause and effect, and classification as some of his methods in pointing up the problems of alcoholism. This combination of methods of development is clearly evident in every reading in this text.

WRITING

Although you have already been engaged in writing (freewriting, making notes, listing ideas), the process becomes more concentrated as you undertake a rough draft. (Of course, some writers *start* here.) As you write, work quickly without deliberating over mechanics, spelling, word choice, or sentence variety. Cross out, write over, leave blanks, circle parts to change later, but get words down on paper. *Now* the process of rewriting starts, and you need to repress that fatal urge to go back over what you have written and merely correct the spelling and mechanics. The rough draft is the beginning. The real work comes in the successive drafts of the rewriting process. (Some writers, of course, approach writing differently and insist on perfecting their work word by word and sentence by sentence.)

REWRITING

Many student writers, in the crush of weekly assignments, make a few cursory changes in their first rough drafts and turn them in, believing they have truly revised their papers. For most writers, however, thorough revision is one of·the most crucial aspects of writing. The commitment to and quality of the rewriting process is usually what distinguishes good writing from poor writing. Even professional writers spend many hours reworking their material. (In fact, many of them put in regular eight-hour sessions at their typewriters — rewriting, restructuring, adding, or eliminating ideas — and consider it a successful day if they have produced 500 words that satisfy them.) Ernest Hemingway, for example, rewrote the ending of *A Farewll to Arms* thirty-nine times "to get it right."

The process of revising ("re-seeing") involves fundamental reworking rather than "merely correcting." It will require a careful review of your thesis to make sure that it is challenging and that you do not stray from your subject. You will need to thoroughly evaluate your supporting data to be sure they are sufficient and convincing.

Developing Paragraphs and Transitions

Some instructors will urge you to use the topic sentence (the controlling idea of a paragraph — see Glossary) as the first sentence of each paragraph (see Swanson and McGowan, Unit II). Others will allow you considerable freedom as long as the paragraph itself is unified and fully developed. Paragraph length, of course, can vary from five or six sentences to a dozen or more sentences, all of which amplify the topic sentence.

Paragraphs generally, though not always, introduce a new idea. Some writers, however, may take several paragraphs to exapnd on one single point. Paragraphs can also serve as transitions, or as visual relief from a rather long paragraph. In any

438

case, all paragraphs should relate to the thesis and be tied to other paragraphs by transitional words, phrases, and sentences.

Transitions provide important landmarks in leading your reader from one word, sentence, paragraph, or idea to the next. (See Glossary on coherence and connectives.) The effective use of pronouns (*he, they, it*), adverbs (*therefore, however, nevertheless*), conjunctions (*and, but, for*), as well as other transitional words and phrases, give unity and coherence to your writing. (See Unit III, Carson and Galbraith's effective use of transitions.) Too little attention to transitions makes for choppy, confusing writing.

Peer Editing

All writers need feedback for their work. Even professional writers get feedback from fans, editors, literary critics, bookstore sales. If class meetings are too brief to allow time for peer editing, make up your own out-of-class group in which you critically evaluate each other's papers. Get your roommate or a colleague at work to read your work. Solicit valid, constructive criticism. Look skeptically at the vague, general comments of "Yeah, that's nice," or "OK, it looks good," which tell you little about how to improve your writing. Ask your readers to describe or summarize what each paragraph says. That way they don't have to "judge," and confusing passages are quickly identified. Conscientiously taking your turn as editor also pays dividends; in helping a classmate, you profit as well by sharpening your editing ability — a talent that can increase your marketability after college.

You're wise to ask for suggestions early, rather than fifteen minutes before the paper is due, when it is too late to make substantial revisions. Seek assistance from your instructors and seriously study their criticism of earlier papers. After all, their primary purpose is to help you to improve. And do take advantage of the Writing Centers that most colleges have established to provide additional writing help for any interested student. Also, don't forget to read your paper aloud to make sure it sounds "right."

Polishing

As you proceed to polish your work, liven up your writing by devoting special attention to style (see Glossary). Try to do the following:

Add Impact: Find concrete words to replace abstract words (see Glossary), and work in some figures of speech (similes, metaphors, analogies — see Glossary). Delete every word, phrase, or sentence that does not advance your thesis or is unnecssary (See Galbraith and Medawar, Unit III).

Check for Precision: Use specific detail (see Swanson, Unit II), and incisive, exact word choice to make each commonplace experience unique. Use strong verbs: replace inactive verbs such as *is, are, were* with vital, active verbs. Search for the precise verb (or adjective or noun) that expresses a whole idea.

Spark Reader Interest: Vary sentence lengths, combining some long sentences with short ones for emphasis. Vary a repetitive subject, verb, object order (see Glossary on inversion). Begin some sentences with modifiers. Use a noun clause as a subject or complement; compound the subject, verb or complement.

Subordinate less important ideas in a sentence in order to highlight your main idea (see Glossary).

Let writing techniques that are exemplified in this text work for you. Parallel construction can be one of your greatest assets (see Glossary). Not only is it "correct" sentence structure, but it also serves to emphasize and underscore what you are saying; in addition it is pleasing to the ear (see Lincoln, Unit III, and balanced parallelism and antithesis in Glossary). Allusions also can be very effective (Olsen, Unit I; Swanson, Unit II; Galbraith, Unit III).

Now your final task is to proofread your work meticulously to eliminate errors in mechanics. Typos and misspellings denote carelessness in writing, in thinking, and in research.

Actually, good writers are probably never completely satisfied with their finished product. But they usually know when it is "right." True, writing is a long, often frustrating process, but the same glow of self-confidence that one gains from a successful performance on the athletic field or on an auditorium stage can be your reward for the patience, effort, and persistence that you have put into your writing. Writing well means more than just a grade in college. It makes you a more interesting person. It is your latchkey to promotion, commendation, job insurance, success, and, most important of all, self-knowledge.

BRIEF NOTES ON RESEARCH

Although "scholarly" research writing involves a rather elaborate process of library work, interviews, surveys, or laboratory work, and very careful, specialized documentation (citation of the original source of the material), the library itself can open up a whole new world of fascinating information. There's something innately challenging about extensive reading on a subject that truly interests you, discovering information new to you and to most of your friends, developing an interest or a specialty of your own, and sharing that exciting information with others through writing about it. Many of the readings in this book beg you to investigate them further — in the library, in interviews with members of the faculty, or in surveys of your peers.

For example, the Postman selection may prompt you to undertake a research paper about the ways in which Americans' TV viewing habits are being reflected in their culture and values. Using the Skolnick article as a start, you might want to write an investigative paper about the breakdown of the nuclear family in America. Journals are garnering considerable attention these days, and after reading Hoffman and Swanson in Unit II, you may want to check into the wealth of materials in your library or city or state archives. There you'll discover scores of diaries and letters written by pioneers, explorers, presidents, scientists, soldiers, or even college students of the 1880s and 1890s (sometimes in the original handwriting).

Where does the researcher start in a library? For college papers the material found in *encyclopedias* is usually much too general; however, encyclopedia articles often include bibliographies that could be very helpful. No doubt you have used the *card catalog* in high school and already know it indexes books by author, title, and subject. You also are probably familiar with *Readers' Guide to Periodical Literature* and have used it as a reference to articles in popular magazines that have been indexed according to subject and, now and then, by author. The *New York Times Index* is a reference for articles in that newspaper. However, more specialized and scholarly articles will be found in *Social Science Index, Humanities Index, Book Review Digest* (where you must know the publication date and look at that particular volume in order to locate a review), *Psychological Abstracts, Business Periodicals Index, Public Affairs Information Service Bulletin,* and *Historical Abstracts,* as well as dozens of other reference sources.

Each reference work has directions for its use in the introductory pages. Few contain the information itself but instead refer you to magazine articles, books, newspapers, pamphlets, or bulletins. Librarians can direct you to reference works in your particular field and to specialized and general computer searches that may be available in your library.

As you locate your sources, you are wise to make up bibliography cards citing the *author's name,* the *title,* the *place of publication,* the *publisher* and the *date of publication,* for books, and the *author's name,* the *title of the article,* the *name of the magazine, the volume number,* the *month and date* of the *issue* in which you find the material, and the *exact page numbers* of a *periodical.* Take notes carefully. For best results use only one side of the note card, being sure to *put the material entirely* in *your own words,* or to *quote exactly.* Use the ellipsis (. . .) for a word or a sentence that you omit. Be sure to record the *exact page number* on each card to insure accurate citations in your final paper.

Writing an investigative paper or a paper that involves documentation requires much the same process as other papers. In addition, however, you must be very careful to credit sources *exactly* and to take the utmost precaution to avoid plagiarism. In typing the final paper, you are well aware that all quotations must be documented. However, many students do not realize that the sources for *all* facts, statistics, and even ideas that you did not know before you started writing must be cited. Failure to credit any ideas obtained from another source constitutes *plagiarism.*

Suppose, for example, you are preparing a research paper on a comparison of the styles of Poe and Hemingway, and you encounter the following sentence in your reading of Pickering and Hoeper's *Literature.* (A sample bibliography entry for this source is listed later in these "Notes.")

In comparing the style of Poe to the style of Hemingway, for example, we can see a movement toward less formality and more concrete diction, as well as simpler syntax; the differences reflect the modern tendency toward realism in fiction.

1. If you use the sentence verbatim in your paper, you enclose it in quotation marks, and cite the source and exact page number.

2. If you omit *any* word or words, you must use the quotation marks *and* the ellipsis (. . .) for each omission. For example: "In comparing the style of Poe to the style of Hemingway, for example, we can see a movement toward less formality . . . as well as simpler syntax; the differences reflect the modern tendency toward realism in fiction." (As with the preceding example, you must again cite the source and exact page number.)

3. If you put the sentence entirely in your own words, you *still* must cite the source and page number of that idea. To avoid plagiarism you must *not* simply rearrange a few words (even though you cite the source). For example, you would be "borrowing" too much from the original if you were to write: "The differences reflecting the modern tendency toward realism in fiction can be observed by comparing the style of Poe to the style of Hemingway, where we see a movement toward less formality, more concrete diction, and a simpler syntax." Furthermore, it is plagiarizing to piece together phrases from the original and use them as your own words. You must use quotation marks around any distinctive words or phrases from the original.

When you are involved with a subject that is totally new to you, almost every sentence will need a citation. (Some sentences may require several sources). If you are in doubt about whether the word or sentence needs to be credited, ask your instructor. It is much better to use more documentation rather than less in order to protect yourself from plagiarism.

A handbook can give you the exact form for bibliography and "in-text" citations. Some professors, however, may still expect the now outdated "end-notes" or "footnotes." Be sure to check on the preferred format.

These are two generally accepted forms for bibliography entries taken from the 1984 *MLA Handbook for Writers of Research Papers:*

> *Book:* Pickering, James H., and Jeffrey D. Hoeper, eds. *Literature.* New York: Macmillan, 1986.
>
> *Magazine:* Johnson, Paul. "Marxism's Secret Stigma." *Commentary* Apr. 1984: 100–109.

A word of caution, however. There are many forms of documentation; sometimes as many as five or six different forms may be used on a single campus. Therefore, be sure to check in any class about the exact form that particular professor requires. Professional journals refuse to accept articles that do not adhere to their special form of documentation. In turn, failure to use the exact form preferred by your professor can result in a failing grade. The differences in documentation may seem minimal; however, they are important in academic circles. Sloppy or inaccurate documentation or failure to meticulously proofread an investigative paper usually indicates careless research and is downgraded accordingly.

This is, of course, a very brief summary of the library research process. However, it should be enough to familiarize you with basic research techniques. Often even a small amount of library research can make a great difference between a paper that generalizes and an effective paper built around specific facts and detail.

Jeffrey Potter

Jeffrey Potter received his B.S. in journalism from Michigan State University in 1983. The following series of writings is based on an editorial assignment for the school newspaper on a topic of his own choosing: (a) two pages of Potter's prewriting, brainstorming notes; (b) three pages of his first draft with editorial notes to himself and revisions; (c) the published editorial, which, Potter relates, he was not completely satisfied with; (d) his revised version of the three final paragraphs; (e) his remarks about how he composes/revises and his reasons for the postpublication changes.

You can learn a great deal about the writing process from a careful study of these documents. Note the germ of Potter's thesis in his prewriting notes. It is necessarily vague, abstract; but examine how he makes it concrete in the printed version and clarifies and adds emphasis in the postpublication revision. Note his choice of words; short, concise sentences; his allusions; figures of speech. Assess the tone.

DOCUMENT 1

1.

(School's a place for learning about a whole lot
more'n statistics. It's a place for learning about
society.

At school red tape hits us hard. We learn all
about pressure & relaxation — that dropping the
ball occasionally & getting a bad grade isn't the end
of anything (besides naiveté).

(What diff. is a 3.1 gonna make when — even if we
kill ourselves trying — we might've had a 3.3? No
one can tempt most of us w/ the prospect of high
honors, etc., anyway. Don't got a chance! But they
try. Too bad.

• School is where
  1. it's heaped on
  2. we learn to resist — adjust
        Despite the parental units.
  Because such is our world:
  1. B.S.
  2. Commands & Choices

(Our <u>particular</u> major is hardly impt — my
internship taught me that! we get "trained"
upon being hired, anyway. Bosses hardly worry
about our little <u>particulars</u>.

• School's not for sitting quietly. @ School <u>anyone</u>

can get into the why-fors of human history on any
scale—from the classics to analysis. Students treat
their world-class library like it's a torture
chamber from Grade School! (Back then things
were diff.) But you don't need a GPA to learn. No
one admits that.

2.

At State we present cards, ID & proof of honor like
we never imagined.
To get a degree, in short, we learn to fit in.
⎯→ BUT THAT BETTER NOT BE ALL!!

• The concept isn't explicit but to rise above mass
society we must work something out for ourselves.
(I spose they don't care if you make, those SOB's,
they have all the strings: w/o this, this, this, you
be impotent, boy.)
Work it out w/ peers, profs, resources, the system,
the opposite sex . . . the same sex. . . .
We must solve these problems. It's not explicit.
Someone should come out & say it better. More
often. We forget.
In the end we find something private, can't be
transmitted over any radio wave. It'll be a
commitment, a failing, a friggin' success. It'll be
home again. Ours. Theirs. It'll be for us. In about 4
yrs. In about average. OR it won't be nothin'
OK—Formalize this. Pick One topic. 〔Grades〕
Anecdotes.—Specific. Give it a Beat.
GRADES Find MSU Med Sch requirements (ph.
office for top ten criteria) Inspirational Prof
Lombardin mention his name? GET TO WORK!

DOCUMENT 2

JEFF POTTER
J-412 MURRAY 12/6/82
TOPIC: MSU & GRADES
FOR THE STATE NEWS---JUST BEFORE FINALS

Students should not let finals tear at their
we
souls. Even so, most of us know the inner

struggle, the straining for or crying over symbolic

445

differences like the abyss ~~that can~~ separat*ing* numbers

such as 2.5 and 3.0.

    ~~Everyone~~ *The world* shouts at us: "be all that you can

be!"--- *but* ~~get~~ get grades lower than are expected of you,

~~however,~~ and you'll be sorry. Potential employers

will see ~~the number~~ *a GPA* and know the intent of our

heart. Surely parents do.

    Parents can sense the friends, the ~~extraneous~~

~~activity~~ *action*, the daydreaming---the fun, the life---that

separates a 3.1 from a 3.2. Oh, how we know it... we

remember the futile late nights, ~~and~~ the botched

footnotes... we're blushing even now.

    It's easy to forget that jobs are won with more

than ~~strait-laced applications~~ *grades* when ~~kids are~~ *we* figuring*e*

~~their grades~~ *them* to the hundredths.

   ②The MSU medical school uses ten interdependent

factors in judging students who apply. ①Grades are

only ~~one factor.~~ one factor. (Read ① then ②)

    Most often personal ~~interactions~~ *ity* and personal

interactions determine whether one applicant among

many who are qualified gets the job. Company

recruiters are coming more ~~and more~~ up front about

this. Employers talk ~~a lot~~ about new applicants

"fitting into the family."

Some of us know students who had a family member die while they were away to school. ~~The~~ A

mourner's grades often plummet. Then, just as often, *Sometimes they work themselves into a kind* they kick themselves for poor performance~~)~~ ~~By all~~ *of numbness and their grades skyrocket.* ~~means they should ease up.~~ Something much more *unfortunately they do not realize that* important than Statistics 101 is happening in their

life. *Take note: An important collegiate* ~~The~~ point is don't be caught burrowing and

shutting yourself,in, or scheming like a job-hungry

coyote to bag The Grade.

Most employers treat their new-found graduates *anyway* like fresh-scrubbed cubs~~.~~ Then they set about

training us to the real work, their work. ~~The~~ college

education becomes a background, a base. "kid, you

don't know nothin'," and regardless of whether *likely* that's true, you'll/hear it soon after getting hired.

A lot of these good-intentioned bosses are over 40 *will soon leave* and they never had ~~the~~ what you ~~recently left behind~~:

The Rite of Passage called MSU.

This passage sometimes brings to us what are

known as "bad semesters," where the bookin'-

machine suddenly winds down on its own, ~~maybe~~ to

recover or rest or blow off, ~~nor~~ or maybe to encourage

its owner to take a look inside.

SAMPLE STUDENT PAPER: AN EDITORIAL

But ~~Try to~~ take those finals *anyway*. take them well, because

grades are important. But grades don't determine

values.

when

A Michigan Supreme Court judge died ~~recently~~ *Blair Moody, Jr.*

last year

~~and~~ the Detroit Free Press said this about him: *would be "wrote"*

"Someone once said you can never construct a system

so perfect that good men do not have to exert *Needs explaining*
Remember the
system isn't
themselves to keep it working. Justice Moody was a *"them"; it's*
you. Flawed.
good man, he pushed himself to make the system *Own up to it*
but never
work as justly and efficiently as possible." *bow to it;*
it's half-
busted and
A philospher who ~~once taught~~ *teaches* at MSU, and who *you've much*
to learn
useless tends to criticise teachers who ~~force~~ *encourage* students to *before you go*
clause, *out and*
a tangent regurgitate flurries of ~~specialized~~ facts for tests, *give it hell.*
– strike
it! expounds on this thought: A child can memorize

every fact about its sexuality. But until it grows up

and understands relationships it can't understand sex.

Becoming the Good Man requires such a

breakthrough and growing up. College can provide

the atmosphere, grades can't.

Add ¶S *A society deposits us here to make*
the change from dreamer to manager. But we
mustn't compromise our souls. The diploma
no longer means much, but we might.
The college atmosphere – w/ its
~~beautifully endless supply~~ *thrushing young*
community and professors and their attendant
resources – will never again be so
accessible to us. Through college we
can complete the modern rite
of passage.

448

VIEWPOINT: GRADES
Finals Aren't the Big Finale
Jeff Potter

Students should not let finals tear at their souls. Even so, we know the   1
inner struggle, the straining for or crying over symbolic differences like the
abyss separating such numbers as 2.5 and 3.0.

The world shouts at us: Be all that you can be!—but get grades lower than   2
are expected of you and you will be sorry. Potential employers see a GPA and
know the intent of our heart. Surely parents do.

Parents can sense the friends, the action, the daydreaming that separates a   3
3.1 from a 3.2. Oh, how we know it . . . we remember the futile late nights,
the botched footnotes . . . we're blushing even now. And it is easy to forget
that jobs are won with more than grades when we figure them to the hundredths.

The MSU medical school uses ten interdependent factors in judging   4
students who apply. Grades are only one factor. Most often personality and
personal connections determine who gets the job among many who are
qualified. Company recruiters talk about an applicant's ability to "fit into the
family."

Some of us know students who had a family member die while they were   5
away to school. A mourner's grades often plummet; then just as often they kick
themselves for poor performance. Sometimes, though, they work themselves
into a kind of numbness and their grades skyrocket. Unfortunately, they don't
realize something much more important than statistics is happening in their life.

Take note: Don't be caught burrowing and shutting yourself in, or   6
scheming like a job-hungry coyote to bag The Grade. Employers treat their
new-found graduates like fresh-scrubbed cubs anyway. Then they set about
training us to the real work, their work. "Kid, you don't know nothin'," true,
false, or said in jest, you will hear it soon after getting hired. The undergrad
education becomes a background, a base.

A lot of these good-intentioned bosses are over 40, experts, war vets, what   7
have you, but many never had what you will soon leave: The Rite of Passage
called MSU.

This passage sometimes brings us to bad terms, where the bookin'-machine   8
suddenly winds down on its own to recover or rest or blow off, or maybe to
encourage its owner to take a look inside. So, take those finals. Take them
well, because grades are important. But grades do not determine values.

When Michigan Supreme Court Justice Blair Moody, Jr. died last year, the   9
Detroit Free Press said this about him: "Someone once said you can never
construct a system so perfect that good men do not have to exert themselves to

---

Potter is a senior majoring in journalism who says he occasionally gets low grades.

keep it working. Justice Moody was a good man; he pushed himself to make the system work as justly and efficiently as possible."

A philosopher who teaches at MSU expounds on this thought: A child can memorize every fact about its sexuality. But until it grows up and understands relationships it cannot understand sex. Becoming the Good Man requires such a breakthrough and growing up. College provides the atmosphere, grades cannot.

DOCUMENT 4

REFINED DRAFT

But take those finals anyway. Take them well, because grades are important. But grades don't determine values.

When Michigan Supreme Court Justice Blair Moody died last year the Detroit Free Press said this about him: "Someone once said that you can never construct a system so perfect that good men do not have to exert themselves to keep it working. Justice Moody was a good man; he pushed himself to make the system work as justly and efficiently as possible." Remember, the system is not them; it's you. Flawed. You made it and you keep it going. Own up to it, but never bow to it: it is half-busted and you have much to learn before you go out to give it hell.

A philosopher who teaches at MSU expounds on this thought: A child memorizes every fact about its sexuality; but until it grows up and understands relationships it cannot understand sex. Becoming the Good Man requires just such a breakthrough and growing up. College can provide the atmosphere, grades cannot.

After all, society puts us here to make just such

a change. From dreamer to manager. But in so doing we must never compromise our souls. A diploma no longer means much; but we might! We have these four years to solve the problem. The college atmosphere---with its thirsting young community and professors and their attendant resources---will never again be so accessible to us. It provides the stuff of the modern Rite of Passage. Grades cannot.

###

DOCUMENT 5

EXPLANATION

Why did I make these changes? The first drafts were diluted intolerably. I had to cut off straying grafs and sentences, and I had to make the essay concise. Repetition lurks everywhere in my first drafts, so a lot of common sense condensing clarifies the theme and makes it read faster. I get off my main thought and start writing about God every few paragraphs, or I'll get an interesting flash connection in my head and introduce it, then explain . . . Ugh, those lobes just have to go: an essay should be like an arrow.

I wanted to strengthen connections I had in the editorial that had their solidity only in my head. With the first change (the so to the but in paragraph eight) I wanted readers to understand the notion of humane education; but I also wanted them to know that discipline, and so grades, is important to

451

achieve. A small change, but it made the connection better.

I added those sentences to the end of the judge quote because I wanted to strengthen the connection of the man (any man) to the system. Talk about the system needing good men wasn't enough. We are resonsible for the system: it's ours. And no one should ever feel inferior to it: no one is inferior to their nose or appetite, are they? (Fear of those things is another story.) It is important to get the man over, and admitting of his creation. onto the end

Lastly, I added a graf because I didn't connect Justice Moody to sex well enough before. I had to reinforce the connections between Society-Good Man-Growing Up. Students must realize that college matters, but that merely college-plus-grades equals zero. I'm writing about soul. Work + Soul equals Life after college, Life after Marriage. I'm writing about the end of that pest, alienation. So I added the graf.

P.S. The reporter's conventions allow for a great way to write drafts. Triple spacing, narrow margins and no worries about typing mistakes lets a write "cut-and-paste" easily with a big, fat pencil.

QUESTIONS ON CONTENT: (IN DOCUMENT 3)

1. What is Potter's thesis and how does his title suggest it?
2. In document 4, last paragraph, Potter writes about the college atmosphere and "attendant resources." What important resource do you think Potter is referring to? Where in document 1 does he perhaps reveal what he has in mind?

3. What is meant in paragraph 7 by "The Rite of Passage" (see its repetition in document 4)?

4. What is the meaning of the last line in document 3?

QUESTIONS ON WRITING STRUCTURE AND STRATEGY:

1. What idea appears throughout the editorial to provide coherence?

2. What kind of support does Potter use to support his thesis?

3. Note his choice of words: in paragraph 1, why is "abyss" an appropriate word when referring to student concern over grades? Is it used ironically? In paragraph 5, why is the word "skyrocket" appropriate? What is the connotation of the word? In paragraph 6, what is the connotation of "job-hungry coyote"? Is it appropriate? What is Jeff conveying to the reader by the use of this term? In the same paragraph, what is the connotation of "fresh-scrubbed cubs"? Why is it appropriate in this context?

4. How is the Moody obituary related to the philosopher's comment (i.e., why are they coupled)? Is it clearer in the postpublication revision?

WRITING ABOUT READING

Sometimes during your writing course you will probably be given free rein to write about almost any topic you choose, as was Jeff Potter in the preceding selection. On other occasions you will be asked to respond to a particular reading, as, for example, the class assignment that prompted Jo Harris's paper. In asking for your response, your instructor may ask for a critical paper (which can be either antagonistic or laudatory), a personal response, or a specific response to a question or series of questions (such as many of those following the readings in this text).

Writing about reading, for example, responding to what you have read, involves (a) understanding, (b) analyzing, and (c) reacting to what you read. Therefore, as you read (preferably at least a day before you begin writing) in preparation to responding to a selection, react to what you are reading — question ideas that seem confusing or illogical, pencil in (if it is your personal copy of the article) examples from your own experience that corroborate or contrast with the author's ideas, mark passages that impress or repel you.

In the next few days, as you reread, continue penciling in marginal notes. Recheck the headnotes and questions following each selection. Examine the author's purpose, thesis, tone, organization, methods of development, supporting material, and word choice.

In developing your response, avoid a humdrum repetition or summary of exactly what the author has said in the original article — or play or novel. Instead, you may briefly identify the author and title of the selection and highlight key ideas or the specific one you intend to criticize, defend, analyze, or expand upon (see Argumentation in the Rhetorical Index). Sometimes the source of the article, the publication date, or the time, place, or conditions under which the selection was written are important details needed to orient your reader (see Harris's opening sentence).

Your response may take many forms. For example, you may present an analytic response. That is, you may devote your response to examining errors in the writer's logic, the lack of convincing support (examples, facts or statistics, authority, reasons, specific incidents, or descriptive details), or the author's unrealistic expectations, biases, lack of knowledge about the subject. You may also choose to analyze the style, organization, or development of the author. Whatever you do, be sure your analysis is not superficial, that it probes beneath the surface, and that it treats the subject in depth.

Rather than analyzing the selections, you may decide to support the author's contentions or, as Harris does, synthesize the author's ideas. Your response could supplement a point made by the author by providing additional insights, noting examples from your own experience (which many of our review questions suggest), examining related problems, or citing research data. You might develop your response by making complex material more personal, more palatable, or more applicable to a different audience. Whatever your choice, support your statements with evidence that is pertinent, accurate, and adequate.

The following student essay is a response to the Reverend Martin Luther King, Jr., selection in Unit III. Her annotated first drafts help clarify her particular process in developing her response.

Jo D. Harris

Jo D. Harris is a nontraditional, part-time student at Michigan State University. She plans to pursue a degree in English as soon as her husband completes medical school and her youngest son enters first grade. She works full time. In the following five documents, we follow her through the writing process as she completes an assignment calling for a response to a reading of the Reverend Martin Luther King, Jr.'s "Letter from Birmingham Jail". Harris's response is in the form of a summary: (a) two pages in which Harris tells how she went about writing her paper, illustrating that there is no one way to go about writing a paper; (b) two pages of Harris's first draft, a combination outline and mapping exercise; (c) four pages of Harris's second draft; (d) three pages of Harris's third draft, copy submitted to her instructor containing his comments and her own penciled notes for changes; and (e) three pages of her final draft. Observe how the organization outlined in document II is carried through all drafts.

DOCUMENT 1

The moment I was assigned to write about Dr. King's letter from the Birmingham jail (about a week and-a-half before it was due), I ran a mental check on my "time budget." (Let's see . . . Annette's baby shower is Monday night so I'll have to work on the first draft this weekend, do revisions on Tuesday, then let it rest till Thursday. I can review it Thursday night after the kids are in bed, and type it up Friday on my lunch hour. I'll think over the "final draft" next weekend and make any necessary revisions, and—voila—hand it in on Monday.) So even with working full time, caring for my family, and leading a social life I'd arranged a compatible but flexible time schedule for writing the paper.

For the first couple of days I explored the subject without putting pen to paper. By coincidence, the week I wrote the paper was the week of Dr. King's birthday celebration. I watched the television specials and read the newspaper articles, gathering as much insight into his philosophy as possible. I discussed his ideas with my husband, friends and co-workers—anybody who was willing to listen to me. Sharing these ideas with the people around me activated my "inner dialogue." I found myself pondering brotherhood while doing the dishes; I argued against segregation while driving to work in the morning. By the time I was ready to sit down and write, I'd formed a rough outline in my mind.

I began by identifying the three groups of people (white moderates, complacent blacks, white church leaders) criticized by King for their refusal to fight segregation. Then I took each group, and with supporting quotes from the text, described and explored the reasons for his unhappiness with them. I had to do some introspective exploration to come up with the conclusion. What was the essential message in King's letter to the clergy? What message did I gather from the TV reports and newspaper articles? I realized that he wasn't just a black minister fighting segregation. He was a humanitarian struggling for dignity and equality for all men.

Then the outline was complete, and all I had to do was write the paper in a way that would be clear to the reader. That's the part that took some floor-walking, hair-tearing, and lots of revising. I used the deadline as a constructive tool—it forced me to sit down, produce, and write. I tried certain words and phrases; I discarded them and retrieved them; I arranged and rearranged till I was somewhat satisfied (I call this process "knit one, purl two").

As I said, I was "somewhat satisfied." There gets to be a point when you simply run out of time and ideas, when the words begin to blur, and you just have to turn it in, hoping for the best. I think the best of writers think to themselves, "Gee, if I just had another week. . . ."

DOCUMENT 2
DRAFT 1
OUTLINE

King - due Monday

Letter from birmingham jail

And we still have 2 ways to go.

To whom? What for? (What's the issue?)

457

P. 179 "Shallow understanding from people of good will is more frustrating than absolute misunderstanding from people of ill will.

To his fellow clergymen (read pgs. 170, 171 for context) Issue: he's angry at their criticism for (outside agitators) condoning civil disobedience. Unhappy with those. equal rights! who won't help "the cause". Who?

1. white moderates - concerned about keeping the status quo; concerned about keeping civil laws - see pg. 175. election of A. Boutwell as mayor. (". . . . dedicated to the maintenance of the status quo.) Expresses dismay that we are "moving w/ jet-like speed toward gaining political independence, but we still creep at horse and buggy ~~speed~~ pace toward gaining a cup of coffee at a lunch counter." ⟶ leads to "wait" (pg. 176) Well-meaning people - passive whites more concerned with maintaining the status quo, smoothing ruffled feathers. Use example on pg. (Broken promises) 173. ¶ 7 - racist signs removed, then put back up.)

they settled for a sort of negative peace

2. Oppressed blacks - so downtrodden, so used to segregation - wills broken. Won't protest against racial injustice, won't help bring about social change; denial of responsibility - letting down their brothers. pgs 180,181 A few actually profit from segregation (academic and/or economic reasons) become insensitive to the issue. King feels caught between the "do-nothingness" of the complacent negro and bitter

hatred of the black nationalist (violent) - <u>both</u>

<u>hamper the fight for racial equality</u>.

3. <u>Church leaders</u> - King's disappointment that

their failure to see the immorality of racial

segregation, racial inequality - goes against the

Christian philosophy. (How could people who call

themselves "Christians" stand by and watch

injustice?). Sees the Christian church as having

become weak, as "standing behind stained-glass

windows" Where is the "true" sacrificial spirit of the

Christian church? Boils down to a lack of moral

conviction.

↓

Now that we've got "who" - we need "why?" What's

King's point? [We all share a <u>moral responsibility</u>:]

Use statement on pg 178, ¶ 4 - "We are caught in"

All men are created equal. <u>Everyone</u> should want

racial equality. By not reaching for it, by sitting

passively by and not doing anything, we're hurting

ourselves.

↑
nice conclusion

DOCUMENT 3
DRAFT 2
TITLE

When King wrote, "shallow understanding from
people of good will is more frustrating than absolute

misunderstanding from people of ill will" - he was unhappy with white moderates who were content with segregation, blacks who were so oppressed that they grew used to segregation, and white church leaders who wouldn't upset the status quo, wouldn't take a strong stand against immoral (unjust?) laws. They would not confront the issue, would not demand of their leaders a resolution to the problem. Because King felt this resolution was urgent, the reluctance of these people was intolerable. So he unleashed a rebuke of people who could not see that any strong stand for equal rights would help to create a positive tension bring the issue into focus, and force a settlement.

King was frustrated with the white moderates. The opposed the demonstrations at Birmingham (a common attitudes shared by whites throughout the south). They were concerned about the breaking of civil laws, whether they were just or unjust - or whether they were the very cause of the unrest they opposed. They seemed only to understand that this discontent was disrupting the status quo. In an attempt to pacify the colored community, local businessmen negotiated to remove degrading racial signs. A few were removed, but were put back up. This broken promise made it increasingly apparent that white leaders were more concerned with pacifying the local blacks than doing anything about unjust laws. Those who did seem to understand the plight of the Negroes appeared sympathetic but demonstrated limited comprehension of the desperation of the situation by advising colored people to "wait for a more convenient season" to struggle for equal rights. They thought (mistakenly) that time eventually cures all ills; that even after 340 years of repression, blacks should patiently (!!) wait longer for equality. As Dr. King wrote about the white moderates, ". . . . they become the dangerously structured dams that block the flow of social progress."

He was also unhappy with Negroes who had become so oppressed and drained of self-respect that they lost their racial pride. Segregation was a way of life; no one wanted to cause trouble by breaking a white law. There were also a few middle-class blacks who actually found profit by segregation, and because of academic or economic reasons they were content to leave things (~~as they were~~ *alone*). King saw that these complacent people had grown immune to the discrimination suffered by the people of their own race. He was concerned that passive acceptance of racial injustice and refusal to support nonviolent protest would be hamper the fight for equality. He must have viewed this inaction as a betrayal of all blacks by a few self-centered brothers.

And - finally - his greatest disappointment was in the failure of white church leaders to take a strong stand against such blatantly immoral - but legal - treatment of fellow human beings. He couldn't comprehend that people who <u>professed</u> to be Christians could advocate (ignore?) violent injustice taking place under their very noses. He wrote, ". . . . all too many. . . . have been more cautious than coro courageous and have remained silent behind the anesthetizing security of stained-glass windows." He showed his disillusionment when he wrote: (Pg. 184, ¶ 37). So by the church's refusal to lack of moral conviction and refusal to take a stand against injustice, they seem to advocate racial inequality. King's unhappiness came from the realization that today's Christians - who should have been his <u>strongest</u> allies - had strayed so far from the true sacraficial spirit of the early Christians.

Kings frustration with the moderate, the complacent, and the passive citizen was born of a desire to see <u>all</u> men benefit from equality. As he stated in paragraph 4, "we are caught in an inescapable network of mutuality, tied in a single garment of density. Whatever affects one directly, affects all indirectly." In other words, the attainment of racial equality would ultimately benefit every American - indeed, the essay implies that it's every person's moral obligation to do his part in reaching that goal. However, a person's refusal to share in that responsibility would not only hamper social reform, but eventually work against the person himself. And <u>this</u> is what King sought to change.

461

DOCUMENT 4

THE "PEACE" OF PASSIVE MISUNDERSTANDING

① When Dr. King wrote from his jail cell in Birmingham that "shallow understanding from people of good will is more frustrating than absolute misunderstanding from people of ill will", he expressed his unhappiness with white moderates who seemed content with segregation, with complacent Negroes who became so oppressed that they grew used to segregation, and with white church leaders who refused to upset the status quo by taking a strong stand against immoral and unjust laws. These passive people who would not confront the problem of racial inequality refused, by their very passivity, to demand of their leaders a resolution to the problem. And in light of the urgency felt by Dr. King, this reluctance to get involved was intolerable. Despite the letter's gentle tone King unleashed a scathing rebuke of people who could not see that any strong stand—for or against equal rights—would help to create a positive tension, bring the issue into focus, and ultimately force a settlement. The very recalcitrance of these passive citizens appeared to be an endorsement of segregation.

② Consider King's frustration with the white moderates. They expressed their dismay at the demonstrations in Birmingham—undoubtedly a common attitude shared by other white communities across the nation, wherever racial unrest flared. Their concern seemed to be centered around the

462

breaking of civil laws; little thought was given to
whether those laws were just or unjust, or that such
laws might be the underlying cause for black
discontent. They seemed only to understand that
this discontent was disrupting the status quo. In one
superficial attempt to pacify Birmingham's ~~colored~~ **black**
community, local merchants negotiated to remove
degrading racial signs; indeed, a few were removed,
but were eventually put back up. Such a broken
promise made it increasingly apparent that white
leaders were more concerned with pacifying the local
blacks than rectifying unjust laws. The moderates
who did seem to understand the plight of the Negroes
appeared sympathetic, but demonstrated limited
comprehension of the situation's desperation by
advising colored people to "wait for a more
convenient season" to struggle for equal rights. They
held the mistaken notion that time eventually cures
all ills; that even after 340 years of repression,
blacks should patiently wait longer for equality. ~~As~~
Find another quote- pg. 175, ¶13 - perfect!!
~~Dr. King wrote about white moderates, ". . . they~~
~~become the dangerously structured dams that block~~
~~the flow of social progress."~~

not exactly accurate; the dams are law and order divorced from justice.

③ Dr. King also expressed his unhappiness with
persecuted?
Negroes who had become so oppressed and drained of
self-respect that they lost their racial pride.
for them
Segregation/was a way of life; no one wanted to cause
trouble by breaking a white law. There were also a
few middle-class blacks who actually found profit by
segregation, and because of academic or economic

reasons they were content to leave things alone.
King saw that these complacent people had grown
immune to the discrimination suffered by people of
their own race.] He was concerned that this
acceptance of racial injustice and refusl to support
nonviolent protest would hamper the fight for
equality. (And undoubtedly he viewed this inaction
as a ~~betrayal of all blacks by a few self-centered brothers.~~ *(Clarify ¶ 4)*

Good point—but what is unspoken is MLK's unwillingness to chide them too severely. He forgives those who have borne so much their weakness—but the weakness of those who have borne nothing is another matter.

④ Perhaps Dr. King's greatest disappointment was
in the failure of white church leaders to take a
strong stand against such blatantly immoral — but
legal — treatment of fellow human beings. He found
it incomprehensible that people who professed to be
Christians could, in all good conscience, ignore — or
even advocate — the violent injustice taking place
under their very noses. He wrote, " . . . all too
many. . . . have been more cautious than
courageous and have remained silent behind the
anesthetizing security of stained-glass windows." He
voiced his disillusionment with the Christian church
when he wrote:

True enough but long quotes intimidate reader. Writers should prefer short ones or they should paraphrase or prepare the reader to see exactly what's significant in the quote with as precise as possible a characterization of the quote.

There was a time when the church was very
powerful—in the time when the early Christians
rejoiced at being deemed worthy to suffer for what
they believed. In those days the church was not
merely a thermometer that recorded the ideas and
principals of popular opinion; it was a thermostat
that transformed the mores of society. . . . Things
are so different now. So often the contemporary
church is a weak, ineffectual voice with an uncertain

sound. So often it is an arch-defender of the status quo. Far from being disturbed by the presence of the church, the power structure of the average community is consoled by the church's silent — and often even vocal — sanction of things as they are.

(5) So by the lack of moral conviction and its refusal to take a stand against injustice, the white church seemed to advocate racial inequality. Dr. King's unhappiness came from the realization that today's Christians — people who should have been his strongest allies — had strayed so far from the true sacrificial spirit of the early Christians.

This could use more development. What sacrifice is called for? Pg. 84, ¶37 describes what I mean.

(6) Dr. King's frustration with the moderate, the complacent and the passive citizen was born of a desire to see all men benefit from equality. As he stated in paragraph four, "We are caught in an inescapable network of mutuality, tied in a single garment of density. Whatever affects one directly, affects all indirectly." In other words, the attainment of racial equality would ultimately benefit every American — indeed, the essay implies that it's every person's moral responsibility to do his part in reaching that goal. However, a person's refusal to share in this responsibility would not only hamper social reform, but eventually work against the person himself. And this is what Dr. King sought to change.

good

I think you've successfully made the transition from personal to "academic" writing — and with no loss of a strong, personal voice.

THE "PEACE"
———— OF PASSIVE MISUNDERSTANDING ————

When Dr. King wrote from his jail cell in Birmingham that "shallow understanding from people of good will is more frustrating than absolute misunderstanding from people of ill will," he expressed his unhappiness with the white moderates who seemed content with segregation, with the complacent Negroes who became so oppressed that they grew used to segregation, and with the white church leaders who refused to upset the status quo by taking a strong stand against immoral and unjust laws. These passive people who would not confront the problem of racial inequality refused, by their very passivity, to demand of their leaders a resolution to the problem. And in light of the urgency felt by Dr. King, this reluctance to get involved was intolerable. Despite the letter's gentle tone King unleashed a scathing rebuke of people who could not see that *any* strong stand—for or against equal rights— would help to create a positive tension, bring the issue into focus, and ultimately force a settlement. The very recalcitrance of these passive citizens appeared to be an endorsement of segregation.

Consider King's frustration with the white moderates. They expressed their dismay at the demonstrations in Birmingham—undoubtedly a common attitude shared by other white communities across the nation, wherever racial unrest flared. Their concern seemed to be centered around the breaking of civil laws; little thought was given to whether those laws were just or unjust, or that such laws might be the underlying cause for black discontent. They seemed only to understand that this discontent was disrupting the status quo. In one superficial attempt to pacify Birmingham's black community, local merchants negotiated to remove degrading racial signs; indeed, a few were removed, but were eventually put back up. Such a broken promise made it increasingly apparent that white leaders were more concerned with pacifying the local blacks than rectifying unjust laws. The moderates who did seem to understand the plight of the Negroes appeared sympathetic, but demonstrated limited comprehension of the situation's desperation by advising colored people to "wait for a more convenient season" to struggle for equal rights. They held the mistaken notion that time eventually cures all ills; that even after 340 years of repression, blacks should patiently wait longer for equality. But to King, like so many of his brothers and sisters, the meaning of "wait" had become "never." Equality wouldn't come with patience. It would have to be demanded by the oppressed.

Dr. King also expressed his unhappiness with Negroes who had become so persecuted and drained of self-respect that they lost their racial pride. Segregation for them was a way of life; no one wanted to cause trouble by breaking a white law. There were also a few middle-class blacks who actually profited by segregation, and because of academic or economic reasons they were content to leave things alone. King saw that they had grown immune to the discrimination suffered by people of their own race. He was distressed by their resigned acceptance of racial injustice and by their unwillingness to support nonviolent protest. Here was yet another frustrating barrier in the fight for equality.

Perhaps Dr. King's greatest disappointment was in the failure of the white church leaders to take a strong stand against such blatantly immoral treatment of fellow human beings. These leaders—professed interpreters of the Christian doctrine—were looked up to and trusted by their communities. Yet by their unwillingness to speak out against injustice, to upset the status quo—by their very lack of moral conviction and refusal to take a stand against inequality—the church appeared to endorse segregation. As King wrote, " . . . all too many . . . have been more cautious than courageous and have remained silent behind the anesthetizing security of stained-glass windows." These church leaders seemed to have forgotten the true sacrificial spirit of those early Christians who voluntarily faced hungry lions or went to the chopping block rather than obey certain Roman laws. Such willingness to engage in civil disobedience and endure persecution helped to bring about some of our most significant social reforms. King realized that the strength of the early Christians came from obedience to the righteous voice of God, and that the weakness of the Southern white church leaders came from obedience to the imperfect voice of society.

Dr. King's frustration with the moderate, the complacent and the passive citizen was born of a desire to see *all* men benefit from equality. As he stated in paragraph four, "We are caught in an inescapable network of mutuality, tied in a single garment of density. Whatever affects one directly, affects all indirectly." In other words, the attainment of racial equality would ultimately benefit every American; indeed, the essay implies that it's every person's moral responsibility to do his part in reaching that goal. However, a person's refusal to share in this responsibility would not only hamper social reform, but eventually work against the person himself. And this self-defeating behavior is what Dr. King sought to change.

QUESTIONS ON CONTENT:

1. What is Harris's thesis? Where does it appear in her paper?
2. What is the meaning of her title and how does it relate to her thesis?
3. What does King see as the failing of the white moderates? Of the blacks? Of the white churches?

QUESTIONS ON WRITING STRUCTURE AND STRATEGY:

1. In which paragraphs does Harris use topic sentences? In what way are they effective or ineffective?

2. How effective is Harris's use of quotations? How does she integrate them into her paragraphs? In her final draft, has she eliminated too much of the King quotation?

3. Could Harris have used more examples? Where in her article? Examples from King? From history? From contemporary life?

4. What is the effect of Harris's short, concluding sentence? Why is the last paragraph a good concluding paragraph?

5. Do you find any examples of "sexist language"? Where?

6. Why do you believe she changed the word "apartheid" in document IV to "segregation" in document V?

7. Pinpoint significant stylistic changes in the text from the third to the fourth draft.

Rhetorical Index

Although each of the writers in this text employs a combination of methods of development, the following index can be used to identify selections illustrating the various methods. A brief description of the method precedes each list.

Analogy

An analogy is an extended comparison between two seemingly different ideas, situations, or subjects with at least a single point of similarity. It may be used to clarify or to persuade. It can help to clarify by explaining the unfamiliar in terms of the familiar. In argumentation, analogy adds conviction and serves as a cogent tactical device by intimating that because of certain resemblances, further similarity is probable. Although sometimes confused with similes and metaphors (in reality they are simple analogies), analogies usually are more extended and involve several bases of comparison. Analogies can be brief statements or extended through several paragraphs. Note, for example, Alda's analogy in paragraph nine of "You Have to Know What Your Values Are." Here Alda compares a man succumbing to a bribe to throw a little poison into a reservoir to unprincipled individuals who are contributing to what he sees as the moral disintegration of today's society. As with most analogies, there are several bases of comparison: the man poisoning the reservoir and unprincipled businessmen and government officials; the reservoir and society; the bribe and personal gain. For other analogies see the following:

Loren Eiseley	Anthony J. Sousa
Roy Hoffman	William Swanson
Neil Postman	George Will

Argumentation

The most complex of these methods, the art of persuasion, encompasses the entire spectrum of organizational methods as well as a host of additional emotional and logical strategies that you can use to win your reader to your point of view.

Argumentation means using *reason* to attempt to change a person's thinking, actions, or beliefs. Inductive reasoning involves providing a large body of evidence that leads the reader to a general conclusion. (See Rodriguez in Unit II) Deductive reasoning reverses the process: a general premise is made, and a conclusion about another person, idea, or situation is deduced. Syllogistic reasoning, a form of deductive reasoning, consists of a major premise, a minor premise, and a conclusion. These are explained in more detail in the Glossary and are exemplified in the Declaration of Independence, in Unit III. (Also see Huxley, in Supplementary Readings.) Inductive and deductive reasoning are not only applicable to argumentation but are valid methods of development in almost any kind of writing.

Although emotional appeals are especially pertinent to persuasion and argumentation, they, along with logical appeals, are pervasive in most writing. Emotional appeals are directed toward the reader's sense of fear, pity, loyalty, pleasure, and self-interest — in fact, all of the emotions.

Because most people fail to respond exclusively to reason or to emotion, the two are usually employed in combination. For example, when you attempt to persuade your roommate or a fellow worker to go out on a blind date, to vote for a particular candidate, or to join a local softball team, you no doubt will employ both emotional as well as logical appeals. Notice that Lincoln in the Gettysburg Address (Unit III) appeals primarily to emotion, the sympathy and patriotism of his listeners, although he does, of course, evoke reason. Jefferson (Unit III), on the other hand, appeals primarily to reason in the Declaration of Independence, but not without tendering certain emotional appeals as well.

In addition to emotional and rational approaches, ethical appeals elicit the reader's confidence in the writer as a person, or in the writer's integrity, fair-mindedness, or intellectual acumen. Writers may refer to their standing in the community, their reputation for honesty, their devotion to country or duty, or their participation in liberal causes. These ethical appeals often establish credence in the writer and his or her cause.

One of the first considerations in the psychology of persuasion is audience sensitivity. Early in the writing process, the writer should attempt to determine the audience's attitude toward the subject. If the audience is apathetic or undecided, the writer's task is to awaken them with startling facts and impressive evidence. If the audience is hostile, the writer uses a conciliatory approach: tries to find some common ground, secures some basic agreement, encourages a sense of fair play.

It may help to consider persuasion and argumentation in terms of good, common sense fortified by integrity. In persuasive or argumentative writing skilled writers find they can be most effective by

1. Stating the proposition clearly and precisely.
2. Studying the evidence to be certain that it is adequate, relevant, unbiased, and logically developed.
3. Anticipating and possibly refuting the reader's objections to the proposition.

Effective writers try to avoid what are known as logical fallacies:

1. Oversimplifying; giving a superficial, simplistic solution to a complex problem.
2. Examining only one aspect of a proposition.
3. Forcing a decision between two choices when more than two courses of actions are possible.
4. Making sweeping generalizations whereby you stereotype or base your conclusions on insufficient evidence.
5. Begging the question — assuming a proposition to be true that actually needs to be proven.
6. Shifting the question — arguing another question or a different aspect of the question, thereby obscuring or dodging the issue.
7. Confusing coincidence with causation.
See the following.

Alan Alda	Tillie Olsen
Arthur Ashe	George Orwell
Rachel Carson	Jesse Owens and Paul G. Neimark
William Faulkner	Neil Postman
John S. Hoppock	Richard Rodriguez
Thomas Jefferson	Anne Roiphe
Barbara Jordan	Priscilla Scherer
Garrison Keillor	Albert Shanker
John F. Kennedy	Jonathan Swift
Martin Luther King, Jr.	Henry David Thoreau
Abraham Lincoln	David Vogel

Cause and Effect

Everyday you employ causal analysis in your thinking, speaking, and writing. "Why won't my car start?" "Why do I have this miserable headache?" "Why am I flunking chemistry?" "Why doesn't Mark call?" These and hundreds of other questions may prompt you to investigate the causes. You reason from cause to effect (and vice versa) when you are attempting to establish some connection between actions, situations, or events to find out how they are related, *why* things happen.

Cause and effect reasoning can be particularly effective in analytical and/or persuasive writing. By amassing facts, statistics, and testimony that lead to a logical conclusion, you make that conclusion convincing for your reader.

In using cause and effect, study your reasoning carefully, testing it for soundness and plausibility. Double-check to verify the accuracy of your facts and statistics and to be sure you are assigning the correct cause to an effect. See the following:

Arthur Ashe	Lance Morrow
Bruno Bettelheim and Karen Zelan	Tillie Olsen
Paul Blumberg	Neil Postman
Jane E. Brody ("Anger")	Arlene Skolnick
Jane E. Brody ("Bulimia")	Graham Spanier
Rachel Carson	David Vogel
John S. Hoppock	Alice Walker
William McGowan	George Will

Classification

Colleges classify students as freshmen, sophomores, juniors, and seniors according to credits completed; the catalog separates courses into departments; professors rank students by grading them; you group your colleagues into brains, jocks, grinds, airheads, and partyers. We are constantly caught up in separating people, things, and ideas into groups based on their similarities and distinguished from other divisions by their differences.

Use classification as a method of clarifying, analyzing, showing relationships, comparing and contrasting, and supporting ideas. Often the classification (e.g., "There are four different types of professors at a university. . . . ") can provide the framework, the organization, and perhaps the coherence for the entire paper. In his "Letter from Birmingham Jail" Martin Luther King, Jr., first classifies laws into just and unjust laws and then proceeds to define each type, a tactic that sets the stage for the whole essay. See the following:

Jane E. Brody ("Anger")	George Orwell
Jane E. Brody ("Bulimia")	Neil Postman
Garrison Keillor	Albert Shanker
Martin Luther King, Jr.	Arlene Skolnick
Lance Morrow	Anthony Sousa
Alleen Pace Nilsen	Graham Spanier

Comparison and Contrast

Comparisons and contrasts permeate almost every aspect of life. In fact, almost every practical decision, almost every conscious action or even inaction (which is

472

in itself a "kind" of action) is based on comparison and/or contrast reasoning: the college dormitory, as well as the major you choose; the clothes, stereo, or car you buy; the pizza, candy bar, or soft drink you consume. Actually, comparison and contrast are two different operations: comparison focuses on *similarities,* whereas contrast examines *differences* between things. They are frequently employed as an excellent means of clarifying, analyzing, explaining, informing, or persuading.

Basically, there are two patterns of organization: (a) *subject by subject,* in which you focus on all aspects of one subject and then concentrate on all the aspects of the second subject; or (b) *point by point,* whereby you focus on one point at a time, examining it first in terms of subject A and then in relation to subject B, alternating back and forth throughout the course of the essay.

The *subject by subject* method is most effective when used with shorter papers in which a small number of aspects are being compared; the *point by point* when the subject is longer and more complex. Either pattern can be successful; the choice is usually determined by the subject and purpose.

When using comparison or contrast, focus on important similarities and/or important differences, compare the same aspects of each subject, and use effective transitions. See the following:

Bruno Bettelheim and Karen Zelan	Priscilla Scherer
Jane E. Brody ("Anger")	Arlene Skolnick
Jean Bethke Elshtain	Lewis Thomas
Thomas Henry Huxley	David Vogel
Lance Morrow	George Will
Horace Porter	

Definition

You work with definitions constantly: whenever you learn the meaning of new words or terms for another course, whenever you look up a word in the dictionary, whenever you say, "What I mean is. . . . " In defining a word or phrase, you set limits to it, clarify its fundamental meaning.

Words can be defined in numerous ways. For example, you can provide a short definition by citing a synonym, antonym, or an example. Or you can write an extended defintion that expands into a paragraph, several pages, or a whole book. When you explain what something is — describe it, compare it, contrast it — you are in a general sense defining it. In defining words or phrases, be sure to consider your audience and its knowledge of the subject carefully. To define words people already know puts them off; to fail to clarify words they do not know confuses them. See the following:

Jane E. Brody ("Bulimia")	Abraham Lincoln
Jean Bethke Elshtain	Lance Morrow

473

William Faulkner   Priscilla Scherer
Thomas Henry Huxley   Anthony Sousa
John F. Kennedy   William Swanson
Martin Luther King, Jr.

Description

A description is a word picture or impression. By using specific detail and vivid language, you help your reader to formulate a sensory image (visual, auditory, tactile, gustatory, olfactory) of something — a sunset, a summer afternoon, freshly baked bread, country music. Most commonly used in combination with other modes, descriptions can enliven writing, add impact and dimension, and help clarify by making the abstract concrete. Effective description (a) maintains a consistent point of view (focal point or perspective), (b) develops one dominant impression (mood, atmosphere, attitude), and (c) employs figurative language — similes, metaphors (see Glossary). See the following:

Jane E. Brody ("Bulimia")   Lance Morrow
Loren Eiseley   Horace Porter
Jean Bethke Elshtain   Richard Rodriguez
Samuel Gompers   Virginia Woolf
Gilbert Highet

Example

When you write to a friend that college is demanding, that your professor is impossible, that the football team is the greatest, you probably back up these statements with specific examples. Successful writers find real or hypothetical examples or illustrations invaluable aids in clarifying, giving meaning to, making concrete a generalization. Not only can examples provide vital support to help prove or disprove a proposition, they also can add considerable color, variety, and interest to your writing. Your examples, of course, should be pertinent, appropriate, and convincing for your reader.

You may organize your examples to lead your reader to a conclusion by citing data and then drawing a conclusion (inductive reasoning, see Glossary), or you may cite a generalization or statement which you support by listing examples (deductive reasoning, see Glossary). Rachel Carson (Unit III) uses deductive reasoning by identifying her thesis, the pollution of our environment through the careless use of pesticides. She then proceeds to support that thesis with a barrage of examples and illustrations. Lewis Thomas (Unit III) in "Nurses" uses inductive reasoning by describing the changing role of nurses and concluding with his controlling idea, a tribute to all nurses. See the following:

Arthur Ashe	H. L. Mencken
Ann Bayer	Lance Morrow
Jane Brody ("Bulimia")	George Orwell
Jane Brody ("Anger")	Horace Porter
Gilbert Highet	Priscilla Scherer
Roy Hoffman	Albert Shanker
John Hoppock	Anthony Sousa
Thomas Henry Huxley	William Swanson
Thomas Jefferson	David Vogel
William McGowan	George Will

Narration

Relating a play-by-play account of a football game, retelling the plot of a movie, reporting your spring break experiences to a classmate all involve narration — the recounting of an experience or an event. It is frequently interwoven with description and can be either factual (such as personal narratives like those of Douglass, Franklin, or Malcolm X, in Unit I) or fictional (as in novels, London, Unit I). Narration can be used to entertain, explain, or convince your reader.

Narrative writing, like any writing, should be tailored to make some meaningful point (recall Christ preached in parables). The experience or event should have changed you in some way, taught you a lesson, impressed you in a significant way.

You may summarize part of the narration or use flashbacks to bridge time spans, to give movement, or to relieve straight chronological reporting. Or, you may dramatize by using action verbs, dialogue, foreshadowing, or suspense to heighten interest. You can show the passage of time, as well as add coherence and clarity to your writing, by using adverbs, such as *now, meanwhile, subsequently, afterward, next, shortly,* or adverbial clauses, such as "after he finally braked to a stop" or "while he waited at the airport." See the following:

Maya Angelou	Malcolm X
Eldridge Cleaver	H. L. Mencken
Frederick Douglass	Tillie Olsen
Loren Eiseley	Jesse Owens and Paul G. Neimark
Jean Bethke Elshtain	Horace Porter
Benjamin Franklin	Richard Rodriguez
Samuel Gompers	Lewis Thomas
Eric Hoffer	Virginia Woolf
Garrison Keillor	Richard Wright
Jack London	

Process

Giving a friend directions to your home, building a sundeck for your home, and learning to water ski are all activities that involve a process, a step by step method to achieve a desired result. Here, more than in any other writing situation, clarity and accuracy are mandatory. Omission of one important step sends your reader back to square one, confused and angry.

In preparing directions, it is absolutely vital to study your audience. How much do they know about the subject? Are they experts or novices? You thoroughly mystify your readers if you write over their heads, and, in turn, you quickly bore them if you are too simplistic. Knowledge of your audience will determine not only your choice of words but also your approach to your subject, your extent and type of detail, and your tone. You are also wise to orient your readers to necessary equipment and to alert them to possible pitfalls. See the following:

John Kenneth Galbraith   William Swanson
Peter Medawar   Marvin H. Swift
Sherry Sweetnam

APPENDIX C

Index to Some Composition Concerns

The following list indexes selections from the text according to major composition concerns and strategies. For an illustration from a selection employing rhetorical questions, allusion, or irony, for example, the reader may quickly refer to selections listed under the appropriate heading. This list is not exhaustive but merely indexes various elements of composition that are especially well executed.

FOCUS

THESIS

Arthur Ashe

Rachel Carson

Frederick Douglass

William McGowan

Malcolm X

ORGANIZATION AND DEVELOPMENT

OVERALL COMPOSITION ADVICE

John Kenneth Galbraith

Peter Medawar

George Orwell

Marvin Swift

TOPIC SENTENCES
Rachel Carson
John Kenneth Galbraith
William McGowan
Peter Medawar
Alleen Pace Nilsen
Priscilla Scherer
Lewis Thomas

METHODS — SEE RHETORICAL INDEX

COMBINATION OF METHODS
Lance Morrow
Anthony Sousa
William Swanson
David Vogel

COHERENCE
Jane Brody ("Anger")
Jane Brody ("Bulimia")
Gilbert Highet
William McGowan

TRANSITIONS
Rachel Carson
John Kenneth Galbraith
Alleen Pace Nilsen
Neil Postman
Arlene Skolnick

INTRODUCTIONS
Jane Brody ("Bulimia")
John Hoppock
William McGowan

CONCLUSIONS
Rachel Carson
Horace Porter
Neil Postman

SUCCINCT CONCLUDING SENTENCES
Samuel Gompers
John Hoppock

478

Arlene Skolnick
Lewis Thomas
Richard Wright

STYLE AND DICTION

ALLUSION
Maya Angelou
John Kenneth Galbraith
Tillie Olsen
Anthony Sousa
Alice Walker

ANTITHESIS
Frederick Douglass
Gilbert Highet
John F. Kennedy

DIALOGUE
Jack London
Jesse Owens
Richard Wright

CONNOTATION AND DENOTATION
Paul Blumberg
Gilbert Highet
Alleen Pace Nilsen
George Orwell
Anthony Sousa

FIGURATIVE LANGUAGE

Discussion of Figurative Language — George Orwell
Paul Blumberg
H. L. Mencken
Lance Morrow
Anne Roiphe
Henry David Thoreau
Alice Walker
George Will
Virginia Woolf

IRONY
  John Hoppock
  Garrison Keillor
  Jonathan Swift

PARALLELISM
  William Faulkner
  Thomas Jefferson
  John F. Kennedy
  Martin Luther King, Jr.
  Abraham Lincoln
  Priscilla Scherer

PERSONAL VOICE
  Arthur Ashe
  Paul Blumberg
  Loren Eiseley
  Martin Luther King, Jr.
  Henry David Thoreau

REPETITION FOR EFFECT
  Alan Alda
  William Faulkner
  John F. Kennedy
  Jesse Owens
  Lewis Thomas

RHETORICAL QUESTIONS
  John Hoppock
  Barbara Jordan
  Alleen Pace Nilsen
  Anthony Sousa
  Sherry Sweetnam
  Alice Walker

SENTENCE LENGTH VARIETY
  Benjamin Franklin
  Lewis Thomas

SPECIFIC DETAIL
  Ann Bayer
  Anne Roiphe

APPENDIX D

Glossary of Terms

Abstract/concrete words: Abstract words are vague, general terms — love, honor, virtue, patriotism — which do not bring pictures to our mind. Concrete words usually produce specific sensory images. Prefer the concrete over the abstract:
"He is six feet tall" instead of "He is a tall man."
"Jane has maintained a 3.95 grade point average during four years of college." instead of "She's a smart girl."

Allusion: An indirect reference to a person, place, or event. Allusions may be made to history, literature (especially Shakespeare, Greek and Roman mythology), the Bible, the contemporary scene (see Galbraith).

"We are all desperately afraid of sounding like Carry Nation."

"But anyone who is not certifiably a Milton had better assume that the first draft is a very primitive thing."

The use of allusions can be a very rewarding technique for writers: (a) allusions provide clarity by succinctly showing relationships or citing examples; (b) they are an economic means of supporting or proving a point because they are basically undeveloped examples or references or illustrations; (c) they sometimes add a scholarly, well-read tone to the writing; and (d) when aptly

483

used, they allow the reader to experience a flush of rapport or even satisfaction upon recognizing the reference (though failure to recognize sometimes makes one feel inadequate or stupid).

Antithesis: A figure of speech in which opposites are paired in similar grammatical constructions, either words, phrases, clauses, sentences, or ideas. Writers use this figure for clarification ("not this, but that") and emphasis. The following example has been endlessly quoted:

> *And so, my fellow Americans: ask not what your country can do for you — ask what you can do for your country.*
>
> JOHN F. KENNEDY, Inaugural Address

Abraham Lincoln also employed antithesis in his Second Inaugural. The second sentence in the following quotation from that speech, only four words, forms a powerful climax.

> *Both parties deprecated war; but one of them would make war rather than let the nation survive, and the other would accept war rather than let it perish. And the war came.*

Lincoln also used antithesis in the "Gettysburg Address":

> *The world will little note nor long remember what we say here but it can never forget what they did here.*

Other examples of antithesis:

> *If a free society cannot help the many who are poor, it cannot save the few who are rich.*
>
> JOHN F. KENNEDY, Inaugural Address

> *The honest man takes pains and then enjoys pleasures; the knave takes pleasures, and then suffers pain.*
>
> BENJAMIN FRANKLIN, *Poor Richard's Almanac*

Balanced parallelism: Achieved by repeating the syntactical construction, thereby creating two coordinate (equal) structures. (See Parallelism for illustrations):
"To be or not to be. . . ."

Colloquial: Informal English characteristic of spoken rather than written English, not considered substandard or illiterate but generally not appropriate to formal, written discourse.

Coherence/Connectives: Coherent writing is writing that hangs together; everything belongs and is connected. Coherence depends not only on unity of subject matter but also on how well the writer has inserted connectives to tie the sentences and paragraphs together. The following analysis of a paragraph from Paul Blumberg's "Snarling Cars" will serve to illustrate how one writer achieves paragraph coherence by carefully constructing his sentences to indicate their relationship to other sentences in the paragraph.

[1]In 1949 the U.A.W.'s research and engineering people published an article, "A Motor Car Named Desire," that called on Detroit to build a small, light, affordable car, suitable for postwar urban America. [2]They cited a contemporary opinion survey taken by the Society of Automotive Engineers, which showed that 60 percent of Americans wanted the U.S. auto industry to produce a small car. [3]Specifically, the U.A.W. proposed a car about 170 inches in length, weighing about 2,000 pounds, with a small six- or four-cylinder engine that would get more than 25 miles to the gallon. [4]In other words, the U.A.W. proposed a car almost identical in conception to the Datsuns, Toyotas, and Hondas now inundating America. [5]Had Detroit heeded the U.A.W.'s advice then, it would now have the experience to meet and beat the small-car competition from abroad, rather than belatedly struggling to catch up. [6]But it ignored the suggestion; in fact, it responded to Walter Reuther's presumption with a bold assertion of executive power meant to keep the union in its place and to protect the principle of managerial prerogative. [7]In its contract with the U.A.W. in 1950, and in every contract thereafter, G.M. inserted a clause stipulating the "Rights of Management." [8]It provided that "the products to be manufactured, the location of plants, the schedules of production, the methods, processes and means of manufacturing are solely and exclusively the responsibility of the Corporation."

Blumberg's article discusses how the managers of the auto industry did themselves in, and the paragraphs preceding this one concern management's decision to build large cars instead of *small* ones. This paragraph is linked to the earlier ones by its reference to *small* cars in the first sentence. The 1949 U.A.W. article, mentioned in this first sentence, calling for the production of small cars, its details and management's reactions to it, becomes the subject of the paragraph. The sponsor of the article and research, the U.A.W., appears in five of the eight sentences; one additional sentence mentions Walter Reuther, president of the U.A.W. These repetitions are constant reminders of the central subject, the U.A.W. proposal. At the same time they serve to cement the sentence relationships. (Keep in mind the value of *repetition* and *connectives* in your own writing.)

"They" in sentence two refers to "U.A.W.'s research and engineering people" in sentence one, the people who prepared the article. The sentence itself provides support for the recommendations in sentence one, namely the call to build a small car.

By beginning sentence three with "Specifically," the writer implies a connection to the preceding sentence and signals that this sentence will list the *details*—the specifics—of the U.A.W. proposal. The sentence lists four details of the proposal.

Sentence four begins with "In other words," again implying that a sentence has preceded this one, and then goes on to give meaning to the details supplied in sentence three. The U.A.W., in other words, had called for the production of the same kind of cars Japan is now exporting to the United States.

Sentence five starts with a conditional clause and draws a conclusion. It is linked to previous sentences by its repetition of "U.A.W." and by including the word "advice," a reference to the U.A.W. proposal ("proposed a car") in sentences four and three and to "article" in sentence one. It also repeats "Detroit," a metonymy for the "auto industry," both of which terms appear in sentences two and one. Had Detroit heeded the U.A.W., Blumberg asserts, there would be no problem with imported small cars.

"But" in sentence six implies that another sentence has preceded it and alerts the reader that the content of the sentence *contrasts* with the content of sentence five. "Suggestion" is a synonym for "advice" in sentence five and for the U.A.W. proposal "proposed" in sentences four and three and to the "article" in sentence one. "It" in both clauses of this sentence refers back to "Detroit" in sentence five. Not only did Detroit reject the U.A.W. suggestion, management boldly asserted its prerogative.

Sentence seven clarifies sentence six by explaining how management insured its prerogative. The repetition of "U.A.W." in this sentence is linked to "Walter Reuther" of the U.A.W. in the preceding sentence and to the "U.A.W." in the earlier sentences. G.M., one of the Detroit auto companies, stipulated the "Rights of Management" in its U.A.W. contract.

The content of sentence eight links to sentence seven because it explains what is meant by "rights of management" in sentence seven. The use of "It" refers back to "clause" in sentence seven.

Not all writers are as careful as Blumberg in constructing and ordering their sentences coherently to aid the reader's comprehension. All his sentences are relevant to the subject and follow in logical sequence. The many *connectives* serve to reinforce the logical sequence and aid the reader in seeing the relationships between the sentences. Thus, *form* reinforces *meaning*.

Coordination/Subordination: Ordinarily important ideas are placed in independent clauses; lesser ideas or modifying ideas in subordinate clauses. Note the two versions of the complex sentence below (one independent clause and one subordinate clause):

When I stopped to tie my shoe lace, a huge truck crashed into the fire hydrant behind me.

Or:

A huge truck crashed into the fire hydrant behind me when I stopped to tie my shoe lace.

The important idea is in the underlined independent clause; the lesser idea is in the subordinate clause. It would be ludicrous to coordinate the two ideas, as in the sentence below (i.e., putting both ideas in independent clauses and joining with a coordinating conjunction):

I stopped to tie my shoe lace, and a huge truck crashed into the fire hydrant behind me.

Manifestly, the second of the two ideas is the more important, and its position in the independent clause should indicate that (i.e., form reinforces meaning). Coordination implies that the joined, or coordinated, elements are of equal importance. (Regard coordinating conjunctions — *and, but, or, nor, for, yet,* and *so* — as the grammatical equivalents of equal signs.)

Coordination and subordination are important concepts to understand when you are combining sentences. If you find that you are stringing out a series of simple sentences, try combining them and making compound sentences or complex sentences.

Two simple sentences: I have completed my homework. Now I have time to help you.

A compound sentence: I have completed my homework, so now I have time to help you.

A complex sentence: Because I have completed my homework, I have time to help you.

Or: I have time to help you because I have completed my homework.

Some of the most common subordinating conjunctions:

after	before	though	when	till	where
although	as	if	unless	whether	because
once	since	that	while	why	

A common student error is to write a subordinate clause as a sentence, resulting in a sentence fragment. Subordinate clauses cannot stand alone; they must be attached to independent clause(s).

In high school I played football. Which was my best sport.

In high school I played football, which was my best sport.

Denotation/Connotation: The dictionary definition of a word is its denotation, but words also have connotations, emotional overtones acquired through years of use and association. You must be aware of the connotation of words, since writers often establish tone and convey style through the connotation of the words they use (see Lance Morrow, "What is the Point of Working?") There is a world of difference between saying, "This is my house" and "This is my home." Both "house" and "home" may denote the same thing, but the emotional aura surrounding the word "home," its connotation, is not conveyed by the word "house." Connotation was important to Abraham Lincoln when he used "Fourscore and seven years ago. . . . " The occasion of the address was a solemn one and called for compatible language and tone. "Fourscore and seven" echoes the language of the Bible, and Lincoln's use of it instead of "Eighty-seven" brought to his address something of the emotion and feeling people associate with the Bible. Lincoln recognized that people respond to words both intellectually and emotionally. Words can also be used for their pejorative connotations. (See Paul Blumberg, "Snarling Cars.")

Diaries/Journals: Although the distinction is sometimes blurred, a "journal" is a notebook of sorts in which one daily records observations, insights, experiences, whereas a diary is primarily a recording of one's daily activities. We suggest that you also use the journal to record new additions to your vocabulary, to list misspelled words, to record quotations and felicitous expressions, unusual phrasings, and so on.

Economy: The omission of every word, phrase, sentence, paragraph, or idea irrelevant to the main idea; a conciseness of expression that contributes to clarity without sacrificing grace or style. To achieve economy, the writer (a) naturally excises any unnecessary word; (b) attempts to use strong verbs and precise nouns and adjectives, making one word do the work of several less exact words; or (c) condenses clauses into phrases or adjectives.

Emphasis: One of several methods employed in writing to make an idea (or word or phrase) stand out. An idea may be emphasized by (a) positioning it first or last in a sentence, paragraph, or paper; (b) allotting it a generous amount of space; (c) repeating the ideas, using similar words or parallel, balanced, or antithetical construction; (d) condensing it into a single terse sentence or epigram; (e) using a particular sentence construction; (f) adding intensifiers (*too, very, much, extremely*); (g) inverting word order; or (h) employing mechanical devices such as paragraphing, dashes, italics, exclamation marks, capital letters.

Euphony: The selection and patterning of words so as to be pleasing to the ear. The skillful writer avoids strident, cacophonous prose and instead orders words for a smooth, pleasant, harmonious presentation (see Sousa, Unit III, for discussion with examples.)

Five W's and How: The journalist's traditional method of establishing the who, what, when, where, why, and how of the subject early in the news story in an effort to quickly orient the reader and clarify the essentials (see McGowan and Brody).

Inductive/Deductive Reasoning/Development: Induction moves from the specific to the general; deductive moves from the general to the specific. In writing, Lewis Thomas's "Nurses" is developed inductively, that is to say he develops a number of particulars before arriving at a general conclusion. The best illustration of deductive development is the Declaration of Independence. See Syllogism, below, for the way an argument is developed. See also Thomas H. Huxley in Supplementary Readings for further discussion.

Inversion: A variation of the normal subject-verb-object sentence order, used as a stylistic device to achieve variety of emphasis.

Normal order: (subject)	(verb)	(object)
He	liked	that
Inverted order: (object)	(subject)	(verb)
That	he	liked
Inverted order: (complement)	(subject)	(verb)
A bargain	it	was, from her viewpoint.

Irony: A figure of speech — more easily detected in the spoken than in the written word — whereby the manner and context in which words are used implies their direct opposite, as when Antony says of Caesar's murderer, "Brutus is an honorable man." Some readers often fail to notice irony either because they are perhaps too literal-minded (hence they take Jonathan Swift's "A Modest Proposal" seriously and are outraged at Swift's recommendation that the starving Irish sell their babies as food for the rich); or they are unused to the subtleties of language. Often, too, they mistake irony for the more familiar sarcasm, which is harsher, more obvious, as when a friend double-crosses you and you respond: "Thank you very much!" Irony involves a disparity between what writers say and what they mean, between what is intended and what happens (sometimes called poetic justice), and in drama between what the audience knows and what particular characters know. See Garrison Keillor's selection on "Shy Rights." We know he does not intend his proposal to be taken seriously, because there is a disparity between what he believes and what he says.

Loose sentence (also cumulative sentence):   One in which the main idea comes early in the sentence. This is the most common type of sentence and is unlike the periodic sentence where the meaning is not clear until the end of the sentence.

Periodic: The world will little note nor long remember what we say here but it can never forget what they did here.

Loose: The world can never forget what they did here as countless speakers will continue to remind us in years to come.

Metaphor: A figure of speech in which an implied comparison is made between one thing and another, "ship of state," "Himalayan praise," "in tune with the times," "mad-dog killer," "wild-cat strike," "powdered snow." (See Orwell for further discussion.)

Metonymy: A figure of speech in which the name of one thing is substituted for that of another to which it has some logical relation: "the crown" for the king; "the bottle" for strong drink; "the Vatican says" for the Pope says; "London says" for the British government says; "Hollywood" for the motion picture industry; "Detroit" for the automobile industry.

Overstatement (hyperbole, hyperbolic):   A deliberate exaggeration, as in "Fail to turn in your paper on time and we'll hang you up by your thumbs for twenty-four hours." Or: "George Whitefield was such a powerful speaker that when he rolled his tongue over the word 'Mesopotamia,' frail women fainted and strong men wept." (Edmund Kean, famous Shakespearian actor, speaking of England's noted evangelist.)

Oxymoron: A figure of speech in which contradictory terms are paired for emphasis. For example: "sweet sorrow," "deafening silence," "terribly happy," "frightfully beautiful," "deliciously painful." Use of such figures, when appropriate, attracts the reader's attention and lends interest and emphasis to the ideas expressed.

Paradox (paradoxical):   An apparent contradiction which is nevertheless true. It can apply to a statement or to a situation: "Paradoxically, he was happiest when he was losing." It is often used to achieve emphasis and draw attention to important ideas (see Galbraith). Frederick Douglass suggests that education can be both a *blessing* and a *curse.* In the context both statements — contradictory through they may be — are nevertheless true.

Parallelism: A rhetorical structure in which similar grammatical constructions of words, phrases, clauses in series are repeated in a sentence or sentences. It is used by writers to gain emphasis, coherence, and euphony (see Jefferson, Lincoln). For effective parallelism equal ideas should be expressed in coordinate constructions. That is, if one element of a parallel construction is a prepositional phrase, then the other equal elements should be prepositional phrases. If one element is an adjective, then other equal elements should be adjectives.

Faulty parallelism: The tour group hated to rush through the Capitol, missing the White House, and after lunch, they had to skip the Supreme Court buildings.

Correct parallelism: The tour group hated rushing through the Capitol, missing the White House, and after lunch, skipping the Supreme Court buildings.

Not only should the constructions be similar, but each component (in both parallel and balanced constructions) should be relatively equal in importance, in number of words, in types of modifiers, and in verb tense. In serial parallelism make sure the elements are in ascending order of importance. A descending order tends to make for humor if the last element is anticlimactic (see Galbraith). The use of parallelism and balance offers several advantages to the writer: (a) The repetition tends to *reinforce* and *emphasize* what is being said; (b) Parallelism provides an economical way to add *support* and *credence* for your thesis by using three or four quick examples in one sentence; (c) The construction helps to *show relationships* by putting equivalent ideas and constructions in parallel, balanced series; (d) it is an excellent stylistic device because it is *euphonious*. It sounds right and creates a certain rhythm that can become even lyrical or poetic at times.

Paraphrase: A restatement *in your own words* of a passage of writing to condense and/or clarify its meaning. In paraphrasing one does not change the meaning, only the words and form or structure. But you do not merely change a word or two; paraphrasing is more like translating. Eliminate all unnecessary material and identify the main and important subpoints. Avoid personal opinion.

Parentheticals: Remarks placed between parentheses or paired dashes (i.e., words, phrases, sentences) set off from the main part of the sentence, either to amplify, rename, repeat differently, or add to what has gone before. See Tillie Olsen for lavish use of parenthetical interrupters. Parenthetical material is generally not considered vital but is of peripheral interest. Many parentheticals tend to slow down the reading, as in the Olsen selection. Many writers prefer paired dashes, if only for aesthetic reasons.

Periodicity/periodic sentence: The periodic sentence produces its effect by withholding its meaning until the end of the sentence. The writer thus builds up suspense in the reader's mind so that all the emphasis falls on the end of the sentence. President John F. Kennedy employed such a sentence in his Inaugural Address:

Let every nation know, whether it wishes us well or ill, that we shall pay any price, bear any burden, meet any hardship, support any friend, oppose any foe to assure the survival and success of liberty.

The first sentence of the Declaration of Independence employs periodicity so that the emphasis falls on the final clause.

491

When in the course of human events, it becomes necessary for one people to dissolve the political bands which have connected them with another, and to assume among the powers of the earth, the separate and equal station to which the Laws of Nature and of Nature's God entitle them, a decent respect to the opinions of mankind requires that they should declare the causes which impel them to the separation.

Point of view: Point of view is the perspective from which a writer communicates and is determined by the grammatical person chosen. It can be in the first person (I), as in Frederick Douglass's account of his life as a slave and his attempt to learn to read and write; in the second person (You), as in Sherry Sweetnam's instructions on how to write effective business communications; and in the third person (It), as in Jane Brody's article on anger or bulimia.

Précis: A concise summary that maintains the focus, organization, and tone of the original document (see Medawar, Unit III).

Rhetorical questions: Questions asked by the writer to which no real answer is expected, or questions which the writer proceeds to answer. They are frequently used to provoke thought, initiate a topic, or stress a point (see Lance Morrow, Unit II).

Satire: A witty or humorous, critical assessment of institution(s) or individual(s), the object of which is to entertain and/or to change for the better. Satire can be literary, dramatic, pictorial, or musical in form, and gentle or biting in tone. It is the most conspicuous feature of the popular television program "Saturday Night Live." Satire also characterizes the so-called "roasts" of politicians and other celebrities. (See Jonathan Swift.)

Sentence variety: Sentences vary in:

1. Purpose (declarative — provides information
       interrogative — asks questions
       imperative — issues commands or requests
       exclamatory — expresses strong feeling, emphatic).
2. Length (long or short).
3. Completeness (full or elliptical).
4. Syntax (simple, compound, complex, compound-complex).
5. Word order (subject-verb-object or inverted: object-subject-verb). For greater variety start sentences with modifiers such as infinitives, participles, and prepositional phrases.
6. Form (loose or periodic).

Sentimentality: Shallow and excessive use of emotion in dealing with an idea or an event. Sentimentality is often seen in some newspaper accounts of deaths

492

or accidents, especially of the young or helpless. Hence the term "sob story," meaning that the writer has gone beyond what the normal reader expects. Sentimentality is also evident in much of television and in many movies.

Simile: A figure of speech in which a comparison is made between two seemingly dissimilar things, usually introduced by "like" or "as." (See Medawar: "Further, writing should be as far as possible natural — that is, not worn like a Sunday suit. . . . " Others: "light as a feather," "mean as a snake," "hot as Hades," "quick as a flash," "like putty in his hands," "like a ribbon of steel." "The Ambassador's elaborate plans to restore the economy of the underdeveloped country were about as effectual as rearranging the deck chairs on the *Titanic*."

Speaking and writing differences: A speaker, just as a writer, must structure a speech with the subject, purpose, audience, and occasion clearly in mind. The latter two, audience and occasion, assume even greater importance for the speaker, inasmuch as in most cases (other than radio and television addresses) the audience is clearly visible, and the occasion is usually specific. Speakers must devote special attention to their audience's (a) knowledge of the subject, (b) background (age, education, religious affiliation, interests, prejudices), and (c) attitude toward the subject — favorable, apathetic, or hostile (see Methods-Argumentation). Logical, emotional, and ethical appeals are important considerations, particularly in persuasive speeches. Here, ethical appeals, the speaker's expertise, background, and character play an even greater role than in writing. Because there is a closer audience relationship, the speaker may effectively employ second person ("you"), and on less formal occasions may assume a more conversational tone. The speaker's chief concern is clarity (there are no opportunities to "reread" and time limits prohibit digressions). The need to be direct and concise usually translates into shorter sentences, as well as a more quickly comprehended vocabulary and sentence construction. Speakers as well as writers must be concerned about euphony, emphasis, stimulating introductions, and memorable, climactic conclusions. (See Alda, Faulkner, Lincoln, Jordan, and Kennedy speeches.)

Style: The characteristic way in which a writer expresses him or herself. Partly conscious and partly unconscious, style is the result of the individual writer's choices: in words, both for their denotation and connotation; in figurative language; in the shaping, length, and variety of sentences; and in the method of development. We catch something of the personality of the writer in his or her style. Style is best illustrated in this text by comparing radically different examples. Tillie Olsen employs a highly elliptical style in *Silences*: long sentences with many parenthetical digressions and truncated sentences. Eric Hoffer, on the other hand, opts for a cleaner, more concise and direct style, more aphoristic. Some of Hoffer's short, pithy sentences are eminently quotable, while Olsen's sentences, rarely short and pithy, are not. On the other

493

hand, Jefferson's style in the Declaration of Independence is an elevated one, solemn, with long sentences, carefully balanced and properly subordinated.

Like Franklin and Hoffer, you can improve your style. When you run across a particularly appealing style, try to emulate it. In time you will evolve your own style made up of elements you pick up from the writers you admire.

Subordination: See Coordination.

Syllogism: (See Jefferson Study Questions for suggestions on how to frame a contemporary argument.) A syllogism is a logical, three-part deductive argument consisting of a *major premise,* a *minor premise,* and a *conclusion.* The following is a categorical syllogism, the type employed in the Declaration of Independence.

> Major premise: All men are mortal.
> Minor premise: Socrates is a man.
> Therefore: Socrates is mortal.

In order to arrive at a valid conclusion, the major premise must be a universal proposition, that is to say, there can be no exceptions.

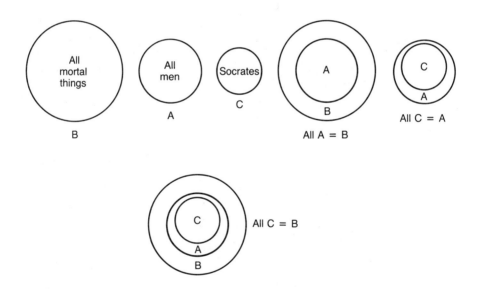

> All of A is contained in B.   All men (A) are mortal (B)
> All of C is contained in A   Socrates (C) is a man (A)
> TF: All of C is contained in B   Socrates (C) is mortal (B)

Argument in the Declaration of Independence

A		B
All people whose governments are denying them their God-given rights.	= (are)	All people who have the right to rebel and change their governments.

C		A
The people of the American colonies today.	= (are)	A people whose government is denying them their God-given rights.

C		B
The people of the American colonies today.	= (are)	A people who have the right to rebel and change their government.

The minor premise is the one the Colonists have to *prove*. To do this the Declaration lists a series of violations. Hence, the conclusion is inescapable: revolution.

Symbol: A person, place, thing, idea, word, and so on to which the writer assigns meaning beyond the literal, or which has acquired such meaning through long usage. See Ann Bayer, where a gesture by the doorman becomes a symbol for the writer. (Many symbols exist in the public mind: for example, the cross upon which Christ was crucified became the symbol for Christianity. Such symbols are, of course, different from those of individual authors.) Leaving home for the first time and going off to school may come to symbolize for you the beginning of a new life.

Thesis: The controlling idea of a composition; a one- or two-sentence assertion about the main point of a paper. Where none exists, in good writing an implicit thesis statement can be framed that sets forth the central point the writer is trying to make (see Writing Process for an extended discussion).

Tone: Tone is a reflection of the writer's attitude toward the subject. In oral communication, one's attitude toward a subject is conveyed in one's tone of voice. In written communication, tone is conveyed in word choice and sentence structure. (In some cases, tone is also conveyed by the unconventional positioning of material on a page: the poetry of E.E. Cummings, for example.) Tone can be serious, frivolous, ironic, satirical, poignant, nostalgic, scientific, objective, colloquial, favorable, unfavorable, optimistic, pessimistic. It may have a biting edge (see Tillie Olsen), or it may project the self-assured tone of Jean Bethke Elshtain. It may be poignant and nostalgic, as in Ann Bayer, or it may be satirical and humorous, as in Garrison Keillor. Tone must be appropriate to the subject, occasion, and purpose.

Topic sentence: A topic sentence is a one-sentence summary of a paragraph. It can be explicit, in which case it is usually the first sentence in the paragraph; or it may be implicit, in which case the reader must mentally form the sentence. Explicit topic sentences serve as a kind of a blueprint for all the other sentences in the paragraph. Each must clarify, amplify, explain, or develop the topic sentence.

Transitions: Words, phrases, clauses, usually used at the beginning of sentences to show relationships, to establish coherence. (Sentences and short paragraphs can also serve as transitions.) Transitional devices may be used to indicate sequence ("first," "second," "third"); to show time relationships "before," "later," "when"); to make comparisons or contrasts ("similarly," "on the other hand," "nevertheless"); to show cause and effect ("therefore," "thus," "consequently"); to exemplify ("for example," "for instance"); to emphasize ("most importantly," "indeed," "even more significant"); to summarize ("in conclusion," "in summary," "in short"), and so on.

Understatement (litotes):   A figure of speech that minimizes for emphasis, as in "You'll have to admit that ten inches of rain in less than twenty-four hours is a bit much." Or: "I would not be displeased in the least if I won the million-dollar lottery."

Unity: In writing, the combination of materials (words, phrases, sentences, paragraphs, ideas) that lead to one overall, holistic effect. The writer must eliminate any extraneous matter that detracts from that design and continuity of purpose.

498

row Hawks," Copyright © 1955 by Loren Eiseley. Reprinted from THE IMMENSE JOURNEY, by Loren Eiseley, by permission of Random House, Inc.; From THE AUTOBI-OGRAPHY OF MALCOLM X with Alex Haley. Copyright © 1964 by Alex Haley and Malcolm X. Copyright © 1965 by Alex Haley and Betty Shabazz. Reprinted by permission of Random House, Inc.; Copyright © 1932 by Alfred A. Knopf, Inc. and renewed 1960 by Edwina C. Rubenstein. Reprinted from COLLECTED POEMS OF ELINOR WYLIE, by permission of the publisher.

Albert Shanker. "Literacy Requires Learning the Culture," by Albert Shanker, from a column entitled "Where We Stand," published in the *New York Times* (August 4, 1985). Reprinted by permission.

Simon & Schuster. "Ray Kroc: Artist of the Hamburger" by George F. Will, from THE PURSUIT OF VIRTUE AND OTHER TORY NOTIONS, pp. 300–303. Copyright © 1982 Reprinted by permission.

Arlene Skolnick. "The Paradox of Perfection" by Arlene Skolnick, Wilson Quarterly (Summer 1980), pp. 113–121. Reprinted by permission.

Graham Spanier. "Outsiders Looking In," by Graham Spanier. Wilson Quarterly (Summer 1980), pp. 122–129. Reprinted by permission.

Time. "What Is the Point of Working?" by Lance Morrow. Copyright 1981 Time Inc. All rights reserved. Reprinted by permission from TIME.

Viking Penguin, Inc. "Nurses," from THE YOUNGEST SCIENCE, by Lewis Thomas. Copyright © 1982 by Lewis Thomas. Reprinted by permission of Viking Penguin, Inc.

Index

To the Student
From the Authors

Just as your writing goes through various revisions, so, too, does a textbook. We have spent several years reworking sections of *Writing for Life* in response to suggestions from students and instructors. Now, your input will be a great help to us in preparing subsequent editions. We would like to know which selections work well, which ones helped you with your writing, which ones are ineffective. We, therefore, would greatly appreciate your taking a few minutes to note your reactions. Please place checks in the appropriate columns and mail your comments to College English Editor, Macmillan Publishing Company, 866 Third Avenue, New York, New York 10022.

Selection	Helped me with my writing	I liked particularly	I didn't like	I didn't read
UNIT I THE WRITER'S MOTIVATION: READING THE SELF-TAUGHT WRITER				
Douglass, "How I Learned to Read and Write"				
Cleaver, "On Becoming"				

Selection	Helped me with my writing	I liked particularly	I didn't like	I didn't read
London, "Martin Decides to Become a Writer"				
Malcolm X, "Words, Words, Words"				
Angelou, "Life Line"				
Franklin, "My Early Beginnings as a Writer"				
Hoffer, "Writing: Not a Rare Talent"				
Olsen, "Silences"				
UNIT II THE WRITER'S CONSCIOUSNESS: ENLARGING OUR WORLD THROUGH READING AND WRITING				
Hoffman, "On Keeping a Journal"				
Swanson "The Mail of the Species"				
Alda, "You Have to Know What Your Values Are"				
Brody, "Bulimia: Binge-Eating Cycles Followed by Purges and Guilt"				
Skolnick, "The Paradox of Perfection"				
Spanier, "Outsiders Looking In"				
Bayer, "After Death, Mememtos That Mean a Life"				
Brody, "Venting Anger May Do More Harm Than Good"				

Selection	Helped me with my writing	I liked particularly	I didn't like	I didn't read
Walker, "In Search of Our Mothers' Gardens"				
Wright, "Genesis of a Writer"				
Porter, Reflections of a Black Son"				
Elshtain, "A Feminist's Journey"				
Rodriquez, "Aria"				
Will, "Ray Kroc: Artist of the Hamburger"				
Morrow, "What is the Point of Working?"				
Ashe, "Send Your Children to the Libraries"				
Hoppock, "The Costs of Drinking"				
Blumberg, "Snarling Cars"				
McGowan, "Iliterasee att Wurk"				
Roiphe, "Confessions of a Female Chauvinist Sow"				
UNIT III WRITING INTHE WORLD OF WORK: READING AND WRITING ACROSS THE PROFESSIONS				
Medawar, "Presentations"				
Swift, "Clear Writing Means Clear Thinking Means. . . ."				
Sweetnam, "How to Organize Your Thoughts for Better Communication"				

INSTRUCTOR'S MANUAL
to Accompany

WRITING FOR LIFE

A WRITER'S READER

Marilyn Mayer Culpepper
Perry E. Gianakos

Michigan State University

Macmillan Publishing Company
NEW YORK

PREFACE

The same commitment to flexibility and practicality in our text
has been a primary concern in our preparation of this manual. First,
for instructors who prefer a topical organization of material, we
provide a thematic table of contents. The major portion of the
manual, however, is devoted to answers to the questions on Content
and Structure and Strategy at the end of each selection. Since
space does not permit our answering all of the questions, we
have attempted to cover some of the more challenging questions,
omitting some questions that are clearly identifiable in the text
or are matters of opinion. Upon occasion we have disregarded the
questions entirely and concentrated on specific   characteristics
or additional points of interest in a selection. The following
section contains the apparatus for the supplementary readings,
including answers and suggestions. (It should be noted that we
are not dogmatic and can easily envison other equally valid answers
to questions. The very controversial nature of some questions
should initiate thoughtful student analysis accompanied by lively
class discussions.)

Because we and many other instructors require research papers
or papers based on sources, we have included a list of research
topics (to supplement suggestions offered in the text itself)
based on subjects that either are spin-offs of reading topics or
are subjects alluded to in the various readings. The concluding
pages of the manual are devoted to suggestions for teaching
organization and for using journals and peer editing as pedagogical
aids for a writing course. A check list for student papers and
exercises that can be photocopied and used in class to point out
common writing errors complete the manual.

Macmillan Publishing Company
866 Third Avenue, New York, New York 10022

Collier Macmillan Canada, Inc.

Printing: 1 2 3 4 5 6 7   Year: 8 9 0 1 2 3 4

ISBN 0-02-341790-0

CONTENTS

iii

Unit III   Writing in the World of Work

THEMATIC TABLE OF CONTENTS

1

2

We start with the "self-taught" writer for two reasons: (1) We often encounter students who do not believe that they can write, who lament "I've always had trouble with English." Reading the experiences of these self-taught writers often spurs students to make a much more deliberate effort to improve their writing skills. If these disadvantaged people can do it, they reason, so can we. (2) We wish to demonstrate to students the power and sense of security one gains with the ability to clearly express oneself. The ability to write empowered these individuals to fulfill their innate potential. Acquiring this ability can do the same for students.

DOUGLASS: Some remarks about slave narratives may be appropriate before assigning the first selection. Douglass' account points up the fact that it was generally considered unlawful to teach slaves to read. Notable too is his mistress' changed attitude once she had been admonished to stop her reading instruction, illustrating how oppression distorts the personality of the oppressor.

Content:

2. Keeping slaves ignorant rendered them more manageable. Douglass sees literacy as a means to freedom.

3. Douglass learned about the "power of truth over the conscience of even a slaveholder."

4. Learning to read had given him a view of his own wretched condition without the remedy.

Strategy:

1a. Repetition of key words and ideas; phrases: "...as I have said...."
 b. "tender heart became stone;" "lamblike disposition gave way to one of tiger-like fierceness."

CLEAVER: Some remarks about the turbulent 60's and early 70's will help set the stage for both Cleaver and Malcolm X. William O'Neill's Coming Apart is a readily available reference.

Content:

2. Douglass is attempting to escape from physical bondage; Cleaver is attempting to free himself from self-imposed psychological bondage.

Strategy:

2. Paragraph two serves as a transition, emphasizes and points up writing as a means to save himself.

4. Paragraph four contains references to youth movements; Cleaver addresses the reader directly.

LONDON: Having gotten a taste of the novel from these selections, many students go on to read the novel. Although Martin Eden is set around the turn of the century, students do not find the story alien to their experience.

Content:

1. Their strange talk sends him to the library to check words; he leaves with new books.

2. Ch. IX, paragraph 5: On return from 8 months at sea, he determines to write: "There was career and the way to win to Ruth."

Strategy:

2. Martin's speech improves as a result of his intensive study while at sea.

3. "...his mind was fallow...ripe for the sowing;" "It had never been jaded by study, and it bit hold of the knowledge in the books with sharp teeth that would not let go."

MALCOLM X: This account begins after Malcolm X's brother had introduced him to Elijah Mohammad of the Black Muslims. During this period the Black Muslims had been spectacularly successful in rehabilitating black convicts and drug addicts. These are the same Black Muslims that the Reverend Martin Luther King, Jr. identifies in his "Letter from Birmingham Jail" as "extremists" (Unit III). They were Black Power advocates and preached a doctrine of racial separation.

Content:

3. After his study of the dictionary, Malcolm X could now understand what he was reading, a new world had opened.

4. His home education gave him "a little bit more sensitivity to the deafness, dumbness, and blindness that was afflicting the black race in America."

Strategy:

1. Malcolm mentions often that he was in prison; he also mentions other convicts, the prison library, guards, etc.

3. See paragraphs 3, 9, 10, 11, 13, 14, 22, 23, 24.

FRANKLIN: To pique student interest in Franklin, we generally start by asking students to speculate on why a person writes an autobiography. What kind of person writes an autobiography? Students may also be interested in contrasting this brief excerpt from Franklin's 18th century Autobiography with Malcolm X's 20th century effort. Interestingly, both authors complain of a want of words, though Franklin's aim here is to develop a style. He approached a solution to his problem through poetry; Malcolm X began copying the dictionary.

Content:

1. Franklin's father dissuades him from becoming a poet, although later Franklin employs poetry in his attempts to improve his style. Prose writing, was, as he writes, "a principal means of my advancement."

2. Franklin learned disputation from reading his father's polemical works. He abandoned it because he found it "disagreeable," "souring and spoiling conversations," etc.

3. From Xenophon he found models of the Socratic method. He practiced it for some time, eventually abandoning it in favor of a more studied diffidence.

Strategy:

1. Students may find Franklin's writing closer to Douglass' than to Malcolm X's. Both reflect an edifying/didactic purpose.

2. It might be useful to contrast Franklin's sentence length with sentences in a contemporary "How To" book.

HOFFER: Students who like this selection will also find Hoffer's other books provocative.

4

Content:

1. No longer able to use his talents to keep records, he turned
   his skill to "writing"--he became a "writer."

2. Hoffer democratically assumes we all have hidden talents,
   and these will manifest themselves if we are able to spread
   expertise in the arts and sciences as we do in mechanics
   and sports.

3. He had to acquire the "taste" for a good sentence. He
   gained that from reading and re-reading Montaigne's essays
   during the time he was snow-bound near Nevada City.

4. He implies that learning to write well is not a rare talent
   --anyone can do it.

Strategy:

1. Hoffer is livelier; his sentences are shorter. Some of his
   sentences have "hooks" in them to attract and delight the
   reader.

2. "Writing was invented not to write books but to keep books."
   "I have always had the feeling that the people I live and
   work with are lumpy with talent."
   "Where the development of talent is concerned we are still
   in the food-gathering stage. We do not know how to grow it."

ANGELOU: Students who like this selection might be interested
in reading the other volumes of her autobiography.

Content:

1. See paragraphs 2 through 5. She is revealed in her love of
   reading and her kindness to Marguerite. Angelou compares
   her to women she has read about in English novels--"who
   walked the moors...like the women who sit in front of
   roaring fireplaces, drinking tea incessantly from silver
   trays full of scones and crumpets."

2. The behavior and speech of each reveal differences in
   educational/social levels.

3. It has to be before the 1954 school desegregation decision,
   before the general use of refrigeration.

4. Her many literary references confirm that she is a voracious
   reader.

Strategy:

1. She wishes to point up the differences in the two households
   and in the two women. Momma is not well-read and takes
   speech literally. Mrs. Flowers is too well-read to do what
   momma did.

OLSEN: Instructors should caution students that Olsen's
elliptical style and her use of many parentheticals tend to slow the
reading. This is her intent, for she has some serious things to
say, and she piles on the documentation to support what she says.

Content:

1. Her thesis is best represented by her remarks in paragraph
   34, the next to last paragraph. Students should be able
   to come up with their own wording.

2. See paragraph 14: Men have also been silenced. Paragraph
   21: She denies that women need necessarily sacrifice claims
   to femininity and family life in order to become writers.

5

3. & 4. See paragraphs 16 through 24.

    Strategy:

    1. She mentions "silences" in paragraphs 2, 10, 13, 14, 30,
        etc.

3. & 4. Her style causes her occasionally to omit subjects and verbs.
         This cuts down on wordiness, but sometimes it may lead to
         confusion, since the reader is not always sure what verb
         she intends. The staccato effect that sometimes results
         from her style reflects conversational speech. Her many
         parentheticals reflect a complex mind at work on a serious
         subject. She has a great deal of information to convey,
         and much of it winds up in her parenthetical remarks.
         Sometimes these remarks are illustrations, examples,
         additional facts, or asides to the reader. Again, her very
         complex style tends to slow the reading, something she
         obviously intends.

    6. Olsen's vocabulary reflects extensive reading, as do her
        many allusions. Her profuse use of allusions suggests that
        she assumes her readers are familiar with most, if not all,
        of them. She is perhaps optimistic in her judgment.

                              Unit II

        In this unit we seek to emphasize the students' growing worlds:
the world of the self--the world of achievement and relationships
and the wider world of social engagement.

        HOFFMAN: The advantages of requiring journals in a writing
course are discussed in the later sections of this manual.

    Content:

    1.-5. Hoffman discovers rich material to write about close at
           home--on campus. The notebooks vividly recall the people,
           times, and events of his youth. In addition he meets a
           younger Hoffman. He calls a notebook a secret garden which
           you can call your own and in which you can frolic and "muse."
           Hoffman urges readers to write with abandon, without the
           fear of prying eyes.

6. & 7. See paragraphs 10 and 11.

    Strategy:

    1. There are several similies (paragraphs 1, 4, and 11);
        metaphors (paragraphs 4, 7, and 9); and allusions in para-
        graphs 4 and 9.

    2. Hoffman speaks of his college days--the girls, professors,
        buildings, and activities. The article was published in
        Newsweek On Campus. He urges students to keep notebooks
        in paragraph 8, and writes of the advantages to students of
        journal keeping. His work choice, tone, and examples
        indicate that he is writing for college students.

        SWANSON: The subject matter here, obviously, needs less analysis
than the style--the real object lesson in this selection. The
article warrants a detailed study of Swanson's use of a variety of
methods of development, of deft touches of humor, and of vivid
figurative language to energize what could have been an otherwise
humdrum topic.

        Letter writing is, of course, a subject all students know
something about; however, saying something of interest and substance
about such a common place subject is quite another thing. Therefore,
in a short in-class writing session, the day before the selection is

assigned, we ask our students to do a journal entry about letter writing. In the next period, after they have read the article, we study the selection with them in detail prior to asking them to revise their writing.

We encourage them (1) to draw on their own originality;(2) to appreciate the need for good organization in almost all types of writing; (3) to note Swanson's methods of development as he _defines_, _compares_, _contrasts_, _classifies_, and _describes_ letters, cites dozens of _examples_, draws _analogies_, suggests a _process_, shows _cause_ _and_ _effect_, _narrates_ about receiving letters, and in the end attempts to _persuade_ his readers; (4) to understand the importance of specific detail and examples to set the tone, to support ideas, and to capture and sustain reader interest (for example: "displayed, envelopeless, under a strawberry magnet on a refrigerator door," or "still damp from the abysmal mimeograph machine "); (5) to see how the allusions to both popular and classical writers add an air of erudition to the writing; and (6) to comprehénd the value of a more precise word (and in Swanson's case a more humorous word) in place of a less expressive more routine word. (For example: "hoard" for save, "torched" for burned, "rife" for full, "heft" for weight.)

Now and in later life students can greatly enhance their sphere of influence through letters which raise spirits--and money, direct action, inspire, forewarn, or charm.

ALDA: The government, the ministry, the military, organized sports, unions are all coming under fire for their moral lapses. After first taking stock of their own values, students can then go on to examine the moral commitment or moral disintegration that they observe in the world around them. (National surveys of students' reasons for coming to college are yielding some primarily materialistic motives these days.)

Content:

1. See paragraph 2. 2. See paragraph 5.

3. We refer to people who say one thing and do another as hypocrites.

4. See last paragraph.

Strategy:

1. The tone of this selection could be considered hortatory. Word choice, examples, and sentence structure convey tone. Alda is speaking to America's future leaders and is urging them to shore up their values.

3. It appears Alda is seeking emphasis.

4. In his final paragraph Alda summarizes the important values in life as he sees them and ties them in with work, the world that is soon to occupy much of the future time and effort of these new college graduates. He achieves unity by tying his conclusion to his introduction.

BRODY (Bulimia): Problems of self-esteem can often turn otherwise rational human beings into victims of bulimia or anorexia nervosa. The problems are so pervasive that it takes little prodding to stimulate a discussion about dieting, nutrition, health fads, and America's growing health concerns.

Content:

1. Brody seems to be saying that bulimia is a growing problem with serious consequences. Her analysis of the problems, dangers, and treatment build to her concluding sentence which appears to be her message.

7

2. See paragraph 9.

3. & 4. See paragraphs 10 through 15.   5. See paragraph 6.

6. See paragraphs 19-22.

Strategy:

1. Brody starts with a confession and a brief case study.

3. Brody uses subject-verb-object sentence structure for clarity.

SKOLNICK: This selection is punctuated with allusions to writers, psychologists. Students might do some additional research/reading.

Content:

1. Skolnick's thesis is generally set forth in paragraph 1.

2. See paragraphs 4 through 7. Popular culture gives us an illusion that conflicts with reality.

3. See paragraphs 29 through 31.

4. See paragraphs 33 & 34.

Strategy:

1. In paragraph 3, Skolnick introduces "ambiguity," which in paragraph 4 prompts a rhetorical question. To illustrate, she quotes from the New Yorker. In paragraph 5, she develops the paradox into "illusion" and "reality." In paragraph 6 she cites illustrations from the popular media. In paragraph 9 she invites the reader to compare the past with the present. She summarizes in paragraph 16 and notes some similarities between the two periods.

2. She uses statistics and historical analysis (colonial and 19th century).

3. The topic sentence in paragraph 3 serves for paragraphs 3 and 4; the TS in paragraph 10 serves for paragraphs 10 through 13.

5. She offers only assertions.

SPANIER: Students will have a wealth of material to drawn on for discussion and writing on the consequences of marriage and divorce in their own families and in those of their contemporaries; on the development of high school liaisons; and on the problems of pre-marital sex, AIDS, "children having children," etc.

Content:

1. See paragraphs 3 through 6.   2. See paragraphs 8 & 9.

3. See paragraph 10.   4. See paragraph 14.

Stragegy:

2. Spanier seems to be analyzing current research on marriage and divorce for a general audience rather than for a specialized audience of social scientists, psychologists, or researchers.

1. Spanier varies his use of introductory topic sentences with rhetorical questions (paragraph 8 & 14), a correction of a popular misconception which leads into paragraph 10, and the notation of just one aspect in paragraph 16 and 17 instead

8

of summary topic sentences.

3. Spanier's tone could be said to be objective and authoritative.

BAYER: This selection hits home with almost all students, and, therefore, instead of answering the review questions, we will simply note our experience in using this selection.

The nostalgia and emotion elicit a certain empathy from the students and inspire them to examine some of their own personal relationships. These relationships are special ones and students can easily come up with specific examples and personal touches that greatly enhance their writing. Since students often do quite well on these papers, they serve as morale builders (for both students and instructors) after a series of discouraging grades and papers.

In discussing the selection, we ask our students to describe Ann Bayer's mother. This exercise underscores the importance of "showing" rather than "telling." Although Bayer does not say "She was imaginative, cultured, likeable, good natured...," students can draw these conclusions for themselves. We then ask students to repeat the exercise by listing some of the characteristics of Bayer herself.

We next ask students to reexamine the selection to discover techniques that Bayer uses that they can effectively employ in their own writing. This leads them to observe Bayer's use of specifics. For example: in paragraph 13 Bayer writes "Other events, public and private, took its place." Inexperienced writers might leave it at that, but Bayer identifies specific events, briefly, economically, without wasting a whole paragraph for each example. Students should note the similes in paragraphs 1, 2, and 8, for example. They should be aware of the very precise word choice in "a favorite customer" in paragraph 8. It was not a manicurist and any customer, but rather a "favorite" customer. They should identify the parallel constructions at the end of paragraph 5, at the end of paragraph 12, and at the beginning of paragraphs 13 and 15. They should note her skillful use of contrasts that contribute so greatly to style and memorability. Instructors might require students to use at least one of these techniques in their papers.

BRODY (Anger): How we handle anger has both short and long range effects on our physical and emotional health as well as on our social relationships. In this selection Brody employs data from recent research and quotations from authorities to buttress her remarks.

Content:

1. Brody points out that "the new view sees anger as often more destructive when expressed than when suppressed....a far more limited role for the ventilation of anger than is now popularly pursued." (See paragraph 4.)

2. In the past, many psychotherapists argued that unexpressed anger could lead to physical ills. (See paragraphs 2 and 3, for example.) The new views on venting anger, particularly its ravaging effects on social interactions, are discussed throughout the rest of the article.

3. See paragraphs 16 and 17. 4. See concluding paragraph.

Strategy:

1. Brody objectively reports the most recent theories on venting anger to readers of her New York Times newspaper column.

9

2. Brody gains credibility and a sense of objectivity through her extensive use of authorities.

WALKER: Walker's essay is a complex one, but students who keep the title in mind as they read should have little difficulty. Phillis Wheatley and the various black women writers/artists mentioned in the essay will make good research topics, furthering the students' knowledge of little known black women artists.

Content:

1. Near the end of the essay this sentence appears, which might well be Walker's thesis: "Guided by my heritage of a love of beauty and respect for strength--in search of my mother's garden, I found my own."

2. Walker's mother's garden--which is obviously a work of creativity--becomes a symbol for the creativity which is passed on from mother to daughter. As a growing entity, the garden is also an appropriate symbol.

3. Black women exhibited creativity in song, in sewing, in quilting, the tasks of their daily lives, etc.

4. During the period of slavery, it was unlawful to teach slaves to read or write (see Douglass, Unit I). In the post-Reconstruction era, the opportunities were lacking since America was still a white dominated and a male dominated culture.

5. "Yet so many of the stories that I write, that we all write, are my mother's stories." (Paragraph 34)

6. "To be an artist and a black woman, even today, lowers our status in many respects, rather than raises it: and yet, artists we will be." (Paragraph 25)

Strategy:

2. See, for example, paragraph 25, where she writes: "When we have pleaded...when we have asked...."

WRIGHT: Wright's struggle to gain access to the library stands in sharp contrast to many of today's students who have little experience with libraries and books.

Content:

1. "Could I ever learn about life and people? To me, with my vast ignorance, my Jim Crow station in life, it seemed a task impossible of achievement. I now knew what being a Negro meant...to feel that there were feelings denied me, that the very breath of life itself was beyond my reach, that more than anything else hurt, wounded me. I had a new hunger."

2. His reading enabled him to understand his mother's suffering, to understand his white boss, etc. "I hungered for books, new ways of looking and seeing. It was not a matter of believing or disbelieving what I read, but of feeling something new, of being affected by something that made the look of the world different."

3. He was originally attracted to Mencken because of his antipathy for the South. He was dazzled by Mencken's style.

4. He opts for learning grammar from his reading rather than from a text. Martin, of course, studied a text.

10

PORTER: Porter's references to authors he read at Amherst include several of the authors whose selections are used in this text: Faulkner, Richard Wright, Tillie Olsen, etc. Paragraph 19 provides some excellent research topics.

Content:

1. See paragraphs 7, 9, and 10. Most of the rest of the selection deals with how his reading and his experiences at Amherst affected his thinking and his behavior.

2. See paragraph 16 through 19. His religion, teachers, fellow students, and guest lecturers helped him through his frustration.

3. See next to last paragraph.

Strategy:

2. Students should familiarize themselves with at least some of the writers Porter alludes to: Ellison, Mailer, Hesse, Beckett, Melville, etc.

ELSHTAIN: This selection offers a good opportunity to point up the difference between "a statement of purpose" and a "thesis."

Content:

1. The dilemma or bind referred to in paragraph 6 is described in paragraph 5, second and third sentences.

2. Paragraph 8: She is conditioned in rural egalitarianism and has lived a life much like that of earlier pioneer women. Paragraph 9: Leaving this environment, she learned that women were supposed to spend their time making themselves attractive to their husbands.

3. See paragraphs 14-16.   4. See paragraphs 19-20.

Strategy:

1. She states the purpose of her talk.

3. She sees the dilemma as a complex issue, not easily resolvable with simple answers.

RODRIGUEZ: This essay is excerpted from a longer one and falls into two parts: Rodriguez's weaning away from Spanish--his assimilation; and his critique of bilingual education. (See Bettelheim & Zelan for their remarks on the conventional bilingualism of Swiss children.)

Content:

2. See paragraph 12: Rodriguez made a distinction between the sound of Spanish (private) and the sound of English (public). The associations of both differ widely and he reacts differently to each. As he says, "...it is not healthy to hear such sounds so often...not healthy to distinguish public words from private sounds so early. I remained cloistered by sounds, timid and shy in public, too dependent on voices at home."

4. The nuns forced the parents to speak English to the children at home. His parents' English seemed to "push him away" rather than embrace him as was the case when they spoke Spanish. See paragraphs 23 & 24.

5. See paragraphs 13 through 15; 25 & 26; 32 through 34.

Strategy:

2. His tone in the first part of the essay is warm and slightly
   sentimental, especially when he speaks of the intimacy
   of Spanish and family. In the bilingual part, he is
   rational and slightly hostile.

3. See Rodriguez's many references to sounds. An aria is
   an operatic solo, a personal song. This essay, so full
   of references to sound, is Rodriguez's Aria, his personal
   experience.

WILL: This selection is a favorite with students. Many of them
have worked at a fast food restaurant at one time or another and can
write volumes about their experiences. We have had some very
enlightening student papers about waiting tables, restaurant
customers, tipping, and the extensive pre-planning for "99¢ Double
Cheese Whopper" Saturdays. Furthermore, the subject matter has
ramifications for students majoring in business, home economy, food
science, accounting, hotel and restaurant administration, and even
engineering.

Content:

1. Some students may argue that Will's thesis is explicit,
   although it is composed of phrases and ideas from throughout the selection. "Ray Kroc [like other mass production
   innovators who acted on the obvious] did not just launch
   a company, he energized an industry...." Others may insist
   that the thesis is implied: Ray Kroc's success was the
   result of his genius for mass production, attention to
   details, and acting on the obvious. This latter thesis
   clues the answers to questions 2 and 4.

5. Will gave Kroc the title because of his romantic outlook
   and his literary style.

Strategy:

1. Will compares Kroc, the entrepreneur, to three of McDonald's
   most familiar products.

2. & 3. They are impressive, add support, and enable readers to
   visualize the statistics in terms of things they can
   identify with.

4. Will's use of the Journalist's Five W's and How would be
   second nature. Perhaps Will's discussion of Kroc's writing
   style could be considered a deviation.

MORROW: In some respects work is much like a besieged fortress
--those who are "in" want "out" and those who are "out" want "in."
Millions of people with jobs live for 5 p.m. and a two-week vacation
in August, while the unemployed become severely depressed, even
suicidal. What's it all for, anyway? Do we work for money, for
security, for a sense of accomplishment, for a sense of worth?
(See Alda)

Content:

1. There could be dozens of phrasings of Morrow's thesis. One
   might be: Although the work ethic is weak now, work is
   still respectable and important as it serves to provide
   basic human needs, such as food and shelter, security,
   friendship, "belongingness," respect, self-actualization
   --and community (see last sentence).

2. The change in attitudes toward work is the basis of much of
   the selection. Some changes noted by Morrow include: the
   prejudice against work as degrading, the virtue of work
   advocated by Luther and Calvin, the enthusiasm for

12

work as a means of upward mobility, etc. Regarding immigrants, see paragraph 14.

3. See paragraphs 13 through 19.

Strategy:

> Morrow's style (see question 2) seems to energize his writing. The interspersion of short paragraphs now and then is typical of journalists' attempts to retain reader interest. Morrow's use of transitions (still, after that now); connectives (and, yet, because); repetition of the wor s "work" and "ethic," and his rhetorical questions ("Has the American work ethic really expired?") help to provide unity and coherence to his writing.

ASHE: Although this article is addressed to blacks, Ashe's advice applies to all athletes longing for careers in professional sports. The subject of sports, a popular one with students, invites discussions about women in athletics, ticket prices, the incredible sales figures for concessions, and intramural sports. Exempting athletes from college rules and admission requirements is drawing considerable attention these days. Students often find themselves quite glib in discussing the commercialization of college athletes, some from the vantage point of their own experience, some from observing their parents or neighbors. Are alums insatiable in their clamor for winning teams? (Remember the Michigan State coach whose alumni wired him "We're behind you--win or tie.") What about special dorms and dining rooms for athletes? What about a lowering of academic standards for athletes? These subjects and other spin-off topics make for lively writing and discussions.

Content:

1. His thesis is his first sentence and is reflected in his title. One part of the thesis is restated in paragraph 3.

2. See paragraph 12. 3. See paragraphs 13-16. 4. See last two paragraphs.

Strategy:

1. Ashe's use of "we blacks," "our black children," his examples of black athletes, and his statistics convince his readers that he is speaking to black parents. (This could be extended to include black teachers, coaches, advisors, and in the long run, black athletes.)

2. Probably nothing but cold, hard facts can convince young hopefuls and their parents that the chances of joining the pros are miniscule.

HOPPOCK: If your students are not already sufficiently alarmed by the high incidence of death and maiming among teenagers from driving while intoxicated, Hoppock's article should certainly hammer home the sad reality.

Content:

1. Hoppock enumerates the costs of drinking to the individuals themselves as well as to innocent victims they maim or kill.

2. He seems to infer that society may contribute to the alcoholic's problems--possibly through advertising, parental and role models' consumption of alcohol, etc. Hoppock certainly contends that the "alcoholic" harms others in addition to himself.

3. See next to last paragraph.

Strategy:

1. & 2. Hoppock piques the reader's interest in his first sentence and then proceeds to frighten his readers with the horrible realities of alcohol related accidents.

   3. He points out the dangers of drunk driving both to the sober driver and to pedestrians.

   5. Although Hoppock does not concern himself with the causes of alcoholism, he clearly relates excessive alcoholic consumption to "death and destruction--of lives, property, relationships." The answer to the questions implied in the title provides the framework for the article and at the same time promotes coherence.

BLUMBERG: This selection is an excellent illustration of how a writer conveys much of his feeling through diction. See Glossary (Connectives/Coherence) for an analysis of how the author achieves paragraph coherence.

Content:

1. See paragraph 2: Detroit marketed its products as "instruments of violence...as vehicles of mayhem and destruction."

2. See paragraph 14.

3. To the manufacturers big cars mean big profits; small cars mean small profits. They rejected the UAW proposal and reasserted management's prerogative to make all such decisions. See paragraph 8.

4. See paragraph 10: "...we'll build these compacts if we have to, but they're going to be the biggest, widest, heaviest, most powerful, most expensive compacts the world has ever seen."

Strategy:

3. He catches the reader's attention with the news item about the Mercury cougar and then links the story to the health of the American auto industry.

4. Reductio ad absurdum (reducing to absurdity)

McGOWAN: Although our students experience aliteracy problems rather than illiteracy problems, many of them testify that some of their colleagues in high school qualified as semi-illiterates. The selection raises serious problems about our country's material excesses compared to our literary incompetencies and provokes challenging discussion and writing about the effectiveness of our school system. Rhetorically the selection is a gem for illustrating clear, well-organized writing employing an explicit thesis and clear topic sentences. The selection "What I Lived For" in the IM, and Rachel Carson's article also provide excellent examples of well-organized writing.

ROIPHE: This selection works well as a foil to some of the feminist writers.

Content:

1. Her thesis is the last sentence in paragraph 3; it is repeated in paragraphs 9, 14 & 15.

2. She discusses female prejudice in paragraphs 4-8.

3. "If we want men to share in the care of the family in a new way, we must assume them as capable of consistent

14

loving tendencies as we."

Strategy:

3. Her title is the other side of the "Male Chauvinist Pig." Women arethe flip side of the coin. The title may appear humorous to some; ardent feminists may be offended.

Unit III

We have organized this unit around the professions rather than across the curriculum in order to acquaint students with writing as a necessary function of life. Some students rather naively think that once they have passed safely through the storm of freshman comp they will never have to struggle with writing again. This unit will demonstrate to all students early in the game that they can expect writing to be critical to the rest of their education and to their future professional lives.
Reading and writing are for life.

MEDAWAR: Many of our science majors are intimidated by writing classes. With sufficient motivation and effort, however, they can frequently not only compete with but actually outdistance their classmates because of their in-depth experience with problem solving, logical analysis, and economy of expression. Medawar speaks to these students in particular. If time permits, this is a good time to secure handouts on suggestions for writing proposals from the office on your campus which handles grant proposals. Although students will not be writing proposals in their immediate future, eventually this type of writing very possibly will become an important part of their professional responsibilities. The materials serve to supplement classroom material, provide good practical advice, and underscore the importance of writing in one's professional life.

Content:

1. Paragraph 3, particularly sentence 2, reiterates the premise of this book. He cites specific models in paragraph 7 and writes about assessing one's sudience in paragraph 9.

3. See paragraphs 9 & 10.   4. See paragraph 11.

Strategy:

1. The vocabulary ("adjudicators," "condign," "prolixity"), the scholarly and scientific allusions (Shaw, Congreve, Russell, Dr. Johnson), and the practical references to and examples of writing in learned journals contribute to the scholarly tone. Subtle traces of humor, tongue-in-cheek phrases, and the interspersion of colloquial language provide light touches throughout the selection.

3. This selection can serve as the basis for an excellent vocabulary exercise. Students can expand their vocabularies studying words in context. (For example: "precosity," "tropes," adjuvant," "etiology," "inimical.")

SWIFT & SWEETNAM: Both of these selections focus on practical, everyday writing in the workplace. Both authors address their writing to professionals seeking clear, direct, effective communication. Swift is directing his remarks to business managers, and the memo in his example is directed to office workers. The writer must be forceful yet diplomatic, a combination which calls for careful revising and rewriting.

Sweetnam, on the other hand, speaks for almost all business communications. Her specific suggestions for "frontloading" are designed to dispatch information clearly and succinctly.

Most students like the practical experience of writing "business" memos and quickly recognize the importance of clarity and exactitude. We have students bring in some examples of vague, circuitous memos and letters and let the class rework them.

Because business communications, as well as personal communications, often involve giving directions--how to operate machinery, how to use a product, how to perform a task--give students some practical experience in writing very succinct, clear directions. Ask them to give directions in less than 150 words on how to use jumper cables to start a stalled car, how to change a tire, or how to make a good pie crust, or....

GALBRAITH: Business Ad students recognize the name of John Kenneth Galbraith and are programmed to accept his advice about writing, if not his ideas about economics. Whatever their majors, however, most students will enjoy comparing the styles of Galbraith, Mencken, Keillor, Swanson, Medawar, etc. as they study the use of humorous touches in writing and as they evaluate when and where they work.

Content:

2. See paragraphs 2 through 5.

Strategy:

2. Many students are unfamiliar with Kerouac and need to understand that Kerouac was a writer during the fifties and sixties whose work met with mixed reviews, some reviewers calling it drivel, others terming it innovative. His harsher critics thought his book On The Road was inspired more by drugs than by talent. In his conclusion Galbraith, with tongue-in-cheek, compares writing on economics with Kerouac's mindless prose, calling it typing rather than writing. This final sentence, therefore, illuminates his title.

3. His "lessons" became the framework for his article.

FAULKNER: Some students often have trouble with this selection because they misinterpret the word "basest" in paragraph three, reading it as if it were "basis." Consequently, they end up with a distorted impression of Faulkner's remarks. We remind students to use their dictionaries.

Faulkner believes that man will not only endure, he will prevail; and that it is the writer's duty to help him prevail by writing about the eternal verities. The fear of nuclear destruction, however, had distracted the writer/artist from his true calling so that he now writes "not of love, but of lust...not of the heart but of the glands."

Faulkner's ostensible audience is the glittering gathering he is addresssing, but he is primarily interested in speaking to the young men and women writers, one of whom, he says, will one day stand where he is now standing.

He particularizes the "old verities and truths of the heart" by naming them: love and honor and pity and pride and compassion and sacrifice. His diction is eloquently elevated and appropriate for what is a very solemn occasion.

SOUSA: Sousa's enthusiasm for his subject is obvious. All the claims he makes for benefits to engineers, of course, apply to all student writers. (A number of engineering schools are now requiring that a certain percentage of a student's grade be based on writing ability.)

16

Content:

1. See paragraph 6: "It will start you on the path of inner development that will produce real changes in the years to come."

    Paragraph 7: Practically, Sousa claims that writing poetry will improve the art of writing.

    Paragraph 8: "Poetry can sensitize one, and provide the image that a man is educated and not merely someone with a degree."

2. See paragraph 33.   3. See paragraphs 16 through 21.

Strategy:

1. The title implies that this is a decidedly non-engineer subject, an uncommon suggestion to make to engineers.

    Sousa employs rhetorical questions throughout and poses the kinds of questions his readers would ask. They appear in paragraphs 2, 3, 5, 14, 21, 22, 23, 32, etc.

THOMAS: Because Thomas writes on a variety of subjects, we encourage students to read other Thomas essays. He has a fine one on "Punctuation."

Content:

1. See paragraph 3: her "usefulness."

2. Relations with doctors have changed; relations are more adversarial (unlike descriptions in paragraphs 1 and 2). Nurses have more administrative tasks, resulting in less personal contact with patients. Their training has been upgraded: they are now college graduates.

Strategy:

1. Paragraphs 1-3 describe his mother's life as a nurse, listing all her duties and ending with her satisfaction. All three paragraphs start with topic sentences. Paragraph 4 introduces his father's opinion of nurses. In paragraph 5 Thomas inserts himself. The essay moves from the past to the present to the future.

2. Parallel construction: paragraph one contains 11 sentences in parallel order; paragraph 5 contains a parallel construction of participial phrases; paragraph 11 contains a parallel construction of subordinate clauses.

3. Placing his thesis at the end makes it less likely that he will turn off those readers unsympathetic to the nurses' plight.

CARSON: Since this selection is so clearly and effectively organized, we have suggested that students hone their writing skills by preparing both an outline and a precis of the chapter. Students need to be reminded of the formal structure of an outline (Roman numerals, capital letters, Arabic numerals, and small letters); the need to adhere to the organization of the original article; the need for major divisions to consist of at least two subdivisions (I. needs II. and A. needs B.); and the need to keep topic headings in a logical balance and in the same grammatical construction. Students will probably be most successful in using a sentence outline.

In writing a precis, students should cover the major points, retain the order and emphasis of the original, attempt to capture the author's style and tone, and strive for accuracy and coherence.

Quotations from the original should not dominate the precis, and if used, should be carefully integrated into the writing.

Content:

1. Carson introduces her thesis in paragraph 2: "The most alarming of all man's assaults upon...." She further refines it in paragraph 9: "...the central problem of our age...." In paragraph 24 she contends: "...we have put poisonous...." In the next to last paragraph she notes the irresponsible use of these chemicals (pesticides). Finally, she concludes by pointing out that we have a right to know the "damaging results of pesticide applications," and determine whether or not to discontinue their use.

2. See paragraph 3, 4, and 5.

3. See paragraphs 14 through 19.

Strategy:

1.-3. Since Carson does not use technical language, we assume she is addressing a general audience rather than a audience of scientists. Carson employs both logic (statistics, facts, authority) as well as emotion (dramatic word choice and examples). Her effective transitions ("another factor," "these invasions," "yet such a world") help to unify her writing.

VOGEL: For students headed for the business school what Vogel says here is vital. For the rest of us--who have a vital stake in the efficient functioning of the American economy--his message is eye-opening.

Content:

1. See paragraph 1: organizational techniques, standardized parts, assembly line, scientific management, corporate organization, and professional management education.

2. See paragraphs 2 through 8.   3. See paragraphs 11 & 13.

4. See paragraphs 14 & 15.

Strategy:

3. Vogel's appeal is over-whelmingly rational and appropriate to the subject. There may be an implicit emotional appeal to the reader's nationalistic sensibilities.

OWENS: Recent movies and extensive TV coverage have created ever greater interest in the Olympics. Students need to know something of the political/social aspects of the Games, particularly the 1936, 1972, and 1980 contests.

Content:

1. See paragraphs 11 through 14.

2. Owens' and Long's common interests included love of family, loyalty to their respective countries, problems about uncertain futures, an ability to see beyond skin color. Owens writes "Thanks to Luz, I learned that the false leaders and sick movements of this earth must be stopped in the beginning, for they turn humanity against itself." Owens learned lessons in brotherhood and sportsmanship that caused him to abhor prejudice in all of its manifestations.

3. Although a move can mean a new beginning, it also means leaving homes, families, friends, security, "roots" behind.

Structure:

1. His rhetorical questions force the reader to think, and this paves the way for his message. He unifies the selection by repeatedly pointing out the unimportance of one's skin color and by concluding "Skin-deep is never beautiful."

3. He uses comparison and contrast; assessments of its validity will vary.

NILSEN: We find students receptive to the idea of eliminating sexism in language. Students enjoy examining their own language and that of their peers, the language of television and writing in newspapers for evidence of sexism in the language.

Content:

1. Feminists are hopeful that by changing the language to eliminate sexism the culture will change in the same way.

2. Answers may very: "A close examination of our language and its usage reveal how really deep-seated sexism is in our communication system."

3. In paragraph 5, a woman's body is considered important, but it is a man's mind which is valued. Paragraph 15: Women are expected to be passive; men to be active.

4. She documents comparisons to food, plants, animals, names, relationships, etc.

Strategy:

1. Since the article appeared in Female Studies, we can expect it to be aimed primarily at female academics or academics interested in feminist studies. However, it is ultimately aimed at all those who are interested in eliminating sexism in American life. Though written by a specialist and appearing in a specialist journal, it is easily understood by the common reader.

2. She reveals a scientific attitude in her thoroughness and in her specificity.

5. The article ends abruptly. Nilsen does not direct her reader's attention back to her implied question at the beginning, namely whether a change in language will affect the culture.

EISELEY: Students who expect an anthropologist's report of a lesson learned on a scientific expedition to be dull reading, replete with technical detail, have a delightful surprise in store in this selection.

Content:

1. a. Anthropological expeditions to collect bones and artifacts of earlier civilizations require money and equipment (see paragraph 3).
b. There was an interchange of services between a zoo abroad and the museum--a "We'll do you a favor and in turn you do us a favor" arrangement (see paragraph 4).
c. The real enemy was the man, not the hand (see paragraph 8).

Structure:

1. At the end of the first paragraph Eiseley makes clear that
    his purpose is to explain why he can never bear to see a
    bird imprisoned.

2. Eiseley uses the analogy of the "assassin" in paragraphs 6,
    8, and 10 to indicate his general distaste for the assignment
    for which he is being paid.

KING: This selection provides the instructor with the opportunity to say something about the civil rights movement in America,
especially the early movement in which Dr. King participated. In
this selection King presents all the arguments against racial
segregation and defends his strategy of civil disobedience. His
justification for civil disobedience may be compared with Thoreau's.
(See student Jo Harris' sample paper responding to this selection
in "The Writing Process.")

Content:

1. King answers the charge that he is an "outsider" in
    paragraphs 2 through 4.

2. The four steps for a non-violent campaign are listed in
    paragraph 6 and explained in paragraphs 7 through 11.

3. King defines "just" and "unjust" laws in paragraphs 15
    through 22.

4. King explains his disappointment with white moderates in
    paragraph 23.

5. King answers the charge of extremism in paragraphs 27
    through 31.

6. King's disappointment with white churches is explained in
    paragraphs 33 through 44.

Strategy:

1. King's appeal to authorities includes Thomas Aquinas, St.
    Augustine, Martin Luther, the Apostle Paul, Paul Tillich,
    Socrates, Jesus, Martin Buber, Lincoln, Jefferson, etc.

3. His tone is serious, passionate, diplomatic. Like all true
    practitioners of civil disobedience King wishes to attract
    the sympathy of the uncommitted. His language is tempered
    accordingly.

GOMPERS: Given Gompers' interest in the education of workers,
especially their economic education, a follow-up on contemporary
union educational activity will make a useful research project.
Have students check the library for any union publications. Then
have them examine the contents to determine the extent to which
unions are interested in educating their members, in economic
facts or in any other area. How well are these publications written/
edited?

Content:

1. Statements may very. "Acquiring an informal education
    requires motivation and opportunity."

2. As Gompers relates, from the New York Sun, in addition
    to information, he "absorbed ideas of style, sentence
    structure, and the use of words."

3. See paragraph 3.

Strategy:

1. Gompers' final remark suggests that he had a working class audience in mind: "All associated effort must have discipline." However, since his Autobiography is a kind of Horatio Alger story, he doubtlessly expected his book to appeal to the common reader.

2. Gompers follows the Journalist's Five W's and How.

POSTMAN: Postman's remarks in this selection are relevant to ideas in the Bettelheim & Zelan selection and to the Albert Shanker selection. From these three readings students may gain some insight into the origin of their own reading and writing problems. All three relate broad critiques of American culture/education.

Content:

1. Postman conjectures, admitting that we will not know for a long time (see paragraphs 1 & 2).

2. See paragraphs 3 through 5. 3. See paragraphs 17 & 18.

4. See paragraphs 12 & 13.

Strategy:

1. Physiological effects are covered in paragraphs 1 & 2 and are based on conjecture. Psychological effects are covered in paragraphs 3 through 6. Postman offers as evidence student behavior. Social effects are covered in the remaining paragraphs. He supports with analysis and examples.

BETTELHEIM & ZELAN: This selection, the Postman, and the Shanker selections constitute an indictment of some contemporary educational practices.

Content:

1. See paragraphs 1 through 3. 2. See paragraphs 4 & 5.

3. See paragraph 7.

Strategy:

1. The short paragraph on the "child's fate" is sufficient to attract the attention of parents. Since the article originally appeared in The Atlantic Monthly, it is aimed at a highly literate audience, at parents who take active interest in their children and their schools.

3. They compare American texts with their Swiss counterparts.

KEILLOR: As an exercise in irony for humorous effect this selection serves as a useful contrast to Jonathan Swift's ironic effort for a more serious effect.

Content:

1. See paragraph 10, 11, 21, 22, & 23. 2. See paragraph 8.

3. He is parodying groups which have launched frivolous campaigns against supposed discrimination: for example--cat lovers who claim discrimination because some localities have passed cat leash laws.

Strategy:

1. Keillor is appealing to a fairly sophisticated audience.

21

Irony is often misunderstood by many who are unfamiliar with it. (Experience with Swift's "A Modest Proposal" is a case in point.)

2. The chief elements of humor are self-depreciation, self-effacement, parody, absurdities.

MENCKEN: If they have not already described their early experiences in learning to read and write, students can use the Mencken article as a model for a paper or journal entry about their early teachers, books, or classes. Mencken's experience offers a startling contrast to what Bettelheim and Zelan relate about today's basal readers.

Content:

1. Mencken's discovery of Huckelberry Finn launched him "upon the career of a bookworm" for the rest of his life. See paragraphs 5 and 12, the first sentence in paragraph 14, and Mencken's concluding sentence.

2. & 3. See paragraph 5.

Strategy:

1. For example, "the neighborhood apprentices to gang life," "the effect is...comparable to that which flows, in later life, out of filling a royal flush or debauching the wife of a major-general of cavalry," or "while my father searched the Evening News hopefully for reports of the arrest, clubbing and hanging of labor leaders." These tongue-in-cheek phrases or statements "show rather than tell," frequently register Mencken's disdain, and become humorous through exaggeration.

3. Mencken's strong verbs ('bscillated," "staggered and stumbled," "blooded") and use of the vernacular ("gob," "as smarties will have guessed by now," "gulp") enliven, add humor, and make memorable his writing.

JORDAN: Jordan's career as an outstanding legislator, both in Texas and in the Congress, and as a distinguished professor at the University of Texas places her in that noble assemblage of American women who have brightened American political life. Instructors might ask students to do some research on other contemporary women political figures.

Content:

1. Because the Harvard team was superior, they should have won. However, the debate was a tie, and therefore Jordan considers that a win for her team (see paragraphs 3 & 4).

2. Thesis: the last sentence might well serve for this excerpt: "The stakes, the stakes are too high for government to be a spectator sport." She describes numerous instances where the input of citizens has been inhibited or abridged.

Strategy:

1. Jordan ingratiates herself with her audience and her hosts.

SCHERER: This selection works especially well when used with the Thomas article on nurses.

Content:

1. See paragraphs 1 through 3. 2. & 3. See paragraphs 4-6.

4. & 5. See paragraphs 7 through 11.

6. See paragraph 9. Nurses are locked into restrictions and hourly wages.

Strategy:

1. Almost all paragraphs are introduced by topic sentences; some follow a brief transitional sentence. Paragraph 5 (which is used for comparison) and paragraph 11, (which concludes with the topic sentence) are exceptions. Scherer uses examples, historical and contemporary facts, and comparisons as support for her assertions.

2. We could call the tone passionate, perhaps even mildly angry.

3. It indicates that times have changed--greatly. And so have nurses and their work.

SHANKER: Shanker's column sets forth the general thesis of E.D. Hirsch, Jr's. Cultural Literacy (1987). This book was widely reviewed/praised for its insights into contemporary problems with public education. See also Diane Ravich, "Sociology for Tots," American Scholar (Summer, 1987), which confirms Hirsch's findings. If you want a scare, see also Allan Bloom's The Closing of the American Mind (1987) for his remarks on students, books, music.

Content:

1. They are culturally illiterate because they and the writer do not share a common background.

2. Extensive knowledge is broad, knowing a little about a great many things. Intensive knowledge involves a great deal of information narrowly focused.

3. Educators are generally prejudiced against memorization. They also overuse contemporary reading material and ignore more traditional readings.

JEFFERSON: We teach the Declaration's ideas (the natural rights doctrine) along with the rhetoric, since we find many students are not fully familiar with the ideas and the way the structure of the document reenforces them. We urge instructors to use the formula outlined in the discussion questions for devising syllogisms on contemporary issues. The syllogism may be taught in connection with Huxley's "The Method of Scientific Investigation."

Strategy:

3. Jefferson offers no proof for his major premise beyond his assertion that it is composed of self-evident truths deduced from natural law. To prove his minor premise, he offers the litany of charges against the King, beginning with paragraph 4 and running through paragraph 25. Some of these, as Jefferson indicates, were deleted by the Congress. All the charges are directed at the King, the Congress desiring to avoid any acknowledgement of parliamentary authority over the colonies.

4. Jefferson uses parallelism throughout: in paragraph 2 sentence 1; paragraph 3, sentences 1, 2, & 3; paragraphs 4-23; paragraph 26.

LINCOLN & HIGHET: Although many students believe they know all there is to know about Lincoln's Gettysburg Address, a serious examination of the phrasing usually brings about a new appreciation and understanding of its eloquence and significance.

Content:

1. & 2. Lincoln has come to dedicate the field as a national

cemetery for those who died in battle. Instead of dwelling on the past and on death, Lincoln asks his listeners to dedicate <u>themselves</u> to the future, to assuring for America "<u>a new birth</u> of freedom" and a truly democratic government. His final words have become a definition of democracy. He moves from past, to present, to future in his three paragraphs.

Strategy:

1. Lincoln speaks of the birth of a new nation, the birth of a new dedication to America's future, and the birth of a new freedom, etc. See Highet paragraph 11.

2. His tone is certainly solemn, hortatory, and patriotic. See Highet regarding Biblical cadences, rhetorical devices, etc.

Highet Content:

2. See paragraphs 10 & 11.

3. See paragraphs 13 through 15.

KENNEDY: Both Kennedy and Faulkner address their remarks to young people, Kennedy more specifically to all American youth and not just to potential artists. Kennedy's speech also conveys an appeal to the idealism of youth, especially in the beginning and closing remarks.

Content:

1. Frost in honored (paragraphs 5 through 8).

2. See paragraph 7.   3. See paragraph 8.   4. See paragraphs 9 & 10.

5. He is addressing the graduating class of Amherst College and beyond that he is speaking to all young Americans. The road he is calling them to might be termed "responsible, engaged citizenship in the service of the Great Republic."

Strategy:

1. For parallel construction, see paragraphs 1, 4, 7, 11 & 12; Antithesis, see paragraphs 5 & 6.

2. Kennedy separates poets in a "free society" from poets "elsewhere."

Supplementary Readings

GEORGE ORWELL

Questions on content:

1. To what does Orwell attribute the degeneration of the English language? Do you believe the same reasons apply today? Explain. Answer: Political and economic concerns, slovenliness and the abuse of language. See paragraph 2.

2. What are dying metaphors? Cite some examples. Do any contemporary ones come to mind? What are they? What are verbal false limbs? Cite examples. Answer: See paragraphs 5-8 where he defines and gives examples.

3. What does Orwell mean by "meaningless words?" What does he mean by "pretentious diction?" Cite examples.

4. What does Orwell mean when he says images in metaphors clash? What is another name for this fault?

5. What is euphemism, and according to Orwell when and/or why is it used?
Answer: See paragraphs 13-15.

7. What is Orwell's opinion of political writing? Is he justified? Explain.
Answer: See paragraph 12.

Questions on writing structure and strategy:

1. Orwell's language is punctuated with figures of speech. What similies and metaphors do you find?

2. What are the chief methods of development?
Answer: He uses cause and effect, examples, description, contrast, analogy.

3. In what ways does Orwell disregard his own advice?
Answer: He often begs the question, assuming to be true what he has to prove is true.

Questions for writing and discussion:

1. Examine a recent paper you have written to detect examples of passive voice, commonplaces at ends of sentences, pretentious diction that could be eliminated.

2. Write a paper in which you support or refute one of the following statements from Orwell's article:
   a. "...language merely reflects existing social conditions and ...we cannot influence its development by any direct tinkering with words or constructions."
   b. "...language is a natural growth and not an instrument which we shape for our own purposes."
   c. "But if thought corrupts language, language can also corrupt thought."

3. Review several issues of your local newspaper, a national newspaper, your school newspaper, textbooks, your own papers, a political speech for the following: dying metaphors, meaningless words, pretentious diction and verbal false limbs.

4. In paragraph 5, Orwell writes that terms like Fascism, socialism, democracy have become meaningless because the different definitions assigned to them are contradictory. In a paper, examine meanings assigned to the terms "liberal" and conservative." See how "liberal" is used; see if you can deduce meanings from the context in which the terms are used. (See The National Review, The American Spectator, The New Republic, The Washington Monthly, The New Leader, The Progressive, Mother Jones. These are all journals of opinion and deal extensively with political issues. See also The Atlantic and Harper's, both general circulation magazines.

5. Examine the language employed in the continuing debate over nuclear power & nuclear disarmament to discover "meaningless words." See newspapers and news magazines, editorials, columns, letters to the editor, etc.

6. You have had advice from Galbraith and Orwell, and English teachers from grade one. What is the best advice you have ever received about writing? What advice would you pass on to a younger sibling? Write a paper.

THOMAS HENRY HUXLEY

Questions on content:

1. What is Huxley's thesis? Why are his examples and reasoning convincing or unconvincing?
   Answer: His thesis is stated in the first paragraph and repeated through the essay. See paragraph 7.

2. How does Huxley define the method of scientific investigation? What is induction? What is a syllogism? What is an hypothesis?
   Answer: See paragraphs 5 & 9.

3. What is the major difference in the way we ordinarily think and act and the way men of science think and act?
   Answer: See last of first paragraph and paragraph 7.

Questions on writing structure and strategy:

1. What methods of development does Huxley use? Which are most effective?
   Answer: Cause and effect, description, comparision/contrast, example, analogy.

2. What is the function of paragraph 7?
   Answer: It serves as a transition.

3. Who is Huxley's audience? How do you know?

4. What transitional devices does Huxley use?
   Answer: "Now," "Well, now...." Rhetorical questions, etc.

Questions for discussion and writing:

1. If, as Huxley says, hypotheses guide most of our daily lives, explain at least three that guide your daily life.

2. Try tracing your alternating use of deduction and induction in arriving at a particular decision.
   Or:
   Write a paper in which you reconstruct your use of induction, deduction, hypothesis, and verification in one of your science classes.
   Or:
   Write a paper in which you reconstruct your use of induction, deduction, hypothesis, and verification on the job.

JONATHAN SWIFT

Questions on content:

1. What problem in Ireland is the speaker addressing and what does he propose to do about it?
   Answer: To reduce the number of Irish children.

2. What groups, in addition to the British government, does Swift satirize?
   Answer: Absentee landlords, Americans, Formosans, the Episcopal Church in Ireland, upper classes in Ireland, anti-Catholics, Protestants, etc.

3. What serious proposals does Swift offer as alternatives? Why does he reject them?
   Answer: See paragraphs 29-30.

Questions on writing structure and strategy:

1. What specific words does Swift use to liken the Irish poor to livestock?
   Answer: "dropped from its dam;" "wives as breeders; "fore and hind quarters of a child;" "carcass of...fat child;" "yearling child," etc.

2. How do they contribute to the tone of the essay?
   Answer: They heighten the irony and intensify the revulsion

against the oppressors of the Irish poor.

3. What types of support does Swift use to back up his arguments?
   Answer: He uses facts, statistics, examples, analysis.

4. Swift uses almost every method of development discussed in the
   Rhetorical Index. Examine the essay and cite at least one
   example of each type of development.

Questions on writing and discussion:

1. Write a proposal of your own (either ironic or serious) about
   a solution to America's homeless, world over-population, or
   world hunger.

2. Swift's "Modest Proposal," although understood to be ironic,
   is too strong for some people. Are some readers so turned
   off by the repulsiveness of the thesis that they are unwilling
   to examine it in any detail or to empathize with the Irish
   poor? Explain.

3. Compare Swift's use of irony with Garrison Keillor's use in
   "Shy Rights: Why Not Pretty Soon?"

HENRY DAVID THOREAU

Questions on content:

1. Why is Thoreau hostile to the government?
   Answer: Thoreau objects to the war on Mexico as a scheme to
   spread slavery. The war and especially slavery are mentioned
   throughout the essay. See paragraph 7 and especially the
   end of paragraph 9.

2. What does Thoreau believe about majority rule? Why do we
   follow the rule of the majority, according to Thoreau?
   Answer: See paragraph 4.

3. What is the difference in men who serve the state with their
   "bodies," with their "heads," and with their "consciences?"
   Which does Thoreau believe is superior?
   Answer: See paragraph 5.

4. What action does Thoreau recommend to those who believe they
   are right and the government is wrong?
   Answer: See paragraphs 8, 14-20, 36-38.

5. What does Thoreau mean when he says "the more money, the less
   virtue?"
   Answer: See paragraph 23.

6. Why does Thoreau say that the constitution is evil?
   Answer: See paragraphs 19, 40 & 43.

7. What is Thoreau's plan for a "peaceable revolution"?
   Answer: See paragraph 22.

Questions on writing structure and strategy:

1. How would you characterize Thoreau's organization in this essay?
   Answer: Though the essay is loose in construction, it is
   developed as a formal argument.

2. Thoreau's style has been described as "aphoristic" (short,
   pithy, memorable and quotable sayings). Point out several.
   (You might have students check dictionaries of quotations to
   see how often Thoreau is quoted.)

3. Do you believe that Thoreau violates Orwell's injunction
   to limit abstractions and generalizations? Explain.

4. How does Thoreau insure coherence?
    Answer: The logic of his argument insures coherence.

Questions for writing and discussion:

1. Explore the implications of Thoreau's remark: "The only obli-
    gation which I have a right to assume is to do at any time
    what I think right " (paragraph 4). Ask yourself if it is
    always so easy to know what is right. What are the difficulties
    in allowing everyone and anyone to adopt this attitude?
    Or:
    Consider this remark by Thoreau: "If I have unjustly wrestled
    a plank from a drowning man, I must restore it to him though
    I drown myself."
    Or:
    "That government is best which governs not at all." Is this
    really possible? Explain.

2. The appeal to "conscience" or "higher law" always presents
    problems to constituted authority. David Bell has made a
    useful distinction between the "ethic of conscience" and the
    "ethic of responsibility." The two are not congruent. Thoreau
    appeals to the "ethic of conscience" when he refuses to pay
    his tax in protest against the Mexican War and slavery. As
    he puts it: "This people must cease to hold slaves, and to
    make war on Mexico, though it cost them their existence as
    a people " (paragraph 9). Can an elected official--the
    President of the United states who has sworn to uphold the
    Constitution--ever do as Thoreau suggests? Or does his oath
    of office make him responsible to others and not to his
    conscience alone? Explain.

3. Compare the stands of Thoreau and the Reverend Martin Luther
    King, Jr. against what they perceived as injustice.

VIRGINIA WOOLF

Questions on content:

1. What is meant by "the Angel in the House?" (Note how Tillie
    Olsen alludes to this phrase.)
    Answer: See paragraph 3.

2. In the first paragraph, what does Woolf mean when she says
    writing is a "harmless occupation?" Is this meant to be
    humorous? Explain. Answers may vary. Woolf is writing
    with tongue-in-cheek.

3. How did her inheritance enable her to overcome "the Angel in
    the House?"
    Answer: See paragraph 3.

4. What additional obstacles does Woolf encounter as a writer?
    Answer: See paragraphs 5 & 6 where she describes the prejudice
    against a woman writer "telling the truth."

5. What does she mean when she says "You have a room of your
    own...."?
    Answer: See paragraph 6: One has achieved financial inde-
    pendence, beholden to no one for financial support.

Questions on writing structure and strategy:

1. Why does Woolf employ understatement (see Glossary) in paragraph
    2? In paragraph 5 when speaking of her own accomplishments?
    Answer: Woolf is very modest and desires to reduce the distance
    between herself and her audience.

2. What is the purpose of paragraph 4?
    Answer: It serves as a transition from her personal experience
    to the universal need for women to express themselves in all

the arts and professions. She encourages them to do so.

3. Pinpoint her use of parallelism. What can you say about her sentence variety?

4. Where and why does she use rhetorical questions?

5. Examine her conclusion. How might you have concluded it more effectively?
   Answer: Her time was up. Answers may vary.

Questions for discussion and writing:

1. Was there or is there an "Angel in the House" in your home? Are you it? What qualifies the person as "the Angel in the House?" Is the angel necessarily female?

2. Write a paper on the obstacles that loom in the way of the professional woman today. Consider children, day-care, competition, discrimination, work hazards, etc.

3. Do some research on "the Bloomsbury group," of which Woolf was a part. Write a paper on your findings.

Research Topics

1. Cultural literacy (Reactions to Hirsch's book)

2. The 1936, or 1972, or 1980 Olympics

3. The Black Muslims

4. The Black Panthers

5. Malcolm X's assassination

6. Franklin D. Roosevelt as a handicapper

7. Handicapper accessibility on your campus/workplace

8. Marian Anderson and DAR's Constitution Hall

9. Eric Hoffer as a longshoreman/philosopher

10. American cars vs. foreign cars; recalls

11. Books that changed your mind

12. Ideas that changed the world

13. Thoreau as a journal keeper

14. Lincoln's wartime letters

15. Student suicides. Why?

16. Students 100 years ago (comparative costs of education, availability of programs)

17. Historical figures associated with your campus/school

18. Insider trading on the stock market

19. The Edsel and other lemons

20. Tom Watson and IBM

21. Malcolm Forbes and business

22. Selecting a computer

23. Female sports figures

24. Women legislators (state, federal)

25. The Bloomsbury Group

26. The Triangle Shirtwaist Fire

27. Sit-down strikes of the 1930's

28. The Hoovervilles of the depression era

29 The Okies of the depression era

30. The Dustbowl of the 1930's

31. See the Horace Porter selection for writers mentioned throughout.

32. See the Angelou selection for writers mentioned in the headnote.

33. Franklin D. Roosevelt and the Supreme Court

34. See the George Will selection, paragraph 5, for business tycoons.

35. See Tillie Olsen selection, paragraph 25, for women writers.

36. Slave narratives

37. Silent Spring 25 years later

38. Learning to write in prison

39. The Outward Bound Program

40. The Ratification of the Constitution

41. Child Abuse

42. Literary figures and journals

43. Letters of famous people

44. Women as business entrepreneurs (or C.E.O.'s)

45. Philanthropic efforts to prevent school drop-outs

46. Literacy programs (High School equivalency programs)

47. The work ethic

48. The myths of drinking

49. Off-the-road vehicles and safety

50. Courtship--then and now

51. A bibliographical essay on recent books on education

52. See Nilsen selection, paragraphs 21-22, for important women

53. Adult education

54. The Boat People and Immigration

55. New American citizens

56. Birth order of siblings

TEACHING ORGANIZATION

Organization seems to be one of the most difficult aspects of writing to impart to students--perhaps because there are so many different ways to organize ideas, or because students often assume the easiest form of organization (chronological) is the best organization.

All too often students do not think their subjects through clearly and go off on vague digressions. Still others by-pass the transitions, repetitions of key words, and summaries that are so vital to the unity and coherence of their writing.

In an attempt to prevent these confusing and irrelevant detours, urge students to review the material on thesis and topic sentences in "The Writing Process" and in the Glossary. Reassure students there are no hard and fast rules for theses and topic sentences and remind them that organization is a considerably different concern in personal narratives and imaginative writing than in a logically developed essay. At the same time, point out that in expository writing, good clear thesis and topic sentences are some of the most important means to fast, effective communication.

31

The following short essay by Nobel Prize winner Bertrand Russell can be used to provide a quick, basic lesson in effective organization and the fundamentals of unity, coherence, and emphasis.

"What I Lived For"

Three passions, simple but overwhelmingly strong, have governed my life: the longing for love, the search for knowledge, and unbearable pity for the suffering of mankind. These passions, like great winds, have blown me hither and thither, in a wayward course, over a deep ocean of anguish, reaching to the very verge of despair.

I have sought love, first, because it brings ecstasy-- ecstasy so great that I would often have sacrificed all the rest of life for a few hours of this joy. I have sought it, next, because it relieves loneliness--that terrible loneliness in which one shivering consciousness looks over the rim of the world into the cold unfathomable lifeless abyss. I have sought it, finally, because in the union of love I have seen, in a mystic miniature, the prefiguring vision of the heaven that saints and poets have imagined. This what I sought, and though it might seem too good for human life, this is what--at last--I have found.

With equal passion I have sought knowledge. I have wished to understand the hearts of men. I have wished to know why the stars shine. And I have tried to apprehend the Pythagorean power by which number holds sway above the flux. A little of this, but not much, I have achieved.

Love and knowledge, so far as they were possible, led upward toward the heavens. But always pity brought me back to earth. Echoes of cries of pain reverberate in my heart. Children in famine, victims tortured by oppressors, helpless old people a hated burden to their sons, and the whole world of loneliness, poverty, and pain make a mockery of what human life should be. I long to alleviate the evil, but I cannot, and I too suffer.

This has been my life. I have found it worth living, and would gladly live it again if the chance were offered me.

As students reread the article they should observe that:

1. Russell introduces his thesis in the opening sentence. (In more elaborate discourse, this would probably be preceded by a sentence or a paragraph designed to grab the reader's attention.)

2. Each succeeding paragraph is initiated by a topic sentence containing one of the key words from the thesis ("love," "knowledge," and "pity"). This repetition of key words obviously serves to unify the essay by relating each paragraph to the thesis.

3. Paragraph four unifies by repeating the first two passions and then contrasting them with the third passion.

4. Each passion is supported with reasons and specific detail.

5. The last sentence of each paragraph summarizes Russell's degree of success in each area.

6. His last paragraph is a terse summary which connotes a tone of satisfaction as well as a sense of finality.

We offer no guarantees; however, students tell us that an examination of   Russell followed by a study of the organization of the McGowan article in Unit I helped them immensely in understanding the basics of organization. (After they examine these two selections, students can move on to Rachel Carson's expert organization of considerably more difficult material in "The Obligation to Endure" in Unit III.)

JOURNAL KEEPING

If you are not already committed to asking students to keep journals, we urge you to try it. Having students keep journals, we find, is an excellent way to encourage frequent writing without adding to our already overwhelming burden of papers.

Although many instructors require journals, they differ greatly in their attitudes toward journal writing. Some instructors place no limitation on topics or procedures; others ask their students to write on assigned topics. We recommend a mix of both practices. However, we are gravely disappointed when students (despite our admonitions) settle for "diaries" in which they simply record their daily (and nightly!) activities. We ask our students to keep journals that are also "notebooks" or "workbooks." We prefer a certain number of pages to be used for "freewriting" on topics of their own choosing, while other pages are to be used for experimenting with different writing techniques (parallel construction, antithesis, similes, metaphors) and different methods of development (comparison, contrast, cause and effect, analogy). In journal entries students can try various styles and strategies without having to write a whole paper on a single method of development, for example. We find students much more inclined to experiment, when they know their "trials" will not jeopardize their grade. Although most journal writing is done out of class, journal writing can be implemented during class time on days when there are no questions and the lecture runs short. Entries may be finished out of class or may be peer edited in class. Examples from magazine and newspaper reading can be taped or stapled in journals. Students can read "one of their best" for the class. When time permits between longer papers, we ask students to turn in entries which we examine carefully and then ask students to revise in their journals. Thus in a sense their journals become their portfolios (along with their papers) of their work for the course.

Journals are, of course, great openers for student conferences, as well as one of the quickest ways to get to know students and to gain insight into some of their writing problems. Some instructors grade the journals, but most of us adopt a more lenient procedure of giving full credit or partial credit based on the number of assigned pages completed and the seriousness of their writing commitment. Some poor writers put some of their best efforts into journal writing and are encouraged by being rewarded for their efforts. We ask students to date their entries, and we check journals several times a term in order to prevent "night before marathons" at the end of the term. (Journals can be checked quickly--albeit casually--during class periods when the students are working on other assignments such as peer editing or in-class writing.)

We assure students that we will not be as meticulous about spelling and mechanics as in their regular papers and that personal entries need not be circulated or read before the class.

The journal entries at the end of each unit should serve both as creative outlets as well as learning experiences and ought certainly to relieve that universal despair over "I can't think of anything to write about in my journal."

JOURNAL EXAMPLES

"What's the big deal? This ain't spring by a long shot. Where's the sun? Hey, I know this is Michigan, but summer is a native albeit only a part-time resident of this state too. I should have stayed in Georgia where it doesn't snow and the june-bugs camp out in the trees and the woods are free of briars. A guy can't even walk the woods in this place. Too cold and too much snow. Complaining about weather is so useless...."

"This is my last day of my journal. When I look back at the first days of this journal, I can see the improvement in my writing. At first I thought this was a stupid idea, but as I look back, I have changed my mind. Writing every day has helped my thoughts. The first in class paper we wrote rattled me. Now, I can stay calm and cool when surprised with a topic. This was exhibited on our first test. I felt in control during the writing portion. This was proven when I received a 4.0. I am going to continue some sort of journal writing. I know that my skills can quickly decline if neglected."

Sounds

"To me one of the most interesting things to do late at night is to just sit quietly and listen to the sounds that float into my room. From the slow humming sound of cars out on the road to the musical symphony provided by several crickets out in the courtyards, they all seem to intrigue me. Inside the dorm the sounds of late night studiers fill the halls with a cacophony of noises, such as shuffling papers, the crackling sound of a pretzel bag being emptied and crumpled, and the droning sound of snoring roommates who don't have journals keep them up all night. I guess listening to sounds late at night is quite off the wall but for me its sort of peaceful."

PEER EDITING

Instructors already aware of the virtues of peer editing can quickly by-pass this section. Others, heretofore dubious or discouraged about using peer editing as a teaching device, may be interested in sharing our experiences.

As with writing, we find students need motivation to become effective peer editors. Students need to be reminded that by developing their editing talents, they not only enable their classmates to achieve better grades, but they in turn become better writers themselves. They need to realize that in the end they must become their own editors, that they must develop a sense of good vs. poor writing, a sense of when writing works and when it doesn't. They also should learn that their editing abilities can be very advantageous in the workplace. A reputation as "editor" among their colleagues may well pay off in promotions later on. Remind them that almost all writing, from Jefferson's drafts of the Declaration to the manuscripts of novelists and professional writers, is subjected to peer editing.

In many respects peer editing sessions can be considered "writing workshops," a perhaps less formidable term. There are various ways these "workshops" can be conducted and instructors need to experiment to discover techniques that work well for them and their particular students. Usually three to four students to an editing group is best, although sometimes one-on-one is more effective. (These "duos," however, can sometimes disintegrate into gossipy "conversations.") Editing can take an entire class period; on other occasions a twenty minute exchange is sufficient time for less comprehensive editing. Even the methods of editing can vary from assignment to assignment.

(1) Students can respond to questions or write extensive critiques.

(2) They can photocopy their papers and bring them to class for in-class or out-of-class editing.

(3) They can make oral presentations and criticisms or pencil in comments and suggestions on the papers themselves.

Even the list of peer editing questions at the end of this manual can be used in different ways. For example, the lead questions ask for detailed answers that may be used in longer editing sessions, while the questions that follow invite short answers to be used when time is at a premium.

Experience has taught us to ask students to initial their peer editing. This raises the level of expectation and lets students know we are concerned about the quality of their editing. When peer editing is successful, students learn there is more to editing than simply correcting grammar and mechanical errors. They then begin to look for the virtues as well as the faults of the papers.

Peer editing thus helps tremendously in providing needed feedback for students and in reducing the student paper load for the instructor. In addition, criticism sometimes bears more weight coming from a colleague than from the instructors who are universally accused of being "picky" and ultra conservative. Then, too, there is that special bonus when students pick up on an idea that we, because of differences in age and perspective, have failed to notice.

PEER EDITING LIST

1. What is the writer's thesis? Is it challenging? Does it make the reader think? Is it a commonplace that needs no proof, no support? Are the subject and the thesis significant? Do they warrant the reader's time? Can the thesis be sharpened in any way?

2. To what specific audience is the writing directed?

3. Why is the introduction challenging or lacklustre? Does it make you want to read on? Could it be improved?

4. Summarize each paragraph in a word, a phrase, or a sentence. Is there a clear, logical organization to the paper? If the paper is chronologically developed, would a topical development be more effective?

5. Which ideas in paragraphs could benefit from more adequate support? (Examples, authority, statistics, etc.) What types of development are employed? Are the writer's points convincing?

6. Why is the conclusion effective or ineffective? Could it be improved?

7. Which sentences reveal the writer's attention to specific detail, precise word choice, strong verbs?

8. Where could the writer use greater sentence variety (more subordination, for example) rather than a repetition of the same subject, verb, object order? Where would more effective parallel construction add emphasis or grace?

9. Where could the writer use more figurative language (similes, metaphors, etc.)?

10. Where are there errors in spelling, punctuation, grammar?

METHODS OF DEVELOPMENT

ARGUMENTATION

USE: To change thinking, action, or beliefs

DO: Use logical, emotional, and ethical appeals

Give special consideration to your reader's background and attitudes

AVOID: Using logical fallacies

COMPARISON AND CONTRAST

USE: To clarify

analyze

explain

inform

persuade

DO: Compare important similarities/differences

Use effective transitions

AVOID: Comparing/contrasting different aspects of two subjects

DEFINITION

USE: To clarify

set limits

DO: Use clear, understandable terms, not more complicated ones

Differentiate clearly between other similar things

AVOID: Giving a circular definition using figurative language

NARRATION

USE: To explain
entertain   (short stories, novels)
convince

DO: Maintain consistent point of view

Develop logical organization

Use adverbs as time indicators

AVOID: Using pointless detail and repetition

PROCESS

USE: To explain
instruct

DO: Make a significant statement

Orient reader regarding equipment, possible pitfalls

Follow orderly sequence of steps

Use meaningful transitions

AVOID: Confusing words, digressions, or omission of steps

METHODS OF DEVELOPMENT

ANALOGY

USE: To compare/contrast

       convince

DO: Make certain two subjects
       have sufficient points of
       comparison

       Use fresh, logical comparisons

AVOID: Mixing metaphors

CAUSE AND EFFECT

USE: To show relationships

       persuade

       explain

DO: Maintain soundness and
       plausibility

       Verify facts/statistics

AVOID: Assigning a single cause
       or the wrong cause to an
       effect

       Oversimplifying or
       overqualifying

CLASSIFICATION

USE: To clarify

       show relationships

       compare and/or contrast

       support ideas

DO: Let it help with organ-
       ization when appropriate

       Main consistent class-
       ification

       Be sure classification is
       complete

AVOID: Overlapping classification

DESCRIPTION

USE: To clarify

       add color, live-
       liness, impact,
       dimension

DO: Fix upon a point of view

       Develop a dominant
       impression

       Use logical organization

       Use figures of speech

AVOID: Adding extraneous detail

EXAMPLE

USE: To clarify

       concretize

       add color, variety,
       interest value

DO·   Use enough examples to be
       convincing

       Use pertinent, appropriate
       examples

AVOID: Overusing examples

We certainly realize that whatever students learn from completing exercises does not necessarily carry over into their writing. However, if students are ever to correct poor habits, they must at least have some idea of what they are doing wrong and of how to go about correcting their mistakes. We, therefore, are including some short exercises that an instructor can photocopy and use as a class exercise or with students experiencing special problems with pronouns, apostrophes, or parallel constructions. Answers appear on page 42. These revisions, of course, represent just one of several options for correcting these sentences.

CORRECT THE FOLLOWING SENTENCES TO ELIMINATE PRONOUN PROBLEMS.

1. When one searches for meaning in life, they must look beyond themselves.

2. Smoking is bad for my health, but I often do it anyway.

3. The book shows us what life is like when you are trapped within your own neurotic phobias.

4. He eventually realized that anyone can become bankrupt regardless of their position in life.

5. Everyone's life has meaning to them.

6. Even though there were no arrests, each person in town had their own viewpoint about the crime.

7. The Puritans were taught to respect the authority of those above him.

8. One definitely needs to keep up with their work in order to get through the first year at college.

9. Once a person has travelled in Europe, they see their own country in a new light.

10. Each of these people, in order to protect themselves from suspicion, threw suspicion on their neighbors.

11. I feel everyone can always improve on their grammar.

12. If a guy does not understand the rules right away, they can be faced with ten weeks of confusion.

13. It can be rather difficult to practice the beliefs that one has been raised with, no matter how definite they feel their morals are.

14. Each teacher is different; they have various methods of teaching and grading.

15. Each of the members of the sorority should do their own thing.

CORRECT THE FOLLOWING SENTENCES FOR APOSTROPHES. SOME SENTENCES
ARE CORRECT; OTHERS MAY HAVE ONE OR MORE ERRORS.

1. The dog chewed its bone.

2. Its too late to make the plane.

3. The girls parents refused to allow her to attend the party.

4. Its often difficult to understand other peoples values.

5. The Smiths were looking for someone to mow their lawn.

6. The Smiths new baby was a boy.

7. After a weeks time, she called her boyfriend.

8. Its a great honor to be in the Womens Hall of Fame.

9. Although I cannot attest to anyones integrity but my own,
   theirs seems more questionable than most peoples.

10. Theres great rejoicing over Karens scholarship.

11. Not one of the students knew the professors grading system.

12. Lets get our watches synchronized.

13. Hes my best friend and role model.

14. The boys are overconfident about their teams potential

15. Babe Ruth is one of Americas most famous athletes.

CORRECT THE FOLLOWING SENTENCES TO ELIMINATE FAULTY PARALLEL CONSTRUCTION. (See Glossary and Index to Some Composition Concerns)

1. I enjoy writing poetry, playing tennis, and music.

2. She was attractive, charming, and a good student.

3. My brother is a great procrastinator, a true friend, and selfish.

4. Keeping a journal seems both worthwhile and a necessity.

5. Karen is a good writer but lacking the experience of a professional.

6. A basketball player must learn how to shoot baskets, guard opponents, and good sportsmanship.

7. For his birthday he wanted a tie, a sweater, a record album, and to go skiing.

8. I was fond, though certainly not in love with, my teacher.

9. In grade school, teachers encouraged me to write short stories, to read poetry, as well as many different exercises relating to reading and writing.

10. My roommate is a guy who falls in love with one girl after another, parties seven nights a week, and his grades are atrocious.

11. Captain Vere had to do three things: obey naval law, thwart any plans for a mutiny, and to maintain his authority.

12. Chaos results when students do not preregister or when registering late.

13. The people knew that in order to attract new business downtown they needed new landscaping, a civic center, to fix up the old storefronts, and build a parking ramp.

14. He went to college to meet new people and for a good education.

15. The professor praised the students for their diligence and because their writing had improved.

16. Julie is a girl with brains and who is very beautiful.

CORRECT THE FOLLOWING SENTENCES TO ELIMINATE MISPLACED MODIFIERS.

1. Being inexperienced, the work proved very difficult.

2. After gently massaging the bruise with soap and water, a cushion of moleskin is carefully applied.

3. When tired and hungry, a mid-morning break is taken at a fast food restaurant.

4. While walking to school, a strange event occurred.

5. Dressed in a white cotton shirt and jeans, the cool breeze chilled her to the bone.

6. Sitting on the end of the dock, the sun was warm and bright.

7. After completing the homework, the test was easy.

8. Knowing little calculus, the assignment was difficult.

9. Tired, after having studied all night for a history exam, the day appeared ominous.

10. Sentimental about family relationships, the reunion would be a great chance to recapture the past.

11. By making three revisions, my paper finally was ready to turn in to the instructor.

12. If adopted, we assume the new tuition hike will cause problems.

Possible Pronoun Problem Revisions: 1. When people search for
meaning in life, they must look beyond themselves. 2. Smoking
is bad for my health but I often smoke anyway. 3. The books show
us what life is like when we are trapped within our own neurotic
phobias. 4. He eventually realized that anyone can become bankrupt regardless of his or her position in life. 5. Everyone's
life has meaning to that person. 6. Even though there were no
arrests, each person in town had his or her own viewpoint about
the crime. 7. The Puritans were taught to respect the authority
of those above them. 8. One definitely needs to keep up with
one's work in order to get through the first year at college.
9. Once people have travelled in Europe they see their own
country in a new light. 10. These people, in order to protect
themselves from suspicion, threw suspicion on their neighbors.
11. People can always improve on their grammar. 12. If a guy
does not understand the rules right away, he can be faced with
ten weeks of confusion. 13. It can be rather difficult to
practice the beliefs that one has been raised with, no matter how
definite one feels his or her morals are. 14. Each teacher is
different; each has various methods of teaching and grading.
15. Each of the members of the sorority should do her own thing.

Apostrophe Revisions: 1. Correct 2. It's 3. girl's 4. It's
and people's 5. Correct 6. Smiths' 7. week's 8. It's and
Women's 9. anyone's and people's 10. There's and Karen's
11. professor's 12. Let's 13. He's 14. team's 15. America's
and no apostrophe in athletes.

Possible Parallel Construction Revisions: 1. I enjoy writing
poetry, playing tennis, and listening to music. 2. She was
attractive, charming, and studious. 3. My brother is a great
procrastinator, a true friend, and an egotist. 4. Keeping a
journal seems both worthwhile and necessary. 5. Karen is a good
writer but lacks the experience of a professional. 6. A basketball player must learn how to shoot baskets, how to guard one's
opponents, and how to practice good sportsmanship. 7. For his
birthday he wanted a tie, a sweater, a record album, and a ski
trip. 8. I was fond of, though certainly not in love with, my
teacher. 9. In grade school, teachers encouraged me to write
short stories, to read poetry, and to do various exercises.
10. My roommate is a guy who falls in love with one girl after
another, parties seven nights a week, and gets atrocious grades.
11. Captain Vere had to do three things: obey naval law,
thwart plans for a mutiny, and maintain his authority. 12. Chaos
results when students do not preregister or when they do not
register on time. 13. The people knew that in order to attract
new business downtown they needed new landscaping, a civic center,
new storefronts, and a parking ramp. 14. He went to college to
meet new people and to obtain a good education. 15. The
professor praised the students for their diligence and for their
improvement. 16. Julie is a girl who has brains and who is
very beautiful.

Possible Misplaced Modifier Revisions: 1. Being inexperienced,
found the work very difficult. 2. After gently massaging the
bruise with soap and water, carefully apply a cushion of moleskin.
3. When tired and hungry, take a mid-morning break at a fast
food restaurant. 4. While walking to school, I encountered a
strange event. 5. Dressed in a white cotton shirt and jeans,
she was chilled to the bone by the cool breeze. 6. Sitting on
the end of the dock, I found the sun warm and bright. 7. After
completing the homework, I discovered the test was easy.
8. Knowing little calculus, I found the assignment difficult.
9. Tired, after having studied all night for a history exam,
I thought the day appeared ominous. 10. Sentimental about
family relationships, I knew the reunion would be a great chance
to recapture the past. 11. By my making three revisions, my
paper finally was ready to turn in to the instructor. 12. If it
is adopted, the new tuition hike will cause problems.

CHECK LIST FOR PAPERS

SUBJECT - THESIS - SUPPORT

1. Is your subject matter challenging and engaging? Do you have a subject worth writing about? Do you really have something to say? Do you have a specific audience and purpose in mind?

2. Do you have a clearly stated or implied thesis?

3. Have you adequately supported your thesis by way of examples, illustrations, statistics, quotations, comparisons, contrasts, etc? Is the support convincing?

4. Do you "show" your readers rather than "tell" them?

5. Have you used adequate specific detail to make your writing clear and interesting? Are all the details relevant? Have you used too much detail so that your writing becomes ponderous or boring?

ORGANIZATION - UNITY - COHERENCE

1. Is your organization clear and effective?

2. Is your paragraphing meaningful?

3. Have you used effective transitions? Between sentences? Between paragraphs?

4. Is the introduction, particularly the first sentence, designed to "hook" your readers--capture their interest?

5. Is your conclusion climactic and emphatic? Does it clearly drive home your message? Have you avoided introducing a new idea here?

STYLE

1. Have you used adequate sentence variety or do most sentences follow the traditional subject, verb, object order without variation? Have you used dependent clauses now and then to subordinate less important ideas, or are all of your sentences simple or compound sentences?

2. Have you eliminated any unnecessary words or phrases?

3. Have you used strong verbs rather than weak verbs such as "is," "am," "are," "was," "were," "have," "been?"

4. Are your adjectives and nouns precise? Have you avoided vague, general, sweeping statements?

5. Have you employed effective parallel construction?

6. Do you use figurative language, such as similes, metaphors, analogies, alliteration, allusions. when they are appropriate and effective?

FINAL EDITING

1. Have you checked for correct spelling, punctuation (especially the apostrophes), subject and verb and pronoun and antecedent agreement?

2. Have you proofread carefully to avoid typos and careless errors?